The third pre-series train (Train 800002) just after arrival at North Pole Train Maintenance Centre, West London, on 24 October 2015, as part of the testing of the Hitachi Class 800/801 trains for the InterCity Express Programme. **HITACHI**

WORKING TOGETHER ON RAIL SOLUTIONS

Industry commentators may well view 2015 as a year of mixed fortunes for the rail industry. On the one hand, the creation of Transport for the North, with a new 'TransNorth' rail system, will dramatically change rail travel in the North and allow regions and cities to pool their strengths.

On the other hand, increased costs at Network Rail have delayed plans for CP5, with further assessments now required on how the UK's infrastructure provider operates and is funded. There has still been an unprecedented level of investment in the railways and High Speed Rail represents a unique opportunity for the UK to showcase its ability to build a modern rail service that links people and cities, delivering a host of economic and passenger

benefits. Hitachi Rail Europe has a significant role to play in High Speed and was proud to launch its Vision for High Speed at 2015's Railtex.

I think it is important to remember that these political developments can sometimes overshadow the achievements that have been made within the industry. For the first time since the late 1950s, the industry is covering its operating costs, with franchises contributing £800million to the Treasury. UK rail manufacturing has witnessed a rebirth in the North East, with Hitachi Rail Europe opening its Rail Vehicle Manufacturing Facility in Newton Aycliffe; and, significant milestones have been reached on key infrastructure projects across the UK, including the completion of 42km

of tunnelling on Crossrail and the opening of the Borders Railway.

Despite concerns across other parts of the manufacturing sector, Hitachi Rail Europe is incredibly proud to be part of what Prime Minister David Cameron described as 'bringing train manufacturing back to the North East'. Our rolling stock business has expanded to offer different trains for different travelling purposes, and the award of our first Traffic Management contract for the Thameslink franchise in June means that we are now a total railway solutions provider in the UK. To support this growth and continue offering innovative solutions for customers, we have developed a strong skills development programme and are a sponsor of a new University

Technical College being built in County Durham.

As central government and devolved transport bodies look to the industry for more support in 2016, helping to tackle the challenges faced around capacity, customer satisfaction, skills and digital solutions, we are better placed than ever to help shape the future of transport in the UK. What we must remember is that the industry needs to collaborate to ensure the best decisions are made for all, especially fare-paying customers.

KAREN BOSWELL
Managing Director
Hitachi Rail Europe

CONTENTS

3   Foreword by Karen Boswell, MD of Hitachi Rail Europe

SECTION 1 - SETTING THE AGENDA - INDUSTRY STRUCTURE

9   Interesting Times for Rail in the UK: Jeremy Candfield, Director General, the Railway Industry Association

10   The Freight Perspective: Maggie Simpson, Executive Director, the Rail Freight Group

11   2016 - Year of Frustration. Business review by Roger Ford, Industry & Technology Editor of Modern Railways

15   Across the industry

■   Department for Transport

■   Scotland and Wales

■   Network Rail

■   Office of Rail Regulation

■   Rail Delivery Group

■   Passenger Focus

■   The privatised rail industry

SECTION 2 - FINANCE AND LEASING

28   Angel Trains

30   Eversholt Rail Group

31   Porterbrook Leasing

33   Britain's rolling stock - who owns it?

■   The ROSCO fleets

SECTION 3 - TRAIN FLEET MAINTENANCE AND MANUFACTURE

40   Knorr-Bremse RailServices

41   New Trains Arriving - Rolling Stock market review by Roger Ford

46   Hitachi

48   Siemens

50   CAF

52   Stadler, GE Transportation, Electro-Motive Diesel

54   Alstom

56   Bombardier

59   Nomad Digital

60   Wabtec Group

SECTION 4 - PASSENGER TRAIN OPERATORS

63   Train operating company index

64   Passenger operator finances: review by TAS's Chris Cheek

71   First Group:

71   Great Western Railway

73   First TransPennine Express

74   First Hull Trains

75   Serco and Abellio:

75   Northern

76   Merseyrail

78   Greater Anglia

79   ScotRail

80   Caledonian Sleeper

81   Govia:

81   GTR (Govia Thameslink Railway)

84   Southeastern

85   London Midland

87   Arriva:

87   Chiltern Railways

88   Arriva Trains Wales

89   CrossCountry

91   Grand Central

92   Stagecoach:

92   South West Trains

93   East Midlands Trains

94   Virgin Trains West Coast

96   Virgin Trains East Coast

97   c2c

98   Eurostar

99   Heathrow Express

100   Eurotunnel

SECTION 5 - FREIGHT AND HAULAGE

103   Construction and Intermodal sustain Railfreight: we analyse the freight market

■   Freight company accounts

112   DB Schenker UK

113   GB Railfreight

HITACHI
Inspire the Next

114 Freightliner
115 Colas Rail Freight
Direct Rail Services
116 Freight and haulage operators

SECTION 6 - INNOVATION AND ENVIRONMENT

118 Knorr-Bremse
119 Community Rail goes international. Modern Railways columnist Alan Williams examines its prospects
122 The Railway Industry Innovation Awards
■ Golden Spanners focus on reliable trains
■ The Golden Whistles awards
■ The Fourth Friday Club
124 Industry exhibitions update

SECTION 7 - KEY PROJECTS AND CONSULTANTS

126 Key projects
■ London Crossrail
■ Intercity Express Programme
■ Thameslink Programme
■ High Speed 2
■ Scotland's rail projects
■ Great Western modernisation
■ Electrification
■ Consultant files – supporting rail developments

SECTION 8 - INFRASTRUCTURE MAINTENANCE AND RENEWAL

134 Ricardo Rail
135 Network Rail efficiency in spotlight
■ Infrastructure review
■ The main infrastructure contractors

SECTION 9 - SIGNALLING AND CONTROL

142 Delta Rail
143 Signalling & control - can the new technology deliver? Roger Ford reports
■ Signalling innovations
150 Thales

SECTION 10 - LIGHT RAIL AND METRO

152 Thales
154 Light rail traffic on a high
■ GB light rail systems reviewed
157 Transport for London
■ London Underground
■ London Overground

SECTION 11 - INTO EUROPE

165 Into Europe - developments in European rail

169 - THE MODERN RAILWAY DIRECTORY

A compendium of more than 2,000 UK Rail businesses, suppliers and industry bodies

The Modern Railway

Editor:	Ken Cordner
Production Editor:	David Lane
Contributors:	Roger Ford
	Alan Williams
	John Glover
	Chris Shilling
	Ken Harris
	Tony Miles
	Chris Cheek
	Keith Fender
Advertisement Manager:	Chris Shilling
Advertising Production:	Cheryl Thornburn
Graphic Design:	Matt Chapman
	Jack Taylor
Managing Director and Publisher:	Adrian Cox
Commercial Director:	Ann Saundry
Project Manager:	David Lane
Executive Chairman:	Richard Cox

The Modern Railway is published by:
Key Publishing Limited, PO Box 100,
Stamford, Lincs PE9 1XP

The Modern Railway is supported by:

Printing:
Printed in England by Gomer Press Ltd, Llandysul Enterprise Park, Llandysul, Ceredigion, SA4 44JL

Purchasing additional copies of *The Modern Railway*:
Please contact our Martin Steele on 01780 755 131
or by email at martin.steele@keypublishing.com
Corporate and bulk purchase discounts are available on request.

Thank you!
We are very grateful to the many individuals from businesses in all sectors of the railway who have kindly provided help in compiling The Modern Railway. Information contained in The Modern Railway was believed correct at the time of going to press in November 2015. We would be glad to receive corrections and updates for the next edition.

Cover photos: Paul Bigland, DLR, Wabtec, Network rail, Network Rail / Phil Adams
ISBN 978-1-910415-30-6

Competing for West Midlands traffic: loco No 68011 heads north from King's Sutton with a Chiltern Railways service from London Marylebone to Banbury on 23 April 2015. **FRASER PITHIE**

HITACHI
Inspire the Next

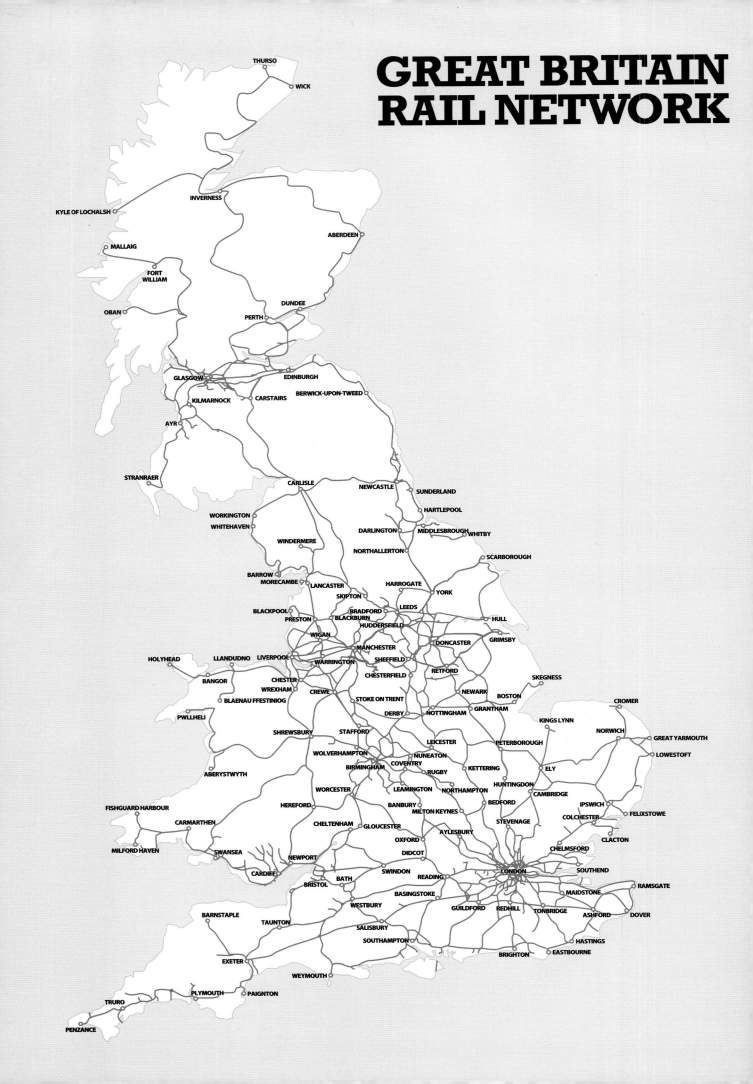

GREAT BRITAIN RAIL NETWORK

SETTING THE AGENDA

IN ASSOCIATION WITH

HITACHI
Inspire the Next

INTERESTING TIMES FOR RAIL IN THE UK

There is reputedly an old curse attributed to the Chinese on the lines of 'May you live in interesting times'. The UK rail industry is certainly living in interesting times at the moment, ranging from the highs of the largest investment programme for a century, to the lows of a sudden and dramatic 'pause' in infrastructure projects, stemming from delays and cost-overruns.

While this is affecting the whole industry, the effect on the supply chain was especially keenly felt. Some suppliers reported a backlog of completed orders which could not be delivered, while others faced a blank order book, despite knowing that products would be required very soon.

These exemplify the fundamental issues generating waste in the supply industry - the unpredictability and volatility of demand and of specifications for products and services. Manufacturers, contractors and consultancies all share this problem. Research that the Railway Industry Association has carried out suggests that additional costs of some 20-30% are regularly incurred.

For the most efficient delivery, what is needed is a clear, robust and deliverable programme, which enables and encourages suppliers to gear up their resources and invest in the necessary skills and training. Responding to short term variations is at best expensive and at worst potentially damaging. As the 'paused' enhancement work gradually gets back under way, it really is essential that a considered and deliverable rolling programme is developed, to provide the assurance that suppliers need if they are to build up the capability required.

However it is not all bad news, as there is still considerable activity across the sector as can be seen by the entries in The Modern Railway directory. A large order book for rolling stock production includes the new inter-city fleets and electric multiple-units for commuter and regional lines, although there is still a large question over how the future need for diesel units will be met. Despite the 'pause' in enhancement projects, Network Rail continues with a high level of maintenance and renewals, as does London Underground, while work in resignalling and station improvements continues apace.

Innovation continues to be a major focus of activity, with enormous scope to gain from technological changes and new processes, and not least in transferring innovation both to and from other sectors. The range of terms now in regular use that would have been unknown a few years ago shows the rapid pace of change: 'Cloud Computing'; 'Big Data'; 'Digital Railway'. We must continue to encourage and support this work if we are to meet the needs of the future, and especially to serve the continuing passenger traffic growth. Some claim that the changes in technology reduce the need to travel, but experience seems to show the opposite: the demand for travel increases alongside the growth in use of mobile devices.

But meeting this ever-increasing demand is not easy. In the supply industry, we are frequently hampered by the continuing problem of skills shortages. Despite the great efforts of the industry focused through the National Skills Academy for Railway Engineering, the recently-opened National Training Academy for Rail and other initiatives, a recent survey of Railway Industry Association members showed that more than half of respondents were suffering from a skills shortage and few expected this to improve in the short term. We must continue with our work in this area, and especially in attracting young people into the industry, highlighting the tremendous and exciting prospects of the major schemes ahead.

Addressing skills issues is also one of the workstreams of the Rail Supply Group, whose activity is now getting firmly under way. Bringing industry together with strong and active support from the Department for Transport and the Department for Business, Innovation and Skills presents a major opportunity to make some radical changes in the ways that industry operates, tackle some of the barriers to efficiency and help us to restore world-class capability in some areas where we have fallen behind other industries.

With a continuing Government focus on achieving major improvements to productivity and the national infrastructure, railways have a really strong role to play and must step up to the plate to deliver. ▓

Jeremy Candfield
Director General
Railway Industry
Association

Station improvement work continues apace across the rail network. Manchester Victoria station was officially reopened on 6 October 2015 by the Transport Secretary, Patrick McLoughlin, following a £44 million upgrade. **DEPARTMENT FOR TRANSPORT**

The intermodal market continues to prosper. Freightliner's Class 86 Nos 86632 and 86622 approach Carluke with the 14.01 Coatbridge to Crewe container train on 22 June 2015. **STEWART ARMSTRONG**

THE FREIGHT PERSPECTIVE

DESPITE TOUGH TIMES IN SOME MARKETS, THE RAIL FREIGHT SECTOR CONTINUES TO PROSPER IN MOST PARTS OF THE UK, AS **MAGGIE SIMPSON**, EXECUTIVE DIRECTOR, RAIL FREIGHT GROUP, EXPLAINS.

2015 turned out to be rather a mixed year for rail freight. From a market perspective, the most obvious difficulties for rail freight in 2015 were the significant fall in coal volumes, especially since April. Whilst decline in this sector has been predicted for a long while, the rate of decline this year has surprised the market, leaving operators struggling with uncertainty in their resource planning. The key driver for this was the near doubling of the 'carbon floor price', a UK Government generation tax which makes it harder for coal power plants to compete against gas and other alternatives.

This rise in the carbon tax, coupled with high transmission charges, has forced Scotland's largest power station, Longannet, to announce its closure from next March, and the future of other coal-powered stations, including Eggborough, is also uncertain.

Over the year, movement of biomass has increased, including the new flow from the Port of Liverpool to Drax which we welcome. However it is highly unlikely that biomass volumes will ever replace coal's role as the main baseload bulk traffic.

The steel market is also in the doldrums. The difficulties were highlighted by the much-publicised closure of the SSI plant in Redcar, while more serious for rail traffic was Tata's decision downscaling Scunthorpe and mothballing Dalzell and Clydebridge. Overall, steel volumes on rail are down as overcapacity in the market keeps prices low and demand is still affected by the worldwide economy.

The on-going situation on the French side of the Channel Tunnel has, understandably, led to a reduction in freight trains travelling between the UK and the Continent. Damage to goods and equipment has been common as migrants seek to hide in curtain-sided containers and on wagons. But the most significant aspect is the unreliability that resulted from delays and cancellations. Some customers switched to alternative (road) routes, with the fear that others will follow as the underlying issues are unlikely to go away any time soon.

There is better news in the construction industry, which is experiencing overall growth and also increasing its use of rail freight. In fact, volumes of stone, sand, cement and other construction products reached a record high in the last financial year. The Rail Freight Group has launched an initiative with the Mineral Products Association to develop the use of rail freight logistics in the construction sector. Steps include a 20% average increase in payload per train within the next five years and aiming to make rail freight the preferred solution for supplying major infrastructure schemes.

The intermodal market is also continuing to prosper with the launch of new services, including the 31st service linking the Port of Felixstowe to inland terminals (in this case BIFT at Birch Coppice) and the new service between Teesport and Mossend and Grangemouth in Scotland. We also welcome the fact that planning consent has been given for Phase 3 at Daventry International Rail Freight terminal and we hope for the same outcome for several other strategic rail freight interchanges presently in the planning system.

These developments clearly demonstrate how rail freight markets are sensitive to Government policies and to Government support. This sets the tone for 2016, when the impact of the three rail reviews from Bowe, Hendy and Nicola Shaw will start to be felt. It is essential that network enhancements for freight, essential for providing capacity for continuing growth, continue to be funded through these reviews - especially the Felixstowe to Nuneaton route but also in relation to paths out of the ports of Southampton and Liverpool.

We are also pressing for a continuous, nationwide operation of critical functions no matter what decisions are taken on devolution of powers to different routes or regions. Transport for the North is now on the way to becoming formalised, and has been very supportive of rail freight to date and we hope to see this continue as it becomes more established. Other regional devolution schemes involving transport, such as Midland Connect, are some way behind but we continue to work with them as well – and all stakeholders – to ensure rail freight is always considered as an integral element in the planning stages, not something to be bolted on afterwards. ∎

2016 – YEAR OF FRUSTRATION

ROGER FORD, INDUSTRY & TECHNOLOGY EDITOR OF *MODERN RAILWAYS*,
EXPLAINS WHY 2016 IS SET TO BE A YEAR OF CONTRASTING FORTUNES

With the third year of Control Period 5 (CP5) starting on 1 April, 2016 was supposed to be the year that the railway began to deliver on the £38.5 billion allocated to Network Rail in the Office of Rail and Road's (ORR's) final determination. While even government ministers refer to the £38.5 billion as 'investment', it covers three categories of spending.

Operations and maintenance – the cost or running the daily railway represents around a third. Another third covers renewals, equivalent to amortisation in a conventional company.

Finally there is the genuine 'investment' in the form of enhancements. For CP5, ORR set enhancement expenditure for the UK network totalled £12.7 billion.

Under its previous status as a company limited by guarantee, Network Rail borrowed to fund enhancements. When a project was completed, its value was transferred to the Regulatory Asset Base (RAB).

At each periodic review, the regulator, ORR, calculates a notional return on the RAB which is added to Network Rail's income for the coming control period and was used to pay the interest on the debt and cover amortisation. This money-go-round resulted in what became known in the railway industry as the 'Network Rail credit card'. If the Department for Transport decided to add some new infrastructure enhancement, Network Rail could borrow the money and add the value of the scheme to the RAB, secure in the knowledge that the next Periodic Review would cover the interest on the loan.

Such funding also provided Network Rail with a means of dealing with project cost over-runs. It could borrow to pay the contractors' bills and put it on the credit card.

UNSUSTAINABLE

But, as the ORR eventually pointed out, this method of funding was unsustainable because the credit card was never paid off. By April 2015, Network Rail's debt stood at £36.5 billion and the RAB at £53 billion.

Matters were brought to a head by the re-classification of Network Rail as a public body. This meant that its debt was transferred to the Treasury's books.

As a result, borrowing on the money markets ended. Instead Network Rail has a loan agreement with the Department for Transport capped at £30 billion throughout CP5. An initial loan £6.5bn was made available in 2014, of which £2.4 billion was used to pay back existing bonds with the remainder funding capital expenditure.

As NR Chief Executive, Mark Carne, explained to the Parliamentary Public Accounts Committee in October 2015, the 'intended flexibility of the regulatory regime' changed following reclassification. Dependent solely on capped Government loans, Network Rail is no longer able to raise additional debt to fund cost increases.

This exacerbated an already serious problem with the rising costs of enhancement projects, electrification in particular. In its HLOS for CP5, DfT had included a number of projects at a very early stage of development.

Ready for the wires: on 21 August 2015 a High Speed Train heads west over the new flyover at Reading, a key part of Network Rail's successful project to improve this busy junction location. Electrification is in place at the new train depot on the right, and is to be installed on the main lines as part of the Great Western electrification project. **PAUL BIGLAND**

Destination Edinburgh: following franchise replacement, the East Coast main line is again the target of the open access entrepreneurs. A reliveried Virgin Trains East Coast diesel High Speed Train stands at Edinburgh Waverley. **VTEC/CHRIS WATT**

Network Rail's Guide to Rail Investment Process (GRIP) process does not provide reliable indicative costs until the end of GRIP Stage3 single option development. Because costs for many schemes proposed for CP5 were still provisional, ORR had to make an indicative allowance for enhancements in its final determination of Network Rail's income. Final approval of the expenditure was then made subject to an Enhancements Costs Adjustment Mechanism (ECAM).

Under ECAM Network Rail would submit the GRIP3 cost of a scheme for ORR to check. If ORR considered the cost 'inefficient' (too high), the allowed expenditure would be reduced. As reported in this space in the 2015 edition of The Modern Railway, ORR had set a deadline of March 2015 for ECAM submissions. Any scheme presented after that was unlikely to be completed before the end of the control period.

But by October 2015 ORR had completed ECAM reviews on only half of the ECAM portfolio - yet the efficient funding determined by then already added up to about 80% of the £21.7bn. Even worse, not only were some submissions to ECAM coming in at higher than expected prices, ORR was seeing cost increases to schemes that had already passed through ECAM. With ORR employing temporary staff to help process ECAM submissions, evaluation is likely to continue throughout 2016.

ELECTRIFICATION SHOCKS

Three high profile electrification schemes typified Network Rail's inability to hold costs. These were the Great Western Electrification Programme

(GWEP), Midland main line (MML) and North Trans-Pennine (NTP).

Reflecting concerns over rising costs, DfT had initiated its own Affordability Review of Network Rail's enhancements. On 25 June 2015 came the announcement that Sir Peter Hendy would take over as Network Rail Chairman when Richard Parry-Jones retired. While Sir Peter's appointment was itself a surprise, there were two shocks in the associated announcement.

Sir Peter's immediate task would be to develop proposals for a revised enhancements programme for CP5. His terms of reference made clear that his remit was to cut-back the enhancements programme for CP5 to include only those schemes which can be delivered within the Regulator's enhancements budget. Schemes which can no longer be afforded within

the funds available, or cannot now be delivered by 2019, will be deferred until funding is available.

With electrification of the Great Western main line a 'top priority', the Transport Secretary ordered Network Rail 'to concentrate its efforts on getting that right'. As a result, the MML and NTP electrification schemes would be 'paused'.

In parallel, the Government commissioned two further reviews, one retrospective, one forward-looking. Dame Colette Bowe was to look at lessons learned from CP5 and make recommendations for better investment planning in future. Her report was also due 'in the autumn'.

High Speed 1 Chief Executive Nicola Shaw was given the remit to 'develop recommendations for the longer-term future shape and financing of Network Rail'. Subsequently Ms Shaw

commented that re-privatisation could not be ruled out. Ms Shaw's detailed report 'with implementation proposals' is scheduled to be completed 'by the time of the budget in spring 2016'. The likely date for the budget is sometime in March.

POLITICS

In pausing the two northern electrification schemes, the politics of rail investment had not been taken into account. NTP was a key element of the Chancellor of the Exchequer's vision of an industrial and commercial revival aimed at creating a Northern Power House. Following the decision to pause the two electrification schemes, opposition MPs took to taunting the Chancellor on his 'Northern Power Cut'.

At the end of September, the Chancellor reacted, ordering an immediate 'un-pause' of both the NTP and MML electrification schemes. With MML budgeted at around £1.3 billion and the NTP electrification and route upgrade under development, the un-pause threw a couple of spanners into Sir Peter's already herculean task.

Civil servants and Sir Peter were not happy, but DfT was told that the un-pause was non-negotiable for political reasons. On 29 September Sir Peter wrote to the Transport Secretary with his formal advice on options for restarting the two electrification schemes. His letter was a masterclass in coded criticism of an overtly political decision. It concluded, 'I am continuing work to set out the already evident likely funding shortfall in CP5', adding 'I understand the Government acknowledge that un-pausing now will create further significant spending pressure'.

TABLE 1: COMPARISON OF EAST COAST AND GREAT WESTERN ELECTRIFICATION (GW INITIAL PROGRAMME DATES)

	ECML	GWML
Date approved	July 1984	July 2009
Initial Service (note 1)	April 1989	December 2016
GWML Bath Corridor to Bristol		May 2017
Completed (note 2)	October 1991	December 2017
Project timescale	86 months	100 months
Single Track km (stkm)	1810	981
Masts/foundations	28000	19000
Clearance (bridges/structures)	157	161 (note 3)
Stations	9 (note 4)	57
Electrification cost (£ million 2014-15 prices)	810	2,915
Cost per stkm (£)	447,573	2,971,254
Cost of GWML at ECML rates (£m)		439

1) ECML - Leeds. GWML Oxford/Bristol Parkway
2) ECML -Edinburgh. GWML Cardiff
3) Plus 64 track lowers
4) Major stations only

UNAFFORDABLE

Before the un-pause, the 'unaffordable in CP5' category in Sir Peter's review had included TransPennine and Midland Main Line electrification plus the MML capacity enhancements, upgrading Reading-Ascot to take 10 car trains and Wessex capacity enhancements. A surprising inclusion was IEP readiness work on the East Coast main line plus the London North Eastern traction power supply upgrade. Also facing deferral were the Anglia Great Eastern upgrade and remodelling of the Ely North junction where three lines converge.

Since the un-pause, the pressure on Network Rail's fixed budget has continued to grow. Project timescales are equally important. On 21 October Network Rail revealed a new cost estimate for GWEP of £2.5 billion to £2.8 billion at 2012 prices.

At the same time Network Rail was unable to give a completion date for GWEP. Under the original programme, electric services between London and Bristol Parkway, plus Newbury and Oxford, were due to start with the May 2017 timetable.

With under a quarter of the piled foundations for the Overhead Line Electrification support masts installed, and in many cases test pits having to be dug by hand to avoid cutting through buried signalling cables, GWEP is already at least a year late.

OPERATING SUCCESS

Against this background of infrastructure cost over-runs, delayed schemes and unaffordable projects being slipped back to CP6 (2019-2024), the passenger train operating companies continue to see rising ridership and revenues. The use of Direct Award Franchise Agreements to extend selected existing franchises has created a steady programme of replacement franchise bidding.

One victim of the re-classification of Network Rail was the 'Deep Alliance' with South West Trains. This was an agreement between two private companies able to share commercial risk. However, with Network Rail a government body it has no 'skin in the game' and the Alliance was 're-shaped'.

Fortunately, the spirit of the Alliance lives on in four core areas where joint working continues. These are operational control, performance management, planning and the management of Waterloo station under an Alliance Governance Board.

In Scotland, the award of the replacement franchise mandated the formation of a deep alliance with Network Rail. This is now in place under Managing Director Phil Verster.

CHALLENGE

Highlighting the buoyant passenger market, open access operators are not only flourishing but seeking to provide new services. The most recent statistic for the first quarter of 2015-16 showed year-on-year revenue growth for long-distance franchised operators of 6.6%. Contrast this with 17.5% revenue growth for the open access operators, which is particularly noteworthy against the background of an increase in timetabled train kilometres of only 0.2%.

Early 2016 is likely to see a landmark decision in the long running battle between the franchised operators, supported by the DfT, and the open access sector. In the early days of privatisation, open access was province of small start-up companies. But over the years they have been absorbed by major transport groups, adding financial backing and commercial credibility to innovative service proposals.

Ironically, franchise replacement means that once again the East Coast main line is the target of the open access entrepreneurs. Bidders for the Intercity East Coast franchise had to offer proposals for a new timetable with more frequent services exploiting the availability of the Hitachi-built

TABLE 2: RISING COST OF GREAT WESTERN ELECTRIFICATION
(2014-15 PRICES)

	PROJECT COST £M	£/SINGLE TRACK KM
July 2009	625	637,100
July 2011	850	866,460
January 2013	910	927,625
2013/2014	1,380	1,406,730
December 2014	1,700	1,732,925
October 2015	2,915	2,971,254

Wires up: a revised enhancements programme for Control Period 5, including new electrification projects, has been in preparation. Improvements to electrification at Chadwell Heath are under way in this Easter 2015 engineering project. **NETWORK RAIL/PHIL ADAMS**

Intermodal is now much the biggest sector in UK railfreight. Direct Rail Services' Class 66s Nos 66434 and 66425 power through Holytown with the 06.16 Daventry-Mossend Tesco intermodal train on 18 June 2015. **STEWART ARMSTRONG**

Intercity Express Programme (IEP) fleets from 2020.

This meant that new franchisee, Virgin Trains East Coast (VTEC), had to apply for the necessary Long Distance High Speed (LDHS) paths in the May 2020 timetable. But, seeing an opportunity, two open access operators have also applied for paths for two radically different services.

Alliance Rail is backed by German Railways through its UK group Arriva, which already operates the Grand Central services on the ECML. It is proposing to run 3hr 45min London-Edinburgh services using new Alstom Pendolino tilting trains under the Great North Eastern Railway brand. In August 2015, Alliance's application to run London-Blackpool services on the West Coast main line, as Great North Western Railway, was approved by ORR. This is also based on acquiring new Pendolinos.

First Group, which owns ECML open access operator Hull Trains, is proposing a rail version of the low-cost airlines, also for London-Edinburgh. First would use Hitachi AT300 (IEP-based) sets with single-class travel and ultra low fares.

CAPACITY

Central to this battle is Network Rail's ability to provide the eight paths per hour which could accommodate both VTEC and one open access operator. This is complicated by the fact that in determining the potential

capacity Network Rail does not have an integrated timetable to model.

Following detailed analysis completed in October 2015, Network Rail was still unable to confirm whether it would be possible to accommodate 8 LDHS services per hour once various enhancements (Table 3) had been delivered. The open access applicants continue to point out that certain hours in the current timetable already accommodate 8 LDHS paths/hr.

However the greatest threat, to both VTEC's IEP timetable and the open access aspirants, is the likelihood that the Hendy Review will delay the planned ECML capacity upgrades.

COAL DECLINE

For the railfreight market, 2016 will be a year of transition as external factors slash the railway's traditional baseload – coal. Statistics for the first quarter of 2015-16 revealed that coal movements had fallen year-on-year by 61% to 640 million net tonne-km. This was

the lowest volume since ORR records began in 2002. The importance of coal to the railfreight market was reflected in total freight net tonne-km for the quarter declining by 17.7%.

ORR gave a number of reasons for the abrupt decline in coal traffic, explored in more detail in the Freight and Haulage section of this publication. These include 'the doubling of the UK's carbon top-up tax since April 1 2015', which has reduced output of coal-fired plants. The closure of Hatfield Colliery also contributed.

ORR believes that the fall in coal traffic is a sign of worse to come. Electricity generating companies planning to close coal-fired power stations such as Ferrybridge and Longannet during 2015-16 have begun gradually reducing their reliance on coal, cutting deliveries.

Once the leader, coal is now third in the freight commodities league table, behind domestic intermodal (34.7% of total freight traffic) and

construction (22.7%). While too much should not be read into one quarter's figures, year on year, domestic intermodal traffic was also down 1·4% in Q1 2015-16. ORR suggests this may have been due to a tailing-off of the 'boost' provided in 2014-15 by clearing more routes to the W10 loading gauge to accommodate larger containers, as well as the opening of the Ipswich Chord which provides a direct route from Felixstowe port to the Midlands.

STARK CONTRAST

Overall, the contrast in fortunes on either side of the wheel rail interface has never been so stark. While Network Rail faces a cost, delivery and performance crisis, the passenger market continues its relentless growth with record numbers of new trains entering service providing desperately needed capacity which the infrastructure cannot accept. A year of frustration indeed. ■

TABLE 3: ECML CAPACITY ENHANCEMENTS PROPOSED

LOCATION	AVAILABILITY DATE	COST (£M)
Huntingdon-Woodwalton four-tracking	Jan 2021	86.52
Fletton-Peterborough speed improvements	Apr 2018	13.62
Werrington grade separation	Dec 2020	96.20
Doncaster bay platform and signalling	Dec 2016	21.17
York North throat	Dec 2020	8.76
Northallerton to Newcastle Freight Loops	Mar 2020	65.2

Plus London King's Cross remodelling (a renewal project)

HITACHI
Inspire the Next

ACROSS THE INDUSTRY

DEPARTMENT FOR TRANSPORT

The Department for Transport (DfT) is the government body, 'responsible for setting the strategic direction for the rail industry in England and Wales – funding investment in infrastructure through Network Rail, awarding and managing franchises, and regulating rail fares'. The DfT also encourages the use of new technology such as smart ticketing and the maintenance of high standards of transport safety and security.

Following the failed attempt to let the West Coast main line franchise in 2012, and subsequent enquiry and review, franchising programme has been redesigned with a single responsible Director. All rail activity is now overseen by a single Director General.

Established in April 2014, the DfT's Rail Executive's high-level structure was altered from November 2014, with changes to the split of functions across directorates, based on initial experience. The Office of Rail Passenger Services was relaunched as the Rail Executive - Passenger Services, to make clear the governance arrangements and that it was part of the Rail Executive. The DfT says the new organisation has adopted an integrated, market-based approach, intended to enhance its ability to take a long-term, strategic view of the railway, promote collaborative working and facilitate the development of a solid knowledge base.

The Rail Executive leads on the sponsorship of major rail projects including Crossrail, Thameslink and the Intercity Express Programme, as well as DfT's interest in Network Rail's investment programme. The Executive also takes the lead on policy and funding for the rail sector, and the sponsorship of Network Rail.

HS2 is being developed by the DfT and High Speed 2 Ltd, an executive non-departmental public body (NDPB). The DfT's HS2 Group is responsible for ensuring that the HS2 programme meets its demanding timetable and delivers long-term strategic national planning for this major addition to national infrastructure. There is close working between HS2 Group and the Rail Executive.

The conditions attached to individual rail franchises vary, but in general invitations to bidders specify frequency levels and carrying capacity to be provided, punctuality and reliability standards, and the control of some fares levels.

The train operating companies also commit themselves to financial regimes. Typically, these require less subsidy as time progresses, or paying an increased premium. They may also undertake specific enhancements, such as train fleet renewals.

Franchise bid evaluation is based on two basic principles. First is the decision on what the Department should buy and on what commercial terms to give the best outcome - for example, evaluation based on financial result has been widened to include a weighting of the quality of what bidders are intending to provide. Second is the need to retain the confidence of all the parties involved.

PERMANENT SECRETARY
Philip Rutnam
DIRECTOR GENERAL, HIGH SPEED 2 David Prout
RAIL EXECUTIVE DIRECTOR GENERAL Bernadette Kelly
MD, PASSENGER SERVICES
Peter Wilkinson

TRANSPORT SCOTLAND

Transport Scotland is an agency of the Scottish Government, whose purpose is to increase sustainable economic growth through the development of national transport projects and policies.

Transport Scotland's Rail Directorate is responsible for managing the ScotRail and new Caledonian Sleeper franchises; relationships with Network Rail and the Office of Rail and Road; sponsoring major rail projects, including the Edinburgh-Glasgow Improvement Programme (EGIP) and the Borders Railway; advising Ministers on investment priorities; working with the UK government on cross-border services, including high-speed rail; and leading policy development.

Aims included in the Scottish High Level Output Statement for 2014-19 include hourly services between Aberdeen and Inverness taking around 2hr; Highland main line development to provide an hourly Inverness-Perth

ATOC's Rail Settlement Plan allows passengers to buy tickets to travel on any part of the network from any station. This is the ticket hall at Cardiff Central. **ARRIVA TRAINS WALES**

service with extensions to either Glasgow or Edinburgh; and electrifying 100 single track km per annum when EGIP work is finished.

There are funding schemes for stations, freight, network improvements and level crossings, while passenger and train handling capacity at the main Edinburgh and Glasgow stations is clearly a concern. Transport Scotland also co-ordinates the National Transport Strategy and is responsible for the national concessionary travel scheme.

The Glasgow area is the largest commuter operation outside London and its users account for about 60% of railway passengers in Scotland.

CHIEF EXECUTIVE Roy Brannen
DIRECTOR OF RAIL
Aidan Grisewood
DIRECTOR OF TRANSPORT POLICY Donald Carmichael

TRANSPORT WALES

Since 2006 the Welsh Government (WG) has been responsible for management and funding of the current Wales & Borders rail franchise which continues until 2018. Rail franchising will be fully devolved to the WG from 2017. Rail infrastructure is non-devolved, but the WG identifies priorities to inform Network Rail and UK and Wales government investment plans.

The Welsh Government Transport company was formally incorporated in April 2015 as a not-for-dividend, wholly-owned subsidiary. By being not-for-dividend, and 'most likely' taking revenue fare risk, the WG envisages it will free up more money to run services: or alternatively, even without further powers to run a completely not-for-dividend system, that a concession service with a capped profit margin could be developed.

Phase Two work for an integrated Metro system, estimated to cost £500m-£600m, for the Cardiff Capital City Region is expected to be an integral part of WG negotiations for the new Wales rail franchise – the funding estimates include £125m pledged by the UK government for the Valleys Lines electrification, though overall options being explored for the Metro include light rail, heavy rail, bus rapid transit and trams. The WG has been exploring the possibility of a single contract linking delivery of the Metro and operation of the rail franchise, and the WGTC's initial priority is to provide advice and technical expertise for both.

WG has also been in discussions with the Department for Transport to ensure that long distance rail services operated by other franchises meet the needs of people travelling to and from Wales.

An expert panel has been appointed to advise during rail franchise negotiations and development of the Metro: David Stevens, Chief Operating Officer at Admiral; Andrew Haines, Chief Executive at the Civil Aviation Authority and former MD at South West Trains and First Group; and Chris Gibb, former MD at Virgin Trains and Wales & Borders Trains.

DIRECTOR GENERAL, ECONOMY, SCIENCE AND TRANSPORT James Price

LOCAL TRANSPORT AUTHORITIES

Passenger Transport Executives (PTEs) are statutory bodies, funded by a combination of local council tax and government grant, which provide, plan, procure and promote public transport in six of England's largest conurbations: Greater Manchester (Transport for Greater Manchester), Merseyside (Merseytravel), South Yorkshire (SYPTE), Tyne & Wear (Nexus), West Midlands (Centro) and West Yorkshire (West Yorkshire Combined Authority).

PTEs are responsible to Combined Authorities (CAs) - district council leader-led bodies which co-operate on strategic decisions on key areas like transport. In West Yorkshire the PTE has been absorbed into the CA. Centro is responsible to an integrated transport authority, and a CA is expected to be established in 2016. Some CAs have a

The Borders Railway was officially opened on 9 September 2015 by Her Majesty the Queen, who travelled on a steam hauled train along the route and unveiled a plaque at Tweedbank, accompanied by Scotland's First Minister, Nicola Sturgeon, and HRH The Duke of Edinburgh. The 35 miles from Edinburgh to Tweedbank is the northern part of the former Waverley route to Carlisle. **SCOTTISH GOVERNMENT**

wider geographical coverage than the former metropolitan areas.

Merseytravel itself lets and manages the concession (not franchise) for Merseyrail Electrics. The Northern and TransPennine franchises provide local rail services in all the PTE areas other than the West Midlands.

The government in October 2014 announced the creation of a new body called Transport for the North (TfN) – a partnership between England's northern city region authorities, government and national transport agencies. Initially, the city regions have been acting collectively as TfN, working with Local Enterprise Partnerships (LEPs), government and national agencies through a Partnership Board.

TfN is to become a statutory body with its transport policies and investment priorities set out in a long-term strategy, with £30m of additional funding pledged by government over three years to support its running costs and work programme. It is planned to be the first of a series of Sub-National Transport Bodies which could be established at the request of local areas in England, as advisory bodies which could later gain decision making and delivery powers.

Government is to work with TfN on plans to transform east-west rail connections as a new 'TransNorth' network, linking Liverpool, Manchester, Leeds, Sheffield, Newcastle and Hull. Options range from radically upgrading existing routes to building new lines. Smart and integrated ticketing across bus, tram, metro and rail services is also a government priority.

The DfT agreed in March 2015 to devolve more power to Rail North, representing 29 local transport authorities in the north of England, in the management of the Northern and TransPennine Express franchises (new contracts for both due in 2016). The DfT and Rail North have a joint strategic board and management team based in Leeds.

Increased local powers over transport for Greater Manchester, with a devolved and consolidated transport budget, were announced by the government in November 2014, and similar proposals for the Sheffield and Tyne & Wear city regions were announced in autumn 2015. In the West Midlands, 14 Metropolitan District, Shire and Unitary local transport authorities are working towards devolution of the region's rail network as West Midlands Rail.

In other areas of England, for now, the Local Transport Authority is either the Unitary Authority or County Council. LEPs - business-led bodies designed to promote local economic growth - have produced Strategic Economic Plans in collaboration with local authorities, which set out, among other things, priorities for transport investment, and bid for funding from the Local Growth Fund.

The Passenger Transport Executive Group, PTEG, is a non-statutory body bringing together and promoting PTE and wider urban transport interests.
TRANSPORT FOR THE NORTH CHIEF EXECUTIVE David Brown
PTEG CHAIR Jon Lamonte

NATIONAL INFRASTRUCTURE COMMISSION

The National Infrastructure Commission (NIC) was created following an announcement by the Chancellor of the Exchequer in October 2015, and is later to be put into statute. It is 'an independent body that enables long term strategic decision making to build effective and efficient infrastructure for the UK'. It reports to the Treasury.

The NIC's role is to deliver a long-term plan and assessment of national infrastructure needs early in each parliament. It will be overseen by a small board, appointed by the chancellor, and able to commission research and call for evidence from public sector bodies and private sector experts.

The Treasury said that NIC's initial focus will be on transforming the connectivity of the Northern cities, including high speed rail (HS3); setting priorities for future large-scale investment in London's public transport infrastructure; and how to ensure investment in energy infrastructure can meet future demand most efficiently.

- Investment in rail network (26p)
- Maintaining track and trains (22p)
- Industry staff costs (25p)
- Interest payments and other costs (9p)
- Leasing trains (11p)
- Fuel for trains (4p)
- Train company profits (3p)

The Department for Transport's January 2015 presentation of how a rail passenger's pound is spent.

SOURCES: Network Rail and The Rail Delivery Group

The NIC was also to begin work on a national infrastructure assessment, looking ahead 30 years.
CHAIRMAN Lord Adonis

EUROPEAN UNION

In the last 20 years, the European Commission has been active in restructuring the rail transport market and strengthening the position of railways. Efforts have been concentrated on: opening the rail transport market to competition; improving interoperability and safety of national networks; and developing rail transport infrastructure.

Four railway 'packages' aimed to open up the international rail freight market, provide a legally and technically integrated railway, and revitalise international passenger services by extending competition and interoperability. They also introduced standards and authorisation for rolling stock and independent management of infrastructure.

COMMONS TRANSPORT COMMITTEE

The Transport Committee is appointed by the House of Commons to examine the expenditure, administration and policy of the Department for Transport and its associated public bodies.

During the course of a year, the Committee will consider around 20 topics on which they will call formally for written evidence from interested parties. Formal reports are made to the House, which are published together with a verbatim report of the evidence sessions and the main written submissions.
CHAIR Louise Ellman

NETWORK RAIL

Network Rail (NR) is the infrastructure manager of the national network. Formed in October 2002, the company owns, operates, maintains and develops the national railway infrastructure of Great Britain. This consists of the track, signals, bridges, viaducts, tunnels, level crossings and electrification systems, of

which it is the monopoly owner. It also owns and operates 18 large stations. With a few minor exceptions, the others are owned by NR, but primary responsibility for day-to-day operations is that of the main TOC serving the station, to which the station is leased.

The task is the delivery of a safe, reliable and efficient railway network. From 1 September 2014, Network Rail was reclassified from the private to the public sector. It retains commercial and operational freedom to manage the railway infrastructure, but borrowings are constrained by the requirements of HM Treasury.

Network Rail Ltd is licenced by the Secretary of State for Transport. The company is accountable to its train and freight operator customers through their access contracts and to the Office of Rail and Road.

In conjunction with stakeholders, the company's Long Term Planning Process predicts future demand, agrees priority uses for the capacity available and assess value for money options for investment.
CHAIRMAN Sir Peter Hendy CBE
CHIEF EXECUTIVE Mark Carne

OFFICE OF RAIL AND ROAD (ORR)

The Office of Rail Regulation changed its name to the Office of Rail and Road, to reflect new responsibilities as the independent monitor of Highways England from 1 April 2015.

A non-ministerial government department, ORR holds the railway industry to account to meet the priorities of the governments in England, Scotland and Wales. It regulates health and safety performance, holds Network Rail and High Speed 1 to account on performance, service, and value for money, and ensures that the rail industry is competitive and fair. The ORR has concurrent jurisdiction with the Office of Fair Trading to investigate potential breaches of the Competition Act 1998 in relation to railways.

HM Railway Inspectorate (HMRI) is part of ORR and its inspectors and policy advisors develop and deliver the safety strategy. ORR is the enforcement authority for the Health & Safety at Work Act 1974 and various railway specific legislation. ORR is led by a Board appointed by the Secretary of State for Transport.

The principal economic regulatory functions are to regulate Network Rail's stewardship of the national rail network, to licence train and other operators of railway assets, and to approve track, station and light maintenance

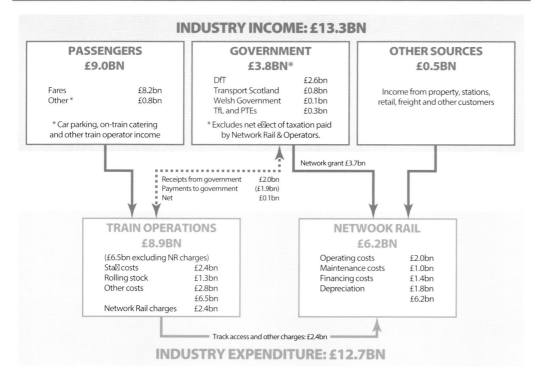

INDUSTRY INCOME, EXPENDITURE AND GOVERNMENT FUNDING IN 2013-14

INDUSTRY INCOME: £13.3BN

PASSENGERS £9.0BN

Fares	£8.2bn
Other *	£0.8bn

* Car parking, on-train catering and other train operator income

GOVERNMENT £3.8BN*

DfT	£2.6bn
Transport Scotland	£0.8bn
Welsh Government	£0.1bn
TfL and PTEs	£0.3bn

* Excludes net effect of taxation paid by Network Rail & Operators.

OTHER SOURCES £0.5BN

Income from property, stations, retail, freight and other customers

Network grant £3.7bn

Receipts from government	£2.0bn
Payments to government	(£1.9bn)
Net	£0.1bn

TRAIN OPERATIONS £8.9BN

(£6.5bn excluding NR charges)	
Staff costs	£2.4bn
Rolling stock	£1.3bn
Other costs	£2.8bn
	£6.5bn
Network Rail charges	£2.4bn

NETWOOK RAIL £6.2BN

Operating costs	£2.0bn
Maintenance costs	£1.0bn
Financing costs	£1.4bn
Depreciation	£1.8bn
	£6.2bn

Track access and other charges: £2.4bn

INDUSTRY EXPENDITURE: £12.7BN

HITACHI Inspire the Next

The £44m facelift of the Grade-II listed Manchester Victoria station, officially opened by the Transport Secretary in October 2015, included restoration of this famous façade. **DEPARTMENT FOR TRANSPORT**

depot access arrangements. ORR also regulates High Speed 1.

ORR oversees Network Rail's delivery of the regulatory outcomes specified in five-year Control Periods (currently 2014-19, Control Period 5). These include the scope for further efficiency gains and performance improvements, and the need for investment in more capacity.
CHAIR Anna Walker
CHIEF EXECUTIVE Richard Price

RAIL DELIVERY GROUP

The Rail Delivery Group (RDG) was set up in 2011 to bring together the owners of Britain's passenger train operating companies, freight operators and Network Rail to provide leadership to Britain's rail industry. In 2013 the structure of the group was formalised through the incorporation of a new membership condition into the licences of Network Rail and passenger and freight operators. Some of its policy formulation and communications functions were undertaken prior to 2013 by the Association of Train Operating Companies (ATOC).

RDG says its strategy is to strengthen the benefits brought about by the range of commercial operators on a single network by co-ordinating solutions to cross-industry challenges in partnership with government,

regulators and industry suppliers to the benefit of customers.
CHIEF EXECUTIVE Paul Plummer

ATOC

The Association of Train Operating Companies (ATOC) acts as a clearing house for passenger train operators through the Rail Settlement Plan. This allows passengers to buy tickets to travel on any part of the network from any station. It also provides the National Rail Enquiry Service (NRES) and runs a range of discounted and promotional railcards for the public and also staff travel facilities.

There is also an operations, engineering and major projects team that supports scheme members in delivering a safe, punctual and economic railway.
CHIEF EXECUTIVE Paul Plummer

RAIL FREIGHT GROUP

The Rail Freight Group is a representative body for rail freight in the UK, with a membership which includes some of the biggest names in logistics along with many smaller companies, all of whom contribute to the success of rail freight. Its members include ports, terminal operators, property developers, equipment suppliers and support services.

Since 1991, the RFG has been working to increase the amount

of goods conveyed by rail. It seeks to achieve this in three ways: by campaigning for a policy environment that supports rail freight; promoting the rail freight sector, and supporting members as they grow their businesses.
CHAIRMAN Lord Berkeley
EXECUTIVE DIRECTOR
Maggie Simpson

FREIGHT ON RAIL

Freight on Rail, a partnership between the rail trade unions, the rail freight industry and Campaign for Better Transport, works to promote the economic, social and environmental benefits of rail freight, both nationally and locally. It advocates policy changes that support the shift to rail and provides information and help on freight related issues.

HIGH SPEED 1

HS1 Ltd is the long term concession holder of HS1, the 109km high speed rail line connecting London St Pancras International with the Eurotunnel boundary. The 30 year concession to operate, maintain and renew the railway continues until 2040, when asset ownership reverts to the government.

The delivery of operations and maintenance responsibilities is achieved principally through contracts with Network Rail (High Speed) Ltd.

HS1 stations are London St Pancras International, Stratford International, Ebbsfleet International, and Ashford International. All have both domestic and international platforms, but international trains have yet to serve Stratford.

Present operators are Eurostar for international services under an open access arrangement, and Southeastern for domestic operations as part of its franchise agreement. Vehicles operating on HS1 must be specifically authorised.

Ashford Area Signalling Centre is the location of the traffic, signalling and electrical controls and the communications centre for HS1.

HS1 Ltd is policed by the Office of Rail and Road, with a Control Period 2 (2015-2020) beginning on 1 April 2015. In their review, ORR was required to approve HS1's operating, maintenance and renewal costs and the resultant Track Access charges. They approved HS1 Ltd's reductions of 12%-13% for passenger services, and 20% for freight.

Revenue earning freight traffic is restricted to a six hour night time slot as conventional freight trains are limited to 140km/h.

In 2014-15, HS1 Ltd generated net income of £11.5m, which is £9.1m higher than assumed in the Access Charges Review for 2010-15. Significant passenger and freight growth resulted in increased demand for train paths and

This is an exciting time for High Speed rail in the UK

Visit our website to view our vision for High Speed and become part of the Hitachi design journey...

HITACHI
Inspire the Next

hitachirail-eu.com  @HitachiRailEU

A new entrance onto St Thomas Street in Southwark will be part of the transformation of London Bridge station, which is being rebuilt by Network Rail as part of the Thameslink Programme. The new station entrance facades have been installed as pre-cast sections, from Thorp Precast Ltd, with brickwork to match the rest of the viaduct. The remaining arches have had their decorative brickwork and pediments restored. **NETWORK RAIL**

HS1 Ltd achieved greater efficiencies than originally assumed.

BRITISH TRANSPORT POLICE

British Transport Police (BTP) is the specialised police service for Britain's railways, funded by the train operating companies. BTP provides a service to rail operators, staff and passengers throughout Britain, as well as London Underground, the Docklands Light Railway, Glasgow Subway, Midland Metro, London Tramlink and Emirates AirLine. Over 2,900 officers police Britain's rail network.

The British Transport Police Authority sets the strategic targets for BTP. These are keeping the railway running, making the railway safer and more secure, delivering value for money, and promoting confidence in use of the railway. It monitors BTP's performance and sets the budget. Both organisations are responsible to the DfT.

The 2013-19 strategic plan addressed 'a period that will require unprecedented change in railway policing to provide exceptional service quality at reduced cost', and with rising passenger numbers, an increase in demand for BTP's services

is expected. BTP has restructured from seven areas into three larger divisions, aiming to deliver a more efficient force, generating savings to reinvest in more officers.

Depending on devolution legislation, the BTP in Scotland is expected to become part of Police Scotland.
CHIEF CONSTABLE Paul Crowther

RAILWAY INDUSTRY ASSOCIATION

The Railway Industry Association (RIA) is the representative body for UK-based suppliers of equipment and services to the world-wide rail industry, with services including Representation of the supply industry's interests, Technical activities, Exports Support, Improvement Initiatives, and Skills & Recruitment.

It has around 200 member companies across the whole range of railway supply. RIA is an active member of UNIFE, the trade association for the European railway supply industry.

RIA members represent the greater part of the UK railway supply industry. This includes the manufacture, leasing, component supply, maintenance

and refurbishment of rolling stock, the design, manufacture, installation, maintenance and component supply of infrastructure, and specialist expertise in consultancy, training, project management and safety.
DIRECTOR GENERAL
Jeremy Candfield

RAIL SUPPLY GROUP

The Rail Supply Group comprises ministers, rail industry business leaders and senior representatives from the Department for Transport and the Department for Business, Innovation and Skills.

RSG has been developing an industrial strategy for the rail supply chain, with a clear implementation plan. RSG's vision is for the British rail industry, by 2025, to: more than double export volumes; attract the very best UK talent to create a sustainable skills base and to develop new technologies; harness the energy, drive and innovation of small and medium sized businesses to meet the needs of the global railway market; be a global leader in High Speed Rail; and have an entrepreneurial supply chain that constantly innovates to meet customer needs, from urban to intercity networks.

THE RAIL ALLIANCE

The rail sector's largest dedicated b2b networking organisation, the Rail Alliance aims to bring customers, suppliers and supply chain opportunities together and support members with mentoring, marketing intelligence and networking opportunities. It also aims to help organisations fulfil their business potential and be the essential business resource for any ambitious organisation involved in the rail sector, whether already in rail or looking to break into this growth market. It works to provide regular networking opportunities; advertise and promote members' services and capabilities; promote the membership internationally; develop a mentoring, education and training programme; and develop relationships between the research and technology community and industry to promote best practice and innovation.

RSSB

RSSB is a not-for-profit company owned by major industry stakeholders. Its primary purpose is to support continuous improvement in the level of safety in the rail industry, drive out unnecessary cost and improve business performance.

Key activities of RSSB include the support of cross-industry working

groups; the management of system safety; the management of industry-wide programmes of research and development, in cooperation with the Department for Transport, Network Rail and others; and developing the content of Railway Group Standards (RGS) and the Rule Book.

This includes the development of the industry's Safety Risk Model (identifying all significant risks), a Precursor Indicator Model (risk from train accidents) and the SPAD ranking methodology (risk from passing signals at danger).

Other activities are funded by member levies. Five Committees manage Interfaces between Vehicles and, separately, Structures, Track, Train Energy, Train Control & Communications, and Other Vehicles.

RSSB is registered as the Rail Safety & Standards Board: it does not use the full name as its status and activities have changed over time.
CHIEF EXECUTIVE Chris Fenton

TECHNICAL STRATEGY LEADERSHIP GROUP

The Technical Strategy Leadership Group (TSLG) is a cross-industry RSSB-facilitated expert body with representatives from Network Rail, train and freight operating companies, rolling stock leasing companies, suppliers, Transport Scotland, and the university sector through Rail Research UK Association.

TSLG is responsible for developing the Rail Technical Strategy (RTS) and ensuring the 30 year vision for the railway system forms part of forward planning and supports the rail business.

TSLG sponsors activities including research (with a dedicated fund for projects and programmes); overseeing the rail industry's vehicle/infrastructure Systems Interface Committees (SICs); enabling innovation; working with others in the transport sector to stimulate new ideas (including co-funding and competitions with Innovate UK, and setting up a Transport Systems 'Catapult'); and inputting technology development proposals to industry planning.

RSSB's Future Railway Programme was has cross industry support through the TSLG. It promotes innovation by supporting cross-industry demonstrator projects and seeking out innovative ideas and proposals.

RAIL ACCIDENT INVESTIGATION BRANCH

The Rail Accident Investigation Branch (RAIB) is the UK's statutory

SIEMENS

siemens.co.uk/mobility

Evolution in motion

The next generation is here today

The Desiro family of award winning trains is joined by the next generation.

The Desiro City, the UK's first second generation platform, is state-of-the-art, energy efficient, reliable, flexible, lightweight and environmentally friendly – and it's here today.

With a focus on quality and excellence for both train operators and passengers, Siemens' trains travel over 60 million miles per year in Britain. So if you are looking for a partner you can rely on, look no further. The new Desiro City: setting the benchmark for commuter rail services in the UK.

independent body for investigating accidents and incidents occurring on railways and tramways, with operational centres in Derby and Farnborough. It is part of the DfT but functionally independent.

The RAIB's role is to investigate the causes of railway accidents and incidents where it believes this will bring safety learning to the industry; identify risks which may lead to a similar accident or make an accident worse and making recommendations to prevent reoccurrence; increasing awareness of how railway accidents happen; co-operating with other investigation organisations nationally and internationally to share and encourage good practice. Where appropriate, results of investigations are published.

RAIB is not a prosecuting body and does not apportion blame or liability.

ACTING CHIEF INSPECTOR Simon French

TRANSPORT FOCUS

Transport Focus - formerly Passenger Focus - is the independent, consumer watchdog for Britain's rail passengers, as well as England's bus, coach and tram passengers (outside London), and, since March 2015, users of England's Strategic Road Network.

It aims to make a difference for transport users and be useful to those in government and the transport industry who make major decisions about services and infrastructure, using evidence to drive change for the better.

Transport Focus is responsible for the National Rail Passenger Survey (NRPS), an Official Statistic, which is seen as the key measure of passenger satisfaction, embedded in rail franchise contracts and bonus schemes.

Key objectives for 2015-16 include strengthening the passenger voice in rail franchise replacement and monitoring; enhancing the usefulness and value for money of NRPS and other

surveys; and handling cases where rail companies and passengers are deadlocked following a complaint.

It is structured as an executive non-departmental public body. Transport Focus is sponsored and substantially funded by the Department for Transport.

CHIEF EXECUTIVE Anthony Smith

ASSOCIATION OF COMMUNITY RAIL PARTNERSHIPS

The Association of Community Rail Partnerships (ACoRP) is a federation of over 50 community rail partnerships and rail promotion groups. It is focused on practical initiatives, which add up to a better and more sustainable railway. Improved station facilities, better train services and improved integration with other forms of transport are central to the work of ACoRP and its members.

Partnerships bring together a wide range of interests along rail corridors,

and some have been instrumental in achieving spectacular increases in use of rail through innovative marketing, improved services and better station facilities.

GENERAL MANAGER Neil Buxton

DERBY & DERBYSHIRE RAIL FORUM

The Derby & Derbyshire Rail Forum (DDRF) dates from 1993 and represents over 100 businesses across the East Midlands. These employ over 25,000 people and contribute an estimated £2.6bn to the local economy. The area is reckoned to contain the largest cluster of rail companies in the world.

As well as providing a collective voice and promoting the area's rail industry, DDRF holds quarterly networking meetings and an annual conference. DDRF has dedicated local support from local authorities and industry groups.

CHAIRMAN Colin S Walton

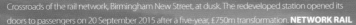

Crossroads of the rail network, Birmingham New Street, at dusk. The redeveloped station opened its doors to passengers on 20 September 2015 after a five-year, £750m transformation. **NETWORK RAIL**

THE INSTITUTION OF MECHANICAL ENGINEERS

The Railway Division of the Institution of Mechanical Engineers (IMechE) was founded in 1969. Its scope covers research, design, development, procurement, manufacture, operation, maintenance and disposal of traction, rolling stock, fixed equipment and their components within rail, rapid transit and all forms of rail-borne guided surface transport.

CHIEF EXECUTIVE Stephen Tetlow

RAILWAY CIVIL ENGINEERS ASSOCIATION

The Railway Civil Engineers Association (RCEA) was founded in 1921. An Associated Society of the Institution of Civil Engineers, its members are involved in the development, design, construction or maintenance of railway infrastructure. It exists to foster continuing professional development and the exchange of knowledge and experience.

Presentations, meetings and visits take place on current projects and issues and interests cover heavy rail, light rail and metro systems.

SECRETARY Greg James

PERMANENT WAY INSTITUTION

The Permanent Way Institution (PWI) promotes and encourages the acquisition and exchange of technical and general knowledge about the design, construction and maintenance of every type of railed track.

The PWI holds local meetings in all its geographically-based Sections, as well as arranging technical conferences and visits. Its textbooks have been the industry standard works for over half a century and members receive a widely consulted Journal.

CHIEF EXECUTIVE OFFICER David Packer

INSTITUTION OF RAILWAY SIGNAL ENGINEERS

The Institution of Railway Signal Engineers (IRSE) was formed in 1912. Its objective was and remains the advancement of the science and practice of railway signalling, telecommunications and allied disciplines. It is the professional institution for all those engaged in or interested in such matters and aims to maintain high standards of knowledge and competence within the profession. IRSE is an international organisation, active throughout the world.

CHIEF EXECUTIVE & GENERAL SECRETARY Francis How

INSTITUTION OF RAILWAY OPERATORS

The Institution of Railway Operators (IRO) exists to advance and promote the safe and reliable operation of the railways by improving the technical and general skills, knowledge and competence of all those thus engaged.

At the heart of the IRO's educational provision is its Professional Development Programme, run in conjunction with Glasgow Caledonian University. This comprises the Certificate and Diploma of Higher Education in Railway Operational Management and the Degree in Railway Operational Management, all delivered through the combination of on-line learning and direct tutorials.

Through its seven Area Councils, the IRO provides a full programme of local events and visits.

CHIEF EXECUTIVE Fiona Tordoff

INSTITUTION OF ENGINEERING AND TECHNOLOGY

The Railway Network of the Institution of Engineering and Technology (IET) covers the electrical engineering aspects of the promotion, construction,

THE PRIVATISED RAIL INDUSTRY

Until 1994, the nationalised British Railways Board (BRB) operated what became known as the vertically integrated railway. The Board itself provided the infrastructure, owned the trains and operated the services.

Under the Railways Act 1993, these and other functions were separated. The ownership of the infrastructure went to a new company, Railtrack, subsequently privatised. All operators paid Railtrack access charges for the use of the track, signalling and electrification systems.

Passenger train operations were split into what initially were 26 separate franchises. They were the subject of competitive tendering, mostly for a seven year term. Franchise awards took into account the additional services and investment commitments of each bidder, and whether that company would require a subsidy or would pay a premium to the government over the franchise term.

The passenger stations were owned by Railtrack, but all except the very largest were run by the Train Operating Companies (TOCs).

The passenger rolling stock became the property of three rolling stock companies (ROSCOs), which then leased the stock to the TOCs. The aim was to surmount the problem of relatively short franchise terms and asset lives of 30 years or more.

The freight companies were also privatised, but they owned the locomotives and any wagons which were not privately owned by customers.

Franchising was carried out by the Office of Passenger Rail Franchising (OPRAF) and various aspects of the industry including licensing were carried out by the independent Rail Regulator plus the Health & Safety Executive.

The Association of Train Operating Companies (ATOC) was created to manage passenger railway affairs such as running the National Rail Enquiry Service (NRES), Railcard schemes, and settling accounts between companies.

The last franchises were let very shortly before the 1997 General Election, which brought a change of government from Conservative to Labour. Labour said it wished to improve overall direction and planning in the industry, and created the short-lived Strategic Rail Authority (SRA). But other problems afflicted the industry, in particular the inability of some franchisees to make the financial returns they had expected, plus the level and quality of maintenance and investment by Railtrack.

Rising traffic levels and the operation of many more trains led to performance problems. These became chronic following the Hatfield derailment of 2001, caused by poor track quality. The result, according to SRA Chairman Sir Alastair Morton, was that 'the system suffered a collective nervous breakdown'. This led to huge political and media driven criticism, the downfall of Railtrack, and a strong move to centralisation.

Over time, many of the franchises, including the management buy-outs, were acquired by groups active in the bus industry. More recently, franchise ownership has extended to companies based in France, Germany, the Netherlands and Hong Kong.

The cost of the railway to the public purse rose fast, not least with the West Coast Route Modernisation. When the Rail Regulator ruled in 2003 on the level of access charges needed to fund Railtrack's successor, Network Rail, this proved too much. This became a charge funded by government, since the TOCs were protected by an indemnity clause in their contracts.

The Railways Act 2005 abolished the SRA with most of its functions transferred to an enlarged Department for Transport. Safety policy, regulatory and enforcement functions are now the responsibility of the Office of Rail and Road (ORR - formerly Office of Rail Regulation). Separately, the government set out what Network Rail was expected to deliver for the public money it receives in a High Level Output Statement (HLOS) plus a Statement of Funds Available (SoFA). The access charges review process was amended, and there was some transfer of powers and budgets to Scotland, Wales and London.

regulation, operation, safety and maintenance of railways, metros, tramways and guided transport systems. IET takes the view that transport is a system and that developments in one area will have impacts in others, also that new technology requires a long term policy goal and incentives for its use.
CHIEF EXECUTIVE & SECRETARY
Nigel Fine

CHARTERED INSTITUTE OF LOGISTICS AND TRANSPORT (UK)

The Chartered Institute of Logistics and Transport (CILT UK) is the professional body for individuals and organisations involved in all aspects of transport and logistics. It is not a lobbying organisation, aiming to provide a considered and objective response on matters of transport policy. Through a structure of forums and regional groups, it provides a network for professionals to debate issues and disseminate good practice. There is a very active Strategic Rail Policy Group and another on Light Rail & Trams.
CHIEF EXECUTIVE Kevin Richardson

YOUNG RAIL PROFESSIONALS

Young Rail Professionals (YRP) was founded in 2009 to bring together young people from across the railway industry. The YRP cover all aspects, from engineering to asset management, train operations, strategic planning, rolling stock design, maintenance, franchising, regulation and marketing.

For those starting out in their careers, Young Rail Professionals provides networking and professional development opportunities to enhance and inspire (as well as entertain) its members. The YRP also runs an ambassadors' programme, providing opportunities for its members to visit schools, colleges and universities to attract the next generation into a dynamic rail industry.

YRP has seven regions and more than 3,000 members. It is run by volunteers and delivers at least 50 events a year nationwide, thanks to the support of its corporate members.
CHAIRMAN Stephen Head

REF

The REF (Railway Engineers' Forum) is an informal liaison grouping of the railway interest sections of the professional institutions listed immediately above. As a non-political body, the REF aims to provide a common view on railway topics and a co-ordinated response to requests for professional comment. The

New track being laid at Norton Bridge using a New Track Construction machine as part of of Network Rail's £250m Stafford area improvement work. The final phase of the programme is the new rail-over-rail flyover at Norton Bridge, creating a grade separated junction for the route towards Stoke on Trent, which is due to be completed for Easter 2016. **NETWORK RAIL**

REF also organises multi-disciplinary conferences and produces a monthly resumé of professional meetings around Britain, which is available on its own website and also those of its constituent bodies.
CHAIRMAN Andrew Boagey

RAILWAY STUDY ASSOCIATION

The Railway Study Association (RSA) provides a forum for the exchange of experience, knowledge and opinion on issues relating to all aspects of the railway industry, and the part played by railways in the total transport scene. RSA members have a wide range of backgrounds and expertise, embracing operations, engineering, business planning, project management, marketing and consultancy.

The Association's calendar of events including evening lectures in London, regional meetings in Birmingham, an Annual Dinner, a Presidential address and an overseas study tour. These provide opportunities for learning, professional development and networking. The President for 2015-2016 is Karen Boswell of Hitachi Rail Europe.
CHIEF EXECUTIVE Alex Warner

NSARE

The National Skills Academy for Railway Engineering (NSARE) is responsible for developing and implementing a unified railway engineering skills strategy for the whole industry, to ensure that the training capability and capacity meets future needs. Activities include forecasting skills requirements, accreditation of training organisations, standardisation of course content, services for employers and training companies, and promoting careers in the railway industry.
CHIEF EXECUTIVE & COMPANY SECRETARY Neil Robertson

RAIL RESEARCH UK ASSOCIATION

Rail Research UK Association (RRUK-A) is a partnership between the British rail industry and UK universities. Its aims are the support and facilitation of railway research in academia; common understanding of research needs to support the rail network and its future development; identification of research, development and application opportunities in railway science and engineering; and provision of solutions to the rail industry.

The core activities of RRUK-A are funded by RSSB and Network Rail. It is managed by an executive committee comprising the two industry funders and eight elected university representatives.

RAILWAY RESEARCH IN BIRMINGHAM

The Birmingham Centre for Railway Research and Education brings together a multi-disciplinary team from across the University to tackle fundamental railway engineering problems. The team actively engages with industry, other Universities through RRUK-A, and international partners. Its mission statement refers to the provision of fundamental scientific research, knowledge transfer and education to the international railway community.

INSTITUTE OF TRANSPORT STUDIES, UNIVERSITY OF LEEDS

The Institute of Transport Studies at Leeds is the largest of the UK academic groups involved in transport teaching and research. For more than two decades, a principal interest has been the economics of rail transport. Key research topics include demand forecasting and travel behaviour, infrastructure cost modelling, efficiency analysis and pricing, project appraisal methodology, off-track and on-track competition, and transport safety. Research is sponsored by a wide variety of clients, including the Department for Transport, the European Commission and the Engineering and Physical Sciences Research Council.

THE INSTITUTE OF RAILWAY RESEARCH (IRR)

The Institute of Railway Research (IRR) within the School of Computing and Engineering at The University of Huddersfield is a world leading centre in the field of railway engineering and risk.

Its research has helped to improve the knowledge of the way in which railway vehicles interact with the track including key performance aspects such as suspension performance, wheel-rail contact, traction and braking. ■

FINANCE AND LEASING

IN ASSOCIATION WITH

Rail People
Real Expertise

Rail People
Real Expertise

As one of the UK's leading train leasing specialists, Angel Trains is passionate about financing and delivering high quality, modern assets to our customers and we are committed to providing innovative solutions to modernise and improve the UK's train fleet.

Angel Trains was created in 1994 as one of the three rolling stock companies in preparation for the privatisation of the UK rail industry. We now own and maintain over 4,300 passenger vehicles in the UK, representing around 34% of the nation's rail stock, which are leased to all 19 franchised and open access operators in the UK.

We employ around 120 professional, technical and support staff at our headquarters in Victoria, London and at a second office in Derby and have invested £3.5 billion in new rolling stock and refurbishment programmes over the last 21 years.

In August of this year, two of our existing shareholders, AMP Capital and PSP Investments, substantially increased their respective interests in Angel Trains. This has given us a strong and fully resourced platform to continue our significant investment, in both our current fleet and new trains, as we work with the government and industry to deliver rolling stock solutions that meet the needs of passengers now and in the future.

The new Class 350/4s for First TransPennine Express make up one of Angel Trains' newest fleets. No 350406 is seen in central Manchester.

WHAT WE DO

Angel Trains bridges the worlds of finance and the operational railway. We attract the necessary finance to procure, refurbish and enhance rolling stock to meet the needs of the UK's Train Operating Companies (TOCs) and ultimately to passengers of the UK railway.

Angel Trains has a track record of investing in assets central to the future of the UK rail industry, consistent with our proactive long-term approach to fleet strategy. This disciplined and focussed approach has enabled us to procure and invest in a high quality and diversified portfolio of high-speed trains, regional, and commuter passenger multiple units. We place great importance on long-term asset stewardship, so the value of the asset can be consistently delivered and optimised throughout its lifecycle, delivering value for UK rail users.

VALUE TO UK INVESTMENT

As a conduit for private sector funding into the UK railway, we have acted as an enabler for £3.5bn of investment in new trains and the modernisation of its existing rolling stock. By taking long-term investment decisions in core UK infrastructure assets, we transfer risk away from the public sector. In addition, Angel Trains also invests around £80 million per annum in the ongoing maintenance of the fleets, which is channelled through our supply chain, who range from large companies to specialist SMEs across the UK.

We are also proud that our business directly and indirectly supports more than 2,500 skilled jobs across the UK.

RAIL PEOPLE, REAL EXPERTISE

We employ a strong and committed team with extensive rail experience and trusted relationships within the industry. Angel Trains has strength in finance, engineering, commercial and customer service.

We have assets in all stages of the lifecycle and the strength of our company lies in our structured approach to the stewardship of our rolling stock from cradle to grave. Angel Trains works through the various stages in rolling stock asset life, and through its staff, provides the different skills needed throughout. The rolling stock asset life and the necessary skills that we provide are outlined below:

Specification – We have engineers who are able to write and evaluate technical and performance specifications of new rolling stock to ensure Angel Trains only invests in assets that will be desirable to lessees in the long-term.

Procurement – Our commercial and procurement experts use the specifications to negotiate competitive terms from manufacturers and maintainers.

Project Management – Our project managers take procurement contracts and ensure timely delivery of goods and services.

Performance Growth – We work with suppliers to ensure that rolling stock is not only delivered but properly commissioned to ensure that performance grows to optimum levels and continues throughout its asset life.

Fleet Management – Our engineers ensure that a detailed understanding is retained in Angel Trains and all performance issues

Southeastern Class 465/2 Networker EMU, leased from Angel Trains, next to the Shard at London Bridge.

and changes of maintenance plans are accurately documented, so that assets can transfer from one lessee to another with comprehensive knowledge databases.

Maintenance Management – Our contract managers and planners ensure that documentation is kept up to date throughout the asset life, that vehicle maintenance is carried out in a timely manner, and that maintenance is delivered to the right quality and safety levels.

Refurbishments & Enhancements – Our team of experts ensure that any planned changes to rolling stock meet either customer or owner requirements and are carried out in a professional manner with a view to maximising asset value for the longer term.

Continuous Service Operation – With detailed knowledge of our assets, we are able to consider future developments such as obsolescence,

environmental performance, and other legislative changes.

Disposal – Our procurement specialists deal with the responsible disposal of assets when the time comes.

DIVERSITY – WOMEN IN RAIL

Angel Trains is wholly committed to supporting the diversification of the rail industry's workforce and is dedicated to encouraging more women to view the UK rail sector as a long-lasting career option. Angel Trains is a proud sponsor of the Women in Rail group which was founded by Adeline Ginn, General Counsel at Angel Trains, to provide networking opportunities and support for all women in the rail industry, promoting rail as an attractive career choice and to develop strategies for engaging young people to consider a career in rail.

Angel Trains owns the Virgin Trains fleet of 56 Alstom Pendolino tilting trains.

THE FUTURE OF UK ROLLING STOCK

Angel Trains is already investing in and developing the capabilities of our fleets to meet growing passenger demands for decades to come. While we are ready for what the future holds, we understand

the need to manage costs according to customer demand. We are planning a long-term steady flow of work and innovations that incorporates new technologies to ensure Angel Trains plays its part in the transformational change in the UK railway. ▓

Eversholt Rail is to procure and finance 173 new Hitachi AT300 vehicles, worth £361m, for Great Western Railway. The bi-mode trains will run on West of England services, primarily from London Paddington to Plymouth and Penzance. **HITACHI**

Eversholt Rail Group's passenger rolling stock portfolio comprises around 3,500 passenger vehicles, of which over 3,100 are electric-powered. Eversholt Rail also owns 83 freight locomotives.

The group was acquired in April 2015 by CK Investments S.A R.L., a company jointly owned by Cheung Kong Infrastructure Holdings Limited and Cheung Kong (Holdings) Limited. It was previously owned by the Eversholt Investment Group, a consortium of STAR Capital Partners, 3i Infrastructure plc and Morgan Stanley Infrastructure Partners, which purchased the group from HSBC at the end of 2010. The transaction valued Eversholt's gross assets at approximately £2.1 billion. The Eversholt Rail Group brand replaced that of HSBC Rail in 2010. The name echoes that originally given to the business - Eversholt Leasing - when privatised.

In July 2015, Eversholt Rail signed a contract with Great Western Railway to procure and finance 173 new Hitachi AT300 vehicles, worth £361m. The fleet will comprise 22 five-car and 7 nine-car trains, and is scheduled to enter service by December 2018. The bi-mode trains will run on West of England services, primarily from London Paddington to Plymouth and Penzance. The transaction marks a further involvement with Hitachi after Eversholt's role in the funding and introduction of the Class 395 fleet for HS1.

Eversholt Rail awarded Wabtec a £60m contract to refurbish Class 321 electric multiple-units in May 2015. The Class 321 'Renatus' builds on the Class 321 Demonstrator programme that showed how a high-quality refurbishment and enhancement programme on an existing proven fleet can deliver a passenger experience comparable with a new train at a lower cost. Passenger and train operator feedback from over 15 months of intensive commuter service operation of a Class 321 Demonstrator train has been instrumental in developing and refining the scope of Renatus.

The scope of works includes new air-conditioning and heating systems; new seating throughout; larger vestibules for improved boarding and alighting; Wi-Fi enabled for passengers and operator; improved space allocation for buggies, bicycles and luggage; passenger power sockets throughout; new, energy efficient lighting; one accessible toilet and a second controlled emission toilet on each 4-car unit; complete renewal and remodelling of all interior surfaces.

Eversholt Rail committed to this investment ahead of the new East Anglia franchise being let. This phase of the contract is for the initial tranche of 30 Class 321s, with the first 10 units being delivered into service with Abellio Greater Anglia by October 2016 and the remaining 20 units being offered for service when the new East Anglia franchise starts.

The programme will be delivered from a multi-million pound dedicated new production facility in Doncaster using state of the art systems and processes.

The Class 321 Demonstrator was also been fitted with a new traction system in 2015, by Vossloh Kiepe UK Limited at Network Rail's Innovation and Development Centre, Old Dalby. The re-traction includes four new-design AC motors, new auxiliaries and new braking systems. Testing is to conclude in spring 2016. This is a further investment of £5.5m by Eversholt Rail to integrate this pre-series upgrade. The project scope includes design, production, type testing, combined testing, unit fitment, track testing and approvals.

Eversholt Rail sold its freight wagon fleet of 920 wagons and 63 containers in March 2015 to Nacco, owned by US transportation finance group CIT. The vehicles range from container flats and autoballasters to coal and aggregate hoppers and box wagons.

For the new Siemens Desiro City trains for Thameslink, Eversholt signed a long-term agreement to provide project and asset management services to Cross London Trains, the consortium providing the new fleet. Services under the 22 year agreement include project management during the build and delivery of the rolling stock, and then long-term asset management, including both technical and commercial support to Cross London Trains. With more than 16 years' experience in procurement, and through-life asset management of new rolling stock, and maintenance and enhancements of existing stock, the company believes the Cross London Trains agreement provides a significant opportunity to utilise its proven skills and expertise for the benefit of new entrants to the market.

Other current projects include upgrading and overhaul of Class 334, Class 365, Class 322, Class 321/9 and Class 318 EMUs and Class 91 locomotives. ■

SENIOR PERSONNEL
EVERSHOLT RAIL

CHIEF EXECUTIVE OFFICER
Mary Kenny
CHIEF OPERATING OFFICER
Andy Course
CHIEF FINANCIAL OFFICER
David Stickland
HEAD OF RELATIONSHIP DEVELOPMENT Stephen Timothy

porterbrook

Porterbrook is one of the three major Rolling Stock Companies (ROSCOs), and has owned and leased rolling stock and related equipment for over 20 years. The company has invested over £2.7 billion in new trains for the UK rail industry.

The business has continued to build its portfolio during 2015 with the acquisition of 116 Class-387/1 vehicles, with orders in place for a further 220 Class 387 vehicles. These builds, when delivered will, mean that since privatisation Porterbrook has procured over 2,200 passenger rolling stock vehicles, giving a portfolio of more than 4,000 passenger vehicles and over 1,400 freight locomotives and wagons in use across the UK rail network.

Beyond new rolling stock procurement, Porterbrook has continued to invest in its rolling stock, re-tractioning a significant proportion of its conventional EMU fleet and undertaking projects such as trialling a mechanical transmission as an option for its DMU vehicles going forward. These activities are intended to improve train sustainability, both from an environmental and performance perspective.

The re-tractioning works that commenced in 2015 on Porterbrook's Class 455 and Class 323 fleets are targeting a number of performance considerations. The replacement of the traction equipment on the Class 455 fleet will allow the introduction of regeneration and improved maintenance periodicities, while the Class 323 enhancement deals with both obsolescence and reliability concerns. These projects will continue into 2016, and Porterbrook will continue to look to identify further innovative enhancement opportunities for its EMU fleet that reflect customer needs and aspirations.

The mechanical transmission trial currently being undertaken on a South West Trains leased Class 158, is achieving significant fuel consumption savings which will be considered across other its diesel fleet applications.

During 2015 Porterbrook also undertook the development of a Class 144 Pacer unit to identify how this type of vehicle, and similar age Diesel Multiple Units could potentially be enhanced to meet future customers' expectations. The '144 Evolution' was modified to achieve Passengers of Reduced Mobility Technical Specification for Interoperability (PRM TSI) compliance as well as bringing some other enhancements, such as WiFi, to customers. The unit returned to service and feedback on its deployment will be utilised in the development of future Class 143 and Class 144 offers, while also providing valuable intelligence for other enhancement programmes that the company is considering. In recognition of the 2020 deadline for compliance with PRM TSI accessibility regulations, Porterbrook has embarked upon a programme of work to ensure that its fleet can continue to operate beyond this threshold. These workstreams ramped up in 2015 with Class 319, 455, 456, 150, and 156 fleets all receiving attention. Further activity is planned in 2016 and beyond in this area as other overhaul programmes commence.

Employing a team of 100 professional staff with expertise in areas of Finance, Engineering, and Asset Management Porterbrook's extensive experience and knowledge of the rail industry gives the company a strong base to deliver value for money for the services being offered.

Porterbrook recognises that over the next few years further high levels of investment are required across the UK rail industry for new train projects and on-going vehicle enhancements to support the ever increasing demands being placed on the industry. The business is well placed to support these requirements, whether it is undertaking engineering improvement work and carrying out PRM compliance modification of existing stock, or procuring new vehicles, with the commitment of the company's owners and management to maintain its position as a leading player in this market.

While developing the business, the company is also committed to supporting its people and the future of the industry. In this area the company offers an accredited graduate training scheme providing a comprehensive rail industry based training programme, which is helping bring dynamic new professionals into the UK rail industry. ▓

Porterbrook's orders for Class 387 have reached a total of 336 vehicles. This Class 387/1 train is in service on Thameslink.

HITACHI
Inspire the Next

We believe the best way to know how a train is running is to ask it.

What tells you the most about your fleet's performance? A maintenance check? A chat with the driver? A vehicle breakdown? At Angel Trains, we're investing in what we believe is a much better source of information - remote diagnostics. Using a sophisticated monitoring system, remote diagnostics gives you real time analysis via GSM/3G. It can highlight degrading components and report on how well the vehicle is running. So you can plan solutions before the train has even reached the depot.

See what the UK's biggest rolling stock asset manager can do for you.

Rail People
Real Expertise

BRITAIN'S ROLLING STOCK
WHO OWNS IT?

ROLLING STOCK ALLOCATION ON THE NATIONAL NETWORK

Three rolling stock leasing companies (ROSCOs) own 92% of the passenger rolling stock on the British main-line railway network.

The three ROSCOs were established at railway privatisation in 1994 to take over ownership of this rolling stock from the nationalised British Rail, and the ROSCOs were sold to the private sector, with their initial fleet leases in place.

The aim was for each ROSCO to have a reasonably diversified portfolio, with comparable fleets allocated to each. Larger fleets of a single type were divided, but smaller fleets were allocated to a single ROSCO. This gave each a range of customers and gave most train operating companies (TOCs) a relationship with at least two ROSCOs.

Table 1 shows how different types of passenger rolling stock

were allocated to the three ROSCOs. Approximately 38% of passenger rolling stock was allocated to Eversholt, 32% to Angel and 30% to Porterbrook. By 2009, ex-British Rail rolling stock formed approximately 60% of the passenger fleet, and by March 2015 this stock formed 52% of a fleet that had grown to 12,775 vehicles, with the rest purchased since privatisation. About 1,260 new vehicles entered service during Control Period 4 (2009-2014).

In 2009 Angel had a 36% share of the total rolling stock, Porterbrook

32% and HSBC (Eversholt) 29%: by March 2015, these figures were 34%, 31% and 27% respectively.

Details of passenger rolling stock ordered since privatisation are shown in the opening article in the Train Fleet Manufacture and Maintenance section of this publication.

With the five-digit series for individual vehicle numbers becoming overloaded, six-digit vehicle numbers have been introduced, first for the new Class 387 Electrostar electric multiple-units.

OTHER OWNERS

Another substantial lessor of rolling stock to franchised TOCs is Voyager Leasing. It was established to lease a new fleet of 'Voyager' trains to Virgin CrossCountry Trains. It is a subsidiary of the Royal Bank of Scotland Group (RBS), but ownership of the trains is equally split between Halifax (now part of Lloyds Banking group) and RBS.

Voyager Leasing originated when NatWest bank was appointed to arrange funding for the new fleet of 78 Voyager trains. The operating lease was arranged by a NatWest subsidiary,

TABLE 1 - ALLOCATION OF PASSENGER VEHICLES AT PRIVATISATION

ROSCO	DMU	EMU	HST VEHICLES*	TOTAL
Angel	1,039	2,010	531	3,580
Eversholt	0	2,864	1,366	4,230
Porterbrook	681	1,699	948	3,328
TOTAL	**1,720**	**6,573**	**2,845**	**11,138**

*Diesel High Speed Trains - power cars and coaches. *Source - Competition Commission*

Northern neighbours: trains from the TransPennine and Northern franchises pass at Huddersfield on 11 June 2015. On the left, TransPennine's Eversholt-owned Class 185 No 185108 has departed with a service for Scarborough, while (right) Northern's Angel-owned Class 142 'Pacer' No 142091 approaches the station. **PAUL BIGLAND**

Lombard Leasing Contracts Ltd, later renamed Voyager Leasing. When NatWest was acquired by RBS (at that time the parent of Angel Trains), in order to reduce RBS's exposure to Virgin Trains, the CrossCountry fleet was evenly split and half the vehicles were sold to Halifax. RBS and Halifax then entered into head lease arrangements with Voyager Leasing.

Voyager Leasing has not undertaken any other leasing business. Though it had the same parent company as Angel Trains - RBS - it remained largely separate. It contracted Angel Trains to provide technical and other support, but these arrangements ended in 2008 when Angel was sold to a consortium of investors. Most of the Voyager fleet is now leased by the new CrossCountry franchise, held by DB group company Arriva.

RBS also owns 24 Docklands Light Railway vehicles under a finance lease signed in April 2005.

QW Rail Leasing, a joint venture between Sumitomo Mitsui Banking Corporation and National Australia Bank, leases Class 378 electric multiple-units to London Overground Rail Operations Limited (LOROL) for Transport for London's London Rail Concession. It also owns the 57 additional carriages used to increase all the trains to 5-car length in 2015.

Some relatively small quantities of passenger rolling stock are owned by TOC groups, most notably First Group which owns 12 HST power cars and 42 trailer vehicles, while Arriva owns Mk3 vehicles used on Chiltern Railways' London-Birmingham and Arriva Trains Wales' north-south Wales services, with others in reserve.

Connex Leasing Limited purchased rolling stock for the Southeastern / SouthCentral franchises, which its parent group originally won. These vehicles were subsequently purchased and leased by HSBC (now Eversholt). Wiltshire Leasing was a subsidiary of Great Western Holdings, set up to finance new Class 175s for its North Western franchise and new Class 180s for Great Western. These vehicles were subsequently purchased and leased by Angel.

Six Class 43 HST power cars and 24 trailers used by Grand Central were purchased in 2010 by Angel Trains from Sovereign Trains, a ROSCO within the same group as Grand Central.

Heathrow Express trains were purchased by the airport company, including the five 5-car Class 360/2 electric multiple-units used for Heathrow Connect services.

Clean face: CrossCountry Voyagers, owned by Voyager Leasing, pass at Bristol Temple Meads on 18 August 2015. On the left, Class 221 No 221133 has its windscreen cleaned, while Class 220 No 220028 waits on the right. **PAUL BIGLAND**

FREIGHT LOCOS

The three main ROSCOs lease out large fleets of freight and general purpose locomotives, as shown in the tables. Other leasers include Beacon Rail, RBS and Macquarie European Rail.

Ex-British Rail freight locomotives were transferred to the ownership of English, Welsh & Scottish Railway (now DB Schenker) or to Freightliner at privatisation. Significant numbers of freight locomotives, some ex-British Rail, are owned by freight operating companies including Colas Rail, Mendip Rail and Direct Rail Services. In 2011, Class 66 locomotives were purchased from Eversholt Rail Leasing by GB Railfreight (4 locos) and Colas (5 locos), with five more purchased from Porterbrook by GBRf. In 2013, GBRf purchased three Class 66s from the Netherlands. After a flurry of purchases in 2014, Colas Rail's fleet grew to, three Class 47s, ten Class 56s, ten Class 60s, five Class 66s and (leased from RBS/ Lombard) ten new Class 70s; and by late 2015 Colas had nine Class 37s.

In February 2014 GB Railfreight announced it would purchase a total of 21 new Class 66 locomotives from Electro-Motive Diesel Inc (EMD), and purchase 16 Class 92 electric

Evening light: Angel-owned Class 150 No 150106 brings up the rear of an early-evening Great Western train bound for Bristol Temple Meads at Oldfield Park, east of Bath, on 18 August 2015. **PAUL BIGLAND**

locomotives from its parent company, Europorte, a subsidiary of Groupe Eurotunnel. Nine existing GBRf Class 66s were sold to and leased back from Beacon Rail. In August 2014, GBRf confirmed the purchase of a Class 59 locomotive, 'Yeoman Highlander', from German-based Heavy Haul Power International. Seven further Class 66s were ordered by GBRf in late 2014.

Several specialist companies including Harry Needle Railroad Company, Electric Traction Ltd, Europhoenix, and UK Rail Leasing also have smaller fleets of locomotives

which are hired to UK freight and passenger operators.

Alpha Trains - formerly Angel Trains International - manages a fleet of approximately 360 locomotives and 270 passenger trains in continental Europe. A subsidiary acquired 202 locomotive and passenger rolling stock assets from The Royal Bank of Scotland (RBS) at the end of 2013. The vehicles had been managed by Alpha Trains on behalf of RBS since a consortium of investors acquired Angel Trains from RBS in August 2008.

CROSS LONDON TRAINS

Cross London Trains is a consortium comprising Siemens Project Ventures GmbH, Innisfree Ltd and 3i Infrastructure Plc set up to finance and purchase Class-700 Desiro City trains from Siemens for the Thameslink rail franchise. The first was delivered in 2015.

Eversholt Rail was appointed to provide project and asset management services to Cross London Trains, including project management during the build and delivery of the rolling stock, and then long-term asset management, including both technical and commercial support.

MACQUARIE EUROPEAN RAIL

In November 2012, Macquarie Group announced that Macquarie Bank Limited had established a new business, Macquarie European Rail, and agreed to acquire the European rolling stock leasing business of Lloyds Banking Group.

The business comprises several portfolios of rolling stock, including 30 four-car Class-379 EMUs operated by Greater Anglia, and a UK rail

freight portfolio, leasing 19 Class-70s to Freightliner, 26 Class-66s to Freightliner (some of them in Poland), and 14 Class-66s to Direct Rail Services, as well as the former CB Rail business, with locomotives, passenger trains and wagons on operating lease to operators in Europe.

Lloyds was also part of the consortium that purchased Porterbrook Leasing in 2008 but it exited from the consortium in 2010. Lloyds has an interest too in Voyager Leasing.

BEACON RAIL

Beacon Rail Leasing Limited was established in January 2009 by BTMU Capital Corporation as its business entity for freight rolling stock leasing in the European market. In May 2014, Pamplona Capital Management announced the purchase of Beacon for a consideration of approximately $450 million.

Headquartered in London with offices in Boston and Rotterdam, Beacon's portfolio includes 148 locomotives, 944 freight wagons, and 20 passenger train units (owned or on order in December 2014), with leases in the UK and continental Europe.

In Britain, Beacon Rail leases ten Class 66s to Freightliner and five Class 66s to Direct Rail Services. Two Class 66s, transferred from Germany, entered service with GBRf in 2013, and a further nine GBRf Class 66s were sold to Beacon and leased back to GBRf in 2014.

Beacon Rail has worked with Direct Rail Services on the development of Vossloh Eurolight diesel locomotives for the UK: 15 of these Class 68s were ordered in January 2012 in a contract worth roughly Euro 50 million, with a further 10 ordered in September 2014, and another seven in July 2015. An order for ten electric/diesel dual-mode Class 88 locomotives from Vossloh was announced by Beacon and DRS in September 2013.

Beacon's first passenger trains were acquired in 2012 - twenty Class-313 dual-voltage electric multiple-units, retained by HSBC when it sold rolling stock company Eversholt Rail. The GTR (Southern) TOC leases 19 of the Class 313s, and Network Rail leased the 20th as a test train for European Train Control system equipment.

In July 2015, Beacon bought 17 EMD Class 66 and 10 Siemens Eurorunner ER20 diesel locomotives from Mitsui Rail Capital Europe.

CALEDONIAN RAIL LEASING

Hitachi Rail Europe and Abellio announced in March 2015 that they had signed a contract for provision and maintenance of 70 new electric multiple-unit trains for the ScotRail franchise.

The contract is financed by Caledonian Rail Leasing Ltd, a Special Purpose Vehicle created by SMBC Leasing, involving KfW IPEX-Bank of Frankfurt and RBS/Lombard. KfW IPEX-Bank's contribution amounts to £140m. The order has been placed by leasing company SMBC Leasing (UK) Ltd.

The 46 three-car and 24 four-car AT200 EMU trains are being procured for the Edinburgh-Glasgow and Stirling–Alloa/Dunblane lines and will go into service in late 2017. The contract also comprises a 10-year maintenance deal, with plans to service the trains at depots in Edinburgh.

The first seven trains are scheduled to be built in Hitachi's Kasado factory in Japan, with the remaining 63 being built in its Newton Aycliffe train manufacturing facility in the UK.

This was the first contract for Hitachi's recently launched AT200 commuter train.

CALEDONIAN SLEEPERS RAIL LEASING LTD

The fleet of 75 new Caledonian Sleeper coaches will be built and manufactured by CAF for introduction into service in April 2018.

The project is being funded with £60m from Scottish Ministers, with additional financing by Caledonian Sleepers Rail Leasing Ltd, a subsidiary of Lombard North Central plc, part of RBS. Overall the contract is valued at approximately Euro 200m for CAF.

CAF will continue to support the new fleet with a contract to supply and manage spares, while the coaches will be maintained by Alstom.

ROLLING STOCK - SIMPLIFIED GUIDE TO CLASSES

Multiple units are trains of self-propelled vehicles with driving cabs, usually comprised of one to five carriages. They can be coupled together (in 'multiple') to form longer trains. The main groups of ex- British Rail diesel multiple-unit (DMU) are:
- Class 142-144 'Pacers' - 4-wheeled bus-based trains.
- Class 150-159 'Sprinters'. Class 150 is the most basic, with Class 153 / 155 / 156 'Super Sprinters' for longer cross country services, and Class

158 / 159 Express units. Class 165 Networker Turbo and Class 166 Network Express fulfill similar roles.

Post privatisation, the main DMU designs were Class 170-172 Turbostars (and similar Class 168) built by Bombardier Transportation, and less numerous Class 175 Coradia designed by Alstom. Class 180 is an Alstom design for express services, and Class 185 a Siemens design introduced for TransPennine Express. Class 220, 221 and 222 'Voyagers' and 'Meridians', built by Bombardier, also operate InterCity services.

Electric multiple-unit (EMU) Classes 313-315, 455, 456, 465, 466, 507 and 508 are ex-British Rail inner-suburban trains; Class 317-323, 365 and 442 are outer-suburban/long-distance types.

The main post-privatisation EMUs built by Alstom are Classes 334 and 458; by Bombardier, Classes 357, 375-379, the new Class 387 and Crossrail's forthcoming Class 345; by Siemens, Classes 332, 333, 350, 380, 444 and 450, and the new Desiro City Class 700. 70 new Hitachi 'AT200' EMUs are on order for ScotRail.

The main electric locomotive designs are Class 91, built for East Coast high-speed services, designed for 140mph (225km/hr) running in semi-permanent 'InterCity225' (IC225) train formations; and Classes 86 and 90, used for both passenger and freight work.

The West Coast main line's Pendolino electric tilting trains (built by Alstom) are known as Class 390 and the Hitachi-built Southeastern high-speed EMUs using High Speed 1 are Class 395. The new Hitachi trains for the InterCity Express Programme are Classes 800 (bi-mode) and 801 (electric).

The dominant freight diesel locomotive type is the Class 66 from General Motors / Electro-Motive Diesel, designed for 75mph freight work. The Class 67 is a mixed traffic express locomotive from the same stable, and Class 57 is a rebuilt ex-British Rail freight and passenger locomotive. Class 70 is the General Electric PowerHaul design operated by Freightliner and Colas. New Vossloh diesels for DRS are Class 68, and Vossloh dual-modes for DRS are Class 88.

Class 43 is the power car (locomotive) type used at both ends of diesel 'InterCity125' High Speed Trains: the ROSCOs also own substantial numbers of IC125 and IC225 passenger vehicles. ∎

Leaning to the curve: Porterbrook's Class 158/0 No 158702 stands at Croy with the 12.48 Glasgow Queen Street to Dunblane ScotRail service on 8 April 2015. **STEWART ARMSTRONG**

THE ROSCO FLEETS

MULTIPLE-UNIT VEHICLES, HST POWER CARS, AND LOCOMOTIVES OF THE THREE MAIN ROLLING STOCK LEASING COMPANIES (ROSCOS) - LISTED BY ROSCO AND TRAIN OPERATING COMPANY

porterbrook

Class	No. of vehicles
ARRIVA TRAINS WALES	
Class 143	22
Class 150/2	72
Class 153	3
C2C RAIL	
Class 357	184
CHILTERN	
Class 168/0	20
Class 168/1	17
Class 168/2	21
Class 168/3	10
CROSSCOUNTRY	
Class 170 (2 Car)	26
Class 170 (3 Car)	48
Class 43 HST Power Car	5
EAST MIDLANDS TRAINS	
Class 43 HST power car	24
Class 153	11
Class 156	22
Class 158	18

Class	No. of vehicles
GREATER ANGLIA	
Class 153	5
Class 156	18
Class 170 (2-car)	8
Class 170 (3-car)	24
Class 90	15
GREAT WESTERN	
Class 43 HST Power Car	22
Class 57	4
Class 143	10
Class 150	34
Class 153	5
Class 158	43
GTR - SOUTHERN	
Class 171 (2-car)	20
Class 171 (4-car)	24
Class 377	834
GTR - THAMESLINK	
Class 319	244
Class 377	128
Class 387	116
LONDON MIDLAND	
Class 139	2
Class 153	8

Class	No. of vehicles
Class 170 (2-car)	34
Class 170 (3-car)	18
Class 172 (2-car)	24
Class 172 (3-car)	45
Class 319	16
Class 323	78
Class 350/2	148
NORTHERN	
Class 144	56
Class 150	22
Class 153	8
Class 155	14
Class 156	36
Class 158	24
Class 319	80
Class 323	51
SCOTRAIL	
Class 158	80
Class 170 (3-car)	150
SOUTH WEST TRAINS	
Class 158	22
Class 159	90
Class 455	364
Class 456	48
Class 458	180

Class	No. of vehicles
TRANSPENNINE	
Class 170	8
VIRGIN TRAINS EAST COAST	
Class 43 HST power car	9
FREIGHTLINER	
Class 66	35
Class 86	10
Class 90	10
NETWORK RAIL	
Class 43 HST Power Car	3
DIRECT RAIL SERVICES	
Class 57	21
GB RAILFREIGHT	
Class 66	9

Class	No of vehicles
CHILTERN	
Class 168	9

HITACHI
Inspire the Next

Ready for a new challenge?

Rail Technical Services
Technical support to the rail industry worldwide.

serco

Four unique disciplines, one first class service.

Serco Rail Technical Services (SRTS), a division of Serco Ltd are a leader in the provision of rail technical expertise, providing an extensive package of first class services to customers around the world, from four disciplines:

- Engineering
- Non-Destructive Testing and Training
- Raildata
- Strategic Asset Solutions.

Our **Engineering** team are a leading independent provider of vehicle and infrastructure test and monitoring services, specialising in bespoke instrument installations and analysis techniques. We are at the forefront of in-service overhead line monitoring for the rail industry and have considerable expertise in testing and commissioning for the introduction of new vehicle fleets. To complement our engineering services, SRTS provide component metallurgical analysis and material suitability advice and our considerable rail experience reinforces our position, as a leading, independent specialist within the industry.

Our **Non-Destructive Testing** (NDT) engineers provide the rail industry with business critical NDT production, consultancy and training services. We also offer independent bearing

failure analysis and bearing related training support, at our dedicated training facilities, or at customer sites if required.

Our **Raildata** specialists have been providing professional data management services to the UK's rail industry, its suppliers and contractors since the mid 1990's. We offer a full suite of data management services that are widely recognised as providing industry 'best practice'.

We are a leading provider of asset management services to the rail sector. Our **Strategic Asset Solutions** (SAS) team provides asset risk management services, applying proven techniques from other high integrity and safety-critical industries. We provide services for individual clients as well as collaborating in industry research projects covering a variety of areas. Through the development and application of the VTISM model, SAS also helps stakeholders understand the impact of different train designs, track maintenance and renewal strategies on whole life costs. VTISM has become an important tool for the GB rail industry, maintaining a world lead in track and wheelset deterioration modelling and whole life costing.

Ultimately we aim to help our rail customers be successful and this is achieved by drawing on our 60+ specialist rail engineering and operations staff and bringing it to bear on our customers' business challenges.

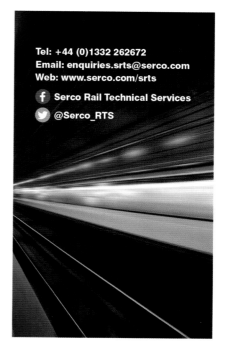

Tel: +44 (0)1332 262672
Email: enquiries.srts@serco.com
Web: www.serco.com/srts

f **Serco Rail Technical Services**
🐦 **@Serco_RTS**

All Pacer railbuses are due to disappear from the Northern franchise. Angel-owned No 142051 awaits its departure time as the 10.20 to Huddersfield at Halifax on 17 August 2015. **PAUL BIGLAND**

EAST MIDLANDS TRAINS
Class 222	143

GREATER ANGLIA
Class 321	376

GTR - GREAT NORTHERN
Class 313	132
Class 321	52
Class 365	160

GTR - SOUTHERN
Class 170	12
Class 455	184

LONDON OVERGROUND
Class 315	68

MTR CROSSRAIL
Class 315	176

NORTHERN
Class 158	20
Class 321	12
Class 322	20

SCOTRAIL
Class 170	15
Class 318	63
Class 320	66
Class 321	21
Class 334	120
Class 380	130

SOUTHEASTERN
Class 375	438
Class 376	180
Class 395	174
Class 465	388

TRANSPENNINE EXPRESS
Class 185	153

VIRGIN TRAINS EAST COAST
Class 91	31

FREIGHTLINER
Class 66	56

GB RAILFREIGHT
Class 66	27

angel Trains
Rail People
Real Expertise

Class	No of vehicles
ARRIVA TRAINS WALES	
Class 142	30
Class 153	5
Class 158	48
Class 175 (2-car)	22
Class 175 (3-car)	48
C2C RAIL	
Class 357/2	112
CHILTERN	
165/0 (2-car)	56
165/0 (3-car)	33
172	8
CROSSCOUNTRY	
Class 43 HST power car	5
EAST MIDLANDS TRAINS	
Class 153	6
Class 156	8
Class 158	32

GRAND CENTRAL
Class 180	25
Class 43 HST power car	6

GREATER ANGLIA
Class 317/5	60
Class 317/6	96
Class 317/7	4
Class 317/8	24
Class 360	84

GREAT WESTERN
Class 150	46
Class 153	9
Class 165/1 (2-car)	40
Class 165/1 (3-car)	48
Class 166	63
Class 180	25
Class 43 HST power car	86

GTR - GREAT NORTHERN
Class 317/1	48

GTR - SOUTHERN
Class 442	120

HULL TRAINS
Class 180	20

LONDON MIDLAND
Class 150	6
Class 350/1	120
Class 350/3	40

LONDON OVERGROUND
Class 172	16
Class 317/7	32
Class 317/8	24

MERSEYRAIL
Class 507	96
Class 508	81

NORTHERN
Class 142	158
Class 150	94
Class 153	11
Class 156	56
Class 158	52
Class 333	64

SCOTRAIL
Class 156	96
Class 158	14
Class 314	48

SOUTH WEST TRAINS
Class 444	225
Class 450	508

SOUTHEASTERN
Class 465/2	64
Class 465/9	136
Class 466	86

TRANSPENNINE EXPRESS
Class 350/4	40

VIRGIN TRAINS EAST COAST
Class 43 HST power car	22

VIRGIN TRAINS WEST COAST
Class 390	574

DB SCHENKER
Class 66	249
Class 67	30

HITACHI
Inspire the Next

TRAIN FLEET MAINTENANCE AND MANUFACTURE

IN ASSOCIATION WITH

RailServices offer extensive in-house expertise across a wide range of systems including train door systems.

KNORR-BREMSE
RailServices

CAPACITY

With the largest total facilities of their kind in the UK, with a combined area of some 420,000 square metres, Knorr-Bremse RailServices has the capacity to deliver solutions to train owners and operators based in the UK and Ireland.

The impressive RailServices facilities located at Springburn near Glasgow and Wolverton near Milton Keynes can deal with a wide range of Customer requirements, undertaking major "whole train" and systems refurbishment projects which improve and enhance existing rail stock.

CAPABILITY

RailServices possesses not only the capacity but also the capability to deliver support and solutions for customers. This capability is made possible by a highly skilled and experienced work force numbering over 1000 who work across the four major UK facilities. In-house expertise in engineering, project management, operations, purchasing and quality enables RailServices to respond to enquiries quickly. RailServices uses its extensive experience, gained through working across a wide range of rail vehicle maintenance services and original equipment supply projects, to offer customers proven but innovative solutions.

FLEXIBILITY

RailServices considers flexibility to be at the core of its proposition. Individual services can be demanded from the huge range available and provided to customers as and when needed or RailServices can manage the entire assets of the operator against pre-agreed targets, improving visibility and minimising lead times.

The types of service offered by RailServices include; vehicle overhaul, refurbishment, upgrade, re-livery and incident repair (on all EMUs/DMUs, coaching stock, light rail, locomotive and special vehicle types). In addition there are a wide range of flexible service types available to customers, including the overhaul, repair and refurbishment of components, passenger and freight wheel sets and bogies, gear box, transmission, rail plant and peripheral equipment.

Services offered "in-house" at either of the RailServices UK sites can also be provided at customers' own locations and facilities if required. These include a 24 hour, 364 day incident and rectification service. Following a request for assistance with incident or rectification, RailServices will visit the customer's site within 24 hours of the call and can transport and deliver the vehicle to a location as required. RailServices can also offer customers RAIB investigation quarantine berths if they are required.

Components can also be supplied to customers whether the components are overhauled, especially manufactured, re-manufactured or from the original systems manufacturer.

The extensive Knorr-Bremse Rail Group portfolio of systems and products is, of course, also available from RailServices.

ADDED VALUE

RailServices works in close partnership with customers to develop a deep understanding of their objectives. Continuous improvement through close collaboration enables RailServices to deliver improved visibility and open communications, resulting in strong working relationships and shared benefits.

RailServices can offer a wide choice of internal enhancement options, including on-board Wi-Fi connectivity, power and USB charge points, LED lighting, air conditioning, CCTV, passenger information and counting, bicycle and luggage storage and improved toilets. These options come together to provide a cost effective and service enhancing offer for passengers. The outcome is a refurbished fleet of trains with a passenger environment that has an "as new" look and feel, delivering a much improved travelling experience.

RailServices can also deliver significant added value to your project, due to extensive systems experience. The Knorr-Bremse systems portfolio includes air supply, braking systems and ancillary equipment, condition based maintenance, electrical components, electronic control and management, fire protection, HVAC, power converters, power supply, sanding, train doors (internal and external), wheel slide and wash and wipe systems.

This in-house expertise and experience results in deep understanding of how to deliver a successful system upgrade and provides the optimal solution based on customers' specific requirements. When combined with innovative new systems such as the iCOM Condition Based Maintenance system, improved in-service performance reliability is achieved which maximises asset availability and reduces costs for operators.

Significant investment in process improvements and robust, quality and customer focused Key Performance Indicators, are also delivering significant benefits to our business operations with industry leading levels of delivery performance and productivity now being achieved.

RailServices views its role as one of working together with and supporting the customer to keep their trains safe, reliable, available and importantly, in revenue earning service. It certainly has the capability and capacity to do just that. ∎

RailServices has the capacity to deliver wheelset solutions for UK based customers, with high throughputs, minimum lead times and optimised logistics.

RailServices deliver an enhanced travelling experience for passengers with an "as new" look and finish.

HITACHI
Inspire the Next

NEW TRAINS ARRIVING

PROMISES ARE STARTING TO TURN INTO HARDWARE, REPORTS **ROGER FORD**, INDUSTRY & TECHNOLOGY EDITOR OF *MODERN RAILWAYS*

For train operators and their passengers, 2016 will be the year when promises start to turn into hardware. In addition to first deliveries of long-promised new trains, major upgrades of existing fleets will be appearing on the rails.

Of the three state-procured 'mega-contracts', the first examples of both Siemens' Class-700 Desiro City EMUs for Thameslink and Hitachi's 800-Series bi-mode diesel-electric multiple units for the Great Western Railway have been delivered and are on test.

Bombardier completed the test body-shell for its Class 345 Aventra EMU for Crossrail in September 2015.

First of the 'big three' to enter revenue earning service will be the Thameslink sets, due to appear on the route during the first half of this year. Delivery of the 1,140 vehicles in 8 and 12 car formations will continue,

with Great Northern receiving its first trains in 2017. The full fleet will be available for the new 24 trains/hr Thameslink service with the December 2018 timetable.

As with the Bombardier Aventra stock for Crossrail, the Desiro City is optimised for the metro-style service through the central core. This has meant compromises when it comes to provision for the long-distance commuter duties outside London to Brighton, Bedford, Peterborough and Cambridge.

When the Department for Transport ordered the Class 700 fleet, the specification did not include Wi-Fi, seat-back tables or at-seat power sockets in Standard class. In February 2015 DfT announced that £50 million would be made available to install Wi-Fi on rolling stock operated by Govia Thameslink Railway plus three other franchises.

While installing Wi-Fi on the Class 700 units would not be an issue, power sockets would involve what Siemens terms a 'significant' weight gain. As we went to press, the practicality of adding seat back tables was also being discussed.

For the other two fleets, May 2017 is the critical date. Under the Intercity Express Programme (IEP), the Hitachi-led Agility Trains consortium

is due to supply 866 vehicles to Great Western Railway (GWR) and Virgin Trains East Coast (VTEC) under separate contracts.

This total train service provision deal is based on payment per diagram. If a train is unavailable and a service is cancelled, there is no payment. Responsible for the contracts are two subsidiaries, Agility Trains West (ATW) and Agility Trains East (ATE).

TABLE 1: CROSSRAIL SERVICE INTRODUCTION

STAGE	SERVICE INTRODUCTION	DATE
1a	Test rolling stock. Liverpool St- Shenfield	From Dec 2016
1b	Passenger service starts Liverpool St-Shenfield	May 2017
2	Paddington-Heathrow	May 2018
3	Paddington (Crossrail)-Abbey Wood	December 2018
4	Paddington (Crossrail) -Abbey Wood & Shenfield	May 2019
5	Maidenhead & Heathrow - Abbey Wood & Shenfield	December 2019

The Docklands Light Railway has been considering a new generation of rolling stock to meet the continuing growth in passenger demand. Class 'B90' vehicles, such as No 23 seen here at Canary Wharf, are likely to be replaced. **DLR**

First to enter service will be the ATW units for GWR, based at a new depot at Stoke Gifford Bristol and Old Oak Common. Currently being delivered are 36 five car bi-mode diesel-electric multiple units which are scheduled to enter service with the May 2017 GWR timetable.

It was intended that 21 nine-car EMUs for the London-Bristol-Cardiff-Swansea services would follow in the first half of 2018. However, because of the delay to the GWML electrification, DfT is considering changing the contract so that these trains will also be delivered as bi-modes.

Delay to electrification also means that the planned 2017 timetable will have to be diesel operated. With the reduced power of the Class 800 units under diesel power, an interim timetable, without the planned journey time reductions, may have to be introduced.

Also in May 2017, Crossrail runs its first passenger service with Class 345 between Liverpool Street and Shenfield. This route was taken over from the Greater Anglia franchise by Crossrail last year and will be used for testing the new trains before trial services start.

MORE ORDERS

As predicted in last year's overview, the change in franchising procurement to include a value on quality improvements continues to encourage rolling stock investment.

TABLE 2: ROLLING STOCK ORDERS AND PROSPECTS

FLEET	CLASS NO	TYPE	QUANTITY (VEHICLES)	FORMATION	MANUFACTURER	FUNDER	STATUS (NOV 2015)
IEP (GWML)	800/801	AT300 EMU/bi-mode	369	(note 1)	Hitachi	Agility Trains West	Delivering
IEP (ECML)	800/801	AT300 EMU/bi-mode	497	(note 2)	Hitachi	Agility Trains East	Ordered
Great Western Rly	802	AT300 Bi-mode (note 3)	173	5 car and 7 car	Hitachi	Eversholt Rail	Ordered
Thameslink	700	Desiro City EMU	1140	8 & 12 car	Siemens	Cross London Trains	Delivering
Crossrail	345	EMU	594	9 car	Bombardier	DfT/TfL	Ordered
Govia Thameslink (note 4)	387/1	EMU	116	4 car	Bombardier	Porterbrook	Delivered
GWR	387	Electrostar EMU	32	4 car	Bombardier	Porterbrook	Ordered
LOROL (note 5)	378	Electrostar EMU	57		Bombardier		Delivered
GTR (Gatwick Express)	387/2	EMU	108	4 car	Bombardier	Porterbrook	Delivering
SWT (HLOS build)	707	Desiro City EMU	150	5 car	Siemens	Angel Trains	ordered
Caledonian Sleeper		Sleepers	75		CAF	Lombard	Ordered
ScotRail	AT200	EMU	234	3 & 4 car	Hitachi	Caledonian Rail Leasing (6)	Ordered
ScotRail	AT200	EMU	30	3 car	Hitachi		Option (note 7)
LOROL (note 8)	Aventra	Aventra EMU	180	4 car	Bombardier	TfL	Ordered
Porterbrook (note 16)	387	Electrostar EMU	80		Bombardier	Porterbrook	Ordered
TOTAL (incl. options)			**3835**				
ORDERS PENDING							
GTR (Class 313 replacement)		EMU	150	6 car	Bombardier/Siemens/CAF		Bidding
Merseyrail (note 9)		EMU	150	3 car			OJEU issued
Merseyrail (note 10)		EMU	180	3 car			OJEU issued
LU Northern Line (note 11)		Tube Stock	30	6 car		TfL	OJEU issued
LU Northern Line (note 12)		Tube Stock	270	6 car		TfL	OJEU issued
LU Jubilee Line (notes 13, 14)		Tube Stock	126	7 car		TfL	OJEU issued
TOTAL (main line, incl options)			**4315**				
STATED REQUIREMENTS							
Essex Thameside capacity		EMU	68	4 car			Franchise commitment
Northern Pacer replacement		DMU	120				Franchise requirement
MAXIMUM TOTAL			**4503**				
PROVISIONAL							
First Group (ECML)	AT300	EMU	25	5 car			
Alliance Rail open access ECML	390	EMU	108	9 car			
Alliance Rail open access GWML	390	EMU	24	6 car			
East Anglia Franchise (note 15)		EMU	210				
Hull Trains open access (note 17)	AT300	Bi-mode	25	5 car	Hitachi		
POSTPONED							
Trans Pennine Express electrification		EMU	150	5 car			
Midland Main Line electrification		EMU	175	5 car			

1 56 x 5 car bi-mode: 21 x 9 car EMU

2 12 x 5 car EMU: 30 x 9car EMU: 10 x 5 car bi-mode

3 For West of England IC125 replacement.

4 110mph dual-voltage, for Thameslink pending new fleet

5 Lengthening existing fleet to 5-car

6 SMBC Leasing:KfW IPEX Bank:RBS/Lombard

7 Subject to three year franchise extension option

8 Greater Anglia Inner suburban, Gospel Oak-Barking, Euston-Watford

9 Max train length 60 metres

10 Option for up to 60 units to support possible extension of network

11 Firm requirement

12 Total of potential options

13 Could include retractioning of exisiting fleet

14 Option

15 Intercity spec for 'Norwich in 90'

16 Customers to be confirmed

17 Dependent on track access extension

HITACHI
Inspire the Next

ScotRail has ordered 234 EMU vehicles from Hitachi in a mixture of three and four car units. The first are for the Edinburgh-Glasgow electrification programme routes which will see the debut of Hitachi's new AT200 outer-suburban EMU for the UK.

In England, the new Thameslink Southern & Great Northern franchise, won by Govia Thameslink Railway, includes a commitment to replace the Class 313 dual-voltage EMU fleet which operates services through the tunnel section into Moorgate. Similarly the replacement Essex Thameside franchise, better known as c2c, includes a growth build of 17 four car units.

REPEAT ORDERS

Significantly, DfT also authorised mew rolling stock in the First Great Western Direct Award franchise extension. The IEP deal does not include West of England services and a decision was needed on whether to upgrade and life extend the existing IC125 fleet or go for new build.

In July 2015 FGW (subsequently re-branded as Great Western Railway) received DfT approval to acquire 29 IEP bi-mode derivatives in five and seven car formations. Designated AT300, this is Hitachi's commercial version of the IEP, priced at just over £2 million per vehicle.

This order highlighted Hitachi's conservative approach to engine rating with the IEP bi-mode units. The nominal maximum power from the MTU engine is 700kW (940hp) but in IEP this is reduced to 560kW (750hp), reflecting the penalties for unreliability in the IEP availability-based IEP contracts.

At this rating IEP would be unable to keep to time over the West of

The 'Norwich in 90min' aspiration could result in a new fleet of inter-city electric multiple units, replacing the current loco hauled trains. Abellio Greater Anglia's Class No 90001 at Crown Point depot, Norwich. **TONY MILES**

England gradients. As a result, the engines in the GWR AT300 will run at the full output. Fuel tanks will also be larger to provide the necessary range.

With Hitachi's Newton Aycliffe assembly plant fully occupied with IEP and the ScotRail AT200 order, the AT300s will be assembled in Japan, although retaining equipment supplied by European sub-contractors for IEP.

Meanwhile, following Siemens' order from South West Trains for a repeat of the Thameslink Desiro City design, reported last year, Bombardier has received the first order for its standard UK EMU.

In competitive procurement against Hitachi and CAF of Spain, Bombardier's Aventra won the £260 million contract for 45 EMUs for service on the Liverpool Street to Enfield Town, Cheshunt and Chingford routes and between Romford and Upminster, which became part of the TfL network in May 2015. The contract will also provide sets when electrification of the Gospel Oak-Barking line is commissioned.

Bombardier is also to build a final order of 20 more Class 387 Electrostars, an order announced by Porterbrook in November 2016. It said a number of parties had expressed an interest in leasing them, notably Rail for London but also established operators and prospective bidders of upcoming franchises.

UPGRADES

Meanwhile, facing competition from new build, the Rolling Stock Companies are seeking to protect their existing assets with increasingly ambitious upgrades to the ex-British Rail EMU fleets which continue to form the basis of many commuter services.

South West Trains is replacing the existing electro-mechanically controlled traction packages fitted to the Class 455 inner suburban EMU fleet with modern three-phase drives from Vossloh Kiepe. Following acceptance testing with two pre-series conversions, series production starts at Eastleigh works in January and will run until October 2016.

This timescale is critical, because SWT is due to receive the first

TABLE 3: PASSENGER TRAIN ORDERS 2007-13

OPERATOR / FINANCIER	CLASS	VEHICLES	MANUFACTURER	DELIVERED
London Midland / Porterbrook	350/2	148	Siemens	2009
Southern / Porterbrook	377/5	92	Bombardier	2009
Southeastern (HS1) / Eversholt	395	174	Hitachi	2009
London Overground / QW	378	228	Bombardier	2011
London Overground / Angel	172/0 DMU	16	Bombardier	2010
ScotRail / Eversholt	380	130	Siemens	2010
London Midland / Porterbrook	139*	2	Parry People Movers	2008
Virgin West Coast / Angel	390	106	Alstom	2012
Greater Anglia / Lloyds	379	120	Bombardier	2011
London Midland / Porterbrook	172/2 and /3 DMU	69	Bombardier	2011
Chiltern / Angel	172/1 DMU	8	Bombardier	2011
Southern / Porterbrook	377/6	130	Bombardier	2013
Southern / Porterbrook	377/7	40	Bombardier	2014
London Midland / Angel	350/3	40	Siemens	2014
TransPennine / Angel	350/4	40	Siemens	2014

*LPG/flywheel hybrid drive railcars.

All are electric multiple-units except where shown (DMU - diesel multiple-unit)

HITACHI
Inspire the Next

CLASS 321 'RENATUS' SPECIFICATION

New air-conditioning and heating systems

New seating throughout

Larger vestibules for improved boarding and alighting

Wi-Fi enabled for passengers and operator

Improved space allocation for buggies, bicycles and luggage

Passenger power sockets throughout

New, energy efficient lighting

One PRM-TSI compliant accessible toilet plus a second controlled emission toilet on each unit

Complete renewal and remodelling of all interior surfaces

Siemens Class 707 in December 2016. The converted Class 455 fleet will require less maintenance, releasing capacity at Wimbledon depot and allowing the new Class 707 fleet to be maintained within the existing facilities.

Another example of the impact of competition is the decision by Eversholt Rail to upgrade 10 of Abellio Greater Anglia's Class 321 EMUs to the 'Renatus' specification by the end of the current 'short' franchise in October 2016. These vehicles are part of a £60m modernisation programme which will see Wabtec Rail upgrade 30 of the four-car units.

Wabtec Rail is investing in a multi-million pound new production facility at its Doncaster works dedicated to the Class 321 programme. The first unit is scheduled to return to early this year

Eversholt Rail has committed to this investment ahead of the new East Anglia franchise being let. While Abellio Greater Anglia will have the first 10 units in service by October 2016, the remaining 20 units in the programme are being offered to the bidders for the replacement franchise.

Meanwhile, under a £5.5m contract, Eversholt's Class 321 Renatus demonstrator has been fitted with a new traction package by Vossloh Kiepe UK at Network Rail's Rail Innovation and Development Centre at Old Dalby. As with the Class 455 re-traction programme, Vossloh Kiepe will provide new inverters supplying AC traction motors in the existing bogies. New auxiliaries and regenerative braking will also be fitted. Testing is currently under way.

PRESSURE

In London, rolling stock manufacturers are warning of a potential 'bidding overload' as projects slip back, notably the Invitation to Tender for the Jubilee and Northern Line additional trains originally due to have been issued in 'early 2015', but deferred until the end of the year.

Bidding for the New Tube for London (NTfL) train fleet has also been deferred as a result of the delay to the Sub Surface Lines resignalling programme. Originally planned for 'early 2015' the invitation to tender was expected to be issued early in 2016.

In May 2015, TfL subsidiary DLR Ltd opened discussions with manufacturing industry on a new generation of rolling stock to meet the continuing growth in passenger demand. To provide maximum capacity the DLR interior design is likely to follow that for NTfL. As a result NTfL and the DLR fleet procurement exercises are now likely to run in parallel.

Other major LU rolling stock contracts in the same timeframe include the proposed Central Line re-tractioning and the Jubilee Line mid-life overhaul.

Overall, the rolling stock market, both for new build and for life extension and upgrades, faces a busy 2016, with assured demand for the next three years. And that is before work to modify the 5,000-vehicle-strong ex-BR fleets for PRM-TSI accessibility compliance for operation beyond the January 2020 deadline, and the start of European Train Control System fitment is taken into account. ∎

TABLE 4: PASSENGER TRAIN ORDERS FROM PRIVATISATION (1994) TO 2007

ORIGINAL CUSTOMER	MANUFACTURER	TYPE	NO OF VEHICLES	DELIVERY	FUNDER
Anglia Railways	Bombardier	Class 170 DMUs	32	2000	P
Arriva Tr Nthn	Siemens/CAF	16x4-car Class 333 EMUs	64	2000-04	A
c2c	Bombardier	74x4-car Electrostar EMUs	296	1999-2001	P,A
Central Trains[a]	Bombardier	23x2-car, 10x3-car Class 170 DMUs	76	2000-04	P
Central/Silverlink	Siemens	30x4-car Class 350/1 (West Coast route)	120	2004-05	A
Chiltern Railways	Bombardier	Class 168 DMUs	67	1998-2005	P, H
Connex (Southeastern)	Bombardier	Electrostar EMUs	618	2000-05	H
Connex / Southern	Bombardier	28x3-car, 154x4-car Electrostar EMUs	700	2002-05	P
First N Western	Alstom	16x3-car, 11x2-car Class 175 DMUs	70	2000	A
Gatwick Express	Alstom	8x8-car Juniper EMUs	64	1999	P
First Great Eastern	Siemens	21x4-car Desiro EMUs	84	2002	A
First Great Western	Alstom	14x5-car Class 180 DMUs	70	2000-01	A
Heathrow Connect	Siemens	5x5-car Class 360/2 EMUs	25	2005-06	T
Heathrow Express	CAF/Siemens	9x4-car, 5x5-car EMUs	61	1998-2002	T
Hull Trains	Bombardier	4x3-car Class 170 DMUs	12	2004	P
Hull Trains	Bombardier	4x4-car Class 222 DMUs	28	2005	H
Midland Mainline	Bombardier	17x2-car, 10x1-car Class 170 DMUs	44	2000-04	P
Midland Mainline	Bombardier	16x4-car, 7x9-car Class 222 DEMUs	127	2004-05	H
ScotRail	Alstom	40x3-car Class 334 Juniper EMUs	120	1999-2000	H
ScotRail	Bombardier	55x3-carClass 170 Turbostar DMUs	165	1999-2005	P, H
Southern	Bombardier	Class 170 DMUs	42	2003-04	P
South West Trains	Siemens	127 x 4-car Class 450 Desiro EMUs	508	2002-07	A
South West Trains	Bombardier	9x2-car Class 170 DMUs	18	2000-02	A
South West Trains	Siemens	45x5-car Class 444 Desiro EMUs	225	2002-05	A
TransPennine	Siemens	51x3-car Class 185 Desiro DMUs	153	2005-06	H
Virgin CrossCountry	Bombardier	40x5-car, 4x4-car tilting DEMUs	216	2001-03	V
Virgin CrossCountry	Bombardier	34x4-car non-tilting DEMUs	136	2000-02	V
Virgin West Coast	Alstom	53x9-car Pendolino trains	477	2001-05	A

[a] Plus 1x2-car and 2x3-car originally ordered by Porterbrook for spot hire

V Halifax Bank of Scotland and Royal Bank of Scotland.

T Owned by Heathrow Express.

A Angel Trains

P Porterbrook

H HSBC Rail (Eversholt)

Hitachi will deliver 110 Class 800/801 trains from its new Rail Vehicle Manufacturing Facility in Newton Aycliffe.

HITACHI
BRINGING RAIL MANUFACTURING BACK TO ITS BRITISH BIRTHPLACE

Hitachi Rail Europe (HRE) has enjoyed an incredibly busy 2015, signing new contracts across its rolling stock and traffic management businesses, beginning testing of its InterCity Express trains, launching its concept for the British Bullet Train, and opening a state-of-the-art rail vehicle manufacturing facility in Newton Aycliffe, which marks the start of a new era in building world-leading trains here in the UK. This is alongside continuing to deliver exceptional performance for the Class 395 'Javelin' fleet which has dramatically reduced journey times between London and Kent since its introduction in 2009. With everything Hitachi does, the company continues to be guided by its customers, developing innovative technological solutions which exceed expectations, unlock new opportunities and positively contribute to society.

In November 2014, Hitachi unveiled the first pre-series Class 800/801 train for the Department for Transport's £5.7bn InterCity Express Programme (IEP) at Hitachi Rail's manufacturing facility in Kasado, Japan. In March 2015, this first pre-series Class 800/801 train was greeted upon arrival at the Port of Southampton by Rail Minister Claire Perry, Japan's Ambassador to the UK and partners at Great Western Railway and Virgin Trains East Coast. The arrival of this train was a double celebration of the excellence of Hitachi's British and Japanese engineers as well as the precursor to a new era of train travel in the UK.

Whilst the arrival of the first pre-series train marked a new beginning for the InterCity Express Programme, 3 September heralded the launch of Hitachi Rail Europe's manufacturing in the UK. On this day, the Prime Minister opened Hitachi's £82m Rail Vehicle Manufacturing Facility in Newton Aycliffe, alongside VIPs including the Chancellor of the Exchequer, Transport Secretary, Rail Minister, Japanese Ambassador, senior representatives of the North East and the rail industry. Together with around 670 guests, Hitachi celebrated the return of rail manufacturing to its British home in the North East.

Hitachi Rail Europe will deliver 110 of the 122 Class 800/801 trains from this facility, which will serve the Great Western and East Coast main lines. These trains will enter passenger service in 2017 and 2018 respectively. The IEP trains represent a step-change in travel for fare-paying customers, who will enjoy more comfortable, reliable and faster travel. They provide generous legroom, improved Wi-Fi access and, as well as delivering environmental benefits, will reduce wear and tear on the country's rail infrastructure.

To enable world-class maintenance and service delivery for the IEP trains for 27.5 years, Hitachi has invested in the new-build, upgrade and refurbishment of a network of train maintenance centres across the UK, from Scotland to the West Country. The extensive work being undertaken nationwide reached a milestone of its

Vision for High Speed - Hitachi has developed a conceptual train interior for which the central focus is user experience.

HITACHI
Inspire the Next

own in January, with a 'topping out' ceremony to mark the completion of the external frame of the train maintenance building at Stoke Gifford, near Bristol. This important work continues at a number of sites across the country (see maintenance map). Hitachi's Ashford Train Maintenance Centre, which supports the Class 395 'Javelin' trains, has set the highest standards for maintenance and service delivery, and the IEP centres will see advanced engineering and systems rolled out across the UK.

Newton Aycliffe will also be the home of production for the 70 AT200 EMU commuter trains that Hitachi Rail Europe is manufacturing for the Abellio ScotRail franchise. From 2017, these trains will run between Edinburgh and Glasgow, and Stirling, Alloa and Dunblane. Also in 2015, Hitachi Rail Europe signed new contracts to deliver new intercity trains for the South West of England and an innovative Traffic Management System to drive capacity efficiencies for Thameslink in the London Bridge area.

VISION FOR HIGH SPEED

With long term planning and investment at the heart of its vision for the future of rail, Hitachi Rail Europe showcased the value it places on innovation with the global launch of its Vision for High Speed at the 2015 Railtex. The vision encompasses Hitachi's expertise in delivering rolling stock for HS1 and the iconic Shinkansen trains in Japan. Following extensive user research and passenger studies, Hitachi has developed a conceptual train interior for which the central focus is user experience.

The design draws upon key influences from existing and influential rolling stock in the UK and looks forward to address the needs of future passengers, providing a train that has the flexibility to grow and evolve with society. Design influences have been extended beyond rail to also examine the automotive and aeronautical industries, creating a balance between comfort, speed, efficiency and aesthetics. Hitachi is aiming to deliver a new future for rail in the UK with a total digital railway system, making the customer's journey seamless, door to door, from buying the ticket to boarding the train and staying updated throughout the journey.

Hitachi Rail Europe's long-term investment in its supply chain and people lies at the heart of its long-term commitment to the UK. Hitachi held two recruitment fairs in February, which saw 2,000 tickets

HITACHI TRAIN MAINTENANCE CENTRES

sell out in a few short hours. Visitors had the opportunity to find out what it means to work for Hitachi Rail Europe, the company's cultural values and also to learn about the wide range of roles the company will be recruiting in the North East, ranging from procurement to advanced manufacturing, quality assurance and human resources.

The industry has recognised the commitment that Hitachi Rail

Europe is making to the UK. Against a backdrop of European expansion, it has won several accolades demonstrating the breadth of its offer. These include the Human Factors and Ergonomics Society 2015 Stanley Caplan award, heralding inclusive design innovation for the Class 800/801 interiors for the InterCity Express Programme, the RailStaff Awards Depot Team of the Year for the Ashford Train

Maintenance Centre, and the National Rail Awards Outstanding Personal Contribution in Rail for Managing Director Karen Boswell.

Hitachi Rail Europe looks forward to building on these achievements and showcasing its commitment to the UK rail manufacturing in 2016 by collaborating with industry and the government to deliver the best rail services and experience for fare paying customers. ▪

SIEMENS IN THE UK

Over the past 170 years, Siemens has established itself as a leader in sustainable and innovative development within the UK rail industry. Today, the company employs approximately 14,000 people across 13 factories around the UK. It supplies products and equipment for multiple and varied projects across the country such as the London Thameslink Programme which has included the construction of two depots at Three Bridges and Hornsey, the upgrades on the London Underground (New Tube for London) and a National Training Academy for Rail (NTAR) in Northampton. In addition, Siemens continues to manufacture and maintain world-class trains operating in and around London, including the new Eurostar fleet.

NATIONAL TRAINING ACADEMY FOR RAIL (NTAR)

It is estimated that an additional 4,000 rail engineers are needed over the next five years to develop and

The National Training Academy for Rail opened to the first intake of students in October 2015.

maintain advancements in the UK rail industry. It is with a view to nurturing the development of the engineering talent pool and securing the UK's capacity for future rail expansions that Siemens runs extensive, high quality training programmes. The National Training Academy for Rail (NTAR) is just one of a number of Siemens' training initiatives alongside the 'Trailblazer'

apprenticeship programme, The Curiosity Project - which aims to reach 5 million children by 2016 - and Inspire Engineering.

NTAR is a joint project between Siemens, the National Skills Academy for Railway Engineering (NSARE), the Department for Business Innovation and Skills (BIS) and the Department for Transport (DfT). The Academy, which

opened to the first intake of students in October 2015, offers 20,000 man days of training per year and will act as a central national 'hub' supplemented with regional facilities around the country with a view to bridging the skills gap emerging in the UK rail industry.

In addition to providing 50% of the funds for the innovative project, Siemens provides valuable industry experience in terms of the nature and depth of the training courses. The flagship traction and rolling stock training centre combines state-of-the-art facilities with elements of both practical and classroom-based teaching to ensure that the highest standard of training is available to students from across the rail industry. Training is aimed at all levels within the UK rail industry, from apprenticeships to the upskilling of existing employees, focusing on evolving a number of areas such as 'fly-by-wire' electronic controls.

'NTAR's aim is to collaborate very strongly to encourage training

The new Eurostar e320 trains are entering commercial service.

Aerial view of the new Three Bridges depot for the Class 700 Thameslink trains.

market expertise and contributions from different suppliers' says Simon Rennie, General Manager of NTAR. 'Our goal is to bring the best knowledge together in one community – offering them a fabulous facility for optimal learning

that adopts and reinforces NSARE's accreditation and skills recording, ensuring professional excellence and a return on their training investment.'

THAMESLINK PROGRAMME

The Government-sponsored Thameslink Programme aims to provide a comprehensive overhaul of transport links and improve reliability on north-south travel throughout London. In 2013, Siemens plc, alongside Cross London Trains (XLT), was awarded the contract for supply of 115 Class-700 Desiro City trains to be used along the routes.

The Thameslink fleet will comprise 55 12-carriage and 60 8-carriage vehicles, totalling 1,140 carriages. Such an expansion will increase capacity along the route allowing for up to 1,754 and 1,146 passengers on the 12- and 8-carriage trains respectively. These state-of-the-art trains will first begin operation in 2016 on the Bedford to Brighton Line and will then gradually be rolled out across both the Thameslink and Great Northern (London to Peterborough/Cambridge) routes by 2018.

The Class 700 Desiro City continues the tradition of state-of-the-art trains and cutting-edge technology from Siemens, being approximately 25% lighter and 50% more energy efficient than previous generations. These trains will be faster and more spacious than previous generations offering a greater number of seats, improved access for people with reduced mobility and increased luggage space – ensuring a significantly

A new Class 700 Desiro City train for Thameslink, seen at the new Three Bridges depot.

improved travel experience for passengers. The addition of CO_2 sensors for automatic temperature regulation, real time updates and travel information as well as leading-edge driver control will help increase reliability across the line. An increase from 16 to 24 trains per hour in each direction at peak times will provide a London Tube-like service and greatly improve efficiency.

As part of the Thameslink contract, Siemens has built two new state-of-the-art depots at Three Bridges and Hornsey to house and maintain the new fleet. The depots include top of the range equipment such as an automatic inspection facility which will allow for timely and efficient train maintenance. A full cab simulator will also provide all drivers with the specialist training for the new trains. The Three Bridges depot is complete and already home to two of the new

trains, the facility in Hornsey is due for completion in early 2016.

EUROSTAR E320

To wrap up a stellar year for Siemens, the end of 2015 sees the introduction of the Eurostar e320 train into commercial service.

The world-class reputation of the Eurostar fleet will be bolstered by the introduction of the improved trains, which are a fourth generation train of the Siemens Velaro family. In order to ensure continued excellence and smooth journeys between the UK and continental Europe, these trains will be able to travel up to 200mph or 320 km/hr, 20km/hr faster than the current fleet. The e320 will also increase passenger capacity per train by 20% and passengers will benefit from a beautifully re-crafted interior that makes passenger comfort a priority. ■

CAF CONTINUES TO WIN NEW ORDERS IN THE UK

CAF- Construcciones y Auxiliar de Ferrocarriles, S.A. - has secured a number of further new orders in the highly competitive UK market. CAF is currently developing the new trains for the Caledonian Sleeper service linking Fort William, Aberdeen, Edinburgh and Glasgow to London via the West Coast main line.

These units comprise 5 types of cars arranged in up to 16-car trains. Specifically, the new fleet features First and Standard Class Cars, Lounge Car and Sleeper Cars. Significant improvements include en-suite berths, Pod Flatbeds used for the first time in rail, and a brasserie-style Club Car. In addition, these new cars feature passenger accessibility enhancements. The new fleet, representing an investment of over £100m, is expected to be introduced by the summer of 2018.

Additionally, CAF are undertaking the Enterprise Refurbishment Project in partnership with NI Railways and Irish Rail. The project includes the refurbishment and upgrade of the Enterprise fleet operating between Belfast and Dublin. The work involves interior and exterior overhaul of 28 coaches, 4 generator vans and 6

CAF has successfully delivered 20 Class-4000 trains that operate alongside 23 Class 3000 trains for Translink / Northern Ireland Railways.

locomotives which go together to make up 4 fully formed train rakes. CAF's scope of work includes the installation and integration of a modern Train Control and Monitoring System (TCMS), Seat Reservation System (SRS) and the replacement of the existing Passenger Information System (PIS) as well as material supply and technical support.

CAF is widely known for its role in the provision of the iconic Heathrow Express fleet operating between Heathrow Airport and Central London. Elsewhere in the UK, CAF has

successfully delivered 20 Class-4000 trains that operate alongside 23 Class 3000 trains for Translink / Northern Ireland Railways, as well as Urbos trams to Birmingham and Edinburgh. Additionally, Class 333s operate in Northern England - they are almost identical to the Heathrow Express trains but with a modified interior layout.

Iarnród Éireann also uses Mark 4 carriages built by CAF. These seven eight-car trainsets were built with 422 seats in each. They operate between Dublin and Cork with a Driving Van

Trailer and are capable of achieving speeds of up to 125mph.

As a result of its commitment to R&D, and long-standing experience, CAF has developed the OARIS solution, a family of very high-speed trains capable of reaching 350km/h. Designed with exceedingly reliable in-house technology, this family of trains features the ultimate in design, accessibility, safety and comfort.

Its highlights are:

- Flexible interior layout, to vary the seating capacity and services according to requirements.

CAF Urbos 3 trams at Midland Metro's Wednesbury depot. **CENTRO/CAF**

HITACHI
Inspire the Next

- Variable configuration with 4, 6 and 8 car solutions.
- Multivoltage current collection (1.5 and 3kV DC, 15 and 25kV AC).
- Multi-signalling options.
- Cross-border interoperability.
- High reliability, and low operating and maintenance costs.
- Gauge change option: 1,435-1.688mm.
- Complete user accessibility from different platform levels.

CAF continues to expand its business through both acquisition and organic growth with the turnover of Euro 1.4 billion and a backlog of Euro 5.3 billion. Currently employing over 8000 people in the design, manufacture and maintenance of subsystems for the global rail market, CAF has major production facilities in Spain, Brazil, Mexico, France and USA.

Reflecting its growing involvement in the after-sales market, CAF has maintenance operations throughout Spain, in major cities including Madrid, Barcelona, Bilbao and Sevilla. Other major global maintenance operations are based in Belfast, Auckland, Mexico City, Sao Paulo, Buenos Aires and Lisbon. In total CAF operates out of more than 40 maintenance locations.

A snapshot of other recent orders includes: 35 x 8 car EMUs for CPTM in Sao Paulo, Brazil; 3 x 5 car trams for the city of Cagliari in Italy, with option for a further 6 trams; 12 x 7

A CAF Edinburgh Tram calls at Edinburgh Park. **TONY MILES**

car trams for the city of Freiburg in Germany; 20 x 4 driverless metro trains for Helsinki, Finland; a turnkey project to build the first phase of the circular light metro line for the city of Kaohsiung in Taiwan utilising CAF's unique 'ACR' (catenary free) technology; Oslo Airport Link trains using the OARIS platform; 118 EMU trains for the Netherlands; trams for Luxembourg, Saint Etienne and Utrecht.

However, CAF doesn't just deliver trains. For example, CAF delivered Line 1 of the Suburban Railway which links the city of Mexico with

CAF has supplied new Urbos trams to Budapest, Hungary which at 56 metres are the longest trams in the world.

four neighbouring regions, supplying not only new trains, but 27km of new railway, including stations, bridges, signalling and electrification.

CAF has supplied new Urbos trams to Budapest, Hungary which at 56 metres are the longest trams in the world. ■

NEW BUILD LOCOS
FOR THE UK

The first of the second batch of Stadler Variobahn trams for London Tramlink, No 2560, on a trial run at the just-completed second Tramlink platform (No 10b) at Wimbledon, on 2 November 2015. The contract for the four new vehicles was worth £10.2m: they are being bought under an option in the contract which saw six new Variobahns delivered in 2012. **TRANSPORT FOR LONDON**

STADLER TO BUY VOSSLOH RAIL VEHICLES BUSINESS

With significant orders for the UK currently in production, a contract for the sale of Vossloh's Rail Vehicles business unit to Stadler Rail AG was signed on 4 November 4, 2015.

Stadler will pay Euro 48 million and take over debt liabilities of Euro 124 million. The transaction was still subject to merger control and other clearances, with completion targeted for the first quarter of 2016, but backdated to July 2015.

Rail Vehicles, with headquarters in Valencia, is one of three Vossloh's Transportation business units. Business operations include the development and production of innovative diesel-electric locomotives and light rail vehicles. In financial year 2014, sales of Euro 223.2million were achieved and in the first nine months of 2015 sales amounted to Euro 182.4 million.

All of Rail Vehicles' proven functions are planned to remain in Valencia and it is also intended to strengthen the location as a centre of competence for locomotive engineering.

The Valencia plant is currently building versions of the Vossloh Eurolight diesel locomotives for Beacon Rail and Direct Rail Services the UK: 32 of these Class 68s have been ordered. An order for ten electric/diesel dual-mode Class 88 locomotives from Vossloh was also placed by Beacon and DRS.

Change of ownership of Vossloh Locomotives in Kiel and Vossloh Electrical Systems (formerly Vossloh Kiepe), headquartered in Düsseldorf, is also envisaged, with the objective of finding a suitable buyer for both businesses by the end of 2017.

Stadler Rail Group has locations in Switzerland, Germany, Poland, Hungary, the Czech Republic, Italy, Austria, the Netherlands, Belarus, Algeria and the USA. It has a workforce of around 6,000 people. Its best-known vehicle series are the articulated multiple-unit train GTW, the Regio-Shuttle RS1, the FLIRT, the double-decker multiple-unit KISS and the high-speed train EC250, and in light rail the Variobahn (as delivered to London Tramlink) and Tango. The Metro is another addition for the underground/commuter rail market (13+24 vehicles sold).

Stadler has been reported to be considering the possibility of a UK version of its GTW articulated multiple-unit.

ELECTRO-MOTIVE DIESEL

GB Railfreight announced in February 2014 a deal with Electro-Motive Diesel Inc to purchase a further 13 Class-66 locomotives, and seven further Class 66s were ordered by GBRf in late 2014.

The purchases will take GB Railfreight's Class-66 fleet to 78 locomotives. The locomotives were secured ahead of the change in EU emissions legislation which, from January 2015, sees new regulations coming into force that could impact the ability to obtain compliant and affordable locomotives.

Electro-Motive Diesel was acquired by Progress Rail Services, a wholly-owned subsidiary of Caterpillar Inc, in 2010 from previous owners Greenbriar Equity Group and Berkshire Partners. EMD became a wholly-owned subsidiary of Progress Rail, creating a global locomotive manufacturing and rail services company.

Progress Rail Services is one of the largest providers of rail and transit products and services in North America, including: locomotive upgrade and repair; railcar remanufacturing; trackwork; rail welding; rail repair and replacement; signal design and installation; maintenance of way equipment; parts reclamation and recycling.

UK company EMDL - a subsidiary of Electro-Motive Diesel - signed a 10-year contract with GBRf in 2012 to maintain its fleet of Class 66 locomotives – the company's first full-maintenance contract.

The company provides all post delivery services, including commissioning, locomotive modification and maintenance of EMD locomotives in Europe, Scandinavia and parts of the Middle East.

EMDL has invested in a new maintenance and warehouse facility, with new cranes and wheel lathe, at its Doncaster base.

CLASS 70S FOR COLAS

Ten GE Transportation UK PowerHaul Series locomotives joined the Colas Rail Freight fleet in 2014, bringing the total of these Class 70 locomotives in operation in the UK to 29.

Freightliner Group placed the original order for these locomotives in 2007, partnering with GE on the new design configured to take into account current and future requirements for efficiency, emissions control and safety.

The 129-ton PowerHaul Series locomotive is designed to generate more horsepower and tractive effort while lowering fuel consumption and greenhouse gas emissions. The locomotive features several leading technologies to achieve this performance including a V16-cylinder, twin-turbo PowerHaul series engine - a product of Ecomagination, a GE-wide initiative to help meet customer demand for more energy-efficient products.

GE's unique AC individual-axle traction-control technology enables the PowerHaul Series to haul heavier loads by significantly reducing slippage on start-ups, inclines and sub-optimal track conditions. The PowerHaul Series also features dynamic braking in addition to air brakes to provide smoother handling when hauling heavier loads. ■

An Alstom-built Pendolino lifted on the Mechan jacks at Alstom's Manchester Traincare Centre. **TONY MILES**

ALSTOM FOCUSED ON RAIL TRANSPORT

Alstom became entirely refocused on rail transport following the sale in November 2015 of its energy activities (power generation and grid) to General Electric, and acquisition from GE of its signalling activities.

In the UK, Alstom operates from 12 sites and employs more than 2,500 people. Around a third of all rail journeys in the UK are made on Alstom rolling stock. Signalling Solutions Ltd is its integrated signalling business which holds three of the eight UK licenses for interlocking.

Alstom has full service provision and technical support contracts with a number of train and metro operating companies, notably for the Alstom-designed and built Pendolino fleet for Virgin. Alstom built several current fleets of trains running on the London Underground and provides maintenance for the Northern Line fleet.

Preston is its UK centre for spare parts logistics, supply, overhaul, modernisation and life extension of traction systems and components, and supply of innovative new products such as energy-efficient traction drives and remote condition monitoring systems.

NOTTINGHAM

The first Alstom trams to be delivered to the UK are the 22 Citadis trams ordered by Nottingham Express Transit (NET) for the tramway extension project, which opened on 25 August 2015.

As part of the Tramlink consortium, Alstom was also awarded the contract to maintain the trams, including the 15 Bombardier trams already in service. Refurbishment worth over £300,000 has been carried out for the existing fleet.

Alstom also built the two new lines, with overhead wires, track and signalling, with its consortium partner Vinci Construction / Taylor Woodrow.

Alstom's unique Appitrack machine was used for the first time in the UK on NET. Appitrack can lay the platform and insert the shoes for the rails with total accuracy, at rates averaging 150 metres a day.

PENDOLINO

A new bogie facility, opened within Alstom's traincare centre in Longsight, Manchester, is in action as part of the fourth heavy overhaul of the Pendolino fleet.

The facility is capable of overhauling up to 22 Pendolino bogie sets, which incorporate a complex tilt mechanism, every week. The H4 overhaul of the Pendolino fleet is being carried out at

Alstom's Manchester and Liverpool sites and is expected to run until March 2016.

Other systems and components overhauled during the work include heating, ventilation and air conditioning systems, doors, pantographs, transformers, and traction control.

Alstom has also invested £1.3m in its facilities in Manchester and Preston to improve logistics and distribution: £1m in building new warehousing at Longsight, designed as a storage facility for the bogie workshop, and £300,000 on new facilities at its Preston parts and modernisation facility. 'Lean Lift' technology was introduced at Preston to ensure a quicker end product and pick the right part first time, every time.

Alstom has been awarded a 15-year service contract, worth Euro 125m, by Serco to maintain passenger cars on the Caledonian Sleeper trains, including the new fleet from 2018 - mainly at Alstom Polmadie (Glasgow) and Wembley (London) traincare centres.

UNDERGROUND

The London Underground Northern Line mid-life project is a refurbishment of the Alstom-built fleet comprising upgrades to the interior and exterior of the 106 trains, which Alstom completed in 2015. The programme included 3.7 million items replaced on the fleet.

Alstom will continue to maintain the Northern Line trains until at least 2027 after Transport for London decided in September 2015 to retain its 1995 private finance initiative contract with Alstom for train provision and maintenance.

ELECTRIFICATION PROGRAMME

ABC Electrification (Alstom, Babcock and Costain) won its first contract in 2013, a £48m project for the third phase of the West Coast power supply upgrade – then ABC was appointed in 2014 as one of four suppliers to deliver Network Rail's £2 billion electrification programme. The total contract for ABC is estimated at around £900 million over an initial seven year term. ABC was awarded two out of the six areas.

The ATC joint venture (Alstom, TSO and Costain) has been awarded the contract to fit out and commission track and power equipment in the Crossrail tunnels under London. The contract is worth over Euro 350 million.

Crossrail's contract for high voltage traction power supply, valued at about £15m, was awarded to the AC Joint Venture (Alstom and Costain) – as was the non-traction high-voltage power supply contract (value about £25m). ■

UK MANAGING DIRECTOR, ALSTOM TRANSPORT
Terence Watson

Bombardier is to deliver the new fleet of trains for the prestigious London Crossrail project.

BOMBARDIER
UK RAIL ENGINEERING AND MANUFACTURING

Bombardier Transportation, the rail division of Bombardier, has around 3,500 employees at eight sites and 23 service locations across the UK. The company has important sites at Crewe, Plymouth, Derby and Burton on Trent. It also operates from several locations in and around London, including its heavy maintenance depot at Ilford.

Bombardier's Derby site, which has produced a significant proportion of the UK's latest technology rolling stock for both main line train operations and London Underground, forms part of the world's largest cluster of rail companies.

Bombardier has built, or has on order, around 60% of the UK's modern-era rolling stock and the company maintains around a third of the UK fleet. With its global centre of excellence for rail engineering and aluminium car body manufacture in Derby, Bombardier is also the only company that both designs and manufactures trains in the UK. Bombardier's trains are in operation throughout the UK, including on West Coast and CrossCountry services, East Midlands, ScotRail, Greater Anglia, including Stansted Express, Chiltern Railways and many London operations including London Overground,

London Underground, London Midland and Southern rail routes.

In the light rail sector, the Flexity family of tram and light rail solutions ranges from 100% low-floor trams to high-capacity light rail vehicles as well as dual-mode solutions. Bombardier has supplied light rail vehicles and trams for Blackpool, Manchester, Nottingham and for London Tramlink. Bombardier also provided the state-of-the-art driverless vehicles for the Docklands Light Railway.

Bombardier is the world's leading provider of people mover systems and its Innovia people mover vehicles are in operation at Gatwick and Heathrow (Terminal 5) airports.

Bombardier supports train operators throughout the UK with a comprehensive range of fleet maintenance services, technical and materials support and vehicle upgrade solutions. The purpose-built maintenance depot at Central Rivers provides overnight maintenance for the Voyager fleet, while maintenance crews throughout the country support train operators 24/7 to ensure excellent reliability and availability for their fleets. Sites at Ilford and Crewe provide heavy maintenance services that add value and extend the life of rolling stock assets in the UK.

At its Plymouth site, Bombardier's rail control solutions business manufactures a range of railway signalling products for the UK and the global market, with a portfolio including train detection systems and associated test tools, signals, European Rail Traffic Management System (ERTMS) products, and level crossings, including enhanced user worked crossings.

Bombardier latest products include the Orbita predictive maintenance tool and Aventra, an energy-efficient and technology leading electric multiple-unit (EMU).

In July 2015, Bombardier signed two contracts, valued at approximately £358 million, with Transport for London (TfL) to build and maintain 45 four-car new Aventra EMUs for London Overground, with 20-metre long vehicles. The contracts also include an option for up to 24 additional trains.

Bombardier is also to deliver 27 new four-car trains for Govia Thameslink Railway (GTR), for operation on the Gatwick Express under a £145 million contract. The new Class 387/2 Electrostar trains have additional features for the rail-air route. 29 4-car Class 387/1 trains, the first 110mph Electrostars, entered

service in 2015 on GTR's Thameslink route. These are later planned to transfer to Great Western Railway, supplemented by eight more Class 387s ordered by GWR. Bombardier is also to build 20 further Class 387 Electrostars, an order announced by Porterbrook in November 2016.

Bombardier is the supplier of 191 trains for the Sub Surface Lines (SSL) upgrade - the Metropolitan, District and Circle, Hammersmith and City lines - built at Derby, and the first trains on the London Underground system to feature air-conditioning and walk through gangways. LU's Victoria Line service has been provided entirely by new Bombardier trains since July 2011.

In February 2014, in the 175th year of train manufacture in the city of Derby, Bombardier received the contract to deliver the new fleet of trains for the prestigious London Crossrail project. The contract is for the delivery and maintenance of 65 new trains - based on the Aventra EMU product platform - and a new maintenance depot at Old Oak Common. ■

MANAGING DIRECTOR AND HEAD OF PROJECTS, BOMBARDIER TRANSPORTATION UK
Richard Hunter

HITACHI
Inspire the Next

Your Dedicated Rail Partner

To discover what a partnership with Yellow can do
for your business, call: **+44 (0)1332 258865**

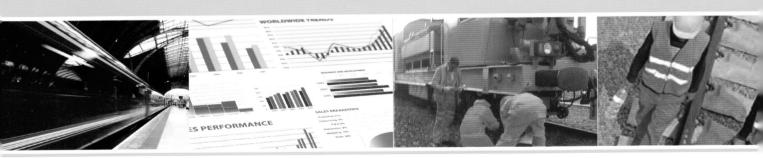

www.yellow-group.com

PIONEERING
THE DIGITAL TRAIN

Nomad Digital is the world's leading provider of wireless connectivity and Information and Communications (ICT) solutions to the rail industry. Its comprehensive portfolio of connectivity technology enables operators to significantly enhance the passenger experience, while delivering improved levels of reliability, safety and operational efficiency. Nomad's solutions include market leading connectivity and WiFi, Passenger Information Systems (PIS), on-board entertainment platforms, Remote Online Condition Monitoring (ROCM) and Reliability Centered Maintenance (RCM).

Headquartered in the UK, Nomad Digital's solutions have been deployed by operators across Europe, North America, the Middle East, Asia and Australia and currently serve more than 50 customers in over 20 countries, supported by a global network of staff and offices. Nomad's technology is used on more than 11,000 connected vehicles worldwide, providing infotainment to over 1.7 billion passengers each year. Customers include the world's leading transport operators, manufacturers and maintenance providers, on both refit and new-build projects.

Overall, Nomad systems are deployed on nearly 50% of all connected rail vehicles worldwide and in the UK, Nomad's passenger WiFi services are deployed on 75% of all UK WiFi connected trains.

Dual advertising screens.

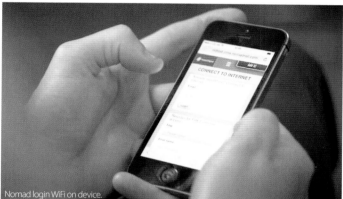
Nomad login WiFi on device.

OBIS controller.

NEXT GENERATION COMMUNICATIONS

Nomad is the pioneer of a unified and fully integrated multi-bearer on-train communications platform that enables superior bandwidth, high-availability and inter-connectivity for on-board systems, devices and applications - driving the modernisation of operations and maintenance of train fleets throughout the world.

Nomad's communications platform is intelligent, driven to maximise access and extract the value of on-board data. It is

the cornerstone that provides operational, financial and experiential benefits for operators and passengers alike. Nomad designs, builds and operates all its turnkey solutions with a complete life cycle perspective. This enables future-proof designing and scalability to adapt to developing market and operator needs. It is the fundamental building block for all connected services on-board, today and in the future.

ENHANCING PASSENGER SERVICES

In an increasingly digital age, people expect to be able to access WiFi and digital content, such as information and entertainment, whenever and wherever they are and being on the train is no exception.

Nomad provides innovative real-time passenger solutions via both passenger devices and/or vehicle displays. This covers an extensive

range of passenger services including internet access, travel information, entertainment delivery and security applications. Nomad's solutions currently inform and entertain 4 million passengers daily across the world.

INTELLIGENT FLEET MANAGEMENT

Providing rail operators with a real-time fleet-wide view of how numerous on-board systems and isolated components are performing in the field is a growing trend within the rail industry.

Nomad not only provides remote connectivity to previously offline digital and analogue legacy systems, but also brings the know-how and tools to extract and interpret critical operational data. This enables operators to perform real-time analysis on-board, automatically issue alerts of impending equipment failures and feed the relevant information in real-time to the operations departments and maintenance depots. Using Nomad's powerful on-shore tool, historical diagnostic data is available for analysis at any time in order to support improved decision making.

Intelligent Fleet Management is delivered by Nomad Tech, a business created as a joint venture with EMEF, the Portuguese Railways company for rolling stock maintenance and therefore benefits from many years of practical experience in railway maintenance operations.

DELIVERING GLOBAL TECHNOLOGY 'FIRSTS'

Nomad has demonstrated its position at the forefront of global ICT for the railways with technology firsts including: the provision of the world's first seamless tunnel connectivity passenger WiFi solution; the first on-board movie-on-demand service to passengers using WiFi; first seamless train-station platform WiFi session handover and the world's first real-time automated integrated passenger information portal and PIS. ■

HRH The Princess Royal opened a new workshop at Wabtec's Doncaster facility in September 2015, and viewed production of Class 458/5 EMUs. **WABTEC**

WABTEC GROUP BOOSTS CAPACITY

HRH The Princess Royal opened a new workshop at Wabtec's Doncaster facility in September 2015. Creation of the new shop was driven by the growth in demand for refurbishments and upgrades on a range of fleets for various rolling-stock owners and the company's need to add extra capacity on its 22 acre site alongside the East Coast main line.

The project on show when Princess Anne visited the site was the Class 321 'Renatus' overhaul for owner Eversholt, which is to be carried out in the new shop. This project covers 30 EMUs currently in service with Abellio Greater Anglia.

The Wabtec Group has the combined resources to provide an all-encompassing range of services to the UK rail industry. It is part of Wabtec Corporation, a worldwide leading supplier of value-added, technology-based products and services for rail, transit and other industries.

The group includes Wabtec Rail Limited, Wabtec Rail Scotland, Brush Traction, LH Group, including the Hunslet Engine Company, and now Fandstan Electric Group whose brand names include Brecknell Willis.

Based at Barton under Needwood in Staffordshire, LH is a leading supplier of multiple unit passenger rail products and services. A key part of the company's activities is the overhaul of rail vehicles, engines and transmission systems. The Hunslet Engine Company is renowned throughout the world as

a designer and manufacturer of quality industrial shunting, tunnelling and specialised locomotives.

Through Wabtec Rail Limited's works at Doncaster and Wabtec Rail Scotland's works at Kilmarnock in Scotland, the Group undertakes the refurbishment and maintenance of railway rolling stock, locomotives, passenger trains and freight wagons. Brush Traction's facilities at Loughborough provide locomotive overhauls, services and aftermarket components, including traction motors, electrical control systems and wheelsets.

In 2014 Wabtec Corporation acquired Fandstan Electric Group, the leading rail and industrial equipment manufacturer - expanding high-technology content on rail vehicles and providing another entry into the infrastructure segment of the market. The company's highly engineered products include pantographs, third rail shoe gears, electrical contacts and brush holders, and its brand names include Brecknell Willis, Stemmann Technik and Transtech.

Brecknell Willis Composites specialises in structural phenolic resin mouldings. Recent rail production includes cab ends for Bombardier Electrostars and interior panels for Tyne & Wear Metrocars being refurbished at Wabtec, Doncaster. Fandstan Electric has about 1,000 employees and operations in the UK, Europe, China, Australia, and the US.

Other major refurbishment and overhaul contracts presently under way at Wabtec's Doncster works include creation of six additional Class 458 EMUs for Porterbrook, South West Trains and Alstom - reconfiguring the Class 458 fleet into 5-car units and incorporating equipment from the Class 460 fleet previously used on Gatwick Express.

Modernisation and conversion work on Class 73 electro-diesel locomotives for GB Railfreight, including fitting them with more powerful 1,600hp MTU engines, is currently under way at Brush - giving them up to 25 more years in service, according to GBRf. The '73/9s' are to work on infrastructure monitoring and railhead treatment duties for Network Rail and, under GBRf's contract with Caledonian Sleepers, power sleeper trains on the diesel-hauled parts of their routes in Scotland.

Brush has also refurbished four Class 92 electric locomotives for GBRf's Caledonian Sleepers contract, and has been carrying out exams and half-life engine overhauls on Freightliner Class 66 locomotives. A series of overhauls and examinations for Porterbrook owned DMUs including Class 170 and Class 158 are among other contracts.

Further conversions and modernisation of Mk3 coaches for Great Western have been carried out at Wabtec Rail Scotland in Kilmarnock, with 18 Trailer Firsts

converted to First/Standard composite vehicles and 23 to full Standard class. Assembly of container carriers in permanent twin and triple-wagon formations for Freightliner and GB Railfreight via VTG has also been underway.

Wabtec also refurbished Mk3 vehicles for Chiltern Mainline services, fitting them with external sliding plug doors, with driving-van trailer vehicles also undergoing overhaul and modification.

Refurbishment and overhaul of electric multiple-unit fleets by Wabtec for Eversholt is also under way.

Other major recent contracts include the 'as new' refurbishment of Tyne & Wear Metrocars for DB Regio Tyne & Wear Ltd. These were constructed between 1977 and 1979, and Wabtec has extended their lives by a further 15 years.

In October 2015, Wabtec Corporation signed an agreement to acquire the Faiveley family's 51% share of Faiveley Transport as part of a proposed acquisition valued at US$1.8bn. Wabtec said its strategic combination with Faiveley Transport would create one of the world's largest public rail equipment companies, with revenues of about US$4.5 billion.

Faiveley Transport products include air conditioning, power collectors and passenger information systems; passenger access systems and platform doors; braking systems and couplers. ∎

PASSENGER TRAIN OPERATORS

IN ASSOCIATION WITH

SIEMENS

modern railways

News, Views and Analysis on Today's Railway...

Established for 50 years, Modern Railways has earned its reputation in the industry as a highly respected railway journal. Providing in-depth coverage of all aspects of the industry, from traction and rolling stock to signalling and infrastructure management, Modern Railways carries the latest news alongside detailed analysis, making it essential reading for industry professionals and railway enthusiasts alike.

REGULAR FEATURES INCLUDE:

NEWS EXTRA
National and international news on the latest developments in the railway industry, including traction and rolling stock; infrastructure; signalling and control.

INFORMED SOURCES
Roger Ford, the rail industry guru: his widely-acclaimed 'Informed Sources' column strips away the PR hype to reveal what is really happening in the industry.

TRACKWATCH
An in-depth look at changes on the national rail network.

MOVING WHEELS
Keep informed on the changes to rolling stock with the latest fleet news.

AND MUCH MORE!

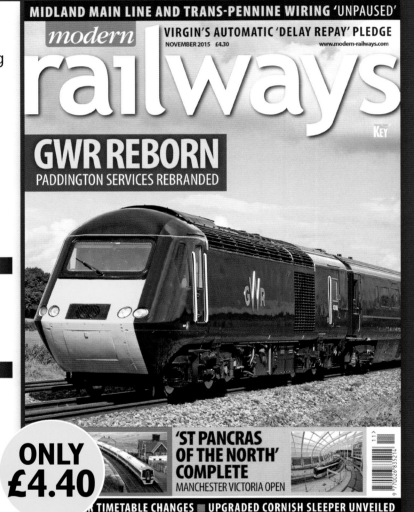

MIDLAND MAIN LINE AND TRANS-PENNINE WIRING 'UNPAUSED'

modern railways

VIRGIN'S AUTOMATIC 'DELAY REPAY' PLEDGE

NOVEMBER 2015 £4.30   www.modern-railways.com

KEY

GWR REBORN
PADDINGTON SERVICES REBRANDED

ONLY £4.40

'ST PANCRAS OF THE NORTH' COMPLETE
MANCHESTER VICTORIA OPEN

TIMETABLE CHANGES ■ UPGRADED CORNISH SLEEPER UNVEILED

1298/15

AVAILABLE MONTHLY
From WHSmith and other leading newsagents

For latest subscription deals visit
www.modern-railways.com

TRAIN OPERATING COMPANIES - INDEX

COMPANY	OWNING GROUP	NEW FRANCHISE START [D]	PAGE NO
Great Western	First	Mar 2019	p71
First TransPennine Express	First/Keolis	Apr 2016	p73
*First Hull Trains	First	-	p74
Northern Rail	Serco/Abellio	Apr 2016	p75
*Merseyrail (a)	Serco/Abellio	July 2028	p76
GreaterAnglia	Abellio	Oct 2016	p78
*ScotRail	Abellio	Apr 2015	p79
Caledonian Sleeper	Serco	March 2015	p80
Govia Thameslink Railway (GTR)	Govia	Sept 2014	p81
Southeastern	Govia	June 2018	p84
London Midland	Govia	Oct 2017	p85
Chiltern Railways	Arriva	Dec 2021	p87
Wales & Borders (c)	Arriva	Oct 2018	p88
Cross Country	Arriva	Oct 2019	p89
*Grand Central	Arriva	-	p91
South West Trains	Stagecoach	June 2017	p92
East Midlands Trains	Stagecoach	Mar 2018	p93
Virgin Trains West Coast	Virgin/Stagecoach	Sept 2017	p94
Virgin Trains East Coast	Stagecoach/Virgin	March 2015	p96
c2c	National Express	Nov 2014	p97
*Heathrow Express	Heathrow airport	-	p99
*Eurostar	London & Continental (DfT)	-	p98
*Eurotunnel	-	-	p100
*London Overground Concession (b)	LOROL (MTR and Arriva)	November 2016	p160
*MTR Crossrail (TfL Rail)	MTR Crossrail	2023 (option to 2025)	p160

Not franchised by Department for Transport.
(a) concession agreement with Merseytravel.
(b) concession agreement with Transport for London.

(c) franchising expected to be fully devolved to Welsh Government in 2017.
(d) as planned in Department for Transport programme, July 2015, or by other authorities.

Standing at Glasgow Central on 18 June 2015, in new and not-so-new liveries, are ScotRail's Nos 156437, 314211, 314206, 156449, 314202, and 156477. **STEWART ARMSTRONG**

PASSENGER OPERATOR FINANCES

CHRIS CHEEK OF PASSENGER TRANSPORT SPECIALISTS TAS
FINDS GROWTH BECOMING MORE PATCHY, AS HE ANALYSES
TRAIN OPERATING COMPANIES' FINANCIAL PERFORMANCE

This year 2014/15 saw the long sequence of growth in rail demand maintained, but it slowed a little, driven by a continuing but still rather patchy economic recovery. Four straight quarters of growth throughout 2014/15 were aided no doubt by a rather more benign winter that lacked the catastrophic storms which severed parts of the network completely a year earlier.

Growth in both the InterCity and regional markets was once again slightly slower than London & the South East, reflecting the fact that economic growth continues to be dominated by what is happening in the capital and the home counties which surround it.

The national patronage totals for the twelve months ended 31 March 2015 show the number of passenger journeys rising to 1,654 million, up by 4.2%. Passenger kilometres travelled rose by 4.6% to 62.3 billion.

Looking at the individual sectors, passenger journeys on the London and South East routes grew at the fastest rate, winning another 48 million journeys a rise of 4.3%, taking the total to 1,155 million. It is a measure of the growth we have seen that this is higher than the total carried by the whole network as recently as 2006/07.

The longer distance operators experienced slightly slower growth, winning an extra five million passenger journeys, a rise of 4.0%. This took the total to 134.2 million. Growth was maintained on the regional networks a very sluggish period a couple of years ago: an extra fourteen million journeys were made, taking the total to 365 million, also growth of 4%.

On the revenue front, all three sectors saw growth during 2014/15, as total railway revenue hit £8.8 billion 7.3% up on the previous year. Regional routes gained 7.8%, commuter services 7.3% and InterCity services 7.0%. After taking inflation into account, revenue was ahead in real terms by around 4.8%.

This growth is not, however, generally reflected in train operator profits: the benefits have mainly gone straight into the Whitehall pot: DfT Rail earned enough in premium payments to cover the hefty subsidies paid to the regional franchises and still have £142m over. Mind you, this is down on the £420m surplus that arose in the previous year, largely thanks to higher subsidies in the regions.

OPERATOR PROFITS

According to the latest analysis from passenger transport specialists TAS, profits at Britain's privatised train operating companies improved in 2013/14. Overall, the figures show that operating profits rose by 14.8% during the year, marking the first rise for five years.

A busy scene at Leeds station, which was undergoing refurbishment in late 2015 to improve concourse capacity. It is a focal point of the Northern and TransPennine Express franchises, whose passenger income has seen significant increases. The two are to operate under new franchises from 2016. **NETWORK RAIL**

a year earlier. Pre-tax profits were therefore 17% lower at £290.9m (2013: £258.6m). Pre-tax profit margins were 2.7% (previous year: 2.4%).

Total capital expenditure by the TOCs during the year fell by 4%, from the previous year's £139.2m to £133.6m. The value of net assets employed by the operators more than trebled, up from £48.7m to £183m.

As is often the case, however, there were sharp variations between different rail industry sectors and between train operators. Overall, two of the 19 TOCs made an operating loss, down from three last year. London Midland recorded a loss of 1.8%, worse than the previous year's 0.3%, while Chiltern also increased losses, recording 1.3% up from 0.3% a year earlier.

InterCity operators saw margins unchanged at 1.2%. Total turnover amongst the companies rose by 1.8% to £3,827m, whilst operating costs rose by the same amount to £3,781m. The resulting operating profit of £45.4m compared with £44.0m in 2012/13. Biggest earner in all this was the Department for Transport, which extracted £346m in net premium payments from these operators during the year though this was down from £457m in 2012/13.

Operators in London and the South East saw margins inch ahead, but saw profits fall by 48%. Again, the government was a big winner, extracting premium payments worth £658m (last year: £720m) from the sector as a whole: only Southeastern and London Midland are now in receipt of subsidy from DfT, with

London Overground getting its £28.7m subvention from Transport for London.

Turnover at these commuter companies rose by 7.6%, taking the total to £4,827m, whilst operating costs rose by 7.4% to £4,751m. The resulting operating profit of £76.1m compared with £62.5m in the previous year, at a margin of 1.6% (last year: 1.4%). Margins remain well below the peak they hit before the recession this was the 4.8% achieved in 2006/07.

The regional franchises also saw a small rise in profit levels though interestingly it remains the case that those TOCs most heavily reliant on public funding also deliver the highest returns. Turnover rose by 8.9% to £2,216m, whilst operating costs were 8.6% higher, totalling £2,109m. Operating profits were 15.6% up at £106.4m (last year £92.0m), at a margin of 4.8% (4.5%). As usual, this sector consumed the bulk of the subsidy paid to train operators, soaking up £1,146m worth of taxpayer funding, up from £863m in 2012/13.

Individually, the most profitable TOC was the Merseyrail Electrics operation, which returned an operating margin of 10.1%. Next came TransPennine Express on 7.8% followed by National Express Group's surviving franchise, c2c Rail, on 6.1%.

In the summaries below, figures are extracted from accounts lodged at Companies House. Practice concerning the declaration and calculation of different cost and revenue items varies between train operators. This occasionally makes interpretation and reconciliation difficult: major issues are noted in the brief commentaries.

LONG DISTANCE OPERATORS

CROSS COUNTRY

The company stayed in the black, albeit at a lower margin, during the year as revenue support from the Department for Transport was again payable, offsetting the premium payable by the company. The structure of the accounts was changed, so that no split between track access and train leasing costs was provided.

DfT support was worth a total of £113.7m during the year, up from £80.3m in 2012. Offsetting this was a premium payable to DfT under the franchise agreement of £85.0m (previous year: £53m). Passenger revenue grew by £18.3m (4.2%).

PERIOD TO:	31/12/2013	31/12/2012
	£000	£000
Turnover	552,536	501,577
Operating Costs:	540,449	485,527
Operating Profit:	12,087	16,050
Operating Margin:	2.2%	3.2%
Turnover per Employee	£325,980	£306,026
Track Access	0	98,345
Rolling stock lease	0	50,574
Rail contracts	269,615	0
Franchise premium payments	85,000	53,000
Revenue Grant	113,711	80,287

FIRST GREAT WESTERN

The company improved its result during the year, returning to the black after previous losses. However, the margins remain very tight indeed. This came despite the severe weather at the start of 2014, which caused the breaches of the main line in Devon and in Somerset.

The analysis covers all the train operating companies (TOCs) lodging accounts with financial year ends between 31 December 2013 and 30 June 2014. Across the franchised train operating companies as a whole, turnover was up by 5.7% at £10,870m, whilst operating profits totalled £228m (last year: £199m on £10,280m), to give an operating margin of 2.1% (last year: 1.9%).

Operating costs reached a total of £10,642m, 5.6% higher than the 2012/13 total of £10,082m. The bulk of the increases were driven by a rise in the cost of track access charges, which totalled £1,675m in these accounts, up from £1,541m in the previous year.

The companies continued to be net earners of interest during the year a figure that now includes pension scheme income. Proceeds earned rose as investment returns improved. The total was just £62.9m, up from £50.2m

2013-14 was the last full year of public sector operation of East Coast as Virgin Trains East Coast (VTEC) took over in March 2015. A Class 91 locomotive is seen in VTEC livery at King's Cross. **VTEC**

Passenger income has risen at Arriva Trains Wales: the next franchise is due to begin in 2018 and will be procured by the Welsh government. A pair of Pacer trains passes the Millennium stadium in Cardiff: the city's core route is undergoing modernisation to improve capacity. **NETWORK RAIL.**

In addition to the profit shown, an exceptional item saw £4.6m worth of unused provisions written back to the profit and loss account.

PERIOD TO:	31/03/2014	31/03/2013
	£000	£000
Turnover	1,067,970	1,130,274
Operating Costs:	1,062,722	1,140,976
Operating Profit:	5,248	(10,702)
Operating Margin:	0.5%	-0.9%
Turnover per Employee	£201,504	£222,451
Track Access	169,514	138,655
Rolling stock lease	72,413	69,553
Revenue Grant	177,394	269,905

EAST COAST

The company improved its results during the year, as revenue growth moved slightly ahead of increased costs. This proved to be the last full year of public sector ownership as the Stagecoach/Virgin joint venture took over in March 2015. Key to the level

of the operating costs, though, was another substantial £206m premium payment to government. Passenger revenue grew by £28.6m (4.4%).

PERIOD TO:	31/03/2014	31/03/2013
	£000	£000
Turnover	717,456	692,498
Operating Costs:	712,069	688,085
Operating Profit:	5,387	4,413
Operating Margin:	0.8%	0.6%
Turnover per Employee	£247,399	£241,541
Track Access	66,916	48,839
Rolling stock lease	65,011	83,026

VIRGIN TRAINS WEST COAST

The company saw profits dip sharply during the year, which was the first full year of the Interim Franchise Agreement which ran from November 2012 until November 2014. This provided for a margin of 1% of revenue. Passenger revenue growth of £55.6m (6.1%) contributed to the

profits earned. In the event, a new agreement replaced the interim one from 22 June 2014 and runs until 31 March 2017, offering a more commercial margin in exchange for greater risks.

PERIOD TO:	31/03/2014	31/03/2013
	£000	£000
Turnover	990,546	966,651
Operating Costs:	986,763	946,281
Operating Profit:	3,783	20,370
Operating Margin:	0.4%	2.1%
Turnover per Employee	£333,181	£331,613
Rolling stock lease	318,792	302,333
Track Access	186,222	156,215
Franchise premium payments	97,472	131,366

EAST MIDLANDS TRAINS

The company improved its performance during the year, increasing profits by more than one third, as above-inflation revenue growth including £12.2m from

passengers (3.8%) - outstripped the rise in costs.

PERIOD TO:	26/04/2014	30/04/2013
	£000	£000
Turnover	498,420	469,127
Operating Costs:	479,474	455,294
Operating Profit:	18,946	13,833
Operating Margin:	3.8%	2.9%
Turnover per Employee	£239,395	£228,175
Track Access	89,973	76,485
Rolling stock lease	27,891	27,856
Franchise premium payments	132,620	114,716
Revenue Grant	138,040	121,927

LONDON AND SOUTH EAST OPERATORS

C2C RAIL

The company saw profits fall during the year as operating costs rose ahead of income. The original franchise agreement expired on 26 May 2013 and was replaced by

HITACHI
Inspire the Next

in October 2015), the company's operating performance deteriorated during the year, as increased operating costs outstripped the otherwise strong revenue growth. This included £12.5m worth of extra passenger income (8.1%).

PERIOD TO:	31/12/2013	31/12/2012
	£000	£000
Turnover:	169,419	155,575
Operating Costs:	171,545	156,000
Operating Profit:	(2,126)	(425)
Operating Margin:	-1.3%	-0.3%
Turnover per Employee	£217,483	£203,101
Rolling stock lease:	21,348	19,161
Track Access	41,996	36,663
Revenue Grant	0	0

FIRST CAPITAL CONNECT

The company improved its performance during the year, though margins remained very narrow. This was the last full year of trading as the company's operation of the Thameslink/Great Northern franchise ceased in September 2014, when it was handed over to Govia, the joint venture between Go-Ahead and Keolis.

PERIOD TO:	31/03/2014	31/03/2013
	£000	£000
Turnover	653,801	604,332
Operating Costs:	640,454	599,269
Operating Profit:	13,347	5,063
Operating Margin:	2.0%	0.8%
Turnover per Employee	£261,103	£249,827
Rolling stock lease	57,145	57,522
Track Access	67,090	56,102
Franchise premium payments	254,376	228,245
Revenue Grant	59,600	45,900

GREATER ANGLIA

This was the company's second full year of trading, having taken over the franchise from National Express in February 2012. The company just stayed in the black during the year, as strong revenue growth, including £84.8m (13.8%) from passengers, was outstripped by slightly higher rises in operating costs.

PERIOD TO:	31/12/2013	31/12/2012
	£000	£000
Turnover	680,790	569,635
Operating Costs:	680,789	564,945
Operating Profit:	1	4,690
Operating Margin:	0.0%	0.8%
Turnover per Employee	£231,877	£198,756
Rolling stock lease	134,544	121,348
Track Access	93,252	70,941
Revenue Grant	35,874	12,225

LONDON MIDLAND

The company's performance deteriorated sharply during the year as the previous year's small profits turned into losses. In addition, an exceptional charge of £3.0m was incurred from restructuring costs, both front line staff and head office personnel.

PERIOD TO:	28/06/2014	29/06/2013
	£000	£000
Turnover	376,346	356,756
Operating Costs:	383,065	356,299
Operating Profit:	(6,719)	457
Operating Margin:	-1.8%	0.1%
Turnover per Employee	£158,662	£153,774
Track Access	95,145	85,293
Rolling stock lease	53,891	52,463
Revenue Grant	55,903	58,383

LONDON OVERGROUND

The company saw profits dip sharply during the year as revenue growth failed to keep pace with rising operating costs. The company expanded after the year end, taking over the operation of services from Greater Anglia between Liverpool Street and Enfield Town, Cheshunt (via Seven Sisters) and Chingford, together with the Romford to Upminster line with effect from 31 May 2015 until the end of the concession in November 2016.

PERIOD TO:	31/03/2014	31/03/2013
	£000	£000
Turnover	131,715	126,829
Operating Costs:	130,646	120,388
Operating Profit:	1,069	6,441
Operating Margin:	0.8%	5.1%
Turnover per Employee	£111,812	£104,991
Track Access	14,168	12,486
Rolling stock lease	2,100	2,088
Revenue Grant	101,460	98,507

SOUTHERN

The company improved its result during the year as above-inflation 6.6% revenue growth kept ahead of rising cost levels. This was the penultimate year of the franchise which was merged into the new Thameslink/Great Northern business in the summer of 2015.

PERIOD TO:	28/06/2014	29/06/2013
	£000	£000
Turnover	775,717	725,591
Operating Costs:	746,662	708,695
Operating Profit:	29,055	16,896
Operating Margin:	3.7%	2.3%
Turnover per Employee	£194,269	£180,675
Track Access	153,106	143,560
Rolling stock lease	122,355	110,898
Revenue Grant	9,415	0

SOUTHEASTERN

The company improved its results sharply during the year, recording quadrupled operating and pre-tax profits on the back of £29.9m worth of extra passenger revenue (4.3%). However, margins started from a very low base and remained very tight.

PERIOD TO:	28/06/2014	29/06/2013
	£000	£000
Turnover	771,241	764,151
Operating Costs:	758,008	761,641
Operating Profit:	13,233	2,510
Operating Margin:	1.7%	0.3%
Turnover per Employee	£199,752	£200,934
Track Access	307,977	304,044
Rolling stock lease	143,990	144,363

SOUTH WEST TRAINS

The company improved its performance very slightly during the year, as turnover growth including a £29.9m (4.3%) increase in passenger revenue - just outstripped the rise in costs.

an interim agreement based on profit shares at given percentages starting at 10% and rising to 100% depending on thresholds reached. This lasted until the new franchise agreement commenced in November 2014.

PERIOD TO:	31/12/2013	31/12/2012
	£000	£000
Turnover	142,657	137,360
Operating Costs:	133,950	127,801
Operating Profit:	8,707	9,559
Operating Margin:	6.1%	7.0%
Turnover per Employee	£238,159	£239,721
Track Access	15,307	12,144
Rolling stock lease	27,538	23,344
Revenue Grant	0	0

CHILTERN

After discounting the costs and income related to the latest phase of Project Evergreen (the extension to Oxford which partially opened

TAS - THE PASSENGER TRANSPORT SPECIALISTS

For 25 years, TAS has been providing research, analysis and advisory services to a huge range of organisations involved in passenger transport - including government at national, regional and local level, together with operators of rail, light rail and bus and community transport services.

TAS's market-leading market intelligence reports have achieved a worldwide reputation for being the definitive analysis of the financial and market performance of the UK's rail, light rail and bus industries, being widely quoted by government, the media and academics. These are now available online via the popular and successful TAS Business Monitor subscription service.

Passenger transport in all its forms is about delivery providing services and networks that get customers to where they want to be quickly, comfortably and above all safely, whilst at the same time delivering value for money to customers and stakeholders.

TAS is an employee-owned company that exists to help transport providers to deliver these services and to deliver continuous improvement in today's demanding and ever-changing world.

For further details, visit *www.tas.uk.net*

PERIOD TO:	26/04/2014	27/04/2013
	£000	£000
Turnover	1,125,707	1,044,910
Operating Costs:	1,106,152	1,027,563
Operating Profit:	19,555	17,347
Operating Margin:	1.7%	1.7%
Turnover per Employee	£244,188	£229,046
Track Access	101,532	89,099
Rolling stock lease	111,667	109,481
Revenue Grant	160,245	133,457

REGIONAL, SCOTLAND AND WALES

ARRIVA TRAINS WALES

The company improved its performance slightly during the year as revenue growth edged ahead of cost increases with passenger income up by 5.0% and subsidy by 9.4%.

PERIOD TO:	31/12/2013	31/12/2012
	£000	£000
Turnover	307,428	287,210
Operating Costs:	288,793	270,069
Operating Profit:	18,635	17,141
Operating Margin:	6.1%	6.0%
Turnover per Employee	£152,570	£143,462
Rolling stock lease	40,140	40,176
Track Access	70,002	52,863
Revenue Grant	162,854	147,522

FIRST SCOTRAIL

This was the penultimate year of the franchise, which transferred to Abellio on 1 April 2015. The company improved its profitability by more than half during the year as subsidy rose by over a third and passenger revenue growth of 6.1% was achieved.

PERIOD TO:	31/03/2014	31/03/2013
	£000	£000
Turnover	855,164	778,672
Operating Costs:	838,192	767,752
Operating Profit:	16,972	10,920
Operating Margin:	2.0%	1.4%
Turnover per Employee	£178,867	£166,954
Rail contracts	425,240	375,458
Revenue Grant	506,433	447,196

FIRST TRANSPENNINE

Following the sharp fall in turnover and profits last year, following a new franchise extension deal with DfT, the company improved its performance during the year.

Revenue grew at a faster rate than operating costs, though margins remain below the levels previously earned by the company. Subsidy rose once more, and passenger income was 6% up.

PERIOD TO:	31/03/2014	31/03/2013
	£000	£000
Turnover	266,205	241,472

Southeastern has seen improved financial results, but currently faces the challenges of operation during the Thameslink Programme modernisation works. It is the operator of high-speed domestic services over High Speed 1, using Hitachi Class 395 trains, one of which is seen at St Pancras International. **HITACHI**

Operating Costs:	245,312	224,866
Operating Profit:	20,893	16,606
Operating Margin:	7.8%	6.9%
Turnover per Employee	£234,335	£226,947
Track Access	59,699	48,438
Rolling stock lease	61,477	62,758
Revenue Grant	65,654	52,354

MERSEYRAIL ELECTRICS

The company continued to trade profitably, albeit at slightly lower margins as costs grew at a slightly faster rate than revenue.

PERIOD TO:	04/01/2014	05/01/2013
	£000	£000
Turnover	144,853	135,224
Operating Costs:	130,192	121,400
Operating Profit:	14,661	13,824
Operating Margin:	10.1%	10.2%
Turnover per Employee	£117,195	£109,582
Track Access	13,941	11,281
Rolling stock lease	12,368	12,218

NORTHERN RAIL

The company saw a small increase in cash profits during the year, but traded at slightly lower margins, as revenue growth failed to keep pace with changes in cost levels. Subsidy payments were 9% up but passenger revenue was 5.8% higher.

PERIOD TO:	04/01/2014	05/01/2013
	£000	£000
Turnover	642,401	592,458
Operating Costs:	607,164	558,928
Operating Profit:	35,237	33,530
Operating Margin:	5.5%	5.7%
Turnover per Employee	£128,429	£121,405
Track Access	129,496	100,319
Rolling stock lease	37,588	37,168
Revenue Grant	356,185	324,111

NON-FRANCHISED OPERATORS

EUROSTAR INTERNATIONAL

The company saw a very small reduction in profitability during the year, as costs rose more quickly than revenue.

PERIOD TO:	31/12/2013	31/12/2012
	£000	£000
Turnover	882,200	829,400
Operating Costs:	829,000	776,400
Operating Profit:	53,200	53,000
Operating Margin:	6.0%	6.4%
Turnover per Employee	£543,227	£499,940
Track Access HS1	67,800	71,800
Track Access - Europe	92,200	82,200
Track Access Eurotunnel	221,100	206,500

GRAND CENTRAL

The company commenced the operation of a fifth daily departure on the Sunderland service in December 2012 and a fourth daily departure on its West Yorkshire service a year later. This helped to drive strong revenue growth which led to sharply improved operating and pre-tax profits. The result

was further assisted by an exceptional credit of £37.7m, after the write-off of inter-company debts.

PERIOD TO:	31/12/2013	31/12/2012
	£000	£000
Turnover	32,670	27,071
Operating Costs:	29,221	27,346
Operating Profit:	3,449	(275)
Operating Margin:	10.6%	-1.0%
Turnover per Employee	£284,087	£237,465

HULL TRAINS

The company improved its results sharply during the year, as revenue grew at a rate above inflation, whilst operating costs fell. The company was fully acquired by FirstGroup later in 2014, as the holding company bought out co-founders Renaissance Trains.

PERIOD TO:	31/03/2014	31/03/2013
	£000	£000
Turnover	23,824	22,762
Operating Costs:	21,676	22,383
Operating Profit:	2,148	379
Operating Margin:	9.0%	1.7%
Turnover per Employee	£224,755	£212,729
Rolling stock lease	1,908	2,462

PASSENGER OPERATOR ARTICLES

In the following pages, statistics for train operating companies (TOCs) are drawn from data published by the Office of Rail Regulation and Department for Transport (DfT).

Punctuality figures are the Public Performance Measure annual average - for long distance operators, the percentage of trains arriving within ten minutes of planned arrival time at final destination; and for London & South East operators and regional, Scotland and Wales operators, the percentage

arriving within 5min of planned arrival time.

The subsidy figures include franchise payments and revenue support: negative values mean the DfT was receiving payments. Network grant figures are DfT estimates based on each TOC's share of track access charges. Network Rail receives network grant in lieu of fixed track access charges that it would otherwise receive from franchised train operators.

modern railways*insight*

THE DEFINITIVE ONLINE GUIDE TO THE UK RAIL INDUSTRY

IRECTORY • REFERENCE • OPINION • REVIEW

Brought to you by the team behind Modern Railways magazine, Modern Railways Insight provides strategic information on the UK rail industry. Registered users have access to detailed information from over **2,750** rail businesses.

Split into 126 key areas it provides invaluable coverage of:

- **Policy and Finance**
- **Rolling Stock**
- **Infrastructure**
- **Train Operations**
- **Customer Interface**

Our extensive database includes:

- **Full Company Listings**
- **Profiles**
- **Route Maps**
- **Contracts**
- **Statistics**

1293/15

The answer to all of your information needs

Whether your background is in operations, manufacturing, maintenance, telecommunications, human resources or any other area of the industry, Modern Railways Insight will revolutionise the way in which your business uses UK rail industry data.

For just £695* for a single user, or just £49.95 with multiple licence purchases†, our detailed database could transform the way in which you operate.

To arrange your personal demonstration, contact David Lane today on mri@keypublishing.com, call 01778 420888/07795 031051 or visit:

First

- HULL TRAINS
- FIRST GREAT WESTERN
- FIRST TRANSPENNINE EXPRESS

HITACHI
Inspire the Next

FIRSTGROUP

FirstGroup operates the Great Western Railway (GWR) and First TransPennine Express (FTPE) franchises and the open-access First Hull Trains. The group also operates London Tramlink on behalf of Transport for London, and Heathrow Connect jointly with Heathrow Express. First's other major operations are in UK Bus and North America.

In March 2015 the DfT extended the GWR contract until at least 1 April 2019 (with a further year at the DfT's discretion), and First TransPennine Express until the start of a new franchise, expected on 1 April 2016. First is one of three shortlisted bidders.

Revenue in First's UK Rail division was £2,207.1m in 2014/15 (2013/14: £2,870.1m), reflecting a reduction in First ScotRail subsidy (this franchise ended on 31 March 2015), the end of revenue support at Great Western, and the end of the First Capital Connect (Thameslink and Great Northern) franchise in 2014. Operating profit was £74.1m (2013/14: £55.2m), representing a margin of 3.4% (2014: 1.9%). The group continued to benefit from robust growth in passenger volumes, which increased by 4.2% in the year.

Since 2005 the group's franchises have received more than 250 awards, including recognition for GWR's work in partnership with Network Rail to keep the west moving after unprecedented flood damage in 2014; and for the 'Building a Greater West' marketing campaign. FTPE has achieved Investors in People Gold status and became the first rail company to win the British Quality Foundation UK Excellence Award.

The group is embracing new technology to enhance the customer experience. The customer app for its operating companies has been downloaded more than one million times, and it has led one of the largest roll outs of free Wi-Fi on the UK rail network.

UK RAIL MANAGING DIRECTOR
Steve Montgomery

GWR

DIRECT AWARD UNTIL 1 APRIL 2019

The Greater Western franchise was rebranded from First Great Western to Great Western Railway (GWR) and a new green livery introduced, to coincide with the Department for Transport's (DfT's) new five-year Direct Award to First Group from 20 September 2015 to 30 March 2019. The company said, 'It means we no longer behave as a franchisee, but as a custodian - responsible for reinvigorating the west by returning the railway to its former glory.'

The franchise began operation on 1 April 2006, combining the previous Great Western inter-city, London and Thames Valley, and West Country regional franchises. Its routes are from London Paddington across the South and West of England and South Wales.

In 2011 a contractual three-year franchise extension was not taken up by FirstGroup, and the DfT planned a longer term franchise to help deliver route electrification to Bristol, Swansea, Oxford and Newbury; as well as Crossrail and introduction of the new Hitachi Intercity Express Programme (IEP) electric and bi-mode trains. After the DfT paused its franchising programme in October 2012, a series of contract extensions followed. The latest direct award, until March 2019, could have a possible extension of up to a year.

With IEP introduction, the new award period is due to see withdrawal of the diesel High Speed Train fleet, and re-allocation of diesel multiple-units (DMUs) when electric multiple-units are brought into service on newly electrified routes.

KEY STATISTICS
GREAT WESTERN

	2013-14	2014-15
Punctuality	87.9%	88.9%
Passenger journeys (millions)	99.7	103.7
Passenger km (millions)	5,785.0	5,940.9
Timetabled train km (millions)	43.0	42.9
Route km operated	1,997.2	1,997.2
Number of stations operated	206	206
Number of employees	5.353	5,705
Subsidy per passenger km (p)	-1.3	-1.0
Network grant / pass km (p)	5.3	5.3

The 29 new Class-387 four-car EMUs temporarily in service with Thameslink will transfer to GWR, supplemented by eight more Class 387s from Bombardier. Their acceleration and ability to run at 110mph will help them operate between IEPs on the fast lines. 21 Class-365 EMUs will also transfer from GTR. Class 165 and 166 'Turbo' DMUs displaced from the Thames Valley will move to be based at Bristol for services to Cardiff, Portsmouth, Taunton, Westbury, Weymouth, Gloucester, Worcester and Cheltenham. The Class 158s currently on many of these services will move to Devon and Cornwall,

In the new GWR green livery, an HST lead by power car No 43187 passes the strengthened section of sea wall at Dawlish with the 08.44 Penzance-Paddington on 2 October 2015. **STEWART ARMSTRONG**

bringing improvements for Exeter Central-Barnstaple (hourly), Exmouth-Paignton (2 trains/hr), and a much enhanced service between Exeter, Plymouth and Penzance. With changes to the inter-city network, this will give Cornwall's main line a half-hourly service. Class 143, 153 and 150/1 fleets will be released; some Class 150/2s will be retained for Devon and Cornwall local services, following accessibility modifications and fitting of WiFi and at-seat charging points.

After extensive evaluation, GWR concluded that West of England inter-city services will be best served by a new fleet of seven nine-car and 22 five-car AT300 trains from Hitachi - similar to the IEP bi-mode trains, but using higher engine operating power for the more demanding gradients. The 5-car sets will be able to work in pairs, dividing to serve a wider range of destinations. GWR's

premium 'Pullman' food offer is planned to be retained on the IEPs and AT300s as long as it remains popular.

In 2015 an increase in Standard-class capacity (almost 3,000 more seats a day) on High Speed Trains was completed, through converting some First class carriages. 4,500 more peak-time seats were previously provided by FGW in summer 2012, by rebuilding disused buffet cars.

A £146.6m package of rail improvements for Cornwall is seeing a major upgrade to the Night Riviera London-Penzance sleeper trains, improved signalling on the main line, and enhancements to the traincare centre in Penzance.

FGW has seven train maintenance and servicing depots; Old Oak Common, London; Laira, Plymouth; St Philips Marsh, Bristol; Long Rock, Penzance; Landore, Swansea; Exeter; and Reading. A new

depot at Reading, to replace the existing facility as a result of the infrastructure remodelling, opened in 2013.

The FGW diesel multiple-unit fleet has these 2-car units: Class 143 (8 units), Class 150/1 (17), Class 150/2 (19), Class 158 (2), Class 165/1 (20); and 3-car units: Class 150/0 (2), Class 158 (13), Class 165/1 (16), Class 166 (21); plus 14 Class-153

single-car units. There are five five-car Class 180 trains.

The HST fleet has 119 Class 43 power cars and 442 Mk3 coaches (12 of the power cars and 42 Mk3 vehicles are owned by FirstGroup).

There are 20 Mk3 Sleeper vehicles and four Class 57/6 locomotives mainly used on sleeper trains. ■

SENIOR PERSONNEL
GREAT WESTERN RAILWAY

MANAGING DIRECTOR Mark Hopwood (in photo)
ENGINEERING DIRECTOR AND DEPUTY MD Andrew Mellors
ALLIANCE & PROGRAMME DIRECTOR Richard Rowland
FINANCE DIRECTOR Ben Caswell
COMMERCIAL DEVELOPMENT DIRECTOR Matthew Golton
DIRECTOR OF SALES & MARKETING Diane Burke
DIRECTOR OF HR Sharon Johnston
DIRECTOR, COMPLIANCE, SUSTAINABILITY & ENVIRONMENT Joe Graham

First TransPennine Express

DIRECT AWARD UNTIL APRIL 2016

The TransPennine Express (TPE) franchise holder since 1 February 2004 has been a joint operation by First Group (55% share) and Keolis (45%). French Railways (SNCF) is a major shareholder in Keolis. First TransPennine Express (FTPE) runs inter-city train services linking Liverpool and Manchester with Leeds, York and the Northeast, and with Sheffield and Doncaster, and the Lake District. In 2006/07 it took over the Manchester Airport-Blackpool North and Manchester-Glasgow/Edinburgh routes.

Initially the franchise was awarded for eight years with an optional five-year extension. In 2011 the Department for Transport (DfT) announced an extension to 2014 or 2015, then, following the DfT franchising review, a new direct award was scheduled. This was agreed in March 2015, running to April 2016, so that the next TPE and Northern franchises will start at the same time, allowing some transfer of routes, and management of both by a formal partnership of the DfT and Rail North, a consortium of local transport authorities: this team is planned to be based in Leeds.

Routes planned to transfer from TPE to Northern are: Manchester Airport-Blackpool North, Oxenholme-Windermere, and Lancaster to Barrow-in-Furness. Depending on Manchester-York electrification plans, the York-Scarborough route was also being considered for transfer.

Bidders shortlisted for the new franchise were First Group;

Siemens-built First TransPennine Express Class 350/4 electric and (right) Class 185 diesel multiple-unit trains at Ardwick depot, Manchester, which was adapted to accommodate the electric trains as well as the earlier diesel fleet. **SIEMENS/FTPE**

KEY STATISTICS
FIRST TRANSPENNINE EXPRESS

	2013-14	2014-15
Punctuality (0-10min)	90.4%	88.6%
Passenger journeys (millions)	26.1	28.6
Passenger km (millions)	1,663.3	1,850.8
Timetabled train km (millions)	17.4	20.1
Route km operated	1,250.5	1,411.4
Number of stations operated	30	30
Number of employees	1,175	1,240
Subsidy per passenger km (p)	3.7	2.3
Network grant / pass km (p)	6.8	5.9

a Keolis/Go-Ahead joint venture; and Stagecoach.

TPE achieved an 85% passenger satisfaction rating in the spring 2015 National Rail Passenger Survey, but passengers have commented that the increase in numbers travelling affected satisfaction with seating capacity and luggage space. The £60m fleet of 10 four-car Class 350/4 Desiro EMUs, fully deployed from May 2014, enabled a new timetable providing 90,000 extra seats a week.

They have taken over most Manchester Airport-Glasgow/Edinburgh services and released Class 185 DMUs to provide additional capacity on other services, and to work a new service between Liverpool and Newcastle from May 2014. The Manchester-Scotland route has 15 daily services each way, a 36% increase in frequency. An additional 50,000 seats a week were added between Manchester and Leeds, with five trains an hour. The new Liverpool-Newcastle service via Manchester Victoria gave significant journey time reductions.

Further timetable improvements are planned for the next franchise with additional capacity on many routes.

Since the franchise began, annual passenger journeys have increased from 13.5 million to almost 29m, with underlying income growth significantly ahead of industry average. FTPE has been particularly successful in developing advance purchase ticket sales. In 2013/14 it had the second highest seat occupancy of UK operators and the company calculates that taxpayer subsidy as a proportion of farebox revenue is down by 80%.

With its network serving a number of student centres, FTPE has targeted the student market with initiatives including 50% discount on its own advance purchase fares with 16-25 Railcards.

In 2013/14 the train company became the first to have a fully adaptive website which worked on PC, mobile and tablet. Since spring 2015, it has rolled out free WiFi at many of its major stations.

In December 2014, FTPE was awarded the British Quality Foundation 'Excellence 600' award, the first train company in the UK to achieve this.

The ten 110mph Siemens Class 350/4 four-car Desiro EMUs and 51 three-car 100mph Siemens Desiro DMUs are supplemented by four 2-car Class 170 Turbostar DMUs whose transfer to Chiltern Railways has been deferred. With five Class 170s moving to Chiltern in May 2015, capacity has been maintained through daily hire of six Class 156 DMUs from Northern Rail. ■

SENIOR PERSONNEL
FIRST TRANSPENNINE EXPRESS

MANAGING DIRECTOR Nick Donovan (in photo)
COMMERCIAL DIRECTOR Darren Higgins
FLEET DIRECTOR Paul Staples
PROGRAMME DIRECTOR Chris Nutton
OPERATIONS DIRECTOR Paul Watson
FINANCE DIRECTOR Liz Collins
HUMAN RESOURCES DIRECTOR Sue Whaley
CUSTOMER SERVICE DIRECTOR Kathryn O'Brien

First ⑦ Hull Trains

NON-FRANCHISED INTERCITY TRAIN COMPANY

Celebrating its 15th anniversary on 25 September 2015, First Hull Trains is a non-franchised ('open access') inter-city train company operating between Hull and London King's Cross, calling at Brough, Howden, Selby, Doncaster, Retford and Grantham. In February 2015 the company launched a new direct service from Beverley to London King's Cross, the first ever.

In its first year the company carried just 80,000 passengers between Hull and London on three daily services. Now it runs 90 trains to London per week, with annual passenger journeys totalling around 880,000.

The company is now a fully owned subsidiary of FirstGroup, which held an 80% share after purchasing the previous parent company, GB Railways. In August 2014, FirstGroup acquired the remaining 20% share from original promoters of Hull Trains.

In 2002 the Rail Regulator awarded the company 10-year rights, until May 2010. A £36m investment in a new fleet of 4-car Class 222 'Pioneer' trains in 2005 was followed by a new leasing deal with Angel Trains for four 5-car Class 180s in their place, delivering an extra 500,000 seats a year.

Following regulatory decisions on East Coast main line capacity, First Hull Trains was granted firm rights for seven weekday and five weekend return services until December 2014. Further negotiations brought an extension until the end of 2016, in exchange for a commitment to undertake a train refurbishment programme and other improvements. In January 2015, the company's track access agreement was extended by three years, until December 2019.

In September 2015, Hull Trains announced a plan for a new fleet of five five-car Hitachi bi-mode trains, similar to InterCity Express Programme trains, valued at £68m. Each train would have 320 seats, compared to 266 on the existing Class 180. They would be capable of running at up to 225 km/hr and using electric traction on the East Coast main line. This was linked to an application to the Office of Rail and Road for a ten-year track access extension until December 2029.

Humber Local Enterprise Partnership (LEP) and Hull City Council continue to develop plans for electrification of the Hull-Selby line, to create fully electrified routes from Hull to London, and to Leeds and Manchester. A £7.5m grant was allocated in the 2014 Growth Deal funding by the Department for Transport, following negotiations with the LEP and City Council. This followed a £2.5m DfT grant to fund a feasibility study into the project.

2012 and 2013 saw significant investment in engineering overhauls on the Class 180 train fleet, with modifications to design implemented in conjunction with Angel Trains. In late 2015, the Miles per Technical Incident figure for the fleet stood at 19,564 (moving annual average) which is 'best in class'.

A new commercial strategy has delivered increasing market share, with particular success in growth at Retford and Grantham of 16% and 17% respectively (2014/15). For two years, Hull Trains has topped the National Passenger Survey for passenger satisfaction, at 96%.

Innovations include new M-ticketing technology, with 13% of sales via the Hull Trains App in 2014/15. In 2014, Hull Trains was the first operator to introduce free 4G-enabled single-sign-up WiFi on all its trains, and in April 2015 the company launched another industry-first, on-board information screens with real-time train information. ∎

KEY STATISTICS
FIRST HULL TRAINS

	2013-14	2014-15
Punctuality (0-10min)	82.0%	88.3%
Passenger journeys	774,159	c860,000
Timetabled train km (millions)	1.48	1.54
Staff employed	106	110

SENIOR PERSONNEL
FIRST HULL TRAINS

MANAGING DIRECTOR Will Dunnett (in photo)
DIRECTOR, OPERATIONS & CUSTOMER EXPERIENCE Joel Mitchell
FINANCE MANAGER Glenn McLeish-Longthorn
HEAD OF ENGINEERING Jonathan Plowright
HEAD OF HR & PEOPLE SUPPORT Deborah Birch

Hull Trains' Class 180 No 180113 heads for King's Cross, passing Harringay on 27 March 2015. **TONY MILES**

SERCO AND ABELLIO

A 50-50 partnership of Serco and Abellio (formerly NedRailways) holds the Northern Rail and Merseyrail franchises. Abellio alone has the Greater Anglia franchise, won the new ScotRail franchise from April 2015, and was shortlisted in August 2014 for the new Northern Rail franchise. Serco won the new franchise for the Caledonian Sleeper from March 2015. An Abellio/ Stagecoach joint venture was shortlisted in June 2015 for the new Greater Anglia franchise.

Serco, an international service company, operated, maintained and supported the Docklands Light Railway in London from 2006 until December 2014. Serco began operating and maintaining the new Dubai Metro in 2009, and in 2013 won a contract to operate the Dubai Tram for five years. A Serco-led consortium in 2015 signed a contract with the Saudi Railway Company for management and technical support for operations on the North South Railway (total value to Serco, approx £120m over five years). Serco Rail Technical Services offers services including vehicle testing and condition monitoring. In 2014 Serco's share of Northern Rail revenue was £288.7m (2013: £325.2m) and profit after tax was £6.5m (2013: £12.4m).

Abellio is the international passenger transport subsidiary of the Dutch national railway company, Nederlandse Spoorwegen. Its 20,000 people provide rail, bus and tram services to over one million customers in the UK, Germany and in the Netherlands each day.

MD SERCO TRANSPORT
David Stretch
MD, RAIL, SERCO GROUP
Steve Butcher
MD, ABELLIO UK
Dominic Booth

NEW FRANCHISE PLANNED FROM 2016

A new nine-year Northern franchise (with possible year's extension) is planned to begin in April 2016. The Department for Transport (DfT) shortlisted three groups for the new franchise in August 2014: Abellio, Arriva, and Govia.

The DfT in 2012 granted a continuation of Serco and Abellio's Northern Rail's franchise (originally awarded in December 2004) from 15 September 2013 until 1 April 2014. Then in March 2014 the DfT announced a further Direct Award agreement, to operate until the new franchise begins, at the same time as the new TransPennine Express franchise.

Northern runs inter-urban, commuter and local train services for northwest and northeast England, Yorkshire, and Humberside, and Serco and Abellio previously secured a two-year extension in 2010, triggered by improved punctuality and reliability.

The new franchise Invitation to Tender in February 2015 specified that the 'Pacer' railbus trains should be withdrawn and at least 120 new coaches provided for electrified routes. Higher quality rolling stock was specified for services such as Blackpool North-Manchester Airport and Nottingham-Leeds.

The new franchise will be managed by a formal partnership of the DfT and Rail North, a consortium of 30 local transport authorities: this team is planned to be based in Leeds, to use local knowledge and liaise with local transport authorities, while drawing on DfT Rail Executive support functions.

Services transferring from TransPennine Express (TPE) to Northern are Manchester Airport-Blackpool North, Oxenholme-Windermere, and Lancaster to Barrow-in-Furness. York-Scarborough may also

On the first day of electric trains between Liverpool and Manchester Airport, 5 March 2015, 'Northern Electric' Class 319 No 319363 runs between Manchester Oxford Road and Piccadilly with an airport-bound service. **TONY MILES**

transfer, subject to confirmation of Manchester-York electrification plans. A transfer planned from Northern to a re-let East Midlands Trains franchise (due in 2017) is Cleethorpes to Barton-on-Humber.

A one third increase in capacity compared with May 2014 is expected on the Northern franchise. An additional 200 services on Mondays to Saturdays will see frequencies doubled in many cases, with around 300 extra services on Sundays.

'Driver Controlled Operation' is planned to be introduced on at least 50% of train miles by 2020. The DfT plans that the second member of on-train staff will be freed to serve passengers and collect fares, while ensuring on-train safety. While trains could be operated without a second staff member, the DfT said, the franchisee would not be obliged to do so, and a second member of staff should be provided unless collection of revenue, and passenger security and information could be maintained.

Since the Serco/Abellio franchise began in 2004, Northern has provided a more punctual and reliable railway, increasing PPM punctuality from 83.7%, to 91%

KEY STATISTICS
NORTHERN

	2013-14	2014-15
Punctuality (0-5min)	91.0%	90.9%
Passenger journeys (millions)	94.0	96.4
Passenger km (millions)	2,210.5	2,276.5
Timetabled train km (millions)	44.8	45.3
Route km operated	2,734.3	2,734.3
Number of stations operated	463	463
Number of employees	4,980	5,051
Subsidy per passenger km (p)*	7.8	4.9
Network grant / pass km (p)	15.9	10.9

not including PTE grants (5.4p per km in 2014-15)

in 2014, with passenger numbers growing by nearly 50%. The Northern fleet has grown by nearly 20%. Introduction of GPS tracking on the Scarborough to Hull route has seen performance improve by up to 3%.

Against a 'no growth, no investment' franchise specification, it attracted over £100m of external investment. Serco and Abellio have invested over £33m. Northern operates over 2,500 services each weekday.

Northern supports 18 Community Rail Partnerships, promoting rural lines and bringing the railway and local communities closer together. A Community Ambassadors Scheme has been created to promote the use of local rail services with Black and Minority Ethnic and socially excluded groups.

Northern operates a diverse fleet of diesel multiple-units: 79 Class-142, and 13 two-car and 10 three-car Class 144 'Pacers'; 58 Class-150s; 7 Class-155s; 42 Class-156s; 37 two-car and 8 three-car Class-158s; and 18 single car Class-153s. There are eight

Class-321/322 electric multiple-units and 16 Class-333s operated in West Yorkshire, with 17 Class-323s used mainly in Greater Manchester.

With electrification from Manchester to Liverpool via Newton-le-Willows ready from March 2015, three refurbished 'Northern Electrics' Class 319 EMUs, transferred from Thameslink, were available. This increased to 10 as Wigan and Manchester Victoria were added to the electric network in May 2015. Liverpool-Preston services were next to go electric, with the '319' fleet increasing to 20 by December. Driver-only-operated on Thameslink, the '319s' have been modified for driver and conductor operation.

With TPE's Class 170 DMUs being transferred to Chiltern Railways, Northern, TPE and the DfT co-operated to provide alternative trains from May 2015. 20 rather than 14 Class-319 EMUs were to be in use in the North West by the end of 2015, with Northern providing six Class 156 DMUs to TPE. Two loco-hauled sets hired from Direct Rail Services

were introduced on the Cumbrian Coast route.

Northern's main maintenance depots are at Newcastle (Heaton), Manchester (Newton Heath),

Leeds (Neville Hill) and a new depot opened in 2011 at Liverpool (Allerton). Alstom's West Coast Traincare maintains the Class 323s at Manchester. ■

SENIOR PERSONNEL
NORTHERN

MANAGING DIRECTOR Alex Hynes (in photo)
CUSTOMER SERVICE DIRECTOR Natalie Loughborough
DIRECTOR OF OPERATIONS Paul Barnfield
DIRECTOR OF ENGINEERING Stuart Draper
PLANNING AND PROGRAMMES DIRECTOR Rob Warnes
SAFETY AND ENVIRONMENT DIRECTOR Andrea Jacobs
COMMERCIAL DIRECTOR Richard Allan
TRANSITION DIRECTOR Lee Wasnidge
FINANCE DIRECTOR Chris Harris
HUMAN RESOURCES DIRECTOR Adrian Thompson

 ## Merseyrail

25-YEAR CONCESSION FROM JULY 2003

The Merseyrail electric network is one of the most heavily used outside London, with almost 800 trains carrying about 110,000 passengers on an average weekday, on 15min train frequencies, increasing to 5min on city centre sections. Nearly half of Merseyrail passengers are daily users.

Merseytravel, the transport executive body, manages the unique operating concession for this 75-mile, self-contained network of 750V DC, third-rail electrified railway, for the Liverpool City Region Combined Authority.

The 25-year contract, with a total value of £3.6bn, was awarded in 2003

to the Serco and Abellio joint venture 'Merseyrail Electrics 2002', subject to five-yearly reviews. Merseytravel livery is carried on trains and stations. Average fares are among the cheapest in the country, with rises capped at the Retail Price Index level.

The Northern Line links Southport, Ormskirk and Kirkby to Hunts Cross, and the Wirral Line serves West Kirby, New Brighton, Chester, Ellesmere Port and a central Liverpool loop line - 6.5 miles in tunnel with four underground stations in Liverpool and one in Birkenhead.

Merseytravel announced the go-ahead in October 2015 for a major project to replace the train fleet by the end of the decade. New electric trains are to be capable of operation beyond

the Merseyrail 750V DC system. The new trains project is valued at about £430m, including work on power supplies, stations and depots. £65m in Merseytravel reserves is allocated,

with the rest expected to come from public sector or European Investment Bank borrowing. Merseytravel expects to procure the trains under a build and maintain contract, and to own the

KEY STATISTICS
MERSEYRAIL

	2013-14	2014-15
Punctuality (0-5min)	95.8%	95.6%
Passenger journeys (millions)	42.7	44.3
Passenger km (millions)	661.2	695.7
Timetabled train km (millions)	6.4	6.4
Route km operated	120.7	120.7
Number of stations operated	66	66
Number of employees	1,242	1,251
Subsidy per passenger km (p)	12.7	12.4

Merseyrail's Class 508 No 508122 arrives at Hunts Cross in the morning peak on 30 May 2014. **TONY MILES**

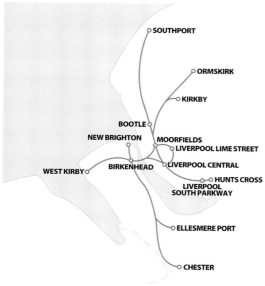

trains which would be leased to the train operator.

Growth and operational efficiencies are expected to help recover additional costs – as is improved reliability. The new trains are expected to achieve close to 40,000 miles per casualty, compared with 10,000 miles on the existing fleet – so an initial fleet of around 50 trains of 60-metre length to replace the existing 59 trains is thought realistic. A larger fleet would be required for future demand and network extensions. More standing room could increase capacity from 303 to 480 passengers per train and driver-controlled operation is anticipated with guards redeployed.

50 of the current fleet of 59 three-car Class 507 and Class 508

trains (built in 1978-79) are required in service each day. A further, £8.5m refurbishment of the trains is continuing, with work on the interiors complementing the new exterior livery. £5.5m has come from rolling stock company Angel Trains, through a revised lease agreement with Merseytravel. £3m has been provided by Merseyrail shareholders, Abellio and Serco.

The new exterior livery features six different themes that reflect attributes of the Liverpool city region, including tourist attractions, shopping and sport. The work is being undertaken at Merseyrail's own depots at Kirkdale and Birkenhead North.

A wide range of service improvement and expansion plans in

the Liverpool City region have been put forward in a 30-year strategy, including improved links to cities and towns further afield for both Merseyrail and other rail routes in the region. Electrification of the Ormskirk-Preston, and Kirkby-Wigan lines, and a new rail service for Skelmersdale, are outlined, and the Wrexham-Bidston line could also be improved and incorporated into the Merseyrail Wirral line. Some options could require dual-voltage Merseyrail trains.

A £40m-plus overhaul for all five underground stations began with £20m of improvements completed in 2012 at Liverpool Central, the network's busiest station, and the underground station with the highest footfall outside London. The Wirral line platform at the final station in the package, Moorfields, was upgraded in 2015, and Network Rail has secured an additional £4.4m to replace nine of the station's escalators.

The funding package was shared between Network Rail, Merseytravel and the European Rail Development Fund.

At Central, transformation of the concourse was carried out by Merseyrail and contractor Strategic Team Group, while Network Rail and contractor Morgan Sindall improved the platforms, escalators and passageways. The station has gained an additional lift, replacement escalators to the Northern Line; additional platform space; and improved toilets and waiting areas. A clear glazed roof and glass external walls allow natural lighting.

Commissioning of the GSM-R leaky feeder radio system within Merseyrail's tunnels was completed in 2014, the final part of Network Rail's nationwide GSM-R train radio roll out.

Merseyrail retained the title as top regional performer in the Spring 2015 National Rail Passenger Survey, and the operator has excellent results for public performance measure punctuality, typically averaging over 95%.

Merseyrail has nine 'Mtogo' stores, combined retail outlet and ticket offices tailored to suit both large and smaller stations. Mtogo is aimed at enhancing the customer experience and making passengers feel more secure. ■

SENIOR PERSONNEL
MERSEYRAIL

MANAGING DIRECTOR
Jan Chaudhry-van der Velde (in photo)
DEPUTY MANAGING DIRECTOR Andy Heath
ENGINEERING DIRECTOR Mike Roe
CUSTOMER SERVICES DIRECTOR Kaj Mook
SAFETY AND ASSURANCE DIRECTOR Zoe Hands
FINANCE AND COMMERCIAL DIRECTOR Paul Bowen
DIRECTOR OF HUMAN RESOURCES Jane English

abellio greateranglia

NEW FRANCHISE
UNTIL OCTOBER 2016

The Greater Anglia franchise was awarded to Abellio from 5 February 2012 for 29 months, a relatively short term, as the DfT prepared for revisions in franchising policy. In April 2014 a new short franchise was agreed, which runs from July 2014 until 15 October 2016.

The agreement with the DfT included a package of over £20m in service enhancements by Abellio Greater Anglia (AGA), including: additional train services between Cambridge and Stansted Airport; and between Norwich and Sheringham with a year-round hourly Sunday service introduced in October 2014. Norwich-Lowestoft now has an hourly service, and two additional services run on the Norwich-London route on summer Sundays. AGA also introduced Delay Repay online for season ticket holders. AGA has extended Oyster pay-as-you-go to customers along the Hertford East line; opened a new Stansted Express customer service desk at Liverpool Street station and recruited a team of 56 on board cleaners.

Services between Liverpool Street and Enfield Town, Cheshunt (via Seven Sisters) and Chingford, as well as Romford-Upminster, transferred to London Overground from 31 May 2015. Liverpool Street-Shenfield stopping services switched to operation by MTR Crossrail, under TfL Rail branding, on the same date.

A £12m major refresh is being undertaken on the Mk3 carriages on Norwich-London inter-city services, to include controlled emission toilet (CET) tanks. Seven catering vehicles are being converted to offer 44 Standard instead of 24 First class seats, continuing to offer the existing catering service. All of the fleet will have been refurbished by the end of the franchise. Work to refurbish the company's five Class 153 units was completed in February 2015 and work

Class 90 No 90010 propels the 12.00 Liverpool Street-Norwich at Ingatestone on 9 August 2015. The train is the former West Coast set on hire from Porterbrook to provide cover during overhauls. **ANTONY GUPPY**

has started on a £1m programme to refresh the 24 Class 317/6 EMUs.

In June 2015 AGA announced that ten of its Class 321 EMUs are to be fully refurbished in a £60m major upgrade programme delivered in partnership with Eversholt Rail. Work will deliver new, more comfortable seating; air conditioning and a new heating system; larger vestibules for improved boarding and alighting, power sockets and wi-fi and an upgrade to on-board monitoring systems to improve reliability. Work is being carried out by Wabtec Rail. AGA is also carrying out a refresh for 40 Class 321s, with new seat covers and better lighting. Along with work carried out on the 17 Class 321s which transferred from London Midland, this means that 67 of the 94 Class 321s will have received customer-focused improvements.

AGA became the first operator in the country to fit a Driving Van Trailer with new equipment that helps to help tackle low adhesion in autumn by applying gel to tracks. Following positive results the programme is being extended to some EMUs.

AGA has made consistent improvements in punctuality since taking the franchise over working more closely with Network Rail through an alliance to deliver improved performance. An agreement with Network Rail has ensured a revised approach to engineering work, significantly reducing disruption at weekends and in 2014 a joint investment of £1m was announced to raise performance standards. AGA continues to work with the DfT, Network Rail and other stakeholders as part of the Great Eastern rail campaign, to develop plans to improve journey times and service.

An extensive programme to improve stations has brought work including new secure cycle

compounds, upgraded waiting rooms, and, at 35 stations, new customer information screens. Major work is ongoing to improve Chelmsford, Norwich and Cambridge stations and improvements are being delivered at Ipswich station under the DfT's National Stations Improvement Programme. Burnham station house has undergone complete refurbishment and the building has been leased to the council and local artists.

Renewed focus on marketing to encourage more passenger journeys includes an innovative partnership with Visit East Anglia. AGA is strengthening its commitment to the Community Rail Partnerships by increasing its funding contribution by 20%.

KEY STATISTICS
ABELLIO GREATER ANGLIA

	2013-14	2014-15
Punctuality	91.7%	91.1%
Passenger journeys (millions)	135.2	143.4
Passenger km (millions)	4,350.3	4,524.0
Timetabled train km (millions)	33.8	34.0
Route km operated	1,611.0	1,611.0
Number of stations operated	167	167
Number of employees	3,008	3,118
Subsidy per passenger km (p)	-3.7	-4.1
Network grant / pass km (p)	4.7	5.8

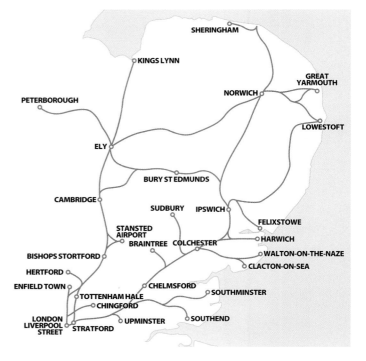

HITACHI
Inspire the Next

Greater Anglia's main train depots are at Ilford, Norwich and Clacton, with cleaning and stabling at other locations. The fleet of four-car electric multiple-units, based at Ilford, is made up of 46 Class 317s (317/5: 15 trains; 317/6: 24; 317/7: one train; 317/8: 6 trains), 94 Class 321s, 21 Class 360s and 30 Class 379s. The diesel fleet has five single-car Class 153s, nine Class 156s, four two-car Class 170s and eight three-car Class 170s. The locomotive-hauled fleet is comprised of 15 Class 90 locos, 15 Mk3 Driving Van Trailers and 118 Mk3 coaches. There are also 10 Mk3s and a DVT on hire from Porterbrook (formerly used on West Coast) as cover during overhauls. Two Class 08 shunters are hired, and 2 Class 37 locomotives and 3 Mk2 carriages hired from DRS are used on Norwich-Great Yarmouth/Lowestoft services.

SENIOR PERSONNEL
ABELLIO GREATER ANGLIA

MANAGING DIRECTOR Jamie Burles (in photo)
OPERATIONS DIRECTOR Peter Lensik
CUSTOMER SERVICE DIRECTOR Andrew Goodrum
FINANCE DIRECTOR Adam Golton
ENGINEERING DIRECTOR Kate Marjoribanks
ASSET MANAGEMENT DIRECTOR Simone Bailey
HR AND SAFETY DIRECTOR Michelle Smart
COMMERCIAL DIRECTOR Andy Camp

SEVEN-YEAR FRANCHISE FROM 1 APRIL 2015

Abellio was awarded the new ScotRail franchise by the Scottish Government in 2014, beginning operation on 1 April 2015. The franchise is for seven years, with a three-year extension available, subject to performance.

Abellio ScotRail has established a deep alliance with Network Rail, led by a single managing director, which is expected to deliver improved performance and efficiencies. The ScotRail livery and colour scheme incorporates Scotland's national flag, the Saltire, and continues irrespective of franchise operator.

On 6 September 2015 the Borders Railway opened, restoring train services between Edinburgh and Galashiels and Tweedbank after more than 40 years. The line includes 30 miles of new railway with seven new stations. Ridership has exceeded expectations, with ScotRail working to find spare trains to strengthen services.

As part of the revised Edinburgh-Glasgow Improvements Programme (EGIP), platforms at Glasgow Queen Street station are being extended to accommodate longer trains. Completion of EGIP will enable the Edinburgh-Glasgow journey-time, worked by new 4-car EMUs, to be cut to 42min, the best ever. Completion of the programme to electrify the Cumbernauld line enabled electric trains to be introduced on the route in May 2014, with many trains operating via Glasgow Queen Street low level as an extension of existing Springburn-Dalmuir services.

A Smart Flex-Carnet ticket is planned by Abellio, allowing part time commuters to benefit from reduced price travel. A new Super Off-peak Smart fare will be introduced on suburban routes, providing discounts of up to 20% on existing off-peak prices at times when services are lightly used. New advance fares between any two Scottish cities will start at £5 for Standard class.

With electrification of the Edinburgh-Glasgow and Stirling-Alloa-Dunblane routes, deliveries will start from December 2017 of a new fleet of 46 three-car and 24 four-car Hitachi AT200 electric trains (Class 381). Abellio says it will order a further 10 three-car units if granted the three-year franchise extension. These new 100mph trains will feature air conditioning, at-seat power sockets, wi-fi and table seating. From 2018 Glasgow-Alloa journeys will fall to 45min.

Abellio also intends to replace Class 170 DMUs on many long distance services from December 2018 with refurbished diesel High Speed Train sets in four-car or five-car formations, providing an overall increase in seats of more than 33%. The vehicles will have new seats, tables, floor coverings and wi-fi, with buffet and at-seat trolley service. Fastest journeys between

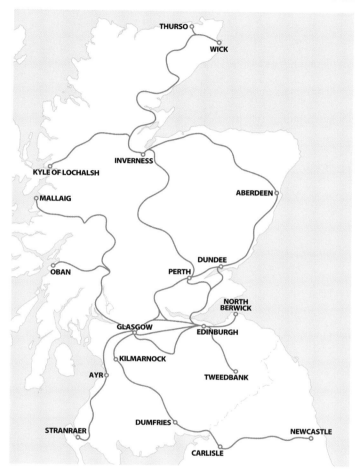

Class 320 No 320316 arrives at Greenfaulds on 16 April 2015 with the 12.22 Cumbernauld-Dalmuir ScotRail service. **STEWART ARMSTRONG**

KEY STATISTICS
SCOTRAIL

	2013-14	2014-15
Punctuality (0-5min)	91.4%	90.5%
Passenger journeys (millions)	86.3	92.7
Passenger km (millions)	2,827.5	3,020.7
Timetabled train km (millions)	45.3	46.4
Route km operated	3,065.8	3,065.8
Number of stations operated	347	347
Number of employees	4,845	4,966
Subsidy per passenger km ()	17.5	8.6

Operator until 31 March 2015: First ScotRail

SENIOR PERSONNEL
SCOTRAIL ALLIANCE

MANAGING DIRECTOR Phil Verster (in photo)
COMMERCIAL DIRECTOR Cathy Craig
OPERATIONS DIRECTOR Perry Ramsey
ENGINEERING DIRECTOR Angus Thom
CUSTOMER EXPERIENCE DIRECTOR Jacqueline Taggart
INFRASTRUCTURE DIRECTOR David Dickson
CLIENT & COMMUNICATIONS DIRECTOR Rob Shorthouse
SAFETY, SUSTAINABILITY & ASSURANCE DIRECTOR David Lister
PROGRAMMES & TRANSFORMATION DIRECTOR Ian McConnell
HR DIRECTOR Julie McComasky
FINANCE DIRECTOR Kenny McPhail

Glasgow and Inverness are planned to fall below 3hr. Abellio will also adopt a new approach to train maintenance, with monitoring equipment on more trains.

ScotRail is also progressing a major investment programme for flagship stations including Aberdeen, Inverness, Perth and Stirling.

The ScotRail fleet has 2-car diesel multiple-units of Class 156 (48 trains) and Class 158 (48 trains). 3-car DMUs are of Class 170/3 (4 trains), and Class 170/4 (51). 3-car electric multiple-units are of Class 314 (16 trains), Class 318 (21), Class 320 (22), Class 334 (40). There are 22 three-car and 16 four-car Class 380 EMUs. The fleet is maintained

at Edinburgh Haymarket, Glasgow Eastfield, Shields Road and Corkerhill, and Inverness depots. The Hitachi AT200s are to have a new depot at Millerhill near Edinburgh. HSTs will be maintained at Inverness, Haymarket and Craigentinny.

Seven Class 321 units cascaded from London Midland are being reformed to three-car units to

match the existing Class 320 sets and provide additional capacity for Glasgow suburban services. Two Class 68-hauled trains are hired from DRS for peak runs on the Fife Circle.

After acquisition of the new and additional trains, existing trains leaving the franchise are expected to be 10 Class-156, eight Class-158 and 34 Class-170. ■

CALEDONIAN SLEEPER

15-YEAR OVERNIGHT SERVICE FRANCHISE

Caledonian Sleeper is the new 15-year standalone franchise for the overnight services between London and Scotland. The franchise was awarded to Serco Caledonian Sleepers Limited in May 2014 and it took over the operation (which was previously part of ScotRail) on 31 March 2015. The franchise is expected to deliver revenues of up to £800m over the 15 years, of which approximately £180m will be in the form of franchise payments, according to Serco. A 'gain share' agreement has been reached

with Transport Scotland 'to incentivise performance improvements'.

Trains run nightly (except Saturday night) and operations comprise two services: the Lowland Sleeper which operates services to/from Glasgow and Edinburgh; the Highland Sleeper which operates services to/from Aberdeen, Inverness and Fort William. Passengers can continue to use valid daytime tickets on the Caledonian Sleeper on the West Highland Line between Glasgow Queen Street and Fort William (both directions), and also between Kingussie and Inverness (northbound only).

A new fleet of 72 coaches, to be built by CAF, should start entering service in the summer of 2018. Valued at approximately

£150m, the new fleet is being part-funded by a £60m grant from the Scottish government. The vehicles will include en-suite berths in a premium business class, reclining seats that can be repositioned as flat beds, and a brasserie-style Club Car. Serco pledged a broad partnership with Scottish suppliers to offer an 'outstanding hospitality service that is emblematic of the best of Scotland': hotel and catering company Inverlochy Castle Management International will support the operation. An updated sales and reservation system with a 'broader range of fares' is planned to drive growth in passenger numbers, both among UK residents and international tourists.

Currently the Sleeper fleet comprises 22 Mk2 coaches providing seated accommodation and 53 Mk3 sleeper cars.

Serco has agreed contracts with Alstom for rolling stock maintenance and GB Railfreight to provide traincrew and traction. GBRf plans to use a refurbished fleet of Class 92 locomotives for the main legs of the journey over the WCML to Glasgow/Edinburgh with rebuilt Class 73/9 locomotives for non-electrified sections to Fort William, Inverness and Aberdeen. Class 67 locomotives hired from DB Schenker Rail continue until the Class 73s are ready to take over. Three locomotives hired from the AC Locomotive Group, Nos 86101, 86401 and 87002, are used as back-up and for empty stock workings. Problems with the Class 92 locomotives, principally due to some issues with the 25kV power supply north of Crewe, saw the locomotives temporarily replaced by Class 90 locomotives hired from DBS and Freightliner. ■

NEWCOMER: Class 92 No 92038 in new Caledonian Sleeper livery powers the 2014 Inverness, Fort William and Aberdeen to London Euston service through Berkhamsted on 11 April 2015. **KEN BRUNT**

SENIOR PERSONNEL
CALEDONIAN SLEEPER

MANAGING DIRECTOR
Peter Strachan (in photo)
GUEST EXPERIENCE DIRECTOR
Ryan Flaherty

HITACHI
Inspire the Next

GOVIA

Govia is responsible for nearly 30% of national passenger rail journeys and its subsidiary GTR is the UK's busiest rail operator. Other rail franchises it operates are Southeastern and London Midland.

Govia is a joint venture partnership between British company The Go-Ahead Group and Keolis. Go-Ahead, the 65% majority partner, employs 26,000 people in UK rail and bus.

Keolis - in which French Railways (SNCF) is a major shareholder - operates trains, buses and metros across the world. Another joint venture, between FirstGroup and Keolis, has held the TransPennine Express franchise since 2004.

Go-Ahead operated the Thames Trains franchise from 1996 to 2004 and Govia the Thameslink franchise from 1997 to 2006.

Govia was awarded the Integrated Kent franchise, operated as Southeastern, in 2006. In November 2007 it began operating the new West Midlands franchise, as London Midland.

The GTR (Govia Thameslink Railway) franchise started on 14 September 2014, incorporating Thameslink and Great Northern routes. In July 2015 Southern and Gatwick Express services joined GTR.

In the DfT's revised franchising programme, a Southeastern direct award contract was agreed, running until 24 June 2018. The London Midland franchise was extended until March 2016, and in summer 2015 the DfT indicated that a new direct award contract was planned to run to October 2017.

Govia was shortlisted in 2014 for the Northern franchise, and in another joint venture with Keolis (Keolis is the 65% majority shareholder) was shortlisted to bid for TransPennine Express.

GTR

SEVEN-YEAR MANAGEMENT CONTRACT

The Thameslink, Southern, Great Northern (TSGN) franchise, operated by Govia from 14 September 2014 as Govia Thameslink Railway (GTR), replaced the previous Thameslink & Great Northern franchise held by First Capital Connect (FCC). From 26 July 2015, the franchise was further enlarged when it incorporated Southern and Gatwick Express which had previously been operated as a separate franchise by Govia. A number of stations on the Catford loop and the operation of Sevenoaks-Blackfriars services transferred from the Southeastern franchise to TSGN in December 2014.

The basis of the franchise is a seven year management contract: this means that Govia passes ticket revenue directly to the government.

The arrangement was chosen because of the extensive work being carried out on the Thameslink route through the centre of London, including resignalling of the central part of the route, and the extensive rebuilding of London Bridge station. From its start, the franchise used separate branding for Thameslink and Great Northern, with each service group having its own website. The Southern and Gatwick Express brands have been retained since they joined the new franchise: the GTR name is not used on trains or stations.

The Thameslink and Great Northern routes connect important regional centres north and south of London such as Peterborough, Cambridge, Bedford, Luton and Brighton. They provide rail links to Gatwick and Luton airports, and to Eurostar at St Pancras International. From 2018, Farringdon station will provide an interchange between Thameslink and Crossrail, bringing connections to Heathrow Canary Wharf and central London.

KEY STATISTICS
GTR - THAMESLINK & GREAT NORTHERN

	2013-14	2014-15
Punctuality (0-5min)	86.1%	85.2%
Passenger journeys (millions)	117.8	123.8
Passenger km (millions)	3,848.2	3,975.5
Timetabled train km (millions)	25.1	26.0
Route km operated	494.1	547.2
Number of stations operated	75	81
Number of employees	2,541	2,610
Subsidy per passenger km (pence)	-5.3	-4.5*
Network grant / pass km (p)	2.9	5.0*

First Capital Connect franchise until 14 September 2014.

* period from 14 September 2014.

The Southern franchise was operated by Govia from August 2001. Originally branded as South Central, Govia took over the franchise from Connex South Central. In June 2008 the franchise was expanded with the addition of Gatwick Express, with the Gatwick Express branding for this London Victoria-Gatwick Airport service being retained. Some Gatwick Express trains are extended to serve Brighton in peak periods. Govia won a franchise renewal in September 2009.

GTR (Thameslink) Class 387/1 No 387123 at Blackfriars, bound for Bedford on 24 June 2015. **TONY MILES**

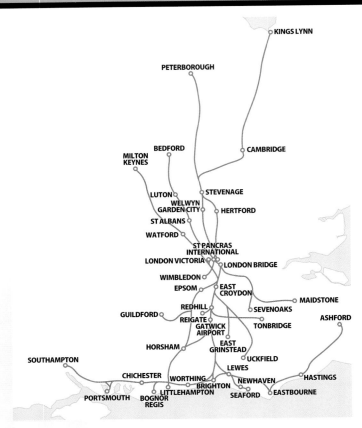

from July 2015, Govia's revenue from franchise payments is estimated to be about £1.1bn. Target operating profit margins average about 3% over the life of the franchise and there are performance regimes in place to incentivise or penalise Govia to meet a range of service quality targets (including for punctuality, customer experience at stations and on train, and revenue protection). In addition to performance regimes, Govia can also achieve bonus payments for delivery of key performance milestones in the Thameslink Programme. Govia will work with the DfT to generate passenger revenue of an estimated £12.4bn over the life of the franchise.

NEW TRAINS

Govia has committed to the procurement of around £430m of investment over the life of the franchise, including significant investment in rolling stock and franchise improvements. Major projects include the introduction of three new train fleets for Thameslink, Great Northern and Gatwick Express, providing 26% more carriages and 10,000 additional seats on trains to London in the morning peak, and additional services.

The franchise is playing a crucial role in delivering the government's

£6.5bn Thameslink Programme - the major infrastructure project that will allow up to 24 trains per hour to travel in each direction on the core of the network, between Blackfriars and St Pancras. New tunnels will carry trains from the Great Northern route to join the Thameslink route at St Pancras. The franchise will introduce new Class 700 'Desiro City' trains, totalling 1,140 carriages and being constructed by Siemens, on the Thameslink network. The first train was delivered to the new Three Bridges depot in July 2015, with the depot itself formally opened by the Secretary of State for Transport on

Southern services operate into London Bridge and London Victoria from South London and the South Coast, and between Milton Keynes and Croydon via the West London Line.

GTR is the largest rail franchise in the UK in terms of passenger

numbers, trains, revenue and staff, it is forecast to carry 273m passenger journeys per year, employ around 6,500 people, and generate annual passenger revenues of £1.3bn. In the first full year to June 2016, which includes the Southern franchise

GTR (Southern) Class 455 No 455834 passes Thameslink Programme work in progress on the Southeastern lines at London Bridge on 23 May 2015. **NETWORK RAIL**

15 October 2015. Another new depot for the trains is at Hornsey, alongside the main Great Northern depot.

The Class 700s will start running on the Bedford to Brighton line in spring 2016, and should then be introduced on the London King's Cross to Cambridge, King's Lynn and Peterborough routes later in the year.

29 new Class 387/1 EMUs entered service on the Thameslink route in 2014/15, an interim measure to allow the cascade of Class 319 trains to other parts of the country, meaning that by spring 2015 almost every Bedford-Brighton service was being worked by an air-conditioned Class 377 or 387 Electrostar EMU. When Class 700 trains enter full service, the Class 387s will also be redeployed elsewhere.

In November 2014, GTR announced that it had signed a £145.2m order for 108 new Class 387/2 sets to replace the 1980s-built Class 442 Gatwick Express fleet in 2016. The new trains will operate in 12-car formations at peak times, and feature better-configured luggage space, free wi-fi, and power points. On-board screens will provide better onward travel information including Tube service updates, and additional on-train staff are planned to provide travellers with help and information.

Govia is also to procure a fleet of 25 six-car air-conditioned 'Metro' EMUs to replace the 40-year-old Class 313s currently operating on the route between Moorgate, north London and Hertfordshire in 2018. The trains will be fitted with real-time information screens, and will be fully accessible for disabled passengers.

The majority of the Class 365 fleet is to be transferred for use elsewhere

GTR (Great Northern) Class 365 No 365517 at Harringay, bound for King's Cross on 27 March 2015. **TONY MILES**

in the UK, and Great Northern services to Cambridge and King's Lynn will be handed over to Class 377 EMUs transferred from Southern. There is also a commitment to bring in longer trains on the diesel operated Uckfield and Ashford-Hastings lines: four 3-car Class 170s transferred from ScotRail in April 2015 for modification to make them compatible with the existing Class 171 fleet. Work to extend 12 station platforms on the Uckfield line in preparation for 10-coach trains began in September 2015.

Work continues to improve the existing train fleet, and during 2015 GTR brought in the first upgraded Class 319 and Class 365 sets with wheelchair-friendly toilets and other accessibility improvements, including door sounders and automated public address and electronic information screens.

SERVICE RECAST

The Gatwick Express timetable will be changed to see a half-hourly through service between Brighton, Gatwick Airport and London Victoria (a key part of the business case for the new trains), alternating every 15min with services between Gatwick and Victoria only. A recast of the Brighton main line timetable in December 2015 foreshadows many service changes planned for the full 2018 Thameslink timetable. The new off-peak timetable on the route is intended to create a more evenly spaced, more punctual service and also to help with better performance during the evening peak, which has been a major challenge since the start of service alterations for Thameslink Programme work at London Bridge.

Since January 2015 all Thameslink services have been running via Elephant & Castle as the London

Bridge route is not available until the completion, in 2018, of work to rebuild the station and the tracks serving it.

December 2015 also sees the opening hours of the Moorgate branch extended on weekdays, and trains will also serve it at weekends. The completion of track work north of Ely by May 2017 is planned to enable off-peak King's Lynn-London King's Cross services to go half-hourly.

In 2018, with the ending of the London Bridge blockade, the high frequency service through the Thameslink core will be launched. Initially at 21 trains/hr, it is planned to grow to 24 by the end of the year. New Thameslink services will include fast trains between Cambridge and Brighton, which will link Cambridge and Gatwick in about 1hr 40min. Other services include Peterborough-Horsham via Gatwick Airport. Service frequency for Hertford North and

KEY STATISTICS
GTR - SOUTHERN

	2013-14	2014-15
Punctuality (0-5min)	85.8%	83.1%
Passenger journeys (millions)	181.8	188.6
Passenger km (millions)	4,548.5	4,715.5
Timetabled train km (millions)	37.8	37.8
Route km operated	666.3	666.3
Number of stations operated	156	156
Number of employees	4,045	4,202
Subsidy per passenger km (p)	-3.6	-4.0
Network grant / pass km (p)	4.0	3.8

Welwyn Garden City will be increased with trains to Moorgate increasing from 12 to 14 an hour in the high peak. GTR has begun a £9.8m investment in staff training and development and has launched the UK's biggest driver recruitment and training programme.

The new franchise has committed to deliver smartcard ticketing across the franchise area, using the 'Key' smartcard already established on Southern. In autumn 2015 it was launched for season ticket holders on Thameslink and Great Northern services. Oyster pay-as-you-go is also to be extended to Epsom, Gatwick Airport, Luton Airport Parkway, Welwyn Garden City and Hertford North. Evening restrictions on off-peak fares that First Capital Connect introduced will remain through the first part of the franchise.

Single-leg pricing is to be introduced, benefiting passengers making journeys that are 'peak' in one direction and 'off-peak' in the other: 'super off peak' fares are to become available during the week in the north part of the franchise from 2018. GTR is also carrying out extended trials of flexible season tickets for part-time workers, utilising smartcard technology, and cheaper advance tickets will be introduced.

GTR is also to deliver £50m of station improvements, with every station seeing a level of upgrading based on its condition. St Albans, Luton and possibly Stevenage will get high levels of refurbishment and an additional fund for improvements to small stations is pledged, with community involvement also encouraged. The DfT is requiring 'first to last train' staffing at the 101 busiest stations which have more than a one million passenger footfall per year at the start of the franchise, and free wi-fi will be rolled out at 104 stations. Gatelines will be introduced at 21 stations.

Almost £1m of accessibility improvements have been made in recent years to stations across the Southern network. Southern also delivered a £1.5m, 500-space cycle hub at Brighton station. The secure-entry facility also includes a coffee shop, maintenance and repair workshop, showers, changing rooms and accessible toilets. 50 electric vehicle charging points were installed across the Southern network.

A number of job seekers in Luton have been taking part in Southern's Princes Trust 'Get into Railway' 4-week programme and its success should see the scheme rolled out onto the Great Northern and Southern networks in 2016.

GTR's Passenger Service Directors (PSDs) are empowered to lead all aspects of service delivery within their directorates, responsible for drivers, conductors and station staff within their areas.

At the start of November 2015 the Thameslink, Southern and Great Northern train fleet had the following 3-car electric multiple-units (EMUs): 44 Class-313 (Great Northern), 19 Class-313 (Southern); 28 Class-377/3.

4-car EMUs are: 12 Class-317/1, 12 Class-319/0, 6 Class-319/2; six Class-319/3; 38 Class-319/4; 13 Class-321; 40 Class-365; 23 Class-377/5; 75 Class-377/4; 15 Class-377/2 (9 Thameslink, 6 Southern); 64 Class-377/1; 29 Class-387/1; and 46 Class-455.

5-car EMUs are 24 Class-442; 26 Class-377/6; 8 Class-377/7.

DMUs are 10 Class-171/7 (each with 2 cars); and 6 Class-171/8 (4 cars). ■

SENIOR PERSONNEL
GOVIA THAMESLINK RAILWAY

CHIEF EXECUTIVE OFFICER Charles Horton (in photo)
CHIEF OPERATING OFFICER Dyan Crowther
CHIEF FINANCIAL OFFICER Wilma Allan
COMMERCIAL DIRECTOR David Innis
ENGINEERING DIRECTOR Gerry McFadden
PROGRAMME DIRECTOR Keith Wallace
INTEGRATION DIRECTOR Jonathan Kennedy
HEAD OF SAFETY AND SUSTAINABILITY Colin Morris

PASSENGER SERVICE DIRECTORS:
GREAT NORTHERN Keith Jipps
THAMESLINK Stuart Cheshire
SOUTHERN MAINLINE David Scorey
SOUTHERN METRO Alex Foulds
GATWICK EXPRESS Angie Doll

southeastern.

DIRECT AWARD
UNTIL JUNE 2018

The Southeastern franchise serves Kent, south east London and part of East Sussex and includes high-speed domestic services on High Speed 1 (HS1). 80% of its passengers are commuters and its service is heavily geared to meet a huge and growing demand for peak period services.

After being awarded an initial six-year franchise from 1 April 2006, Southeastern was granted a two-year extension to 12 October 2014 after performance targets had been met. Under the DfT's revised franchising programme, a new direct award contract until June 2018 was agreed. It covers the duration of the Thameslink Programme infrastructure upgrade and London Bridge rebuild, with, in turn, Charing Cross and then Cannon Street services not stopping at London Bridge.

The new agreement included commitments to more high-speed services with extra peak capacity, and new journey opportunities designed to help passengers during the three year rebuild of London Bridge. Changes include faster peak trains for Hastings, direct services between Maidstone East and Canterbury West, more services between Dartford and London Victoria and a new Blackfriars-Maidstone East service. In December 2014 a small number of Catford Loop services were incorporated into the GTR Thameslink service group.

Extra staff have been deployed on gatelines at key stations and more customer service staff are on hand at key stations throughout the major timetable changes to help passengers with information and provide advice on alternative travel options.

Innovative ticketing changes include the extension of the Transport for London Oyster system to Dartford and Swanley, and between St Pancras International and Stratford International.

Southeastern has also been working to increase Off-Peak travel, with Advance tickets and online discounts.

Station improvements include 63 additional ticket machines, deep cleaning of all stations and a £4.8m programme including repainting all managed stations. Long-line information systems have been upgraded and improvements carried out to the company's Eyewitness and CCTV monitoring service.

Southeastern believes one of the key factors of passenger satisfaction on the network is information

KEY STATISTICS
SOUTHEASTERN

	2013-14	2014-15
Punctuality (0-5min)	89.0%	89.3%
Passenger journeys (millions)	178.6	185.8
Passenger km (millions)	4,347.2	4,514.5
Timetabled train km (millions)	38.2	37.7
Route km operated	748.3	748.3
Number of stations operated	173	176
Number of employees	3,866	4,065
Subsidy per passenger km (p)	2.2	0.7
Network grant / pass km (p)	5.5	5.1

Passing work in progress on the new Crossrail interchange at Abbey Wood, Southeastern's Class 465 No 465002 heads an 8-car formation towards Dartford on 1 October 2015. **CROSSRAIL**

provision, which has been improved by the creation of a new and improved journey planning app, 'On Track', and by adding 20 customer information screens at key stations across the network. Tablets issued to train crew and gateline staff provide live information and put them in a better position to assist passengers during disruption. Southeastern's Twitter team saw followers leap from less than 20,000 to more than 90,000 in a year.

Class 375 trains, which account for a third of Southeastern's rolling stock, are undergoing a mid-life refresh, which includes new seats and carpets, new interior paintwork, better toilets and a total exterior repaint similar to the Class

395 high-speed trains' colour scheme. First class seating is being moved from the ends of the trains to central carriages so that more Standard class seating can be provided.

An improved score in overall customer satisfaction was recorded during the mid 2015 National Rail Passenger Survey, the second successive rise. Southeastern was one of only three train operators in London and South East to see a rise in overall customer satisfaction. The independent Institute of Customer Service in 2015 also rated Southeastern as the second most improved company nationally.

Southeastern's commitment to reducing traction energy has seen the

increased use of regenerative braking, the re-training of drivers and the promotion of eco-driving techniques supported by the creation of an award for good driving. A 'driving energy further' initiative has reduced carbon emissions by 42,000 tonnes of CO_2, saving around £6.2m. Southeastern was also the first stand-alone train company to commit to the '10:10' carbon reduction commitment. 70% of all waste is now recycled (up from 10% in 2006).

Southeastern runs a completely electric train fleet. Maintenance is carried out at Slade Green near Dartford (suburban) and Ramsgate (main line), with smaller depots for maintenance and cleaning at Ashford, Grove Park and Gillingham. Hitachi's depot at Ashford maintains the 29 Class-395 six-car high-speed trains. The remainder of the fleet is made up of 10 three-car and 102 four-car Class 375s; 36 five-car Class 376s; 147 four-car Class 465s; and 43 two-car Class 466s.

SENIOR PERSONNEL
SOUTHEASTERN

MANAGING DIRECTOR David Statham (in photo)
ENGINEERING DIRECTOR Mark Johnson
PASSENGER SERVICES DIRECTOR Barbara Thomas
TRAIN SERVICES DIRECTOR Richard Dean
HR DIRECTOR Scott Maynard
FINANCE DIRECTOR Elodie Brian

london midland

DIRECT AWARD UNTIL OCTOBER 2017 PLANNED

The London Midland (LM) franchise began on 11 November 2007, combining the former Silverlink franchise's County routes and most of Central Trains. The company has two brands, London Midland City (West Midlands conurbation and the wider region, with Centro's Network West Midlands brand prominent) and London Midland Express (longer distance West Coast main

line - WCML - routes connecting London Euston, the Midlands and Northwest).

Following its review of franchising, the DfT extended LM's franchise by 28 weeks until March 2016, prior to a new direct award contract planned to run to October 2017, according to a DfT programme issued in summer 2015. A grouping of West Midland shire and unitary authorities has been in discussion with the DfT over a staged approach to management devolution of West Midlands services in future franchises.

KEY STATISTICS
LONDON MIDLAND

	2013-14	2014-15
Punctuality (0-5min)	85.9%	88.0%
Passenger journeys (millions)	64.0	65.3
Passenger km (millions)	2,363.7	2,373.0
Timetabled train km (millions)	25.7	25.9
Route km operated	898.8	898.8
Number of stations operated	148	148
Number of employees	2,401	2,353
Subsidy per passenger km (p)	2.8	2.7
Network grant / pass km (p)	6.1	7.6

LM's timetable structure introduced in 2008 includes through services between Birmingham and London, and a new service between London and Crewe via the Trent Valley and Stoke-on-Trent. 37 new Siemens Class 350/2 Desiro electric trains were introduced, and Class 172 Bombardier Turbostars replaced most Class 150 Sprinters from 2011. Seven Class 321 EMUs retained to increase capacity between Watford Junction and London Euston were replaced by Class 319s in 2015.

A joint initiative with Siemens upgraded the Class 350/1 EMUs to run at 110mph, to cut WCML journey times and introduce additional services. Phase two of the project, for trains of 8 to 12 vehicles to run at 110mph, was completed in 2014. 110mph running allows some services to avoid Northampton and cut journey times to London by up to 30min, and capacity was created for an extra hourly Milton Keynes-London train, off-peak.

Ten new 110mph Class 350/3 Desiros were delivered in 2014. Seven are allocated to the WCML, providing around 4,000 more peak seats per day in and out of Euston, and the other three release Class 323s to provide extra Birmingham Cross-City services.

From December 2014 WCML routes have had more lengthened trains, changes to calling patterns, further 110mph operation, and additional services. In May 2015, LM reduced many of its Birmingham/Crewe-London fares.

Meters on all LM's Class 323 and Class 350 EMUs monitor how much

Arriving at Rugby with a train for London Euston, No 350373 is one of London Midland's 110mph Class 350/3 trains built in 2014. **TONY MILES**

electricity is used and the amount regenerated in braking. The data can be analysed to help with driving in a more energy efficient way.

A commitment to addressing passenger needs, raising punctuality and reducing cancellations was the basis of a 'Strong Foundations' programme implemented in 2013. Work has included building resilience into timetables so LM is better prepared to address challenges such as major public events.

LM's Public Performance Measure figures have shown progress, with the September 2015 score reaching 89.6% and a Moving Annual Average of 87.6% - an improvement on the 2014

figure, given the ongoing challenge of running many services on the highly congested WCML.

A £2 million Park & Ride extension constructed by Centro in 2015 provides 55 additional parking spaces at Four Oaks, near Sutton Coldfield, with an additional car park deck.

London Midland has four heads of route who have overall responsibility for the West Coast main line, Birmingham Snow Hill services, Regional, and Cross City services. They focus on train performance, customer service and passenger information, as well as working closely with Network Rail and other partners.

London Midland has taken advantage of the DfT's National Station Improvement Programme (NSIP) to benefit 21 stations. This was achieved through £1.2m of NSIP funds and an additional £2.5m of outside funding. In a £100m investment package in north Worcestershire, Network Rail installed a new 3km section of double track in summer 2014, allowing LM to run three services an hour between Barnt Green and Redditch.

Work is also underway on a £17.4m replacement station at Bromsgrove, with four platforms, supported by

electrification between Bromsgrove and Barnt Green, which will enable Cross-City services to be extended to the new station. The new Stratford-upon-Avon Parkway station opened in 2013, and new stations have been constructed at Ricoh Arena and Bermuda Park, on the on the Coventry-Nuneaton line. The new Northampton station was completed in December 2014, and a new station for Kenilworth is being developed, with construction due to begin in late 2015.

LM is now working with industry partners to develop a new depot at Duddeston to absorb an expected capacity uplift. Existing main depots are at Northampton, and Birmingham's Tyseley and Soho.

The diesel train fleet consists of: Class 172 Turbostars (12 two-car and 15 three-car), Class 170 Turbostars (17 two-car and six three-car), Class 150 Sprinters (3 two-car); Class 153 (8 single-car), Class 139 (2 single-car, LPG/flywheel-powered Parry People Movers).

The electric train fleet mainly has four-car trains: four Class 319, 30 Class-350/1, 37 Class-350/2, and 10 Class 350/3 Desiros; plus 26 three-car Class-323s. ∎

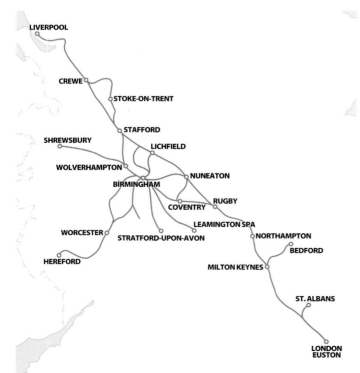

SENIOR PERSONNEL

LONDON MIDLAND

MANAGING DIRECTOR Patrick Verwer (in photo)
FINANCE & CONTRACTS DIRECTOR Ian McLaren
PASSENGER SERVICES DIRECTOR Tom Joyner
COMMERCIAL DIRECTOR Richard Brooks
ASSET MAINTENANCE DIRECTOR Neil Bamford
GENERAL MANAGER, WEST COAST Sean McBroom
GENERAL MANAGER, WEST MIDLANDS Mark Goodall
HEAD OF OPERATIONS John Robson

HITACHI
Inspire the Next

ARRIVA

Arriva is the division of the German state rail group Deutsche Bahn (DB) responsible for regional passenger transport outside Germany, since DB acquired Arriva plc in 2010. In 2014, 45,700 (full time equivalent) employees operated in 14 countries, with revenue of Euro 4.49billion and operating profit (EBITDA adjusted) of Euro 498m (2013: Euro 467m).

Arriva UK Trains operations cover about 14% of the UK passenger network. CrossCountry and Arriva Trains Wales franchises were won prior to 2010, and DB has run Chiltern Railways since acquiring its parent Laing Rail in 2008. Open-access train company Grand Central was acquired in 2011.

Also involved in the Laing acquisition was the London Overground (LO) concession, awarded in 2007 to London Overground Rail Operations Ltd (LOROL), a joint venture of Laing with Hong Kong's MTR. A two-year extension to November 2016 was confirmed in 2013. In June 2015 Arriva and MTR, independently, were among four groups invited to tender for a new LO concession. Arriva operates a seven-year Tyne & Wear Metro contract for Nexus, the Passenger Transport Executive, covering train services, fleet maintenance and modernisation, and station management.

The train maintenance, overhaul and servicing company Arriva TrainCare (formerly LNWR) is based in Crewe, with other locations at Bristol, Eastleigh, Cambridge and Tyne Yard.

Alliance Rail Holdings (ARH), acquired by DB in 2010, undertakes strategic development work for Grand Central and other proposed open-access services. The Office of Rail and Road gave ARH approval in August 2015 for six daily Great North Western Railway return services between London and Blackpool: planned to start from December 2017 using 6-car Alstom Pendolino trains.

ARH is seeking to introduce a two hourly Great North Eastern service from London to Bradford and Ilkley, calling at Leeds and a new 'parkway' station to the east. Services to Scunthorpe, Grimsby and Cleethorpes, using new build Hitachi Super Express Trains or equivalent, are also being pursued – as is an hourly King's Cross-Edinburgh service taking 3hr 43min, operated by 9-car Alstom Pendolinos, their ability to tilt giving a time advantage.

ARH is also evaluating other open access opportunities and supporting Arriva companies on track access matters.

UK Trains operating profit (EBITDA adjusted) in 2014 was Euro 67m (2013: Euro 62m). In 2015, Arriva selected Fujitsu to provide the rail industry's first smartphone-based ticket issuing system, STARmobile.

MD, ARRIVA UK TRAINS Chris Burchell
MD, ALLIANCE RAIL Ian Yeowart

Chiltern Railways

20 YEAR FRANCHISE FROM FEBRUARY 2002

Chiltern Railways reached a major milestone on 25 October 2015 with the first trains running on a new route from Oxford Parkway to London Marylebone via Bicester – fastest journey, 56min.

The £320m project includes a £130m investment from Chiltern. First conceived in 2002, it finally achieved Transport & Works act approval in 2013. The single-track Oxford-Bicester branch has mostly become a double-track main line, with new stations at Oxford Parkway (at Water Eaton Park & Ride) and Bicester Village, close to the previous Bicester Town. A 0.75-mile chord has been constructed to link the Oxford-Bicester route to the Chiltern main line at Bicester. The final section from Oxford Parkway to Oxford's existing station is planned to open in Spring 2016. Proposals for a further extension, south of Oxford to Cowley, are under development. An £87m Oxford-route design-and-build contract was awarded to Carillion and Buckingham Group in March 2014. A collaboration with Network Rail has overseen this, and also coves the first phase of work on East West Rail (Oxford-Bicester-Bletchley-Bedford/Milton Keynes, with Chiltern services planned to be extended north from Aylesbury to the new route, and run to Bletchley and Milton Keynes).

The Oxford service is part of the current development package, Evergreen 3, for which funding of about £259m from Network Rail is to be repaid by the train operator over 30 years. With this project, Chiltern says a total of £600m will have been invested since the start of its original franchise in 1996.

The first part of 'Evergreen 3' was launched in 2011, with new London-Birmingham 'Mainline' services offering fast journeys to London Marylebone (fastest train from Birmingham Moor Street in 98min, as at October 2015) and simplified fares. Free Wi-Fi is offered, and on selected Mainline trains a Business Zone offer a cost efficient alternative to First class. Over

In Mainline livery, Chiltern's Class 168 No 168218 leaves Birmingham Moor Street with the 15.12 Birmingham Snow Hill-London Marylebone on 20 September 2014. **TONY MILES**

KEY STATISTICS
CHILTERN RAILWAYS

	2013-14	2014-15
Punctuality (0-5min)	94.9%	95.0%
Passenger journeys (millions)	22.8	23.6
Passenger km (millions)	1,198.0	1,221.0
Timetabled train km (millions)	10.9	10.8
Route km operated	341.2	341.2
Number of stations operated	32	32
Number of employees	780	780
Subsidy per passenger km (p)	-0.4	-2.5
Network grant / pass km (p)	5.3	3.8

50 miles of track were upgraded for 100mph, with key junctions improved.

The £80m 'Evergreen 2', completed in 2006, was a Design, Build, Finance & Transfer project, improving capacity for 20 trains per peak hour to use Marylebone. 'Evergreen 1' doubled single track between Aynho Junction and Princes Risborough. Aylesbury Vale Parkway, 3km north of Aylesbury, designed to serve housing development and park-and-ride, opened in 2008. Warwick Parkway, the first non-Railtrack station delivered on the rail network, opened in 2000.

Chiltern in 2013 became the first operator to roll out 'App and Go' tickets, with mobile ticketing company Masabi. On-phone tickets can be scanned at barriers.

Nine 2-car Class 170/3 diesel multiple-units are transferring to

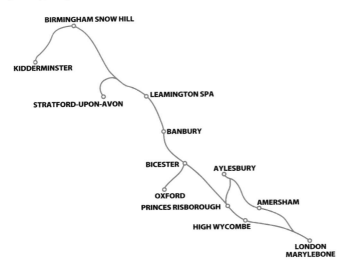

SENIOR PERSONNEL
CHILTERN RAILWAYS

BUSINESS DEVELOPMENT DIRECTOR Graham Cross
CUSTOMER SERVICES DIRECTOR Jennifer Payne
ENGINEERING DIRECTOR David Penney
OPERATIONS AND SAFETY DIRECTOR Andrew Munden
COMMERCIAL DIRECTOR Thomas Ableman
HR DIRECTOR Rebecca Ward
FINANCE DIRECTOR Duncan Rimmer

Chiltern to enlarge the fleet. A refurbishment contract for the first five – reclassified '168/3': was won by Wabtec / Brush prior to introduction of the Oxford services. Four '170s' were to remain with TPE temporarily. The four locomotive-hauled Mainline trains of Mk3 coaches underwent major refurbishment by Wabtec, including new power-operated bodyside doors, and controlled-emission toilets. From 2014, Direct Rail Services (DRS) is providing six new Class 68 locomotives for these trains, replacing Class 67s hired from DB Schenker.

The Class 168 'Clubman' diesel multiple-units have also been refurbished by Wabtec with the Mainline silver livery, in a £5.3m programme. There are ten 4-car and nine 3-car Class 168s, used for longer-distance services. A fifth loco-hauled train is used for commuter services. Four new two-car Class 172 DMUs went into service in 2011. There are 28 two-car and 11 three-car Class 165 'Turbo' trains. Two refurbished Class-121 single-car diesels are used on Aylesbury-Princes Risborough shuttles. The main maintenance depot is at Aylesbury, with another at Wembley, and a redeveloped Banbury depot is expected to open by 2017.

Awarded in 2002 by the former Strategic Rail Authority, Chiltern Railways' unique 20-year franchise (with a five-year extension option) is linked to delivery of investment. ■

ARRIVA
Trains Wales
Trenau Arriva Cymru

15 YEAR FRANCHISE FROM DECEMBER 2003

Arriva Trains Wales/Trenau Arriva Cymru (ATW) includes national, regional and local routes within Wales; through services to Birmingham, Chester, Manchester and Cheltenham; and the 'Borders' route via Shrewsbury. The 15-year Wales & Borders franchise commenced on 7 December 2003, and in April 2006 the Welsh Government (WG) took responsibility for it, gaining powers to fund improvements.

Rail franchising is to be fully devolved from the Department for Transport (DfT) in 2017, and the Welsh Government Transport company, a not-for-dividend, wholly-owned subsidiary, was established in April 2015. It is to provide advice and technical expertise for the Metro system planned for the Cardiff region, including Valleys-lines modernisation and electrification, as well as specifying and procuring the next rail franchise, from 2018.

A completely 'not-for-dividend' franchise has been discussed, but a concession award with a capped profit margin is another option not requiring further WG powers. Alternative contractual models for the Valleys electrification were being considered, including a single contract to operate the Wales & Borders franchise, and deliver the Metro (for which light and heavy rail and bus rapid transit are options).

Contrary to assumptions of little growth, there has been more than a 60% increase in journeys on the franchise since 2003, and PPM performance has improved from around 80% to 93%. ATW has invested more than £30m in train maintenance and improvements, station upgrades, ticketing, information and security, and government has funded additional trains and stations.

Current enhancements include a £220m modernisation, to improve capacity and flexibility, bringing an extra four trains per hour through the Cardiff area. A new station opened in 2013 at Energlyn near Caerphilly.

A new Ebbw Vale town station opened in May 2015, with 1.3 miles of new track from Ebbw Vale Parkway, after the WG provided £11.5m funding. A new Pye Corner station on the Ebbw Vale line was funded by £2.5m from the DfT New Station Fund and £1m from the WG. The Wales Stations Improvement Programme

KEY STATISTICS
ARRIVA TRAINS WALES

	2013-14	2014-15
Punctuality (0-5min)	93.1%	93.0%
Passenger journeys (millions)	29.9	30.8
Passenger km (millions)	1,167.2	1,197.7
Timetabled train km (millions)	24.3	24.3
Route km operated	1,670.5	1,623.8
Number of stations operated	245	244
Number of employees	2,072	2,050
Subsidy per passenger km (p)	13.2	8.5

An Arriva Trains Wales Class 175 train passes Ferryside between Llanelli and Carmarthen. **ARRIVA TRAINS WALES**

has seen major enhancements at Swansea and Chester, with Port Talbot and Aberystwyth benefitting in the next round.

A recent £44m project to double part of the Wrexham-Chester line is designed to give capacity for an extra train each way every 2hr. This should assist with a 16min reduction in Holyhead-Cardiff journeys, along with improved signalling on the North Wales coast line and improved line speeds south of Wrexham. Doubling of five miles of Swansea-Llanelli single track was completed in 2013.

Four additional Aberystwyth-Shrewsbury trains were introduced

from May 2015, as a three-year WG-funded trial, with extra commuter trains for the Heart of Wales line. The WG funded five extra daily trains for Fishguard, from 2011, now extended until 2018.

A loco-hauled express with restaurant service links Holyhead with Cardiff via Wrexham, and another loco-hauled train, boosting services between North Wales and Manchester from December 2014, was enabled by a £1.2m deal with the DfT, involving a change of control fee paid by Deutsche Bahn after acquiring Arriva plc.

Apart from the Class-67-loco-hauled trains, long-distance services

SENIOR PERSONNEL
ARRIVA TRAINS WALES

MANAGING DIRECTOR Ian Bullock (in photo)
OPERATIONS AND SAFETY DIRECTOR Claire Mann
CUSTOMER SERVICES DIRECTOR Lynne Milligan
MIKE TAPSCOTT Projects Director
FLEET DIRECTOR Matt Prosser
HUMAN RESOURCES DIRECTOR Gareth Thomas
FINANCE DIRECTOR Rob Phillips

use 24 Class-158 diesel multiple-units and 27 Class-175s. A fleet of 30 Class-142/143 Pacer railbuses is mainly used in the Cardiff area. There are also 36 Class-150s and 8 single-car Class-153s.

Most of the fleet is based at Cardiff Canton, with a £3million facility at Machynlleth servicing Class 158s, while Class 175s are maintained at manufacturer Alstom's Chester depot. ■

crosscountry

EXTENDED AWARD TO OCTOBER 2019 PLANNED

The CrossCountry (XC) network is the most extensive GB rail franchise, stretching from Aberdeen to Penzance, and from Stansted to Cardiff. Arriva's franchise, starting on 11 November 2007, was due to run until 31 March 2016. The Department for Transport (DfT) in 2013 announced a proposed extended award, running until October 2019 according to the July 2015 rail franchise schedule.

There are regular half-hourly services on key route sections, including Birmingham to Bristol, Reading, Manchester, Sheffield and Leicester; hourly direct services between Bristol and Manchester; hourly through services for all destinations between Plymouth and Edinburgh (via Leeds),

Southampton, Reading and Newcastle (via Doncaster), Bournemouth and Manchester, Cardiff and Nottingham, Birmingham and Stansted Airport. CrossCountry trains via Motherwell and Edinburgh connect Glasgow with Northeast England, Yorkshire, the Midlands and Southwest. Britain's longest direct train service is CrossCountry's 08.20 Aberdeen to Penzance (774 miles).

CrossCountry has introduced a series of commercial innovations, including pioneering print-at-home tickets. XC Advance tickets can be delivered to an app and displayed for inspection.

Travellers can register for alerts when advance tickets become available, and students can receive an extra 10% discount on XC Advance tickets. The 'Advance Purchase On the Day' (APOD) initiative enables purchase of discounted advance purchase

fares (and seat reservations on many services) on the day of travel, up to 10min before boarding a train – via website, mobile app, or a call centre. It won the Passenger Experience award at the 2014 Rail Industry Innovation Awards, organised by *Modern*

Railways. The DfT in January 2015 confirmed that APOD could continue on a permanent basis, following a successful trial involving 150,000 journeys since 2013.

CrossCountry operates 34 Class-220 (4-car) and 23 Class-221 Voyager trains

KEY STATISTICS
CROSSCOUNTRY

	2013-14	2014-15
Punctuality (0-10min)	86.7%	88.8%
Passenger journeys (millions)	34.2	35.4
Passenger km (millions)	3,247.2	3,367.2
Timetabled train km (millions)	32.7	32.7
Route km operated	2,710.1	2,710.1
Number of stations operated	0	0
Number of employees	1,705	1,756
Subsidy per passenger km (p)	1.0	-1.4
Network grant / pass km (p)	8.7	6.5

SENIOR PERSONNEL
CROSSCOUNTRY

MANAGING DIRECTOR Andy Cooper (in photo)
COMMERCIAL DIRECTOR David Watkin
CUSTOMER SERVICE DIRECTOR Jeremy Higgins
PRODUCTION DIRECTOR Will Rogers
HR DIRECTOR Maria Zywica
FINANCE DIRECTOR Jonathan Roberts

(most 5-car); 29 Class-170 Turbostar diesel multiple-units (16 x 3-car, 13 x 2-car) and 5 High-Speed Trains.

Since the beginning of the franchise CrossCountry has carried out £40m worth of improvements to its fleet, with reconfiguration to provide additional seating and luggage space producing a 35% increase in capacity on principal routes in the evening peaks. The Voyager fleet has won the *Modern Railways* 'Golden Spanner' for the most reliable InterCity train for six consecutive years.

The HSTs were fully refurbished by Wabtec at Doncaster, with a number of additional trailers converted from loco-hauled vehicles. MTU engines were fitted to the power cars.

The Class 170 Turbostars operate on Cardiff/Birmingham-Nottingham/ Stansted Airport/Leicester routes. Various sub-classes were configured to a standard layout (120 seats in the two-car and 200 in three-car units) during a refurbishment by Transys Projects (now Vossloh Kiepe UK). The Class 170 fleet won the 2014 *Modern Railways*

'Golden Spanner' for the most reliable new generation DMU.

Work in conjunction with Nomad Digital to equip all HSTs and Voyagers with wi-fi was completed in 2012, and then extended to Turbostar trains. At-seat catering is provided on most services, providing hot and cold refreshments appropriate to the time of day. A new range including hot meals was introduced, with pre-ordering, in 2015 on Edinburgh-Plymouth and Manchester-Bournemouth routes.

CrossCountry has achieved EFQM 'Recognised for Excellence' status- the first Arriva train company to gain the maximum '5 star' rating: and was also awarded the 2013 British Quality Foundation prize for 'Excellence in Employee Engagement'.

Installation of the Energymiser driver advisory system by Arriva began with CrossCountry in 2014. It is designed to maximise train performance and reduce fuel consumption and emissions. A forward-facing CCTV system has also been installed on all trains to monitor the rail infrastructure. ▨

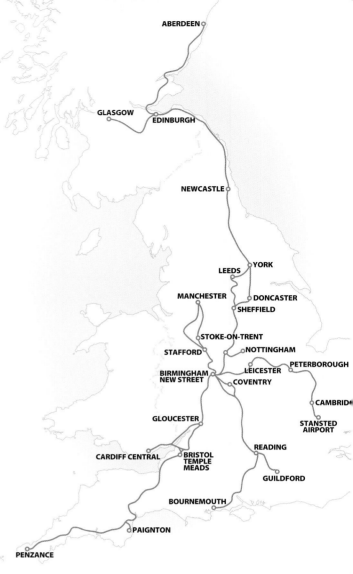

A CrossCountry Class 170 Turbostar bound for Nottingham passes Severn Tunnel Junction on 26 January 2015. **NETWORK RAIL**

HITACHI
Inspire the Next

Grand Central's Class 180 No 180112 heads north through Doncaster. **TONY MILES**

OPEN ACCESS OPERATOR ON TRACK TO 2026

Grand Central Rail (GC) is beginning a further programme of investment in its fleet and at stations after being awarded an extended access contract, by 10 years, until 2026.

GC's first open access service, from Sunderland to London King's Cross, was launched in December 2007: a three trains a day service began in July 2008. By 2012, GC was running five return journeys. The West Riding service started in May 2010, offering three trains a day between Bradford Interchange and King's Cross (calling at Halifax, Brighouse, Wakefield Kirkgate, Pontefract Monkhill and Doncaster – and from December 2011, Mirfield). GC was permitted a fourth Bradford service from December 2013.

A series of changes in ownership culminated in GC becoming part of Arriva in November 2011. GC has invested over £40m of private capital in trains and people, as well as covering its start-up costs, with a £400,000 programme of investment in stations up to 2014. Notable among improvements to stations through partnerships has been

the transformation of Wakefield Kirkgate: once dubbed by former transport minister Lord Adonis as the worst medium sized station on the network. A fresh investment programme, including in station and depot facilities, will continue into 2017, aiming for more reliable trains and more efficient operations.

2015 saw continuation of rapid journey growth, especially on the West Riding route, driven by more services, improved awareness, and the increased availability of Advance fares. The company has seen growth in First Class, with more competitively priced tickets. An exclusive partnership with the National Union of Students offers discounted Advance tickets. Carnet tickets for frequent travellers have been reformulated and made available via more channels.

With a total staff of 135, Grand Central Rail has created more than 65 jobs in Sunderland, 44 in Bradford and 22 in York – it emphasises these are skilled, permanent positions.

GC is to take over the five Class 180s currently working with First Great Western from December 2016. They may be sub-leased back to FGW for a period, before GC begins operating a uniform fleet of Class 180s after 2017, when its three Class 43 High Speed Trains will be retired. A Class 180

refurbishment programme began in 2015. GC currently leases five Class 180 and three HSTs from Angel Trains.

All West Riding services are presently worked by Class 180s, and the North Eastern route is shared between '180s' and HST sets. In 2010 the 21 HST vehicles (6 Class 43 power cars and 15 Mk3 coaches) were sold by GC sister company Sovereign Trains to Angel Trains, which agreed to invest in a substantial engineering programme, to improve performance and reliability. This included installation of new MTU engines in power cars. GC agreed to lease the sets until at least December 2016.

Working with Angel, First Hull Trains and First Great Western, Grand Central entered into a unique technical support contract with Alstom which covers all Class 180s. This is delivering significant improvements in arrangements for maintenance, including fitment of remote conditioning monitoring

equipment on key systems. Northern Rail maintains Grand Central's trains at Heaton depot, Newcastle and provides riding inspectors to check on trains en route. Two '180s' are serviced overnight at Crofton, Wakefield, by Bombardier.

GC is the UK's most trusted long-distance rail company, according to research by Passenger Focus. The spring 2015 National Rail Passenger Survey found 94% of its passengers were satisfied, or very satisfied.

GC manages a Facebook page and Twitter feed, responding to passenger feedback, helping with queries and sharing information.

GC's award-winning Station Ambassador scheme was extended during 2014: voluntary representatives help passengers mainly on Sundays when booking offices are closed and most disruption due to engineering work occurs.

The PPM punctuality statistic for 2014-15 was 88.2% (2013-14: 80.7%). ▪

SENIOR PERSONNEL
GRAND CENTRAL

MANAGING DIRECTOR Richard McClean (in photo)
CHIEF OPERATING OFFICER Sean English
FLEET DIRECTOR Dave Hatfield
COMMERCIAL DIRECTOR Louise Blyth
FINANCE DIRECTOR Mark Robinson
STAKEHOLDER AND ENGAGEMENT MANAGER Alex Bray
HEAD OF HR Stewart Dew

STAGECOACH AND VIRGIN

Stagecoach Group is an international public transport company with extensive operations in the UK, mainland Europe, USA and Canada. The group employs around 38,000 people, and operates bus, coach, rail, and tram services in regulated and deregulated markets.

It directly runs the South West Trains and East Midlands Trains franchises. Stagecoach Supertram holds a 27-year concession until 2024 for Sheffield's 28km light rail network.

Stagecoach and Virgin Group have two rail franchise joint ventures. Stagecoach is the majority shareholder (90%) in the new Virgin Trains East Coast franchise, and has a 49% shareholding in Virgin Rail Group, which operates the West Coast rail franchise.

Stagecoach UK rail subsidiaries' revenue for the year to 30 April 2015 was £1,478.4m (previous year: £1,252.0m) and operating profit was £26.9m (previous year: £34.3m). Stagecoach's 49% share of Virgin Rail Group operating profit was £28.0m (previous year: £2.6m) – a new commercial franchise (with Virgin Rail Group taking most revenue/cost risk) began in June 2014, replacing a management contract.
CHIEF EXECUTIVE Martin Griffiths

SOUTH WEST TRAINS

10-YEAR FRANCHISE FROM FEBRUARY 2007

The South West Trains (SWT) franchise, held by Stagecoach, began on 4 February 2007, combining the previous SWT and Island Line (Isle of Wight) franchises. The Department for Transport (DfT) announced in July 2015 that, instead of an extension that had been considered, the franchise would end in June 2017.

An alliance between SWT and Network Rail in 2012 introduced a single management team aiming to create better working relationships between the two companies. In June 2015, SWT and Network Rail announced that the alliance would be reshaped, with Network Rail reintroducing its own Route Managing Director and commercial arrangements, though a joint executive team would continue. The integrated control centre and 'one station' team at Waterloo, integrated capacity and planning teams, and the joint performance team remain in place. A new Basingstoke Campus and Route Operating Centre was officially opened in November 2015, providing 5,000 sq m of training space for Network Rail and South West Trains staff - the first to provide for both organisations under one roof.

The biggest investment made to the network since the 1930s is set to provide 30% more capacity for passengers at peak times, with stations on suburban routes having their platforms extended for longer trains. Introduction of 108 additional refurbished electric multiple-unit carriages has progressed. In September 2015, the last of 48 refurbished Class 456 vehicles were delivered. Introduction of 60 additional Class-458/5 carriages was expected to be completed in early 2016: Class 460 (former Gatwick Express) vehicles are being used to extend and supplement SWT's Class 458 sets. In 2014, SWT announced a £210m contract for 30 new 5-car

A South West Trains Class 455 EMU leaves Vauxhall, nearing its London Waterloo terminus. A new platform surface has reduced the step for passengers and increased safety at Vauxhall. **NETWORK RAIL/SOUTH WEST TRAINS**

Desiro City trains, with manufacturer Siemens and leasing company Angel Trains. All are due in service by early 2018, providing for more than 18,000 extra peak passengers a day.

In March 2015, a £50m package of benefits for customers was agreed by the DfT - including additional off-peak capacity, more car parking, a new website and mobile app, new 'customer ambassadors', and new ticket machines including 90 with direct video links.

Improved services for the West of England from December 2015 include 800 additional seats every weekday between Waterloo and Somerset, and new services from Waterloo to Bruton and Frome for the first time ever.

In March 2015, a £2m project on the Island Line was completed ahead of schedule. The work followed storm damage and included essential track maintenance. The 8.5-mile line is worked by five ex-London Underground Class 483 2-car EMUs.

The DfT said in September 2015 that it expects to ask bidders for the next franchise to suggest how to turn the Island Line into a separate and self-sustaining business, reducing running costs (currently £4m a year, with income of £1m) – perhaps with an investment partner or social enterprise approach.

SWT secured a share of £60m to improve accessibility at a number

HITACHI
Inspire the Next

of stations by 2019 and major improvements were delivered at Twickenham ahead of the Rugby World Cup 2015.

Main train depots are at Wimbledon, Salisbury and the Siemens-built Desiros, Northam near Southampton. Upgrading to facilities at Wimbledon and Farnham will cater for additional vehicles. At Wimbledon traincare depot around £6m has been invested, with a new bogie drop system for bogies and other equipment to be detached.

The electric multiple-unit fleet has 45 Class 444 five-car Siemens Desiro trains (designed for longer distance services), 127

Class 450 four-car Desiros, and 91 pre-privatisation Class 455s being upgraded with new traction equipment to help improve reliability. The 24 two-car Class 456s transferred from Southern to SWT in 2014. 30 three-car Class 159 and 11 two-car Class 158 diesel multiple-units are used on non-electrified routes from Southampton and Basingstoke to Salisbury and beyond.

At the *Modern Railways* Golden Spanner awards in November 2014, for the 10th year in a row, the Class 158/159 diesel trains won the award for the most reliable former British Rail DMU. The Class 455 EMUs also won a Golden Spanner. ■

SENIOR PERSONNEL
SOUTH WEST TRAINS

MANAGING DIRECTOR Tim Shoveller (in photo)
CUSTOMER SERVICE DIRECTOR Arthur Pretorius
COMMERCIAL DIRECTOR James Vickers
OPERATIONS DIRECTOR Mark Steward
SAFETY & ASSURANCE DIRECTOR Sharon Vye-Parminter
FINANCE DIRECTOR Andy West
HR DIRECTOR Kelly Barlow

KEY STATISTICS
SOUTH WEST TRAINS

	2013-14	2014-15
Punctuality (0-5min)	89.7%	90.1%
Passenger journeys (millions)	222.8	229.9
Passenger km (millions)	6,045.8	6,222.0
Timetabled train km (millions)	39.5	39.5
Route km operated	944.7	944.7
Number of stations operated	186	186
Number of employees	4,827	4,760
Subsidy per passenger km (p)	-5.2	-6.0
Network grant / pass km (p)	4.1	3.9

EAST MIDLANDS TRAINS

DIRECT AWARD
UNTIL MARCH 2018

The East Midlands franchise, awarded to Stagecoach, began operations on 11 November 2007, combining the previous Midland main line franchise with Central Trains' eastern section. It was due to continue until 1 April 2015, subject to a performance review after six years.

The Department for Transport (DfT) in September 2015 announced a new Direct Award contract, running until March 2018, and Stagecoach has committed to £150m in premium payments to the government. The DfT can extend the award by up to a year. A £13m package of improvements

for passengers includes a freeze on Anytime fares to London; 250,000 discounted tickets; an automatic refunds system; improved on train wi-fi; a new mobile app; £250,000 for Community Rail partnerships; and more seats and services, particularly between Nottingham and Lincoln. The second London-Sheffield train per hour, previously supported by South Yorkshire Passenger Transport Executive and Yorkshire Forward, will continue without this local funding.

In May 2015, EMT introduced improved weekday services between Nottingham, Newark Castle and Lincoln - the Castle line - with over £2m in local and government funding. Many stations now have more weekday services than ever before.

The timetable improvements were developed and funded in partnership with the DfT and county, city and district councils, business groups and Local Enterprise Partnerships.

Parkway Railink, providing a shuttle service between East Midlands Parkway station and East Midlands Airport, was introduced in March 2015, in a partnership between EMT, the airport, Rushcliffe Borough Council and Elite Cars. Single journeys are fixed at £6.

A new station building and 1,000 space car park for Wellingborough are included in the major Stanton Cross housing and commercial development which got under way in March 2015. Significant station improvements have been led by the Nottingham Hub redevelopment, with extensive remodelling and resignalling in a £100m project. £50m of improvement to the station itself created a new, glass-fronted southern concourse, with fully accessible

KEY STATISTICS
EAST MIDLANDS TRAINS

	2013-14	2014-15
Punctuality	91.3%	92.1%
Passenger journeys (millions)	24.1	25.5
Passenger km (millions)	2,231.8	2,353.7
Timetabled train km (millions)	22.0	22.2
Route km operated	1,549.8	1,549.8
Number of stations operated	89	89
Number of employees	2,052	2,061
Subsidy per passenger km (p)	0.2	-3.5
Network grant / pass km (p)	8.0	6.3

Power car No 43081 is on the rear of an EMT HST set waiting to depart from Nottingham for London St Pancras. **TONY MILES**

connections with the car park and tram network.

Derby station's forecourt was transformed in a £2.7m scheme, with a new transport interchange. Other schemes include the £100,000 project to improve Chesterfield station, and a £250,000 project at Lincoln.

36 of EMT's stations have now been awarded Secure Station Accreditation by the DfT and British Transport Police (BTP), and 30 car parks now have Park Mark security status. EMT secured £1.4m in DfT funding in 2015 to improve cycle facilities.

The June 2015 National Passenger Survey showed overall satisfaction with EMT has continued to rise, reaching 9% higher than the national average. It has also continued to be

the most punctual long distance train operator, for the sixth year in a row.

In partnership with Network Rail, EMT worked on a £70m line speed improvement scheme on the Midland main line to enable trains to run at up to 125mph on some sections, with almost 160 miles of track upgraded. From December 2013 the average journey between Sheffield and London was reduced by 7 minutes and between Nottingham and London by 5 minutes. Electrification and further improvements are planned. EMT's fastest Sheffield-London train covers the journey in 2hr, the fastest from Nottingham to London is 1hr 31min.

A £30m programme to refurbish all trains was completed in 2012. It included the £10m refurbishment of 25 two-car Class 158 sets, a £5m

project to refurbish the 17 Class-153 and 15 Class-156 sets, while a £9m programme for the InterCity 125 High Speed Train (HST) fleet brought updated interiors, and technical modifications to increase reliability. Class 222 Meridian trains were refurbished in a £6m project. CCTV has been installed on all trains. The Energy Saving Mode on Meridian trains allows some engines to be

turned off when stationary, resulting in reduced noise and emissions.

EMT has 10 HSTs (plus one set of coaches on hire to Virgin Trains East Coast), formed of eight coaches and two power cars per train: there is a pool of 24 power cars. The Class 222 Meridian fleet was reorganised in 2008 to form six 7-car and seventeen 5-car sets, and four additional 4-car Class 222s were transferred from Hull Trains. ■

SENIOR PERSONNEL
EAST MIDLANDS TRAINS

MANAGING DIRECTOR Jake Kelly (in photo)
SAFETY & OPERATIONS DIRECTOR Ian Smith
CUSTOMER EXPERIENCE & COMMERCIAL DIRECTOR Neil Micklethwaite
ENGINEERING DIRECTOR Tim Sayer
FINANCE DIRECTOR Tim Gledhill
HR DIRECTOR Kirsty Derry

WEST COAST DIRECT AWARD UNTIL SEPTEMBER 2017

The Virgin Trains West Coast intercity franchise is run by Virgin Rail Group - a joint venture between Virgin Group (51%) and Stagecoach Group (49%). Main routes are from London Euston to Glasgow, Liverpool, Manchester and Birmingham. Following the collapse of Railtrack and reduction in scope for the West Coast Route Modernisation, the original terms were replaced by an interim agreement in 2002 and then by a new deal, agreed with the Department for Transport (DfT) in December 2006.

This arrangement was extended from March 2012 to December 2012 as the DfT revisited terms for a new franchising competition. Then a 'pause' was announced in October 2012 after the West Coast franchising process was challenged and cancelled. Virgin was awarded an interim extension, with DfT taking revenue and cost risk, but a new Direct Award franchise took effect from 22 June 2014. This was due to run until 31 March 2017, when the next competed franchise would start: the July 2015 DfT rail franchise schedule shows it running until September 2017 though this was still to be formally agreed.

Virgin Trains was to pay a guaranteed premium of £430m

(about £155.3m a year) under the new contract, if the economy performs as expected. If returns exceed expectations, government

will take an increasing share. Virgin committed to convert Coach G on all 21 nine-car Pendolinos from First to Standard class, and all trains

KEY STATISTICS
VIRGIN TRAINS WEST COAST

	2013-14	2014-15
Punctuality (0-10min)	85.8%	84.8%
Passenger journeys (millions)	31.9	34.5
Passenger km (millions)	6,215.4	6887.9
Timetabled train km (millions)	35.8	35.7
Route km operated	1,190.9	1,264.9
Number of stations operated	17	17
Number of employees	2,999	3,114
Subsidy per passenger km (p)	-1.6	-1.4
Network grant / pass km (p)	4.5	6.1

MANAGING DIRECTOR Phil Whittingham (in photo)
EXECUTIVE DIRECTOR, OPERATIONS AND PROJECTS Phil Bearpark
GROUP COMMERCIAL DIRECTOR (WITH EAST COAST) Graham Leech
PROJECT DIRECTOR Samantha Wadsworth
EXECUTIVE DIRECTOR, CUSTOMER EXPERIENCE Steve Tennant
COMMERCIAL OPERATIONS DIRECTOR Peter Broadley
MARKETING DIRECTOR Katie Knowles
CUSTOMER STRATEGY DIRECTOR Bob Powell
EXECUTIVE DIRECTOR, HR Patrick McGrath
EXECUTIVE DIRECTOR, FINANCE Mark Whitehouse

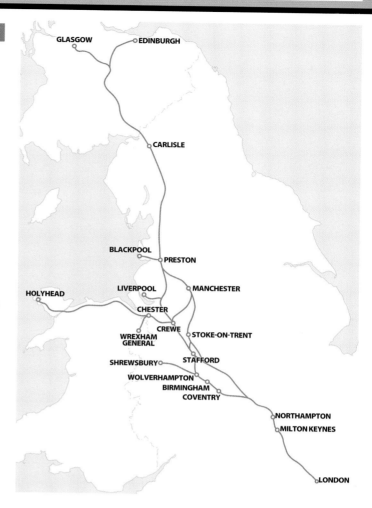

are to be equipped with superfast wi-fi, which Network Rail intends to support with trackside infrastructure - deploying 4G technology will enable Virgin to provide free wi-fi.

The deal also includes more than £20m on modernising stations; an upgraded website; more staff on stations; increased emphasis on apprenticeships and traineeships; a pledge to have 10% more small and medium enterprises in the supply base; a commitment to make station and training centre facilities available for community use; plus a range of environmental commitments.

The 'VHF' (Virgin High Frequency) timetable, introduced in 2008 after the West Coast Route Modernisation, sees nine Virgin trains departing from London every hour in the off-peak periods, and 11 in the peak.

The company introduced direct trains between London and Shrewsbury and Blackpool from December 2014, using existing train paths south of Preston or the West Midlands.

A new programme of 'Virgin Trains Escapes' is aimed at stimulating leisure travel and rewarding existing customers, while for the May 2016 timetable further service enhancements are being developed. The corporate market saw a 9% increase in 2014-15: the development of Virgin's 'Brain on the Train' may enable at-seat ordering of refreshments.

Virgin has launched the industry's first automatic 'delay repay' system, with passengers on delayed trains who booked through Virgin's website receiving their refund automatically.

Demand projections led the DfT to sanction capacity increases in 2008, when train lessor Angel Trains signed contracts with Alstom for four new 11-car Pendolinos and two extra cars for 31 existing trains (106 additional vehicles in all), along with a 10-year maintenance regime, worth a total of £1.5bn. The project was completed in December 2012.

Virgin's train fleet comprises 35 eleven-car and 21 nine-car Pendolino electric tilting trains, and 20 five-car Class-221 diesel Super Voyager units. In September 2015 the West Coast and East Coast Virgin franchises launched a joint advertising campaign, 'Be Bound for Glory', the largest in the company's history. ∎

Virgin 'Voyager' No 221102 at Shrewsbury, which along with Blackpool made a return to the Virgin Trains map in 2014. **TONY MILES**

EIGHT-YEAR FRANCHISE UNTIL 31 MARCH 2023

Virgin Trains East Coast (VTEC) began operating the InterCity East Coast franchise on 1 March 2015. It took over from the Directly Operated Railways business East Coast which had been running the service group for the Department for Transport (DfT) since November 2009.

The franchise is due to run until 31 March 2023, with option of a one-year extension at the DfT's discretion. VTEC is a joint venture between Stagecoach (90%), and Virgin (10%). The new franchise includes a commitment to deliver £2.3bn in real terms in premium payments to the DfT and the company says it is set to see more than £140m invested in delivering an improved service and a more personalised travel experience.

Principal services operate between London and Aberdeen, Edinburgh, Newcastle, York, and Leeds. Less frequent trains run to Inverness, Glasgow, Skipton, Bradford, Harrogate, Hull and Lincoln. After introducing a new daily service to Sunderland via Newcastle and another to Stirling from December 2015, VTEC proposes to extend several trains from Newcastle to Edinburgh in May 2016, and extend services that terminate at Newark and York to Lincoln and Harrogate respectively. From May 2019 the company plans half-hourly limited-stop services to Edinburgh with a small fleet of 7-car InterCity 225 sets, with regular weekday London-Edinburgh train taking just 4hr, calling only at Newcastle. Additional and faster services between Leeds and London are also planned for 2019, many with a journey time of about 2hr; along with new direct Middlesbrough-London services, two-hourly direct Bradford-

Harrogate-Lincoln-London trains, and new direct peak-time Huddersfield-London services. Improved Saturday and Sunday timetables are to see more frequent and faster Leeds-London trains, faster journey times for Edinburgh-Newcastle-London, a two-hourly Harrogate-London direct service, and a two-hourly direct Lincoln-London service.

From 2018 the company will begin to introduce the 65 Hitachi 'Super Express' InterCity Express Programme electric and bi-mode trains. Meantime the existing trains with be refreshed in a £13.4m programme. By 2020 the franchise promises a 50% increase in capacity, with 12,200 additional seats.

The new franchisee announced a range of improvements for passengers including a 10% cut in Standard Anytime fares on long-distance journeys to and from London and Stevenage; a new website, interactive touchscreen information points at major stations, smartphone apps, portable technology for staff, and improved on-train WiFi as well as free WiFi at all stations. New technology will also allow at-seat food ordering and more simple ticket purchase and reservations backed by a new Nectar loyalty programme. An improved on-board service will be provided with additional staff presence. Fresh cooked breakfasts for First class passengers are one of a series of catering improvements planned.

VTEC plans investment of over £25m in stations and car parks with new open plan customer zones introduced for combined ticket purchase and information. First Class lounges are to be upgraded, with local businesses and community groups able to use selected lounges free of charge in the evenings.

A £1m annual budget is allocated to customer service initiatives and the company plans to introduce 30 security and revenue officers who are also special constables.

VTEC also plans a range of measure to improve accessibility, transport integration and sustainability. New electronic information boards will be provided at stations, with interactive touchscreens at key locations providing up-to-the minute information, including about onward transport. Customer action teams will be on hand to help provide extra customer service during times of disruption. Car-club and car-sharing schemes will have dedicated websites: environmental measures are aimed at delivering a 20% reduction in passenger and vehicle CO2 emissions and a 22% reduction in water consumption.

VTEC's fleet has 31 Class-91 electric locomotives powering 30 rakes of Mk4 coaches. 32 Class-43 power cars power 14 diesel High Speed Train sets, with one more set hired in from East Midlands Trains. ∎

KEY STATISTICS
EAST COAST

	2013-14	2014-15
Punctuality (0-10min)	84.2%	88.6%
Passenger journeys (millions)	19.9	20.7
Passenger km (millions)	5,107.8	5,297.7
Timetabled train km (millions)	22.0	22.0
Route km operated	1,480.6	1,480.6
Number of stations operated	12	12
Number of employees	3,031	3,065
Subsidy per passenger km (p)	-4.0	-5.1*
Network grant / pass km (p)	3.7	5.1*

*Virgin Trains East Coast from 1 March 2015. * up to 1 March 2015.*

SENIOR PERSONNEL
VIRGIN TRAINS EAST COAST

MANAGING DIRECTOR David Horne (in photo)
COMMERCIAL DIRECTOR Suzanne Donnelly
PEOPLE DIRECTOR Clare Burles
ENGINEERING DIRECTOR Jack Commandeur
MAJOR PROJECTS DIRECTOR Tim Hedley-Jones
MARKETING & SALES DIRECTOR Danny Gonzalez
CUSTOMER EXPERIENCE DIRECTOR Alison Watson
SAFETY & OPERATIONS DIRECTOR Warrick Dent

Map stations: INVERNESS, CARRBRIDGE, AVIEMORE, KINGUSSIE, NEWTONMORE, ABERDEEN, STONEHAVEN, BLAIR ATHOLL, PITLOCHRY, MONTROSE, ARBROATH, DUNKELD, DUNDEE, GLENEAGLES, PERTH, LEUCHARS, DUNBLANE, STIRLING, KIRKCALDY, INVERKEITHING, GLASGOW, FALKIRK, DUNBAR, EDINBURGH, MOTHERWELL, BERWICK-UPON-TWEED, ALNMOUTH, MORPETH, NEWCASTLE, SUNDERLAND, DARLINGTON, NORTHALLERTON, HARROGATE, SKIPTON, YORK, HORSFORTH, SELBY, KEIGHLEY, HULL, BRADFORD, LEEDS, BROUGH, WAKEFIELD, DONCASTER, RETFORD, LINCOLN, NEWARK NORTH GATE, GRANTHAM, PETERBOROUGH, STEVENAGE, LONDON

HITACHI
Inspire the Next

c2c

15-YEAR FRANCHISE
UNTIL NOVEMBER 2029

National Express Group (NX) has operated the 'c2c' Essex Thameside franchise since 2000, and won a new 15-year term starting on 9 November 2014, which will see new trains and extra services, and a range of customer service initiatives.

From December 2015, a new timetable provides over 20% more services in total in the AM peak, and 30% more services in the PM peak. West Ham, the second-busiest c2c destination, has 75% more peak services. About a quarter of weekend trains call at Stratford, for access to Westfield shopping centre, and Liverpool Street, offering new connections. By the end of the franchise, there are to be 25,000 additional seats serving London in the morning peak every week.

17 new trains (68 carriages) are to be introduced from 2019, increasing capacity by over 4,500 seats a day. As part of a £12m upgrade of existing trains, 20% of them (17 trains becoming Class 357/3) will each provide room for 150 more people by creating more standing space, and will be focused on the shortest peak journeys.

There will be automatic compensation for registered smartcard customers for delays over 2min. Registered customers will also receive personalised performance reports, and passengers have the right to be sold the cheapest ticket for any c2c journey, or be compensated.

Every station has been staffed from first until last train since September 2015, and CCTV will be renewed and expanded. c2c is the first train operator to have full smart ticketing coverage, and improvements to

A Class 357 train in service with c2c near Limehouse **TONY MILES**

wi-fi, information and stations are under way.

c2c's new live app won the Passenger Experience award at the *Modern Railways* 2015 Railway Industry Innovation Awards. It is the first from a UK rail company to offer a postcode journey planner, and from 2016 will be the platform for automatic compensation for delays.

NX will pay around £1.5bn to the Department for Transport (DfT) over the 15 year franchise. Based on DfT methodology, net present value was estimated at £1.1bn.

While NX was shortlisted in June 2015 for the new Greater Anglia franchise, the c2c franchise is the only one it currently holds. NX became responsible for c2c in 2000, when it took over Prism Rail after financial problems at other Prism franchises. The franchise had been awarded in May 1996 in a 15-year deal. The

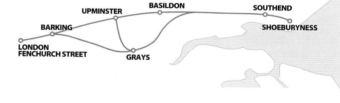

company adopted the 'c2c' name in 2002, and suggested it could indicate 'coast to capital' or 'commitment to customers'. During DfT reviews of rail franchising, two short term c2c contracts spanned the 2011-14 period.

Passenger demand broke records for c2c during the London 2012 Games, with 1.96m journeys during the 17 days of the games.

c2c holds the UK record for any four-week performance period, at 98.8% by the Public Performance Measure, and also holds the record for punctuality on a moving annual average (97.5%).

Bombardier Transportation provides maintenance for the 74 four-car Class 357 trains, mainly at East Ham depot, under a 10-year contract signed in 2015, valued at approximately £143m. It contains an incentivised

performance regime and incorporates Bombardier's Automatic Vehicle Inspection System, using cameras and sensors to analyse vehicle condition, helping reduce component usage and maintenance interventions while increasing utilisation.

c2c works in an alliance with Network Rail, building since 2012 on an established partnership, which includes joint signalling and operating control.

Driver-only operation (DOO) is used for trains of up to 8 cars: DOO of 12-car trains is to be introduced from 2016 when additional platform monitors are fitted.

Funding for a new station at Beam Park, between Dagenham Dock and Rainham, was allocated by Transport for London in 2015 to support plans for residential development. ■

KEY STATISTICS
C2C

	2013-14	2014-15
Punctuality (0-5min)	96.7%	96.9%
Passenger journeys (millions)	38.8	40.8
Passenger km (millions)	1,044.4	1084.5
Timetabled train km (millions)	6.5	6.5
Route km operated	115.5	115.5
Number of stations operated	25	26
Number of employees	762	706
Subsidy per passenger km (p)	-0.4	-1.7
Network grant / pass km (p)	3.9	4.4

SENIOR PERSONNEL
C2C

MANAGING DIRECTOR Julian Drury (in photo)
DELIVERY DIRECTOR Kevin Frazer
COMMERCIAL DIRECTOR Clare McCaffrey
FINANCE DIRECTOR Richard Bowley
MD, RAIL, NATIONAL EXPRESS GROUP Andrew Chivers

New Eurostar 'e320' train. **SIEMENS/EUROSTAR**

INTERNATIONAL INTER-CITY TRAINS

The UK government announced in February 2015 the £757 million sale of its entire interest in Eurostar International Limited (EI), the cross-channel passenger train operator.

A consortium comprising Caisse de dépôt et placement du Québec (CDPQ) and Hermes Infrastructure acquired the government's 40% stake in Eurostar for £585.1m. Eurostar also agreed to redeem the government's preference share, providing a further £172m for the exchequer.

SNCF (French Railways) holds 55% of EI, and SNCB (Belgian Railways) 5%. A shareholders' agreement in 2015 has seen SNCF take sole managerial control of Eurostar, subject to conditions set by the European Commission to avoid obstruction to future competitors. These include access to train paths, as well as to ticketing, information services and station facilities, and to maintenance centres.

Eurostar links St Pancras International, Ebbsfleet International, and Ashford International in the UK with Paris, Brussels, Lille, Calais, Disneyland Resort Paris, and the French Alps. An all-year direct service between London and Lyon, Avignon and Marseille launched in May 2015. In partnership with international operator TGV Lyria, connections are available via Lille to Geneva, as well to Swiss ski resorts in winter.

Eurostar in 2013 announced an agreement with Netherlands Railways to launch direct, 4hr London-Amsterdam services from December 2016, using new trains compatible with the Netherlands' high-speed infrastructure. Eurostar plans two services a day, calling at Antwerp, Rotterdam, and Schiphol Airport.

Eurostar marked its 20th year of operation in 2014. Launched by state railway companies, the British interest was sold to London & Continental Railways (LCR) when chosen as Channel Tunnel Rail Link developer by the government in 1996. As it prepared to sell the Channel Tunnel Rail Link (High Speed 1 - HS1), the government took control of LCR in 2009, and in 2010, a new standalone joint venture company, EI, replaced the unincorporated joint venture of the three national companies.

In 2010 Eurostar announced a £700m investment in its fleet, with £600m to purchase 10 new 'e320' trains and £100m for refurbishment of its existing fleet. In November 2014, an additional seven e320 trains (UK Class 374) were ordered, bringing the overall investment in the fleet to over £1bn. The Siemens-Velaro-based 320km/hr trains are the same length as existing trains (400m), with about 150 more seats. Nomad Digital is supplying onboard wi-fi on new and existing fleets.

The first of the original 'Trans Manche Super Trains' to be refurbished (now known as 'e300' after the 300km/hr top speed) entered commercial service in summer 2015, with the first e320s planned to be in service in late 2015. About 14 'e300s' (UK Class 373) are expected to remain in service alongside the 17 'e320s'.

European Train Control System signalling is to be provided at Ashford station, so that e320 trains, which lack the UK's Train Protection & Warning System, can continue to call. The European Commission and South East Local Economic Partnership (through the Local Growth Fund) will each provide half of the £4m required.

A programme of station improvements saw the London St Pancras ticket office relocated and improvements to the business lounge in Brussels-Midi station in 2014, with Lille Europe and Gare du Nord, Paris also due to benefit. A new design of uniform for Eurostar staff was introduced in 2014.

In 2014, passenger numbers rose by 3% to 10.4m (2013: 10.1m) bringing the total number of passengers travelling on Eurostar since the start of services in 1994 to over 150m. 2014 sales revenues increased by 1% to £867m (2013: £857m). The number of business travellers increased by 4% compared with 2013. Like-for-like operating profit was up 2% in 2014 to £55.0m (2013: £54.0m). In Quarter 2 of 2015, a record number of passengers in a quarter - 2.8m - was recorded.

Following major disruption to services during adverse winter weather in December 2009, new investment of £28m was committed, to improve resilience of trains, as well as passenger care, and communication systems inside and outside the Channel Tunnel.

Record journey times were achieved on special runs before normal services began on HS1, the new line from London to the Channel Tunnel, in 2007: Paris-London, 2hr 3min, and Brussels-London, 1hr 43min. HS1, with its new London St Pancras terminal, saw journey times cut by about 20min. The London-Paris non-stop timing is now 2hr 16min.

The flagship Business Premier class features a guaranteed boarding service; express check-in; three course meals developed in partnership with Culinary Director, Raymond Blanc; on-board taxi bookings; and exclusive business traveller facilities at main stations. Standard Premier is a 'mid-class' designed for cost-conscious business travellers, and others who want extra space and service.

Under its Tread Lightly environmental plan, Eurostar has set targets of reducing carbon dioxide emissions per traveller journey by 35%, with a 25% cut in wider Eurostar business emissions, alongside studies of Eurostar's direct and indirect carbon footprint, and Sustainable Travel Awards to promote local initiatives in the UK, France and Belgium. ▪

SENIOR PERSONNEL
EUROSTAR

CHIEF EXECUTIVE OFFICER Nicolas Petrovic (in photo)
CHAIRMAN Clare Hollingsworth
OPERATIONS DELIVERY DIRECTOR Frank Renault
COMMERCIAL DIRECTOR Nicholas Mercer
SERVICE AND PEOPLE DIRECTOR Marc Noaro

HITACHI
Inspire the Next

Heathrow Express

FAST AIR-RAIL LINK

A fast and frequent service between Heathrow and London Paddington, Heathrow Express trains depart every 15min each way, for most of the day, taking just 15min to/from Terminals 2-3.

Heathrow Express is a private train operating company and subsidiary of the airport owner: its infrastructure within the airport was built as part of a long-term strategy to increase public transport use for airport access. 69% of customers are estimated to be business passengers.

A separate Heathrow rail infrastructure management is to be set up when Crossrail replaces Heathrow Connect, with access charges, set by the Office of Rail Regulation, paid by Heathrow Express, and by TfL for Crossrail which will run four trains an hour to Terminal 4.

ADComms is installing GSM-R radio coverage in Heathrow's rail tunnels, to provide one of the first European Train Control System level 2 systems in the UK, for the Crossrail project.

A total of 5.83 million passengers travelled on Heathrow Express in 2014 and the stopping service Heathrow Connect carried 0.46m. The combined total was down by 0.9% compared with 2013, due to service disruption for Crossrail engineering works.

Trains reach the airport on a dedicated line, tunnelling from near Hayes & Harlington on the Great Western main line, for about 3.5km

to Heathrow Terminals 2-3 and about 6.5km to Terminal 4 (both opened in 1998). A 1.8km extension to Terminal 5 opened in 2008.

Terminal 5 station has two platform spaces for western rail links: a proposed link via Staines was shelved in 2011, but a new study of southern rail access was begun by the Department for Transport in 2014. Plans for a 5km link to the Great Western main line towards Reading are being taken forward for possible completion in 2021.

Terminals 2-3 and 5 (Terminal 1 is closed) have a direct Heathrow Express service. A regular shuttle runs between Terminal 4 and Terminals 2-3. The Class 332 electric trains are owned (under a leaseback arrangement) by Heathrow, and were built by Siemens in partnership with CAF of Spain.

Heathrow Express launched new branding and a train refurbishment programme in 2012, a £16m project. The major refurbishment, with input from Siemens and Interfleet Technology, was completed in 2013. Designs by the Tangerine agency aim to create an airliner ambience. Internet access is available throughout the journey. Heathrow Express was the first UK train company to launch an app which allows users to buy a ticket and receive it on a phone. A new version was launched in February 2015.

Tata Communications' branded Heathrow Express trains entered service in June 2015, starting a campaign that will see the company wrap the entire fleet.

Pre-purchased fares (late 2015) for Express Class are £21.50 single, £35

return (£29.50/£53 First Class). Tickets can be purchased on-board trains, with an extra £5 charge in Express Class. Promotional fares for two or more passengers travelling together were introduced in 2012, and a trial of new Advance purchase fares began in September 2015. Since March 2015, accompanied children travel free.

An online partnership with Aer Lingus allows customers to book Heathrow Express travel with flights, and travellers can arrange flights and connecting travel via Great Western and Heathrow Express, in partnerships with Singapore Airlines and British Airways.

Heathrow Connect was introduced in 2005, representing a £35m investment by Heathrow, in partnership with FirstGroup, aimed at providing access to the airport for London and Thames Valley residents and airport workers. Trains run generally half-hourly between Paddington and Terminals 1-3 (32min journey), calling at five stations. Fares are aligned with price-sensitive and local markets: a London-Heathrow single (late 2015) is £10.10. Trains and on-board staff are supplied by Heathrow Express, and between Paddington and Hayes & Harlington, operation is by Great Western. Between

Hayes & Harlington and Airport Junction, open-access rights apply. Heathrow Connect uses five 5-car Class 360/2 trains built by Siemens.

The 14 Class-332 Heathrow Express trains generally run in pairs, making up eight or nine-car trains. (Five additional carriages, valued at £6m, increased five trains to five-car length.) Siemens carries out train maintenance, with reliability standards specified in the contract. The purpose-built depot is at Old Oak Common, near Paddington.

After trials at Terminal 5, platform gap-fillers to reduce the risk of stepboard accidents were installed at all Heathrow Express stations in 2015.

In 2014, according to the airport company's accounts, the revenue of its Heathrow Express segment was £129m (EBITDA £6m), compared with £124m in 2013 (EBITDA £6m).

Heathrow Express Public Performance Measure punctuality (moving annual average) for 2014/15 was 92.6%. Heathrow Express has 450 employees. It achieved an overall satisfaction rating of 94% in the spring 2015 National Rail Passenger Survey.

Of the 84 train drivers employed by the firm, 34, or 40.5%, are female, by far the highest proportion of female drivers in the UK rail industry. ▪

SENIOR PERSONNEL
HEATHROW EXPRESS

BUSINESS LEAD AND COMMERCIAL DIRECTOR Fraser Brown (in photo)
OPERATIONS DIRECTOR Keith Harding
ENGINEERING MANAGER Mark Chestney

Heathrow Express Class 333 (right) and Heathrow Connect Class 360 trains at their Old Oak Common depot in August 2015. **SIEMENS/HEATHROW EXPRESS**

CROSS-CHANNEL AND RAIL FREIGHT GROUP

Groupe Eurotunnel operates the Channel Tunnel – which has twin railway tunnels and a service tunnel - under a 100-year concession signed in 1986 with the French and British governments. Terminals at Folkestone and Coquelles provide car, coach and lorry access to shuttle trains. International passenger and freight trains also run through the Tunnel.

Eurotunnel's international rail freight subsidiary, Europorte, includes operations in France and the British operator GB Railfreight.

Summer 2015 saw Eurotunnel break new traffic records for its Le Shuttle Passenger service, with almost 658,000 vehicles carried in July and August. On 15 August more than 17,000 vehicles travelled, the highest ever daily traffic in the 21-year operating history of the Tunnel. Additional security has been provided after the migrant crisis in the Calais area in 2015 saw incursions onto Eurotunnel infrastructure, with disruptions to traffic, fatalities and injuries.

Eurotunnel's consolidated revenues for 2014 amounted to Euro 1.207 billion, an increase of 7% compared to 2013. Operating profit increased by 11% to Euro 334m.

Eurotunnel is pursuing application of European interoperability specifications, one aim being that rail freight trains can run in the Tunnel without the specialised Class 92 locos. Tests with new-generation Siemens Vectron and Alstom Prima II locomotives were conducted in 2012 and 2013 to check compatibility with Tunnel systems. Europorte has also encouraged the idea of a piggyback rail network to carry lorry trailers across Europe and into Britain.

16 Class-92 electric locomotives were bought from Europorte by GB Railfreight in 2014. They are equipped for North of London, Tunnel and North of France 25kV 50Hz pantograph supply; and for the UK 750V-DC third-rail network.

Eurotunnel in 2015 sold two ferries, following the end of their lease to independent operator MyFerryLink, after the UK Competition Commission confirmed its decision to prohibit their operation. Eurotunnel proposed to retain a third ferry for freight operations, catering for cargo not permitted in the Tunnel.

Headed by a 5.7MW Brush-built locomotive, a Eurotunnel shuttle train undergoes maintenance. **EUROTUNNEL**

The basis of Channel Tunnel track access charges was challenged by the European Commission in 2013: in April 2014, this was dropped after the extension of the ETICA programme (Eurotunnel Incentive for Capacity Additions) to support new rail freight services, plus reduction of some off-peak tariffs for rail freight.

The UK and French regulators, the Office of Rail and Road (ORR) and Araf, took over responsibility for access and charges in the Channel Tunnel (apart from Le Shuttle) from the Intergovernmental Commission (IGC) in June 2015, pledging to ensure fair competition, full transparency, and non-discriminatory access. IGC continues to have responsibility for security.

Cross-Channel rail freight saw 14% more trains in 2014 and tonnage increased by 21%, attributed to intermodal and automobile components flows combined with the ETICA scheme. An increase of Euro 20m in Europorte's revenues (8%) in 2014 is attributed mainly by new contracts started in 2014 and by the extension of the Network Rail contract in the United Kingdom. A 2011 European Railway Agency report found passenger trains with distributed traction (rather than power cars at train ends) could be permitted in the Tunnel, as required by Eurostar and Deutsche Bahn plans for new trains and new international passenger services. In

June 2013, the Intergovernmental Commission granted Deutsche Bahn a certificate to operate passenger services through the Tunnel, though by late 2015 firm proposals had not been made.

Four SAFE fire-fighting points, installed in the tunnels in 2011, are designed to suppress fires on lorry shuttles, and hot-spot detectors are used on lorries.

Eurotunnel has nine passenger shuttles for cars and coaches (one was restored in 2012 after being out of use), and 15 lorry shuttles. Each 800-metre long shuttle has two locomotives.

Shuttle locos have three bogies, each with two motorised axles for good wheel/rail adhesion. There are 45 locos of 7MW rating, many uprated from 5.7MW, with 13 remaining at 5.7MW. There are also seven Krupp/MaK diesel auxiliary locos. Eurotunnel increased the top speed of its shuttles from 140km/h to 160km/h in 2012.

Under a strategy of increasing market share from 38% to 45% by 2020, Eurotunnel plans to expand lorry capacity by 20% and aims to improve quality of service, with up to eight departures per hour in each direction, instead of six today. It has ordered three new lorry shuttles (valued at Euro 40m) from WBN Waggonbau Niesky for delivery by 2017. Terminal capacity is being enlarged in a Euro 30m programme.

A 1,000MW electrical interconnector between Great Britain and France is under development by ElecLink, a Eurotunnel joint venture with STAR Capital.

Mobile phone services were provided inside the North running tunnel (usual direction UK to France) in 2014 with the help of three UK telecom operators and equipment supplier Alcatel-Lucent. The South tunnel was equipped in 2012 by French operators. 4G mobile services were also introduced in 2014. ∎

SENIOR PERSONNEL

EUROTUNNEL

CHAIRMAN AND CHIEF EXECUTIVE
Jacques Gounon (in photo)
CHIEF OPERATING OFFICER Michel Boudoussier
COMMERCIAL DIRECTOR Jo Willacy
CHIEF FINANCIAL AND CORPORATE OFFICER François Gauthey
BUSINESS SERVICES DIRECTOR Patrick Etienne
DIRECTOR OF ETHICS AND SAFETY Philippe de Lagune
CHIEF OPERATING OFFICER, EUROPORTE Pascal Sainson

HITACHI
Inspire the Next

FREIGHT AND HAULAGE

IN ASSOCIATION WITH

Wabtec
GROUP

CONSTRUCTION AND INTERMODAL
SUSTAIN RAILFREIGHT...

...AS COAL FALLS OFF A CLIFF. THE MODERN RAILWAY'S RAILFREIGHT REVIEW ANALYSES BIG CHANGES IN RAILFREIGHT GEOGRAPHY

It's been a long time coming, and some thought it would never arrive, but there's no doubt that the days of coal-fired electricity generation are numbered and that the decline of railborne coal has well and truly started. Whilst the catastrophic year-on-year drop of 61% in Quarter 1 (Q1) of 2015/16 was, to some degree, a function of artificially high stocks built by the generators in advance of the big increase in carbon tax in April 2015, the number of major power station closures announced in recent months indicates that the eclipse of coal has begun.

Rail's other traditional staple - iron and steel - is also under the cosh and plant closures are the order of the day here too. Praise be, therefore, for the growth in construction materials and intermodal in recent years - without these two growth markets, plus some other bright spots such as automotive, rail freight would be heading rapidly up the proverbial creek without a paddle. With these offsetting positives, in spite of the disaster that was coal, rail freight overall was only 17% down in the quarter and, for all the recent problems,

2014/15 was the second best year since the start of the century, coming in slightly under the preceding year. Even so, the seismic shift in coal means that it now accounts for less than 15% of UK rail freight - in Q1 2015/16 construction was over 60% bigger than coal and intermodal was 2.5 times larger. How times have changed.

As it is, railfreight geography is changing rapidly - and for good. The time-honoured heartland of British Rail's Trainload Freight (TLF) in Yorkshire and the North East will soon be a very pale shadow of its former glory. At the time of privatisation, such was the volume of traffic in this area that the (roughly) equal three-way split of TLF's business led to the creation of Loadhaul, whose home area extended no further than Retford in the south and and Berwick in the north, whereas Mainline's area stretched from the East Midlands across the whole of South East England, and Transrail required vast tracts of the western side of England, plus the whole of Wales and Scotland, to achieve a similar turnover. Furthermore, Loadhaul was the most profitable of the three companies, with

huge tonnages of highly profitable coal to Drax, Eggborough and Ferrybridge, plus iron ore and steel traffic at Lackenby and Scunthorpe. Twenty years on, Eggborough, Ferrybridge and Lackenby have, or shortly will be, closed and Scunthorpe leads a precarious existence. Drax is in the process of switching to biomass and only the petroleum business from Immingham survives in recognisable form.

In contrast, further south, coal activities at West Burton, Cottam and Ratcliffe have so far survive unscathed and the construction business from Leicestershire and the Mendips to the South East is booming. Also in the South East, Deep Sea containers at Felixstowe and Southampton have also grown, and continue to grow, substantially. In the west, Fiddlers Ferry and Aberthaw continue as does the South Wales steel industry. With Deep Sea growth and the rise of domestic intermodal - most of which is associated with DIRFT at Daventry - the West Coast main line (WCML) is a key, and very busy, freight artery. So it is that one can travel down the

East Coast main line (ECML) from Doncaster to Berwick upon Tweed and not see a single freight train, whereas on the WCML, Midland main line (MML) and the Great Western (GWML), even a relatively short journey will journey will generally yield several freights.

MAIN LINE DISCIPLINE

The general pattern is clear - gone are the areas of intensive local working in closely defined areas. Freight is now about running along the main lines - WCML for intermodal, MML and the GWML for construction materials. The ECML has evolved from being a conveyor belt for bulk materials north of Doncaster to being a significant artery for intermodal south thereof, at least as far as Peterborough. This is associated with the ever increasing importance of Felixstowe - now the biggest railfreight location in the UK, with 31 trains in and out each day. It follows that freight is increasingly competing for paths on the main inter-city routes and no longer enjoys the luxury of a secondary network where it could - to a degree - please itself.

Will daytime freight be able to co-exist with the intensive service of IEPs on the Great Western main line? Freightliner's Class 66 No 66414 passes the new IEP depot at Stoke Gifford, near Bristol Parkway, with the 11.00 Bristol to Tilbury container train on 27 August 2015. **STEWART ARMSTRONG**

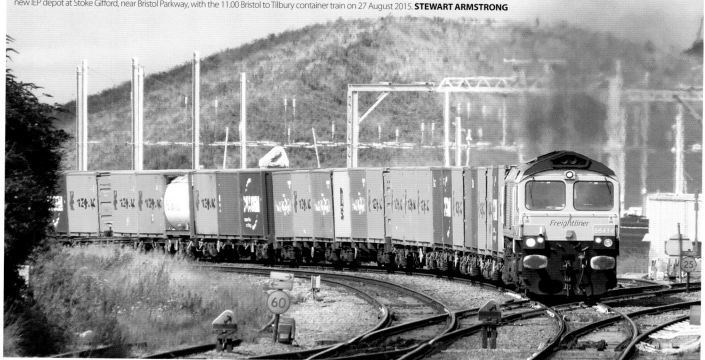

Greater discipline in timetabling and performance is one clear outcome - it was by no means uncommon in years gone by for freights to run hours early or hours late. Now, it is much more likely than not for a freight to appear in its booked path and freight punctuality has, of necessity, reached unprecedented levels. Freight Operating Companies (FOCs) - and customers - have come to realise that a late start, typically waiting for loading to be completed, is very likely to result in a train losing further time due to it being out of path and quickly becoming at least an hour late, worse if it is running close to the peaks. With tight resource planning to achieve lowest cost and thus, in a highly competitive market, keenest price, running an hour or more late can result in losing the next trip, with potentially serious consequences for both FOC and customer.

Even with passenger standards of performance, continued growth in construction and intermodal is putting serious pressure on several routes in terms of current and future capacity. Network Rail's programme of Route Studies (formerly Route

Utilisation Studies - RUSs) is doing a good job in analysing future capacity requirements for all users and outlining possible solutions. Roundly half of the Route Studies have now been out for consultation and, whilst differing somewhat in tone and emphasis, they have each defined a range of strategies to cater for predicted demand - some are relatively straightforward (passenger) train lengthening or timetable modification proposals, others major interventions requiring the expenditure of tens of millions of pounds, usually to eliminate conflicting moves at key junctions by grade separation or to cater for more frequent services by installing extra tracks.

That is very often a case of reinstating what was taken out by BR in the very different, contracting, market of the 1960s, 70s and 80s. Some commentators are wont to criticise such measures as having been short sighted false economy, but there was no rational possibility at the time of the sort of growth we are now seeing and, in most cases, the assets concerned have gone through at least one renewal cycle, so it could be

argued that a worthwhile saving was made. Were it not for a dire shortage of signalling resources, of which more anon, the reinstatement of more complex track layouts would be a straightforward matter. In any event, the lexicon has changed, from singling and dequadrification, to redoubling and requadrification.

WRONG SIGNALS

Network Rail has, it is painfully clear, a wide and serious range of problems in discharging its responsibilities of providing rail infrastructure in an efficient and timely manner. Missed efficiency targets, serious slippage of schemes and the dire performance with electrification are evident for all to see - Peter Hendy has a huge task ahead: good, then, that Network Rail finally has a seasoned transport professional at the helm. It is, however, worth recognising that the problems can, in many cases, be traced back to entirely the wrong signals being sent to suppliers in the electrification and signalling businesses over the past 20 years - Railtrack initially and subsequently Network Rail, at the

most senior levels in engineering, were adamant that diesel and fuel cell would provide the best option for traction and that ERTMS/ETCS would provide all the answers in signalling: how wrong could they be? And now we have the electrification 'factory train' for the GWML.

Commendable as it is to look to new technology as an option, a complex and intensively used system such as the UK rail network is not the place to carry out experiments or trials. Operators require - and customers deserve - a robust infrastructure that delivers fault-free performance day-in, day-out. An Engineering Director's personal pride at being at the cutting edge of technology has no place in the decision-making hierarchy, unspoken or otherwise – operators cry out for tried and trusted kit that works: boring and uninspiring it might be, but running trains to carry freight and passengers is the objective, not professional gratification.

In this context, we must pay tribute to Network Rail's civil engineers and their contractors. Where signalling and electrification schemes collapse

Coal traffic has fallen sharply in 2015. GBRf's rainbow-liveried Class 66 No 66720 passes Freemans Crossing, North Blyth, working 23 loaded coal hoppers from North Blyth to West Burton on 11 June 2015. **BILL WELSH**

in chaos, the civils are delivering major projects on time and to budget. Yes, it would be even better to see lower costs and quicker delivery, but Reading and Norton Bridge are shining examples of how to deliver major capacity-enhancing projects while the railway carries on around them - the classic 'open heart surgery'. The lesson is surely simple - stick to proven solutions, use modern methods wherever they can be trusted and hone the project planning and management to a fine degree. Network Rail's electrification engineers, instead of putting their faith in an unproven factory train, might have been better advised to apply the ECML system and methods to the GWML and simply learn the lessons about stronger catenary in exposed locations.

That more capacity is needed is no longer a matter of debate. From a freight perspective, the priority bar none is Felixstowe. There was much rejoicing in autumn 2015 at the launch of the 31st daily train - a GBRf operation for Maritime Transport to their terminal at Birch Coppice near Tamworth. There are, however, substantial numbers of containers that are daily going out of the gates by road which the customer, let alone the port and the rail industry, would rather see on rail - a major road haulier has instituted a shuttle between Felixstowe and the North West simply because there is insufficient capacity on rail.

KEY SCHEMES

For years Network Rail has been looking at enhancements to the Felixstowe branch to create more paths, but the sad truth is that nothing has happened, nor are spades in the ground even imminent. The latest hiatus is a funding shortfall due to failure to win a hoped-for European grant. The prevarication has to stop - in the context of overall rail funding a shortfall of a few million pounds is lost in the roundings. It is time for Government to instruct Network Rail to implement at least partial doubling of the Felixstowe branch to create desperately needed capacity - it is much the biggest step Ministers could take to increase the amount of freight on rail, as they consistently say they want to do.

In the meantime, Network Rail and the FOCs need to ensure that every single path on the branch is used productively. Light engine movements to/from Ipswich consume capacity - fuelling at Felixstowe would improve productivity and free up paths whilst, in the short term, locos could be moved dead in tow or double head trains rather than waste a valuable path. More radically, why not couple two trains together for the run up the branch? No doubt there would be any number of reasons why not, but SNCF - not noted as the most successful freight operator in Europe - is trialling the concept on main lines, so why not here?

Elsewhere, there are a number of important schemes to create more capacity for freight. Some, like four tracking through Leicester from Syston to Wigston - which will benefit both construction and intermodal - are relatively imminent, assuming that funding does not dry up: others, like remodelling of Basingstoke to ease the path of intermodals heading for Southampton, are making haste slowly. Others still have no clear proposals - even with delays to GWML electrification, all the signs are that the Intercity Express Programme trains will be delivered on time by Hitachi and will go into service using their bi-mode capability rather more extensively than originally envisaged.

The proposed service of seven IEPs an hour in each direction over the largely two-track section from Swindon to Didcot leaves virtually no scope for day time freight, unless the IEPs are heavily flighted to leave a 10-15min slot for a freight path - which is likely to be resisted by passenger service specifiers. The GW Route Study talks vaguely of extending the short four track section westwards from Challow to Swindon, but does so without conviction - and it would be at massive cost. The much cheaper and easier solution of reinstating the one time Up Goods line from Shrivenham to Knighton Crossing - and possibly replicating it on the Down side - seems not to have considered.

In the traditional bulk freight heartland, Wrawby Junction at Barnetby is about to be remodelled under a renewal scheme which will eliminate one of the last major islands of semaphore signalling, but it is hard to see any other locations where coal and steel are dominant justifying major capital expenditure. The once unthinkable prospect of the UK having no coal-fired power stations is now forecast to occur in 2023. Whether that happens remains to be seen, but it is the scenario on which NR and the FOCs have to plan. Yes, margins on the grid for winter 2015/16 are uncomfortably tight but, by a combination of paying eye-wateringly high prices for standby gas generation and enforcing interruptable supply agreements with major industrial users, the signs are that the country will squeeze through a harsh winter without domestic power cuts - at a price.

COAL IMPACT

As well as the closures in Yorkshire mentioned above, by mid 2016 Scotland will be without a coal fired power station - Cockenzie was demolished in autumn 2015 and Longannet is to shut in spring 2016. With coal consumption falling and ample port capacity closer to the remaining English power stations, imports through Hunterston are likely to dwindle and may cease altogether. With much reduced quantities of opencast coal being mined in Ayrshire, there is likely be precious little coal traffic north of the border. Further south, some opencast production continues in Northumberland and South Wales, but the UK's last deep mines (Thoresby, Kellingley and Hatfield) closed in 2015, bringing to a sad end a once great industry on which Britain's economy was built.

The once hopeful development of biomass as a substitute for coal now appears dead in the water. Drax is set to use 50% biomass, supplied from Tyne, Hull, Immingham and (from autumn 2015) Liverpool, but the only other major power station using biomass, Ironbridge, is set to close at the end of 2015 and no other conversions are in prospect. Eggborough's plans were dashed by a change of Government energy policy that peremptorily ended support for biomass, with the result that the station is now to close in 2016. A speculative proposal by a third party to convert Eggborough seems, as we write, to have fallen on stony ground. The substantial investment by the ports - particularly Immingham - in biomass handling facilities seems unlikely to provide much of a return. Fortunately, the rail industry avoided much in the way of abortive investment in biomass, with only GBRf's fleet of wagons being dedicated to the fuel and these are intensively used at Drax.

The implosion of coal volumes noted at the outset has inevitably hit the FOCs hard. GBRf has seen the least impact, having some volume guarantees, while Colas' token presence in coal has ceased. The big impact has, however, been felt by DB Schenker (DBS) and Freightliner Heavy Haul (FHH) - the former at least has a wide traffic base to reduce the overall impact and has had some success in redeploying coal wagons and locos into its buoyant aggregates business. FHH, on the other hand, has been hit very hard with large numbers of coal wagons parked up with no alternative use. Having also lost aggregates business (to GBRf), cement (to Colas) and waste (to DBS), FHH's infrastructure business with Network Rail has held up. Genesee and Wyoming must be dismayed at the setbacks for their new acquisition: but the traditional Freightliner deep sea container business is doing well.

Even before the closure of Eggborough was announced, DBS had already said that it would shed 235 staff, of which the majority were drivers, and this can only continue. Knottingley, in particular, looks to be very exposed, especially as almost all the coal (and biomass) will come from Immingham and could equally well be resourced from there or from Doncaster. Other coal-related traffic such as limestone for flue gas desulphurisation (FGD) and the gypsum by-product from FGD plants is bound, eventually, to decline, although for the moment desulphogypsum is a growth area, with GBRf having secured a contract with Siniat to haul the material from West Burton to Portbury and Ferrybridge. The former replaces imported gypsum but the latter represents another fine example of circumstances overtaking best

One of Colas Rail Freight's refurbished Class 60s on a recently won contract. No 60021 passes Barnetby with 14 VTG Rail UK vehicles working the 08.55 Preston Docks Lanfina-Lindsey Oil Refinery bitumen tanks on 22 May 2015. **BILL WELSH**

laid plans - the plant was built to use desulphogypsum from the adjacent power station, but the announcement that Ferrybridge was to close meant that the locational logic is out of the window and a new long-term rail flow is the result.

STEEL

Similar gloom is descending on the steel business, where DBS remains very much the dominant haulier: Q1 2015/16 was 9% down on the previous year. The 'perfect storm' of soaring energy costs and business rates, a high pound and plummeting world prices due to overcapacity, notably in China, are crucifying the UK steel industry. The pain is particularly acute in the long products sector (girders and plate) centred on the East Coast and in Scotland. Sadly it was no great surprise that the SSI operation at Lackenby ceased production and went into receivership in summer 2015 - the economics of importing every tonne of iron ore and coal and exporting every tonne produced, using expensive UK labour and energy, defied all commercial logic and the receiver

quickly closed the plant. The impact of the SSI closure on the rail industry was minor - at best only one train a day of lime or limestone from Cumbria or Yorkshire passed over Network Rail metals and even this material had latterly moved by road. GBRf was contracted to undertake internal movements within the plant and to Tees Dock, so found itself with surplus staff and a fleet of heavy duty shunting locos that, having been imported from Norway, are out of gauge for the main line network.

Similarly, the direct impact on rail of the Caparo Industries receivership in Autumn 2015 was not great. Some parts of the business were attractive and would find a new owner and, in its own right, the company was not a rail user, albeit it did consume Tata steel, some of which was routed from Scunthorpe and Sheffield via Wolverhampton Steel Terminal.

Much more serious was Tata's decision to scale back Scunthorpe and mothball (almost certainly as a prelude to complete closure) Dalzell and Clydebridge - since the closure of Ravenscraig 20 years ago the Scottish plants had received their slab feedstock

in a daily train, initially from Lackenby and latterly from Scunthorpe. Taken alongside the demise of coal, this renders the 'deindustrialisation' of Scotland in railfreight virtually complete - the only bulk freight remaining north of the border is petroleum from Grangemouth, cement from Dunbar and alumina to Fort William, none of which amounts to more than one or two trains a day. Without intermodal, there would be virtually no revenue-earning freight left in Scotland.

The only consolation from the Tata announcement was that Scunthorpe was not shutting completely - in early 2015 Tata had attempted to sell the plant to Klesch (a Swiss steel trader) but that deal fell through, and insiders feared that complete closure was looming. That Scunthorpe survives as an integrated works is thus a matter of some relief, but when it is said that it is struggling to operate on a cash-neutral (note, not even cash-positive) basis - let alone make a margin or still less a return on the huge amount of capital invested - the scale of the challenge is plain for all to see. Closure of some of the coke ovens will reduce the inbound movement of coal from

Immingham and at least one of the four blast furnaces seems likely to be mothballed, producing a similar impact on iron ore imports. Outbound flows will, it seems, be limited to bloom movements to Ebange in France, via the Channel Tunnel, Skinningrove and the remaining Tata beam mill at Lackenby, plus long welded rail trains for Network Rail. DB Schenker is bound to be hit hard by the steel cutbacks. The large wagon fleet, being mostly of a specialist nature, has very limited scope for redeployment and, with the cutbacks occurring in the same region as the coal closures, thus limiting the ability to move displaced staff to other work, further redundancies seem inevitable. True, tonnages of imported steel to the UK are likely to increase, but rail is not strong in the movement of finished long products and much of the lost tonnage is in raw materials and semi-finished products, which will not now see UK shores.

SOUTH WALES

The other half of Tata Steel's UK business - the flat products (coil) operation centred in South Wales, which Tata regards as core business, has seen cuts

HITACHI
Inspire the Next

there are several trains a week from South Wales to Tilbury for export, mostly made up of tinplate from Trostre - now the only outbound rail traffic from this location.

Elsewhere in South Wales, Celsa continue to produce reinforcing steel at the electric arc furnace at Cardiff, fed by several daily scrap trains from a wide range of sources, mostly in the Midlands plus a couple in Yorkshire, together with Exeter and Swindon. The latter location also forwards scrap to Tata at Port Talbot and to Liverpool for export. Of late, DBS has handled all these flows, an FHH flow from Dagenham having ceased in mid 2015, although at the same time Devon & Cornwall Railways (DCR) resumed the movement of scrap to Cardiff from North East England. Celsa, having initially switched entirely to road for outbound product movements, are now making increasing use of rail, with trainload tonnages to Rotherham and wagonload movements to Scotland and East London on DBS's network service (formerly Enterprise). There are also sporadic movements of scrap from the above sources to Newport docks for export but, sadly, the substantial scrap export facility that has developed at Southampton is entirely road-fed, in spite of having dock lines immediately alongside.

One dock location that continues to generate steel traffic is Boston, which generates a train a day of imported coil to a steel terminal located in the old Metro Cammell works at Washwood Heath. Regular import hauls also run from Immingham to Wolverhampton Steel Terminal and for Otokumpu stainless steel at Tinsley - the only rail activity left at this once major freight hub.

PETROLEUM

Petroleum traffic still features in South Wales despite production ceasing at Murco's Robeston refinery near Milford Haven in mid 2015 - the jetty and storage facilities remain in use for imported product and a daily DBS train continues to run to Westerleigh on the outskirts of Bristol, with an alternate day working running to Theale. Cardiff Docks sees an occasional GBRf train for Greenergy from Port Clarence on Teesside. As noted earlier, a small amount of petroleum business remains in Scotland, with a daily train from Grangemouth to Dalston, near Carlisle, and odd-day workings to locations within Scotland plus Rolls Royce at Derby. Colas displaced DBS at Grangemouth during 2015 and having also won the Dunbar cement traffic

from FHH, is now a major operator in Scotland, albeit it is a small and declining market.

Immingham, however, continues to be the main source of rail-borne petroleum traffic, with up to 5 trains a day from Lindsey refinery, mostly to the Midlands plus a daily train to Westerleigh and three trains a week to Colnbrook. Humber refinery now despatches just one train a day, to Kingsbury. DBS have long held the Immingham business but Colas are making incursions here too - a further blow to DBS in the area. With their various contract wins, Colas overtook DRS as the UK's number four freight operator, after DBS, Freightliner and GBRf, in late 2015. Overall, the Petroleum business was 6% down in Q1 2015/6 compared with the previous year.

UP SIDE

Having dealt with the rather depressing traditional markets of coal and steel and the, at best, static petroleum business, let us turn to the more upbeat side of rail freight. Before concentrating on the big stories of construction and intermodal, it is worth noting that timber shows encouraging signs and that automotive is forging ahead. Colas continue to move healthy volumes of timber to Kronospan at Chirk, with a daily train from Carlisle plus a second service originating at Baglan Bay or Exeter Riverside, the latter having replaced Teigngrace on the Heathfield branch as the loading point for the South West. In addition, there appear to be reasonable prospects of timber returning to Scotland, with lineside loading on the Far North line at Kinbrace.

The British car industry - or at least the German and Japanese-owned plants located in Britain - is doing well, with output at levels not seen since the 'halcyon' days of British Leyland/Rover and Ford. Jaguar Land Rover (JLR - another part of the Tata empire) forwards several trains a day from Halewood, plus one from Castle Bromwich, to Southampton with deep sea exports, while BMW despatches a daily train from Cowley to Southampton and another to Purfleet, the latter with European exports. Conversely, Ford and other marques use rail for import movements through Dagenham, Southampton and Portbury. These run to the North West, Yorkshire and Scotland on a mixture of trainload and network services - DBS are the major player, although GBRf now has a 'foot in the door' at Dagenham.

With the demise of other traffics and the reduction in MOD business due to defence cutbacks, automotive is now much the most important business on DBS's north-south network services, with Warrington continuing to act as a hub, exchanging portions between trains from the South East and the South West destined for Scotland and Yorkshire, as well as detaching local North West traffic.

Particularly encouraging has been the growth of import volumes through Southampton, notably in the form of vans - once manufactured at Eastleigh but now imported through the docks - which are often too high to double deck on road transporters, so are well-suited to rail. Worth noting too, en passant, that DBS's east- west network service along the GWML has Ford automotive components from Bridgend to Dagenham as one of its staple traffics, alongside intermodal chemicals traffic to/from Dow Corning at Barry.

There are, however, still substantial volumes of new cars moving on transporters along the motorways which could, in part at least, be considered rail potential. None of the Japanese-owned plants - Nissan at Sunderland, Honda at Swindon or Toyota at Burnaston - currently use rail, although the first two have done so on occasions in the past. Most of Nissan's output passes via the Port of Tyne and, without a siding, it is a challenging prospect for rail. Likewise Burnaston, at the moment, has no rail connection although a proposed distribution park on an adjacent site may well rectify this omission within five years. The current intensive road shuttle to/from Grimsby - Toyota's chosen port of entry/exit - would appear to offer significant rail potential when this occurs. Honda has access to a rail siding at the edge of its plant on the outskirts of Swindon and sends a lot of transporters down the M4 each day to rail-connected Portbury, but this has so far proved elusive. These and other automotive hauls - notably for Vauxhall and from JLR's Solihull plant - are volume business for which, ultimately, there ought to be a rail solution.

Notwithstanding some success at Southampton and Portbury, the same clearly applies to the remainder of the 1.5 million cars imported into the UK each year, the vast majority into these self same ports. Much to go at, then, in automotive and a key strategic development is set to go live in 2016 - DBS is investing several million pounds in a major import/ export terminal at Barking, the limit of

but the dire prognosis facing the East Coast plants is not replicated in the west. The hot mill at Llanwern has, once again, been mothballed and Shotton's galvanising line has shut - probably for good - but, thus far, the business and its associated rail movements remain largely intact, albeit with volume reductions of around 20%. The changes mean that hot rolled coil (HRC) moves from Port Talbot to Llanwern in lieu of slab, but in the scheme of things this is little more than a wagon management issue. Daily trains of HRC run from Port Talbot to Hartlepool, Corby and Trostre as well the shuttle to Llanwern, with cold reduced coil passing to Shotton, Round Oak (in the West Midlands), Middlesbrough (for Nissan) and Mauberge in France via the Channel Tunnel.

There is also a twice weekly service to Swindon for the BMW body plant and various local shipment moves to ABP Newport and Birdport on the River Usk. Both port facilities, together with ABP Cardiff, are also used to import slab (or HRC) from the sister plant at IJmuiden in Holland when Port Talbot has production problems, which sadly occurs all too frequently. In addition, continental gauge in the UK, capable of handling 150,000 cars a year. This could be a game changer, since traffic to/from the UK will then have access to the massive car carrying wagon fleet of mainland Europe. Instead of a few hundred UK gauge wagons, many thousands of wagons will be available and, moreover, they can be loaded at any continental car plant - as far east as Poland and Turkey - for direct movement to the UK via the Channel Tunnel and HS1. Whilst these wagons could not run north of London to UK production plants it should not prove too difficult to achieve a drive off/drive on transshipment at Barking between UK feeder services and the continental wagons for exports. For sure, wagons returning empty to the continent could be offered at attractive prices and, if import movements switch to the new route, there will be fewer car carriers shuttling between north European ports and the UK, meaning

less outbound shipping capacity for exports: watch this space.

CONSTRUCTION

So, to Construction. A casual observer might think the business was fairly static - the same locations forward the same sort of trains to the same sort of destinations - but the statistics show that volumes are building on long-established routes and additional flows are starting between places that have not previously been linked. Q1 2015/16 was 7% up on the previous year and was an all time record quarter, building on 2014/15 which was itself a record year, over 40% higher than 5 years earlier. With a buoyant construction industry, especially in the South East, organic growth of rail-borne aggregates is strong - new houses and commercial developments need foundations, concrete and roads, all of which requires aggregates. As a result, trains of limestone from the Mendips and granite from Leicestershire are

running to full programmes, as are trains from Thames wharves such as Angerstein, Dagenham and Cliffe. In addition, terminals that formerly received only their limestone or granite by rail are, in many cases, now also receiving other materials such as sand from the Thames or from Dorset.

Gritstone - the very hard material used for its anti-skid properties - is also now often part of the mix, loaded at a variety of locations in South Wales and the Marches for movement to the South East and elsewhere. Geology dictates that gritstone is often located in areas remote from rail and a lengthy road haul from Mid Wales to loading points at Moreton on Lugg, near Hereford, or Shrewsbury is sometimes necessary. Even in South Wales the material has to be roaded from the quarries to railheads at Neath, Cardiff or Machen. However, given the long haul to the areas where gritstone is required, and the lack of a backload for tipper trucks, rail is increasingly the preferred

option with several trains a day heading through the Severn Tunnel to join the procession of Mendip limestone trains on the GWML. In autumn 2015 DBS announced a new flow of Northern Irish gritstone from Avonmouth Docks to Theale for United Asphalt, together with a hardstone flow from Ipswich Docks for the same customer.

A further material in the mix is china clay sand, vast quantities of which are piled high in mid Cornwall following a century of clay extraction. FHH had sporadic moves of china clay sand to London during the Olympic construction phase, but DBS have now started a dedicated service to Bow with a daily train in propsect, worked as far as Exeter in two portions due to restricted loads on the Devon banks.

As well as intensification of use of established terminals, the next generation of aggregates railheads is on the way. Brett Aggregates, a long term user of rail for sea-dredged sand and gravel landed at Cliffe in Kent,

Getting ready for autumn. Direct Rail Services' Class 66 No 66429 with a railhead-treatment wagon transfer from York to Carlisle Kingmoor is seen on the Tyne Valley line near Gateshead Metrocentre on 24 September 2015. **BILL WELSH**

opened a new terminal at Neasden in October 2015 to facilitate the delivery of aggregates into Central London. Hope Construction Materials (HCM) - a Mittal group company formed out the merger of Tarmac and Lafarge at the behest of competition authorities - opened a new terminal at Walsall in autumn 2015, to be served from their Dowlow quarry in the Peak District by DBS. Dowlow - previously owned by Lafarge - has traditionally sent out only a limited amount of construction aggregate by rail, largely to the North West, so this is a significant development by HCM, most of whose rail movements are of cement from the eponymous Peak District works.

In a further northern development, two adjacent Tarmac quarries in North Yorkshire - Arcow and Dryrigg - are to be connected via a new siding on the Settle & Carlisle line at Helwith Bridge near Horton in Ribblesdale. Installed as part of a scheme to reduce the amount of heavy lorry traffic in the Dales and potentially extend the permitted life of the quarries, several hundred thousand tonnes a year are expected to be loaded out of the new siding.

Minerals planning is a major issue and one to which the rail freight industry arguably does not pay sufficient attention. As an example, Oxfordshire County Council's draft minerals plan proposes allowing sand and gravel extraction in virgin countryside along the Thames south of Oxford. The alternative option of increasing importation of crushed rock by rail from the Mendips, plus china clay sand from Cornwall and sea-dredged gravel from the Thames had not been considered. With seemingly no focus from the FOCs or Network Rail, it was left to interested individuals living locally to promote the rail-based alternative to despoiling the landscape. Given that, in Oxfordshire alone, an extra million tonnes of rail business could result, it is not a trivial matter.

Also seeing significant investment and expansion is the cement business. As well as extra volume on existing routes, new facilities are being (re) created - often in areas that were rail-served until the 1980s. The one time car-loading facility, latterly used for loading scrap metal, at Dagenham Dock is to become a new East London railhead for HCM, served from Hope, and it is rumoured that Southampton Bevois Park, once the destination of trains from Castle Cement at Tring, is also been prepared as a new terminal for HCM. These developments supplement the creation of a new cement terminal at Avonmouth for Castle Cement, supplied by a twice weekly train from Clitheroe and over 150 new bogie cement tank wagons are on order for delivery in 2015/6. In another part of the construction supply chain, a new flow of fly ash is moved in tank containers from Drax power station by DBS twice weekly to Appleford in Oxfordshire to supply block plants that previously used ash from Didcot. Logic suggests there is considerable scope to extend the use of such equipment in the cement business and, potentially, bring rail back into play at major works such as Rugby, which currently despatch all of their production by road. Autumn 2015 saw the commencement of a second flow of ash, this time from West Burton power station to a reopened siding at East Peckham in Kent for J Clubb, to supply block plants that formerly used ash from coal-fired power stations on the Thames Estuary.

Household waste is generally considered as part of the construction business and is a market that is seeing profound changes, as recycling and energy from waste (EFW) replace a large proportion of landfill. Thus it is that long standing rail movements from West London to landfill in Oxfordshire and Buckinghamshire will shortly switch to a new EFW plant at Avonmouth - in the short term, until the new plant is commissioned, trains are running to Scunthorpe and even Dunbar for landfill. Similarly, Manchester's waste, long landfilled at Roxby near Scunthorpe, is now mostly moving to an EFW plant at Runcorn, although again in the short term some trains ran to Dunbar. Paradoxically, Liverpool's waste is set to move in two trains a day to an EFW plant on Teesside. However, notwithstanding a minor flow of incinerator ash from Newhaven to Brentford that started in 2014, it seems unlikely that there will be many more new domestic waste flows. What does seem likely to grow is the movement of construction waste from London to a variety of locations for disposal - Calvert is a favourite destination, but a new facility at the former cement works at Foxton in Cambridgeshire opened in mid 2015.

INTERMODAL
For all the welcome and encouraging growth in Construction - which accounted for 23% of UK rail freight movements in Q1 2015/16 - the decline of Coal means that Intermodal is now much the biggest sector in UK rail freight, accounting for almost 35% of the Q1 total. After a couple of flat years, intermodal growth resumed in 2014/15 to produce the best year on record. As noted above, Felixstowe has reached 31 trains a day and a 32nd train was in prospect for early 2016 - not far off double the 18 trains a day out of Southampton, with a mere 5 trains a day running from London Gateway and Tilbury combined.

Rail is strongest with hauls to the M62 corridor - the North West and Yorkshire, where a chain of terminals extend from Liverpool through Manchester to Leeds and Wakefield. An ORR investigation into Freightliner during 2015 concluded that rail is the mode of choice in this market and that road haulage does not provide an effective competitor. It comes as a surprise to some that Scotland is not a major rail market, but the number of containers heading directly to Scotland is small and feeder vessels - from North European ports as much as Felixstowe and Southampton - provide potent competition. North East England displays similar characteristics - relatively small volumes and sea feeders taking a significant share.

There are attempts to replicate the pattern on the west coast and Peel Ports are investing substantial sums to increase the vessel size that can be accommodated at Liverpool. While some volume may be attracted away from rail to coastal feeders, it is hard to see container shipping lines being prepared to divert massively expensive 20,000 TEU (20ft equivalent unit - the standard measure of container capacity) deep sea vessels away from the English Channel. Almost without exception, the strategy is to call at one southern UK port, plus Rotterdam or Antwerp and a north German port - a French port also features in some itineraries. It makes little sense to incur extra sailing time - and cost - to serve a northern port when capacity exists along the English Channel. The additional sailing time up the Thames

One of the remaining petroleum flows in Scotland, while still hauled by DB Schenker. Class 66 No 66192 approaches Cumbernauld with the 08.32 return working to Grangemouth from Dalston on 16 April 2015. **STEWART ARMSTRONG**

to London Gateway appears to be a significant factor in the much slower than planned growth of the new port: what price therefore a diversion to Liverpool? Significantly, similar proposals at Bristol have been quietly dropped.

The main growth opportunity for Deep Sea is with boxes heading to the 'Golden Triangle' - the area roughly bounded by the M1, M6 and the M42, where almost all the retailers have their National Distribution Centres (NDCs). Whereas fast moving goods such as foodstuffs are generally sourced within the UK, or the near Continent, and are routed direct to Regional Distribution Centres (RDCs) for delivery to stores, slower moving items (clothing, consumer durables etc) - very often sourced from the Far East - are taken first to an NDC before being fed to RDCs for onward delivery to stores.

Accordingly, there are substantial numbers of containers moving daily from deep sea ports to the Golden Triangle. Some are already sent by rail to terminals in the West Midlands for onward road delivery, but the cost of the final delivery by road means that road haulage direct from the port is often cheaper. However, where the NDC is located at - or very close to - the railhead, the equation

moves decisively in favour of rail. A recent study found that eliminating, or at least substantially reducing, the on-cost of final delivery means that rail could be up to 40% cheaper than road for a journey from a deep sea port to a Golden Triangle NDC. This is not lost on the logistics community - retailers are, in any event, keen to switch traffic to rail where feasible for environmental reasons and a saving of even 20% is a major incentive.

EXPANSION

As a result, there are three major rail-linked warehousing developments in train for the Golden Triangle, albeit two are to the north of the classic triangle, reflecting a northward expansion of the area in the face of land and labour shortages further south. Prologis have secured planning permission for the third phase of DIRFT at Daventry (on the site of the redundant radio transmitting station near the M1) and will be further extending the internal rail route to a major new intermodal terminal on the site, which will offer 8-9 million sq ft of new warehousing. Further north, Roxhill are going through the planning process for a new site alongside East Midlands Airport which will house 5-6m sq ft and feature a new 3km branch line from

the Nottingham-Burton on Trent line, plus a large intermodal terminal. Slightly further east, alongside the Derby-Stoke line at Etwall, Goodman are proposing to build another 5-6m sq ft with a dedicated intermodal terminal - it is this that could provide a rail facility for the nearby Toyota car plant. Property developers will only spend such substantial sums of money if they are clear that it will provide good returns and will have talked very closely with the retailers and their logistics providers to ensure that the new warehousing will be taken up. The beauty of this from the rail industry - and the Government's - perspective is that the costs, including all the new rail infrastructure, are paid by the developer and FOCs simply need to run trains to the new terminal as and when required by their customers.

There is a further major potential benefit for the rail industry. As noted above, goods move on from the NDCs to RDCs around the country and, with a rail connection at or very close to the NDC, rail is likely to be competitive for journeys of 150 miles or so, not just the 300-350 mile Anglo-Scottish hauls that classically feature. With a typical 1m sq ft NDC sending out almost 200 HGVs a day to its RDCs - and there are (or soon will be)

dozens of such facilities in the Golden Triangle - the market is substantial. Runs to RDCs in the North of England and the South West would be in play and, whilst South Eastern RDCs are arguably too close from the bottom end of the Golden Triangle, rail would certainly be in contention from the new terminals at the northern edge of the triangle.

In any event, as Tesco have shown for some years now, road congestion around and within the M25 means that rail can be an attractive option into the South East, even from Daventry. Indeed, in due course, it may be that RDCs will also migrate to rail-linked sites to take further cost out of the supply chain, but even without this, the advent of rail-connected NDCs will give rail a big boost in the domestic intermodal market. The boost is eagerly anticipated as growth is currently behind the curve of predicated expansion - as is often the case, growth comes not in a smooth line but in a series of steps and the new Golden Triangle terminals look set to deliver a big step up.

NEW TERMINAL

As an indication of things to come, the opening of Sainsbury's new rail-connected NDC at DIRFT 2 in late 2015 led almost immediately to an

additional daily train to Scotland for JG Russell, who operate the Sainsbury rail terminal. Interestingly, the new train is hauled by Freightliner rather than DRS, who operate the other two Russell trains. Coming after the switch of the WH Malcolm Anglo Scottish trains from DRS to DBS a year earlier, this seems to suggest that DRS, the pathfinders in domestic intermodal, now see their core business lying elsewhere. There is also industry speculation that Tesco may also be about to embark on the next stage of rail expansion, with a train to the new terminal at Teesport in prospect. PD Ports opened the facility in mid 2015 and Freightliner immediately transferred their two trains a day from the Wilton terminal which promptly closed. DBS - in conjunction with PD - launched a new service from Teesport to Scotland in late 2015, with some underwritten volume from a major short sea container operator, a crucial component since previous attempts on this axis (notably by W H Malcolm with DRS in 2012/13) foundered when promised

volumes from the short sea operators failed to materialise. Whisky exports are clearly a major traffic, but Tesco and Asda both have large port-centric warehouses at Teesport, so there is also northbound domestic business which a link from Daventry would, no doubt, strengthen.

The Thames provides a similar picture. Tesco's train from Daventry conveys portions for both Barking and Purfleet, from which swap bodies are delivered to stores in London, Essex and Kent. Those handled at Purfleet return north with goods imported from the Continent, either trans-shipped at Purfleet or with the swap body being sent across on the short sea ferry to collect goods from continental suppliers. The frustration is that there are many more short sea containers landed at Purfleet - and Tilbury - for customers other than Tesco that could go by rail but remain stubbornly on road. Given that a significant number head down the M4 to South Wales and the West Country, there ought to be a competitive rail solution,

as there is for deep sea containers from Felixstowe to Bristol and from Southampton to Cardiff.

That importers wish to use rail is evidenced by the interest in and, before the latest migrant crisis developed, growing use of Channel Tunnel rail services. Q1 2015/16 was 7% up on the previous year - it and the preceding quarter were the best recorded since the halcyon days of Channel Tunnel services at the start of the century - building on the success of 2014/15 which was nearly 30% up on the preceding year. The daily Dourges-Barking shuttle service, much of which was taken up by Proctor & Gamble, was developing into a resounding success and will resume as soon as Eurotunnel could provide a reliable passage and a similar shuttle from Benelux and/or Germany is waiting in the wings. With a daily train from Poland is also in prospect, the interruption to services through the Tunnel was thus little short of tragic. Given the determination of migrants, the answer is surely not to stop the trains

in Calais Frethun at all and, if a loco change is necessary, arrange for this to occur elsewhere to allow for non-stop movement through the Calais area. The use of Class 92s deep into eastern France was examined as long ago as the late 1990s.

In conclusion, intermodal is set to expand on all fronts. Deep Sea is growing organically and, with more capacity out of Felixstowe and the new generation of rail-connected Golden Triangle NDCs in prospect, rail market share should grow significantly. Domestic intermodal should also receive a big boost from the rail-connected NDCs, while European movements via the Channel Tunnel and short sea ports offer further potential. This, coupled with the strong growth in aggregates and other construction materials, suggests there is a reasonable chance that the decline in coal can be offset in the years to come, with UK rail freight remaining at broadly current levels – an achievement that would have seemed impossible only a few years ago. ■

FREIGHT OPERATOR FINANCES

The freight industry's recovery from the recession resumed in 2013/14 after the setback of the previous year when profits fell back. In 2013/14, there were rises of 22% in operating and pre-tax profits, according to analysis undertaken by consultants TAS in Rail Industry Monitor.

Cash operating profits rose from the previous year's £52.7m to £64.3m, with margins rising from 6.6% from 5.8%. Not quite back to the 7.2% of two years before, but well on the way.

The combined turnover of the companies analysed was 6.6% higher at £971.5m, whilst the rise in operating costs was 5.7%, taking the total to £907.2m. Unchanged returns on pension scheme assets met that the industry again recorded £0.4m worth of interest earnings. As a result, pre-tax profits improved to £64.7m at a margin of 6.7% (previous year: £53.1m at 5.8%).

TAS also reports on market share, as measured by turnover. DB Schenker's share dipped below 50% for the first time since privatisation – just: market share was 49.9% compared with 50.8% the previous year: it is interesting to reflect that this figure stood at over 80% in the late 1990s. Freightliner was next with 32.3%, down by 0.4%. The two post privatisation new entrants built up their market shares over years. Eurotunnel subsidiary GB Railfreight reached 11.2% - in double figures for the first time on the back of several

new contracts. Meanwhile, the Nuclear Decommissioning Authority's rail arm Direct Rail Services got to 6.7%.

GB RAILFREIGHT

The company, a subsidiary of Eurotunnel since sold by FirstGroup in 2010, recorded more than doubled operating and pre-tax profits as growth in revenue well in advance of the rise in costs was achieved.

The company reports that two contracts were won to shift biomass and for aggregate movements. Meanwhile, activity in the infrastructure sector doubled on the back of a new contract with Network Rail.

PERIOD TO:	31/12/2013	31/12/2012
	£000	£000
Turnover	108,765	90,047
Operating Costs:	96,475	84,783
Operating Profit:	12,290	5,264
Operating Margin:	11.3%	5.8%
Turnover per Employee	£217,530	£211,378

DIRECT RAIL SERVICES

The company continued to expand, growing turnover by over 8%. However, operating costs rose at a faster rate, so that cash profits and margins dipped.

PERIOD TO:	31/03/2014	31/03/2013
	£000	£000
Turnover	64,855	60,014

Operating Costs:	61,622	56,271
Operating Profit:	3,233	3,743
Operating Margin:	5.0%	6.2%
Turnover per Employee	£189,082	£197,414
Revenue Grant	805	805

FREIGHTLINER

The company that specialises in container movements by rail and road saw profits dip by one fifth as revenue growth fell short of the rise in operating costs.

PERIOD TO:	29/03/2014	30/03/2013
	£000	£000
Turnover	184,031	181,091
Operating Costs:	177,911	173,264
Operating Profit:	6,120	7,827
Operating Margin:	3.3%	4.3%
Turnover per Employee	£163,004	£159,692

DB SCHENKER

The company improved its result during the year as revenue growth outstripped cost increases. Profits were boosted further with the disposal of a £151m tranche of railway properties, sold to Network Rail with a book profit of £9.9m. Despite the revenue growth, the company's market share slipped below 50% for the first time ever.

PERIOD TO:	31/12/2013	31/12/2012
	£000	£000
Turnover	445,000	429,000
Operating Costs:	417,000	404,000
Operating Profit:	28,000	25,000
Operating Margin:	6.3%	5.8%
Turnover per Employee	£168,051	£160,734

DB SCHENKER INTERNATIONAL

The company improved its performance sharply during the year, achieving strong revenue growth on the cross-channel routes. However, the business continued to record losses, albeit at a much reduced level.

PERIOD TO:	31/12/2013	31/12/2012
	£000	£000
Turnover	39,372	33,475
Operating Costs:	39,879	35,871
Operating Profit:	(507)	(2,396)
Operating Margin:	-1.3%	-7.2%
Turnover per Employee	£235,760	£190,199
Revenue Grant	0	73

FREIGHTLINER HEAVY HAUL

The company formed to specialise in and compete for bulk trainload movements saw strong growth in turnover, which outstripped increases in the cost of running the business, so that profits improved.

PERIOD TO:	29/03/2014	30/03/2013
	£000	£000
Turnover	129,479	117,350
Operating Costs:	114,300	104,068
Operating Profit:	15,179	13,282
Operating Margin:	11.7%	11.3%
Turnover per Employee	£192,105	£185,680

DB Schenker's Class 59 No 59205 at Westbury with a Whatley Quarry-Dagenham aggregates working on 15 July 2014. **STEWART ARMSTRONG**

DB SCHENKER

5,000 TRAINS PER WEEK

DB Schenker Rail UK Ltd, Britain's largest rail freight operator, runs around 5,000 trains per week and employs more than 3,000 people. It delivers services through four main product groupings - Trainload services, Wagonload services, Terminal operations and International.

The company has focused strongly on developing international logistics. A twice-weekly service between Barking and Wroclaw, Poland accommodates continental gauge wagons using High Speed 1 from the Channel Tunnel. In January 2014 a new service via HS1 was introduced from Spain carrying foodstuffs in refrigerated containers, and automotive components.

In December 2014 DBSR UK took up a 20-year lease on a 34 acre site in Barking to develop its multimodal London Eurohub for import and export of finished vehicles. Initially capable of handling up to 150,000 vehicles per year, it will be the only rail-linked facility of its type in the country, and connected to HS1.

International traffic using classic routes includes a Padua-Hams Hall intermodal service, with some traffic forwarded to Mossend. Steel slabs for rail manufacture are conveyed from Scunthorpe to Ebange in France for Tata Steel, and bottled water from France is brought in to Daventry. A train of china clay slurry for paper-making runs from Antwerp to Irvine and Aberdeen.

Domestic intermodal activity includes a daily Daventry-Grangemouth service for Malcolm Logistics, and Malcolm's established Daventry-Mossend flow, for which a three-year contract was secured in 2014.

Maritime containers are conveyed from Southampton and Felixstowe to Birch Coppice in the Midlands, Doncaster, Trafford Park and Wakefield. In 2013 DBSR UK operated the first train out of the new DP World London Gateway port: by 2015 services were being operated five days per week, with three trains to Trafford Park, Manchester, and two to Wakefield. Traffic is also conveyed to South Wales.

In August 2015 a daily train was launched between PD Ports' new Teesport facility in Middlesbrough and Mossend and Grangemouth, supported by ECS European Containers.

DBSR UK conveys more than 50% of the coal required by Britain's power generation industry. A three-year contract commenced in April 2015 to deliver coal to Drax power station, mainly from Immingham and Kellingley. For biomass high-capacity vehicles have been converted from HTA coal hoppers by subsidiary Axion Rail. DBSR UK now transports some 80% of Drax's biomass requirements. Coal is also carried for industrial users including Tata Steel and Hope Construction Products.

There are flows of petroleum products from Humberside and West Wales, while crude oil from Hampshire is taken to Fawley. Trains to support steel manufacturing serve sites at Scunthorpe, in South Wales and on Teesside. Imported iron ore trains run between Immingham and Scunthorpe, and there is an extensive network of inter-plant services plus trains delivering finished steel products. Scrap metal is also handled. A shuttle service for Tata Steel connects IJmuiden in the Netherlands with Trostre in South Wales to convey steel coils.

Nearly 400 trains a week are run for the construction and waste industries. A contract with Mendip Rail covers quarries of Aggregates Industries (Merehead) and HeidelbergCement subsidiary Hanson (Whatley), some trains using the shippers' own locomotives and wagons.

In September 2015 DBSR UK announced a new five-year contract with Hope Construction Materials to convey aggregates from Dowlow near Buxton to 10 locations, including a new depot in Walsall. An aggregates contract with Cemex includes flows from the Peak District. Lafarge Tarmac's Mountsorrel quarry is served and sea-dredged aggregates are moved from Thames-side terminals for Brett Aggregates and Marcon. A new aggregates contract with United Asphalt and a new ash transport deal with J Clubb were announced in October 2015.

A two-year contract for Cemex began in July 2015, conveying spoil from Willesden to Barrington, Cambridgeshire, to infill a former quarry.

British Gypsum awarded a two-year extension contract in November 2014 to carry gypsum from Drax and Fiddlers Ferry power stations to Kirkby Thore plasterboard plant, Cumbria.

Jaguar Land Rover cars for export are carried from Halewood and Castle Bromwich to Southampton, and BMW Minis from Cowley to Southampton and Purfleet. Imported vehicles from Portbury to Mossend use the residual wagonload network.

The company fulfils a Ministry of Defence haulage contract, some movements incorporating other traffic to form part of the wagonload network. In 2015 a new Royal Mail contract was secured to operate London-Warrington-Glasgow and London-Tyneside postal trains for a minimum of three years using the customer's 15 Class-325 EMUs.

More than 10,000 trains every year are provided to support track renewal, enhancement, maintenance, monitoring and seasonal work programmes. The company also operates 10 Local Distribution Centres for Network Rail.

The UK diesel fleet includes around 180 Class 66 locomotives and up to 26 Class-60s, of which 21 have been overhauled and refurbished. Six Class 59/2s are used on Mendips aggregates and 30 Class-67s often employed on charter or hire passenger services. There are 25 Class-90 electrics and six operational Class 92 dual-voltage locos modified to operate on HS1. The wagon fleet totals more than 7,500. Trials began in May 2015 with two Ecofret triple-platform container wagons developed and produced by VTG Rail.

SENIOR PERSONNEL

DB SCHENKER UK

CHIEF EXECUTIVE OFFICER Geoff Spencer
CHIEF FINANCIAL OFFICER Andrea Rossi
HEAD OF SALES Les Morris
HEAD OF PRODUCTION Graham Young
HEAD OF MAINTENANCE AND INFRASTRUCTURE Andrew Byrne

1,000 TRAINLOADS A WEEK

Part of the Eurotunnel subsidiary Europorte, GB Railfreight continues to see its business grow and in November 2014 celebrated running more than 1,000 trains per week for the first time.

Intermodal services have seen further expansion. In 2015 the company secured its seventh slot for the haulage of maritime containers from Felixstowe, giving it capacity for some 23% of rail traffic at the port. This slot is used for a train running five days per week to Birmingham Intermodal Freight Terminal (BIFT) at Birch Coppice. Other services run from Felixstowe to Doncaster, Hams Hall, Selby and Trafford Park. A key client is Mediterranean Shipping Company (UK), for which a three-year extension contract took effect in February 2014, providing three daily container services from Felixstowe – two to Hams Hall and one to Selby.

In the international sector, GBRf collaborates with sister company Europorte Channel to operate a Daventry-Novarra (Italy) intermodal service via the Channel Tunnel for container shipper DFDS.

GBRf handles up to 30% of the coal moved by rail for power generation in Britain, operating imported flows out of the ports of Tyne, Immingham, Hull and Redcar, as well as carrying domestically mined coal from UK Coal's Potland Burn railhead. Cottam, Drax and West Burton

are among power stations served, while a new contract signed in 2015 covers the movement of coal from Hunterston and the Port of Blyth to Drax until 2017. The company has invested in rolling stock for conveying biomass, moving 1.5 million tonnes annually between Liverpool and Ironbridge for E.ON and a similar volume between Tyne and Drax.

Other bulk traffic flows include petroleum products from Humberside to Cardiff for Greenergy, gas condensate from North Walsham to Harwich for Petrochem Carless and alumina from North Blyth to Fort William for Alcan. For the automotive industry GBRf runs a daily Dagenham-Garston train carrying Ford vehicles.

January 2015 marked the start of a major new contract in the construction materials sector for Aggregate Industries. The five-year deal sees GBRf running five trains each weekday. Lafarge Tarmac is another significant aggregates client.

After successfully transporting gypsum from West Burton to Portbury, Bristol, for plasterboard manufacturer Siniat for one year, GBRf began an expanded five-year contract in August 2015 which also covers shipments from Cottam to the client's plant at Ferrybridge. The company also moves containerised gypsum from Southampton Docks to Mountfield in East Sussex for British Gypsum.

September 2015 saw the commencement of a three-year contract for FCC Environment to convey construction spoil in a daily train from GBRf's new North London

Railfreight Terminal at Cricklewood to Calvert in Buckinghamshire.

The company continues to run infrastructure materials trains for Network Rail and London Underground. For the latter it has an £80 million 10-year contract awarded by the former Metronet in 2006, including operation of a materials depot at Wellingborough. It provides haulage for deliveries of LU's new Bombardier-built 'S' Stock trains and has a contract with Hitachi to facilitate commissioning and testing of Class 800/801 IEP high-speed trains. Other services include provision of traction or traincrew for rolling stock moves and supplying locomotives for infrastructure monitoring trains on the third rail network.

In the passenger sector, since April 2015 GBRf has provided traincrew and traction for the Caledonian Sleeper franchise operated by Serco, under a 15-year contract.

The traction fleet has continued to expand. In late 2015 the number of EMD Class 66s in service stood at 71, with delivery of a final batch of seven due in January 2016. Locomotive No 59003, repatriated after acquisition

from Heavy Haul Power International in Germany, returned to traffic in 2015. Five Class 47s have been hired from Riviera Trains for haulage of gypsum and sand traffic in Yorkshire, eight Class 20s are used for LU stock moves and seasonal work for Network Rail, and there are four Class 08/09 shunters.

Nine Class 92 electric locomotives were operational in 2015, with others to be returned to traffic. Some are used on the Caledonian Sleeper contract, along with two hired-in Class 86s and one Class 87.

A programme by Wabtec subsidiary Brush Traction to refurbish and upgrade 11 of the versatile Class 73 electro-diesels with an MTU 1,600hp engine continued in 2015. The first five are destined mainly for Network Rail infrastructure monitoring and possession work. The remaining six are to operate Scottish domestic legs of Caledonian Sleeper services. In addition, GBRf retains nine Class 73/1 and 73/2 machines.

Growing business in the maritime intermodal sector led to GBRf signing a lease with VTG Rail UK in 2015 for 15 additional Ecofret triple-platform wagons, 18 of these having been ordered the previous year. ∎

SENIOR PERSONNEL
GB RAILFREIGHT

MANAGING DIRECTOR John Smith (in photo)
FINANCE DIRECTOR Karl Goulding-Davis
CHIEF OPERATING OFFICER David Knowles
COMMERCIAL DIRECTOR Phil Webster

GBRf's locomotive No 66751 is a dedicated resource to haul Hitachi Rail Europe's Class 800/801 trains during testing for the InterCity Express Programme. The third pre-series train (Train 800002) is seen just after arrival at North Pole Train Maintenance Centre, West London, on 24 October 2015. **HITACHI**

Class 70 No 70001 passes St Denys with Freightliner's 09.58 Wentloog-Southampton container train on 1 September 2015. **STEWART ARMSTRONG**

Freightliner®

INTERMODAL, HEAVY HAUL AND INTERNATIONAL

In March 2015 a 94% shareholding in Freightliner Group was acquired from investment firm Arcapita by US-based Genesee & Wyoming, which owns or leases 120 freight railroads worldwide. The remaining 6% interest remains with members of Freightliner's management team until 2020, when it too will be acquired by G&W.

Freightliner has two rail operating subsidiaries in Britain: Freightliner Ltd, serving the UK deep-sea container market; and Freightliner Heavy Haul (FHH), specialising in bulk commodities. Freightliner Maintenance Ltd is the group's third UK subsidiary, dedicated to traction and rolling stock maintenance and repair. Subdivisions include Logico, a division of Freightliner Ltd offering intermodal logistics services and bespoke rail space to new markets.

International subsidiaries are Freightliner Australia, Freightliner Poland Ltd, Freightliner DE GmbH (Germany) and European intermodal rail operator ERS Railways BV. ERS also owns 47% of German-based intermodal rail operator boxXpress.de GmbH. In Saudi Arabia, Freightliner is part of a UK consortium awarded a five-year contract in 2015 to provide management and technical support for infrastructure, freight and passenger operations on the Saudi Railway Company's North South Railway project.

FREIGHTLINER LTD

Freightliner Ltd is the UK's largest rail carrier of maritime containers, operating from the four deep-sea ports of Felixstowe, London Gateway, Southampton and Tilbury. Services run to 13 interchanges, eight of which are owned and operated by Freightliner. It moves some 770,000 containers per year on around 100 daily services.

Main locations are:
- Ports: Felixstowe, Garston (Liverpool), Southampton, London Gateway and Tilbury.
- Inland terminals: Birmingham, Bristol, Wentloog (Cardiff), Coatbridge (Glasgow), Doncaster, Leeds, Liverpool and Manchester.
- Independent terminals served include Daventry (DIRFT), Hams Hall (Birmingham), Ditton (Widnes), Scunthorpe and Teesport.

Having introduced services in 2013 from DP World's London Gateway in the Thames Estuary, Freightliner Ltd now runs a daily train from the port. A service from PD Ports' new intermodal rail terminal at Teesport was launched in November 2014.

Freightliner has the largest intermodal contract in the UK, with Maersk Line, the container arm of the Danish conglomerate AP Moller-Maersk, with a multi-year contract signed in 2011 providing committed space for the transport of containers from Felixstowe. In the same year a second 10-year contract with OOCL was concluded.

FREIGHTLINER HEAVY HAUL

Freightliner Heavy Haul (FHH) operates up to 400 trains per week, moving more than 25m tonnes annually. Coal remains the company's largest bulk market, with more than 13m tonnes per year conveyed to UK power stations from import terminals at Hunterston, Immingham, Liverpool and Portbury (Bristol). A coal haulage agreement with EDF Energy was renewed in 2015.

Aggregates sector flows include quarried stone from Tunstead to Bredbury and Brentford and from Mountsorrel to Luton, while limestone is conveyed from Tunstead to several coal-fired power stations for emissions cleaning processes.

Cement from Hope Construction Materials' plant in the Hope Valley is carried to Dewsbury and Theale, and from HolcimLafarge's Oxwellmains facility to Aberdeen, Inverness and Uddingston in Scotland, and south to Seaham. From Tunstead FHH handles cement flows to West Thurrock and Westbury. Potash and rock salt are moved between Boulby on the Cleveland coast and Teesside.

FHH works with Greater Manchester Waste Disposal Authority (GMWDA) and Viridor moving municipal waste from several locations to a Combined Heat and Power plant at Runcorn.

Infrastructure activities for Network Rail include haulage of high-output ballast cleaning and track renewal systems, National Supply Chain services, ballast movements and operation of the major distribution centre at Basford Hall, Crewe. FHH played a prominent role in construction of the Borders Railway in Scotland by providing works trains.

FREIGHTLINER MAINTENANCE LIMITED

Freightliner Maintenance Ltd undertakes repair and maintenance of traction and rolling stock both for group companies and third parties. Its main site is Leeds Midland Road depot, with supplementary facilities at Crewe, Dunbar, Hope and York. There is a dedicated maintenance facility for Freightliner Ltd at Southampton.

Freightliner's UK fleet comprises 118 Class 66 and 19 Class 70 diesels, Class 86 (16) and Class 90 (10) electrics, plus shunters. The Class 70 GE PowerHaul diesel locomotives are mainly used by the intermodal business.

The wagon fleet totals more than 3,100, of which nearly 2,000 are container flats used by Freightliner Ltd. The number of twin-platform Ecofret 'Shortliner' wagons in service, leased from VTG, had risen to 128 in 2015. ∎

DIRECT RAIL SERVICES

A wholly owned subsidiary of the Nuclear Decommissioning Authority (NDA), Direct Rail Services Limited (DRS) was established to provide British Nuclear Fuels Limited with a strategic rail transport service. In this role, it operates trains between UK power station sites and Sellafield, Cumbria. Additional flows link Sellafield with Drigg and Barrow Dock. The company is also active in the general railfreight market, mainly in retail distribution.

Intermodal movements include trains operated for Tesco in conjunction with Stobart Rail from Daventry to Purfleet and Wentloog, plus Daventry-Coatbridge services in collaboration with logistics firm John G Russell. An intermodal service is operated between Grangemouth and Aberdeen carrying mainly Asda supermarket traffic. There is also a daily train of Tesco swap-bodies between Mossend and Inverness.

Services for Network Rail include operation of autumn railhead treatment trains, winter snow clearance movements, provision of traction for infrastructure monitoring trains and haulage of National Supply Chain traffic in northern and central England. DRS also deploys strategically sited Class 57/3 'Thunderbird' locomotives for West Coast main line rescue services.

In the passenger sector the company supplies Belmond Ltd with locomotives for the Northern Belle luxury train, and provides support for TOCs and traction for charter operators. It has its own refurbished Mk2 coaches, some used for a two-year contract from June 2014 with Abellio Greater Anglia to supply locomotives and stock for Norwich area services. Since May 2015 two sets powered by Class 37s have been assigned to Northern Rail Cumbrian Coast services. Six Class 68s are sub-leased to Chiltern Railways for passenger work, while two more are used on Fife-Edinburgh peak services.

The Vossloh-built Class 68 diesel locomotives are spearheading modernisation of the traction fleet. Entering service in 2014, examples have been used on some intermodal services in Scotland and on National Supply Chain trains. In the same year DRS ordered 10 more Class 68s, followed by a further seven in 2015,

Colas Rail's Class 70 No 70809 at Teignmouth with the 09.36 Westbury-Par engineering train on 19 September 2015. **STEWART ARMSTRONG**

DRS's Class 68 No 68007, on hire to ScotRail, approaches Holytown with a Motherwell-Edinburgh empty stock working on 18 June 2015. **STEWART ARMSTRONG**

bringing the total to 32. Also on order from Vossloh are ten bi-mode Class 88 locomotives for delivery from 2016. These will be rated at 5,360hp under a 25 kV AC supply and at 900hp in diesel mode from a Caterpillar 12-cylinder engine, permitting 'last mile' operation away from overhead power supply.

Other types include 19 Class-66s, 12 Class-57/3s and nine Class-57s. There are also nine Class-47s, 36 Class-37s and eight Class-20s. Some are stored or awaiting refurbishment. ■

COLAS RAIL FREIGHT

Colas Rail Freight is part of the Colas Group, a subsidiary of the French-based multinational Bouygues construction and services conglomerate.

Haulage activities to support Network Rail's renewals and enhancements programmes continue to form a key part of the company's portfolio. In 2014 Colas was awarded a £90m haulage contract for 2014-19, mainly for Western and Southern regions but also in Scotland. In addition, engineering materials trains are operated as part of the Network Rail's National Supply Chain, covering Hoo Junction-Whitemoor/Eastleigh, Eastleigh-Westbury and Westbury-Hinksey-Bescot circuits. In September 2015 Colas took over operation of Network Rail's infrastructure monitoring trains.

In January 2015 the company commenced a five-year contract to convey bitumen from Lindsey oil refinery to Total UK's Preston production plant. Also served from Lindsey are Colnbrook, west London and Rectory Junction, Nottingham. Colas has a contract with Air BP to move aviation fuel from the Ineos refinery at Grangemouth to Prestwick Airport and the Rolls Royce factory in Derby. It also hauls petroleum products from the same refinery to Dalston, Cumbria.

Trains of timber for building materials manufacturer Kronospan are operated to Chirk from Baglan Bay in South Wales and Carlisle, supplemented by loads from Exeter and Ribblehead. Steel for the automotive industry originating at Dunkerque, France, is conveyed from Boston docks to Washwood Heath, Birmingham.

Traction developments include commissioning by late 2015 of the last of 10 refurbished Class 60 diesel locomotives acquired from DB Schenker Rail UK, complementing 10 Class-70s received from GE Transportation in 2014. The fleet also includes five Class 66s, three Class 47s, four Class-37s and operational members of a pool of 10 Class-56s. Additional Class 37s were being procured in late 2015.

The Pullman Rail, Cardiff rolling stock overhaul and engineering facility is also part of the group. ■

DEVON AND CORNWALL RAILWAYS LTD

DCR is a freight operating subsidiary of British American Railway Services Limited, which was formed by US shortline railroad holding company Iowa Pacific Holdings.

Other BARS group companies include RMS Locotec Locomotive Hire, RMS Locotec Track Maintenance and RMS Locotec Rail Projects. The group also owns the Dartmoor Railway between Yeoford and Meldon Quarry in Devon and the Weardale Railway linking Bishop Auckland with Wolsingham and Eastgate. Both lines are connected to the Network Rail system.

The company handles short-term flows of scrap metal to the Celsa plant in Cardiff and spoil from Willesden to Calvert. Other recent traffic has included blending coal from opencast sites in northeast England and aggregates from the Peak District. It also undertakes stock moves for train operating companies and supplies locomotives on hire, as well as collaborating with other rail freight operators.

The operational DCR traction fleet comprises five Class 56s and three Class 31s.

RAIL OPERATIONS GROUP

ROG commenced operations in 2015, focusing mainly on train movements relating to rolling stock delivery, testing, maintenance, modification and refurbishment programmes. Clients include rolling stock owners, train operating companies and the supply industry.

A significant contract from Bombardier covers the movement of 112 Southeastern Class 375 EMUs from Ramsgate to Derby and Ilford for refurbishment under a three-year programme. ROG also has a contact to move 124 Abellio Greater Anglia EMUs from Ilford to Doncaster for refurbishment over a two-year period from 2015 and London Midland Class 323s from Soho to Tyseley.

Where haulage is required, ROG hires in traction. For the Class 375 contract, Dellner-equipped DRS Class 57/3s were initially used, then a Class 47 hired from Freightliner, necessitating the use of translator vehicles. In September 2015 ROG announced that it planned to lease two Class 37s from Europhoenix for these movements once they had been equipped with drophead couplers and electrical translating equipment.

WEST COAST RAILWAYS

With its main base at Carnforth and a subsidiary depot at Southall, west London, WCR specialises in operating charter trains both on its own account and for other tour operators, using diesel and steam traction.

In addition to an extensive programme of tours throughout the year, WCR runs two regular seasonal steam-hauled trains – the Fort William-Mallaig 'Jacobite' and the York-Scarborough 'Scarborough Spa Express'. Traction is also occasionally provided for stock and plant moves.

The active diesel fleet includes six Class 37s, 10 Class 47s and seven Class 57s. WCR also manages the operation of steam locomotives belonging to various owners. Its pool of coaching stock numbers more than 80 vehicles including a rake of Metro-Cammell 1960s-built Pullman carriages.

RIVIERA TRAINS LIMITED

Active since 1996, Riviera Trains claims to be the UK's largest and only independent coaching stock provider, supplying both the charter train market and train operating companies when extra short-term capacity is needed, such as during major sporting events. The fleet of around 120 coaches includes later Mk2 air-conditioned stock as well as Mk1 vehicles, among these the 8-coach Royal Scot carmine and cream set.

In addition to providing coaching stock for railtour clients, the company works in association with three principal charter train operators – DB Schenker Rail (UK), Direct Rail Services and GBRf.

Riviera Trains also owns six Class 47 diesel locomotives. In 2015 five of these were on hire to GB Railfreight. Its main base is at Crewe, with some coaching stock housed at Eastleigh.

VICTA RAILFREIGHT

Since it was formed in 1995, Victa Railfreight has been providing a wide range of support services to rail freight customers, operators and suppliers. It operated its first trains over Network Rail infrastructure in January 2015, soon after award of its Train Operators licence. Victa provides transfer shunt operations at Ripple Lane (Barking) for the Dourges-Barking intermodal service, hauled by GB Railfreight via High Speed 1. From the exchange sidings at Ripple Lane, Victa uses diesel traction to move the wagons to the non electrified terminal operated by John G Russell for unloading and reloading with containers. This is all achieved in a four hour window at night, dictated by the limited availability of freight paths on HS1.

In July 2015, Victa Railfreight was awarded a contract by John G Russell for provision of shunting and train preparation services at the new Sainsbury's rail terminal, operated by Russell's, on the DIRFT 2 development at Daventry. ∎

Ready for the off at Carlisle on 23 March 2015 (left) is West Coast Railway Company's Class 57 No 57313 on an Aviemore-Didcot Parkway railtour. Alongside are (centre) Direct Rail Services' Class 66 No 66301 on a Carlisle North Yard-Crewe Basford Hall engineering train, and DB Schenker's Class 67 No 67027 on a Heaton-Derby test train via the Settle & Carlisle line. **BILL WELSH**

INNOVATION AND ENVIRONMENT

IN ASSOCIATION WITH

 KNORR-BREMSE

CREATIVE SOLUTIONS FROM KNORR-BREMSE

Global experience and continuous innovation combined with locally based expertise and capacity means that Knorr-Bremse can offer customers an outstanding range of both system and service solutions.

These systems and services are delivered by a work force of over 1000 based at four major Knorr-Bremse Rail sites which are conveniently located around the UK. From Melksham in Wiltshire, OE systems and support, from Burton-upon-Trent in Staffordshire, HVAC systems and support, and from Springburn in Glasgow and Wolverton in Milton Keynes, specialist rail vehicle maintenance, service and modernisation is available under the RailServices banner.

Knorr-Bremse Rail UK facilities are the local source for the extensive range of products, systems and services that are available from the entire global Knorr-Bremse Rail Group.

EXPERTLY INTEGRATED

Renowned throughout the rail world for its rail braking systems expertise, Knorr-Bremse offers a complete braking system solution. Covering brake control, including the unique, mechatronic EP2002 Distributed Brake Control system, air supply systems, bogie equipment, brake resistors and controllers, sanding systems and wheel slide protection systems, Knorr-Bremse engineers expertly integrate these components to provide the optimum solution for any rail vehicle.

In addition, the Knorr-Bremse Group offers an extensive and globally proven rail portfolio for both on and off board applications. This range includes air conditioning, condition based monitoring, derailment detectors, driver

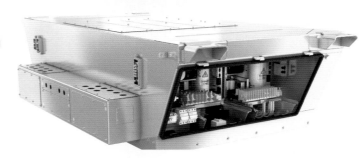

PowerTech are specialists in the design and manufacture of advanced power supply and distribution systems for all types of rail vehicles.

Braking systems from Knorr-Bremse include sanding systems which are expertly integrated to provide the optimum braking solution.

simulators, electrical components, electronic control and management, platform screen systems, power converters, sanding, signalling, train doors (internal and external), wheel slide protection and wash and wipe systems.

This range of rail systems and services from Knorr-Bremse has continued to expand and strengthen recently, with, for example, the addition of PowerTech and Selectron systems to the portfolio. Both of these brands are now fully integrated into the wider portfolio of system solutions that are now on offer to Knorr-Bremse customers based in the UK and Ireland.

PowerTech designs and manufactures advanced auxiliary power supply and distribution systems for all types of rail vehicles. Solutions include compact and lightweight converters, battery charging equipment and complete power supply systems across a range of power outputs for systems including air conditioning, customer power points and on-board digital information systems.

Specialists in electronic control and management, Selectron deliver individually networkable solutions for a wide range of train management

and systems controls which are highly flexible and offer decentralised control. Sub-system management includes illumination, coupling, door and vehicle control systems as well as driver cab displays systems for both digital and analog signal inputs.

INCREASING TRAIN AVAILABILITY

Knorr-Bremse has always been a forward looking Group and a leader in innovation. Recently the Group has been using its technological expertise from around the world to develop systems which can support customers in keeping trains in safe, reliable and cost effective service through the entire life-cycle.

Knorr-Bremse engineers and designers have also recognised that understanding the true status of a train's systems, in real time, can be invaluable for rail operators in increasing train availability. By identifying and addressing any issues before they become major problems, trains can be kept on track, operating safely and in revenue earning service.

Developed by Knorr-Bremse in the UK especially for the UK and Ireland markets, Knorr-Bremse Z300, facilitates both monitoring and control, both in real time, for example the HVAC system. Its modular design uses advanced, web-based smart technology with apps providing advanced condition based maintenance to improve the train's reliability and availability.

The latest development in this area from Knorr-Bremse is iCOM. iCOM identifies the true status of the vital systems on a train, minimising disruption and costs through predicting equipment failures. Detecting, diagnosing and prioritising equipment failures in advance, iCOM can improve both maintenance planning and scheduling. This maximises system and component life whilst increasing train availability. ∎

iCOM identifies the true status of a wide range of on-board systems helping to predict equipment failure.

COMMUNITY RAIL
GOES INTERNATIONAL

BUT IS THE ENTIRE RAILWAY INDUSTRY ONSIDE? COMMUNITY RAIL PARTNERSHIP CHAIRMAN, AND *MODERN RAILWAYS* COLUMNIST, **ALAN WILLIAMS** SUGGESTS SOME TRAIN OPERATING COMPANIES ARE MORE SUPPORTIVE THAN OTHERS, WITH NETWORK RAIL SEEMINGLY THE LEAST CONVINCED.

Like railways themselves, the community rail concept originated in Britain. Or, more precisely, in northern England. The first six 'pilot' schemes created by the then Strategic Rail Authority in 2004 have been followed by further formal designations by the Department for Transport, as part of its Community Railway Development Strategy. Today, there are nearly 40 designated Community Rail lines right across England and Wales – some of them far from being the bucolic rural branch lines many imagine them to be. More recently, Scotland has joined the Community Rail club, with seven lines designated in the last couple of years, and more promised by new ScotRail franchise operator Abellio. There are also over 100 'friends' groups supporting individual stations.

In little more than a decade, community rail has gone from just an idea to being a major element in new franchise proposals, with thousands of unpaid helpers on the ground and enthusiastic support from Ministers.

And now the concept has been exported to Europe.

Based very much on the British model, and with advice from the Devon and Cornwall Rail Partnership, the European Union has set up 'Citizens Rail', with a budget of over Euro 9million, half of which comes from the EU Interreg IVB programme. From a standing start in 2012, projects in France, Germany and the Netherlands are already seeing results, with new services traversing virtually moribund lines across Pays de la Loire, and both additional services on existing lines and re-openings of closed lines on both sides of the border between the Netherlands and Germany.

There is no doubt that the hands-on experience and expertise in low-cost, targeted local promotion that the British partners have been able to offer has aided the rapid start up and implementation of these schemes on the Continent, but together with the rapid progress in Scotland under the aegis of Transport Scotland, it has

The Cambrian lines are covered by one of Wales' Community Rail partnerships. Class 158 No.158840 leaves Machynlleth as No.158828 (right) shunts at the depot. **ARRIVA TRAINS WALES**

also emphasised the frustration with rail bureaucracy many Community rail supporters in England and Wales experience. The Department for Transport's (DfT's) Community Rail Strategy aims to:

- Increase ridership, freight use and revenue,
- Manage costs down,
- Encourage greater involvement of the local community,
- Enable local rail to play a larger role in economic and social regeneration.

Little to complain of there, and everyone in the Community Rail movement I have ever spoken to supports the principles. But delivering them can be rather more difficult. In the past, despite its avowed enthusiasm for Community Rail, the DfT has never required train operating companies (TOCs) to formally support community rail activity as part of their franchise commitments, with the result that there is a considerable disparity in terms of enthusiasm and support – both financial and

practical – across the current clutch of 24 franchised TOCs. As part of its monitoring of designated Community Rail Partnerships, the DfT is constantly urging them to become more actively involved in the operation of the lines they support, but those involved often report that even the more active TOCs, while happy to support the 'soft' aspects of community rail activity, like care of stations and local promotion, baulk at active CRP involvement in timetable or fares issues.

As for Network Rail, since it controversially wound up its Community Rail unit in 2014, despite the touching belief of its senior management that community rail issues could best be dealt with by its various regional units, the reality has been that, in some areas at least, the shutters have come down. Certainly, there has been no NR attendance for the last two years at either of the two Community Rail Partnerships in the north east in which I am involved, despite the fact that many of the issues of concern to our members

around level crossings, speed restrictions, cable theft and the use of redundant buildings, for example (as well as the more mundane, like damaged fences and out of date signage), fall squarely within the remit of Network Rail rather than that of the franchised train operators. This reluctance to become involved – which anecdotal evidence suggests is getting worse – not only makes life more difficult for CRPs but undermines their very credibility. What, ask the representatives of those outside the rail industry in local and regional government, tourism and community groups, is the point of a 'Partnership' if Network Rail, as one of the two most essential parties, consistently refuses to engage?

SHARP FOCUS

This issue will be brought into sharp focus with the award of the new Northern Franchise, starting in April 2016. Eighteen Community Rail Partnerships – almost half of all those designated – are involved in this one

franchise and for the first time, the DfT has formally identified the role of Community Rail in the new franchise. It has made clear that it wants CRPs to 'up their game', suggested that CRPs involved come together in some sort of Community Business Unit, and earmarked a budget to enable them to do so. If successful, this welcome more prescriptive approach will hopefully be part of all future franchises, but is difficult to see how Network Rail's current indifferent approach could then be sustained.

Ironically, given by definition the very local nature of community rail, the post-privatisation fragmentation of the rail industry can be a problem for CRPs in England and Wales. Many find that, even though they have a single sponsor TOC, in order to fully promote their lines, they have to deal with other TOCs, each with their own different priorities, with which they have no formal interaction, and who often have no great financial or service reason to support them. This can be a particular problem where the junction

Devon & Cornwall Community Rail Partnership works to promote travel on the counties' local routes. Service improvements are under way for the Exmouth-Exeter-Paignton 'Riviera Line', with EU Interreg IVB 'Citizens Rail' funding providing assistance. A Class 150 train approaches Lympstone with the 12.13 Paignton-Exmouth Great Western service on 6 December 2014. **STEWART ARMSTRONG**

Abellio Greater Anglia works in partnership with a number of Community Rail groups across Norfolk, Suffolk, Essex and Cambridgeshire, including the Wherry Lines between Norwich, Great Yarmouth and Lowestoft. Class 153 No 153322 leaves Norwich for Lowestoft. **TONY MILES**

station for the rest of the network, and therefore the gateway through which most passengers for a community line travel, is operated by a different TOC to the Community line itself. For example, in the north east alone, the Yorkshire Coast and Esk Valley CRP lines, which are worked by Northern, connect with the national network at Scarborough and Middlesbrough stations respectively, both of which are operated by TransPennine. Likewise Darlington, the gateway for the Bishop Line, also worked by Northern, is operated by Virgin East Coast. Even worse, the recently-designated Tyne Valley line CRP, again worked by Northern, connects Newcastle, also run by Virgin East Coast, and Carlisle, operated by sister company Virgin West Coast. It is hardly surprising that CRPs find that, even though these junction stations are their largest sources of ridership, getting support from the TOCs that run them, who have no proprietary interest in their line and frankly have bigger fish to fry, can be hard work!

In contrast, in Scotland, where the development of Community Rail has been rapid in just the last couple of years, the single operator ScotRail provides nearly all services. I suspect that it is no coincidence that some of the CRPs regarded as the most successful and progressive – those in Devon and Cornwall, East and West Sussex, and East Anglia – all enjoy services provided by the same TOC as the main lines to which they are connected.

OUTPERFORMING

But despite these many and varied complications, and despite in many cases insufficient rolling stock and infrastructure as an inheritance from post-Beeching BR days, ridership on almost all Community Rail lines continues to grow, and many handsomely outstrip growth on the network as a whole.

Passenger satisfaction on CRP lines also consistently outperforms that on other lines, as well as national figures for bus and car travel.

The wholly positive value of Community Rail Partnerships and the volunteers who support them was amply demonstrated by the report of the same name published by the Department for Transport and the Association of Community Rail Partnerships last year, largely dispelling many of the concerns felt across the

community sector that their efforts were not being adequately recognised in political and official circles.

However, one aspect remains of major concern – funding. The Report recognised that continuity of funding, and the uncertainties that surround it, is of increasing concern for CRPs as local authorities and other external supporters reduce or even in some cases completely withdraw financial support as a result of cuts in public sector spending. It is presumably in recognition of this that the DfT has earmarked a budget of £500,000 for support of CRPs in the new Northern franchise, although it is worth noting that even this amount, if spread equally across all the CRPs covered by the new franchise, would provide considerably less than £30,000 each, insufficient alone to guarantee continued employment and support of a Community Rail Officer for three days a week, the minimum said to be necessary for a successful Partnership. With external sources of funding declining and the DfT seeking closer involvement of CRPs with their sponsoring franchise operator, some in the community rail sector believe the time has come for TOCs to fund Community Rail Officers in return for the undoubted additional revenue and general wider support they receive as a result of the activities of CRPs. But it is fair to say that there are

others who believe, probably rightly, that such a direct provision, making them effectively an employee of the TOC, would undermine the whole concept of 'Partnership'.

What is certain is that community rail now needs – and deserves – more support from the wider rail industry in general and Network Rail in particular.

Senior rail managers must stop thinking of community rail activists as a bunch of irrelevant, perhaps irritating, amateurs and start seeing them as a potent untapped resource – in reality, research shows that many community rail supporters are better qualified than average, particularly in activities such as planning, people management, finance and promotion, areas in which the rail industry as a whole does not exactly generally excel.

With the recent spread of the community rail ethos to both Scotland and the Continent, with differing administrative and financial factors contributing to success, it will soon be possible for the first time to make some real comparisons. What a shame it will be if yet another rail innovation conceived and initially developed close to home (think tilting trains, clockface timetables, etc) proves to have been taken up and bettered elsewhere, simply for a lack of commitment and belief on the home front. ■

INNOVATION FOCUSES ON RAIL CHALLENGES

The rebuilding of Birmingham New Street station carried off the Major Projects award. Finishing touches are applied shortly before the September 2016 opening. **NETWORK RAIL**

BIRMINGHAM DEVELOPMENT WINS MAJOR PROJECT AWARD

Intelligent approaches to engineering, information and environmental challenges dominated the winners' roll of honour at the 2015 Rail Industry Innovation Awards - the longest standing award scheme in the industry.

Roger Ford, Industry & Technology Editor of *Modern Railways*, was the compere and Clare Moriarty, the current Director General, DfT Rail Executive, gave the keynote speech. Trophies were presented in seven categories, at the June meeting of the *Modern Railways* Fourth Friday Club.

MAJOR PROJECT

The Major Projects prize goes each year to a project that looms large on the national scene but that also displays commendable innovation. The latest prize went to the rebuilding of Birmingham New Street station, which fits the bill admirably on both scores.

New Street is the crossroads of the national network and its efficient functioning is essential for the network to perform smoothly. The construction programme was extremely complex, both in maintaining a fully functioning transport hub throughout the development works and also in refurbishing a 1960s building. Mechanical and electrical services contractor NG Bailey has met unprecedented challenges during the redevelopment of the station with innovative engineering approaches. The project, backed by Birmingham City Council, Department for Transport, Network Rail and West Midlands transport authority Centro, was delivered by Network Rail alongside its delivery partner Mace.

It was a £600million project for the regeneration of the station, with a further £150million investment in the transformation of the Pallasades

The Innovation Awards trophies. **TONY MILES**

shopping centre into Grand Central Birmingham.

OPERATIONS AND PERFORMANCE

The DayOne software application from Tracsis was the winner of the Innovation Award for Operations and Performance. The rail industry's only real-time attribution and sub-threshold delay software solution, this app aims to engage frontline rail staff and provide those in remote locations of the rail network with real time information on train movements, delays and incidents. Data is available immediately for analysis, and staff can be aware of and react more quickly to an incident or delay.

Highly Commended were BlueCube train systems monitoring from Barnbrook Systems; and a wheel-slide-protection software solution from Siemens, South West Trains and Knorr-Bremse Rail UK.

HITACHI
Inspire the Next

ENVIRONMENT

A project to reduce the environmental impact of traction power supply for light rail vehicles was the winner of the 2015 Innovation Award for the Environment. Squaring up to a challenge from industry body UK Tram, a consortium led by design, engineering and project management consultancy Atkins, supported by Cecence and Brecknell Willis, has applied advanced composite materials in overhead line equipment for light rail systems.

Highly Commended were Southern's environmental programme; and Furrer + Frey's rapid-charge station for battery powered trains.

ENGINEERING AND SAFETY

Rowe Hankins' Intelligent Wheel Flange Lubrication system was the winner of the Innovation Award for Engineering and Safety, sponsored by the Railway Industry Association. With interfaces to train management systems, track balises and GPS, the system has been designed to apply lubrication exactly when and where it is required and in the right amounts, using an on-board dispensing system, making it technically effective and economic.

Highly Commended were the Sirenum competence management and scheduling system used by First Great Western; and the 'concrete bursting' technique employed on London Underground to break out concrete track bases.

PASSENGER EXPERIENCE

The Innovation Award for Passenger Experience was won by the new c2c Live app, which provides customers with a one-stop shop for everything from personalised journey information to buying tickets and paying for car parking. Developed with IBM, it is the first app from a UK rail company to include door-to-door journey planning, providing alerts of disruptions on a journey and giving information on an alternative route.

Highly Commended were Arriva Trains Wales' Mobile Multi Flex ticketing app; and Hull Trains' DERIS project (Darwin-enabled real-time passenger information system) developed by KeTech.

CROSS-INDUSTRY

The award for Innovation in a Cross-Industry Project went to the independently-powered electric multiple-unit (IPEMU) project,

successfully demonstrating the concept of a battery powered train in a cross-industry collaboration between RSSB (through the Future Railway programme), Network Rail, Abellio Greater Anglia, Bombardier and the Department for Transport. Energy storage specialists Valence, FIAMM, and Altairnano have also been involved.

The campaign pursued by CrossCountry, with industry partners, to ensure continuity of skills and competency in train planning was Highly Commended – as was the campaign by Abellio Greater Anglia and partners to optimise the impact of an improved, hourly service on the East Suffolk line.

SMALL SCALE

The Innovation Award for a Small Scale Project was won by a programme of joint working between Abellio Greater Anglia and Network Rail to realise the benefits of 'in service' use of train coasting during engineering work. With the track open but overhead line electrification not energised, a safe area of operation is created both for the equipment being renewed and the train running line which is in use. This reduces disruption for customers, reduces costs and speeds completion.

Highly Commended entries in this category were the Concrete Canvas construction material; and the digital fuel monitoring system in a joint entry from Rubirail, Virgin Trains East Coast, and Angel Trains.

'GOLDEN SPANNERS' FOR ROLLING STOCK EXCELLENCE

The 12th annual review of traction and rolling stock fleet reliability is published in the January 2016 issue of *Modern Railways* magazine. An awards luncheon the previous November - one of the *Modern Railways* Fourth Friday Club events - sees 'Golden Spanners' awarded to the best performers, with gold (best in class), silver (most improved) and bronze (fastest incident recovery) categories.

The brainchild of Roger Ford, Industry & Technology Editor of *Modern Railways*, the annual awards divide the national rolling stock fleet into categories: Pacers; Ex BR electric multiple-units; Ex BR diesel multiple-units; InterCity, New-generation DMUs and New-generation EMUs. Spanners for each category are awarded based on actual performance data, Miles Per

Rowe Hankins' Intelligent Wheel Flange Lubrication system was the winner of the Engineering and Safety award, sponsored by the Railway Industry Association. Stuart Evans (right) and Toni Hankins of Rowe Hankins received the trophy from prize presenter, Jeremy Candfield of the RIA (left). **TONY MILES**

The Passenger Experience award was won by the new c2c Live app. Receiving the trophy are (left) Paul Challis, c2c's Head of Information Services, and Chris Tibbetts, National Express's IT Experience Manager. On the right is prize presenter, Ann Saundry, Commercial Director of *Modern Railways'* publishers Key Publishing. **TONY MILES**

Technical Incident (MTIN). The awards are widely credited within the industry as contributing to improvements in train reliability.

GOLDEN WHISTLES AWARDS

Skilful operators can make the trains run safely and on time – and the best operators deserve recognition.

For this reason the Institution of Railway Operators and *Modern Railways* magazine joined forces to launch the Golden Whistles Awards. These awards acknowledge best practice and congratulate railway operators (including passenger, freight, and London Underground) that have done a good job by rewarding them with that ultimate symbol of smart operating – a whistle!

The Golden Whistles, based on objective data, emulate the successful Golden Spanners Awards already run by *Modern Railways*. There are awards for best performance and most improved performance in several categories, including right-time performance and minimising delays.

Based on nominations from their peers, Golden Whistles are also awarded to the Outstanding Individual Operator of the Year, and Outstanding Operating Team of the Year.

A panel of senior railway executives interpret the data and ensure fair play.

The 2016 Golden Whistles Awards will be presented at the January meeting of the *Modern Railways* Fourth Friday Club.

THE FOURTH FRIDAY CLUB

The *Modern Railways* Fourth Friday Club provides a unique networking forum for executives from all sectors in the railway industry. The club was the idea of *Modern Railways* Editor, James Abbott who is also Club Secretary.

Since the first meeting in 2003, the growing reputation of the Club for attracting senior policy makers and top railway managers as guest speakers has seen membership expand rapidly.

For more information, visit *www.4thfriday.co.uk* ∎

EXCEL LONDON TO HOST
INFRARAIL 2016

Infrarail visitors will be able to learn more about developments in railway infrastructure technology.

Suppliers of the systems, equipment and skills covering all elements of the railway infrastructure sector will be showcasing their capabilities at Infrarail 2016 in London from 12 to 14 April. And with Earls Court now no longer available, the event has a new venue – ExCeL London in the capital's Docklands.

Organised by Mack Brooks Exhibitions and a sister show to Railtex, Infrarail is the leading UK event for railway infrastructure engineers, providing great opportunities for face-to-face meetings with companies covering the entire supply chain. Some 200 firms took part in the last exhibition in 2014, which was visited by more than 5,100 senior managers, technicians and industry specialists.

On display at ExCeL will be systems, equipment and skills covering all elements of the railway's fixed assets. These range from track construction and maintenance, signalling, communications and electrification to installations such as stations and maintenance depots. Also present will be companies providing technical expertise in areas such as consultancy, recruitment and training, occupational health and security.

As well as providing an opportunity to meet suppliers and learn more about their latest innovations, the exhibition will feature its now familiar extensive supporting programme, adding further benefits to those attending. This will include keynote speeches by leading figures shaping the future of the UK rail sector, industry seminars, project briefings and discussion forums – all free to attend and devised to give valuable insights into trends in policy and technology.

Taking place alongside Infrarail will be CITE, the Civil Infrastructure & Technology Exhibition 2016 (*www.cite-uk.com*). The successful pairing of these two events first took place in 2014. A significant number of companies exhibiting at CITE will be active across the entire infrastructure sector, and with both shows sharing the same hall at ExCeL, visitors will be free to move between the two.

Entry to Infrarail will be free for visitors who pre-register online. Registration opens in the weeks leading up to the show. The latest information and Infrarail 2016 news can be found at *www.infrarail.com*.

Railtex, the 13th Exhibition of Railway Equipment, Systems & Services, will return to the NEC Birmingham in May 2017, offering the opportunity to meet thousands of rail professionals at the UK's premier industry meeting place. Stand reservations are already open at *www.railtex.co.uk*. ■

INNOVATIONS AT ELEVENTH INNOTRANS

The InnoTrans trade fair for transport technology takes place every two years in Berlin, and the eleventh InnoTrans will take place from 20 to 23 September 2016.

A unique feature of InnoTrans is its Outdoor Display, where everything from tank wagons to high-speed trains are displayed on 3,500 metres of track.

At the last event 2,761 exhibitors from 55 countries presented their rail industry innovations to 133,595 trade visitors who came from 146 countries.

The five segments at InnoTrans include Railway Technology, Railway Infrastructure, Public Transport, Interiors and Tunnel Construction. InnoTrans is organised by Messe Berlin GmbH.

The InnoTrans Convention includes Dialogue Forums on the main conference theme; exhibitor presentations at Speakers' Corner and CEO Guided Tours which take place on the last day of the show. The supporting programme concludes with the new Conference Corner, a format offering organisers the opportunity to hold their own series of lectures.

RAIL VEHICLE ENHANCEMENTS

With its unique profile, industry-leading speakers and exhibition, RVE 2016 is set to deliver yet another highly successful event for exhibitors and visitors. The free-to-attend event will be held on 6 October 2016 in Pride Park Derby.

The Expo showcases the very latest in technology and the Forum enables delegates to learn about current and new projects. The new venue at the Riverside Centre, first used in 2015, offers the capacity to double the number of exhibitors and quadruple the number of places in the discussion Forum.

RVE's Forum provides inside information from train owners, train operators, refurbishers and maintainers, tier one suppliers and RSSB. The Forum promises to deliver essential information to anyone presently or seeking to supply into the rail industry. *www.rve2016.co.uk*

Zefiro high-speed train from Bombardier and AnsaldoBreda at InnoTrans 2014.

HITACHI
Inspire the Next

KEY PROJECTS
AND CONSULTANTS

IN ASSOCIATION WITH

KEY PROJECTS

MAJOR DEVELOPMENTS ON BRITAIN'S RAIL NETWORK

BORDERS RAILWAY

The Borders Railway project has reinstated a 35 mile rail link from Edinburgh through Midlothian to Tweedbank in the Scottish Borders, the northern part of the Waverley route which was closed completely in January 1969. The line joins the existing network at Newcraighall, and seven new stations have been built at Shawfair, Eskbank, Newtongrange, Gorebridge, Stow, Galashiels and Tweedbank. The mainly single track railway has three dynamic passing loops.

The first trains set off from the new stations on the route on Saturday 5 September 2015, carrying 200 passengers with special 'golden tickets'. The festivities continued on 9 September, when Her Majesty the Queen officially opened the new line, travelling on a steam train along the route.

The £294m line, funded by Transport Scotland and the Scottish Government, was constructed by Network Rail which assumed management of the project in 2011, and design and build contractor BAM Nuttall. AECOM developed the design and provided support during construction and commissioning.

GREAT WESTERN MODERNISATION

The Great Western route modernisation now under way involves electrification, resignalling, the rebuilding of the Reading station area, new trains, and preparation for Crossrail.

The new Thames Valley signalling centre since April 2015 has controlled the route between Swindon and London, and is planned to control an area including Oxford, Gloucester, Bristol and Newbury, associated with revision of track layouts for electrification.

Network Rail in conjunction with Reading Borough Council has enlarged and modernised Reading station, building two new entrances connected by a new footbridge. There are new lifts and escalators and five extra platforms to enhance station capacity. The new station was officially opened by HM The Queen on 17 July 2014.

Grade separation at the eastern end of the station allows trains to and from the Waterloo lines to reach the Relief Lines on the north side of the station.

By elevating the Main lines with the construction of a new flyover west of the station, completed at the turn of 2014/15, flows to and from the line to Basingstoke can cross to the Relief lines towards Didcot without obstructing the Main lines - so removing one of the most restrictive bottlenecks on the whole railway system.

This has required the resiting of the Reading Traincare depot to the north side of the line and west of the station. A new grade separated eastern chord from the Basingstoke direction links with the north side of the station for passenger trains.

INTERCITY EXPRESS PROGRAMME

The first new InterCity Express Programme Class 800 train arrived in the UK in March 2015, with all 122 trains due to be in service by 2020. The first trains are being built at Hitachi's Kasado works in Japan, and 110 trains will be produced at Hitachi's new purpose-built £82 million facility at Newton Aycliffe, Co Durham, opened in September 2015.

The Intercity Express programme comprises the infrastructure, rolling stock and franchise changes needed to replace services currently operated by diesel high-speed trains.

Agility Trains, a consortium of Hitachi Rail (Europe) Ltd and John Laing plc, was appointed preferred bidder in 2009. The fleet will have some electric trains and some with a combination of electric with diesel power under the floor (bi-modes). Part of DfT's interest in the bi-modes is in preserving through services away from the electrified network, without

The Borders Railway was officially opened on 9 September, when Her Majesty the Queen travelled on a train along the route, hauled by A4 Pacific No 60009 'Union of South Africa', photographed arriving at Tweedbank. **SCOTTISH GOVERNMENT**

operating diesel traction under the wires for appreciable distances.

In the initial contract signed in July 2012, Agility Trains was responsible for the construction of 92 complete trains totalling 596 vehicles, together with maintenance depots in Bristol, Swansea, Old Oak Common and Doncaster. Agility is also responsible for maintaining the trains, with the train operating company (TOC) responsible for operations. The TOCs pay Agility a Set Availability Payment for each train that is presented for duty each day and remains reliable during the operational period.

The DfT is providing Agility Trains with a usage guarantee that there will be a franchised operator in place to make use of the trains.

Phase 1 trains will operate on the Great Western and will consist of 21 nine-car electric only trains and 36 five-car bi-mode trains (total 369 vehicles in 57 trains), due to start to enter passenger service in June 2017.

Phase 2 trains will operate on the East Coast franchise and will consist of 12 five-car electric only trains, 30 9-car electric trains, 10 five-car bi-mode trains, and 13 nine-car bi-mode trains (total 497 vehicles in 65 trains), with deliveries from 2018.

The contract to finance, supply and maintain the whole fleet takes the total value of the IEP programme to £5.7bn.

The bi-modes are electric multiple-units with a number of diesel engines located beneath the floors. Driving vehicles are trailers and are equipped with pantographs specially developed by Brecknell-Willis.

The electric units have a single diesel engine to provide full hotel power in case of an overhead line fault, or offer limited traction power.

An additional 29 bi-mode high speed trains, based on the IEP design, but with higher engine operating power to cope with gradients, were approved in July 2015. The 'AT300' trains will run as electric trains between London and Newbury, and have bigger fuel tanks for long distance journeys to Plymouth and Penzance.

CROSSRAIL

The Crossrail project will create a new integrated railway from Reading and Heathrow in the west, through tunnels under central London, with stations at Paddington, Bond Street, Tottenham Court Road, Farringdon, Liverpool Street and Whitechapel. It then divides into two routes, one to Stratford and Shenfield north of

the Thames, and the other to Canary Wharf, Custom House, Woolwich and Abbey Wood to the south. The joint sponsors are the Department for Transport and Transport for London which set up a company, Crossrail Ltd, to act as the delivery agent.

Crossrail is reckoned to be the biggest transport project in Europe. The new railway is expected to support regeneration across the capital and is estimated to add £42bn to the economy of the UK. The total funding envelope available to deliver Crossrail is £14.8bn.

On 4 June 2015, the Prime Minister joined the Mayor of London and Secretary of State for Transport at Farringdon to mark the end of Crossrail tunnelling, which actually ended on 26 May. For almost three years, eight tunnel boring machines had been in operation seven days a week below the streets of London to construct the 42km of new 6.2 metre diameter rail tunnels, at depths down to 42m at Finsbury Circus.

The project at this stage was over 65% complete, with work well underway on planning for and delivering an operational railway.

Network Rail is responsible for the design, development and delivery of those parts of Crossrail on the existing network. This includes the upgrading of 70km of track, redeveloping 28 stations and renewing 15 bridges, as well as removing spoil from the tunnel excavations by rail.

All four tracks will be electrified west of the rebuilt Airport Junction, with signalling renewed. There will be a new diveunder for freight at Acton yard. At Paddington, there will be a major reworking of platforms and interchange between the Crossrail station and main line platforms.

Over 12,000 people were working across 45 Crossrail construction sites in 2015, with a total of 460 apprentices appointed.

Over 60% of Crossrail funding comes from Londoners and London-based business, including contributions from the City of London, Heathrow Airport Ltd, Canary Wharf Group, a London Business Rates Supplement and a planning development levy. The government is providing about £5bn by means of a grant from the Department for Transport. The funding package was designed to strike a fair balance between businesses, passengers and taxpayers.

The trains to operate the Crossrail service have been designated Class 345. These will be 9-car, 205

Creation of the Bermondsey diveunder is a major part of the Thameslink Programme, enabling Thameslink trains to run between the Brighton main line and the core central London route via London Bridge without junctions on the flat. One of the diveunder ramps is under construction in March 2015. **NETWORK RAIL**

The new Birmingham New Street nearing its opening in September 2015, seen from the top of the Rotunda. Its new atrium roof illuminates an enlarged concourse, and the Grand Central Shopping Centre and John Lewis store have been built as part of the development. **NETWORK RAIL**

KEY PROJECTS AND CONSULTANTS

The expansion of through lines at London Bridge station is evident in this July 2015 view of Thameslink Programme work in progress, looking west. The Southern terminal platforms to the left are largely complete, four Southeastern platforms to the right (north) are still in use in their 1970s configuration.
NETWORK RAIL

metre long lightweight sets, with air conditioning and inter-connected walk-through cars. They will be operated at 25kV AC, but with potential for third rail pick up. A contract to design, build and maintain the 65 train sets for 32 years, together with building a new depot at Old Oak Common, has been let by Transport for London to Bombardier. There is an option to buy a further 18 trains. The new trains will be wholly publicly funded and the first is to be delivered from Bombardier's Derby plant in May 2017.

Crossrail's trains will operate in Automatic Train Operation mode with Automatic Train Protection in the central section, but will need to feature existing train protection systems for the Network Rail sections of line, with provision for future use of the European Train Control System.

TfL subsidiary Rail for London (RfL)

will be the infrastructure manager for the central section of the Crossrail central tunnel section. Crossrail route control will be based at Liverpool Street in the first instance, and later at a new centre at Romford.

Operation of services has been let as a £1.4bn concession to MTR Corporation (Crossrail) Ltd for eight years, extendable to 10. On 31 May 2015 MTR took over Liverpool Street-Shenfield services in readiness for the introduction of the new Crossrail trains from May 2017. Full Crossrail operation is due to start in December 2019. MTR is expected to employ around 1,100 staff with up to 850 new posts. This will include almost 400 drivers and over 50 apprenticeships for people from communities along the route.

At peak times, Crossrail is planned to run 12 trains/hr (tph) between Shenfield and central London, calling

at all stations, with an additional service of 6tph between Gidea Park and Liverpool Street main line station. A similar 12tph service will run from Abbey Wood.

The central section from Whitechapel westwards will thus carry 24tph at peak, of which 14tph will terminate at Paddington. During the off-peak, the service through the central area was proposed to reduce to 12tph but a plan for 16tph has been developed.

West of Paddington, Crossrail will provide 10tph on the GWML at peak; this will include 2tph from Reading, another 2tph from Maidenhead, 4tph from Heathrow (vice Heathrow Connect) and 2tph from West Drayton.

In August 2014, the government launched a study into a potential Crossrail extension from Old Oak Common to the West Coast main line.

Diverting some West Coast services to Crossrail would make it easier to redevelop Euston station for HS2.

THAMESLINK

The Thameslink Programme is a £6bn project to deliver a high capacity, north-south spine railway through central London. With a scheduled completion of December 2018, Thameslink will provide greater capacity, higher frequencies, new services and improved access to central London from a range of destinations within London and across southeast England.

Major benefits from the works include a capacity increase in the core section between St Pancras Thameslink and Blackfriars to 24 trains per hour, mostly of 12 cars.

The first main element is to provide platforms to accommodate trains of 12-car, 20-metre vehicles, and remove

HITACHI
Inspire the Next

key capacity bottlenecks. Second is the specification and procurement of new rolling stock, and third refranchising of service operation.

The major works currently under way are centred on London Bridge. Six high level through platforms and nine low-level terminal platforms are being converted to nine high level through platforms and six low-level terminal platforms. A new approach viaduct and two track bridge over Borough High Street, already built, will feed the new high level station tracks. A very large station concourse is being created underneath the tracks at street level, with new entrances both north and south.

A staged work programme started with the terminus platforms (served by Southern), all opened by the end of 2014. During 2015/16, Southeastern's Charing Cross services will not stop at London Bridge, and similarly for Cannon Street services in 2016/17. Thameslink through services are diverted away from London Bridge during the works.

New bi-directional signalling has been installed throughout between Kentish Town and Blackfriars. The European Train Control System (ETCS) is to operate along with automatic train operation.

The order for new Siemens 'Desiro City' trains for Thameslink was placed in June 2013. The first of these Class 700 electric multiple-units was delivered in July 2015 and they will begin to enter service during 2016. The trains consist of 55 twelve-car and 60 eight-car dual-voltage units. They have no intermediate cabs and cannot be split during normal operation. The contract is worth around £1.6bn and includes new depots at Three Bridges and Hornsey, and fleet maintenance.

Thameslink trains from the Great Northern route will join the existing Thameslink route at a grade separated junction in tunnel, just north of St Pancras. On the south side of London, a new grade separated junction at Bermondsey will segregate Thameslink from other services on the London Bridge approaches.

London Bridge is currently used by 56m people every year, and the new station is designed to be used by more than 90m people, as well as providing a destination in its own right.

HIGH SPEED 2

High Speed 2 (HS2) is a planned new north-south railway promoted and built in two phases. HS2 Ltd, the

company responsible for developing and promoting it, is wholly owned by the Department for Transport.

Phase One plans are for a new high-speed line from London Euston to north of Birmingham, where it will link with the existing West Coast main line allowing fast services direct to destinations further north. New high-speed trains are to serve Birmingham city centre (Curzon Street) and an interchange with Birmingham International and Birmingham Airport, designed to serve the wider West Midlands. At Old Oak Common in west London, a new interchange is to connect HS2 with Crossrail, the Great Western main line and the Heathrow Express.

The proposals for Phase Two would see the line extended north and east, to join the West Coast main line south of Wigan and the East Coast main line south of York. On a Manchester leg, the route for consultation had stations at Manchester Airport and Manchester Piccadilly (adjacent to existing station). A separate branch would serve an East Midlands station near Nottingham, Sheffield Meadowhall and Leeds New Lane. Passengers would be able to travel from central London to Birmingham in 49min rather than 1hr 24min today, and from London to Manchester in 1hr 8min (2hr 8min today).

HS2 is designed for a top speed of 250mph. Plans envisage services running at up to 225mph, seen as becoming the standard for new high speed trains. For future operation at 250mph, noise and other impacts would be considered first. New

Transport Secretary Patrick McLoughlin views the cab of an InterCity Express Programme test train during a visit to the Melton Mowbray test site on 21 August 2015. **HITACHI**

stations on the line would be built to accommodate 400m long trains, each capable of carrying up to 1,100 passengers. A 14 trains per hour capability in Phase One (12 in the initial specification), is expected to rise to 18 trains per hour in Phase Two. Network Rail estimates that over 100 cities and towns could benefit from new or improved services as a result of capacity released on the existing rail network.

The government announced in 2013 a potential funding requirement for HS2 of £42.6bn, at 2011 prices (£21.4bn for Phase One and £21.2bn for Phase Two – including a total contingency for both phases of £14.4bn). The target price for construction of Phase One is £17.16bn, with no spending above this without agreement of the DfT, working with the Treasury.

Permission for the scheme to go ahead is being sought through a 'hybrid' Bill process (combination of Public and Private Bill procedures). The Bill for Phase One received its Second Reading in the House of Commons in April 2014, approving it in principle, and then moved to the Select Committee stage, when petitions are heard.

HS2 Ltd Chairman, Sir David Higgins, in October 2014 proposed amendments to Phase Two plans, including consideration of a single redeveloped Leeds station for HS2 and existing railways. While restating support for a Crewe HS2 station, with delivery accelerated to 2027 instead of 2033, he recommended consideration of through HS2 services via existing lines for Stoke on Trent.

New plans for the HS2 station at London Euston were published in

Track lowering in progress to provide clearance for the Great Western electrification at Sydney Gardens, Bath on 25 August 2015. **NETWORK RAIL**

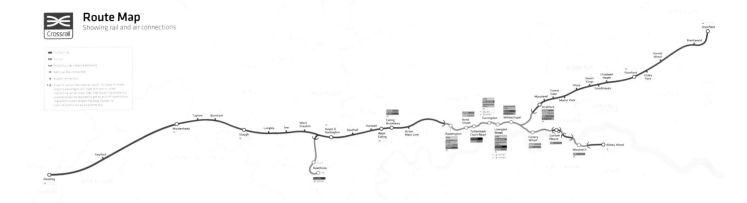

Regional route map (March 2014). **CROSSRAIL**

September 2015. Six high speed platforms would open with Phase One in 2026 and five more in time for opening of HS2 Phase Two routes in 2033 – all at a lower level than existing tracks. 11 domestic platforms would remain. Structural support for future redevelopment above the new platforms is proposed. The government in 2015 also proposed to extend the deep-bore Chilterns tunnel by 2.6km to a new portal just past South Heath to reduce environmental impact.

The bidding process for HS2 Phase One construction began in September 2015, with seven new contracts (total combined value £11.8bn) for the main civils works

on the surface route and tunnels. 50 miles of the second phase of HS2, taking it to Crewe by 2027, were also included (additional value: £1.8bn-£3.3bn).

NORTHERN HUB AND HS3

The Northern Hub upgrading of the rail network will see, alongside electrification of primary routes, improvements including two new platforms at Manchester Piccadilly to allow more trains to run through rather than terminate, and construction of the Ordsall Curve to provide a direct route between Manchester Piccadilly and Manchester Victoria. Selective track doubling is to increase capacity

between Leeds and Liverpool and between Sheffield and Manchester, and Manchester Victoria has been rebuilt, improving interchange. More and faster trains will be able to run on key routes, with more direct rail services to Manchester Airport.

Proposals to improve east-west rail links on the Manchester-Leeds axis (dubbed 'High Speed 3' by the government) were set out by HS2 Ltd Chairman Sir David Higgins in his report, 'Rebalancing Britain', in October 2014. Government and the new Transport for the North (TfN) organisation have set out options for the new 'TransNorth' network, linking Liverpool, Manchester, Leeds, Sheffield, Newcastle and Hull - ranging

from radical upgrades to building new lines. The government said that, working with TfN, it would produce a comprehensive transport strategy for the region, including options, costs and a delivery timetable for the east-west plans (see our 'Across the Industry' section).

BIRMINGHAM NEW STREET

170,000 passengers a day use Birmingham New Street, nearly triple the 60,000 a day it was designed for when it was last rebuilt in the 1960s. The new station can now handle 300,000 a day – it opened in September 2015 after a five-year, £750m transformation.

CONSULTANT FILES SUPPORTING RAIL DEVELOPMENTS

AECOM AND URS

AECOM is a global provider of professional technical and management support services, with international experience of a wide range of rail disciplines, such as systems enhancements, operations, infrastructure maintenance, rail engineering, and policy and strategy. AECOM is a 40% partner in the Transcend joint-venture, providing strategic management services for London Crossrail.

AECOM in 2014 acquired URS Corporation, and the UK rail delivery team numbers 550. Consultancy services cover all aspects of rail infrastructure planning, design, project management, construction supervision and asset maintenance.

ATKINS

Atkins is one of the world's leading design, engineering and project management consultancies, employing some 18,000 people. Atkins is a leader in rail engineering and systems design, providing expertise from experience and in-depth

knowledge. From development and maintenance of existing systems to the implementation of new schemes, it helps clients through the entire project lifecycle to maximise value and outcomes.

Key rail projects include providing architectural and engineering design services on Crossrail, and Atkins is also a route developer for Crossrail 2.

ARUP

Arup is a global firm of designers, engineers, planners and business consultants which provides a full range of professional services. Arup's portfolio includes all modes of rail, ranging from high speed through to urban transport systems and freight.

Projects undertaken by Arup range in scope from master/strategic planning and total rail infrastructure improvement programmes requiring multi-disciplinary teams, to the application of singular, specialist skills such as operations, planning, permanent way, traction power, signalling, communications, acoustics, station design and tunnelling.

BECHTEL

Founded in 1898, Bechtel is a major engineering, construction, and project management company, active around the world. It is part of the Project Delivery Partner team for the central tunnel section of Crossrail, and was selected by Network Rail to provide project management services for the £3.1bn Crossrail and Reading programme. It has successfully delivered some of the largest and most complex rail projects in the world, including the Channel Tunnel and High Speed 1. It is currently also working on London Underground upgrading, the Riyadh Metro, the Rio de Janeiro Metro, and the Dulles Metrorail extension.

CAPITA

Capita provides a range of commercial and project management, engineering, architecture, electrification and plant, permanent way, telecommunications, real estate and environmental services to the rail sector. It has been a key consultant for London's Crossrail, designing the Royal Oak, Woolwich and Plumstead portals, and is one of

the leading consultants on the HS2 design framework and Network Rail's electrification programme. In the past it has also been involved in the design of HS1 and Thameslink.

DELTARAIL

DeltaRail is a specialist software and technology provider partnering with its customers to transform UK transport. It is the largest provider of computerised signalling control systems in the UK and the first to introduce next-generation IT architecture. The company is a British-based SME, located in Derby, employing over 200 highly skilled staff and has invested significantly in R&D. DeltaRail is committed to the Government growth agenda, focusing on highly-skilled SMEs and exports.

CH2M

Employee-owned CH2M is a leading consulting, design, design-build, operations, and programme management companies serving government, civil, industrial and energy clients, employing over 25,000 people worldwide.

HITACHI
Inspire the Next

A spectacular new atrium has been opened up over the concourse, which is now five times the size of London Euston's. The new Grand Central Shopping Centre and John Lewis store have been built as part of the development.

The project was funded by Network Rail, Birmingham City Council, Centro and the DfT and carried out by Network Rail and delivery partner Mace.

EAST-WEST RAILWAY

Chiltern Railways "Evergreen 3', undertaken as a combined project with Network Rail, has built a new chord from south of Bicester North station on to the Bicester-Oxford line which has been upgraded. This enabled new services to be introduced in October 2015 between London Marylebone and a new station at Oxford Parkway - expected to be extended to the existing Oxford station in Spring 2016.

This scheme is linked with the East-West Railway project to restore trains between Oxford, Bletchley and beyond. Consultation was carried out in 2015 on Phase 2, including links from Aylesbury and to Milton Keynes Central. Two shortlisted potential corridors for a link continuing from Bedford to Cambridge, via Hitchin or Sandy, were published in July 2015 for further consideration.

ELECTRIFICATION

Electrification is a central part of the Control Period 5 (CP5, from 2014 to 2019) plans for the rail network, but as reported in our 'Setting the Agenda' article, the programme has been under review, with Great Western main line electrification given priority. After a temporary pause, North TransPennine electrification was anticipated to be reprogrammed for completion by about 2022 and Midland main line by 2023.

New routes in Scotland and Northwest England have however seen electrification completed in 2014 and 2015. The first electric trains ran in service in May 2014 on the Cumbernauld-Glasgow line, the first part of the Edinburgh-Glasgow Improvement Programme (EGIP).

The £80million electrification - covering 50 single track kilometres - was carried out by Carillion Rail and SPL Powerlines, and included electrification of Cowlairs-Springburn and the triangle of lines where the Glasgow-Cumbernauld line meets the Motherwell to Cumbernauld line north of Mossend yard.

Whifflet line electric services began in December 2014 after overhead line electrification was energised in September 2014. The new electrification covers Rutherglen East Junction to Whifflet North

Junction, and Langloan Junction to Coatbridge Junction, joining already electrified routes at each end. Services are now linked into the Argyle line service pattern via Rutherglen and Dalmarnock. The £29.6 million project was realised through an alliance framework agreement between Network Rail and First ScotRail and electrified 25.5 single track kilometres.

In March 2015, electric train services began between Liverpool and Manchester via Newton-le-Willows.

Huyton-Wigan and Ordsall Lane-Manchester Victoria were added to the electric network in May 2015. Liverpool-Preston services were electrified from December 2015.

The electrification of the main Edinburgh to Glasgow line via Falkirk High is anticipated to be completed by December 2016. In November 2014, Network Rail announced the award of £250million alliancing contracts with Costain and Morgan Sindall to deliver the core physical works on the

Artist's impression of the HS2 station at London Euston proposed in September 2015. Six high speed platforms would open with HS2 Phase One in 2026. **HS2 LTD**

Having operated in the UK for over 20 years, it acquired Halcrow in 2011. CH2M provides infrastructure design, engineering and management services and specialised rolling stock services to the rail industry. It is working on iconic infrastructure programmes including High Speed 2 and Crossrail.

SNC-LAVALIN

Interfleet, a member of the SNC-Lavalin Group since 2011, announced its full integration into SNC-Lavalin by January 2016 - aligning business processes, brands and market strategy to offer a larger portfolio of rail and transit expertise and provide an end-to-end client offering. New offices in Derby are the European Centre for SNC-Lavalin.

Founded in 1994, the heritage of Interfleet Technology lies in rolling stock, and it successfully expanded into other areas including infrastructure, rail control systems and strategic transport advisory services.

Some of Interfleet's latest projects have included HS2 – as design and

technical adviser for rolling stock and depots; and Crossrail 2 –assisting in design and development.

JACOBS

Jacobs is one of the world's largest and most diverse providers of technical services. Jacobs UK provides a comprehensive passenger and freight consultancy service to the rail sector covering the full spectrum of infrastructure requirements, from project development, preliminary appraisal and feasibility studies through to detailed design, implementation and operational management advice.

Jacobs was reappointed in 2015 as the sponsors' Project Representative for Crossrail, designed the new Stockley flyover for Crossrail, and won an engineering design framework package for phase two of High Speed 2.

RICARDO RAIL

Formed by the transfer of Lloyd's Register Rail to Ricardo plc in 2015, Ricardo Rail brings together the strengths of each organisation to

help further the safety, quality and performance of the world's rail systems.

Whilst retaining Lloyd's Register Rail's internationally renowned portfolio of assurance and technical consultancy services, this also offer access to Ricardo's world-class engineering capabilities, such as in powertrain and driveline technologies, as well as to the innovation and products that Ricardo has brought to fields such as high-performance vehicles, motorsport and clean energy generation.

MOTT MACDONALD

Mott MacDonald provides rail engineering consultancy and advisory services through teams based in over 35 offices globally.

It has experts in railway systems, rolling stock, rail operations, asset management and infrastructure upgrade and renewal. Examples of its services includes: alignment, trackform, train control, signalling, telecommunications, rolling stock, operations, safety assurance systems, mechanical and electrical systems, traction power, overhead line, human

factors and ergonomics, RAMS, fire engineering, tunnels, bridges, earthworks, stations, intermodal depots, materials handling and freight yards.

NETWORK RAIL CONSULTING

Network Rail's international rail consultancy business sets out to harness the range of skills and experience available within Network Rail to demonstrate British expertise overseas, and be an international ambassador for Britain's rail industry. It also wants to help channel innovation back into Network Rail's core business.

It offers consultancy services across the full spectrum of Network Rail's expertise, including institutional and policy advice, strategic planning, asset management, operations and maintenance, and infrastructure projects.

NICHOLS GROUP

The Nichols Group is a UK consultancy specialising in areas including strategy, programme management and

Edinburgh-Glasgow Improvement Programme. Route clearance works at Winchburgh tunnel were carried out during a six-week blockade in June/July 2015. The Cumbernauld-Greenhill Lower Junction route will also be electrified.

This first phase of the programme will be complemented by the construction of the new Edinburgh Gateway tram interchange station at Gogar, near Edinburgh airport. The second phase includes platform extension work at the concourse end of Glasgow Queen Street and line speed improvements.

Electrification of the lines to Stirling, Alloa and Dunblane (and through Falkirk Grahamston) will form the next step, expected to be completed by December 2018. The Shotts line between Holytown and Midcalder Junctions is expected to be electrified by 2019.

Electrification of the Grangemouth branch is also planned, to be funded from the Scottish Strategic Rail

Freight Investment Fund, which is also expected to contribute to the electrification of the Edinburgh suburban line for freight trains, avoiding Edinburgh Waverley. This is linked with the plan to permit W12 gauge traffic to operate between via the East Coast main line to Carstairs.

In November 2014 the UK government agreed a funding package with the Welsh government on electrification of the south Wales Valley Lines, and the UK government will cover the full costs of electrifying the Great Western main line to Swansea. The UK government would take over sponsorship and fund delivery of the Cardiff-Bridgend section, valued at £105 million, and contribute £125 million towards the costs of the wider Valley Lines electrification scheme.

The Welsh Government will be responsible for sponsorship and delivery of the Valley Lines project, which seems set to be revised.

In another announcement in

The redeveloped Manchester Victoria station, officially opened in October 2015, has an airy new roof, an extended footbridge over the concourse, additional Metrolink platforms and restored Victorian features. Network Rail, Transport for Greater Manchester, principal contractor Morgan Sindall and designer Hyder were among those collaborating on the project. **NETWORK RAIL**

November 2014, £16m of government funding was confirmed to electrify the Windermere branch line. Bolton-Wigan electrification, announced by the DfT in 2013, was awaiting inclusion in delivery plans. A prioritised programme of electrification was published in March 2015 by the North of England electrification task force, set up by the Secretary of State for Transport.

In September 2015, Network Rail awarded a £56.8m contract to electrify the Gospel Oak to Barking line to J. Murphy & Sons, who are expected to subcontract nearly half the work. The line is due to be ready for electric passenger services by the end of 2017, but freight connections were not included in the wiring contract. The deal covers electrification of a 12-mile stretch. ∎

CONSULTANT FILES SUPPORTING RAIL DEVELOPMENTS

project management. The group has advised and assisted in implementing and restructuring major capital rail investment programmes, amongst them TfL's capital programmes, the DfT Intercity Express programme and Thameslink. Nichols has led capital programme reviews for the Office of Rail Regulation, and is a partner in the Transcend team working in programme management for the London Crossrail project.

NORTH STAR CONSULTANCY
With specialist understanding of the rail and air sectors, North Star Consultancy aims to use methodologies that ensure its service meets the needs of the market and allow it to deliver world-class rail and air transport solutions.

Services range from niche specialist consultancy to hands-on delivery and North Star specialises in service concept, operations strategy, start-up and implementation; customer experience; disruption management; and specialist air-rail link advice.

ONYXRAIL
Onyxrail's group provides turnkey projects, engineered products and labour supply, predominantly in the rail industry. Project management and procurement teams, with technology partners, provide a complex range of train enhancements.

Onyxrail also assists higher technology OEMs with route to market services in the UK, and through its sister company provides a range of castings, forgings, fabrications and machined components.

Subsidiary Skills4Rail provides contract staff for variable project requirements, and Onyxrail's events team is also responsible for organising the annual Rail Vehicle Enhancements exhibition and forum.

THE RAILWAY CONSULTANCY
The Railway Consultancy provides consultancy services, both nationally and internationally, in the fields of railway planning, operations, economics, management, strategy and training. Areas of expertise cover both operational and demand planning, and work is carried out for a range of clients, both in the UK and overseas.

Projects it has worked on include feasibility studies, commercial planning, operational planning, management & strategy, audit & assessment, and analysis, research & training.

STEER DAVIES GLEAVE
Steer Davies Gleave is a leading independent transport consultancy providing planning and advisory services to government and business.

Expertise includes rail demand and revenue forecasting, financial modelling, rail operations & costing, rail strategy development & implementation, business case preparation, public consultation, outreach & stakeholder engagement, rail project delivery & appraisal, procurement, rail franchise bidding, specification and evaluation.

TRACSIS
The Tracsis Consultancy Group delivers business critical advice in the rail operations planning, performance and signalling data fields, specifically in Strategic operations and planning advice, timetable design and production, rolling stock diagramming, traincrew diagram optimisation and rostering, operational performance simulation for heavy rail, metros and trams, Schedule 8 and delay attribution analysis, and signalling data analysis.

Tracsis uses industry leading systems such as TrainTRACS for crew optimisation, TracsROSTER for traincrew rostering and TracsRS for rolling stock diagramming.

VOSSLOH KIEPE UK
Vossloh Kiepe UK (formerly Transys Projects Limited) specialises in integration engineering and rolling stock enhancement. Its wide range of capabilities includes engineering, consultancy and design packages,

turnkey solutions, technology enhancements, product support, refurbishment of rail vehicles, and traincare. A major current project is the retractioning of 91 Class-455 units with energy-saving traction equipment, supplied by its German parent company, for Porterbrook Leasing.

WSP AND PARSONS BRINCKERHOFF
WSP has 60 years experience in rail project delivery working across all phases of a project. The design team working on London Bridge station includes a HyderWSP JV and architect Grimshaw.

Parsons Brinckerhoff is a global consulting firm assisting clients to plan, develop, design, construct, operate and maintain critical infrastructure. It is involved in capacity building and development of the rail network, with projects including Northern Hub, Crossrail, Great Western electrification and HS2.

YORK EMC SERVICES
York EMC Services Ltd is an established market leader for the provision of EMC services to the railway industry.

York EMC Services offers a range of consultancy, testing and training services, specifically designed for the railway industry. The company has a solid track record of solving problems and demonstrating EMC for major railway projects around the world.

INFRASTRUCTURE
MAINTENANCE & RENEWAL

IN ASSOCIATION WITH

Ricardo
Rail

Formerly
Lloyd's Register Rail

RICARDO RAIL
VISION FOR A WORLD-CLASS RAIL BUSINESS

Ricardo's TorqStor high-speed flywheel energy storage technology is at the centre of the DDFlyTrain project. This is seeking to identify a technology that could emulate for DMUs the regenerative braking systems found on modern EMUs.

T hough not entirely new to the rail market, the launch of Ricardo Rail in the summer of 2015, following the acquisition of Lloyd's Register Rail, dramatically changed the Ricardo group's standing within the sector almost overnight.

The Shoreham-based engineering business already possessed a small foothold in the rail industry - largely based on transferring capabilities from its automotive origins, such as powertrain and driveline technologies.

But it had been actively looking to build a larger presence within the rail market for some time, and the acquisition of LR's rail division was the opportunity it had been waiting for.

Furthermore, far from reorganising the business, or folding it into an existing rail division, the new acquisition's structures and management were to remain untouched, save for the absorption of Ricardo's smaller incumbent rail division.

SENSE OF CONTINUITY
The result was that, despite the new name, a strong sense of continuity prevailed.

"Ricardo recognised that they were acquiring a successful business that had steadily grown over the past 10 years, and understood our vision

Central to Ricardo Rail's portfolio remain assurance capabilities and technical expertise of complex and critical technologies.

for building a truly world-class rail business", says Martin Giles, Managing Director of Ricardo Rail in the UK and part of the management team that transferred from Lloyd's Register.

"As Lloyd's Register Rail, for example, we were recognised for our assurance capabilities as well as our technical expertise of complex and critical technologies.

"As Ricardo Rail, they remain central to our portfolio. For example, we are continuing to perform important assurance roles on projects like Crossrail, Thameslink and the Wales and Western Programme. Our intention is to grow this area for many years to come, including the launch of

a standalone assurance management entity, Ricardo Certification.

"But to those traditional strengths, we now offer access to the ideas and products that Ricardo has brought to fields such as high-performance vehicles, mass-transit and clean energy generation over many years".

EXPLOITING TECHNOLOGY SYNERGIES
And according to Martin, from the earliest stages of the transition, two significant areas of synergy quickly emerged.

"The first was a shared culture. As an established engineering brand themselves, Ricardo shared

our values around quality and innovation, and for providing trusted, independent advice.

"Second, was the opportunity to transfer skills, technologies and innovation between different sectors".

A perfect example is Ricardo's appointment to support the introduction of a driverless bus fleet at Brussels Airport.

Whilst Ricardo's automotive heritage meant it possessed the necessary expertise of passenger vehicles, it was the arrival of the rail business, with its experience of automated train control technologies, that meant the client could be offered a fully integrated proposal. The team are now overseeing the procurement of the bus fleet and the central control centre, as well as assessing the functional safety of the vehicles.

But the potential also exists in the other direction. To take one further example, technology derived from Ricardo's work in Formula 1 could be the key to the development of an energy recovery system for Diesel Multiple Units (DMUs).

In an initiative co-funded by Innovate UK and the RSSB, the DDFlyTrain project was launched in 2013, in partnership with Artemis Intelligent Power and Bombardier Transportation, to identify a technology that could emulate the regenerative braking systems found on modern EMUs.

And at the heart of the project sits Ricardo's TorqStor high-speed flywheel energy storage technology, with initial indications that the retrofit of flywheels to DMUs could lead to fuel savings of up to 10 percent, as well as extend the life of the vehicle's braking components.

INTRIGUING OPPORTUNITIES
"The first six months were about maintaining continuity of core services, and gradually introducing our new capabilities", says Martin.

"Clients are gaining a better understanding of the wider range of skills and capabilities we now offer. They can see the synergies for themselves and are intrigued by the opportunities it is opening up for them." ▪

NETWORK RAIL
EFFICIENCY IN THE SPOTLIGHT

NETWORK OPERATIONS ACCOUNTS FOR A THIRD OF NETWORK RAIL SPENDING

The Office of Rail and Road's (ORR's) assessment of Network Rail's efficiency and financial performance for 2014-2015 highlights that Network Rail's asset management capability is improving, but more work is needed to enhance its capability to manage projects, programmes and portfolios and improve data quality.

Efficiency in its core business of operating, maintaining and renewing its network (excluding enhancements) was below projected levels. Efficiency shortfalls were in part due to renewals work costing more than expected, including for track, signalling and civils. This contributed to Network Rail's financial performance measure ending the year £485m lower than its target in England and Wales and £9m lower than target in Scotland.

Comparative information across Network Rail's route-based management units for expenditure, income, financial performance and asset management was published for the first time. This will enable a more detailed examination of relative performance, helping identify issues which may be emerging at route level to improve future performance.

Network Rail has increasingly devolved operational responsibility to the operating routes in England & Wales and Scotland over the past four years. ORR says it has found that with route management teams taking on more responsibility, they are in some cases making more informed decisions as they have more autonomy to better respond to local requirements. Although Network Rail's corporate centre is still accountable for the performance of the routes, its processes for managing the business in this way are still being developed and ORR comments that this has led to some difficulty in co-ordinating the company's overall business plans.

Network Rail's financial issues have implications for the remainder of Control Period 5 (2014-19), including delivery of performance targets, says ORR, particularly as more money is being spent in CP5 than originally expected. Network Rail was producing a detailed capability improvement plan with clear milestones to ensure it has the right scope in all areas of its business. ORR was to assess the plan and monitor progress against its milestones to ensure the plan meets customers' needs, particularly on the individual routes.

NETWORK RAIL ORGANISATION

Network Rail's operation of the railway is organised by geographic zones or 'Routes'. The Kent and Sussex routes were merged in April 2014 to form a new South East route: the other routes are Anglia, London North Eastern and East Midlands, London North Western, Scotland, Wales, Wessex, and Western.

Network Operations accounts for nearly three-quarters of Network Rail's workforce but less than a third of its spend, a recent National Audit Office (NAO) report confirms, and it is responsible for day-to-day running of the railway, including maintenance, signalling and small renewal projects (which are less than £500,000 in value).

The major components, maintenance and operations, are

The bridge deck of the Scarborough line bridge over the River Ouse in York was removed and a new one installed during a 10-day possession in February 2015. Around 20 other projects between York and Scarborough were also carried out while the bridge work was completed. **NETWORK RAIL**

delivered in-house rather than contracted to external suppliers.

Almost two-thirds of the 25,500 employees in Network Operations were employed on maintenance works in 2013-14. Network Rail needed to reduce the number of staff working on maintenance by 8% and operations staff by 16% over Control Period 5 to meet efficiency saving targets. But the NAO points out that, overall, staff in Network Operations will increase, by an expected 900 in CP5, to maintain completed infrastructure projects such as Great Western main line electrification, and to provide additional co-ordination staff at headquarters. The new National Centre in Milton Keynes unites many of Network Rail's national teams and functions under one roof to support the new, more powerful business units.

Network Rail is increasing maintenance capability at both supervisor and operative level to reduce reliance on subcontractors providing extra labour and overtime.

Its route-based structure is intended to achieve financial efficiencies by enabling work to be better co-ordinated, and provide more direct accountability to customers and users of the railway.

Each of Network Rail's eight routes is responsible for:
- Day-to-day operations;
- Maintenance and asset management;
- Planning when large infrastructure projects can be delivered.

Each route has a managing director who reports to Network Operations and Network Rail's board. They also liaise closely with the main train operating companies on their route.

Network Rail has agreed with several train operating companies on new ways of working ever closer - 'alliances' in different forms, depending on the kind of railway in each area and the views of the operator.

Successful delivery of the Offering Rail Better Information Service (ORBIS) programme, to improve asset information, is thought to be key to delivering efficiencies as better information is intended to improve decision-making and lead to more effective maintenance and renewals work.

INFRASTRUCTURE PROJECTS

Network Rail has also moved to a new, commercially focused,

Colas Rail's Plasser & Theurer 08-4x4/4S-RT Switch & Crossing tamper No DR73907 at work on the new Stockley viaduct, for Crossrail services to operate to and from Heathrow. **NETWORK RAIL**

regionally based projects delivery business – Network Rail Infrastructure Projects – with four regional Directors and three programme Directors responsible for delivery of major renewal and enhancement work in their area. They manage their own profit and loss and could be charged with winning work under a proposed new competitive structure.

There is also a focus on developing the client capability within Network Rail to clearly define project outputs and work with delivery organisations much earlier in the project lifecycle. These changes should enable improved specification of output requirements, better integration of these into route plans, and greater discipline in the interface with the delivery team. This in turn should help to facilitate greater innovation, including through earlier engagement with the supply chain and through improved project-based partnerships with customers.

It was also intended to invite other organisations to tender for work in competition with Infrastructure Projects, enabling benchmarking of capital project delivery.

Network Rail Consulting was established in 2012, aimed at bringing further skills into the company, with further opportunities to benchmark against market competitors.

HIGH OUTPUT

Network Rail expanded its track renewal programme in 2015 by purchasing a new £50m ballast cleaner, as it welcomed more than 500 employees, previously contractors, into the company.

The new ballast cleaning system 5 (BCS5) incorporates measures to reduce workforce exposure to ballast dust, including mist-based suppression systems. The new cleaner is designed for 'third-rail' operation, allowing the conductor rail to safely remain in place throughout the cleaning process. Purchased from Plasser & Theurer, the purpose-built kit and associated support plant are due to be delivered in 2016.

In March 2015 the Network Rail high output track renewals team completed the transfer of more than 500 AmeyCOLAS contractor

staff, bringing them in-house and marking the largest people transfer into Network Rail since the phased in-sourcing of maintenance activities began in 2005.

BCS5 consists of an RM900 high output ballast cleaner; new ballast power wagon; spoil power wagon; consolidation machine (in-train tamping with double bank dynamic action); and 44 MFS conveyor spoil / new ballast wagons. Support plant comprises: two 09-3X dynamic tamper / track stabiliser machines; a 'third rail' compatible 09-2X dynamic tamper / track stabiliser machine; a USP5000 ballast regulator machine; and a first-of-type third-rail ballast regulator machine.

LABOUR CODE OF CONDUCT

Network Rail awarded a new series of contracts with contingent labour

NETWORK RAIL TRACK DELIVERY PARTNERS 2014-19

PLAIN LINE (CONVENTIONAL), FIVE-YEAR DEALS:
Babcock: Western, Wales and Wessex / Scotland / LNW South – c.£200m.
Carillion: LNW North / LNE and East Midlands – c.£100m.
Colas: Kent and Sussex / Anglia – c.£75m.

SWITCHES & CROSSINGS, TEN-YEAR DEALS:
Amey Sersa: North alliance (Scotland / LNE and EM / LNW North) – up to £400m.
Colas URS: South alliance (Anglia / Kent and Sussex / Western, Wales and Wessex / LNW South) – up to £400m.

The high output track renewals programme is being taken in house from 2015.

The electrification programme is expected to contribute to an overall increase in the number of Network Rail's maintenance workers. **NETWORK RAIL / PHIL ADAMS**

suppliers from April 2015, to provide workers across the network with a total minimum spend of £450m over five years.

The awards see a strategic change in the number of suppliers from 57 to 20. Four core suppliers will provide 70% of the workforce supported by a number of smaller specialist suppliers.

A new code of conduct for labour requires suppliers to provide a competent and more professional contingent labour workforce, investing in training and development.

It also requires them pay as a minimum, the London living wage within Greater London; minimise travel time; adopt Network Rail's lifesaving rules, and 'speak-out' systems; and provide all equipment and protective clothing free-of-charge to workers.

INFRASTRUCTURE CONTRACTORS

Network Rail carries out the bulk of maintenance work in-house, and is taking additional work in house during Control Period 5, but it has relied on contractors for track renewals and infrastructure projects work, and work on stations and structures, and aims to reinvigorate relationships with suppliers for CP5. Some of the main

contractors are featured below.

AMEY

Amey's rail sector services include design, advisory and inspection services in signalling, electrification and power, track and civil engineering structures, as well as installation, renewals and enhancements services. Amey is part of Ferrovial, the major European services and construction group.

Amey secured a second consecutive term to 2019 as Network Rail's supplier of civil examinations, (except London North Western, which Network Rail took in-house), and retained a major role in rail structures assessments. The new contracts are worth over £40m a year.

Amey in 2012 won a £700m contract for Great Western main line electrification. In December 2014 a joint venture with Keolis (30:70) took over operation and maintenance of the Docklands Light Railway. Amey also has specialist skills in customer information and security.

BABCOCK RAIL

Babcock Rail - formerly First Engineering - is a leading player in the UK rail infrastructure market and a major track renewals company. It carries out a wide of range of rail infrastructure work, including track renewal, power and signalling contracts, rail property management, on-track plant, civil and structural engineering, and training services.

The ABC Electrification joint venture of Alstom, Babcock and Costain secured two of Network Rail's National Electrification Programme framework contracts covering the Central (London North Western, South) and Wales and Western regions. These have an estimated value of £900m, shared equally by the partners. Babcock has had further success on the Edinburgh Glasgow Improvement Programme, winning a number of work packages both independently and with the ABC joint venture.

Babcock is also delivering conventional plain line track works across three regions, and the has also seen strong demand for overhead line and special project works.

BALFOUR BEATTY

Balfour Beatty Rail is a leading UK rail infrastructure supplier, and Balfour Beatty's Construction and other businesses are involved in several major UK rail projects. From feasibility studies, planning and design through to implementation and asset management, Balfour Beatty Rail provides multi-disciplinary rail infrastructure services across the lifecycle of rail assets.

Involvement in Crossrail includes a contract valued at over £130m to build two miles of the route and Abbey Wood station, and a to upgrade a 12 mile section between West Drayton and Maidenhead. Bombardier Transportation in 2015 awarded Balfour Beatty a £12.5m contract to build a production and testing facility at Derby for new trains ordered for Crossrail.

Balfour Beatty is delivering the track remodelling for the London Bridge area as part of the Thameslink programme, a contract worth circa £50m. Track Partnership, a collaboration with London Underground, is working to transform track renewal delivery. Balfour Beatty won the contract in 2015 to deliver the new Edinburgh Gateway rail/tram interchange station valued at £25m.

BAM NUTTALL

BAM Nuttall was Network Rail's

main contractor for the delivery of the new Borders Railway, and is to deliver the £170m Aberdeen-Inverness rail upgrade.

BAM Nuttall also won the Network Rail civils contract to build a dive under at Acton freight yard in Ealing for Crossrail. It was principal contractor for repairing the main breach of the Dawlish sea wall in 2014. Network Rail appointed BAM Nuttall as its Sussex region multifunctional framework contractor for CP5, a deal worth around £276m. A Taylor Woodrow Construction / BAM Nuttall JV is TfL's main contractor for the reconfiguring of Victoria Tube station.

CARILLION

Carillion plc is one of the UK's leading support services and construction companies, holding a share in a seven-year, £2bn electrification framework for Network Rail, in partnership with the Austrian firm SPL Powerlines. It covers the Central (East Midlands) and Scotland & North East regions. The partnership has opened training centres for rail engineers to develop skills needed to help deliver the electrification programme.

The £87m contract to design and construct Chiltern Railways' route between London Marylebone and Oxford and the western section of the East West Rail scheme was awarded in 2014 to a joint venture between Carillion and Buckingham Group Contracting.

The first of Network Rail's new mobile maintenance trains (MMTs), built by Robel, was introduced in 2015. A large, extendable work area allows access to the track below, and provides cover, floodlighting and protection from passing trains.

A UK joint venture, Infrasig, combines Bombardier technology for both conventional and ETCS signalling solutions with the UK rail experience of Carillion to deliver signalling and multi-disciplinary projects. It received a framework contract for the development and design of the European Train Control System (ETCS).

Network Rail in 2013 awarded Carillion the contract to electrify the Cumbernauld-Glasgow Queen Street line, a £40m contract for over 50km of railway.

Carillion's £120m Key Output 2 contract for Thameslink involves fitting

out of twin 650 metre tunnels and connecting the East Coast main line to Thameslink. It has also been awarded several Crossrail contracts including the Stockley viaduct, and won a £348m rail engineering framework for the London North Western and East Midlands routes in CP5.

COLAS RAIL

Colas Rail was created in 2007 after Amec Spie Rail was taken over by the French infrastructure company Colas, part of the Bouygues group. It combines the engineering skills of specialist businesses to provide total solutions in all aspects of railway

NETWORK RAIL'S TOP 20 SUPPLIERS, 2014-15

SUPPLIER	SPEND £	SERVICE
Carillion Construction Ltd	360,847,939	Infrastructure contracting
Siemens Rail Automation Ltd	268,610,824	Signalling infrastructure contracting
BAM Nuttall Ltd	250,109,845	Infrastructure contracting
Balfour Beatty Rail Ltd	241,292,785	Track infrastructure contracting
Eversheds LLP	230,563,258*	Business Consultancy
Costain Ltd	215,153,825	Infrastructure contracting
British Energy Direct Ltd	189,339,207	Utilities Supply
Atkins Ltd	176,429,852	Signalling infrastructure contracting, consultancy services
Amalgamated Construction Ltd	158,536,779	Infrastructure contracting
J Murphy & Sons Ltd	154,818,005	Infrastructure contracting
Amey-Colas	150,671,655	Track infrastructure contracting
Babcock Rail Ltd	148,982,569	Track infrastructure contracting
EDF Energy Customers Plc	133,243,059	Utilities Supply
Signalling Solutions Ltd	121,641,617	Signalling infrastructure contracting
Tata Steel UK Ltd	98,022,077	Steel manufacturer
Amey Rail	96,024,814	Infrastructure contracting
Colas Rail Ltd	93,878,273	Infrastructure contracting
Geoffrey Osborne Ltd	89,610,525	Infrastructure contracting
DB Schenker Rail (UK) Ltd	86,709,778	Rail logistics
VolkerFitzpatrick Ltd	75,798,516	Infrastructure contracting

*Network Rail points out that a very large proportion of this figure relates to consideration and disbursements paid for property-related transactions, including a significant one-off transaction.

infrastructure, from high speed rail systems to light and urban rail. It is also active in freight train operation (see 'Freight and Haulage' section).

The new Network Rail fleet of mobile maintenance trains introduced in autumn 2015 is operated and maintained by Colas Rail under a three-year contract. Colas's on-track plant fleet includes modern S&C machines, which with additional compact and plain line machines provide Colas with what it believes to be the largest most advanced on-track plant fleet in the UK. In December 2013 it acquired Amey's on-track tamping machines business in a £5m deal.

Colas runs an extensive suite of courses for personnel who work on Network Rail infrastructure, including track safety and permanent way, electrification, safety training, and railway operations.

As part of a Multi Asset Framework Agreement, a joint venture between Colas Rail and Morgan Sindall has been awarded a £20m project by Network Rail to refurbish roof spans one to three at Paddington station. Other work the Colas Rail and Morgan Sindall joint venture has undertaken includes the circa £35m Swindon to Kemble Redoubling.

A £5m contract to renew the Glasgow Subway depot's track ramps and turnout chambers was awarded to Colas Rail in February 2015, and Colas Rail is part of an alliance with Skanska, Aecom and Mott MacDonald appointed for remodelling of Waterloo station.

COSTAIN

Costain is carrying out the major station redevelopment at London Bridge as part of the congestion-busting Thameslink programme, a contract worth circa £400m.

Costain, in the ATC joint venture with Alstom and TSO, has been awarded a contract worth approximately £300m to design, fit-out and commission the railway systems in Crossrail's tunnel network. Under the contract, ATC will design and install track, overhead lines and mechanical and electrical equipment to fit out the 21km of twin tunnels currently being bored under the streets of London. A joint venture with Alstom was awarded the £15m contract for the design, construction and commissioning of the system that will provide traction power for the trains in the central tunnelled section of the Crossrail scheme. Through other joint ventures Costain

is reponsible for construction of two Crossrai stations.

The ABC Electrification Joint Venture with Alstom and Babcock has won contracts for the electrification of the London North West (South) route (£435m), Edinburgh to Glasgow Improvement Programme (£75m) and Welsh Valley Lines (£450m).

Costain and Morgan Sindall were appointed to work with Network Rail to develop in-depth plans for the electrification of the main Glasgow-Edinburgh line and other major projects that form part of EGIP.

SPENCER

Spencer Group is one of the UK's largest privately owned multidisciplinary engineering businesses. Spencer Rail Infrastructure provides quality multi-disciplinary engineering services to the UK and international markets - supporting and enhancing the operational infrastructure of heavy rail and light rail networks.

Recent projects include the design, construction and fit out of a new modular design building to house the Thames Valley Signalling Centre; a £30m project to extend station platforms on South West Trains routes; the design and build

of an architecturally award winning station at St Helens Central; design and construction of a major new rail depot facility on behalf of East Midlands Trains; the major remodelling at Gravesend, and the new Ipswich chord project, new stations at Apperley Bridge and Kirkstall Forge, and upgrading of New Cross Gate depot.

Spencer Rail was named as a principal contractor on the £150m Multi-Asset Framework Agreement for Scotland, covering upgrading and building platforms, bridges, crossings and signalboxes, as well as electrifying railways. Spencer is also delivering projects under a revised multi-asset framework agreement in East Anglia and Kent.

VOLKERRAIL

VolkerRail, part of the Netherlands-based Volker Wessels group, is a comprehensive multi-disciplinary rail infrastructure contractor, and also specialises in electrification, HV power distribution, signalling, plant and welding, track construction, renewals and maintenance; and metro and light rail projects.

The overall railway capability is enhanced by the plant division, with a large fleet of on-track plant, including Kirow rail mounted cranes.

VolkerRail, as part of the M-Pact Thales consortium with Laing O'Rourke and Thales UK, was awarded contracts to provide Manchester Metrolink Phase 3a and 3b extensions. It is part of the Staffordshire Alliance with Network Rail, Laing O'Rourke and Atkins delivering the Stafford Area Improvements Programme.

Sister company VolkerFitzpatrick carried out a Network Rail contract for a major enhancement of Gatwick Airport station, and has been constructing two Thameslink deports, three IEP depots, and Ilford Yard depot for Crossrail, and completed Siemens' Temple Mills depot, and Reading depot, as well as the third rail terminal at Felixstowe port.

A framework agreement covering enhancements, buildings and civils work on Network Rail's Anglia route in CP5 was also awarded to Volker Fitzpatrick (estimated value £480m), and it won the contract to construct the new Lea Bridge station in north east London. Volker Rail won the CP5 London North Western renewal and enhancement framework, plus a £61m electrification and plant framework. It was also awarded the second part of the Sheffield Supertram rail replacement project. ∎

Network Rail's new RM900 high output ballast cleaner will be similar to its previous acquisitions but adapted for operation on third-rail electrified lines. **NETWORK RAIL**

SIGNALLING AND CONTROL

imagine the journey

IN ASSOCIATION WITH

DeltaRail

A 21ST CENTURY CONTROL CENTRE

MODERN RAILWAYS' **ROGER FORD** RECENTLY VISITED THE NETWORK RAIL SIGNALLING CONTROL CENTRE AT MARYLEBONE TO SEE THE LATEST SIGNALLING CONTROL TECHNOLOGY FROM DELTARAIL, IECC SCALABLE. HERE'S WHAT HE SAW.

DeltaRail's Scalable version of its Integrated Electronic Control Centre (IECC) went live at Marylebone in 2015, controlling part of Network Rail London North Western's Chiltern route towards Banbury. It is the first live application of DeltaRail's 'Reconfigurable' workstations. This refers to the ability of any workstation to control any selected section of route.

During commissioning, the reconfigurable function allowed the whole route to be controlled from a single workstation, but in daily operation Marylebone IECC controls the southern part of the Chiltern route through two workstations. The southern 'desk' covers Marylebone to just south of Princes Risborough, the northern one continues to Aynho Junction - fringing with Banbury South.

There are also fringes with London Underground (at Harrow-on-the-Hill and Amersham) and electric token working with Claydon Junction signalbox for the freight line at Aylesbury. The IECC has also been upgraded to support the new Evergreen 3 line to Oxford and the future East West Rail.

The full suite of facilities which DeltaRail can provide with IECC Scalable is still being explored. Like a smartphone, there is the ability to add applications at a future date.

One app already on trial is the docking tool to improve handling of platform changes at Marylebone. At present a signaller has to access the Train Timetable Processor (TTP), make the changes, save the new schedule and close the TTP software down, after which the Enhanced automatic route setting runs the revised schedule.

Contrast this with DeltaRail's docking tool, which is already running on the company's Scalable Traffic Management System (TMS) demonstration suite at Derby. This allows the signaller at the Scalable

User worked crossings: the finger is pointing at the small yellow rectangles denoting such crossings, with a green triangle calling for the signaller's attention.

workstation to call up any train's headcode and make the changes instantly. Interfacing with the daily service plan produced by train operating companies is another function being considered.

A demonstration at the simulator of Scalable at work finds that a familiar, off -the-shelf, mouse and standard keyboard are used. Routes are set using the traditional Entry/Exit. But with Scalable, when you click on the entry signal, the exit signals of all potential routes (or available platforms) start flashing,

The right mouse button opens up a range of utilities, such as putting a 'reminder' on a signal. For example, if there is a report of a trespasser on the line, the protecting signal can be set at danger with a reminder added. When a train stops the signaller can warn the driver and then allow the train to proceed at low speed by manually over-riding the reminder, but the signal will then revert to danger.

Another popular feature is 'drag and drop'. Holding down the left mouse button and dragging the cursor highlights the section within the area selected. A right click calls up a drop-down menu, listing the equipment within the area. Select 'set reminder' and a reminder is placed on all the signals. This is particularly valuable when emergency maintenance work is being carried out at a junction, say. Instead of setting each signal individually, one click, and a job which could take 45-50 seconds is almost instantaneous.

A related facility can store the sections covered by standard engineering possession areas, which can be implemented at the click of a button which applies reminders and sets the signals.

Another enhancement, using the ability to store and call-up data, is infrastructure details. Suppose a message comes in about a bridge strike. Within the 'alarm' tabs on the signaller's display is a 'search' facility.

Enter the bridge number, and the cursor goes straight to it. A right click calls up a drop-down menu, listing the protecting signals, which can then be set at danger individually or using drag and drop. Compare that with getting out the hard copy list of bridges and locations.

ACI – Automatic Code Insertion – was a feature of Classic IECC from the start. When a train arrived at a terminal station, ACI checked the next working of a train against the Train Service Database (TSDB) and inserted the outgoing headcode for automatic route setting to use. For this to happen the TSDB has to contain the relevant 'associations'; that is, identifying the outgoing working of each incoming train. Establishing these associations is a time-consuming process, especially where the associations are many.

A later version, WACI ('W' for Waterloo where it was first commissioned), works on a one-in/one-out basis. If 1A16 arrives in Platform 4 at 14.00 and 1A23 leaves from the platform at 14.15, then WACI assumes it's the same train, provides the association, and inserts the headcode accordingly.

Two years ago, DeltaRail was commissioned to provide an enhanced version of WACI, able to handle features such as splitting and joining of trains. So if Train A comes in, it becomes Train C for the outward working. But WACI knows that before the outward working can leave, Train B will come in and couple with Train A to form train C. If operators subsequently replatform the incoming train, enhanced WACI maintains the association. Which also avoids confusing the customer information systems.

At somewhere like Waterloo or Liverpool Street, associations that would take hours or days to enter into the TSDB can be done in minutes by WACI. ∎

The Thameslink Programme will see the first application anywhere of ETCS with ATO. The first area to be resignalled as part of this project was London Bridge (Southern), controlled from this new workstation at Three Bridges. **NETWORK RAIL**

SIGNALLING & CONTROL
CAN THE NEW TECHNOLOGY DELIVER, AND WHEN?

ROGER FORD, INDUSTRY & TECHNOLOGY EDITOR OF *MODERN RAILWAYS* MAGAZINE, EXPLORES THE STATE OF PLAY WITH NEW SIGNALLING TECHNOLOGY

Network Rail is planning to spend £3.3 billion on signalling renewals over the five years of Control Period 5 (1 April 2014 to 31 March 2019), as Table 1 shows. This is just under £1bn more than in CP4.

Table 2 breaks down the expenditure into Signalling Equivalent Units (SEU). An SEU is a component of a signalling project such as a signal head or point end.

As the table shows, conventional multiple-aspect colour light signalling dominates renewals for the rest of CP5. However in the final year (2018-19), a significant proportion of renewals is planned to use the European Train Control System (ETCS).

Network Rail has specified Level 2 ETCS, which provides cab-signalling, allowing conventional colour light signals to be dispensed with. A screen on the driver's desk, known as the Driver Machine Interface (DMI), shows the driver the 'limit of movement authority', the distance the route is clear ahead. Also indicated is the target speed, and when the driver needs to brake approaching a stop or a speed restriction. ETCS also provide Automatic Train Protection (ATP).

Currently Siemens is suppling ETCS for the Thameslink Central tunnel section under a three stage re-signalling strategy. First, new multiple-aspect signalling is being be installed. ETCS Level 2 will then be overlaid, using the same safety interlockings. Finally Automatic Train Operation (ATO) will be added to the ETCS and the colour light signals removed.

This will be the first application anywhere of ETCS with ATO, which is essential if the central core is to handle 24 trains/hr. The Thameslink project has been using Network Rail's ETCS National Integration Facility (ENIF) at Hitchin, with the test track near Hertford North, for system integration. The ENIF Class-313 ETCS test train made its first runs through the Central core in October last year.

TRAFFIC MANAGEMENT SYSTEM (TMS)

A new Traffic Management System (TMS) being supplied by Hitachi Information Control Systems Europe, will complete the signalling through the central core. Valued at £24m, the contract will provide a 'plan/re-plan' facility which will advise signallers on routing strategies during service perturbations.

Other functions will include providing data to the route setting system which will generate the codes for the ETCS ATO. There will also be interfaces with the server for the Connected Driver Advisory System (C-DAS) on the Thameslink Class 700 trains and the DARWIN passenger information system database.

Signallers for the West Hampstead, King's Cross and London Bridge areas will receive plan/re-plan recommendations through a Signallers' Advisory Display (SAD). This is likely to a dynamic version of the 'simplifier' already used in control centres to show signallers the sequence of trains in the timetable database.

TABLE 1: SIGNALLING EXPENDITURE IN CONTROL PERIOD 5

CONTROL PERIOD RESIGNALLING SPEND (£M)	2014-15	2015-16	2016-17	2017-18	2018-19	CP4 TOTAL	CP5 TOTAL
Pre-efficient expenditure	827	888	845	731	636		3,927
Efficiency Saving	8.50%	4.50%	5.10%	4.20%	4.70%		24.20%
Post-efficient expenditure	757	776	701	581	482	2,421	3,296

Source: Office of Rail and Road

IMAGINE
THE JOURNEY

Transformed by our world-class
digital technologies

www.deltarail.com

A new signal gantry installed at London Bridge In December 2014 as part of the Thameslink Programme redevelopment. **NETWORK RAIL**

CROSSRAIL

While Crossrail interfaces with conventional signalling at both portals, the tunnel sections will use Siemens' Trainguard Computer Based Train Control (CBTC) system. As with Thales' London Underground sub-surface lines resignalling, radio transmission will be used, in this case with Siemens' Vicos operations control system. In addition to the central tunnels, the CBTC will also be fitted to the eastern extension to Abbey Wood.

On the surface sections, the Great Western main line will have ETCS Level 2, while the Anglia lines with have the Train Protection Warning System (TPWS). Dynamic switchover between the three control systems is planned. Train builder Bombardier has already ordered the module developed by Mors Smitt which can read both ETCS balises and TPWS grids and reconfigure the cab display automatically.

MAIN LINE ETCS

Under the current route modernisation, the Great Western main line is next in line to receive ETCS. As with Thameslink, ETCS Level 2 will be an overlay on the conventional resignalling. Before the 2015 review of Network Rail's enhancements programme, ETCS was due to be commissioned between 2018 and 2020, with colour-light signals removed some time after 2025.

Planned as Network Rail's first signal-free ETCS route was the southern end of the ECML between London and Doncaster. This priority was determined by the need to renew existing signalling equipment installed in the 1980s. Service entry was from 2020.

With ETCS and TMS forming the basis of Network Rail's new Digital Railway (DR) concept, the renewals-led programme has been under scrutiny. DR is based on an economic model with priority determined by the business cases for individual Rail Operating Centre (ROC).

A new ETCS/TMS deployment programme will be needed to make the business cases. This programme will see ETCS and TMS implemented, together with signalling renewals, on a ROC-by-ROC basis. It will inform the industry's Initial Business Plan for the next Control Period (2019-2024).

New signalling installed during major works at Watford Junction at the turn of 2014/15, part of the major Watford area remodelling. The signalling system was commissioned by contractor Siemens and control transferred from Watford Junction power signalbox to Wembley Mainline signalling control centre. **NETWORK RAIL**

TABLE 2: SIGNALLING RENEWALS IN CONTROL PERIOD 5

	2014-15	2015-16	2016-17	2017-18	2018-19	TOTAL
Conventional resignalling (SEU)	1,742	2,769	2,559	1,715	1,048	9,832
ETCS resignalling (SEU)	0	80	115	146	868	1,209

SEU = Signalling Equivalent Unit
Source: Office of Rail and Road

PROCUREMENT

With the placing of the Thameslink contract with Hitachi, the TMS procurement process and the three contracts to develop demonstration suites formally ended. Under the only other contract to be let, Thales is providing basic TMS systems to the Cardiff and Romford ROCs.

At the Cardiff ROC, TMS was to be added to the Newport workstations. Transfer of the existing Upminster Signalling Centre to the new Romford ROC building is now expected by the end of 2016. However control of the rest of the Anglia network is not expected to transfer to Romford until after 2020.

TMS procurement is now an 'open market', according to Network Rail. While new contracts are unlikely in the near future, experienced TMS suppliers who were not included in the initial programme will now be able to bid.

While traffic management on Network Rail is paused, systems are being ordered elsewhere. In 2015, Nexus ordered a new TMS for the Tyne & Wear Metro from DeltaRail. This will provide a digital control system at the Metro control centre which will interface with new train radios, the Positive Train Identification system (which routes trains automatically), and the interlockings. The new system will also enhance customer information on the busiest light rail system in the UK outside London.

According to Nexus, the DeltaRail system was selected for its ease of integration with the existing management systems and the ability to manage operations with the company's flexible workstation environment. Flexible allocation of control between workstations is a feature of DeltaRail's new Scalable Integrated Electronic Control Centre. First commissioned at Marylebone IECC in 2015, IECC Scalable is also being implemented at the TVSC under the GWML resignalling programme.

COMMISSIONING

Meanwhile Network Rail and its contractors are facing challenges with resignalling schemes in Control Period 5. Commissioning of a number of major schemes was awaited, for example Phase 2 of the East Kent Resignalling programme.

This is part of a £149m project covering 33 route miles, including the new station for Rochester, with control transferred from existing boxes to the East Kent Signalling Centre at Gillingham.

Now scheduled for 2016 is the transfer of the area controlled by the Swindon power signalbox on the Great Western main line to the new Thames Valley Signalling Centre (TVSC) at Didcot.

LONDON UNDERGROUND

As London Underground's experience with the Sub-Surface Lines (SSL) resignalling has demonstrated, introducing new signalling and control technology, even when the system is already in service elsewhere, has to be approached with care.

A contract with Thales for the complex network made up of the Circle, District, Metropolitan and Hammersmith & City lines was signed in August 2015. Valued at £760m, what TfL terms 'the main benefits' are due to be delivered by 2022.

Because of the complexity of the track work, Thales' has switched from track-mounted transmission of data to trains to its radio-based system. This will provide 32 trains/hr during peak periods in central London, increasing capacity by an average of a third on the four lines. First to benefit will be the Circle Line in 2021 with additional peak time services. The final improvements will be delivered during 2023, with a further boost to peak and off-peak frequency on the Metropolitan Line. ■

Life expired signals are removed at Stratford, as part of a resignalling project under of the Stafford Area Improvements Programme, carried out by an alliance of Network Rail, VolkerRail, Laing O'Rourke and Atkins. **NETWORK RAIL**

The new signalling centre at Three Bridges is planned eventually to control all the railway from London Victoria and London Bridge stations, along the length of the main line to Brighton and the south coast, and large areas either side in both Sussex and Surrey. **NETWORK RAIL**

HITACHI
Inspire the Next

SIGNALLING INNOVATIONS

Out with the old. Work on signals above the former Up Charing Cross line near London Bridge at Easter 2015, during tack remodelling as part of the Thameslink Programme. **NETWORK RAIL**

SIGNALLING SOLUTIONS BECOMES ALSTOM COMPANY

Balfour Beatty announced the sale of its 50% interest in the joint venture, Signalling Solutions Ltd to Alstom in May 2015, making Alstom the sole owner of the company. It was established in 2007 as a 50:50 joint venture for activity in the UK and Ireland.

Since its formation in 2007 Signalling Solutions Ltd has expanded four-fold to become a market leader in the provision of train control solutions, offering a complete range of services from design to full project delivery.

In March 2015 Network Rail awarded Signalling Solutions a contract worth Euro 54 million to deliver a signalling system for Crossrail East Anglia section. The contract covers the design, manufacture, supply, installation, testing and commissioning of the signalling control system, using Alstom's Smartlock interlocking technology.

The work will cover the route from Pudding Mill Lane Junction near Startford to Shenfield. The project is due for completion in August 2018.

ATKINS INNOVATES

Atkins' signalling team has developed a range of innovations designed to save time on outline design phase and shave 30% off the programme timetable for resignalling schemes.

This includes introduction of a new software package to assess assets along the project route. Working with Gioconda Limited, virtual reality software was created which allows the signal designer at the outline design stage to do everything they could if they were on-site but in a fraction of the time. Signal sighting can usually take up to nine months for a project of the size of East Kent Resignalling Phase 2, covering 33 route miles: but the software solution saw the work completed in just four weeks by one person at their computer without the need to go on-site.

This pioneering solution cut six months from the outline design phase and also made savings in terms of site protection staff while significantly reducing occupational health issues associated with travelling to and from site and working in an operational railway environment. The HD video that was produced was distributed to the design, construction and testing teams so that their site visits could be dramatically reduced too.

The Gioconda software is also being rolled out on resignalling schemes in Feltham and Norwich-Yarmouth/Lowestoft.

WESTRACE IN NORWAY

The introduction of Trackguard Westrace Mk2 concluded Siemens Rail Automation's work on Oslo Metro's Kolsåsbanen extension, providing interlocking and control for the upgrade of Avløs depot. Covering a number of complex interfaces, Siemens' work included the signalling application design, building the data templates, the provision of interlocking and signalling equipment and all installation and testing. The company also provided commissioning support to the client, as well as comprehensive, site-based training for the control centre operators and system maintainers.

Already proven in service on a number of projects worldwide (including the rail depot to the west of Reading station in the UK, the Auckland Project in New Zealand and on metro applications in Singapore), Trackguard Westrace Mk2 provides higher capacity than the Mk1 system and, with a straightforward migration path, its additional processing power delivers faster cycle times. The system architecture also allows for the distribution of input and output modules, remotely from the interlocking, together with a 'hot swap' capability for processor modules. For the maintainer, Trackguard Westrace Mk2 has an enhanced visual diagnostics system for maintenance and fault-reporting and its advanced design means that there is a reduced spares-holding requirement. ■

SIGNALLING RENEWALS AND ENHANCEMENTS

Network Rail awards the majority of signalling renewals and enhancements across England, Scotland and Wales through framework agreements of up to seven years that were established in 2012.

The frameworks were awarded to Siemens Rail Automation (formerly Invensys Rail), Signalling Solutions, and Atkins.

The framework agreements form the backbone of a programme to modernise and maintain safety-critical railway signalling systems and are designed to deliver efficiency savings across the company's signalling work bank over the next seven years, through further reductions in unit costs.

Network Rail said that the length of the agreements, coupled with a visible workload, would provide stability throughout the supply chain, and drive cost savings and innovation.

The frameworks incorporate collaborative working in order to deliver the necessary efficiencies. Integrated design teams and a reduction in man-marking will remove costly duplication of effort, while smoothing of peaks and troughs in Network Rail's work bank will allow better use of suppliers' resources.

The frameworks appointed both a primary and secondary supplier for each area. This provides the flexibility needed to meet the significant increase in volumes required over the life of the framework and provides an alternative in each area if the primary supplier does not have the capacity. The agreements also provide the option to competitively tender up to 20% of the predicted workload each year.

During an engineering possession at London Bridge for the Thameslink Programme, signalling work is completed before a section of realigned track is tamped in May 2015. **NETWORK RAIL**

THALES TPWS MK4
ORDERS TOP 700 SYSTEMS TO BE DELIVERED BY 2018

The latest Mk4 Train Protection & Warning System from global transportation systems provider Thales, has topped the 700 mark with orders of the system to be delivered between now and 2018. Hitachi, Siemens, Vivarail and Stagecoach Supertram are just some of the customers that will experience the benefits of the improved technology that has been rolling out since early 2015.

Thales has been at the forefront of providing and supporting Train Protection and Warning Systems in the UK since 1996, with its solution fitted to around 98% of the rolling stock vehicle cabs in the UK since national roll-out commenced in 2001. Since then there has been a dramatic improvement in network safety as a direct result of the system being in place, mainly through a reduction in the number of Signals Passed at Danger (SPADs).

The TPWS control unit is at the heart of the trainborne equipment, operating the automatic warning system in the event that the overspeed sensor detects that a train is not slowing as it should in response to a red signal. It will also trigger the train stop function and apply the brakes of the train in this scenario, as well as automatically alerting the driver in the cab via the driver machine interface (DMI) that it is doing so.

The TPWS Mk4 is a generic product with configurable interface options developed to support a range of

Thales compact AWS LED Indicator Unit.

Thales TPWS Mk4 Control Panel.

Thales joint TPWS Mk4 Control Unit.

The separate TPWS Mk4 Audio Annunciator.

European Train Control System (ETCS) solutions. With a specific transmission module solution of this version, all the original product features remain, but there is an additional interface with the European Vital Computer (EVC), part of the ETCS.

However, the real benefits of the Mk4 system are that it also provides enhanced fault finding functionality through its library of voice announcements, enabling depot maintenance staff to quickly identify and make right any problem that may be resulting in a fault. This capability greatly reduces fault finding time and allows the vehicle to get back into service sooner. Additionally, a further benefit for retrofit customers is that the peripherals, such as the under-vehicle antennas, don't need to be changed, leaving just the cab equipment to be

upgraded – a far less intrusive and more time efficient enhancement.

Space-saving benefits are also delivered by the Mk4 technology as the new AWS LED Sunflower indicator module that replaces the old AWS alarm and indicator unit is far more compact, taking less space in the driver's desk, and the now separate annunciator unit can be placed elsewhere, releasing even more valuable space. The control unit is also able to display the TPWS functions on the ETCS DMI screen, taking away the need for a control panel or Sunflower indicator module, thus furthering the benefit of reduced space requirements on the driver's cab desk.

Finally, the On-Train Monitoring and Recording (OTMR) unit now connects via a serial interface rather than a parallel one, which enables more data to be sent, while reducing the amount of wiring required. ■

SUPPORT

Thales continues to support its customer base of operators, builders & maintainers, with its Support centre in Crawley offering Evaluation/Repair/Calibration services, First of Class testing services, and a TPWS Technical helpline.
Helpline: 07977 241602
E-mail: *Robert.wheeler@thalesgroup.com*

TPWS has brought a dramatic improvement in network safety. **S. KNAPP**

LIGHT RAIL
AND METRO

IN ASSOCIATION WITH

THALES

Thales has been awarded the vital modernisation contract for the signalling and train control system on the next four London Underground lines. **GEORGE S BLONSKY - CAPA PICTURES, COPYRIGHT THALES**

COLLABORATIVE CAPACITY DELIVERY COMING TO THE NEXT FOUR LINES

Global transportation systems provider Thales was awarded the vital modernisation contract for the signalling and train control system on the next four London Underground 'sub surface' lines by Transport for London in August 2015. This next major phase of the Underground's upgrades will see significant improvements realised, with faster, more frequent and more reliable journeys for millions of passengers who use the Circle, District, Hammersmith & City and Metropolitan lines to move around the capital.

The overall Four Lines Modernisation (4LM) programme, including the introduction of new trains, will boost capacity by an average of a third; a 65% uplift on the Circle and Hammersmith & City lines, 27% on the Metropolitan line and 24% on the District. The main benefits will be delivered by 2022, when the frequency of trains running during peak periods will increase to 32 trains per hour in central London – a train every two minutes - with frequency increases at other times as well.

These improvements follow the successful upgrades of other Tube lines in recent years, including the Jubilee (2012) and Northern Lines (2014), both of which use the Communications based train control (CBTC) technology from Thales. As a result, the Northern Line, one of London's oldest and busiest lines, now operates with an extra 12,500 passengers each hour - a capacity uplift of 20%, with the additional benefit of an 18% reduction in journey times.

The 'One Team' approach established amongst the Jubilee Line upgrade team and further developed by the Northern Line modernisation team (which achieved delivery six months ahead of programme and under budget), continues on 4LM. The Thales and LU project employees are fully committed to the partnership and are co-located, making it easier to work together to resolve issues and challenges more efficiently, and allow the teams to work together in a more effective and productive way.

The Thales contract incorporates automatic train protection, operation, route setting and supervision to replace existing signalling, with moving-block signalling - key to increasing line capacity. The Thales Seltrac (CBTC) system will be introduced first on the Circle Line in 2021, with additional frequent services at peak times. During 2023, the final improvements will be delivered, with a further boost to peak and off-peak frequency on the Metropolitan Line. Confidence that the high level of reliability required can be achieved has been provided by Transport for London's analysis of the Thales automatic train control solution, based on real in-service data gathered from increasing experience of Thales systems. This includes the Jubilee and Northern Lines, together with the Docklands Light Railway, where Seltrac has been installed since 1994 and was upgraded in 2007 to deliver a 50% capacity increase as part of platform extensions and other upgrade work.

The modernisation will lead to the service control staff for all four lines being brought together into a single control facility at Hammersmith with modern facilities and control techniques. These lines are currently controlled by staff at 13 different locations across London.

Patrice Caine, Chairman and Chief Executive Officer of Thales said: 'We are delighted to have been selected by Transport for London and to continue to bring our global expertise in the field of transportation systems to the London Underground. Our technology is in operation on over 80 metro lines in 40 of the world's largest cities, including New York, Dubai, Shanghai and Hong Kong. If the Jubilee and Northern lines' success is any indicator, future travellers on the Circle, District, Hammersmith & City and Metropolitan lines will experience; faster journeys, reduced over-crowding and increased service reliability. Once completed, 60 per cent of the London Underground will have been modernised using Thales signalling technology.'

Once the Four Lines Modernisation is completed, 60 per cent of the London Underground will have been modernised using Thales signalling technology.

A Bombardier 'Flexity 2' tram passes Blackpool Pleasure Beach en route to Starr Gate. **S. KNAPP**

Glasgow's unique Subway reaches its 120th anniversary in 2016. The route has remained unchanged, but the system is now in the middle of a substantial upgrade, with passenger numbers and revenue rising. Meanwhile in Edinburgh, there is again discussion of a tram route extension.

On the eight light rail systems in England, 240 million passenger journeys were made in 201415, a gain of 5.6% over 2013/14. London dominates in passenger journey numbers, with the Docklands Light Railway accounting for 46.0% of the total for England and London Tramlink coming in at 13.5%. Other strong performers were Tyne & Wear Metro at 15.9% and Manchester Metrolink, with its fast growing system, at 13.0%.

The remaining four English systems carried 11.6% of all passengers. Two of

these, Nottingham Express Transit and Midland Metro, have more recently opened extensions, but in 201415 engineering work for extension and improvement seems to have contributed to a decline in usage on Midland Metro and in Sheffield. Blackpool Tramway also saw custom fall away, attributed to new restrictions on non local concessionary passes. The RotherhamSheffield Tram Train project is still some way from commissioning. Assuming at least technical success, where else in Britain might one find possible applications? Not the least of the problems is the mismatch in some cities between light and heavy rail vehicle floor height.

Those travelling the furthest were the riders on Manchester Metrolink and Midland Metro, both 10.5km, with Tyne & Wear Metro at 8.5km. All three have lengthy sections which were formerly part of the national rail system.

The rest, including the DLR, come in at around 5km.

System capacity, as on the national system, can be a major concern. Is the answer longer trains (and all that goes with that), more frequent trains (which may require more sophisticated signalling), or new lines?

LIGHT RAIL AND METRO NETWORKS

KEY STATISTICS	2013/14	2014/15
Passenger journeys (millions)	4.3	4.1
Passenger km (millions)	20.5	18.1
Passenger revenue (£m 2014/15 prices)	6.1	5.6

Blackpool has the sole surviving first generation tramway in Britain: 18km from Starr Gate to the Fleetwood Ferry

terminus. The infrastructure and trams are owned by Blackpool Borough Council, operated under contract by municipally owned Blackpool Transport Services Ltd.

The whole system was closed for total reconstruction, reopening in April 2012. Of the costs of £102m, roughly £33m was required for the trams.

The new Starr Gate depot accommodates the 16 Bombardier 'Flexity 2' trams, each with five articulated sections. They are 32.2m long; each has 74 seats and a standing capacity of 148; they are fully accessible with level access at the 37 stops. Nine 1934 doubledeckers have been upgraded for seasonal operations, and there is also a heritage fleet.

Private/public body Transport for Lancashire (TfL) plans a new tramway branch to Blackpool North station, with a £16m contribution anticipated from the Department for Transport. Light rail conversion of the Blackpool South heavy rail line has been under study.

KEY STATISTICS	2013/14	2014/15
Passenger journeys (millions)	101.6	110.2
Passenger km (millions)	536.9	593.6
Passenger revenue (£m 2014/15 prices)	135.3	143.8

The Docklands Light Railway in London opened in 1987, with 11 two section cars and routes to Tower Gateway, Stratford and Island Gardens. Successive extensions have taken the system length to 38km with 45 stations, with 149 cars built by Bombardier in Belgium or Germany from 1991 onwards. Each is 28.8m long and trains are formed of up to three of the two section articulated vehicles. The main depot is at Beckton, with a subsidiary depot at Poplar.

This 750V DC third rail electrification uses underside contact. The DLR has many grade separated junctions, keeping operational conflicts to the minimum, and automatic operation uses Thales's Seltrac moving block system.

Growth is expected to continue, with the opening of Crossrail causing a temporary fall for about four years before it resumes.

Seven stations have contributed half of this growth: Woolwich Arsenal, Stratford, Bank, Canning Town, Shadwell, Heron Quays and Lewisham. Woolwich accounts for around 10% of DLR journeys.

Since December 2014 the operating concession has been held by Keolis Amey Docklands and continues until April 2021. The company is paid a fixed fee for operation to agreed levels and standards of service, with adjustments for performance. While separate construction / operation concessions for the Woolwich Arsenal line have been terminated by agreement, the Lewisham extension remains in the hands of City Greenwich Lewisham Railway until the contract expires, also in 2021.

Double tracking between Bow Road and Stratford by 2019 will allow frequency to be increased to 20 trains/hr. Some DLR trains are being converted to longitudinal seating to increase capacity and the older fleet of B92 cars is planned to be replaced and the fleet expanded from 2020. A number of service enhancements and station upgrades are planned, particularly to serve Royal Docks development. Custom

House will become a DLR interchange with Crossrail.

The Mayor's 2050 transport 'vision' proposals include replacing the Tower Gateway terminus with a through station on the Bank route.

KEY STATISTICS 2014/15 (10 MONTHS)	
Passenger journeys (millions)	4.1
Passenger km (millions)	1.1
Passenger revenue (£m 2014/15 prices)	6.6

Edinburgh Trams entered public service on 31 May 2014, running the 14km between the Airport, Edinburgh Park, Haymarket, St Andrew Square (for Waverley) and York Place. Endtoend journey time is about 35min.

The much debated overall project costs were £776m, consisting of £440m for infrastructure, £104m for utilities, £65m for the trams and £167m for project management, land, design and legal costs.

The twenty seven 42.8m seven section trams built by CAF in Spain are the longest operating in Britain; they are based at Gogar depot. Ten or so trams, ordered when the system was to be much larger, are surplus to requirements, but their dimensions mean they cannot be used easily on other British systems.

An outline business case was published in June 2015 for a route extension beyond York Place. The destination choices are between Newhaven, Ocean Terminal or the Foot of Leith Walk. Of these, Newhaven looks likely to provide the best benefit:cost ratio. However, there is at this stage no commitment and no funding.

The council has set up a new integrated organisation, Transport for Edinburgh, initially a holding company for the local authority owned operators of Lothian Buses and Edinburgh Trams.

A tram/mainline rail interchange is under construction at Gogar near Edinburgh airport.

KEY STATISTICS	2013/14	2014/15
Passenger journeys (millions)	12.7	13.0
Passenger km (millions)	40.6	41.3
Passenger revenue (£m 2014/15 prices)	16.2	17.8

The Glasgow Subway has 15 stations and runs for 10.6km in a complete circle. A round trip takes 24 minutes to complete and trains

Glasgow Subway modernised Hillhead station: SPT

run every four minutes at peak. It is wholly underground, apart from the depot at Broomloan which is on the surface. Two separate running tunnels (inner and outer circle) are to the restrictive diameter of 3.35 metres, and track gauge is 1,220mm (4ft 0in).

This is a unique combination in global as well as British terms, which requires the design of bespoke rolling stock. The threecar trains are a mere 38.3 metres long.

The Subway opened as a cable hauled system on 14 December 1896. It was electrified in 1935 and was totally refurbished in 1980. It is owned and operated by Strathclyde Passenger Transport (SPT).

The present modernisation covers a number of strategic areas: modernisation of working practices; new smartcard ticketing; new automated trains and signalling; refurbished stations with platform edge doors and improved accessibility; and renewing track and improving the tunnel infrastructure.

The total cost of £288m is being funded with a grant of £246m from Transport Scotland, the balance by SPT. Completion is due in 2018/19. The gains are seen in terms of cost reductions, higher patronage and wider economic benefits.

KEY STATISTICS	2013/14	2014/15
Passenger journeys (millions)	31.2	32.3
Passenger km (millions)	162.4	178.3
Passenger revenue (£m 2014/15 prices)	23.9	24.4

The core of London Tramlink comprises underused or disused heavy rail lines around Croydon which were converted to light rail, with a new fourth line to New Addington.

The core of the system is a oneway street level loop around central Croydon, which gives access to West Croydon rail and bus stations and East Croydon station. The system is 28km long and became fully operational in May 2000. There are 39 stops. Electrification is at 750V DC, fed from 13 substations.

The original fleet consisted of 24 three section trams, each 30.1m long. These are C4000 pairs of articulated cars built by Bombardier in Vienna. An additional six 32.4m long Variobahn trams with five sections have been delivered by Stadler, with a further four following in 2015/16 for the expanded Wimbledon services.

Operation is by Tram Operations Ltd, a First Group subsidiary. In July 2014, TfL triggered a halfway break

HITACHI
Inspire the Next

of interest in a new contract to operate and maintain Metrolink from July 2017. Four operators have been shortlisted to take over Manchester's Metrolink light rail network from 2017.

KeolisAmey, National Express, Transdev and incumbent RATP Dev have all prequalified to bid to operate and maintain the system for 10 years when the current contract ends in July 2017.

In 2014, the Treasury confirmed earnback funding for a new branch from the existing Eccles line to Trafford Centre as part of the devolution deal for Greater Manchester Combined Authority. Completion is planned for 2020. It could later continue to Port Salford.

There is also renewed interest in a Wythenshawe loop, on the Airport line, which could serve the proposed HS2 station near the airport as well as Wythenshawe hospital.

KEY STATISTICS	2013/14	2014/15
Passenger journeys (millions)	4.7	4.4
Passenger km (millions)	49.1	46.1
Passenger revenue (£m 2014/15 prices)	8.1	7.7

Midland Metro's 20.4km Line 1 opened in 1999, mostly over the former Great Western Railway route between Birmingham Snow Hill and Wolverhampton. 2.3km into Wolverhampton is on street. Services are operated for Centro by National Express West Midlands.

A 1.4km extension, constructed by Balfour Beatty, is due to open in December 2015. This runs from Snow Hill via a new £9m viaduct to a terminus in Stephenson Street (outside New Street station) in Birmingham. Four new stops include one to replace the original terminus within Snow Hill station.

A further extension from Stephenson Street to Centenary Square is later to continue to Five Ways and Edgbaston. A short extension is also planned to Wolverhampton main line station. A new Eastside Line 2 is to run to Moor Street, Curzon Street (for HS2) and Digbeth.

A new tram fleet of 21 Urbos3 trams built by CAF is now in service, and there is an option for four more. Extensive depot alterations have been necessary at Wednesbury. The 33m length of the new trams compares with the 24m of the 16 they have replaced. The number of seats remained the same at 52, with much increased

standing capacity, so each can carry around 200 people, rather than the 150 of their predecessors which were all mothballed by August 2015. Electrification is 750V DC overhead.

![NET logo]

KEY STATISTICS	2013/14	2014/15
Passenger journeys (millions)	7.9	8.1
Passenger km (millions)	35.7	43.4
Passenger revenue (£m 2014/15 prices)	8.4	8.8

After the opening of its £570m package of extensions on 25 August 2015, Nottingham Express Transit (NET) consists of three lines.

Line 1 opened in 2004 and runs from Nottingham's main line station to Hucknall, via the city centre. A short branch leads to Phoenix Park. The depot is at Wilkinson Street.

The new Line 2 continues south, bridging the main line and runs 7.6km to Clifton South. Line 3 diverges from Line 2 south of the railway and runs for 9.8km to Toton Lane, about 2km short of the planned HS2 station. The 32km system with 51 stops is more than double the length of the original Line 1.

The original fleet consisted of 15 articulated fivesection vehicles of 33.0m, built in Derby by Bombardier in 2002/03. The advent of Lines 2 and 3 saw a further build of 22 five section low floor Alstom Citadis 302 trams in 2013/14. The total fleet is now 37 strong and cars have around 56 seats. Electrification is at 750V DC.

Line 1 serves five Park & Ride (P&R) sites, at Hucknall, Phoenix Park, Moor Bridge, The Forest and Wilkinson Street. Clifton South on Line 2 is also a P&R site with over 1,000 parking places, while Line 3 has over 1,200 spaces at its Toton Lane terminus. In all, NET serves around 5,400 parking spaces.

Construction funding for Lines 2 and 3 was a grant of £480m by government; separately, Regional Funding Allocations included £7.8m for preparation work. Approval was linked to the introduction of a workplace parking levy.

The PFI concession to finance, build, operate and maintain NET Lines 2 and 3, as well as take over the operation and maintenance of Line 1 for 22 years, was awarded to the Tramlink Nottingham consortium in 2011. This consists of tram builder Alstom, operators Keolis and Wellglade (parent of bus company TrentBarton), Vinci, and Investors OFI InfraVia and Meridiam Infrastructure.

clause in Bombardier's 30year fleet maintenance contract, and brought the work inhouse.

The £30m Wimbledon Tramlink Project will enable a 12 trams/hr service between Wimbledon and Croydon by converting some single track to double and providing a second platform for trams at Wimbledon by 2016. A new loop to the east of central Croydon is planned to allow more trams to run on eastern routes, without reversing at East Croydon or using the congested town centre lines.

Other proposals, up to 2030, include another turning loop west of Croydon, additional trams, a second platform at Elmers End, extensions to South Wimbledon and Sutton, and more doubletracking.

Metrolink

KEY STATISTICS	2013/14	2014/15
Passenger journeys (millions)	29.2	31.2
Passenger km (millions)	303.0	325.9
Passenger revenue (£m 2014/15 prices)	52.7	56.8

Manchester's original Metrolink, completed in 1992, was created by converting the Bury and Altrincham lines to light rail and linking them using citycentre street running.

Transport for Greater Manchester's (TfGM's) system has grown substantially, with the latest section to open from St Werburgh's Road to Manchester Airport on 3 November 2014. It was completed a year ahead of schedule by the MPT consortium (Laing O'Rourke, VolkerRail and Thales), and took the network length to 92km (57 miles). The airport contributed to the cost of this line. The series of network expansions, which saw the addition of routes to AshtonunderLyne, East Didsbury, and Oldham & Rochdale, has resulted in a network roundly three times the extent of the original.

To handle an increased flow of trams through the city centre and help reliability, a 1.6km Second City Crossing is under construction from Deansgate Castlefield via St Peters Square to Victoria station, due to open in 2017.

A new fleet of M5000 'Flexity Swift' trams built in Austria by Bombardier from 2009 runs all services. These are 28.4m sixaxle vehicles in two sections and have a capacity of 200 or so passengers. The order is now for a total of 120 cars, all of which will be in service by the end of 2016. They are housed at Queen's Road and Trafford Bar depots.

The present operator is Metrolink RATP Dev Ltd, whose 10 year concession was sold on by Stagecoach in 2011. TfGM has invited expressions

A Sheffield Supertram at the Cathedral stop. **DEPARTMENT FOR TRANSPORT**

Stagecoach

SUPERTRAM

KEY STATISTICS	2013/14	2014/15
Passenger journeys (millions)	12.6	11.5
Passenger km (millions)	81.5	74.6
Passenger revenue (£m 2014/15 prices)	14.1	12.6

The Supertram network was completed in 1995, with about half of the 29 route km fully segregated, and the rest streetrunning. Geometry is tight, with a minimum horizontal curve radius of 25m and vertical curve of 100m. Maximum gradients are 10%.

Services are operated by Stagecoach from the City Centre to Middlewood in the north with a spur to Meadowhall Interchange. In the south the route is to Halfway, with a spur to Herdings Park.

There are 25 three section Siemens/Duewag cars, each of 34.8m. Vehicles have 88 seats, with space for around 200 standing.

The £60m Tram Train project is to test the operation of specialist tramwaytype vehicles over conventional railway from Rotherham and then continuing on the Sheffield tram network. The trials are being led by South Yorkshire transport executive in conjunction with the Department for Transport, Northern Rail, Network Rail, and Stagecoach Supertram.

From a new terminus at Rotherham Parkgate Retail Park, services will use a heavy rail route towards Sheffield, calling at their own new section of platform at Rotherham Central and joining the Supertram network via a 400 metre link in the Tinsley area at Meadowhall South where there will be a new platform. Network Rail is electrifying its part of the route at 750V DC overhead. Platform height will be 385mm above rail level.

Seven 37.2m Citylink tramtrain vehicles are being built by Vossloh in Valencia, with 750V DC and 25kV AC capability, to accommodate future main line electrification. Three vehicles will provide the basic service, with three to strengthen existing tram services, and one maintenance spare.

Services are now expected to begin in 2017, and the pilot project is to run for two years, with a view to permanent operation.

M METRO

KEY STATISTICS	2013/14	2014/15
Passenger journeys (millions)	35.7	38.1
Passenger km (millions)	295.4	324.8
Passenger revenue (£m 2014/15 prices)	45.9	47.9

Tyne & Wear Metro represents the first real excursion into light rail systems in Britain. Based on the reuse of rundown suburban lines around Newcastle which had once been electrically operated, it linked them through new underground construction in the city centre and a new bridge over the River Tyne.

The initial 56km system opened in stages from 1980 to 1983. Its early popularity can be judged by a high of 59.1m passenger journeys made in 1985. Extensions to Newcastle Airport in 1991 and Sunderland/South Hylton in 2002 produced 78km of route.

The Metro displays elements of light rail, heavy underground metro, and longerdistance urban and interurban operation. There is mixed use with National Rail operators from Pelaw to Sunderland.

A 90 strong fleet of six axle Metrocars was built by MetroCammell in 1980. A refurbishment programme covers 86 cars; each seats 64 and they normally run in pairs. The cars are 27.8m long and the depot is at Gosforth. Electrification is at 1,500V DC overhead.

From a low in 2000/01 of 32.1m passenger journeys, the usage figures for 2014/15 show a welcome improvement to 38.1m.

DB Regio Tyne & Wear won the operating concession which started in 2010 and runs until 2017, extendable to 2019. Nexus Rail, owned by the Passenger Transport Executive, continues to own the Metro and sets fares and services. It pays DB Regio a performance based fee, and has responsibility for infrastructure. Contractingout of operations was a requirement of a £580m government funding package, providing £230m for operating subsidy over nine years from 2010 and £350m for the 11year Metro 'All Change' renewal and modernisation.

In 2014, Nexus launched a major consultation on Metro Strategy 2030. 'Fleet renewal will require major capital investment, and depending on passenger demand and the availability of funding, there may be scope to extend the reach of Metro beyond its current sphere of operation and the boundaries of Tyne & Wear to more fully reflect travel pattern across the wider region.' A wide range of technical options and suitability for various operational scenarios was discussed. The 'core' demand forecast for passenger journeys in 2030 is over 20m more than at present.

THE STOURBRIDGE SHUTTLE

PreMetro Operations Ltd (PMOL) are the service providers of the complete service on the 1.2km Network Rail branch between Stourbridge Junction and Stourbridge Town. With two fourwheeled Parry People Mover railcars, the company styles itself as 'the smallest Train Operating Company in the UK'. PMOL runs the branch for franchise holder London Midland, employs the operating staff and maintains the trains.

This Ultra Light Rail operation commenced in 2009. The Parry People Movers (Class 139) use flywheel stored energy charged by a small Ford engine. The 21seat (and one wheelchair space) vehicles are 8.7m long and weigh a modest 12.5 tonnes. Carrying capacity totals about 60 and they have a maximum speed of 45mph. With a running time of 3min, one train can make six return trips in the hour. Reliability is better than 99% and around 500,000 passengers a year are now carried.

UKTRAM LTD

UKTram Ltd represents the industry in dealings with government and statutory bodies. The aim is the development of a coordinated and structured approach within the industry. Ownership is in equal shares by the Passenger Transport Executive Group, the Confederation of Passenger Transport UK, the Light Rapid Transit Forum and London Tramlink.

Separate groups consider promotion, operation, marketing, standards and heritage issues. Guidance notes provide promoters with practical help in preparing schemes, reducing development costs and making the business case.

UKTram's Low Impact Light Rail scheme, funded by Innovate UK and the DfT, is developing a series of projects to improve the cost effectiveness and reduce the impact of light rail. ∎

HITACHI Inspire the Next

TRANSPORT *for* LONDON

Transport for London (TfL) is a statutory body, under the Greater London Authority Act 1999, which gives the Mayor a general duty to promote and encourage safe, integrated, efficient and economic transport facilities and services to, from and within London.

TfL's role is to implement the Mayor's transport strategy and manage services for which the Mayor is responsible. Currently there are 8.4 million people living in the capital; this is expected to become 10m in the 2030s.

London Underground – nicknamed the Tube though not all its lines are in deep Tube tunnels - is the principal rail operation. In the 2013/14 year, the Underground carried a record 1,305m people, up from 1,265m in 2012/13. That is a far cry from the low of a mere 498m journeys in 1982, three decades ago. Over four million passengers a day is likely to become the norm, which gives an additional urgency to the upgrade programme of replacing life-expired assets with modern technology, which in turn allows capacity to be increased.

TfL receives part of its income in government grant. The Chancellor of the Exchequer confirmed a six-year settlement in 2013. Investment grant of £925m in 2015/16 would rise to £1,007m in 2020/21, with annual borrowing of over £600m for capital investment.

The Mayor committed to efficiencies totalling £9.8bn to 2017/18. He said the grant settlement for 2015-16 represented a reduction of support for TfL of 8.5%.

TFL COMPANIES

Several TfL companies have public transport responsibilities related to rail. London Underground Ltd is responsible for operating the Underground network and serves 270 stations. Docklands Light Railway Ltd owns the land on which the DLR is built and is responsible for the operation of the railway.

Transport Trading Ltd is the holding company for all TfL's operating transport companies, and receives fare revenue. By law, TfL can only carry out certain activities through a limited liability company which is a subsidiary, or which TfL formed alone or with others. Rail for London Ltd (London Rail), Docklands Light Railway Ltd and Crossrail Ltd are three; others include the London Transport Museum.

KEY STATISTICS
LONDON UNDERGROUND

	2013/14	2014/15
Passenger journeys (millions)	1,265	1,365
Passenger km (millions)	10,422	10,847
Passenger revenue (£m 2014/15 prices)	2,287	2,410

SENIOR PERSONNEL
TRANSPORT FOR LONDON

COMMISSIONER Mike Brown (in photo)
MANAGING DIRECTOR, FINANCE Steve Allen
MANAGING DIRECTOR, CROSSRAIL 2 Michele Dix

The 'New Tube for London', being developed by TfL, as visualised by transport design specialists PriestmanGoode. **TFL**

Alstom completed a two-year mid-life refurbishment programme on London Underground's 106 Northern Line trains in April 2015 – here the final train receives a brush up at Morden depot. TfL decided in September 2015 to retain its Northern Line train service contract with Alstom until 2027. **ALSTOM/TFL**

London Underground's Chief Operating Officer is responsible for the running of the Underground and nearly 12,000 operational and support staff.

Line General Managers are responsible for day-to-day management and performance, the Network Services division aims to deliver long-term improvements to the overall operating performance, while Operational Upgrades staff are the Chief Operating Officer's representatives on matters affecting the operational railway. Their task is to ensure that what is delivered is fit for purpose and that he is ready to accept new assets and systems into use.

OBJECTIVES

LU's fundamental objective is to provide a safe and reliable service. This means properly and correctly trained staff, assets that consistently perform well, and an ability to recover swiftly from delays when they do occur.

This results in a number of challenges. These are to deliver a safe service day-in, day-out, irrespective of the reliability of ageing and often obsolete assets, to use the investment programme to make good deficiencies in asset quality, and to build in sufficient new capacity to meet future demand expectations. In addition, customer service standards need to be retained.

Table 1 shows the 15 busiest stations on the system. The figures represent the annual usage during 2014, being the summated totals of entry and exit counts taken on different days throughout the year. Passengers interchanging between lines are excluded.

In this group, Canary Wharf alone has a single Underground line. This station, together with Stratford and Hammersmith, are the only ones featured here which are outside the central area.

Only seven Underground stations were recorded as having an annual entry/exit count of less than one million passengers a year.

This is a story of sustained growth, as Table 2 shows.

PEAK AND OFF PEAK

Table 3 sets out the maximum number of trains needed to maintain the service at various time periods. Noticeable is the varying extent to which the numbers required reduce from the Monday to Friday peak to the midday period. Thus the Bakerloo or the Circle/Hammersmith & City lines, which are largely urban in character, show less change compared with, say, the District or the Metropolitan. Overall, 84% of the trains in service at 09.00 are still running at 12.00.

The Saturday service requires 87%, while Sundays still need as many as 83%.

The time of day or day of the week is thus becoming far less important in terms of service provision, though this does not take direct account of how full those trains are. Even so, fares policies to encourage passengers to travel off peak cannot form much of a solution to system capacity problems.

TRANSFORMATION OF THE TUBE

The key elements of the 'Transforming the Tube' programme are to replace most train fleets, replace signalling assets, reduce the backlog of track investment, renew infrastructure assets, and to upgrade stations. Collectively, this will result in a more reliable system, with additional capacity, featuring the modern features that passengers have come to expect.

By the end of the current programme, the Underground will have delivered up to an additional 30% capacity. Beyond this, there is a continuous requirement to keep assets in good repair.

London Underground has contracted with Otis for procurement and maintenance of new escalators throughout their 30 year life. At least 50 heavy duty metro-type will be installed over the next 10 years, with a further 57 for Crossrail. The whole life cost of a single escalator is around £2.5m.

Balfour Beatty has a £220m contract until 2016 to carry out track renewal work on the Bakerloo, Central and all sub-surface lines. This covers

replacement of ballasted track, points and crossings, all ancillary signalling and drainage works.

SUB-SURFACE LINES

Recent years have seen standardised rolling stock types on the Circle, Hammersmith & City, District and Metropolitan lines. The re-equipping of these, the sub-surface lines, with new 'S-stock' from Bombardier in Derby will be completed during 2016. The result will be a virtually uniform fleet of 191 new air-conditioned walk-through trains, of 8-car sets for the Metropolitan (S8) and 7-car for the rest (S7).

To replace outdate signalling equipment on the sub-surface, a £760m contact has been let to Thales for a radio-based version of the Seltrac control system used on the Jubilee and Northern lines, for completion by 2023. This is to increase line capacities by around one third. One target is 32 trains/hr (tph), each way, the Circle Line.

Other work on the sub-surface railway, which constitutes nearly 40% of the total, has included strengthening power supplies, lengthening platforms, laying new track, and rebuilding rolling stock depots.

NORTHERN TO BATTERSEA

Northern Line Upgrade 1 is now under way. This is a 3.2km tunnelled extension from Kennington to Battersea, with an intermediate station at Nine Elms. It will branch off from the terminal loop beyond the Charing Cross line platforms at Kennington. A Transport & Works Act Order was made in November 2014. Ferrovial Agroman Laing O'Rourke has the design and build contract and opening in 2020 is anticipated. The cost will be around £1bn, funded entirely by developers.

NEW TRAINS

More trains are needed not only for the Northern Line to Battersea (Upgrade 1) but also for increasing the Jubilee Line maximum service frequency from 30tph to 36tph (planned for 2019), and the Northern Line Upgrade 2. This latter will result

TABLE 1: LU STATION USAGE IN MILLIONS – TOP 15 IN 2014

Oxford Circus	98.51m
King's Cross St Pancras	91.98m
Waterloo	91.49m
Victoria	86.23m
London Bridge	74.98m
Liverpool Street	73.66m
Stratford	59.31m
Bank & Monument	52.31m
Canary Wharf	51.81m
Paddington	49.28m
Leicester Square	43.31m
Piccadilly Circus	42.93m
Euston	41.33m
Green Park	39.83m
Hammersmith (both stations)	38.98m
TOTAL, TOP 15 STATIONS, 2013	**935.94M**

(LU annual station usage, entries and exits combined)

TABLE 2: USAGE OF TOP 15 STATIONS, 2010-2014

YEAR	USAGE, MILLIONS	AS INDEX
2010	768.71m	100
2011	821.78m	106.9
2012	851.76m	110.8
2013	881.09m	114.6
2014	935.94m	121.8

HITACHI
Inspire the Next

TABLE 3: UNDERGROUND LINES – TRAINS REQUIRED

LINE	MON-FRI (09.00)	MON-FRI (12.00)	SAT (MAX)	SUN (MAX)
Bakerloo	32	29	29	27
Central	79	66	72	61
Circle/Hammersmith & City	33	32	31	31
District	75	62	64	64
Jubilee	58	48	49	49
Metropolitan	48	36	36	36
Northern	96	80	80	80
Piccadilly	78	68	76	68
Victoria	39	32	32	32
Waterloo & City	5	3	3	no service
Total trains	543	456	472	448
As index	100	84	87	83

* outside autumn 'leaf fall' timetable period

(maximum number of trains required, by line, on Mon-Fri, Sat and Sun: October 2015)

in all trains from Morden running via Bank and all those from Battersea/Kennington via Charing Cross, but retaining the Camden Town junctions. This increases services from 22/26tph to 28/32tph (2021).

It is intended to order 34 trains in late 2016. A further six would be required for Northern Line Upgrade 3, turning it into two fully separated lines, each able to offer between 33 and 36tph. Extensive prior works are needed at Camden Town in particular.

'New Tube for London' – future upgrading of the remaining deep-level Tube lines - has the Piccadilly at the top of the list (replacing '1973 stock'), since it provides the greatest benefits. The Bakerloo (1972 stock) and Central (1992 stock) lines will follow, and the Waterloo & City.

The programme expects to deliver high capacity walk-through trains with air-cooled saloons and capable of fully automatic operation. In prospect is 33-36tph on the Piccadilly, 27tph on the Bakerloo, 33-36tph on the Central and up to 30tph on the Waterloo & City.

These trains will be to a common design, with around 2,500 vehicles needed. Uniform fleets allow trains to be transferred between lines if requirements change over time. A mock up of the New Tube for London, designed by PriestmanGoode, was exhibited in autumn 2014.

STATIONS

A major programme is creating joint stations for the Underground and Crossrail - including Paddington, Bond Street, Tottenham Court Road, Farringdon (already enlarged for Thameslink), Moorgate, Liverpool Street and Whitechapel.

Major works are also under way at several other stations, such as

Victoria, where long standing capacity problems can result in closure of the station at peak times.

More modest works include the installation of CCTV, public address, communications equipment and fire systems, as well as passenger help points, new electronic information displays in ticket halls and on platforms, improved seating and lighting, as well as tactile strips and colour-contrasted handrails for the visually impaired. Platform cooling schemes for the deep Tube lines continue to be tested.

FARES AND TICKETING

The fares system on all TfL services is dominated by the Oyster smartcard. This stores prepaid value which can be used to pay-as-you-go, topped up by the user as necessary with additional payments. Oysters can also be loaded with period Travelcards. Contactless payment bank

cards can now be used for journeys that accept Oyster and have quickly become popular. Cash fares remain available, but are priced to discourage usage.

Use of ticket offices by passengers has fallen steadily, and nearly all are being closed. At stations which see much tourist traffic, Visitor Information Centres are being introduced. Staff remain on hand at entry/exit gates to provide assistance.

All night services were planned for the main sections of five Tube lines on Friday and Saturday nights from September 2015. The proposal was postponed due to lack of agreement with trade unions.

CROXLEY LINK

The Croxley rail link will re-route the double track Watford branch of the Metropolitan over a new viaduct and a station at Cassiobridge, to join the

trackbed of the long disused Croxley Green national railway branch. After calling at another new station at Watford Vicarage Road, trains will join the existing London Overground lines to Watford High Street and Watford Junction.

TfL now has full responsibility for delivering this project. The capital cost is expected to be £284.4m; this compares with an estimate of £116m when the scheme was initiated in 2011. Funding is by DfT (38.6%), TfL (16.4%), Hertfordshire LEP (30.9%), Hertfordshire County Council and Watford Borough Council (14.1%). Any cost over-run will be the responsibility of TfL.

Completion and opening is expected in 2019/20, when the present Watford (Metropolitan) station will close.

BAKERLOO EXTENSION

A proposal to extend the Bakerloo Line southwards would see it run from Elephant & Castle to New Cross Gate in tunnel, routed via either the Old Kent Road or Camberwell, then to Lewisham and over the National Rail surface line to Hayes and/or Beckenham Junction. Bromley town centre is also a possible final destination.

Public consultation in 2014 brought support for the principle of an extension, but different views on the detail. 'If a decision is made to progress the scheme, and the funding secured', says TfL, 'construction could start in 2023 with services running by around 2030'.

LONDON RAIL

Transport for London's London Rail deals with the National Rail network in London. Tasks include overseeing

A London Underground S stock train at Hammersmith. **LONDON UNDERGROUND**

SENIOR PERSONNEL
LONDON OVERGROUND RAIL OPERATIONS

MANAGING DIRECTOR Peter Austin (in photo)
OPERATIONS DIRECTOR Stuart Griffin
FLEET DIRECTOR Peter Daw
CUSTOMER SERVICE DIRECTOR David Wornham

KEY STATISTICS
LONDON OVERGROUND

	2013/14	2014/15
Punctuality (0-5min)	95.8%	95.0%
Passenger journeys (millions)	135.7	140.1
Passenger km (millions)	840.4	863.2
Timetabled train km (millions)	8.1	8.1
Route km operated	124.0	124.0
Number of stations operated	57	57
Number of employees	1,129	1,157

major new rail projects related to London Overground, managing the Overground concession and also the operation of the Docklands Light Railway and of London Tramlink. It also supports and develops Crossrail and Thameslink, and supports Network Rail's contribution to an integrated public transport system.

LONDON OVERGROUND

The London Overground emulates the frequency and service quality of the Underground on a network of improved/extended former National Rail lines, including an orbital route. The operator, London Overground Rail Operations Ltd (LOROL), is a 50/50 consortium of the Mass Transit Railway of Hong Kong and Deutsche Bahn: its concession awarded by TfL has been extended until November 2016. Shortlisted bidders for a new concession from 2016 are Arriva; LoKeGo (joint venture of Keolis and Go-Ahead); Metroline Rail (owned by Singapore transport group ComfortDelGro); and MTR Corporation. TfL controls fares, service levels and procurement of rolling stock.

Because of the Overground's popularity, its Class 378 trains have been extended in 2014-15 from 4-car to 5-car units through new deliveries from Bombardier. A further upgrade to 6 cars and other capacity measures are being considered.

Dual voltage AC/DC electric trains are needed to operate Stratford to Richmond, plus Willesden Junction to Clapham Junction, but DC-only units for all services over the East London line and for Euston to Watford. At present, diesel units operate between Gospel Oak and Barking but the electrification of this line is under way, with electric operation expected by 2018.

From 31 May 2015, services previously operated by Abellio Greater Anglia between Liverpool Street and Enfield Town, Cheshunt (via Seven Sisters) and Chingford, along with Romford-Upminster, become part of the London Overground network.

Stopping services between Liverpool Street and Shenfield switched to operation under TfL Rail branding on the same date, in preparation for introduction of Crossrail services in 2017. They are run by the MTR Corporation company which won the operating concession for Crossrail.

45 new four-car trains will be delivered by Bombardier for West Anglia operations in 2018, though there is an option to increase the number to allow other planned service enhancements. They will be used also on Gospel Oak-Barking and Euston-Watford Junction services. Station capacity enhancement is planned and funded at stations such as West Hampstead, Hackney Central and Dalston Kingsland.

The Mayor and many Greater London Assembly members have argued for the devolution to TfL of decision making and on funding allocations on London's National Rail services. However, London's political boundaries bear very little relationship to railway geography.

The future control of National Rail services elsewhere in what might loosely be called the London area seems most likely to be related to the renewal programme for the existing franchises, or major investments such as Crossrail 2.

BARKING RIVERSIDE

There are plans for the Gospel Oak-Barking service to be extended along the Tilbury line corridor, branching to a terminus at Barking Riverside to serve new housing.

The Mayor has suggested this line could later be extended across the Thames to Thamesmead and to Abbey Wood.

OLD OAK COMMON

The proposed station for High Speed 2 at Old Oak Common will need access to and from local rail services. Besides platforms on the Great Western for Crossrail and perhaps inter-city operations, TfL proposes a new London Overground interchange.

CROSSRAIL 2 AND 3

The proposed Crossrail 2 route would connect destinations across the south east, linking stations in Surrey and Hertfordshire on a general southwest to northeast axis. The current route, now safeguarded, would connect Wimbledon with New Southgate and Tottenham Hale through new tunnels with stations at Tooting Broadway, Clapham Junction, King's Road, Victoria, Tottenham Court Road, Euston St Pancras, Angel, Dalston and Seven Sisters.

Services would continue from Wimbledon on the routes to Epsom, Chessington South, Surbiton and Twickenham using lines presently served by South West Trains, or from Tottenham Hale on the Lea Valley line served by Greater Anglia to Cheshunt and beyond. New Southgate would provide interchange with the Great Northern line.

More detailed engineering work is presently underway. Completion of this £20bn project would not be until the early 2030s.

Crossrail 3 has been sketched out in the Mayor's infrastructure plan for 2050 as an east-west route.

LONDON TRAVELWATCH

London Travelwatch is a statutory consumer body sponsored and funded by the London Assembly. It promotes integrated transport policies and presses for higher standards of quality, performance and accessibility. It also deals with user complaints.

Chief Executive: Janet Cooke. ■

SENIOR PERSONNEL
MTR CROSSRAIL

MANAGING DIRECTOR Steve Murphy (in photo)
TRAIN SERVICE DELIVERY DIRECTOR Andy Boyle
HR AND OPERATIONS DIRECTOR Claire Mann
ENGINEERING DIRECTOR Kev Jones
CONCESSION DIRECTOR Mark Eaton
PROGRAMME DIRECTOR Nigel Holness
CUSTOMER EXPERIENCE DIRECTOR Paul Parsons

A London Overground Class 378 EMU at Stratford. **TONY MILES**

INTO EUROPE

IN ASSOCIATION WITH

CAF

I GROW UP...

...I WON'T BE RAPED, BEATEN OR SCARED

I WILL BE SAFE WITH A HOME AND A FAMILY WHO LOVE ME

Joseph is seven and lives alone on the streets of Nairobi. Every day he fights for his life. Pimps, drug dealers, and thieves abuse him. They take everything he has. His body, his food, his childhood.

We can stop this abuse for good.

If you donate, we can help children like Joseph, tonight, next month, forever.

£16 DOUBLED TO £32 COULD PAY FOR A RESCUE WORKER FOR TWO DAYS

Donate online at **www.ifigrowup.org.uk**   #ifigrowup

Matching your donations with

YOUR DONATION WILL
BE DOUBLED BY THE
UK GOVERNMENT

Fighting for street children

INTO EUROPE

KEITH FENDER, EUROPE EDITOR OF *MODERN RAILWAYS*, REVIEWS DEVELOPMENTS ON THE CONTINENT'S RAILWAYS

Completion of one of the most significant new railway lines in Europe for over a century will take place in 2016, when the 57km long Gotthard base tunnel in Switzerland opens in June for trial running. Full opening in December, it will shorten the distance across the Alps by 31km, offering a nearly level route capable of 250km/hr and reduce passenger journey times by around 50min; Zürich to Milan journey times are expected to reduce to around 3hr for Eurocity trains operated by tilting Pendolino trains.

New open access operator: the first of the MTR Express 'Flirt 3' trains at Gothenburg on 19 April 2015 with a service from Stockholm. **KEITH FENDER**

EUROPEWIDE INFRASTRUCTURE INVESTMENT

The impact of the Gotthard base tunnel will be felt much more widely than in the Swiss Alps. Work to enhance capacity in both Germany and Italy has been underway for many years - with the route from central Germany via Karlsruhe to Basel earmarked for quadrupling. Much of this has been done, but some of the enhancements such as the new Ceneri base tunnel in Switzerland will not be complete until 2020 at earliest.

Elsewhere in Europe, Spanish infrastructure manager ADIF announced early in 2015 it intended to open around 800km of new high speed routes during 2015. The 24.7km Pajares base tunnel will not open until 2016 at earliest, equipped initially only for Iberian broad gauge trains.

In France the eastern extension of LGV Est Européenne is due to open in April 2016, connecting Strasbourg with the existing line, which opened in 2007. In December 2015 the German high speed network grew by 123 km when the new line connecting Erfurt to Halle (Saale) and Leipzig opened: the remainder of the new line connecting Erfurt with Nuremberg opens in 2018. In Zürich the new cross city Durchmesserlinie, part opened in 2014, was completed in October 2015, from December 2015 long distance trains will use the route as well.

MORE EUROPEAN FUNDING

During 2015 the EU Commission allocated nearly Euro 90bn via the Connecting Europe Facility funding programme, Regional Development funding, and the Cohesion Fund available mainly to newer and poorer EU States. This should offer a major boost to the TEN-T programme - a series of prioritised transport corridors, where rail transport is the major beneficiary. The EU Commission estimates the programme will create up to 10 million jobs and grow Europe's GDP by 1.8% by 2030.

The TEN-T programme includes all the major rail projects underway in Europe. Construction continues on many, but some will start commercial operation in 2016, the most important being 'Rail Baltica', the European standard-gauge railway between the Baltic States, connecting Tallinn, Riga, Kaunas and Poland. The first section of standard-gauge from the Polish border to Lithuania's second city Kaunas was used for the first time in August 2015. Through trains between Kaunas and Warsaw should start during 2016.

Other major projects which will be under construction in 2016 include the fixed Fehmarnbelt crossing between Denmark and Germany; the Brenner base tunnel between Austria and Italy; the Semmering base tunnel and Koralm Tunnel / HSL in Austria; the Lyon-Turin high speed line and 57km-long base tunnel between Italy and France; the Ceneri base tunnel in Switzerland; and the Stuttgart 21 and Stuttgart to Ulm high speed projects in Germany.

The first Pesa-built 'Gama' for PKP IC, No SU160 001, arrives in Lublin with a train from southeast Poland on 13 August 2015. **KEITH FENDER**

Leased from new rolling stock leaser ELL (European Locomotive Leasing), Siemens Vectron No 193214 arriving at Hranice na Morave on 11 August 2015 with a Regiojet service from Prague. **KEITH FENDER**

Planning for future new lines funded via the EU programme is underway for the proposed high-speed lines between Dresden and Prague plus Lisbon-Madrid. Planning and construction of new 1,435mm-gauge connections between Barcelona/Valencia and the Portuguese Atlantic port of Sines will begin in 2016. In addition many hundreds of kilometres of main lines will be rebuilt, and some equipped with ETCS in eastern Europe, especially Poland, Romania, Czech Republic and Slovakia.

HIGH SPEED DEVELOPMENTS

New high speed train fleets which started in service during 2015 will expand their coverage in 2016 as more are delivered. The 50 ETR1000 Bombardier/Ansaldo (Hitachi)-built Zefiro high speed trains for Trenitalia will replace older trains operating high speed services on the Turin-Milan-Rome-Naples axis. Currently operating at 300km/hr, approval for 360km/hr operation is expected during 2016. Italian open access high speed operator NTV overcame financial problems and restructured its workforce during 2015 - it too is set on expansion, ordering eight new 250km/hr Pendolino trains from Alstom in late 2015 for delivery in 2017.

During 2015 DB finally started operation of its new Siemens built Velaro-D high speed trains on international services from Germany to Paris: operation to Brussels is expected to begin during 2016. In Turkey the first of 16 similar Velaro trains for national operator TCDD started operation in 2015 - the rest of the fleet, designated HT80000, should be delivered in 2016-2017. Eurostar obtained approval for use of its new Velaro e320 trains in France in late 2015, enabling the trains to start operation between London and Paris.

The French Post Office ended its use of the only high speed freight trains in the world - the postal TGV trains, replaced by a new distribution network that still uses rail.

LONG DISTANCE

Open access competition has spurred innovation for some long distance operators.

In Sweden, MTR subsidiary MTR Express started operation of Stockholm to Gothenburg trains, using a fleet of new Flirt EMUs supplied by Stadler during 2015. MTR is considering additional routes in Sweden and elsewhere for new services. In Austria, open access operator Westbahn ordered a further ten 'Kiss' double deck EMUs from Stadler to expand services from 2017 onwards. In neighbouring Slovakia, Czech operator Regiojet started operating three daily train pairs on the country's main route between Bratislava and Košice, using leased Vectron MS locos built by Siemens. In late 2015, Regiojet threatened to withdraw the services due to what it termed unfair competition from Slovak national operator ZSSK. Regiojet's Czech domestic open access rail services are now running at a profit. Smaller Czech open access operator Leo Express also extended one service into Slovakia to Košice, operating overnight using Stadler built Flirt EMUs. Another international open access operator Thello (joint venture between Trenitalia and French group Transdev) increased services on the Nice to Milan route with three train pairs daily from April 2015.

In Poland plans to part privatise long distance operator PKP Intercity were announced, following from the successful privatisation of several PKP subsidiaries including PKP Cargo. PKP IC has now introduced all 20 of its non-tilting Alstom-built Pendolino EMUs and from December 2015 and during 2016 it plans to introduce 20 Pesa-built 'Dart' 8-car EMUs and 20 Stadler 8-car 'Flirt' EMUs, replacing large numbers of conventional loco operated trains.

In France, long-distance services branded Intercités (also known as the Trains d'Equilibre du Territoire (TET)) seem to be in terminal decline on most routes. A long-awaited report by the Duron Commission set up by the French government offered little respite, or prospect of open tendering or open access type operations in advance of the 2020 deadline envisaged by the EU Commission. Despite orders for some new trains (34 Coradia Liner bi-mode units being delivered by Alstom in 2017), there are plans to liberalise the French long distance coach market, and huge growth has been seen in internet-organised car sharing for intercity journeys in France. These factors are unlikely to assist the long-term future of the TET network and line closures seem likely.

In Germany, passenger data for 2014, issued in 2015, showed overall

public transport usage is the highest ever recorded, but long distance rail traffic was down despite growth in regional and urban rail usage. Long distance coaches, liberalised in 2013, saw passenger numbers double from 8.2m in 2013 to an estimated 19m in 2014. Rather than trim services (as it seems France will do) Germany's main operator DB announced an ambitious multi-year expansion of services, with Intercity services returning to many smaller cities after a two decade absence, and a doubling of frequencies to half hourly on main ICE high speed routes connecting the biggest cities. New trains, in the form of the delayed Bombardier Twindexx double deck Intercity trains (plus new Traxx locos) - now known as IC2 by DB - will enter service in 2016, initially on the Leipzig-Bremen-Norddeich intercity route. More trains, serving more cities directly, and lower advance fares are the main parts of DB's response to coach competition.

Open access competitors for DB in Germany plan to increase services in 2016, with existing (Köln-Hamburg) operator HKX extending some services to and from Frankfurt, meanwhile new entrants derschnellzug and Locomore are both planning to start services from Stuttgart during 2016 to Hamburg/ Aachen and Berlin respectively. In 2015 RDC Deutschland's (the German subsidiary of US rail investor RDC) proposed operation of the car carrying service linking the North German island of Sylt (which only has a rail connection to the rest of Germany) with the mainland was the subject of legal challenges, which appeared to have left both DB and RDC with some but not all paths to operate trains from December 2015.

The Czech government intends to tender some long-distance routes during 2016. Czech Railways received the first of the 14 dual voltage (25kv AC/3kV DC) long distance EMUs on order from Škoda; ten 5-car and four 3-car EMUs are due for delivery in 2016 to replace loco-operated semi fast trains.

REGIONAL SERVICES

National Express, via its German rail subsidiary, won both contracts from an EU wide tender to operate the five route Nuremberg S-Bahn (Stadt Bahn / City Railway) system from December 2018 until December 2030. Assuming legal challenges are overcome in 2016, National Express will order 38 five-car type-7Ev EMUs to be built in the Czech Republic by Škoda. National Express and Abellio shared three major contracts for the new RRX network serving the Ruhr area from 2018 with a fleet of 82 part double deck four-car Desiro HC EMUs, built and maintained by Siemens on behalf of a new local government owned rolling stock company.

During 2015 a wide variety of new EMU and DMU vehicles were delivered for regional operators across Europe, mostly in Germany, Austria, Italy and France. The Bombardier Regio2N semi double deck articulated EMU entered service in several areas of France, while over 100 Alstom-built Regiolis EMUs were introduced in many French regions. In Austria the first of the Siemens Cityjet Desiro-ML EMUs were delivered and in Germany large numbers of new Bombardier Talent 2, Alstom Coradia Continental and Stadler KISS EMUs had been delivered (and, for a change, pre-authorised for use) for new contracts starting in December 2015. In Italy, Alstom-built Jazz EMUs were delivered throughout 2015 as were Pesa-built Swing DMUs.

In Russia, delivery of Desiro-Rus EMUs built entirely in Russia began and Siemens agreed a 40 year maintenance contract for the eventual fleet of 294 trains. Delivery of Stadler Kiss EMUs to Russian operator Aeroexpress was deferred due to the steep decline in the value of the Russian Rouble - some of the trains were quickly re-liveried and sold to Azerbaijan, arriving within weeks of the order in time to operate services during the 2015 European Games held in Baku in May.

Stadler announced the first order for electro-diesel bi-mode versions of its Flirt EMU when five 3-car trains were ordered for services from Turin to Aosta in northwest Italy. Dutch operator NS ordered 58 Flirts for delivery from 2016 without tendering the order, citing an urgent need for new trains! The Luxembourg government approved the purchase of 11 more Kiss EMUs from Stadler to add to the eight in service with CFL since late 2014.

Polish manufacturer Pesa suffered a setback when 12 'Link' DMUs supplied to Netinera for use in Germany were not approved for use and alternate trains sought from Alstom instead. Pesa does still have a substantial contract with DB for Link DMUs for use by DB Regio, the first of these is due to enter service in late 2016.

Cross-border regional services connecting the Czech Republic with neighbouring Poland and Germany were due to be improved in December 2015, with the line between Selb in Bavaria and Cheb in Czech Republic re-opened for the first time in 70 years and a two hourly service provided; another line connecting the Czech Republic with Saxony had re-opened in June 2015, again repairing a gap in the network dating back to WWII. In Poland the longest new railway for several decades opened, serving the airport in Gdansk as part of a major investment in the suburban railways in the Gdynia-Gdansk conurbation.

The long term future of many regional services in Romania were questioned by a government study that suggested several thousand kilometres of the network should be closed; services had been seriously disrupted on many lines when the county's second biggest operator Regiotrans was forced to withdraw its (largely ex SNCF) DMU fleet in March 2015. Services resumed on most lines after several weeks.

MIGRANT CRISIS

From mid 2015 passenger services across Europe were disrupted by huge numbers of migrants attempting to travel from the Middle East to Europe. The civil war in Syria, now in its fourth year has resulted in around 4 million people seeking refuge in neighbouring countries - and many have decided to move to Europe seeking sanctuary or a new life there. Increasing numbers of those seeking to travel led to re-imposition of border controls and removal of services on several international routes such as Munich to Vienna. Railway operations from the Aegean to Calais have been impacted by the growing refugee crisis.

FREIGHT - PRIVATISATION GAINING PACE?

The majority of SNCB Logistics, the freight business of Belgian Railways, was sold to private equity group Argos Soditic during 2015. The new owners announced plans to invest in the launch of new products and services, including quicker direct rail connections such as Swiss Xpress - direct services between Belgium and Switzerland. In Portugal the privatisation of CP Cargas was finalised, with shipping line

Now a more common sight following privatisation of SNCB Logistics. One of its Traxx multi-system locos, No 2817, heads east near Buir in Germany on the line from Aachen to Köln with an eastbound wagonload service on 15 September 2010. **KEITH FENDER**

New Vossloh Tramlink tram in service in Rostock on 21 August 2015. **KEITH FENDER**

Mediterranean Shipping Company (MSC) becoming the new owner. Several governments in eastern Europe have continued their efforts to privatise rail freight companies, with operators in Greece, Croatia and Bulgaria all for sale but little or no progress made.

Recently privatised PKP Cargo started an acquisition programme, buying 49% of Polish domestic open-access operator Pol-Miedź Trans and 80% of AWT, the Czech Republic's second-largest rail freight operator. Significant Polish open access operator Lotos Kolej is to be part sold via a stock market flotation by its owner, oil firm Lotos, during 2016.

German logistics firm Rhenus expanded during 2015 by acquiring the majority of pan EU freight operator Crossrail and 50% of Austrian international operator LTE. In Italy private operator CFI bought fellow Italian operator RailOne making CFI one of the biggest private operators in southern Europe.

The 1,524mm gauge Finnish rail freight market saw its first on-rail competition in 2015: despite the market being formally 'open' since 2007 no competitors to VR had emerged. New private operator Fennia Rail started operations with three CoCo diesel locos built by Czech diesel loco specialist CZ Loko.

In Russia modernisation of Russian Railways' (RZD) loco fleet continued with both new electric and diesel locos delivered, including the first of 68 new CoCo+CoCo 2TE25KM double-unit diesel-electric locos. In response to falling demand for new freight rolling stock (most of which is privately owned), the Russian government instructed RZD to offer lower freight rates for traffic in modern wagons. In Germany DB Schenker is undertaking a programme to replace braking components on over 20,000 wagons to reduce noise from freight trains. Lower track access charges are applied to trains fitted with the new 'whisper brakes'.

LOCO VOLUMES PICK UP

PKP IC will receive the last of ten new diesel locos built by Pesa during 2016 - the Pesa Gama diesel is fitted with a 2,400kW MTU 4000R84 engine and is being used for semi fast passenger trains on non-electrified routes. Bombardier delivered Traxx-ME (Multi Engine) locos to DB and rolling stock company Paribus in Germany, and Vossloh delivered more Euro4000 CoCo diesels to Europorte and other operators in France.

Siemens won orders for its Vectron family of electric locos from leasers - especially MRCE, Railpool and ELL - plus PKP Cargo in Poland. Deliveries of the pre-series 1,524mm-gauge Vectrons for VR in Finland began during 2015. Vectron locos were approved for use in Italy during 2015. Bombardier sold Traxx locos in multiple configurations, including the new diesel engine fitted Traxx Last Mile, to Railpool and other leasing companies.

INDUSTRY EXPANSION AND CONSOLIDATION

During 2015 Alstom became a transport specialist following the sale of most of its power generation sector activities to GE in the USA. Italian train manufacturer Ansaldo Breda became part of Hitachi Europe adding assembly plants in continental Europe to the new one opened in September 2015 in the UK, Hitachi also acquired part of signalling firm Ansaldo STS and launched a tender to buy the remainder of the company.

German rail manufacturer Vossloh announced plans to divest its rail vehicles, locos and traction businesses to focus solely on infrastructure and service activities. The sale of the Valencia loco/vehicle factory to Stadler was announced in late 2015, and sale of the Vossloh Locomotives and Vossloh Electrical (ex Kiepe) businesses is likely during 2016.

Bombardier announced in mid 2015 that a part flotation of its Transportation business was planned to raise funds for investment in Bombardier's civil aircraft programme, in late 2015 this appeared to be on hold after the Quebec Government in Canada (where Bombardier is based) offered to fund investment in the aerospace activity.

LIGHT RAIL AND METRO

In Düsseldorf the new 3.4km cross city underground Wehrhahn Line was delayed - the opening was postponed from 2015 to February 2016. In the southeast corner of Germany the newest tram-train system centred on the Saxon city of Chemnitz was due to begin operation in December 2015, with electro-diesel bi-mode LRVs built by Vossloh taking over some services to non-electrified parts of the region's rail network. Planning has begun for the first Hungarian tram-train system centred on Szeged.

Multiple orders for trams were placed during 2015, amongst the biggest Bombardier won a Euro 562m contract to supply up to 156 low-floor Flexity trams to Vienna. Leipzig tram operator LVB became the third German operator to order Tramino trams from Polish manufacturer Solaris. LVB tendered for up to 41 trams and will initially order five costing Euro 7·7m to replace old Czechoslovak built Tatra T3 vehicles. In Rostock all the old Tatra trams were replaced by new Vossloh built Tramlink LRVs.

As in previous years, new metro construction saw additional lines open in 2015 - the second line of the Warsaw metro, operated by Siemens Inspiro EMUs, opened after delays in March 2015, while in Bulgaria the extension of the Sofia metro to the city's airport opened. In Italy metro extensions, often under construction for several years, opened in Rome and Milan during 2015, with further extensions likely to open in 2016. Work on the ambitious plans for new metro and tram routes around and in Paris has progressed, with construction work starting on the new Metro Line 15. ■

DIRECTORY

THE UK RAIL INDUSTRY IN YOUR HANDS

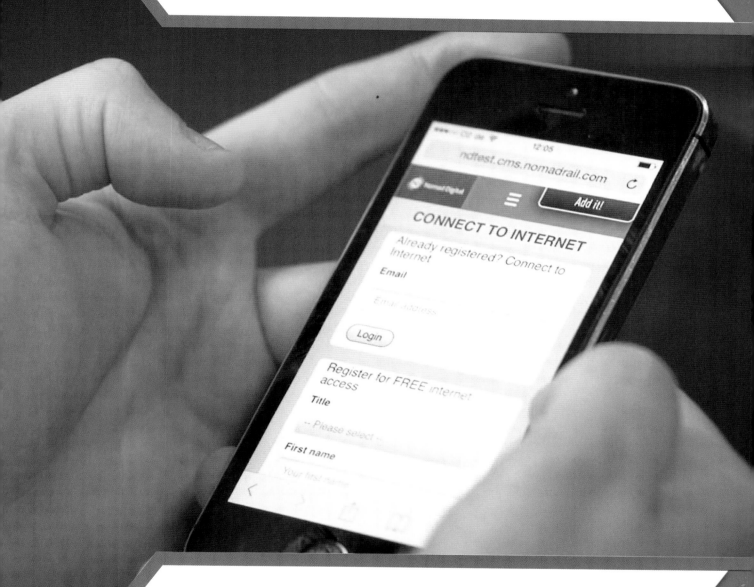

IN ASSOCIATION WITH

1st Solutions
1st Solutions House,
Cwm Cynon Business Park,
Mountain Ash, CF45 4ER
T: 0844 561 7419
F: 0844 561 0933
E: info@1sets.co.uk
W: www.isets.co.uk

1stinrail
1D North Crescent,
Cody Road,
London, E16 4TG
T: 0845 527 8440
F: 0845 527 8441
W: www.1stinrail.co.uk/

360 Vision Technology Ltd
Unit 7, Seymour Court,
Manor Park,
Runcorn,
Cheshire, WA7 1SY
T: 0870 903 3601
F: 0870 903 3602
E: info@ipx360solutions.com
W: www.360visiontechnology.com

3D Laser Mapping
1a Church St,
Bingham,
Nottingham, NG13 8AL
T: 0870 442 9400
F: 0870 121 4605
E: info@3dlasermapping.com
W: www.3dlasermapping.com

3M CPPD
Standard Way,
Northallerton,
N.Yorks, DL6 2XA
T: 01609 780170
F: 01609 780438
W: www.copon.co.uk

3M United Kingdom PLC
3M Centre, Cain Rd,
Bracknell,
Berks, RG12 8HT
T: 01344 858704
E: railsolutions@mmm.com
W: www.3m.co.uk/railsolutions

3Squared
Fountain Precinct,
Balm Green,
Sheffield, S1 2JA
T: 0333 121 3333
E: info@3squared.com
W: www.3squared.com

5PL
T: 01832 734055
E: office@5pl-uk.com
W: www.5pl-uk.com/

A & J Fabtech Limited
700 Bretton Way,
Bretton Park Industrial Estate,
Dewsbury,
West Yorkshire, WF12 9BS
T: 01924439614
E: info@ajfabtech.com
W: www.ajfabtech.com

A Belco Electrical Engineering
Jubilee Ind. Est., Ashington,
Northumberland, NE63 8UG
T: 01670 813275
F: 01670 851141
E: sales@a-belco.co.uk
W: www.a-belco.co.uk

Aardvark Site Investigations Ltd
See Screwfast Foundations Ltd

Aaron Rail
Pepper House, Pepper Road,
Hazel Grove,
Stockport, SK7 5DP
T: 0161 638 3283
E: enquiries@aaronrail.co.uk
W: www.aaronrail.co.uk

AATI Rail Ltd
11 Swinborne Drive,
Springwood Ind. Est,
Braintree, Essex, CM7 2YP
T: 01376 346278
F: 01376 346666
E: info@aati.co.uk
W: www.aati.co.uk

AB Connectors Ltd
Abercynon,
Mountain Ash,
Rhondda Cynon Taff, CF45 4SF
T: 01443 743403
F: 01443 741676
E: sales@ttabconnectors.com
W: www.ttabconnectors.com

AB Hoses & Fittings Ltd
Units 6-7, Warwick St Ind Est.,
Chesterfield,
Derbyshire, S40 2TT
T: 01246 208831
F: 01246 209302
E: info@abhoses.com
W: www.abhoses.com

ABA Surveying
Lansbury Est.,
Lower Guildford St, Knaphill,
Woking, Surrey, GU21 2EP
T: 01483 797111
F: 01483 797211
E: info@abasurveying.co.uk
W: www.abasurveying.co.uk

Abacus Lighting Ltd
Oddicroft Lane,
Sutton-in-Ashfield,
Notts, NG17 5FT
T: 01623 511111
F: 01623 552133
E: sales@abacuslighting.com
W: www.abacuslighting.com

ABB Ltd
Tower Court,
Foleshill Enterprise Park,
Courtaulds Way,
Coventry, CV6 5NX
T: 02476 368500
E: lv.enquiries@gb.abb.com
W: www.abb.com/railway

Abbey Pynford Foundation Systems Ltd
IMEX,
First Floor,
West Wing,
575-599 Maxted Road,
Hemel Hempstead,
Herts, HP2 7DX
T: 0870 085 8400
F: 0870 085 8401
E: info@abbeypynford.co.uk
W: www.abbeypynford.co.uk

Abbeydale Training Ltd
26 Stonewood Grove,
Sheffield, S10 5SS
T: 0114 230 4400
E: abbeydale.training@btconnect.com
W: www.abbeydaletraining.co.uk

Abbott Risk Consulting Ltd
10 Greycoat Place,
London, SW1P 1SB
T: 020 7960 6087
F: 020 7960 6100
E: rail@consultarc.com
W: www.consultarc.com

ABC Electrification
Myson House,
Rugby,
Warks, CV21 3HT
T: 01788 545654
E: jo.evans@chq.alstom.com
W: abcel.co.uk/

Abellio
1 Ely Place,
2nd Floor,
London, EC1N 6RY
T: 020 7430 8270
F: 020 7430 2239
E: info@abellio.com
W: www.abellio.com

Abellio Greater Anglia
11th Floor, One Stratford Place,
Montfitchet Rd,
London, E20 1EJ
T: 020 7904 4031
F: 020 7549 5999
E: contactcentre@abelliogreateranglia.co.uk
W: www.abelliogreateranglia.co.uk

Abellio ScotRail
Customer Relations,
PO Box 7030,
Fort William, PH33 6WX
T: 0344 811 0141
E: customer.relations@scotrail.co.uk
W: www.scotrail.co.uk/

ABET Ltd
70 Roding Rd, London Ind. Park,
London, E6 4LS
T: 020 7473 6910
F: 020 7476 6935
E: sales@abet.ltd.uk
W: www.abetuk.com

Abloy UK
Portobello Works,
School St, Willenhall,
West Midlands, WV13 3PW
T: 01902 364500
F: 01902 364501
E: sales@abloy.co.uk
W: www.abloy.co.uk

ABM Precast Solutions Ltd
Ollerton Rd, Tuxford,
Newark, Notts, NG22 0PQ
T: 01777 872233
F: 01777 872772
E: precast@abmeurope.com
W: www.abmeurope.com/

Abracs Ltd
Abracs House, Unit 3,
George Cayley Drive,
Clifton Moor,
York, YO30 4XE
T: 01904 789997
F: 01904 789996
E: abracs@abracs.com
W: www.abracs.com

ABS Consulting
EQE House,
The Beacons,
Warrington Rd, Birchwood,
Warrington, WA3 6WJ
T: 01925 287300
F: 01925 287301
E: enquiriesuk@absconsulting.com
W: www.eqe.co.uk

Abtus Ltd
Falconer Rd,
Haverhill,
Suffolk, CB9 7XU
T: 01440 702938
F: 01440 702961
E: chris.welsh@abtus.com
W: www.abtus.com

Acal BFI UK Limited
3 The Business Centre,
Molly Millars Lane,
Wokingham, RG41 2EY
T: 01189788878
E: sales-uk@acalbfi.co.uk
W: www.acalbfi.co.uk

Access IS
18 Suttons Business Park,
Reading,
Berks, RG6 1AZ
T: 0118 966 3333
F: 0118 926 7281
E: carol.harraway@access-is.com
W: www.access-is.com

Acetech Personnel Ltd
Pembroke House,
Pegasus Bus. Park,
Castle Donnington,
Derby, DE74 2TZ
T: 01509 676962
F: 01509 676867
E: rail@acetech.co.uk
W: www.acetech.co.uk

Achilles Information Ltd (Link-Up)
30 Park Gate,
Milton Park,
Abingdon,
Oxon, OX14 4SH
T: 01235 820813
F: 01235 838156
E: link-up@achilles.com
W: www.achilles.com

ACIC International Ltd
14 Blacknest Business Park,
Blacknest, Nr Alton,
Hants, GU34 4PX
T: 01420 23930
F: 01420 23921
E: sales@acic.co.uk
W: www.acic.co.uk

ACM Bearings Ltd
Derwent Way,
Wath West Ind Est,
Rotherham, S Yorks, S63 6EX
T: 01709 874951
F: 01709 878818
E: sales@acmbearings.co.uk
W: www.acmbearings.co.uk

ACO Technologies Plc
ACO Business Park,
Hitchin Rd,
Shefford,
Beds, SG17 5TE
T: 01462 816666
F: 01462 815895
E: technologies@aco.co.uk
W: www.aco.co.uk

ACOREL S.A.S
Technopar Pole 2000,
3 Rue Paul Langevin,
07130 St Peray, France
T: 0033 475 405979
F: 0033 475 405771
E: info@acorel.com
W: www.acorel.com

Acorn People
7 York Rd,
Woking,
Surrey, GU22 7XH
T: 01483 654463
F: 01483 723080
E: sarah.griffiths@acornpeople.com
W: www.acornpeople.com

ACT Informatics Ltd
One St Peters Rd,
Maidenhead,
Berks, SL6 1QU
T: 0870 114 9800
F: 0870 114 9801
E: admin@act-consultancy.com

Acumen Design Associates Ltd
1 Sekforde St,
Clerkenwell,
London, EC1R 0BE
T: 020 7107 2900
F: 020 7107 2901
E: info@acumen-da.com
W: www.acumen-da.com

Adaptaflex
Station Rd,
Coleshill,
Birmingham, B46 1HT
T: 01675 468222
F: 01675 464276
E: sales@adaptaflex.com
W: www.adaptaflex.com

ADAS UK Ltd
Woodthorn,
Wergs Rd,
Wolverhampton, WV6 8TQ
T: 01902 754190
E: david.middleditch@adas.co.uk
W: www.adas.co.uk

THE 2016 MODERN RAILWAY DIRECTORY - THE MOST COMPREHENSIVE DIRECTORY OF BUSINESSES INVOLVED IN THE OPERATION OF THE UK RAIL INDUSTRY

KEY TO SYMBOLS

TRAIN OPERATORS
Passenger and Freight Train Operators, TOC Owning Groups, Railway, Metro and Tramway Operators, Rail Tour Operators, Passenger Transport Authorities/Executives, Freight Forwarders/Brokers.

ROLLING STOCK MANUFACTURE, SUPPLY AND DELIVERY
Locomotive, Light Rail, Metro, Carriage and Wagon Manufacture, Locomotive, Wagon and Coaching Stock Hire, Chartering, Rolling Stock Leasing Companies, Rolling Stock Delivery.

INFRASTRUCTURE
Infrastructure Maintenance and Renewal, Lineside Equipment, Construction Projects, Electrification, Electrical Components Misc.,Trackwork, Ground Protection and Safety, Workshop Equipment, Fencing & Security, Lighting (except rolling stock), Platforms, Access Systems, Walkways & Gantries, Cable Management, Power Supply, Carriage Washing, Freight Terminals, Level Crossings and Associated Components, Passenger Information Displays, Signs and Notifications, Car Parking, Cleaning, Weighing & Lifting, Grafitti Removal, Pest Control, Ticketing, CCTV, Public Address, Test Facilities, Fares and Collection. Customer Accessibility, Route Management and Ownership, Noise and Vibration Control.

INFRASTRUCTURE MATERIAL SUPPLIES
Civil Engineering, Projected Developments , Buildings & Building Refurbishment, Plant, Tools, Architects, Surveying, Welding, Paints & Coatings, Clothing & Boots, Chemicals and Lubricants, Scaffolding and Safety Netting., Temporary Bridges, Roads, Buildings and Containers, Flooring.

ON TRACK PLANT & MISCELLANEOUS
On Track Plant Manufacturers, Misc.

ROLLING STOCK MAINTENANCE/PARTS
Locomotive, Carriage and Wagon Maintenance, Component supply, Lighting and Cabling, Decals and Transfers, De-Icing, Sanding, Upholstery, Disposal, Textiles, Fuel Technology, In Train Entertainment, Train Monitoring Systems, Train Branding ,Vinyls and Wraps, Depot Equipment, Weighing & Lifting , Carpeting. & Insulation.

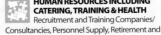

HUMAN RESOURCES INCLUDING CATERING, TRAINING & HEALTH
Recruitment and Training Companies/ Consultancies, Personnel Supply, Retirement and Convalescence, Catering.

SIGNAL & TELECOMMUNICATION
S&T Installation and Equipment, Wireless Technology and Datacoms, Training Simulators.

PROFESSIONAL ADVICE, CONSULTANCY AND SERVICES
Consultants, Legal Services, Economists, Industry Reporting, Insurance, Accreditation & Compliance, Verification & Validation, Assessment, Test & Development, Systems & Software, IT Services, Architects and Design Agencies, Surveying, Data Management, Financial Services, Property, Solutions and Turnkey Providers, Mapping, Vehicle Acceptance, Video & Film Production, Photography, Journey Planning, Conferences & Exhibitions, Specialist Media, Project Management, Marketing, PR & Branding, Weather Forcasting, Simulation, Drugs and Alcohol Testing, Research Organisations, legal and administrative services.

INDUSTRY AND REGULATORY BODIES
Trade Associations, Alliances and Authorities, Advisory Boards, Government Departments, Customer Organisations, Accident Investigators, Campaigning Organisations, Passenger Watchdogs, Trade Unions, Port Authorities and Development Agencies.

ROAD TRANSPORT SERVICES
Conferences Heavy Haulage, Replacement Buses and Vehicle Hire

AECOM

AECOM provide consulting services for transit, intercity passenger rail and long-haul freight rail lines, as well as port cargo and bulk intermodal transfer facilities. We develop projects with a focus on safety, supply chain efficiency, and the long-term operations and maintenance requirements.

Ian Hay, Director and Head of Rail
Transportation
T: +44 (0)141 354 5722
M: +44 (0)7713 887 135
E: ian.hay@aecom.com
aecom.com/transportation

Adeo Construction Consultants
Unit 16, Oakhurst Business Park,
Wilberforce Way,
Southwater,
Horsham, RH13 9RT
T: 01403 821770
F: 01403 733405
E: enquiries@adeo.uk.com
W: www.adeo.uk.com

Adien Ltd
Delta Court, Sky Business Park,
Robin Hood Airport,
Doncaster, DN9 3GB
T: 01302 802200
F: 01302 802201
E: info@adien.com
W: www.adien.com

Adrian Phillips Engineering Ltd
Unit 1, Pontewnydd Ind. Est,
Pontypool,
Torfaen, NP4 6YW
T: 01495 764409
F: 01495 753417
E: info@phillipsengineering.co.uk
W: www.phillipsengineering.co.uk/

ADT Fire & Security
Security House, The Summit,
Hanworth Rd,
Sunbury on Thames, TW16 5DB
T: 01932 743229
F: 01932 743047
W: www.adt.co.uk/

Advance Consultancy Ltd
St Mary's House, Church St,
Uttoxeter, ST14 8AG
T: 01889 561510
F: 01889 561591
E: enquiry@advance-consultancy.com
W: www.advance-consulting.com

Advance Training & Recruitment Services
2nd Floor,
Stamford House,
91 Woodbridge Rd,
Guildford, GU1 4QD
T: 01483 361061
F: 01483 431958
E: info@advance-trs.com
W: www.advance-trs.com

Advanced Handling Ltd
Northfields Ind. Est,
Market Deeping,
Peterborough, PE6 8LD
T: 01778 345365
F: 01778 341654
E: sales@advancedhandling.co.uk
W: www.advancedhandling.co.uk

Advanced Selection Ltd
Cooper House,
The Horsefair, Romsey,
Hants, SO31 8JZ
T: 02380 744455
F: 01794 518549
E: sam@advancedselect.co.uk
W: www.advancedselect.co.uk

Advantage Technical Consulting
See Atkins

Advante Strategic Site Services
4th Floor, Phoenix House,
Christopher Martin Rd,
Basildon, SS14 3HG
T: 01268 280500
F: 01268 293454
E: sales@advante.co.uk
W: www.advante.co.uk

AECOM
AECOM House,
63-77 Victoria St,
St Albans,
Herts, AL1 3ER
T: 0141 354 5722
E: ian.hay@aecom.com
W: www.aecom.com

Aedas Group Ltd
5-8 Hardwick St,
London, EC1R 4RG
T: 020 7837 9789
F: 020 7837 9678
E: london@aedas.com
W: www.aedas.com

AEG Power Solutions Ltd
Vision 25, Innova Park, Electric Ave,
Enfield, Middx, EN3 7GD
T: 01992 719200
F: 01992 702151
E: kevin.pateman@aegps.com
W: www.aegps.com

Aegis Engineering Systems Ltd
29 Brunel Parkway,
Pride Park,
Derby, DE24 8HR
T: 01332 384302
F: 01332 384307
E: info@aegisengineering.co.uk
W: www.aegisengineering.co.uk

AEI Cables Ltd
Durham Rd, Birtley,
Chester-le-Street,
Co. Durham, DH3 2RA
T: 0191 410 3111
F: 0191 410 8312
E: info@aeicables.co.uk
W: www.aeicables.co.uk

Aerco Ltd
16-17 Lawson Hunt Ind. Park,
Broadbridge Heath, Horsham,
W. Sussex, RH12 3JR
T: 01403 260206
F: 01403 259760
M: 07767 002298
E: chenderson@aerco.co.uk
W: www.aerco.co.uk

Aerial Facilities Ltd
Aerial House, Asheridge Rd,
Chesham, Bucks, HP5 2QD
T: 01494 777000
F: 01494 777002
E: sales@aerial.co.uk
W: www.aerialfacilities.com

Aerosystems International
See BAE Systems

AES
The Old Warehouse, Park St,
Worcester, WR5 1AA
T: 01905 363520
E: contact@aesco.co.uk
W: www.aesco.co.uk

Agant Ltd
T: 020 8123 9401
E: contactus@agant.com
W: www.agant.com

AGC AeroComposites Derby
Unit 10a, Sills Rd,
Willow Farm Business Park,
Castle Donington, DE74 2US
T: 01332 818000
F: 01332 818089
E: sales@paulfabs.co.uk
W: www.agcaerocomposites.com

AGD Equipment Ltd
Avonbrook House, 198 Masons Rd,
Stratford Enterprise Park,
Stratford upon Avon,
Warks, CV37 9LQ
T: 01789 292227
F: 01789 268350
E: info@agd-equipment.co.uk
W: www.agd-equipment.co.uk

Aggregate Industries UK Ltd
Bardon Hill, Bardon Hill Quarry,
Coalville, Leics, LE67 1TL
T: 01530 510066
F: 01530 510123
E: corporate.communications@aggregate.com
W: www.aggregate-uk.com

Aggreko UK Ltd
2 Voyager Drive, Cannock, Staffs,
WS11 8XP
T: 08458 247365
F: 01543 437772
E: enquiries@aggreko.co.uk
W: www.aggreko.co.uk

Agility Trains
7th Floor, 40 Holborn Viaduct,
London, EC1N 2PB
T: 020 7970 2700
E: enquiries@agilitytrains.com
W: www.agilitytrains.co.uk

Aikona Management Ltd
Windsor House, Lodge Place,
Sutton, SM1 4AU
T: 020 8770 9393
F: 020 8770 9555
E: training@aikona.com
W: www.aikonatraining.com

Ainscough
Bradley Hall, Bradley Lane, Standish,
Lancs, WN6 0XQ
T: 0800 272 637
F: 01257 473286
E: heavy.cranes@ainscough.co.uk
W: www.ainscough.co.uk

Airex Composite Structures. Airex AG
Park Altenrhein, Altenrhein, 9423,
Switzerland
T: 0071 858 4848
F: 0071858 4858
E: acs.info@airexcomposite structures.com
W: www.airexcomposite structures.com

Airquick (Newark) Ltd
Brunel Business Park,
Jessop Close, Newark,
Notts, NG24 2AG
T: 01636 640480
F: 01636 701216
E: info@airquick.co.uk
W: www.airquick.co.uk

Airtec International Ltd
40 Couper St,
Glasgow, G4 0DL
T: 0141 552 5591
F: 0141 552 5064
E: akilpatrick@airtecintl.co.uk
W: www.airtecinternational.com

AKT II
100 St John Street,
London, EC1M 4EH
T: 020 7250 7777
F: 020 7250 5555
W: www.akt-uk.com/

Alan Dick Communications Ltd
Unit 11, Billet Lane,
Normanby Enterprise Park,
Scunthorpe, DN15 9YH
T: 01724 292200
F: 01724 292556
E: robert.illsley@alandickcomms.com
W: www.alandick.com

Albatros UK
Unit 9, Garamonde Drive,
Clarendon Ind Park, Wymbush,
Milton Keynes, MK8 8DF
T: 01908 305740
F: 01908 577899
E: sales@raildoorsolutions.co.uk
W: www.albatros-uk.co.uk

Alcad
1st Floor, Unit 5,
Astra Centre,
Edinburgh Way, Harlow,
Essex, CM20 2BN
T: 01279 772555
E: carter.sarah@alcad.com
W: www.alcad.com

Alcatel-Lucent
Voyager Place, Shoppenhangers Rd,
Maidenhead, SL5 2PJ
T: 01628 428221
F: 01628 428785
E: olivier.andre@alcatel-lucent.com
W: www.alcatel-lucent.com/railways

Alcoa Fastening Systems (Huck)
Unit 7, Stafford Park 7,
Telford, TF3 3BQ
T: 01952 204603
E: matthew.dowd@alcoa.com
W: www.afsglobal.net

Alcontrol
Units 7&8, Hawarden Business Park,
Manor Rd, Hawarden, Deeside,
Flintshire, CH5 3US
T: 01244 528700
F: 01244 528701
W: www.alcontrol.com

Alere Toxicology
Harbour Quay, 100 Prestons Rd,
London, E14 9PH
T: 020 7712 8000
F: 020 7712 8001
E: sales@medscreen.com
W: www.maritime.aleretoxicology.co.uk

Alfred Bagnall & Sons (North)
6, Manor Lane, Shipley,
West Yorks, BD18 3RD
T: 01274 714800
F: 01274 530171
E: info@bagnalls.co.uk
W: www.bagnalls.co.uk

Alfred Mc Alpine Plc
See Carillion Rail

All Clothing & Protection Ltd
Units 6&7, Manor Park Ind Est,
Station Rd South, Totton,
Hants, SO40 9HP
T: 02380 428003
F: 02380 869333
E: sales@allclothing.co.uk
W: www.allclothing.co.uk

Allan Webb Limited
Bonds Mill, Stonehouse, GL10 3RF
T: 01453824581
E: info@smartditch.co.uk
W: www.allanwebb.co.uk

Allelys Heavy Haulage
The Slough,
Studley,
Warks, B80 7EN
T: 01527 857621
F: 01527 857623
E: robert@allelys.co.uk
W: www.allelys.co.uk

Allen & Douglas Corporate Clothing
See Sartoria Corporatewear

Alliance Rail Holdings
88 The Mount,
York, YO24 1AR
T: 01904 628904
E: info@alliancerail.co.uk
W: www.alliancerail.co.uk

Allies & Morrison
85 Southwark St,
London, SE1 0HX
T: 020 7921 0100
F: 020 7921 0101
E: info@alliesandmorrison.com
W: www.alliesandmorrison.com

Alltask Ltd
Alltask House,
Commissioners Rd,
Rochester, Kent, ME2 4EJ
T: 01634 298000
E: nick.covell@alltask.co.uk
W: www.alltask.co.uk

Alltype Fencing Specialists Ltd
Ye Wentes Wayes, High Rd,
Langdon Hills,
Essex, SS16 6HY
T: 01268 545192
F: 01268 545260
E: sales@alltypefencing.com
W: www.alltypefencing.com

Alonyx Ltd
The Mills, Canal St, Derby, DE1 2RJ
E: alexbrain@alonyx.com
W: www.alonyx.com

Alphatek Hyperformance Coatings Ltd
Head Office & Works, Unit A5,
Cuba Ind. Est, Bolton Rd North,
Ramsbottom, Lancs, BL0 0NE
T: 01706 821021
F: 01706 821023
E: railcoatings@alphatek.co.uk
W: www.alphatek.co.uk

Alstom Transport
PO Box 70,
Newbold Rd, Rugby,
Warks, CV21 2WR
T: 01788 545654
F: 01788 546440
E: jo.doxey@transport.alstom.com
W: www.transport.alstom.com

Altran UK Ltd
2nd Floor Offices,
22 St Lawrence St,
Southgate,
Bath, BA1 1AN
T: 01225 466991
F: 01225 496006
E: info-uk@altran.com
W: www.altran.co.uk

Alucast Ltd
Western Way, Wednesbury, W. Midlands, WS10 7BW
T: 0121 556 6111
F: 0121 556 6111
E: aes@alucast.co.uk
W: www.alucast.co.uk

Aluminium Lighting Company (ALC)
Croeserw Industrial Estate,
Eastern Avenue, Crymmer,
Port Talbot, SA13 3PB
T: 01639852502
E: sales@alulight.co.uk
W: www.aluminium-lighting.com

Aluminium Special Projects Ltd (ASP Group)
Unit 39, Second Ave,
The Pensnett Estate, Kingswinford,
W.Midlands, DY6 7UW
T: 01384 291900
F: 01384 400344
E: david@aspgroup.co.uk
W: www.aspgroup.co.uk

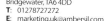

Aluminium Structures
Unit 5a, Aviation Park, Flint Rd,
Saltney Ferry, Chester, CH4 0GZ
T: 01244 531889
F: 01244 539412
E: info@allystructures.co.uk
W: www.allystructures.co.uk

Alvey & Towers
Bythorn House, 8 Nether St, Harby,
Leics, LE14 4BW
T: 01949 861894
E: office@alveyandtowers.com
W: www.alveyandtowers.com

Amalgamated Construction Ltd (AMCO)
Whaley Rd, Barugh,
Barnsley,
S.Yorks, S75 1HT
T: 01226 243413
F: 01226 320202
E: info@amco.co.uk
W: www.amco-construction.co.uk/

Amaro Group Ltd
Corsair Building, Marconi Way,
Rochester, Kent, ME1 2XX
T: 0845 207 1190
E: wendy.meakins@amarogroup.co.uk
W: amarogroup.co.uk/

Ambersil (CRC UK)
Ambersil House, Wylds Road,
Bridgewater, TA6 4DD
T: 01278727272
E: marketing.uk@ambersil.com
W: www.ambersil.com

Ambirad Ltd
Fens Pool Avenue,
Brierley Hill,
West Midlands, DY5 1QA
T: 01384 489700
F: 01384 489707
E: ambiradsales@nordyne.com
W: www.ambirad.co.uk

AMCL Systems Engineering Ltd
221 St John St,
Clerkenwell,
London, EC1V 4LY
T: 020 7688 2828
F: 020 7688 2829
E: sky.crockford@amcl.com
W: www.amcl.com

AMEC Environment & Infrastructure UK
Atlantic House,
Imperial Way,
Reading, RG2 0TP
T: 0800 371733
E: info.ukenvironment@amec.com
W: www.amec-ukenvironment.com/

Ameron UK Ltd
Bankside,
Hull, HU5 1SQ
T: 01482 341441
F: 01482 348350
E: sales.uk@ameron-bv.com
W: www.ameron-bv.com

Amery Construction Ltd
Amery House,
Third Way,
Wembley,
Middx, HA9 0RZ
T: 020 8903 1020
F: 020 8903 1560
E: reception@ameryrail.co.uk
W: www.ameryrail.co.uk

Amey
The Sherard Building,
Edmund Halley Rd,
Oxford, OX4 4DQ
T: 01865 713100
F: 01865 713357
E: ais@amey.co.uk
W: www.amey.co.uk

Amicus
See Unite - The Union

AMOT
Western Way,
Bury St Edmunds,
Suffolk, IP33 3SZ
T: 01284 762222
F: 01284 760256
E: info@amot.com
W: www.amot.com

Amphenol Ltd
Thanet Way, Whitstable,
Kent, CT5 3JF
T: 01227 773200
F: 01227 276571
E: info@amphenol.co.uk
W: www.industrial-
amphenol.com

AMPL Ltd
See Carillion Rail

Amplicon Liveline Ltd
Centenary Industrial Estate,
Hollingdean Rd,
Brighton, BN2 4AW
T: 01273 570220
F: 01273 570215
E: sales@amplicon.com
W: www.amplicon.com

AMT Sybex Ltd
The Spirella Building, Bridge Rd,
Letchworth Garden City,
Herts, SG6 4ET
T: 01462 476400
F: 01462 476401
E: info@amt-sybex.com
W: www.amt-sybex.com

Amtrain Midlands Ltd
A38 Southbound, Fradley,
Lichfield, Staffs, WS13 8RD
T: 01283 792633
F: 01283 792622
E: info@amtrain.co.uk
W: www.amtrain.co.uk

Anchor Systems (Europe) Ltd
Unit 45, Rowfant Business Centre,
Wallage Lane, Rowfant,
West Sussex, RH10 4NQ
T: 01342 719362
F: 01342 719436
E: info@anchorsystems.co.uk
W: www.anchorsystems.co.uk

Anders Elite Ltd
Dashwood House, 69,
Old Broad St,
London, EC2M 1NQ
T: 020 7256 5555
F: 020 7256 9898
E: rail@anderselite.com
W: www.anderselite.com

Anderton Concrete Products Ltd
Units 1 & 2,
Cosgrove Business Park, Soot Hill,
Anderton, Northwich,
Cheshire, CW9 6AA
T: 01606 79436
F: 01606 871590
E: sales@
andertonconcrete.co.uk
W: www.andertonconcrete.co.uk

Andrew Muirhead & Son Ltd
273-289 Dunn St,
Glasgow, G40 3EA
T: 0141 554 3724
F: 0141 554 3724
E: sales@muirhead.co.uk
W: www.muirhead.co.uk

Andrews Signs and Engravers
Units 5 & 6,
Rawcliffe Industrial Estate,
Manor Lane, York, YO30 5XY
T: 01904 658322
E: sales@andrewssigns.co.uk
W: www.railsigns.com

Andromeda Engineering Ltd
5th Floor, Horton House,
Exchange Flags, Liverpool, L2 3PF
T: 0151 244 5472
E: info@andromedauk.com
W: www.andromedauk.com

Andy Waters Rail Safety
Cwm Elan, Cherry Tree Lane,
Botesdale, Diss,
Norfolk, IP22 1DL
T: 01379 898918
M: 07713656355
E: andy@watersrailsafety.co.uk
W: www.watersrailsafety.co.uk/

Angel Trains Limited
123 Victoria St,
London, SW1E 6DE
T: 020 7592 0500
F: 020 7592 0520
E: communications@
angeltrains.co.uk
W: www.angeltrains.co.uk

Anixter
3 Edmund St,
Sheffield, S2 4EB
T: 0114 275 5884
F: 0114 275 7169
E: enquiries@
anixteradhesives.com
W: www.infast.com

Anixter (UK) Ltd
Unit A, The Beacons,
Birchwood Park,
Birchwood, Warrington,
Cheshire, WA3 6GP
T: 0870 242 2822
F: 01925 850292
E: railsales@anixter.com
W: www.anixter.com

Ansaldo STS
8-10 Great George St,
London, SW1P 3EA
T: 020 7340 6100
E: info@ansaldo-sts.com
W: www.ansaldo-sts.com/

Anstee & Ware Ltd - Midlands
Unit 15, Willow Rd,
Trent Lane Industrial Est,
Castle Donington,
Derbys, DE74 2NP
T: 01332 850346
M: 01332 850686
E: john.alden@ansteeware.co.uk
W: www.ansteeware.co.uk

Antagrade Electrical Ltd
Victoria Building, Lewin St,
Middlewich,
Cheshire, CW10 9AT
T: 01606 833299
F: 01606 836959
E: enquiries@antagrade.co.uk
W: www.antagrade.co.uk

Antal International Network
170 Lanark Rd West,
Currie,
Edinburgh, EH14 5NY
T: 0870 428 1745
F: 0870 428 1745
E: edinburgh@antal.com
W: www.antal.com

Antislip Antiwear Treads Int.
See AATI Rail Ltd

AP Diesels Ltd
25a Victoria Street,
Englefield Green,
Egham,
Surrey, TW20 0QY
T: 01784437228
E: office@apdiesels.com
W: www.apdiesels.com

AP Webb Plant Hire Ltd
Common Rd,
Stafford, ST16 3DQ
T: 01785 241335
F: 01785 255178
E: mail@apwebbplanthire.co.uk
W: www.apwebbplanthire.co.uk

APB Group Ltd
Ryandra House,
Ryandra Business Park,
Brookhouse Way,
Cheadle, Stoke-on-Trent,
Staffordshire, ST10 1SR
T: 01538 755377
F: 01538 755010
E: apbgroup@aol.com
W: www.apbgroup.co.uk

APD Communications Ltd
Newlands Centre,
Inglemire Lane,
Hull, HU6 7TQ
T: 01482 808300
F: 01482 803901
E: info@apdcomms.com
W: www.apdcomms.com

Aperio Ltd
See Fugro Aperio Ltd

Apex Cables Ltd
St Johns Rd,
Meadowfield Ind Est,
Durham, DH7 8RJ
T: 0191 378 7908
F: 0191 378 7809
E: apex@apexcables.co.uk
W: www.apexcables.co.uk

Application Solutions (Safety & Security) Ltd
Unit 17, Cliffe Ind. Est,
Lewes,
E Sussex, BN8 6JL
T: 01273 405411
F: 01273 405415
E: contactus@asl-control.co.uk
W: www.asl-control.co.uk

Applied Card Technologies Ltd
Langley Gate,
Kington Langley, Chippenham,
Wilts, SN15 5SE
T: 01249 751200
F: 01249 751201
E: info@weareact.com
W: www.weareact.com

Applied Inspection Ltd
Bridge House, Bond St,
Burton upon Trent, DE14 3RZ
T: 01283 515163
F: 01283 539729
E: ted@appliedinspection.co.uk
W: www.appliedinspection.co.uk

APT Skidata Ltd
The Power House, Chantry Place,
Headstone Lane, Harrow,
Middlesex, HA3 6NY
T: 020 8421 2211
F: 020 8421 3951
E: d.murphy@aptskidata.co.uk
W: www.aptcontrols-group.co.uk

Aqua Fabrications Ltd
Belmont House, Garnett Place,
Skelmersdale, Lancs, WN8 9UB
T: 01695 51933
F: 01695 51891
E: sales@aquafab.co.uk
W: www.aquafab.co.uk

Aquarius Railroad Technologies Ltd
Old Slenningford Farm,
Mickley, Ripon,
N Yorks, HG4 3JB
T: 01765 635021
F: 01765 635022
E: enquiries@railrover.com
W: www.railrover.com

Arbil Lifting Gear
Providence St, Lye,
Stourbridge,
West Midlands, DY9 8HS
T: 01384 424006
F: 01384 898814
E: info@arbil.co.uk
W: www.arbil.co.uk

Arcadia Alive Ltd
Parkfield House, Park St,
Stafford, ST17 4AL
T: 0845 260 0126
F: 01785 214921
E: talk@arcadiaalive.com
W: www.arcadiaalive.com

Arcadis EC Harris
10 Furnival St,
London, EC4A 1YH
T: 020 7216 1000
E: kimberley.richardson@
echarris.com
W: www.arcadis-uk.com

Archer Safety Signs
Unit 6 Daniels Way,
Hucknall,
Nottingham, NG15 7LL
T: 0115 968 1152
F: 0115 976 1110
E: sales@archersafetysigns.co.uk
W: www.archersafetysigns.co.uk

Archerdale Ltd
Hirstwood Works,
Hirstwood Road,
Shipley,
West Yorkshire, BD18 4BU
T: 01274595783
E: sales@archerdale.com
W: www.archerdale.com

Arco Ltd
Head Office, PO Box 21,
Waverley St,
Hull, HU1 2SJ
T: 01482 222522
F: 01482 218536
E: sales@arco.co.uk
W: www.arco.co.uk

Areva Risk Management Consulting Ltd
Suite 7, Hitching Court,
Abingdon Business Park,
Abingdon, Oxon, OX14 1RA
T: 01235 555755
F: 01235 525143
E: abingdon@arevarmc.com
W: www.arevarmc.com

Arlington Fleet Services Ltd
Railway Works, Campbell Rd,
Eastleigh, Hants, SO50 5AD
T: 02380 696789
F: 02380 629118
E: info@arlington-fleet.co.uk
W: www.arlington-fleet.co.uk

ARM Engineering
Langstone Technology Park,
Langstone Rd, Havant,
Hants, PO9 1SA
T: 02392 228283
F: 02036 978 434
E: ibe@arm.co.uk
W: www.arm.co.uk

Arriva CrossCountry
See CrossCountry

Arriva plc
1 Admiral Way,
Doxford International
Business Park,
Sunderland, SR3 3XP
T: 0191 520 4000
F: 0191 520 4001
E: enquiries@arriva.co.uk
W: www.arriva.co.uk

Arriva TrainCare
Crewe Carriage Shed,
Off Weston Road, Crewe,
Cheshire, CW1 6NE
T: 01270 508000
E: info@arrivatc.com
W: www.arrivatc.com

Arriva Trains Wales
St Mary's House, 47 Penarth Rd,
Cardiff, CF10 5DJ
T: 03333 211202
E: customer.relations@
arrivatrainswales.co.uk
W: www.arrivatrainswales.co.uk

Arrow Cleaning & Hygeine Solutions
Rawdon Rd, Moira, Swadlincote,
Derbys, DE12 6DA
T: 01283 221044
F: 01283 225731
E: sales@arrowchem.com
W: www.arrowchem.com

Arrowvale Electronics
Arrow Business Park,
Shawbank Rd, Lakeside, Redditch,
Worcs, B98 8YN
T: 01527 514151
F: 01527 514321
E: sales@arrowvale.co.uk
W: www.arrowvale.co.uk

Artel Rubber Company
Unit 11, Waterloo Park,
Wellington Rd, Bidford on Avon,
Warks, B50 4JH
T: 01789 774099
F: 01789 774599
W: www.artelrubber.com

Artelia International
26-28 Hammersmith Grove,
Hammersmith, London, W6 7HA
T: +44 20 8237 1800
F: +44 20 8237 1810
W: www.uk.arteliagroup.com

Arthur D Little Ltd
Unit 300, Science Park, Milton Rd,
Cambridge, CB4 0XL
T: 01223 427100
F: 01223 427101
E: info.adl@adlittle.com
W: www.adl.com

Arthur Flury AG
Fabrikstrasse 4,
CH-4543 Deitingen,
Switzerland
T: 0041 32613 3366
F: 0041 32613 3368
E: info@aflury.ch
W: www.aflury.ch

Arthur J Gallagher
International Division,
The Walbrook Building,
25 Walbrook,
London, EC4N 8AW
T: +44 (0)20 7204 6000
E: ukenquiries@ajg.com
W: www.ajginternational.com

Arup
The Arup Campus,
Blythe Gate,
Blythe Valley Park,
Solihull,
West Midlands, B90 8AE
T: 0121 213 3412
F: 0121 213 3001
E: rail@arup.com
W: www.arup.com/rail

ASCO Numatics
Pit Hey Place,
West Pimbo,
Skelmersdale,
Lancs, WN8 9PG
T: 01695 713600
F: 01695 713633
E: enquiries.asconumatics.uk@
emerson.com
W: www.asconumatics.eu

Ashley Group
8 Kimpton Link, 40 Kimpton Road,
Sutton, Surrey, SM3 9QP
T: 020 8644 4416
F: 020 8644 4417
E: info@ashleygroup.co.uk
W: www.ashleygroup.co.uk

Ashtead Plant Hire Co Ltd (APlant)
102 Dalton Ave,
Birchwood Park,
Birchwood,
Warrington, WA3 6YE
T: 01925 281000
F: 01925 281001
E: enquiries@aplant.com
W: www.aplant.com

Ashurst
Broadwalk House,
5 Appold St,
London, EC2A 2HA
T: 020 7859 1897
F: 020 7638 1112
E: email@ashurst.com
W: www.ashurst.com

ASL Contracts
See Pitchmastic PmB Ltd

ASLEF
75-77 St Johns St, Clerkenwell,
London, EC1M 4NN
T: 020 7324 2400
F: 020 7490 8697
E: info@aslef.org.uk
W: www.aslef.org.uk

Aspin Foundations Ltd
The Freight Yard, Hemel Station,
London Rd, Hemel Hempstead,
Herts, HP3 9BE
T: 01442 236507
F: 01442 239096
E: info@aspingroup.com
W: www.aspingroup.com

Aspire Rail Consultants
See Keltbray Aspire Rail Ltd

Asset international Structured Solutions
Stephenson St,
Newport, NP19 4XH
T: 01633 637505
F: 01633 290519
E: koh@assetint.co.uk
W: www.assetint.co.uk

Angel Trains Limited
123 Victoria Street
London SW1E 6DE
T: 020 7592 0500
E: communications@angeltrains.co.uk

www.angeltrains.co.uk

angel Trains
Rail People
Real Expertise

Asset-Pro Ltd
Concorde House,
24 Cecil Pashley Way,
Shoreham Airport,
W.Sussex, BN43 5FF
T: 0845 120 2046
F: 01444 448071
E: info@asset-pro.com
W: www.asset-pro.com

Associated British Ports
Aldwych House,
71-91 Aldwych,
London, WC2B 4HN
T: 020 7406 7853
F: 020 7430 1384
E: pr@abports.co.uk
W: www.abports.co.uk

Associated Rewinds (Ireland) Ltd
Tallaght Business Park,
Whitestown,
Dublin 24,
Republic of Ireland
T: 00353 1 452 0033
F: 00353 1 452 0476
E: sales@associatedrewinds.com
W: www.associatedrewinds.com

Associated Train Crew Union
DBH Serviced Business Centres Ltd,
Longfields Court,
Middlewoods Way,
Carlton,
Barnsley, S71 3GN
T: 01226 630166
E: headoffice@atcu.org.uk
W: www.atcu.org.uk

Association for Project Management
150 West Wycombe Rd,
High Wycombe,
Bucks, HP12 3AE
T: 01494 460246
F: 01494 528937
E: info@apm.org.uk
W: www.apm.org.uk

Association of Community Rail Partnerships (ACoRP)
The Old Water Tower,
Huddersfield Railway Station,
St Georges Sq,
Huddersfield, HD1 1JF
T: 01484 548926
F: 01484 481057
E: info@acorp.uk.com
W: www.acorp.uk.com

Association of Railway Training Providers (ARTP)
Kelvin House,
RTC Business Park,
London Rd,
Derby, DE24 8UP
T: 01332 360033
F: 01332 366367
E: info@artp.co.uk
W: www.artp.co.uk

AC:·:RP
Association of Community Rail Partnerships

The Old Water Tower, Huddersfield Railway Station
St. Georges Square, HUDDERSFIELD, HD1 1JF
01484 548926
E: info@acorp.uk.com W: www.acorp.uk.com
'New Life for Local Lines'

Association of Train Operating Companies (ATOC)
2nd Floor, 200 Aldersgate St,
London, EC1A 4HD
T: 020 7841 8062
E: enquiry@atoc.org
W: www.atoc.org

AST Language Services Ltd
Unit 8, Ayr st,
Nottingham, NG7 4FX
T: 0115 970 5633
F: 0845 051 8780
E: office@astls.co.uk
W: www.astlanguage.com

AST Recruitment Ltd
First Floor, Chase House,
Park Plaza, Heath Hayes, Cannock,
Staffs, WS12 2DD
T: 01543 331331
E: iperry@ast-recruit.com
W: www.astrecruitment.co.uk

Astrac Safety Training Solutions Ltd
Unit 2, Victoria Rd, Stoke on Trent,
ST4 2HS
F: 01782 411490
E: train@astractraining.co.uk
W: www.astractraining.com/

At Source QX Ltd
18 Eve St, Louth, Lincs, LN11 0JJ
T: 01507 604322
F: 01507 608513
E: mick@sourceqx.com
W: www.protecthear.co.uk

ATA Rail
See TQ Technical and Vocational

ATEIS UK Ltd
10 Hacche Lane Business Park,
Pathfields, South Molton, Devon,
EX36 3LH
T: 0845 652 1511
F: 0845 652 2527
E: neil.voce@ateis.co.uk
W: www.ateis.co.uk

Athena Project Services
Mill Lane, Barrow on Humber,
North Lincs, DN17 7BD
T: 01469 533333
F: 01469 532233
E: david.tyerman@athenaprojectservices.com
W: www.athenaprojectservices.com

Atkins
Euston Tower, 286 Euston Road,
London, NW1 3AT
T: 020 7121 2000
F: 020 7121 2111
E: rail@atkinsglobal.com
W: www.atkinsglobal.com

ATL Transformers Ltd
Hanson Close, Middleton,
Manchester, M24 2HD
T: 0161 653 0902
F: 0161 653 4744
E: sales@atltransformers.co.uk
W: www.atltransformers.co.uk

Atlantic Design Projects Limited
Branch Hill Mews,
Branch Hill,
London, NW3 7LT
T: 020 7435 1777
E: cg@atlanticdesign.uk.com
W: www.atlanticdesign.uk.com

Atlantis International Ltd
See Karcher Vehicle Wash

Atlas Copco Compressors Ltd
Swallowdale Lane,
Hemel Hempstead,
Herts, HP2 7HA
T: 01442 261201
F: 01442 234791
E: general.enquiries@uk.atlascopco.com
W: www.atlascopco.co.uk

Atlas Rail Components
See AUS Ltd

ATOS Origin
4 Triton Square,
Regents Place,
London, NW1 3HG
T: 020 7830 4447
E: ukwebenquiries@atos.net
W: www.atos.net/transport

Aura Graphics Ltd
Venture House,
2 Arlington Square,
Downshire Way,
Bracknell, RG12 1WA
T: 0845 052 5241
F: 0845 052 5242
E: info@auragraphics.com
W: www.auragraphics.com

AUS Ltd
1 Dearne Park Ind Est,
Park Mill Way,
Clayton West,
Huddersfield, HD8 9XJ
T: 01484 860575
F: 01484 860576
E: sales@aus.co.uk
W: www.aus.co.uk

Austin Reynolds Signs
Augustine House,
Gogmore Lane,
Chertsey,
Surrey, KT16 9AP
T: 01932 568888
F: 01932 566600
E: sales@austinreynolds.co.uk
W: www.austinreynolds.com

Autobuild Ltd
See Pelma Services and Autobuild Ltd

Autoclenz Holdings Plc
See REACT Beyond Cleaning

Autodrain
Wakefield Rd,
Rothwell Haigh,
Leeds, LS26 0SB
T: 0113 205 9332
F: 0113 288 0999
E: mark@autodrain.net
W: www.autodrain.net

Autoglass
1 Priory Business Park,
Cardington,
Bedford, MK44 3US
T: 01234 273636
E: debbie.barnes@autoglass.co.uk
W: www.autoglass.co.uk

Autoglym PSV
Works Road,
Letchworth Garden City,
Herts, SG6 1LU
T: 01462 677766
F: 01462 686565
E: npro@autoglym.com
W: www.autoglymprofessional.com/psv/trains.asp

Autolift GmbH
Mayrwiesstasse 16,
5300 Hallwang,
Salzburg, Austria
T: 0043 662 450588 11
F: 0043 662 450588 18
E: a.foelsce@autolift.info
W: www.autolift.info

Avery Weigh-Tronix
Foundry Lane, Smethwick,
West Midlands, B66 2LP
T: 0845 3070314
F: 0870 9050085
E: info@awtxglobal.com
W: www.awtxglobal.com

Avondale Environmental Services Ltd
Fort Horsted,
Primrose Close,
Chatham,
Kent, ME4 6HZ
T: 01634 823200
F: 01634 844485
E: info@avondaleuk.com
W: www.avondaleuk.com

Axiom Rail
Whieldon Road, Stoke on Trent,
ST4 4HP
T: 07801 905 799
E: sales@axiomrail.com
W: www.axiomrail.com

Axion Technologies
Lokesvej 7-9, 3400 Hillerød,
Denmark
T: 0045 721 93500
F: 0045 721 93501
E: info@axiontech.dk
W: www.axiontech.dk

Axis Communications (UK) Ltd
Ground Floor, Gleneagles,
Belfry Business Park, Colonial Way,
Watford, WD24 4WH
T: 01923 211417
F: 01923 205589
E: pressoffice@axis.com
W: www.axis.com/trains

Axminster Carpets Ltd
Woodmead Rd, Axminster,
Devon, EX13 5PQ
T: 01297 630686
F: 01297 35241
E: sales@axminster-carpets.co.uk
W: www.axminster-carpets.co.uk

Axon Bywater
See Bywater Training Ltd

Azea Ltd
6 Dilton Terrace, Amble, Morpeth,
Northumberland, NE65 0DT
T: 01665 714000
E: info@azea.co.uk
W: www.azea.co.uk

AZPML
55 Curtain Road,
London, EC2A 3PT
T: 020 7033 6480
F: 020 7033 6481
E: lon@azpml.com
W: www.azpml.com

Aztec Chemicals
Gateway,
Crewe, CW1 6YY
T: 01270 655500
F: 01270 655501
E: info@aztecchemicals.com
W: www.aztecchemicals.com

Babcock Rail
Kintail House, 3 Lister Way,
Hamilton International Park,
Blantyre, G72 0FT
T: 01698 203005
F: 01698 203006
E: shona.jamieson@babcock.co.uk
W: www.babcock.co.uk/rail

Experience a First Class service from Europe's leading Transportation Branding supplier
info@auragraphics.com
0845 0525 241
www.auragraphics.com
aura Graphics

Bache Pallets Ltd
Bromley St, Lye,
Stourbridge,
West Midlands, DY9 8HU
T: 01384 897799
F: 01384 891351
E: mike@bache-palletsltd.co.uk
W: www.bache-pallets.co.uk

BAE Systems
Marconi Way, Rochester,
Kent, ME1 2XX
T: 01634 844400
F: 01634 205100
E: john.hawkins@baesystems.com
W: www.baesystems.com/hybridrive

Baker Bellfield Ltd
Display House,
Hortonwood 7, Telford,
Shropshire, TF1 7GP
T: 01952 677411
F: 01952 670188
E: sales@bakerbellfield.co.uk
W: www.bakerbellfield.co.uk

Bakerail Services
4 Green Lane, Hail Weston,
St Neots, Cambs, PE19 5JZ
T: 01480 471349
F: 01480 218044
E: info@bakerailservices.co.uk
W: www.bakerailservices.co.uk

Baldwin & Francis Ltd
President Park, President Way,
Sheffield, S4 7UR
T: 0114 286 6000
F: 0114 286 6059
E: sales@baldwinandfrancis.com
W: www.baldwinandfrancis.com

Balfour Beatty Ground Engineering
Pavilion B,
Ashwood Park,
Ashwood Way,
Basingstoke,
Hants, RG23 8BG
T: 01256 400400
F: 01256 400401
E: neil.beresford@bbge.com
W: www.bbge.com

Balfour Beatty Rail
1st Floor, Kingsgate,
High Street, Redhill,
Surrey, RH1 1SH
T: 01737 785000
F: 01737 785100
E: info@bbrail.com
W: www.bbrail.co.uk/

Balfour Kilpatrick Ltd
Lumina Building,
40 Aislie Rd,
Hillington Park,
Glasgow, G52 4RU
T: 0141 880 2001
F: 0141 880 2201
E: enquiry@balfourkilpatrick.com
W: www.balfourkilpatrick.com

Ballast Tools (UK) Ltd
7 Pure Offices,
Kembrey Park,
Swindon, SN2 8BW
T: 01793 697800
F: 01793 527020
E: sales@btukltd.com
W: www.btukltd.com

Ballyclare Ltd
Union House,
Hempshaw Lane,
Stockport,
Cheshire, SK1 4LG
T: 0161 412 0000
F: 0161 412 0001
E: info@ballyclarelimited.com
W: www.ballyclarelimited.com

BAM Nuttall Ltd
St James House,
Knoll Rd,
Camberley,
Surrey, GU15 3XW
T: 01276 63484
F: 01276 66060
E: headoffice@bamnuttall.co.uk
W: www.bamnuttall.co.uk

Bam Ritchies
Glasgow Rd,
Kilsyth,
Glasgow, G65 9BL
T: 01236 467000
F: 01236 467030
E: ritchies@bamritchies.co.uk
W: www.bamritchies.co.uk

R Bance & Co
Cockrow Hill House,
St Mary's Rd,
Surbiton,
Surrey, KT6 5HE
T: 020 8398 7141
F: 020 8398 4765
E: admin@bance.com
W: www.bance.com

Bank of Scotland Corporate
155 Bishopsgate,
London, EC2M 3YB
T: 020 7012 8001
F: 020 7012 9455
W: www.bankofscotland.co.uk/corporate

Baqus Group Plc
2/3 North Mews,
London, WC1N 2JP
T: 020 7831 1283
F: 020 7242 9512
E: enquiries@baqus.co.uk
W: www.baqus.co.uk

Barcodes For Business Ltd
Buckland House,
56 Packhorse Rd,
Gerrards Cross, SL9 8EF
T: 01753 888833
F: 01753 888834
E: info@barcodesforbusiness.co.uk
W: www.barcodesforbusiness.co.uk

Bardon Aggregates
See Aggregate Industries UK Ltd

Barhale Construction Plc
Unit 3, The Orient Centre,
Greycaine Rd,
Watford,
Herts, WD24 7GP
T: 01923 474500
F: 01923 474501
E: samantha.davis@barhale.co.uk
W: www.barhale.co.uk

Barker Ross Recruitment
24 De Montford St,
Leicester, LE1 7GB
T: 0800 0288 693
F: 0116 2550 811
E: people@barkerross.co.uk
W: www.barkerross.co.uk

Barnbrook Systems Ltd
25 Fareham Park Rd,
Fareham,
Hants, PO15 6LD
T: 01329 847722
F: 01329 844132
E: sales@barnbrook.co.uk
W: www.barnbrook.co.uk

Barnshaw Section Bending Ltd
Tipton Rd, Tividale,
Oldbury,
West Midlands, B69 3HY
T: 0121 557 8261
F: 0121 557 5323
E: tony.farrington@barnshaws.com
W: www.barnshaws.com

Basic Solutions Ltd
See LNT Solutions Ltd

H S Bassett
Coronet Way, Enterprise Park,
Morriston, Swansea, SA6 8RH
T: 01792 790022
F: 01792 790033
E: info@hsbassett.co.uk
W: www.hsbassett.co.uk

BATT Cables
The Belfry,
Fraser Rd, Erith,
Kent, DA8 1QH
T: 01322 441165
F: 01322 443681
E: battindustrial.sales@batt.co.uk
W: www.batt.co.uk

BCM Glass Reinforced Concrete
Unit 22, Civic Industrial Unit,
Whitchurch,
Shropshire, SY13 1TT
T: 01948 665321
F: 01948 666381
E: info@bcmgrc.com
W: www.bcmgrc.com/railhome

Beacon Rail Leasing Ltd
111 Buckingham Palace Road,
Victoria,
London, SW1W 0SR
T: 0207 340 8500
E: rail@beaconrail.com
W: www.beaconrail.com

Beakbane Bellows Ltd
Stourport Rd,
Kidderminster,
Worcs, DY11 7QT
T: 01562 820561
F: 01562 820560
E: info@beakbane.co.uk
W: www.beakbane.co.uk

Bearward Engineering Ltd
Main Road,
Far Cotton,
Northampton,
Northamptonshire
T: 01604 762851
F: 01604 766168
E: sales@bearward.com
W: www.bearward.com

Bechtel Ltd
11 Pilgrim Street,
London, EC4V 6RN
T: 020 7651 7777
F: 020 7651 7972
E: jgreen2@bechtel.com
W: www.bechtel.com

Beck & Pollitzer
Burnham Rd, Dartford,
Kent, DA1 5BD
T: 01322 223494
F: 01322 291859
E: info@beck-pollitzer.com
W: www.beck-pollitzer.com

Becorit GmbH
PO Box 189, Congleton,
Cheshire, CW4 7FB
F: 01270 269000
E: becorit@btinternet.com
W: www.becorit.de

Beejay Rail Ltd
79 Charles St,
Springburn,
Glasgow, G21 2PS
T: 0141 553 1133
F: 0141 552 5333
E: info@beejayrewinds.com
W: www.beejayrewinds.com

Belden Solutions
Suite 13, Styal Rd,
Manchester, M22 5WB
T: 0161 498 3724
F: 0161 498 3762
E: info@belden.com
W: www.belden.com

Bell & Pottinger
E: info@bell-pottinger.com

Bell & Webster Concrete Ltd
Alma Park Rd,
Grantham,
Lincs, NG31 9SE
T: 01476 562277
F: 01476 562944
E: bellandwebster@eleco.com
W: www.bellandwebster.co.uk/

Belmond Luxury Trains
Shackleton House,
4 Battle Bridge Lane,
London, SE1 2HP
T: 020 3117 1300
F: 020 7921 4708
E: help@belmond.com
W: www.belmond.com/luxury-trains

Bender UK Ltd
Low Mill Business Park,
Ulverston,
Cumbria, LA12 9EE
T: 01229 480123
F: 01229 480345
E: info@bender-uk.com
W: www.bender-uk.com

Bentley Systems International Limited
2 Park Place,
Upper Hatch Street,
Dublin 2,
Republic of Ireland
T: (+353) 1 436 4600
W: www.bentley.com

Bentley Systems UK Ltd
North Heath Lane,
Horsham,
W Sussex, RH12 5QE
T: 01403 259511
W: www.bentley.com

Bernstein Ltd
Unit One, Tintagel Way,
Westgate, Aldridge,
West Midlands, WS9 8ER
T: 01922 744999
F: 01922 457555
E: sales@bernstein-ltd.co.uk
W: www.bernstein-ltd.co.uk

Berry Systems
Springvale Business & Industrial Park, Bilston,
Wolverhampton, WV14 0QL
T: 01902 491100
F: 01902 494080
E: sales@berrysystems.co.uk
W: www.berrysystems.co.uk

Best Impressions
15 Starfield Rd, London, W12 9SN
T: 020 8740 6443
F: 020 8740 9134
E: talk2us@best-impressions.co.uk
W: www.best-impressions.co.uk

Bestchart Ltd
6A Mays Yard, Down Rd,
Horndean, Waterlooville,
Hants, PO8 0YP
T: 023 9259 7707
F: 023 9259 1700
E: info@bestchart.co.uk
W: www.bestchart.co.uk

Beta Technology
Barclay Court, Heavens Walk,
Doncaster Carr, Doncaster,
South Yorkshire, DN4 5HZ
T: 01302 322633
E: info@betatechnology.co.uk
W: www.betatechnology.co.uk

BHSF Occupational Health Ltd
Banham Court, Hanbury Rd,
Stoke Prior, Bromsgrove, Worcs,
B60 4JZ
T: 01527 577242
F: 01527 832618
E: admin@bhsfoh.co.uk
W: www.bhsf.co.uk

Bierrum International Ltd
Bierrum House, High St,
Houghton Regis,
Dunstable,
Beds, LU5 5BJ
T: 01582 845745
F: 01582 845746
E: solutions@bierrum.co.uk
W: www.bierrum.co.uk

Bijur Delimon International
Wenta Business Centre,
1 Electric Ave,
Innova Science Park,
Enfield, EN3 7XU
T: 01432 262107
F: 01432 365001
E: chris.riley@bijurdelimon.co.uk
W: www.bijurdelimon.co.uk

Bilfinger
Carl-Reiß-Platz 1-5,
68165 Mannheim,
Germany
T: +49 621 459-0
F: +49 621 459-2366
W: www.bilfinger.com/en/

Bingham Rail
Barrow Rd, Wincobank,
Sheffield, S9 1JZ
T: 0870 774 2341
F: 0870 774 5423
E: info@binghamrail.com
W: www.trainwash.co.uk

Bircham Dyson Bell LLP
50 Broadway,
London, SW1H 0BL
T: 020 7227 7000
F: 020 7222 3480
E: enquirieslondon@bdb-law.co.uk
W: www.bdb-law.co.uk

Birchwood Price Tools
Birch Park, Park Lodge Rd,
Giltbrook, Nottingham, NG16 2AR
T: 0115 938 9000
F: 0115 938 9010
W: www.birdwoodpricetools.com

Birley Manufacturing Ltd
Birley Vale Ave,
Sheffield, S12 2AX
T: 0114 280 3200
F: 0114 280 3201
E: info@birleyml.com
W: www.birleyml.com

Birmingham Centre for Railway Research and Education
University of Birmingham,
Gisbert Kapp Building,
Edgbaston,
Birmingham, B15 2TT
F: 0121 414 4291
E: j.grey@bham.ac.uk
W: www.birmingham.ac.uk/research/activity/railway/index.aspx

Birse Rail Ltd
See Balfour Beatty Rail

Blackpool Transport Services
Rigby Rd,
Blackpool,
Lancs, FY1 5DD
T: 01253 473001
F: 01253 473101
E: enquiries@blackpooltransport.com
W: www.blackpooltransport.com

Blom Aerofilms Ltd
The Astrolabe,
Cheddar Business Park,
Cheddar,
Somerset, BS27 3EB
T: 01934 745820
F: 01934 745825
E: uk.info@blomasa.com
W: www.blomasa.com

Blue I UK Ltd
See Peli Products (UK) Ltd

BMAC Ltd
Units 13-14, Shepley Ind. Est.,
South Shepley Road, Audenshaw,
Manchester, M34 5DW
T: 0161 337 3070
F: 0161 336 5691
E: enquiries@bmac.ltd.uk
W: www.bmac.ltd.uk

BMT Fleet Technology Ltd
12 Little Park Farm Rd, Fareham,
Hants, PO15 7JE
T: 01489 553200
F: 01489 553101
E: uk@fleetech.com
W: www.fleetech.com

BNP Paribas Real Estate
One Redcliff St, Bristol, BS1 6NP
T: 0117 984 8480
F: 0117 984 8401
E: realestate.press@bnpparibas.com
W: www.realestate.bnpparibas.co.uk

BOC
Customer Service Centre,
Priestley Rd, Worsley,
Manchester, M28 2UT
T: 0800 111 333
F: 0800 111 555
E: custserv@boc.com
W: www.bocindustrial.co.uk

Boddingtons Electrical
Prospect House,
Queenborough Lane,
Great Notley,
Essex, CM77 7AG
T: 01376 567490
F: 01376 567495
E: info@boddingtons-electrical.com
W: www.boddingtons-electrical.com/

Boden Rail Engineering
16 Taplin Close,
Holmcroft,
Stafford, ST16 1NW

Bodycote Materials Testing
See Exova (UK) Ltd

Bodyguard Workwear Ltd
Adams St, Birmingham, B7 4LS
T: 0121 380 1308
E: sales@bodyguardworkwear.co.uk
W: www.bodyguardworkwear.co.uk / www.railclothing.co.uk

Bombardier Transportation UK Ltd
Litchurch Lane,
Derby, DE24 8AD
T: 01332 344666
F: 01332 289271
W: www.bombardier.com

Bonar Floors Ltd
See Forbo Flooring Ltd

Bond Insurance Services
Salisbury House, 81 High St,
Potters Bar, Herts, EN6 5AS
T: 01707 291200
F: 01707 291202
E: enquiries@bond-insurance.co.uk
W: www.bond-insurance.co.uk

C F Booth Ltd
Clarence Metal Works, Armer St,
Rotherham, S. Yorks, S60 1AF
T: 01709 559198
F: 01709 561859
E: info@cfbooth.com
W: www.cfbooth.com

Borders Railway Project
Transport Scotland, 7th Floor,
Buchanan House,
58 Port Dundas Rd, Glasgow,
G4 0HS
T: 0141 272 7100
E: bordersrailway@transportscotland.gsi.gov.uk
W: www.bordersrailway.com

Bosch Rexroth Ltd
15 Cromwell Rd, St Neots, Cambs,
PE19 2ES
T: 01480 223253
E: info@boschrexroth.co.uk
W: www.boschrexroth.co.uk

Bosch Security Systems
PO Box 750,
Uxbridge,
Middx, UB9 5ZJ
T: 01895 878094
F: 01895 878098
E: uk.securitysystems@bosch.com
W: www.boschsecurity.co.uk

Boston Marks Insurance Brokers (London) Limited
New Loom House,
101 Back Church Lane,
London, E1 1LU
T: 020 7337 4078
F: 020 7337 4061
E: aorpwood@normanbutcherjonesltd.co.uk
W: www.normanbutcher-jonesltd.co.uk

Bott Ltd
Bude-Stratton Business Park,
Bude,
Cornwall, EX23 8LY
T: 01288 357788
F: 01288 352692
E: i-sales@bottltd.co.uk
W: www.bott-group.com

Bowden Bros Ltd
Brickworks House,
Spook Hill,
North Holmwood,
Dorking, Surrey, RH5 4HR
T: 01306 743355
F: 01306 876768
E: ian.bowden@bowden-bros.com
W: www.bowden-bros.com

Bowen Projects Ltd
1 Portway Close,
Off Torrington Avenue,
Coventry, CV4 9UY
T: 02476 695550
F: 02476 695040
E: s.bowen@bowenprojects.co.uk
W: www.bowenprojects.co.uk

Bowmer & Kirkland Ltd
High Edge Court, Heage, Belper,
Derbys, DE56 2BW
T: 01773 853131
F: 01773 856710
E: general@bandk.co.uk
W: www.bandk.co.uk/

Boxwood Ltd
15 Old Bailey, London, EC4M 7EF
T: 020 3170 7240
F: 020 3170 7241
E: info@boxwood.com
W: www.boxwood.com

Bradgate Containers
Leicester Rd, Shepshed, Leics,
LE12 9EG
T: 01509 508678
F: 01509 504350
E: sales@bradgate.co.uk
W: www.bradgate.co.uk

The Bradley Group
Russell St, Heywood,
Lancs, OL10 1NU
T: 01706 508706
F: 01706 366154
E: pce@johnbradleygroup.co.uk
W: www.johnbradleygroup.co.uk

Branch Line Society
10 Sandringham Rd,
Stoke Gifford,
South Gloucestershire, BS34 8NP
E: tim.wallis@branchline.org.uk
W: www.branchline.org.uk

Brand-Rex Ltd
Speciality Cabling Solutions,
West Bridgewater St,
Leigh,
Lancs, WN7 4HB
T: 01942 265500
F: 01942 265576
E: speciality@brand-rex.com
W: www.brand-rex.com

Bratts Ladders
Abbeyfield Rd,
Lenton Industrial Estate,
Nottingham, NG7 2SZ
T: 0115 986 6851
F: 0115 986 1991
E: stephen@brattsladders.com
W: www.brattsladders.com

Brecknell, Willis & Co Ltd
PO Box 10, Chard,
Somerset, TA20 2DE
T: 01460 260700
F: 01460 66122
E: sales@brecknellwillis.com
W: www.brecknellwillis.com

Brentto Industry
See Onyxrail Ltd

Bridgeway Consulting Ltd
Bridgeway House, Riverside Way,
Nottingham, NG2 1DP
T: 0115 919 1111
F: 0115 919 1112
E: enquiries@bridgeway-consulting.co.uk
W: www.bridgeway-consulting.co.uk

Bright Bond (BAC Group)
Stafford Park 11,
Telford,
Shropshire, TF3 3AY
T: 01952 290321
F: 01952 290325
E: sales@bacgroup.com
W: www.bacgroup.com

Britannia Washing Systems
See Smith Bros & Webb Ltd

Britax PSV Wypers Ltd
Navigation Rd,
Worcester, WR5 3DE
T: 01905 350500
F: 01905 763928
E: enquiries@psv-wypers.com
W: www.psv-wypers.com

British American Railway Services (BARS)
Stanhope Station,
Stanhope,
Bishop Auckland,
Co Durham, DL13 2YS
T: 01388 526203
E: mfairburn@britamrail.com
W: www.rmslocotec.com

British Geological Survey
Kingsley Dunham Centre,
Keyworth,
Nottingham, NG12 5GG
T: 0115 936 3100
F: 0115 936 3200
E: enquiries@bgs.ac.uk
W: www.bgs.ac.uk

British Springs
See GME Springs

British Transport Police (BTP)
25 Camden Rd,
London, NW1 9LN
T: 020 7830 8800
F: 020 7023 6952
E: first_contact@btp.pnn.police.uk
W: www.btp.police.uk

Briton Fabricators Ltd
Fulwood Rd South,
Huthwaite,
Sutton-in-Ashfield,
Notts, NG17 2JW
T: 0115 963 2901
F: 0115 968 0335
E: sales@britonsltd.co.uk
W: www.britonsltd.co.uk

Brixwoth Engineering Co Ltd
Creaton Rd, Brixworth,
Northampton, NN6 9BW
T: 01604 880338
F: 01604 880252
E: sales@benco.co.uk
W: www.benco.co.uk

Broadland Rail
7 York Rd, Woking, Surrey,
GU22 7XH
T: 01483 725999
W: www.broadlandrail.com

Brockhouse Forgings Ltd
Howard St, West Bromwich,
West Midlands, B70 0SN
T: 0121 556 1241
F: 0121 502 3076
W: www.brockhouse.co.uk

Brown & Mason Ltd
Anson House, Schooner Court,
Crossways Business Park, Dartford,
DA2 6QQ
T: 01322 277731
F: 01322 284152
E: b&m@brownandmason.ltd.uk
W: www.brownandmason.com

Browse Bion Architectural Signs
Unit 19/20, Lakeside Park,
Medway City Est, Rochester,
Kent, ME2 4LT
T: 01634 710063
F: 01634 290112
E: sales@browsebion.com
W: www.browsebion.com

BRP Ltd
See Keltbray

Brush Barclay
Caledonia Works,
West Langlands St,
Kilmarnock, KA1 2QD
T: 01563 523573
F: 01563 541076
E: sales@brushtraction.com
W: www.brushtraction.com

Brush Traction
PO Box 17,
Falcon Works,
Meadow Lane,
Loughborough,
Leics, LE11 1HS
T: 01302 340700
F: 01302 790058
E: sales@brushtraction.com
W: www.brushtraction.com

Brush Transformers Ltd
Falcon Works,
Loughborough, LE11 1EX
T: 01509 611511
E: salesuk@brush.eu
W: www.brush.eu/en/38/home/products/transformers

Bruton Knowles
Greybrook House,
28 Brook St,
London, W1K 5DH
T: 0845 200 6489
F: 020 7499 8435
E: patrick.downes@brutonknowles.co.uk
W: www.brutonknowles.co.uk

Bryn Thomas Cranes Ltd
421 Chester Rd, Flint, CH6 5SE
T: 01352 733984
F: 01352 733990
E: dylan.thomas@brynthomascranes.com
W: www.brynthomascranes.com

BSP Consulting
12 Oxford St,
Nottingham, NG1 5BG
T: 0115 840 2227
F: 0115 840 2228
E: info@bsp-consulting.co.uk
W: www.bsp-consulting.co.uk

BTMU Capital Corporation
See Beacon Rail Leasing Ltd

BTRoS Interiors & Cabling
Litchurch Lane,
Derby,
Derbyshire, DE24 8AD
T: 01332 257 500
E: bdm@btros.co.uk
W: www.btros.co.uk

C Buchanan
See SKM Colin Buchanan

Buck and Hickman
Siskin Parkway East,
Middlemarch Business Park,
Coventry, CV3 4FJ
T: 02476 306444
F: 02476 514214
E: enquiries@buckandhickman.com
W: www.buckandhickman.com

Buckingham Group Contracting Ltd
Silverstone Rd,
Stowe,
Bucks, MK18 5LJ
T: 01280 823355
F: 01280 812830
E: mail@\
Buckinghamgroup.co.uk
W: www.buckinghamgroup.co.uk

Buildbase
Gemini One,
5520 Oxford Business Park,
Cowley,
Oxford, OX4 2LL
F: 01865 871700
E: tony.newcombe@buildbase.co.uk

Building Business Bridges UK Ltd
B4 Ashville Centre,
Hampton Park, Melksham,
Wilts, SN12 6ZE
T: 01225 707021
F: 01225 709361
E: hello@bbbuk.co.uk
W: www.bbbuk.co.uk

Bupa – Health Care Service Delivery
Battle Bridge House,
300 Grays Inn Rd,
London, WC1X 8DU
T: 020 7800 6459/ 0845 600 3476
F: 0207 800 6461
E: lampkine@bupa.com
W: www.bupa.co.uk/business/large-business/occupational-health/railways

Bureau Veritas Weeks
Tower Bridge Court,
224-226 Tower Bridge Rd,
London, SE1 2TX
T: 020 7550 8900
F: 020 7403 1590
E: transport.logistics@bureauveritas.com
W: www.bureauveritas.com

Burges Salmon LLP
Narrow Quay House,
Narrow Quay, Bristol, BS1 4AH
T: 0117 939 2000
F: 0117 902 4400
E: email@burges-salmon.com
W: www.burges-salmon.com

Burns Carlton Plc
Simpson House,
Windsor Court,
Clarence Drive,
Harrogate, HG1 2PE
T: 01423 792000
F: 01423 792001
E: contactus@burnscarlton.com
W: www.burnscarlton.com

Butler & Young (BYL) Ltd
Unit 3-4 Jansel House,
Hitchin Road,
Luton, LU2 7XH
T: 01582 404113
F: 01582 483420
E: debbie.clark@byl.co.uk
W: www.byl.co.uk

M Buttkereit Ltd
Unit 2, Britannia Rd Ind. Estate,
Sale,
Cheshire, M33 2AA
T: 0161 969 5418
F: 0161 969 5419
E: sales@buttkereit.co.uk
W: www.buttkereit.co.uk

Bywater Training Ltd
3 Furtho Manor,
Northampton Rd,
Old Stratford, MK19 6NR
T: 01908 543900
F: 01908 543999
E: sales@bywatertraining.co.uk
W: www.bywatertraining.co.uk

C & S Equipment Ltd
15 Wingbury Courtyard,
Leighton Rd,
Wingrave,
Bucks, HP22 4LW
T: 01296 688500
F: 0843 504 4012
M: 07768 366391
E: info@candsequipment.co.uk
W: www.candsequipment.co.uk

C A P Productions Ltd
The Crescent,
Hockley,
Birmingham, B18 5NL
T: 0121 554 9811
F: 0121 554 3791
E: sales@capproductions.co.uk
W: www.capproductions.co.uk

C P Plus Ltd
10 Flask Walk,
Camden,
London, NW3 1HE
T: 020 7431 4001
F: 020 7435 3280
E: info@cp-plus.co.uk
W: www.cp-plus.co.uk

C2C Rail Ltd
2nd Floor,
Cutlers Court,
115 Houndsditch,
London, EC3A 7BR
T: 020 7444 1800
F: 020 7444 1803
E: c2c.customerrelations@nationalexpress.com
W: www.c2c-online.co.uk

C2e Consulting
Ludlow House, The Avenue,
Stratford upon Avon,
Warks, CV37 0RH
E: ed.sharman@c2econsulting.co.uk
W: www.c2econsulting.co.uk

C3S Projects
Canal Mills, Elland Bridge,
Elland, Halifax, HX5 0SQ
T: 01422 313800
M: 01422 313801
E: info@c3s.com
W: www.c3s.com

Cable & Wireless UK
Lakeside House, Cain Rd,
Bracknell, Berks, RG12 1XL
T: 01908 845000
F: 01344 713961
E: companysecretary@cwc.com
W: www.cwc.com

Cable Detection Ltd
Unit 1, Blythe Park,
Sandon Rd,
Cresswell,
Stoke on Trent, ST11 9RD
T: 01782 384630
F: 01782 388048
W: www.cabledetection.co.uk

Cable Management Products Ltd - Thomas & Betts Ltd
CMG House,
Station Rd,
Coleshill,
Birmingham, B46 1HT
T: 01675 468 200
F: 01675 464930
E: info@cm-products.com
W: www.cm-products.com

Cablecraft Ltd
Cablecraft House,
Unit 3,
Circle Business Centre,
Blackburn Rd,
Houghton Regis,
Beds, LU5 5DD
T: 01582 606033
F: 01582 606063
E: claire@cablecraft.co.uk
W: www.cablecraft-rail.co.uk

Cabletec ICS Ltd
Sunnyside Rd,
Weston Super Mare, BS23 3PZ
T: 01934 424900
F: 01934 636632
E: sales@cabletec.com
W: www.cabletec.com

CAF
See Construcciones y Auxiliar de Ferrocarriles SA (CAF)

Calco Services Ltd
Melrose House,
42 Dingwall Rd,
Croydon, CR0 2NE
T: 020 8655 1600
F: 020 8655 1588
E: careers@calco.co.uk
W: www.calco.co.uk

Calmet Laboratory Services
Hampton House,
1 Vicarage Rd,
Hampton Wick,
Kingston upon Thames, KT1 4EB
T: 0845 658 0770
F: 020 8614 8048
E: sales@lazgill.co.uk
W: www.calmet.co.uk

Camira Fabrics Ltd
The Watermill,
Wheatley Park, Mirfield,
West Yorks, WF14 8HE
T: 01924 490591
F: 01924 495605
E: info@camirafabrics.com
W: www.camirafabrics.com/transport

Camlin Rail
31 Ferguson Drive,
Knockmore Hill Ind. Park,
Lisburn, BT28 2EX,
Northern Ireland
T: 028 9262 6982
E: mail@camlinrail.com
W: www.camlingroup.com

Campaign for Better Transport
16 Waterside,
44-48 Wharf Rd,
London, N1 7UX
T: 020 7566 6480
E: info@bettertransport.org.uk
W: www.bettertransport.org.uk

CAN Geotechnical
Smeckley Wood Close,
Chesterfield Trading Est.,
Chesterfield, S40 3JW
T: 01246 261111
F: 01246 261626
E: info@can.ltd.uk
W: www.can.ltd.uk

Cannon Technologies Ltd
Head Office,
Queensway,
Stem Lane, New Milton,
Hants, BH25 5NU
T: 01425 638148
F: 01425 619276
E: sales@cannontech.co.uk
W: www.cannontech.co.uk

Capgemini UK
Forge End, Woking,
Surrey, GU21 6DB
T: 01483 764764
F: 01483 786161
W: www.uk.capgemini.com

Capita Property and Infrastructure Ltd
Capita House, Wood St,
East Grinstead,
W. Sussex, RH19 1UU
T: 01342 327161
F: 01342 315927
E: john.mayne@capita.co.uk
W: www.capitasymonds.co.uk

Capita Architecture
90-98 Goswell Rd,
London, EC1V 7DF
T: 020 7251 6004
F: 020 7253 3568
E: mervyn.franklin@capita.co.uk
W: www.capitaarchitecture.co.uk

Capital & Counties Properties plc (Capco)
15 Grosvenor Street,
London, W1K 4QZ
T: 020 3214 9150
F: 020 3214 9151
E: feedback@capitalandcounties.com
W: www.capitalandcounties.com/

Capital Project Consultancy Ltd (CPC)
See CPC Project Services LLP

Capital Safety Group
Unit 7, Christleton Court,
Manor Park, Runcorn,
Cheshire, WA7 1ST
T: 01928 571324
F: 01928 571325
E: csgne@csgne.co.uk
W: www.uclsafetysystems.com

Captec Ltd
11 Brunel Way,
Segensworth,
Fareham,
Hants, PO15 5TX
T: 01489 866066
F: 01489 866088
E: sales@captec.co.uk
W: www.captec.co.uk

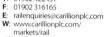

Captrain UK Ltd
2nd Floor,
Asra House,
1 Long Lane,
London, SE1 4PG
T: 020 7939 1900
E: sales@captrain.co.uk
W: www.captrain.co.uk

Cardev International
See Environmental Technologies Ltd.

Carillion Rail
24 Birch St,
Wolverhampton, WV1 4HY
T: 01902 422431
F: 01902 316165
E: railenquiries@carillionplc.com
W: www.carillionplc.com/markets/rail

Carlbro Group
See Grontmij

Carlisle Support Services
800 The Boulevard,
Capability Green,
Luton,
Beds, LU1 3BA
T: 01582 692692
E: info@carlislesupportservices.com
W: www.carlislesupportservices.com

Carlow Precast Tanks UK Ltd
Gunnery House,
The Royal Arsenal, Woolwich,
London, SE18 6SW
T: 01538 753333
F: 0870 493 1409
E: sales@carlowprecasttanks.com
W: www.carlowprecasttanks.com

Carlton Technologies Ltd
Unit 4, Church
View Business Park,
Coney Green Rd,
Clay Cross, Chesterfield,
Derbys, S45 9HA
T: 01246 861330
F: 01246 251466
E: sales@carltontech.co.uk
W: www.carltontech.co.uk

Carver Engineering Services Ltd
11 Brunel Close, Brunel Ind. Est,
Blyth Rd, Harworth,
Doncaster, DN11 8QA
T: 01302 751900
F: 01302 757026
E: sales@carverengineering.com
W: www.carverengineering.com

Cass Hayward LLP
York House, Welsh St, Chepstow,
Monmouthshire, NP16 5UW
T: 01291 626994
F: 01291 626306
E: office@casshayward.com
W: www.casshayward.com

Catalis
See TQ Technical and Vocational

Cats Solutions Ltd
Two Rushy Platt,
Caen View, Swindon,
Wilts, SN5 8WQ
T: 01793 432913
F: 01793 490270
E: sales@cats-solutions.co.uk
W: www.cats-solutions.com

CB Frost & Co Ltd
Green St, Digbeth,
Birmingham, B12 0NE
T: 0121 773 8494
F: 0121 772 3584
E: info@cbfrost-rubber.com
W: www.cbfrost-rubber.com

CCD Design and Ergonomics
Northdown House,
11-21 Northdown St,
London, N1 9BN
T: 0207 593 2900
E: info@ccd.org.uk
W: www.ccd.org.uk

CCL Rail Training
Scope House, Weston Rd,
Crewe, CW1 6DD
T: 01270 252400
E: info@ccltraining.com
W: www.ccltraining.com

CCP Composites
16/32 Rue Henri Regnault,
La Defense 6,
92062 Paris La Defense cedex,
France
T: 00331 4796 9850
F: 00331 4796 9986
E: kevin.louis@ccpcomposites.com
W: www.ccpcomposites.com

CDC Draincare Ltd
Unit 1, Chatsworth Ind. Est,
Percy St, Leeds, LS12 1EL
T: 0845 644 6130
E: enquiries@cdc-draincare.co.uk
W: www.cdc-draincare.co.uk

CDL (Collinson Dutton Ltd)
See GHD Ltd

CDM-UK
PO Box 7035, Melton Mowbray,
Leics, LE13 1WG
T: 01664 482486
F: 01664 482487
E: info@cdm-uk.co.uk
W: www.cdm-uk.co.uk

CDS Rail Ltd
Unit 1, Fulcrum 4, Solent Way,
Whiteley, Hants, PO15 7FT
T: 01489 571771
F: 01489 571985
E: sales@cdsrail.com
W: www.cdsrail.com

Cecence
Unit 2, Centre One, Lysander Way,
Salisbury, Wiltshire, SP4 6BU
T: 01722 327775
E: info@cecence.com
W: www.cecence.com

Cembre Ltd
Dunton Park, Kingsbury Rd,
Curdworth,
Sutton Coldfield, B76 9EB
T: 01675 470440
F: 01675 470220
E: sales@cembre.co.uk
W: www.cembre.co.uk

Cemex Rail Products
Aston Church Rd,
Washwood Heath, Saltley,
Birmingham, B8 1QF
T: 0121 327 0844
F: 0121 327 7545
W: www.cemex.co.uk

Centinal Group
The Brook Works,
174 Bromyard Rd, St Johns,
Worcester, WR2 5EE
T: 01905 748569
F: 01905 420700
E: les@mfhhydraulics.co.uk
W: www.centinalgroup.co.uk/

Central Engineering & Hydraulic Services Ltd
See Centinal Group

Centregreat Rail Ltd
Ynys Bridge, Heol yr Ynys,
Tongwynlais, Cardiff, CF15 7NT
T: 02920 815662
F: 02920 813598
E: rail@centregreat.net
W: www.centregreatrail.co.uk

Centro
Customer Relations,
16 Summer Lane,
Birmingham, B19 3SD
T: 0121 200 2787
E: customerrelations@centro.org.uk
W: www.centro.org.uk

Ch2m Hill
2nd Floor, Quarnmill House,
Stores Rd, Derby, DE21 4XF
T: 01332 222620
F: 01332 222621
E: robert.kaul@ch2m.com
W: www.ch2m.com

Charcon
See Aggregate Industries UK Ltd

Charles Endirect Ltd
Wessex Way,
Wincanton Business Park,
Wincanton, Somerset, BA9 9RR
T: 01963 828400
F: 01963 828401
E: info@charlesendirect.com
W: www.charlesendirect.com

Charter Security Plc
Suite 6, Ensign House,
Admirals Way, London, E14 9XQ
T: 020 7515 0771
E: info@charter-security.co.uk
W: www.charter-security.co.uk

The Chartered Institute of Logistics and Transport (UK) (CILT)
Logistics and Transport Centre,
Earlstrees Court, Earlstrees Rd,
Corby, NN17 4AX
T: 01536 740100
F: 01536 740101
E: enquiry@ciltuk.org.uk
W: www.ciltuk.org.uk

Chase Meadow Consultants
46 Cygnet Rd,
Timothy's Bridge Rd,
Stratford Upon Avon, CV37 9NW
T: 01926 350050
E: enquiries@chasemeadow.com
W: www.chasemeadow.com

CHB & W Buildings & Railway Contractors
Unit 9, Skein Enterprises,
Hodsall St, Sevenoaks,
Kent, TN15 7LB
T: 01732 824687
F: 01732 823285
E: admin@chbw.co.uk
W: www.chbw.co.uk

Chela Ltd
68 Bilton Way, Enfield,
Middx, EN3 7NH
T: 020 8805 2150
F: 020 8443 1868
E: tony.philippou@chela.co.uk
W: www.chela.co.uk

Chester le Track Ltd
See Trainline

Chieftain Trailers Ltd
207 Coalisland Rd, Dungannon,
Co Tyrone, BT71 4DP
T: 028 8774 7531
F: 028 8774 7530
E: sales@chieftaintrailers.com
W: www.chieftaintrailers.com

Chiltern Railways
2nd Floor,
Western House,
Rickfords Hill,
Aylesbury, Bucks
T: 03456 005165
F: 01296 332126
E: marketing@chilternrailways.co.uk
W: www.chilternrailways.co.uk

Chloride Power Protection
See Emerson Network Power

Chubb Systems Ltd
Shadsworth Rd,
Blackburn, BB1 2PR
T: 0844 561 1316
F: 01254 667663
E: systems-sales@chubb.co.uk
W: www.chubbsystems.co.uk

Cintec International Ltd
Cintec House,
11 Gold Tops, Newport,
S.Wales, NP20 4PH
T: 01633 246614
F: 01633 246110
E: johnbrooks@cintec.co.uk
W: www.cintec.co.uk

CIRAS
4th Floor, The Helicon,
One South Place,
London, EC2M 2RB
T: 0203 142 5367
E: info@ciras.org.uk
W: www.ciras.org.uk

CITI
Lovat Bank, Silver St,
Newport Pagnell,
Bucks, MK16 0EJ
T: 01908 283600
F: 01908 283601
E: bdu@citi.co.uk
W: www.citi.co.uk

CJ Architecture
Earl Business Centre, Office 20, E3,
Dowry St, Oldham, OL8 2PF
T: 0161 620 8834
E: enquiries@cjarchitecture.co.uk
W: www.cjarchitecture.co.uk

CJ Associates Ltd
26 Upper Brook St, London,
W1K 7QE
T: 020 7529 4900
F: 020 7529 4929
E: nharrison@cjassociates.co.uk
W: www.cjassociates.co.uk

Clancy Docwra
Clare House, Coppermill Lane,
Harefield, Middx, UB9 6HZ
T: 01895 823711
F: 01895 825263
E: enquiries@theclancygroup.co.uk
W: www.theclancygroup.co.uk

Class 40 Preservation Society (CFPS)
The East Lancashire Railway,
Bolton St, Bury, Lancs, BL9 0EY
T: 07500 040145
F: 0161 740 3300
M: 078 180 40135
E: chairman@cfps.co.uk
W: www.cfps.co.uk

Clayton Equipment
Second Avenue,
Centrum 100 Business Park,
Burton Upon Trent,
Staffordshire, DE14 2WF
T: 01283 524470
F: 01283 524471
E: contact@claytonequipment.co.uk
W: claytonequipment.co.uk/

CLD Fencing Systems
Unit 11,
Springvale Business Centre,
Millbuck Way, Sandbach,
Cheshire, CW11 3HY
T: 01270 764751
F: 01270 757503
E: sales@cld-fencing.com
W: www.cld-fencing.com

CLD Services
170 Brooker Rd, Waltham Abbey,
Essex, EN9 1JH
T: 01992 702300
F: 01992 702301
E: contact@cld-services.co.uk
W: www.cld-services.co.uk

Cleartrack
Salcey-EVL Ltd,
The Old Woodyard,
Forest Rd, Hanslope,
Milton Keynes, MK19 7DE
T: 01908 516250
E: info@cleartrack.co.uk
W: www.cleartrack.co.uk

Clements Technical Recruitment Ltd t/a Clemtech
7 Falcon Court,
Parklands Business Park,
Denmead, Waterlooville,
Hants, PO7 6BZ
T: 023 9224 2690
F: 023 9224 2692
E: rail@clemtech.co.uk
W: www.clemtech.co.uk

Clemtech
See Clements Technical Recruitment Ltd t/a Clemtech

Cleshar Contract Services Ltd
Heather Park House,
North Circular Rd, Stonebridge,
London, NW10 7NN
T: 020 8733 8888
F: 020 8733 8899
E: info@cleshar.co.uk
W: www.cleshar.co.uk

Cleveland Bridge Uk
PO Box 27, Yarm Rd,
Darlington, DL1 4DE
T: 01325 381188
F: 01325 382320
E: info@clevelandbridge.com
W: www.clevelandbridge.com

Clifford Marker Associates
9 Warners Close,
Woodford Green,
Essex, IG8 0TF
T: 020 8504 2570
W: www.cliffordmarkerassociates.com

Clyde & Co LLP
St Botolph Building,
138 Houndsditch,
London, EC3A 7AR
T: 020 7876 5000
E: nigel.taylor@clydeco.com
W: www.clydeco.com

CML
See Construction Marine Ltd

CMS Cameron McKenna
Mitre House,
160 Aldersgate St,
London, EC1A 4DD
T: 020 7367 2113
F: 020 7367 2000
E: jonathan.beckitt@cms-cmck.com
W: www.law-now.com

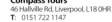

Co Channel Electronics
Victoria Rd,
Avonmouth,
Bristol, BS11 9DB
T: 0117 982 0578
F: 0117 982 6166
E: sales@co-channel.co.uk
W: www.co-channel.co.uk

Cobham Technical Services (ERA Technology Ltd)
Cleeve Rd,
Leatherhead,
Surrey, KT22 7SA
T: 01372 367030
F: 01372 367102
E: era.rail@cobham.com
W: www.cobham.com/technicalservices

Coffey Geotechnics
Atlantic House,
Atls Business Park, Simonsway,
Manchester, M22 5PR
T: 0161 499 6800
F: 0161 499 6802
E: julia_cartmell@coffey.com
W: www.coffey.com

COLAS Rail
Dacre House,
19 Dacre Street,
London, SW1H 0DH
T: 020 7593 5353
F: 020 7593 5343
E: enquiries@colasrail.co.uk
W: www.colasrail.co.uk

Colin Buchanan
See SKM Colin Buchanan

Collis Engineering Civils Division
Salcombe Rd,
Meadow Lane Ind. Est, Alfreton,
Derbys, DE55 7RG
T: 01773 833255
F: 01773 836525
E: sales@collis.co.uk
W: www.signalhousegroup.co.uk

Collis Engineering Ltd
Salcombe Rd,
Meadow Lane Ind. Est, Alfreton,
Derbys, DE55 7RG
T: 01773 833255
F: 01773 520693
E: sales@collis.co.uk
W: www.collis.co.uk

Colman Rail Services
8 Fort House Business Centre,
Primrose Close, Chatham,
Kent, ME4 6HZ
T: 01634 888620
M: 07804 735935
E: clive@colmanrailservices.co.uk
W: www.colmanrail.co.uk

Colour-Rail
558 Birmingham Road,
Bromsgrove, Worcs, B61 0HT
E: colourrail@aol.com
W: www.colourrail.com/

Comech Metrology Ltd
Castings Rd, Derby, DE23 8YL
T: 01332 867700
F: 01332 867707
E: sales@comech.co.uk
W: www.comech.co.uk

Commend UK Ltd
Commend House, Unit 20,
M11 Business Link,
Parsonage Lane, Stansted,
Essex, CM24 8GF
T: 01279 872020
F: 01279 814735
E: sales@commend.co.uk
W: www.commend.co.uk

CommonTime Ltd
15 St Christophers Way,
Pride Park,
Derby, DE24 8JY
T: 01332 542074
E: mike.roberts@commontime.com
W: www.commontime.com

Compass Tours
46 Hallville Rd, Liverpool, L18 0HR
T: 0151 722 1147
F: 0151 722 0297
E: info@compasstoursbyrail.co.uk
W: www.compasstoursbyrail.co.uk

Competence Assurance Solutions Ltd
221 St John St,
Clerkenwell,
London, EC1V 4LY
T: 020 7688 2840
F: 020 7688 2829
E: info@casolutions.co.uk
W: www.casolutions.co.uk

Complete Drain Clearance
49 Weeping Cross,
Stafford, ST17 0DG
T: 01785 665909
F: 01785 664944
E: completedrainclearance@yahoo.co.uk
W: www.completedrainclearance.co.uk

Complus Teltronic
See Commend UK Ltd

Comply Serve Ltd
Number 1, The Courtyard,
707 Warwick Rd, Solihull, B91 3DA
T: 0121 711 2185
E: chris.angus@complyserve.com
W: www.complyserve.com

Comtrol
Unit 6/7 Bignell Park Barns,
Chesterton,
Bicester,
Oxon, OX26 1TD
T: 01869 352740
F: 01869 351848
E: sales@comtrol.co.uk
W: www.comtrol.co.uk

Concrete Canvas Ltd
Unit 3, Block A22, P
ontypridd, CF37 5SP
T: 0845 680 1908
E: info@concretecanvas.com
W: www.concretecanvas.com

HITACHI
Inspire the Next

Conductix-Wampfler Ltd (Insul 8)
1 Michigan Ave, Salford, M50 2GY
T: 0161 848 0161
F: 0161 873 7017
E: info.uk@conductix.co.uk
W: www.conductix.co.uk

Confederation of Passenger Transport UK
Drury House, 34-43 Russell St, London, WC2B 5HA
T: 020 7240 3131
F: 020 7240 6565
E: admin@cpt-uk.org
W: www.cpt-uk.org

Consillia Ltd
See Donfabs and Consillia Ltd

Construcciones y Auxiliar de Ferrocarriles SA (CAF)
The TechnoCentre, Puma Way, Coventry, CV1 2TT
T: 02476 158195
F: 0034 914 366008
E: caf@caf.net
W: www.caf.net

Construction Marine Ltd
The Coach House, Mansion Gate Drive, Chapel Allerton, Leeds, LS7 4SY
T: 0113 262 4444
F: 0113 262 4400
E: info@cml.uk.com
W: www.cml-civil-engineering.co.uk

Containerlift
PO Box 582, Great Dunmow, Essex, CM6 3QX
T: 0800 174 546
F: 0800 174 547
E: joostbaker@containerlift.co.uk
W: www.containerlift.com

Continental Contitech
Chestnut Field House, Chestnut Field, Rugby, Warks, CV21 2PA
T: 01788 571482
F: 01788 542245
W: www.contitech.co.uk

Cook Rail
See William Cook Rail

Cooper and Turner Ltd
Templeborough Works, Sheffield Rd, Sheffield, S9 1RS
T: 0114 256 0057
F: 0114 244 5529
E: sales@cooperandturner.co.uk
W: www.cooperandturner.com

Cooper B-Line
Walrow Ind. Est, Highbridge, Somerset, TA9 4AQ
T: 01278 783371
F: 01278 789037
E: sales@cooperbline.co.uk
W: www.cooperbline.co.uk

creactive design
innovation
engineering
fresh ideas
'The only design team to achieve a 99% customer approval rating for a UK train'
+44 (0) 1926 499 124
www.creactive-design.co.uk

Cooper Bussmann (UK) Ltd
Melton Road, Burton-on-the-Wolds, Leics, LE12 5TH
T: 01509 882737
F: 01509 882786
E: bule.sales@cooperindustries.com
W: www.cooperbussmann.com

Copon E Wood Ltd
See 3M CPPD

Cordek Ltd
Spring Copse Business Park, Slinfold, West Sussex, RH13 0SZ
T: 01403 799600
F: 01403 791718
E: sales@cordek.com
W: www.cordek.com

Corehard Ltd
Viewpoint, Babbage Rd, Stevenage, Herts, SG1 2EQ
T: 01438 225102
F: 01438 213721
E: info@corehard.com
W: www.corehard.com

Coriel Ltd
Nottingham Geospatial Building, Triumph Rd, Nottingham, NG7 2TU
T: 0115 748 4486
E: contact@coriel.co.uk
W: www.coriel.co.uk

Coronet Rail Ltd
See Portec Rail Group

Corporate College
Derby College, Prince Charles Ave, Derby, DE22 4LR
T: 01332 520145
E: enquiries@derby-college.ac.uk
W: www.corporatecollege.co.uk

Correl Rail Ltd
See SGS Correl Rail Ltd

Corus Cogifer
See Vossloh Cogifer UK Ltd

Corus Rail Infrastructure Services
See Tata Steel Projects

Corys T.E.S.S
74 Rue des Martyrs, 38027 Grenoble, France
T: 0033 476 288200
F: 0033 476 288211
E: coryscom@corys.fr
W: www.corys.com

Cosalt Ltd
See Ballyclare Ltd

Costain Ltd - Rail Sector
Costain House, Vanwall Business Park, Maidenhead, Berks, SL6 4UB
T: 01628 842310
E: gren.edwards@costain.com
W: www.costain.com

Covtec Ltd
Allens West, Eaglescliffe Logistics Centre, Durham Rd, Eaglescliffe, Stockton on Tees, TS16 0RW
E: info@covtec.co.uk
W: www.covtec.co.uk

Cowans Sheldon
The Clarke Chapman Group Ltd, PO Box 9, Saltmeadows Rd, Gateshead, NE8 1SW
T: 0191 477 2271
F: 0191 478 3951
E: martin.howell@clarkechapman.co.uk
W: www.cowanssheldon.co.uk

Coyle Personnel Plc
Hygeia, 66-68 College Rd, Harrow, Middx, HA1 1BE
T: 020 8901 6619
F: 020 8901 6706
E: roger@coyles.co.uk
W: www.coylerail.co.uk

CP Films Solutia (UK) Ltd
13 Acorn Business Centre, Northarbour Rd, Cosham, PO6 3TH
T: 02392 219112
F: 02392 219102
W: www.llumar.eu.com

CPC Project Services LLP
5th Floor, Quality House, 5-9 Quality Court, Chancery Lane, London, WC2A 1HP
T: 020 7539 4750
F: 020 7539 4751
E: andy.norris@cpcprojectservices.com
W: www.cpcprojectservices.com

Craig & Derricott Ltd
Hall Lane, Walsall Wood, Walsall, WS9 9DP
T: 01543 375541
F: 01543 361619
E: sales@craiganderricott.com
W: www.craiganderricott.com

Cranfield University
College Rd, Cranfield, Beds, MK43 0AL
T: 01234 750111
E: info@cranfield.ac.uk
W: www.cranfield.ac.uk/soe/rail-investgation

Creactive Design (Transport)
Unit 2 Trojan Business Centre, Tachbrook Park Drive, Warwick, CV34 6RS
T: 01926 499124
E: info@creactive-design.co.uk
W: www.creactive-design.co.uk

Creative Rail Dining
PO Box 10375, Little Waltham, Chelmsford, Essex, CM1 9JW
T: 01245 364051
E: enquiries@crdltd.co.uk
W: www.crdltd.co.uk

Critical Power Supplies Ltd
Unit F, Howlands Business Park, Thame, Oxon, OX9 3GQ
T: 01844 340122
E: sales@critical.co.uk
W: www.criticalpowersupplies.co.uk

Critical Project Resourcing Ltd
116a, High St, Sevenoaks, Kent, TN13 1UZ
T: 01732 455300
F: 01732 458447
E: rail@cpresourcing.co.uk
W: www.cpresourcing.co.uk

Cross London Trains
210 Pentonville Road, London, N1 9JY

Cross Services Group
Cross House, Portland Centre, Sutton Rd, St Helens, WA9 3DR
T: 01744 458000
F: 01744 458099
E: martinclementson@crossgroup.co.uk
W: www.crossgroup.co.uk

CrossCountry
5th Floor, Cannon House, 18 Priory Queensway, Birmingham, B4 6BS
T: 0121 200 6000
F: 0121 200 6003
E: customer.relations@crosscountrytrains.co.uk
W: www.crosscountrytrains.co.uk

Crossrail 2
E: crossrail2@tfl.gov.uk
W: crossrail2.co.uk/

Crossrail Ltd
25 Canada Square, Canary Wharf, London, E14 5LQ
T: 0845 602 3813
E: helpdesk@crossrail.co.uk
W: www.crossrail.co.uk

Crouch Waterfall & Partners Ltd
The Dairy, Greenways Studios, Lower Eashing, Godalming, Surrey, GU7 2QF
T: 01483 425314
F: 01483 425814
E: office@cwp.co.uk
W: www.cwp.co.uk

Crowd Dynamics
21 Station Rd West, Oxted, Surrey, RH8 9EE
T: 01883 718690
F: 08700 516196
E: enquiries@crowddynamics.com
W: www.crowddynamics.com

Croylek Ltd
23 Ullswater Cres, Coulsdon, Surrey, CR5 2UY
T: 020 8668 1481
F: 020 8660 0750
E: sales@croylek.co.uk
W: www.croylek.co.uk

CSC
Royal Pavilion, Wellesley Rd, Aldershot, GU11 1PZ
T: 01252 534000
F: 01252 534100
E: uk-consumer@csc.com
W: www.csc.com

Cubic Transportation Systems
AFC House, Honeycrock Lane, Salfords, Redhill, Surrey, RH1 5LA
T: 01737 782362
F: 01737 789759
E: jennifer.newell@cubic.com
W: www.cubic.com/cts

Cubis Industries
Lurgan, Co Armagh, BT66 6LN
T: 0151 548 7900
F: 0151 548 7184
E: info@cubisindustries.com
W: www.cubisindustries.com

Cubris
Cubris ApS, Ebertsgade 2, 2, DK-2300, Copenhagen S, Denmark
T: 0330 2230 460
E: info@cubris.dk
W: www.cubris.dk/

Cudis Ltd
Power House, Parker St, Bury, BL9 0RJ
T: 0161 765 3000
F: 0161 705 2900
E: sales@cudis.co.uk
W: www.cudis.co.uk

Cummins
Yarm Rd, Darlington, DL1 4PW
T: 01327 886464
F: 0870 241 3180
E: cabo.customerassistance@cummins.com
W: www.everytime.cummins.com

D&D Rail Ltd
Time House, Time Square, Basildon, Essex, SS14 1DJ
T: 01268 520000
F: 01268 520011
E: info@ddrail.com
W: www.ddrail.com

D2 Rail and Civils
1st Floor, Langton House, Bird St, Lichfield, WS13 6PY
E: david@d2railandcivils.co.uk
W: www.d2railandcivils.co.uk

DAC Ltd
Unit 28, Lomeshaye Business Village, Turner Rd, Nelson, Lancs, BB9 7DR
T: 01282 447000
F: 0845 280 1915
E: sales@daclimited.co.uk
W: www.daclimited.co.uk

Dailys UK Ltd
See Novah Ltd

Veolia
5 Limeharbour Court, Limeharbour, London, E14 9RH
T: 01784 496200
F: 01784 496222
E: carol.taylor@dalkia.co.uk
W: veolia.co.uk

Dallmeier Electronic UK Ltd
Dallmeier House, 3 Beaufort Trade Park, Pucklechurch, Bristol, BS16 9QH
T: 0117 303 9303
F: 0117 303 9302
E: dallmeieruk@dallmeier-electronic.com
W: www.dallmeier-electronic.com

Danny Sullivan Group
22 Barretts Green Rd, Park Royal, London, NW10 7AE
T: 020 8961 1900
F: 020 8961 1965
E: enquiries@dannysullivan.co.uk
W: www.dannysullivan.co.uk

Dartford Composites Ltd
Unit 1, Ness Rd, Erith, Kent, DA8 2LD
T: 01322 350097
F: 01322 359438
E: sales@dartfordcomposites.co.uk
W: www.dartfordcomposites.co.uk

Data Display UK Ltd
3 The Meadows, Waterberry Drive, Waterlooville, Hants, PO7 7XX
T: 023 9224 7500
F: 023 9224 7519
E: sales@datadisplayuk.com
W: www.datadisplayuk.com

Data Systems & Solutions
See Optimized Systems & Solutions Ltd

Datasys Ltd
See Tracsis Plc

Datum - Composite Products
22 Longbridge Lane, Derby, DE24 8UJ
T: 01332 751503
F: 01332 385487
E: composites@datum-patterns.co.uk
W: www.datum-patterns.co.uk

David Brice Consultancy
11 Sebastian Ave, Shenfield, Brentwood, Essex, CM15 8PN
T: 01277 221422
F: 01277 263614
E: davidpbrice@aol.com
W: www.bricerail.co.uk

David Brown Gear Systems Ltd
Park Gear Works, Lockwood, Huddersfield, HD4 5DD
T: 01484 465664
F: 01484 465587
E: soldroyd@davidbrown.com
W: www.davidbrown.com

David Lane Publishing
1 West Street, Bourne, Lincolnshire, PE10 9NB
T: 01778 420888
F: 01778 421550
M: 07795031051
E: dave@davidlanepublishing.co.uk

David Simmonds Consultancy
Suite 4, Bishop Bateman Court, New Park Street, Cambridge, CB5 8AT
T: 01223 316098
E: dsc@davidsimmonds.com
W: www.davidsimmonds.com

David Simmonds Consultancy
7-9 North St. David St, Edinburgh, EH2 1AW
T: 0131 524 9475
E: admin@davidsimmonds.com

DB Schenker
Lakeside Business Park, Carolina Way, Doncaster, DN4 5PN
F: 0870 140 5000
E: robert.smith2@dbschenker.com
W: www.rail.dbschenker.co.uk

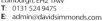

dBD Communications
4 Furlongs, Basildon, Essex, SS16 4BW
T: 01268 449871
F: 01268 442390
E: npurcell@dbdcom.co.uk
W: www.dbdcom.co.uk

DBK Technitherm Ltd
Unit 11, Llantrisant Business Park, Llantrisant, CF72 8LF
T: 01443 237927
F: 01443 237867
E: info-uk@dbk-group.com
W: www.dbktechnitherm.ltd.uk

DC Airco
Opaalstraat 18, 1812 RH Alkmaar, Netherlands
T: 0031 72533 6540
E: info@dcairco.com
W: www.dcairco.com

DCA Design International
19 Church St, Warwick, CV34 4AB
T: 01926 499461
F: 01926 401134
E: transport@dca-design.com
W: www.dca-design.com/

DeltaRail

'Imagine the journey…transformed by our world class technologies'

Delta Rail Group Ltd, Hudson House,
2 Hudson Way, Pride Park, Derby, DE24 8HS

T: 01332 221 000
F: 01332 221 008
E: enquiries@deltarail.com
W: www.deltarail.com

Dedicated Micros
1200 Unit, Daresbury Park,
Daresbury,
Warrington, WA4 4HS
T: 0845 600 9500
F: 0845 600 9504
E: customerservices@
dmicros.com
W: www.dedicatedmicros.com/uk

DEG Signal Ltd
Aspect House, Crusader Park,
Warminster, Wilts, BA12 8BT
T: 01985 212020
F: 01985 212053
E: info@degsignal.co.uk
W: www.degsignal.co.uk

Delay Attribution Board
1 Eversholt St, 8th Floor,
London, NW1 2DN
E: admin@
delayattributionboard.co.uk
W: www.delayattributionboard.
co.uk

Delimon Denco Lubrication
See Bijur Delimon International

Delkor Rail
74 Harley Cres, Condell Park, NSW,
Australia
T: 61 2 9709 2918
F: 61 2 9709 5934
E: george@delkorrail.com
W: www.delkorrail.com

Dellner Couplers UK Ltd
Hearthcote Rd,
Swadlincote,
Derbys, DE11 9DX
T: 01283 221122
E: info@dellner.com
W: www.dellner.com

Delmatic
The Power House,
6 Power Rd,
Chiswick,
London, W4 5PY
T: 020 8987 5900
F: 020 8987 5957
E: sales@delmatic.com
W: www.delmatic.com

Delta Rail Group Ltd
Hudson House,
2 Hudson Way,
Pride Park,
Derby, DE24 8HS
T: 01332 221 000
F: 01332 221 008
E: enquiries@deltarail.com
W: www.deltarail.com

Deltix Transport Consulting
4 Church Hill Drive,
Edinburgh, EH10 4BT
T: 0131 447 7764
M: 07917 877399
E: david@deltix.co.uk
W: www.deltix.co.uk

Deltone Training Consultants
Ground Floor, 42-48 High Rd,
South Woodford,
London, E18 2QL
T: 020 8532 2208
F: 020 8532 2206
E: sales@deltonetraining.com
W: www.deltonetraining.com

Demco
Heyford Close,
Aldermans Green Ind. Est.,
Coventry, CV2 2QB
T: 02476 602323
F: 02476 602116
E: info@mgs.co.uk
W: www.demco.co.uk

Det Norske Veritas
See DNV (Det Norske Veritas)

Department for Transport
Great Minster House,
33 Horseferry Road, London,
SW1P 4DR
T: 020 7944 5409
F: 020 7944 2158
E: fax9643@dft.gsi.gov.uk
W: www.dft.gov.uk

Deploy UK Rail
The Podium, 1 Eversholt St,
London, NW1 2DN
T: 020 7434 0300
E: info@deployuk.com
W: www.deployuk.com

Depot Rail ltd
Mercury House,
Willoughton Drive,
Foxby Lane Business Park,
Gainsborough, Lincs, DN21 1DY
T: 01427 619512
F: 01427 619501
E: sales@drail.co.uk
W: www.depotrail.co.uk

Derby Engineering Unit Ltd
Unit 22, Riverside Park,
East Service Rd, Raynesway,
Derby, DE21 7RW
T: 01332 660364
F: 01332 675191
E: enquiries@
derbyengineeringunit.co.uk
W: www.derbyengineeringunit.
co.uk

The Deritend Group Ltd
Cyprus St, Off Upper Villiers St,
Wolverhampton, WV2 4PB
T: 01902 426354
F: 01902 711926
E: sales@deritend.co.uk
W: www.deritend.co.uk

Design & Projects Int. Ltd
2 Manor Farm, Flexford Rd,
North Baddesley, Hants,
SO52 9FD
T: 02380 277910
F: 02380 277920
E: colin.brooks@
designandprojects.com
W: www.railwaymaintenance.com

Design Triangle Ltd
The Maltings, Burwell,
Cambridge, CB25 0HB
T: 01638 743070
F: 01638 743493
E: mail@designtriangle.co.uk
W: www.designtriangle.com

Designplan Lighting
16 Kimpton Park Way, Sutton,
Surrey, SM3 9QS
T: 020 8254 2000
F: 020 8644 4253
E: sales@designplan.co.uk
W: www.designplan.co.uk

Det Norske Veritas
See DNV (Det Norske Veritas)

Deuta-Werke GmbH
Paffrather Str. 140,
D-51465 Bergisch Gladbach,
Germany
T: 0049 2202 958 100
F: 0049 2202 958 145
E: support@deuta.de
W: www.deuta.de

Deutche Bahn UK
DB Vertrieb GmbH, Suite 6/7,
The Sanctuary, 23 Oakhill Grove,
Surbiton, Surrey, KT6 6DU
W: www.bahn.co.uk

DEUTZ AG - UK & Ireland
Unit 3, Willow Park, Burdock Close,
Cannock, Staffs, WS11 7FQ
T: 01543 438901
F: 01543 438931
E: brocklebank.s@deutz.com
W: www.deutz.de/

Devol Engineering Ltd
Unit 2,
Faulds Park Industrial Estate,
Faulds Park Road, Gourock,
PA19 1FB
T: 01475 657360
F: 01475 787873
E: sales.devol.uk@
jameswalker.biz
W: www.devol.com

Design Triangle Ltd *(col 4 heading)*

Devon & Cornwall Rail Partnership
School of Geography
Earth & Environmental
Studies,
University of Plymouth,
Plymouth, PL4 8AA
T: 01752 584777
F: 01752 233094
E: railpart@
plymouth.ac.uk
W: www.greatscenic
railways.com

Devon & Cornwall Railways
Stanhope Station,
Stanhope,
Bishop Auckland,
County Durham, DL13 2YS
T: 01388 526203
E: documentcontroller@
britamrail.com
W: www.rmslocotec.com
/#/dcr

Dewalt
210 Bath Rd,
Slough, SL1 3YD
T: 01753 567055
F: 01753 521312
E: reply@dewalt.com
W: www.dewalt.co.uk

Dewhurst Plc
Unit 9,
Hampton Business Park,
Hampton Road West,
Feltham,
Middx, TW13 6DB
T: 020 8744 8200
F: 020 8744 8299
E: info@dewhurst.co.uk
W: www.dewhurst.co.uk

Dexeco Ltd
Brickfields Business Park,
Gillingham,
Dorset, SP8 4PX
T: 01747 858100
F: 01747 858153
E: sales@dexeco.co.uk
W: www.dexeco.co.uk/

DG8 Design and Engineering Ltd
Room 7,
The College Business Centre,
Uttoxeter New Rd,
Derby, DE22 3WZ
T: 01332 869351
F: 01332 869350
E: tony.devitt@dg8design.com
W: www.dg8design.com

DGauge Ltd
Innovation Centre,
1 Devon Way,
Longbridge Technology Park,
Birmingham, B31 2TS
T: 0121 222 5662
E: david.johns@dgauge.co.uk
W: www.dgauge.co.uk

Diamond Point
Suite 13, Ashford House,
Beaufort Court,
Sir Thomas Longley Rd,
Rochester, ME2 4FA
T: 01634 300900
F: 01634 722398
E: john.vaines@dpie.com
W: www.dpie.com

DIEM Ltd
Merseyside Office,
11 Jubilee Rd,
Formby,
Merseyside, L37 2HN
T: 01704 870461
E: davidinman@diemltd.co.uk
W: www.diemltd.co.uk

Difuria Ltd
West Stockwith Business Park,
Stockwith Road,
Misterton,
Doncaster, DN10 4ES
T: 01427 848712
F: 01427 848056
E: sales@difuria.co.uk
W: www.difuria.co.uk

Digitals Barriers
Enterprise House,
1-2 Hatfields,
London, SE1 9PG
T: 020 7940 4740
F: 020 7940 4746
E: info@digitalbarriers.com
W: www.digitalbarriers.com/

Dilax Systems UK Ltd
Unit 1, Rankin House, Knowl Hill
Business Park, Roebuck Way,
Milton Keynes, MK5 8HL
T: 01908 208 900
E: info@dilax.co.uk
W: www.dilax.co.uk

Dimension Data
Aldershawe Hall,
Claypit Lane, Wall,
Lichfield, WS14 0AQ
T: 01543 414751
F: 01543 250159
E: enquiries@nextiraone.co.uk
W: www.nextiraone.co.uk

The Direct Group
Unit 2, Churnet Court,
Churnetside Business Park,
Harrison Way, Cheddleton,
Staffs, ST13 7EF
T: 01538 360555
F: 01538 369100
E: dpl@direct-group.co.uk
W: www.direct-group.co.uk

Direct Link North
56 Beverley Gardens,
Wembley,
Middx, HA9 9QZ
T: 020 8908 0638
E: keith.gerry@
directlinknorth.com
W: www.directlinknorth.com/

Direct Rail Services (DRS)
Kingmoor Depot, Etterby Rd,
Carlisle, CA3 9NZ
T: 01228 406600
F: 01228 406601
E: enquiries@drsl.co.uk
W: www.directrailservices.com
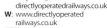

Direct Track Solutions Ltd
Unit C Midland Place,
Midland Way, Barlborough Links,
Barlborough,
Chesterfield, S43 4FR
T: 01246 810198
F: 01246 570926
E: info@
directtracksolutions.co.uk
W: www.directtracksolutions.co.uk

Directly Operated Railways
4th Floor,
Chancery Lane,
London, EC4A 1BL
T: 020 7904 5043
E: enquiries@
directlyoperatedrailways.co.uk
W: www.directlyoperated
railways.co.uk

Discover LEDs
PO Box 222,
Evesham,
Worcs, WR11 4WT
T: 0844 578 1000
F: 0844 578 1111
E: sales@mobilecentre.co.uk
W: www.mobilecentre.co.uk

Discovery Drilling Ltd
32 West Station Yard,
Maldon,
Essex, CM9 6TS
T: 01621 851300
F: 01621 851305
E: enquiries@
discoverydrilling.co.uk
W: www.discoverydrilling.co.uk

DLA Piper UK LLP
Princes Exchange,
Princes Square,
Leeds, LS1 4BY
T: 0113 369 2468
F: 0113 369 2999
E: julie.lang@dlapiper.com
W: www.dlapiper.com

DIAMOND POINT INTERNATIONAL

25 years' experience building **Rugged computers** to Rail industry standards to EN50155, EN50121, RIA12/18. Trackside, on train, under train, WiFi, 3G/4G, Streaming video, Data acquisition and control, EN50155 rugged Ultra Wide Displays and SIL 4 safety critical CCU's

A: Suite 13, Ashford House, Beaufort Court
Sir Thomas Longley Road, Rochester ME2 4FA

T: +44 (0) 1634 300900

E: john.vaines@dpie.com

www.dpie.com

HITACHI
Inspire the Next

DW Windsor

British manufacturer
• Rail-approved exterior lighting
• Complimentary lighting design service

T: 01992 474600 E: light@dwwindsor.co.uk
dwwindsor.com

DMC Group
Unit 17, The Capstan Centre,
Thurrock Park Way, Tilbury,
Essex, RM18 7HH
T: 01375 845070
F: 01375 841333
E: office@dmccontracts.co.uk
W: www.dmccontracts.co.uk

DML Group
See Babcock Rail

DMS Technologies
Belbin's Business Park,
Cupernham Lane, Romsey,
Hants, SO51 7JF
T: 01794 525463
F: 01794 525450
E: info@dmstech.co.uk
W: www.dmstech.co.uk

DNH WW Ltd
31 Clarke Rd, Mount Farm,
Bletchley, Milton Keynes, MK1 1LG
T: 01908 275000
F: 01908 275100
E: dnh@dnh.co.uk
W: www.dnh.co.uk

DNV (Det Norske Veritas)
Palace House, 3 Cathedral St,
London, SE1 9DE
T: 020 7716 6593
F: 020 7716 6738
E: david.salmon@dnv.com
W: www.dnv.com

Docklands Light Railway
Castor Lane, Poplar,
London, E14 0DX
T: 020 7363 9898
F: 020 7363 9708
E: enquire@tfl.gov.uk
W: www.dlr.co.uk

Docmate Services Ltd
18 Alder Tree Rd, Banchory,
Aberdeenshire, AB31 4FW
T: 01330 822620
F: 01330 822620
E: info@docmates.co.uk
W: www.docmates.co.uk

Dold Industries Ltd
11 Hamberts Rd,
Blackall Ind Est,
South Woodham Ferrers,
Essex, CM3 5UW
T: 01245 324432
F: 01245 325570
E: admin@dold.co.uk
W: www.dold.co.uk

Domnick Hunter Industrial Operations
Dukesway,
Team Valley Trading Est.,
Gateshead,
Tyne & Wear, NE11 0PZ
T: 0191 402 9000
F: 0191 482 6296
E: dhindsales@parker.com
W: www.domnickhunter.com

Donaldson Associates
Eastfield,
Church St,
Uttoxeter,
Staffs, ST14 8AA
T: 01889 563680
F: 01889 562586
E: tunnels@
donaldsonassociates.com
W: www.donaldsonassociates.com

Donfabs and Consillia Ltd
The Old Iron Warehouse,
The Wharf,
Shardlow,
Derby, DE72 2GH
T: 01332 792483
F: 01332 799209
E: ian.moss@consillia.com
W: www.trackgeometry.co.uk

Donyal Engineering Ltd
Unit 7,
Hobson Ind Est,
Burnopfield,
Newcastle upon Tyne, NE16 6EA
T: 01207 270909
F: 01207 270333
E: mike@donyal.co.uk
W: www.donyal.co.uk

Dorset Woolliscroft
Falcon Road,
Sowton Industrial Estate, Exeter,
Devon, EX2 7LB
T: 01392 473037
F: 01392 473003
E: info@dorsetwoolliscroft.com
W: www.dorsetwoolliscroft.com

Dow Hyperlast
Station Rd, Birch Vale, High Peak,
Derbyshire, SK22 1BR
T: 01663 746518
F: 01663 746605
E: help@dowhyperlast.com
W: www.dowhyperlast.com

DP Consulting
Unit 4, Tygan House,
The Broadway, Cheam, Surrey
T: 0845 094 2380
F: 0700 341 8557
E: info@dpconsulting.org.uk
W: www.dpconsulting.org.uk

DPSS Cabling Services Ltd
Unit 16, Chiltern Business Village,
Arundel Rd, Uxbridge, UB2 2SN
T: 01895 251010
F: 01895 813133
E: airon.duke@dpsscabling.co.uk
W: www.dpsscabling.co.uk

Dragados S.A.
Regina House, 2nd Floor,
1-5 Queen St,
London, EC4N 1SW
T: 020 7651 0900
F: 020 7248 9044
E: jcruzd@dragados.com
W: www.grupoacs.com

DRail
See Depot Rail ltd

Drum Cussac
8 Hill St, St Helier, Jersey, JE4 9XB
T: 0870 429 6944
F: 01889 562586
E: risk@drum-cussac.com
W: www.drum-cussac.com

Dual Inventive Ltd
Unit 2 Redwall Close, Dinnington,
Sheffield, S25 3QA
M: 07957 880220
E: info@dualinventive.com
W: www.dualinventive.com

DuPont (UK) Ltd
Wedgwood Way, Stevenage,
Herts, SG1 4QN
T: 01438 734061
F: 01438 734836
E: john.hartford@
W: www.rail.dupont.com

Dura Composites
Dura House, Telford Rd,
Clacton-on-Sea,
Essex, CO15 4LP
T: 01255 423601
F: 01255 435426
E: info@duracomposites.com
W: www.duracomposites.com

Durapipe
Walsall Rd, Norton Canes,
Cannock, Staffs, WS11 9NS
T: 01543 279909
E: enquiries@durapipe.co.uk
W: www.durapipe.co.uk

DW Windsor UK
Pindar Rd, Hoddesdon,
Herts, EN11 0DX
T: 01992 474600
E: light@dwwindsor.co.uk
W: www.dwwindsor.co.uk

DWG Infrastructure
141b Derby Rd, Stapleford,
Notts, NG9 7AS
T: 0115 939 5992
E: info@dwguk.com
W: www.dwguk.com

Dyer & Butler Ltd
Mead House, Station Rd, Nursling,
Southampton, SO16 0AH
T: 02380 742222
F: 02380 742200
E: enquiries@
dyerandbutler.co.uk
W: www.dyerandbutler.co.uk

Dyer Engineering Ltd
Solution House, Unit 3,
Morrison & Busty North Ind Est,
Annfield Plain, Stanley,
Co Durham, DH9 7RU
T: 01207 234315
F: 01207 282834
E: paul.dyer@dyer.co.uk
W: www.dyer.co.uk

Dynex Semiconductor Ltd
Doddington Rd, Lincoln, LN6 3LF
T: 01522 500500
F: 01522 500020
E: power_solutions@
dynexsemi.com
W: www.dynexsemi.com

Dywidag-Systems International Ltd
Northfield Rd, Southam,
Warks, CV47 0FG
T: 01926 813980
F: 01926 813817
E: sales@dywidag.co.uk
W: www.dywidag-systems.co.uk

E A Technology
Capenhurst Technology Park,
Capenhurst, Chester, CH1 6ES
T: 0151 339 4181
F: 0151 347 2404
E: john.hartford@
eatechnology.com
W: www.eatechnology.com

E C Harris
ECHQ, 34 York Way,
London, N1 9AB
T: 020 7812 2000
F: 020 7812 2001
W: www.echarris.com

EAL
Unit 2, The Orient Centre,
Greycaine Rd, Watford, WD24 7GP
T: 01923 652400
F: 01923 652401
E: customercare@eal.org.uk
W: www.eal.org.uk

EAO Ltd
Highland House, Albert Drive,
Burgess Hill,
West Sussex, RH15 9TN
T: 01444 236000
F: 01444 236641
E: sales.euk@eao.com
W: www.eao.com

East Lancashire Railway
Bolton St Station, Bury,
Lancs, BL9 0EY
T: 0161 764 7790
E: admin@eastlancsrailway.co.uk
W: www.eastlancsrailway.org.uk

East Midlands Trains
Stagecoach Group,
10 Dunkeld Way, Perth, PH1 5TW
T: 01738 442111
F: 01738 643648
E: mail@stagecoachgroup.com
W: www.stagecoachgroup.com

East West Rail Consortium
E: info@eastwestrail.org.uk
W: www.eastwestrail.org.uk/

Eaton Electrical Ltd
Reddings Lane, Tyseley,
Birmingham, B11 3EZ
T: 0121 685 2100
E: chrisswales@eaton.com
W: www.eaton.com

EB Elektro UK Ltd
Unit 2, Shireoaks Triangle,
Coach Crescent, Worksop,
Notts, S81 8AD
T: 01909 483658
E: william@eb-elektro.co.uk
W: www.eb-elektro.co.uk

Ebeni Ltd
Hartham Park,
Corsham,
Wilts, SN13 0RP
T: 01249 700505
F: 01249 700001
E: john.meredith@ebeni.com
W: www.ebeni.com

EcarbonUK
See Electrical Carbon UK Ltd

Ecebs Ltd
The Torus Building,
Rankine Ave, S
cottish Enterprise
Technology Park,
East Kilbride, G75 0QF
T: 01355 272911
F: 01355 272993
E: enquiries@ecebs.com
W: www.ecebs.com

ECT Group
See British American Railway
Services (BARS)

Ecus Environmental Consultants
Brook Holt,
3 Blackburn Road,
Sheffield, S61 2DW
T: 0114 2669292
E: contactus@ecusltd.co.uk
W: www.ecusltd.co.uk/

Eden Brown
222 Bishopsgate,
London, EC2M 4QD
T: 020 7422 7300
F: 0845 434 9573
E: london@edenbrown.com
W: www.edenbrown.com

Eden Business Analysis Ltd
23 Station Rd,
Upper Poppleton,
York, YO26 6PX
T: 01904 780781
E: neil@edenba.co.uk
W: www.edenba.co.uk

EDF Energy
See UK Power Networks Services

Edgar Allen
See Balfour Beatty Rail

Edif ERA
Cleeve Rd,
Leatherhead,
Surrey, KT22 7SA
T: 01372 367345
F: 01372 367321
E: info@edifera.com
W: www.edifgroup.com

Edilon Sedra
See Tiflex Ltd

Edinburgh Trams Limited
55 Annandale Street,
Edinburgh, EH7 4AZ
T: 0131 475 0177
W: www.http://
edinburghtrams.com

Edmund Nuttall Ltd
See BAM Nuttall Ltd

Edward Symmons
2 Southwark St,
London, SE1 1TQ
T: 020 7955 8454
F: 020 7407 6423
E: info@
edwardsymmons.com
W: www.es-group.com

EFD Corporate
41 Caxton Court,
Garamonde Drive,
Wymbush,
Milton Keynes, MK8 8DD
T: 0845 1285172 / 01908 560669
F: 01908 565672
M: 07827 891705
E: enquiries@efd-corporate.com
W: www.efd-corporate.com

Efficio
22 Long Acre,
London, WC2E 9LY
T: 020 7550 5677
F: 020 7550 5679
E: info@efficioconsulting.com
W: www.efficioconsulting.com/

EFI Heavy Vehicle Brakes
6/7 Bonville Rd,
Brislington,
Bristol, BS4 5NZ
T: 0117 977 7859
F: 0117 971 0573
E: tonyp@efiltd.co.uk
W: www.efiltd.co.uk

Eglin Concourse International
Globe Works,
Victoria Rd,
Sowerby Bridge,
West Yorks, HX6 3AE
T: 01422 317601
F: 01422 833857
E: sales@eglinconcourse.com
W: www.eglinconcourse.com

Eiffage
163 Quai du Docteur-Dervaux,
92601 Asnières-sur-Seine,
Paris, France
T: 0001 4132 8000
F: 0001 4132 8113
W: www.eiffage.com/en/

Elan Public Transport Consultancy Ltd
8 The Grange,
Chesterfield, S42 7PS
T: 0845 123 5733
E: george.watson@elanptc.com
W: www.elanptc.com

Eland Cables
120 Highgate Studios,
53-79 Highgate Rd,
London, NW5 1TL
T: 020 7241 8787
F: 020 7241 8700
E: sales@eland.co.uk
W: www.eland.co.uk

Elcot Environmental
The Nursery,
Kingsdown Lane,
Blunsdon,
Swindon,
Wilts, SN25 5DL
T: 01793 700100
F: 01793 722221
E: peterw@elcotenviro.com
W: www.elcotenviro.com

Eldapoint Ltd
Charleywood Rd,
Knowsley Ind. Prk North,
Knowsley,
Merseyside, L33 7SG
T: 0151 548 9838
F: 0151 546 4120
E: paul.wyatt@eldapoint.co.uk
W: www.eldapoint.co.uk

E-Leather Ltd
Kingsbridge Centre,
Sturrock Way,
Peterborough, PE3 8TZ
T: +44 (0) 1733 843939
F: +44 (0) 1733 843940
E: info@eleathergroup.com
W: info@eleathergroup.com

Electrical Carbon UK Ltd
Office 50, 15 Brynymor Rd,
Swansea, SA1 4JQ
T: 01792 421892
F: 01792 241193
E: sales@ecarbonuk.com
W: www.ecarbonuk.com

Electro Motive
See Progress Rail Services

Electromagnetic Testing Services Ltd (ETS)
Pratts Fields, Lubberhedges Lane,
Stebbing, Dunmow,
Essex, CM6 3BT
T: 01371 856061
F: 01371 856144
E: info@etsemc.co.uk
W: www.etsemc.co.uk

Elite Precast Concrete
Halesfield 9,
Telford,
Shropshire, TF9 4QW
T: 01952 588885
F: 01952 582011
E: sales@eliteprecast.co.uk
W: www.eliteprecast.co.uk

Ellis Patents Ltd
High Street, Rillington,
Malton,
North Yorkshire, YO17 8LA
T: 01944 758395
F: 01944 758808
E: sales@ellispatents.co.uk
W: www.ellispatents.co.uk/

Elmatic
Wentloog Road,
Rumney,
Cardiff, CF3 1XH
T: 029 2077 8727
F: 029 2079 2297
E: petercrisp@elmatic.co.uk
W: www.elmatic.co.uk

Eltek Valere UK Ltd
Cleveland Road,
Hemel Hempstead,
Herts, HP2 7EY
T: 01442 219355
F: 01442 245894
E: steve.pusey@eltekvalere.com
W: www.eltekvalere.com

Eltherm UK Ltd
Liberta House,
Scotland Hill,
Sandhurst,
Berks, GU47 8JR
T: 01252 749910
E: sales@eltherm.uk.com
W: www.eltherm.uk.com

Embed Ltd
Sovereign Court One,
University of Warwick
Science Park,
Sir William Lyons Road,
Coventry, Warks, CV4 7EZ
T: 02476 323251
E: webenquiries@embeduk.com
W: www.embeduk.com

Embedded Rail Technology Ltd
Rosehill House,
Derby, DE23 8GG
E: cp@charlespenny.com

EMEG Electrical Ltd
Unit 3, Dunston Place,
Dunston Road,
Whittington Moor,
Chesterfield,
Derbys, S41 8NL
T: 01246 268678
F: 01246 268679
E: enq@emeg.co.uk
W: www.emeg.co.uk

Emergency Power Systems
See Emerson Network Power

Emergi-Lite - Thomas & Betts Ltd
Bruntcliffe Lane, Morley,
Leeds, LS27 9LL
T: 0113 281 0600
F: 0113 281 0601
E: emergi-lite.sales@tnb.com
W: www.emergi-lite.co.uk

Emerson Crane Hire
Emerson House, Freshwater Road,
Dagenham, Essex, RM8 1RX
T: 020 8548 3900
F: 020 8548 3999
E: liam@emersoncranes.com
W: www.emersoncranes.com

Emerson Network Power
Ebury Gate,
23 Lower Belgrave Street,
London, SW1W 0NR
T: 020 7881 1440
F: 020 7730 5085
E: uk.rail@emerson.com
W: www.emersonnetworkpower.com

Emerson Network Power Chloride Products & Services
See Emerson Network Power

Emico
Forsyth House, 39 Mark Rd,
Hemel Hempstead,
Herts, HP2 7DN
T: 01442 213111
F: 01442 236945
E: contact@emico.co
W: www.emico.co

Enable Access
Marshmoor Works,
Great North Road, North Mymms,
Hatfield, AL9 5SD
T: 0208 2750375
F: 02084490326
E: technical@enable-access.com
W: www.enable-access.com

Enerpac
Bentley Rd South, Darlaston,
West Midlands, WS10 8LQ
T: 0121 505 0787
F: 0121 505 0799
E: info@enerpac.com
W: www.enerpac.com

EnerSys Ltd
Oak Court, Clifton Business Park,
Wynne Ave, Swinton,
Manchester, M27 8FF
T: 0161 794 4611
F: 0161 727 3809
E: enersys.rail@uk.enersys.com
W: www.enersys-emea-rail.com

Engineering Support Group
See ESG

Ennstone Johnston
See FP McCann Ltd

ENOTRAC UK Ltd
Chancery House,
St Nicholas Way,
Sutton,
Surrey, SM1 4AF
T: 020 8770 3501
F: 020 8770 3502
E: sebastien.lechelle@enotrac.com
W: www.enotrac.com

Entech Technical Solutions Ltd
56 Broadwick St,
London, W1F 7AL
T: 0207 434 7370
E: saul@entechts.co.uk
W: www.entechts.co.uk

Entech Technical Solutions Ltd
1st Floor,
Hamilton House,
111 Marlowes,
Hemel Hempstead,
Herts, HP1 1BB
T: 01442 898900
F: 01442 898990
E: info@entechts.com
W: www.entechts.co.uk

Enterprise
See Amey

Enterprise Managed Services Ltd
See Amey

Environmental Management Solutions Group Holdings Ltd (EMS)
Sigeric Business Park,
Holme Lacey Road,
Rotherwas,
Hereford, HR2 6BQ
T: 01432 263333
F: 01432 263355
W: www.ems-asbestos.co.uk/

Environmental Scientifics Group Ltd (ESG)
ESG House,
Bretby Business Park,
Ashby Rd,
Burton upon Trent, DE15 0YZ
T: 01283 554400
F: 01283 554401
E: sales@esg.co.uk
W: www.esg.co.uk

Environmental Technologies Ltd.
Grimbald Crag Road,
Environmental Technologies Ltd.
Grimbald Crag Road
Knaresborough, HG5 8PY
T: 01423 817200
F: 01423 817400
E: admin@ecolube.co.uk
W: www.env-t.com

Envirotech
See LH Group Services

EPC Global
See Talascend Ltd

EQE International
See ABS Consulting

ERG Transit Systems (UK) Ltd
See Vix Technology

Ergonomics & Safety Research Institute (ESRI)
Holywell Building,
Holywell Way,
Loughborough,
Leics, LE11 3UZ
T: 01509 226900
F: 01509 226960
E: esri@lboro.ac.uk
W: www.lboro.ac.uk

Eric Wright Group
Sceptre House, Sceptre Way,
Bamber Bridge,
Preston, PR5 6AW
T: 01772 698822
F: 01772 628811
E: info@ericwright.co.uk
W: www.ericwright.co.uk

ERM Ltd
2nd Floor, Exchequer Court,
33 St Mary Axe,
London, EC3 8LL
T: 020 3206 5401
F: 020 7465 7272
E: nick.cottam@erm.com
W: www.erm.com

Ernst & Young LLP
1 More London Place,
London, SE1 2AF
T: 020 7951 1113
F: 020 7951 3167
E: gfavaloro@uk.ey.com
W: www.ey.com/uk

ESAB (UK) Ltd
Hanover House, Queensgate,
Britannia Rd,
Waltham Cross, EN8 7TF
T: 01992 768515
F: 01992 788053
E: info@esab.co.uk
W: www.esab.co.uk

ESG
Derwent House,
RTC Business Park,
London Rd,
Derby, DE24 8UP
T: 01332 483800
F: 01332 383565
E: sales@esg-rail.com
W: www.esg-rail.com

ESP Systex Ltd
68-74 Holderness Rd,
Hull, HU9 1ED
T: 01482 384500
F: 01482 384555
E: info@espsystex.co.uk
W: www.http://the-espgroup.com

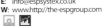

ESR Technology Ltd
410 Birchwood Park,
Warrington,
Cheshire, WA3 6FW
T: 01925 582491
E: info@esrtechnology.com
W: www.esrtechnology.com

ESS Rail
3rd Floor, Regal House,
70 London Rd,
Twickenham, TW1 3QS
T: 0845 245 3000
F: 0845 245 3061
E: john.lynch@essengineering.com
W: www.essengineering.com

Essempy
1 Phoebe Lane,
Church End,
Wavendon,
Bucks, MK17 8LR
T: 01908 582491
E: norman.price@essempy.co.uk
W: www.essempy.co.uk

Essex Medical Testing
104 Haltwhistle Rd,
South Woodham Ferrers,
Essex
T: 01245 426042
F: 01245 425617
E: info@essexmt.co.uk
W: www.essexmedicaltesting.co.uk

ETS Cable Components
Units 4-6,
Red Lion Business Park,
Red Lion Rd, Tolworth,
Surrey, KT6 7QD
T: 020 8405 6789
F: 020 8405 6790
E: sales@etscc.co.uk
W: www.etscc.co.uk

Eurailscout GB Ltd
Unit 2, Kimberley Court,
Kimberley Rd, Queens Park,
London, NW6 7SL
T: 020 7372 2973
F: 020 7372 5444
E: info@eurailscout.com
W: www.eurailscout.com

Euro Cargo Rail SAS
Immeuble la Palacio,
25-29 Place de la Madelaine,
75008 Paris, France
T: 0033 977 400 000
F: 0033 977 400 200
E: info@eurocargorail.com
W: www.eurocargorail.com

Eurochemi
Kingsbury Park,
Midland Rd,
Swadlincote,
Derbys, DE11 0AN
T: 01283 222111
F: 01283 550177
E: info@hkw.co.uk
W: www.eurochemi.co.uk

Eurocom Ltd
W013 to W015,
Westminster Business Square,
Durham Street, Vauxhall,
London, SE11 5JH
T: 020 7820 8344
F: 020 7820 8355
E: comms@eurocomltd.co.uk
W: www.eurocomlimited.com/

Eurolog Ltd
Orlando House,
3 High St,
Teddington, TW11 8NP
T: 020 8977 4407
F: 020 8977 3714
E: info@eurolog.co.uk
W: www.eurolog.co.uk

Europe Rail Consultancy Ltd
North Court,
Hassocks,
West Sussex, BN6 8JS
T: 01273 845583
E: chris.dugdale@europerailconsultancy.com
W: www.europerailconsultancy.com

European Association of Railway Personnel
32 Greet Road,
Lancing,
Sussex, BN15 9NS
T: 01903 521850
E: fam.andrews@yahoo.com

European Investment Bank (EIB)
1 Royal Exchange Buildings,
London, EC3V 3LF
T: 020 7375 9660
F: 020 7375 9699
W: www.eib.org

Europhoenix
Registered Address,
58a High Street,
Stony Stratford, Milton Keynes,
Buckinghamshire, MK11 1AQ
W: www.europhoenix.eu

Eurostar International Ltd
Times House,
Bravingtons Walk,
Regent Quarter,
London, N1 9AW
E: press.office@eurostar.co.uk
W: www.eurostar.com

Eurotech Ltd
3 Clifton Court,
Cambridge, CB1 7BN
T: 01223 403410
F: 01223 410457
E: sales@eurotech-ltd.co.uk
W: www.eurotech-ltd.co.uk

Faiveley Transport Birkenhead Ltd:
Morpeth Wharf, Twelve Quays, Birkenhead, Wirral CH41 1LF
T: 0151 649 5000 **F:** 0151 649 5001
E: john.summers@faiveleytransport.com

Faiveley Transport Tamworth Ltd:
Darwell Park, Mica Close, Amington, Tamworth, Staffordshire B77 4DR
T: 01827 308430 **F:** 01827 308431
E: arnaud.dewally@faiveleytransport.com
W: www.faiveleytransport.com

Faiveley Transport UK provides a comprehensive range of original equipment supply, together with repair and overhaul services, including HVAC, Door Systems, Braking Systems, Couplers, Pantograph, Auxilliary Power Converters, CCTV and Event Recorders.

Eurotunnel
The Channel Tunnel Group Ltd,
UK Terminal,
Ashford Rd,
Folkestone, Kent, CT18 8XX
T: 08443 353535
F: 01303 288784
E: communication.internet@eurotunnel.com
W: www.eurotunnel.com

Eurox
Aqua House, Buttress Way,
Smethwick, B66 3DL
T: 0121 555 7167
F: 0121 555 7168
E: sales.orders@eurox.co.uk
W: www.eurox.co.uk

Eve Trakway Ltd
Bramley Vale,
Chesterfield,
Derbys, S44 5GA
T: 08700 767676
F: 08700 737373
E: mail@evetrakway.co.uk
W: www.evetrakway.co.uk

Evergrip Ltd
Unit 4, Flaxley Rd,
Selby, YO8 4BG
T: 01757 212744
F: 01757 212749
E: sales@evergrip.com
W: www.evergrip.com

Eversheds
1 Royal Standard Place,
Nottingham, NG1 6FZ
T: 0845 497 9797
F: 0845 497 4919
W: www.eversheds.co.uk

Eversholt Rail (UK) Ltd
PO Box 68166, 210 Pentonville Rd,
London, N1P 2AR
T: 020 7380 5040
F: 020 7380 5148
E: wendy.filer@eversholtrail.co.uk
W: www.eversholtrail.co.uk

Evolvi Rail Systems Ltd
3rd Floor,
1 new Century Place, East St,
Reading, RG1 4ET
T: 0871 521 9871
E: accountmanagement@evolvi.co.uk
W: www.evolvi.co.uk

EWS
See DB Schenker

Excalibur Screwbolts Ltd
Gate 3, Newhall Nursery,
Lower Rd, Hockley,
Essex, SS5 5JU
T: 01702 206962/207909
F: 01702 207918
E: charles.bickford@screwbolt.com
W: www.excaliburscrewbolts.com

Exide Technologies
See GNB Industrial Power (UK) Ltd

Exled ITD
Phoenix Mill,
London Rd, Stroud,
Glos, GL5 2BU
T: 01453 456361
F: 01453 756505
E: sales@exled.co.uk
W: www.exled.co.uk

Exova (UK) Ltd
6 Coronet Way,
Centenary Park,
Salford, M50 1RE
T: 0161 787 3291
F: 0161 787 3251
E: steve.hughes@exova.com
W: www.exova.com

Expamet Security Products
PO Box 14,
Longhill Ind. Est. (North),
Hartlepool, TS25 1PR
T: 01429 867366
F: 01429 867355
E: sales@exmesh.co.uk
W: www.expandedmetalfencing.com

Express Electrical
37 Cable Depot Rd,
Riverside Ind Est,
Clydebank, G81 1UY
T: 0141 941 3689
F: 0141 952 8155
E: sales@expresselectrical.co.uk
W: www.expresselectrical.co.uk

Express Medicals Ltd
8 City Business Centre, Lower Rd,
London, SE16 2XB
T: 020 7500 6900
F: 020 7500 6910
E: workhealth@expressmedicals.co.uk
W: www.expressmedicals.co.uk

External Solutions Ltd
Unit 2, 5 Elwes St, Brigg,
North Lincs, DN20 8LB
T: 01652 655933
F: 01652 655966
E: dawn@external-solutions.co.uk
W: www.external-solutions.co.uk

Factair Ltd
49 Boss Hall Rd,
Ipswich,
Suffolk, IP1 5BN
T: 01473 746400
F: 01473 747123
E: enquiries@factair.co.uk
W: www.factair.co.uk

Faithful & Gould
Euston Tower, 286, Euston Rd,
London, NW1 3AT
T: 020 7121 2121
F: 020 7121 2020
E: info@fgould.com
W: www.fgould.com

Faiveley Transport Ltd
Morpeth Wharf,
Twelve Quays,
Birkenhead,
Wirral, CH41 1LF
T: 0151 649 5000
F: 0151 649 5001
E: nigel.bowers@faiveleytransport.com
W: www.faiveleytransport.com

Falcon Electrical Engineering Ltd
Falcon House,
Main St, Fallin,
Stirlingshire, FK7 7HT
T: 01786 819920
F: 01786 814381
E: sales@falconelectrical.com
W: www.falconelectrical.com

Fastrack (Expamet Security Products)
PO Box 14, Longhill Ind. Est. (North), Hartlepool, TS25 1PR
T: 01429 867366
F: 01429 867355
E: sales@exmesh.co.uk
W: www.expandedmetalcompany.co.uk

FCC Construcción
Federico Salmón,
13. 28016,
Madrid, Spain
T: 34 913 595 400
F: 34 913 594 923
W: www.fcc.es/

Federal Mogul Friction Products (Ferodo)
Hayfield Road,
Chapel-en-le-Frith,
Derbys, SK23 0JP
T: 01298 811689
F: 01298 811580
W: www.federalmogul.com

Fenbrook Consulting Ltd
22 Fenbrook Close,
Hambrook,
Bristol, BS16 1QJ
T: 0117 970 1773
E: trevor@fenbrook.com
W: www.fenbrook.com

Fencing & Lighting Contractors Ltd
Unit 21,
Amber Drive,
Bailey Brook Ind Est,
Langley Mill,
Derbys, NG16 4BE
T: 01773 531383
F: 01773 531921
E: info@fencingandlighting.co.uk
W: www.fencingandlighting.co.uk/

The Fenning Lovatt Partnership Ltd
69-71 Newington Causeway,
London, SE1 6BD
T: 020 7378 4812
F: 020 7407 4612
E: mail@fenninglovatt.com
W: www.fenninglovatt.com

Feonic Technology
3e Newlands Science Park,
Inglemire Lane,
Hull, HU6 7TQ
T: 01482 806688
F: 01482 806654
E: info@feonic.com
W: www.feonic.com

Ferrabyrne Ltd
Fort Rd Ind. Est,
Littlehampton,
West Sussex, BN17 7QU
T: 01903 721317
F: 01903 730452
E: sales@ferrabyrne.co.uk
W: www.ferrabyrne.co.uk

Ferrograph Ltd
Unit 1,
New York Way,
New York Ind Park,
Newcastle Upon Tyne, NE27 0QF
T: 0191 280 8800
F: 0191 280 8810
E: info@ferrograph.com
W: www.ferrograph.com

Ferrovial Agroman
10th Floor, BSI Building 389,
Chiswick High Road,
London, W4 4AL
E: pressheadoffice@ferrovial.com
W: www.faukie.com/

Fibergrate Composite Structures
5151 Beltline Rd, Ste 1212,
Dallas, TX 75254,
United States
T: 00 800 527 4043
F: 00 972 250 1530
E: info@fibergrate.com
W: www.fibergrate.com

Fibrelite Composites Ltd
Snaygill Ind. Est,
Keighley Rd,
Skipton,
N Yorks, BD23 2QR
T: 01756 799773
F: 01756 799539
E: covers@fibrelite.com
W: www.fibrelite.com

Field Fisher LLP
Riverbank House,
2 Swan Lane,
London, EC4R 3TT
T: 020 7861 4000
F: 020 7488 0084
E: nicholas.thompsell@fieldfisher.com
W: www.fieldfisher.com

Fifth Dimension Associates Ltd (FDAL)
Suite 18411, 20-22 Wenlock Road,
London, N1 7GU
T: 020 7060 2332
F: 020 7060 3325
E: london@fdal.co.uk
W: www.fdal.co.uk

Findlay Irvine Ltd
Bog Rd, Penicuik,
Midlothian, EH26 9BU
T: 01968 671200
F: 01968 671237
E: sales@findlayirvine.com
W: www.findlayirvine.com

Finning (UK) Ltd
Unit 3,
Triangle Business Park,
Oakwell Way,
Birstall, Batley,
West Yorks, WF17 9LU
T: 0113 201 2065
F: 0113 201 2051
E: oillab@finning.co.uk
W: www.fluid-analysis.com

Fircroft
Trinity House,
114 Northenden Rd, Sale,
Cheshire, M33 3FZ
T: 0161 905 2020
F: 0161 969 1743
E: hq@fircroft.co.uk
W: www.fircroft.co.uk

The Fire Service College
Moreton-in-Marsh,
Glos, GL56 0RH
T: 01608 812130
F: 01608 651790
E: dluff@fireservicecollege.ac.uk
W: www.fireservicecollege.ac.uk

First Choice Protection
See Portwest Clothing Ltd

First Components Ltd
Wallows Ind Est,
Wallows Rd,
Brierley Hill, DY5 1QA
T: 01384 262068
F: 01384 482383
E: info@firstcomponents.co.uk
W: www.firstcomponents.co.uk

First Engineering Ltd
See Babcock Rail

First Hull Trains
Europa House,
184 Ferensway,
Hull, HU1 3UT
T: 03456 769 905
E: customer.services@hulltrains.co.uk
W: www.hulltrains.co.uk

First Procurement Associates
See FPA Consulting Ltd

First Rail Support Ltd
Unit 20,
Time Technology Park,
Blackburn Rd,
Simonstone,
Lancs, BB12 7TG
T: 01282 688110
F: 01282 688141
E: rail.support@firstgroup.com
W: www.firstgroup.com/firstrailsupport

First TransPennine Express
Bridgewater House,
60 Whitworth St,
Manchester, M1 6LT
T: 0345 600 1671
F: 0161 228 8120
E: tpecustomer.relations@firstgroup.com
W: www.tpexpress.co.uk

Firstco Ltd
4 Celbridge Mews,
Royal Oak,
London, W2 6EU
T: 020 7034 0833
F: 020 7229 8002
E: info@firstco.co.uk
W: www.firstco.co.uk

FirstGroup Plc
395 King St, Aberdeen, AB24 5RP
T: 01224 650100
F: 01224 650140
E: corporate.comms@firstgroup.com
W: www.firstgroup.com/corporate

Fishbone Solutions Ltd
25 Statham St, Darley,
Derbys, DE22 1HR
T: 0115 714 3444
F: 020 7942 0701
E: go-fish@fishbonesolutions.co.uk
W: www.fishbonesolutions.co.uk

Fitzpatrick Contractors Ltd
See VolkerFitzpatrick Ltd

FKI Switchgear
See Hawker Siddley Switchgear ltd

FleetwoodMay
Bramble Dene,
35 Cavendish Road,
Woking,
Surrey, GU22 0EP
M: 07836 720537
E: martin@fleetwoodmay.co.uk
W: www.fleetwoodmay.co.uk

Flexible & Specialist (FS) Cables
Alban Point, Alban Park,
Hatfield Rd,
St Albans, AL4 0JX
T: 01727 840841
F: 01727 840842
E: sales@fscables.com
W: www.fscables.com

Flexicon Ltd
Roman Way,
Coleshill,
Birmingham, B46 1HG
T: 01675 466900
F: 01675 466901
E: rail@flexicon.uk.com
W: www.flexicon.uk.com

FLI Structures
Francis & Lewis International,
Waterwells Drive,
Waterwells Business Park,
Gloucester, GL2 2AA
T: 01452 722200
F: 01452 722244
E: m.jones@fli.co.uk
W: www.fliscrewpiles.co.uk

Flint Bishop Solicitors
St Michaels Court,
St Michaels Lane,
Derby, DE1 3HQ
T: 01332 340211
E: info@flintbishop.co.uk
W: www.flintbishop.co.uk

Flir Systems Ltd (UK)
2 Kings Hill Ave,
West Malling,
Kent, ME19 4AQ
T: 01732 220011
F: 01732 843707
E: flir@flir.com
W: www.flir.com

Flotec Rail Division
Unit 8, Pavillion Way,
Loughborough,
Leicestershire, LE11 5GW
T: 01509 230100
M: 07962345387
E: maria@flotechonlinr.com
W: www.floteconline.com

Flowcrete UK Ltd
The Flooring Technology Centre,
Booth Lane,
Sandbach,
Cheshire, CW11 3QF
T: 01270 753000
F: 01270 753333
E: uk@flowcrete.com
W: www.flowcrete.com

Fluke UK Ltd (Tracklink)
52 Hurricane Way,
Norwich, NR6 6JB
T: 020 7942 0700
F: 020 7942 0701
E: industrial@uk.fluke.nl
W: www.fluke.co.uk

Fluor Ltd
Fluor Centre, 140 Pinehurst Road,
Farnborough, Hants, GU14 7BF
T: 01252 291000
F: 01252 292222
W: www.fluor.com

Focus 2000 Infrared Ltd
5a Lodge Hill Business Park,
Westbury-sub-Mendip,
Somerset, BA5 1EY
T: 01749 870620
F: 01749 870622
E: sales@focus2k.co.uk
W: www.focus2k.co.uk

Fone Alarm Installations Ltd
59 Albert Rd North,
Reigate, RH2 9EL
T: 01737 223673
F: 01737 224349
E: enquiries@fonealarm.co.uk
W: www.fonealarm.co.uk

Forbo Flooring Ltd
High Holborn Rd, Ripley,
Derbys, DE5 3NT
T: 01773 744121
F: 01773 744142
E: bob.summers@forbo.com
W: www.forbo-flooring.co.uk

Ford & Stanley Ltd
44 Royal Scot Rd, Pride Park,
Derby, DE24 8AJ
T: 01332 344443
E: daniel.taylor@fordandstanley.com
W: www.fordandstanley.com

Ford Components Manufacturing Ltd
Unit 2,
Monkton Business Park North,
Mill Lane, Hebburn,
Tyne & Wear, NE31 2JZ
T: 0191 428 6600
F: 0191 428 6620
E: shaun.gribben@ford-components.com
W: www.ford-components.com

Foremost Logan Ltd
Kersey Hall, Tannery Rd, Combs,
Stowmarket, Suffolk
T: 01449 742450
F: 01449 771207
E: info@foremostlogan.com
W: www.foremostlogan.com

ForgeTrack Ltd
Thistle House, St Andrew St,
Hertford, SG14 1JA
T: 01992 500900
F: 01992 589495
E: sales@forgetrack.co.uk
W: www.forgetrack.co.uk

Fosroc Ltd
Drayton Manor Business Park,
Coleshill Rd, Tamworth,
Staffs, B78 3XN
T: 01827 262222
F: 01827 262444
E: enquiryuk@fosroc.com
W: www.fosroc.com

Fourth Friday Club
Transport Writing Services Ltd,
PO Box 206,
Tunbridge Wells,
Kent
T: 01892863358
M: 07884232099
W: 4thfriday.co.uk/

Fourway Communications Ltd
Delamere Rd, Cheshunt,
Herts, EN8 9SH
T: 01992 629182
F: 01992 639227
E: enquiries@fourway.co.uk
W: www.fourway.co.uk

FP McCann Ltd
Cadeby Depot, Brascote Lane,
Cadeby, Nuneaton,
Warks, CV13 0BE
T: 01455 290780
F: 01455 292189
E: scarson@fpmccann.co.uk
W: www.fpmccann.co.uk

FPA Consulting Ltd
1 St Andrew's House,
Vernon Gate, Derby, DE1 1UJ
T: 01332 604321
F: 01332 604322
E: johnb@fpaconsulting.co.uk
W: www.fpaconsulting.co.uk

Frankham Consulting Group Ltd
Irene House,
Five Arches Business Park,
Maidstone Rd, Sidcup,
Kent, DA14 5AE
T: 020 8309 7777
F: 020 8306 7890
E: enquiries@frankham.com
W: www.frankham.com

Franklin + Andrews
Sea Containers House,
20 Upper Ground,
London, SE1 9LZ
T: 020 7633 9966
F: 020 7928 2471
E: enquiries@franklinandrews.com
W: www.franklinandrews.com

Frauscher Selectrail (UK) Ltd
Unit 58,
Basepoint Business Centre,
Isidore Rd, Bromsgrove, B60 3ET
T: 01527 834670
F: 01527 834671
E: info@frauscher-selectrail.com
W: www.frauscher-selectrail.com

Frauscher UK
Suite 5, Yeovil Innovation Centre,
Barracks Close, Copse Rd,
Yeovil, BA22 8RN
T: 01935 385905
F: 01935 385901
E: richard.colman@uk.frauscher.com
W: www.frauscher.com

Frazer Nash Consultancy Ltd
Stonebridge House,
Dorking Business Park,
Station Rd, Dorking,
Surrey, RH4 1JH
T: 01306 885050
F: 01306 886464
E: r.jones@fnc.co.uk
W: www.fnc.co.uk

Freeman Williams Language Solutions Ltd
College Business Centre,
Uttoxeter New Rd,
Derby, DE22 3WZ
T: 01332 869342
F: 01332 869344
E: abi@freemanwilliams.co.uk
W: www.freemanwillams.co.uk

Freeths LLP
Cardinal Square, 2nd Floor,
West Point, 10 Nottingham Rd,
Derby, DE1 3QT
T: 0845 634 9791
F: 0845 634 9804
E: mike.copestake@freeths.co.uk
W: www.freeths.co.uk

Freight Europe (UK) Ltd
See Captrain UK Ltd

Freight On Rail
16 Waterside, 44-48 Wharf Road,
London, N1 7UX
T: 020 8241 9982
F: 020 7566 6493
M: 07593 976548
E: philippa@freightonrail.org.uk
W: www.freightonrail.org.uk

FreightArranger Ltd
West View, Brownshill, Stroud,
Glos, GL6 8AQ
T: 01453 367150
W: www.freightarranger.co.uk

Freightliner Group Ltd
3rd Floor, The Podium,
1 Eversholt St, London, NW1 2FL
T: 020 7200 3900
F: 020 7200 3975
E: pressoffice@freightliner.co.uk
W: www.freightliner.co.uk

Frequentis UK Ltd
Regal House, 70 London Road,
Twickenham, TW1 3QS
T: 020 8891 1518
E: marketing@frequentis.com
W: www.frequentis.com

Freshfields Bruckhaus Deringer LLP
65 Fleet St, London, EC4Y 1HT
T: 0207 936 4000
F: 0207 832 7001
E: digitalcommunications@freshfields.com
W: www.freshfields.com

Freyssinet Ltd
Innovation House, Euston Way,
Town Centre, Telford,
Shropshire, TF3 4LT
T: 01952 201901
F: 01952 201753
E: mailto:john.kennils@freyssinet.co.uk
W: www.freyssinet.co.uk

Frontier Economics
71 High Holborn,
London, WC1V 6DA
T: 0207 031 7000
E: transport@frontier-economics.com
W: www.frontier-economics.com/

FS Cables
See Flexible & Specialist (FS) Cables

Fuchs Lubricants (UK) Plc
New Century St, Hanley,
Stoke on Trent, ST1 5HU
T: 08701 203700
F: 01782 202072
E: contact-uk@fuchs-oil.com
W: www.fuchslubricants.com

Fuelcare Ltd
Suite 1, The Hayloft,
Blakenhall Park,
Barton under Needwood,
Staffs, DE13 8AJ
T: 01283 712263
F: 01283 262263
E: sales@fuelcare.com
W: www.fuelcare.com

Fugro Aperio Ltd
Focal Point, Newmarket Rd,
Bottisham, Cambridge, CB25 9BD
T: 0870 600 8050
F: 0870 800 8040
E: info@fugro-aperio.com
W: www.fugro-aperio.com

Fujikura Europe Ltd
C51 Barwell Business Park,
Leatherhead Rd, Chessington,
Surrey, KT9 2NY
T: 020 8240 2000
F: 020 8240 2010
E: sales@fujikura.co.uk
W: www.fujikura.co.uk

Fujitsu
22 Baker Street, London,
W1U 3BW
T: 0843 354 7998
E: askfujitsu@uk.fujitsu.com
W: www.fujitsu.com/uk/industries/rail

Funkwerk Information Technologies York Ltd
See Trapeze Group Rail Ltd

Furneaux Riddall & Co Ltd
Alchorne Place,
Portsmouth,
Hants, PO3 5PA
T: 02392 668624
F: 02392 668625
E: info@furneauxriddall.com
W: www.furneauxriddall.com

Furrer + Frey
Winchester House,
19 Bedford Row,
London, WC1R 4EB
T: 020 3740 5455
E: ndolphin@furrerfrey.ch
W: www.furrerfrey.ch

Furse - Thomas & Betts Ltd
Wilford Rd,
Nottingham, NG2 1EB
T: 0115 964 3700
F: 0115 986 0538
E: enquiry@furse.com
W: www.furse.com

Furtex
See Camira Fabrics Ltd

Fusion People Ltd
2nd/3rd Floor,
Aldermary House,
10-15 Queen St,
London, EC4N 1TX
T: 020 7653 1070
F: 020 7653 1071
E: rail@fusionpeople.com
W: www.fusionpeople.com

Future Rail (formerly Future Welding)
The Rowe,
Stableford,
Staffs, ST5 4EN
T: 01782 411800
E: futureraildesign@gmail.com
W: www.futurerail.co.uk

Gabriel & Co Ltd
1 Cromwell Rd,
Smethwick,
West Midlands, B66 2JT
T: 0121 555 7615
F: 0121 555 1922
E: john.gabriel@gabrielco.com
W: www.gabrielco.com

GAI Tronics (Hubbel Ltd)
Brunel Dr.,
Stretton Business Park,
Burton upon Trent, DE13 0BZ
T: 01283 500500
F: 01283 500400
E: sales@gai-tronics.co.uk
W: www.gai-tronics.co.uk

Galliford Try Rail
Crab Lane, Fearnhead,
Warrington, WA2 0XR
T: 01925 822821
F: 01925 812323
E: ron.stevenson@gallifordtry.co.uk
W: www.gallifordtry.co.uk

Gamble Rail
See Keltbray

Ganymede Solutions Ltd
26 Hershel St,
Slough, SL1 1PA
T: 01753 820810
F: 0870 890 1894
E: gary.hewett@ganymedesolutions.co.uk
W: www.ganymedesolutions.co.uk

Gardiner & Theobald
10 South Crescent,
London, WC1E 7BD
T: 020 7209 3000
F: 020 7209 1840
E: p.armstrong@gardiner.com
W: www.gardiner.com

Gardner Denver Ltd
Claybrook Drive, Washford Ind. Est,
Redditch, Worcs, B98 0DS
T: 01527 838200
F: 01527 521140
E: hydrovane-info.uk@gardnerdenver.com
W: www.gardnerdenver.com/

Garic Ltd
Kingfisher Park, Aviation Rd,
Pilsworth, Bury, BL9 8GD
T: 0844 417 9780
F: 0161 766 8809
E: sales@garic.co.uk
W: www.garic.co.uk

Garrandale Ltd
Alfreton Rd, Derby, DE21 4AP
T: 0800 949 9040
F: 01332 222200
E: sales@garrandale.co.uk
W: www.garrandale.co.uk

GarrettCom Europe Ltd
See Belden Solutions

Gates Power Transmission
Tinwald Downs Rd, Heath Hall,
Dumfries, DG1 1TS
T: 01387 242000
F: 01387 242010
E: mediaeurope@gates.com
W: www.gates.com

Gatwick Express
See Southern/Gatwick Express

Gatwick Plant Ltd
Woodside Works, The Close,
Horley, Surrey, RH6 9EB
T: 01293 824777
F: 01293 824077
E: transport@gatwickgroup.com
W: www.gatwickgroup.com

GAV Access Covers
PO Box 2282, Nuneaton,
Warks, CV11 9ZT
T: 02476 381090
F: 02476 373577
E: gavmet@aol.com
W: www.gav-solutions.com

GB Railfreight
3rd Floor, 55 Old Broad Street,
London, EC2M 1RX
T: 020 7904 3393
F: 020 7983 5113
E: gbrfinfo@gbrailfreight.com
W: www.gbrailfreight.com

GDS Technology Ltd
Unit 6, Cobham Centre,
Westmead Industrial Est, Westlea,
Swindon, SN5 7UJ
T: 01793 498020
E: sales.gdstechnology@gds.com
W: www.gdstechnology.co.uk

GE Transportation Systems
Inspira House, Martinfield,
Welwyn Garden City, Herts,
AL7 1GW
T: 01707 383700
F: 01707 383701
E: getransportationinquiries@ge.com
W: www.getransportation.com

Geatech S.p.A
Via Del Palazzino 6/B,
40051 Altedo (BO), Italy
T: 0039 051 6601514
F: 0039 051 6601309
E: info@geatech.it
W: www.geatech.it

Geismar UK Ltd
Salthouse Rd, Brackmills Ind. Est.,
Northampton, NN4 7EX
T: 01604 769191
F: 01604 763154
E: sales-uk@geismar.com
W: www.geismar.com

Geldards LLP
Number One,
Pride Place, Pride Park,
Derby, DE24 8QR
T: 01332 331631
F: 01332 294295
E: roman.surma@geldards.co.uk
W: www.geldards.co.uk

Gemma Lighting
Unit 3, Marshlands Spur,
Farlington, Portsmouth,
Hampshire, PO6 1RX
T: 0844 856 5201
F: 0844 856 5209
E: marketing@
gemmalighting.com
W: www.gemmalighting.com

GenQuip Plc
Aberafan Rd, Baglan Ind. Park,
Port Talbot, SA12 7DJ
T: 01639 823484
F: 01639 822533
E: sales@genquip.co.uk
W: www.genquip.co.uk

Genwork Ltd
See Bache Pallets Ltd

Geodesign Barriers Ltd
2 Montgomery Ave, Pinehurst,
Swindon, SN2 1LE
T: 01793 538565
E: britt.warg@palletbarrier.com
W: www.geodesignbarriers.com

Geoff Brown Signalling Ltd
The Cottage, Old Lodge,
Minchinhampton,
Stroud, GL6 9AQ
T: 07977 265721
E: geoffbrownsignalling@
btinternet.com

GeoRope
Arumindarrich, West Laroch,
Ballachulish, Argyll, PH49 4JG
T: 01855 811224
E: kam@geo-rope.com
W: www.geo-rope.com

Geosynthetics Ltd
Fleming Rd, Harrowbrook Ind.Est.,
Hinckley, Leics, LE10 3DU
T: 01455 617139
F: 01455 617140
E: sales@geosyn.co.uk
W: www.geosyn.co.uk

Geotechnical Engineering Ltd
Centurion House,
Olympus Park, Quedgeley,
Glos, GL2 4NF
T: 01452 527743
F: 01452 729314
E: geotech@geoeng.co.uk
W: www.geoeng.co.uk

Geotechnics Ltd
The Geotechnical Centre,
203 Torrington Ave, Tile Hill,
Coventry, CV4 9UT
T: 02476 694664
F: 02476 694642
E: mail@geotechnics.co.uk
W: www.geotechnics.co.uk

Getzner Werkstoffe GmbH
Herrenaus, A-6706 Burs,
Austria
T: 0043 5552 2010
F: 0043 5552 201899
E: sylomer@getzner.at
W: www.getzner.at

GGB UK
Wellington House,
Starley Way,
Birmingham Int. Park,
Birmingham, B37 7HB
T: 0121 767 9100
F: 0121 781 7313
E: greatbritain@ggbearings.com
W: www.ggbearings.com/en

GGR Group Ltd
Broadway Business Park,
Broadgate, Chadderton,
Oldham, OL9 0JA
T: 0161 683 2580
F: 0161 683 4444
E: info@ggrrail.com
W: www.ggrrail.com

GGS Engineering (Derby) Ltd
Atlas Works, Litchurch Lane,
Derby, DE24 8AQ
T: 01332 299345
F: 01332 299678
E: sales@ggseng.com
W: www.ggseng.com

GHD Ltd
6th Floor, 10 Fetter Lane,
London, EC4A 1BR
T: 020 3077 7900
E: sue.jackson@ghd.com
W: www.ghd.com

Gifford
See Ramboll UK Ltd

Giken Europe BV
15 Manchester Mews,
London, W1U 2DX
T: 0845 260 8001
F: 0845 260 8002
E: info@giken.co.uk
W: www.giken.com

Gilbarco Veeder-Root
Crompton Close, Basildon,
Essex, SS14 3BA
T: 01268 533090
F: 01268 524214
E: uksales@gilbarco.com
W: www.gilbarco.com

Gioconda Limited
Unit 10, Woodfalls, Gravelly Ways,
Laddingford, Maidstone,
Kent, ME18 6DA
T: 01622 872512
E: mail@gioconda.co.uk
W: www.gioconda.co.uk

GKD Technik Ltd
17 Cobham Rd,
Ferndown Industrial Estate,
Wimborne, Dorset, BH21 7PE
T: 01202 861961
F: 01202 861361
E: nick@gkdtechnik.com
W: www.gkdtechnik.com

GKN Hybrid Power
Po Box 55, Ipsley House,
Ipsley Church Lane, Redditch,
Worcs, B98 0TL
T: 01527 517715
W: www.gkn.com/landsystems/
brands/hybrid-power/pages/
default.aspx

Glasdon UK Ltd
Preston New Rd,
Blackpool,
Lancs, FY4 4UL
T: 01253 600414
F: 01253 792558
E: sales@glasdon-uk.co.uk
W: www.glasdon.com

Gleeds
95 New Cavendish St,
London, W1W 6XF
T: 020 7631 7000
F: 020 7631 7001
E: london@gleeds.co.uk
W: www.gleeds.com

Glenair UK Ltd
40 Lower Oakham Way,
Oakham Business Park,
Mansfield,
Notts, NG18 5BY
T: 01623 638100
F: 01623 638111
E: cbaker@glenair.co.uk
W: www.glenair.com

Glendale
The Coach House,
Duxbury Hall Road,
Duxbury Park, Chorley,
Lancs, PR7 4AT
T: 01257 460461
F: 01257 460421
E: info@glendale-services.co.uk
W: www.glendale-services.co.uk/

Glentworth Rail Ltd
Long Lane, Hawthorn Hill,
Maidenhead,
Berks, SL6 3TA
T: 01628 639823
F: 01628 639823
E: rgraham@william-cook.co.uk
W: glentworthrail.co.uk/

Glide (UK) Ltd
32 Clay Hill, Enfield, EN2 9AA
T: 020 8367 7350
E: info@pigeonglide.com
W: www.pigeonglide.com

Global Crossing (UK) Telecommunications Ltd
See Level 3 Communications

Global House Training Services Ltd
1 Cotswold Close, Bexleyheath,
Kent, DA7 6ST
T: 01322 331617
F: 01322 341817
E: contact@globalhouse.co.uk
W: www.globalhouse.co.uk

Global Rail Support
8 Curzon Lane, Alvaston,
Derby, DE24 8QS
T: 01332 601596
F: 01332 727494
E: ask@globalrailsupport.com
W: www.globalrailsupport.com

Globalforce Group
Custom House, 1-3 Harolds Road,
Harlow, Essex, CM19 5BJ
T: 01279 427898
E: enquiries@
globalforcegroup.co.uk
W: www.globalforcegroup.co.uk

GM Rail Services Ltd
65 Somers Rd, Rugby,
Warks, CV22 7DG
T: 01788 573777
F: 01788 551138
E: dwhitley@gmrail.co.uk
W: www.gmrail.co.uk

GME Springs
Unit C, GME Industrial Estate,
Coventry, CV6 5NN
T: 02476 664911
F: 02476 663020
E: sales@gmesprings.co.uk
W: www.gmesprings.co.uk

GMT Manufacturing Ltd
Old Gorsey Lane, Wallasey,
Merseyside, CH44 4AH
T: 0151 630 1545
F: 0151 639 0510
E: info@gmt.co.uk
W: www.gmt.co.uk

GMT Rubber-Metal-Technic Ltd
The Sidings, Station Rd, Guiseley,
Leeds, LS20 8BX
T: 01943 870670
F: 01943 870631
E: sales@gmt.gb.com
W: www.gmt-rubber.com

GNB Industrial Power (UK) Ltd
Mansell House, Aspinall Close,
Middlebrook, Horwich,
Bolton, BL6 6QQ
T: 0845 606 4111
F: 0845 606 4112
E: sales-uk@eu.exide.com
W: www.gnb.com

GNER
See Alliance Rail Holdings

GNWR
See Alliance Rail Holdings

Go Ahead Group plc
Head Office,
4 Matthew Parker St,
Westminster,
London, SW1H 9NP
T: 020 7799 8999
F: 020 7799 8998
E: enquiries@go-ahead.com
W: www.go-ahead.com

GOBOTiX Ltd
Rural Enterprise Centre,
Battlefield Enterprise Park,
Shrewsbury, SY1 3FE
T: 01743 387030
E: sales@gobotix.co.uk
W: www.gobotix.co.uk/

Golder Associates (UK) Ltd
1 Alie Street, London, E1 8DE
T: (0)20 7423 0940
F: (0)20 7423 0941
W: www.golder.co.uk

Gordon Services Ltd
Unit 8, Dawes Farm, Ivy Barn Lane,
Ingatestone, Essex, CM4 0PX
T: 01277 352895
F: 01277 356115
E: enquiries@
gordonservicesltd.co.uk
W: www.gordonservicesltd.co.uk

GOS Tool & Engineering Services Ltd
Heritage Court Rd,
Gilchrist Thomas ind. Est,
Blaenavon, NP4 9RL
T: 01495 790230
F: 01495 792757
E: enquiries@
gosengineering.co.uk
W: www.gosengineering.co.uk

Goskills
See People 1st

Go-Tel Communications Ltd
See Samsung Electronics Hainan Fibreoptics

Govia
Go-ahead Group Rail,
Go-ahead House, 26-
28 Addiscombe Rd, Croydon,
Surrey, CR9 5GA
E: contact@go-ahead-rail.com
W: www.govia.info

Govia Thameslink Railway (GTR)
1st and 2nd Floor,
Monument Place,
24 Monument Street,
London, EC3R 8AJ
T: 0345 026 4700
W: www.gtrailway.com/

Gradus Ltd
Park Green, Macclesfield,
Cheshire, SK11 7LZ
T: 01625 428922
F: 01625 433949
E: imail@gradusworld.com
W: www.gradusworld.com

GRAHAM
1 Seaward Place,
Centurion Business Park,
Glasgow, G41 1HH
T: 0141 418 5550
E: glasgow@graham.co.uk
W: www.graham.co.uk

Gramm Interlink
17-19 High St, Ditchling,
East Sussex, BN6 8SY
F: 01275 846397
M: 07827 947086
W: www.gramminerlinkrail.co.uk

Grammer Seating Systems Ltd
Willenhall Lane Ind. Est., Bloxwich,
Walsall, WS3 2XN
T: 01922 407035
F: 01922 710552
E: david.bignell@grammer.com
W: www.grammer.com

Gramos Applied Ltd
Orapi Applied Ltd, Spring Rd,
Smethwick, West Midlands,
B66 1PT
T: 0121 525 4000
F: 0121 525 4950
E: info@gramos-applied.com
W: www.gramos-applied.com

Grand Central Railway Co. Ltd.
River House, 17 Museum Street,
York, YO1 7DJ
T: 0345 603 4852
F: 01904 466066
E: customer.services@
grandcentralrail.com
W: www.grandcentralrail.co.uk

Grant Rail Group
See VolkerRail

Grant Thornton UK LLP
Melton St, Euston Square,
London, NW1 2EP
T: 0141 223 0731
E: taylor.ferguson@uk.gt.com
W: www.grant-thornton.co.uk

Grass Concrete Ltd
Duncan House, 142 Thornes Lane,
Thornes, Wakefield, WF2 7RE
T: 01924 379443
F: 01924 290289
E: info@grasscrete.com
W: www.grasscrete.com

Graybar Ltd
10 Fleming Close,
Park Farm Ind. Est,
Wellingborough,
Northants, NN8 6UF
T: 01933 676700
F: 01933 676800
E: sales@graybar.co.uk
W: www.graybar.co.uk

Great Western Railway
Milford House, 1 Milford St,
Swindon, SN1 1HL
T: 0345 7000 125
E: fgwfeedback@firstgroup.com
W: www.gwr.com/

Green Leader Ltd
21 Foxmoor Close, Oakley,
Basingstoke,
Hants, RG23 7BQ
T: 01256 781739
E: nmoore@greenleader.co.uk
W: www.greenleader.co.uk

Greenbrier Europe/ Wagony Swidnica SA
Ul Strzelinska 35, 58-100 Swidnica,
Poland
T: 0048 74 856 2000
F: 0048 74 856 2035
E: europeansales@gbrx.com
W: www.gbrx.com

Greengauge 21
28 Lower Teddington Road,
Kingston-upon-Thames,
Surrey, KT1 4HJ
E: co-ordinator@
greengauge21.net
W: www.greengauge21.net

GreenMech Ltd
The Mill Ind. Park,
Kings Coughton, Alcester,
Warks, B49 5QG
T: 01789 400044
F: 01789 400167
E: sales@greenmech.co.uk
W: www.greenmech.co.uk

Grimshaw Architects
57 Clerkenwell Rd,
London, EC1M 5NG
T: 0207 291 4141
E: info@
grimshaw-architects.com
W: www.grimshaw-architects.com

GripDeck UK
Unit 1, Chancers Farm,
Fossett Lane, Colchester,
Essex, CO6 3NY
T: 01206 242494
F: 01206 242496
E: mail@gripdeck.co.uk
W: www.gripdeck.co.uk

Groeneveld Uk Ltd
The Greentec Centre,
Gelders Hall Rd,
Gelders hall Ind. Est, Shepshed,
Leics, LE12 9NH
T: 01509 600033
F: 01509 602000
E: info-uk@groeneveld-
group.com
W: www.groeneveld-group.com

Grontmij
Grove House,
Mansion Gate Drive,
Leeds, LS7 4DN
T: 0113 262 0000
F: 0113 262 0737
E: enquiries@grontmij.co.uk
W: www.grontmij.co.uk

Groundwise Searches Ltd
Suite 8, Chichester House,
45 Chichester Rd,
Southend on Sea, SS1 2JU
T: 01702 615566
F: 01702 460239
E: mail@groundwise.com
W: www.groundwise.com

GroupCytek
The Oast House,
5 Maed Lane,
Farnham,
Surrey, GU9 7DY
T: 01252 715171
F: 01252 713271
E: projects@groupcytek.com
W: www.groupcytek.com

GT Engineering (Markyate) Ltd
Unit 4, Pulloxhill Business Park,
Greenfield Rd,
Pulloxhill, MK45 5EU
T: 01525 718585
E: sales@gtengineering.co.uk
W: www.gtengineering.co.uk

Gummiwerk
See STRAIL (UK) Ltd

Gunnebo UK Ltd
PO Box 61,
Woden Rd,
Wolverhampton, WV10 0BY
T: 01902 455111
F: 01902 351961
E: marketing@gunnebo.com
W: www.gunnebo.com

Gutteridge, Haskins & Davey Ltd
See GHD Ltd

h2gogo Ltd
The Heights,
59-65 Lowlands Rd,
Harrow,
Middx, HA1 3AW
T: 01494 817174
E: info@h2gogo.com
W: www.h2gogo.com

HaCon (UK)
Luminous House,
300 South Row,
Milton Keynes, MK9 2FR
T: 0845 835 8688
F: 0049 511 33699-99
E: info@hacon.de
W: www.hacon.de

Hadleigh Castings Ltd
Pond Hall Rd, Hadleigh, Ipswich,
Suffolk, IP7 5PW
T: 01473 827281
F: 01473 827879
E: data@hadleighcastings.com
W: www.hadleighcastings.com

Hafren Security Fasteners
Unit 23, Mochdre Industrial Park,
Newtown, Powys, SY16 4LE
T: 01686 621300
F: 01686 621800
E: security@hafrenfasteners.com
W: www.hafrenfasteners.com

Haigh Rail Ltd
Unit 35, Roundhouse Court,
Barnes Wallis Way,
Buckshaw Village, Chorley,
Lancs, PR7 7JN
T: 01772 458000
E: chris@haighrail.com
W: www.haighrail.com

Haki Ltd
Magnus, Tame Valley Ind. Est,
Tamworth, Staffs, B77 5BY
T: 01827 282525
F: 01827 250329
E: info@haki.co.uk
W: www.haki.co.uk

Hako Machines Ltd
Eldon Close, Crick,
Northants, NN6 7UD
T: 01788 825600
F: 01788 823969
E: sales@hako.co.uk
W: www.hako.co.uk

Halfen Ltd
A1/A2 Portland Close,
Houghton Regis, Dunstable,
Beds, LU5 5AW
T: 01582 470300
F: 01582 470304
E: info@halfen.co.uk
W: www.halfen.co.uk

HallRail
See Trackwork Ltd

Halo Rail
See Stewart Signs Rail

Hammond (ECS) Ltd
Canal Road, Cwmbach,
Aberdare, CF44 0AG
T: 01685 884813
F: 01685 888187

Harmill Systems Ltd
Unit P, Cherrycourt Way,
Leighton Buzzard, Beds, LU7 4UH
T: 01525 851133
F: 01525 850661
E: david.flint@harmill.co.uk
W: www.harmill.co.uk

Harmonic Ltd
The Hatchery, Eaglewood Park,
Ilminster, TA19 9DQ
T: 01460 256500
F: 01460 200037
W: www.harmonicltd.co.uk

Harp Visual Communications Solutions
Unit C4,
Segensworth Business Centre,
Segensworth Road, Fareham,
Hants, PO15 5RQ
T: 01329 844005
E: sales@harpvisual.co.uk
W: www.passenger information.com

Harrington Generators International (HGI)
Ravenstor Rd, Wirksworth,
Derbys, DE4 4FY
T: 01629 824284
F: 01629 824613
E: sales@hgigenerators.com
W: www.hgigenerators.com

Harry Fairclough Construction
Howley Lane, Howley,
Warrington, Cheshire, WA1 2DN
T: 01925 628300
F: 01925 628301
E: post@harryfairclough.co.uk
W: www.harryfairclough.co.uk

Harry Needle Railroad Company
Barrow Hill Depot,
Campbell Drive, Barrow Hill,
Chesterfield, S43 2PR
T: 01246 477001
F: 01246 477208
E: info@hnrail.co.uk
W: www.hnrail.co.uk/

Harsco Rail Ltd
Unit 1, Chewton St, Eastwood,
Notts, NG16 3HB
T: 01773 539480
F: 01773 539481
E: uksales@harsco.com
W: www.harscorail.com/

Harting Limited
Caswell Rd, Brackmills Ind. Est,
Northampton, NN4 7PW
T: 01604 827500
F: 01604 706777
E: gb@harting.com
W: www.harting.co.uk

Harvard Engineering plc
Tyler Close, Normanton,
Wakefield, West Yorks, WF6 1RL
T: 0113 383 1000
F: 0113 383 1010
E: johncharles@harvardeng.com
W: www.harvardeng.com

Haskoll
39 Harrington Gardens,
London, SW7 4JU
T: 020 7835 1188
F: 020 7373 7230
W: www.haskoll.co.uk/

Hawker Siddley Switchgear ltd
Unit 3, Blackwood Ind. Estate,
Newport Rd, Blackwood,
S.Wales, NP12 2XH
T: 01495 223001
F: 01495 225674
E: nigel.jones@hss-ltd.com
W: www.hss-ltd.com

Hawkgrove Ltd
The Welsh Mill, Park Hill Drive,
Frome, Somerset, BA11 2LE
T: 01373 710777
E: mike.duberry@ hawkgrove.co.uk
W: www.hawkgrove.co.uk

Hayley Rail
48-50 Westbrook Rd, Trafford Park,
Manchester, M17 1AY
T: 0161 872 7466
F: 0161 877 3005
E: phil.mccabe@ hayley-group.co.uk
W: www.hayley-group.co.uk

HBM Test & Measurement
1 Churchill Court, 58 Station Rd,
North Harrow,
Middx, HA2 7SA
T: 020 8515 6000
F: 020 8515 6002
E: info@uk.hbm.com
W: www.hbm.com

Health, Safety & Engineering Consultants Ltd (HSEC)
70 Tamworth Rd,
Ashby de la Zouch,
Leics, LE65 2PR
T: 01530 412777
F: 01530 415592
E: hsec@hsec.co.uk
W: www.hsec.co.uk

Healthcare Connections Ltd
Nashleigh Court, 188 Severalls Ave,
Chesham, Bucks, HP5 3EN
T: 08456 773002
F: 08456 773004
E: sales@healthcare-connections.com
W: www.healthcare-connections.com

Heat Trace Ltd
Mere's Edge, Chester Rd, Helsby,
Frodsham, Cheshire, WA6 0DJ
T: 01928 726451
F: 01928 727846
E: nil.malone@heat-trace.com
W: www.heat-trace.com

Heathrow Connect
See Heathrow Express

Heathrow Express
The Compass Centre,
Nelson Road, Hounslow,
Middlesex, TW6 2GW
T: 0345 600 1515
W: www.heathrowexpress.com

Heathrow Hub Ltd
60-62, Old London Road,
Kingston on Thames, KT2 6QZ
T: (0) 207 379 5151
E: heathrowhub@maitland.co.uk
W: www.heathrowhub.com

Heavy Haul Power International GmbH
Steigerstrasse 9, 99096 Erfurt,
Germany
T: 0049 361 43046714
F: 0049 361 2629971
E: richard.painter@hhpi.eu
W: www.hhpi.eu

Hedra
See Mouchel

Hegenscheidt MFD GmbH & CO KG
Hegenscheidt Platz,
D-41812 Erkelenz, Germany
T: 0049 2431 86279
F: 0049 2431 86480
E: info@niles-simmons.de
W: www.hegenscheidt-mfd.de

Hellermann Tyton
Sharston Green Business Park,
1 Robeson Way, Altrincham Rd,
Wythenshawe,
Manchester, M22 4TY
T: 0161 947 2200
F: 0161 947 2220
E: sales@hellermanntyton.co.uk
W: www.hellermanntyton.co.uk

Henkel Loctite
Technologies House,
Wood Lane End,
Hemel Hempstead,
Herts, HP2 4RQ
T: 01442 278100
F: 01442 278293
W: www.loctite.com

Henry Williams Ltd
Dodsworth St,
Darlington,
Co. Durham, DL1 2NJ
T: 01325 462722
F: 01325 245220
E: info@hwilliams.co.uk
W: www.hwilliams.co.uk

Hepworth Rail International
4 Merse Rd, North Moons Moat,
Redditch, Worcs, B98 9HL
T: 01527 61243
F: 01527 66836
E: markjones@b-hepworth.com
W: www.b-hepworth.com

Hering UK LLP
Wessex House, Oxford Rd,
Newbury, Berks, RG14 1PA
T: 01635 814490
F: 01635 814491
W: www.heringinternational.com

Herrenknecht AG
Schlehenweg 2, 77963 Schwanau,
Germany
T: 0049 7824 3020
F: 0049 7824 3403
E: info@herrenknecht.com
W: www.herrenknecht.com

Hertford Controls Ltd
14 Ermine Point,
Gentlemens Field, Westmill Rd,
Ware, Herts, SG12 0EF
T: 01920 467578
F: 01920 487037
E: info@hertfordcontrols.co.uk
W: www.hertfordcontrols.co.uk

Hexagon Metrology Ltd
Halesfield 13, Telford,
Shropshire, TF7 4PL
T: 0870 446 2667
F: 0870 446 2668
E: enquiry.uk@ hexagonmetrology.com
W: www.hexagonmetrology. com/uk

HFZ Consulting Ltd
8 Westbury Close,
Bury,
Lancs, BL8 2LW
E: aj@hfzconsulting.co.uk
W: www.hfzconsulting.co.uk

Hid Global

Hiflex Fluidpower
Howley Park Rd, Morley,
Leeds, LS27 0BN
T: 0113 281 0031
F: 0113 307 5918
E: sales@hiflex-europe.com
W: www.dunlophiflex.com

High Speed 1 Ltd
See HS1 Ltd

High Speed 2 Ltd
See HS2 Ltd

High Voltage Maintenance Services Ltd
Unit A, Faraday Court,
Faraday Rd,
Crawley,
West Sussex, RH10 9PU
T: 0845 604 0336
F: 01293 537739
E: enquiries@hvms.co.uk
W: www.hvms.co.uk

Hill Cannon (UK) LLP
Business Centre,
Hartwith Way,
Harrogate, HG3 2XA
T: 01423 813522
F: 01423 530018
E: harrogate@hillcannon.com
W: www.hillcannon.com

Hill McGlynn
See Ranstad CPE

Hilti (GB) Ltd
No1 Trafford Wharf Rd,
Trafford Park,
Manchester, M17 1BY
T: 0800 886 100
F: 0800 886 200
E: gbsales@hilti.com
W: www.hilti.co.uk

Hima-Sella Ltd
Carrington Field St,
Stockport,
Cheshire, SK1 3JN
T: 0161 429 4500
F: 0161 476 3095
E: contactus@hima-sella.co.uk
W: www.hima-sella.co.uk

Hiremasters
See Quickbuild (UK) Ltd

Hitachi Capital Vehicle Solutions Ltd
Kiln House, Kiln Rd,
Newbury,
Berks, RG14 2NU
T: 01635 574640
W: www.hitachicapital vehiclesolutions.co.uk

Hitachi Information Control Systems Europe
Manvers House,
Kingston Rd,
Bradford-on-Avon,
Wilts, BA15 1AB
T: 01225 860140
F: 01225 867698
E: contact_us@ hitachi-infocon.com
W: www.hitachi-infocon.com/

Hitachi Rail Europe Ltd
40 Holborn Viaduct,
London, EC1N 2PB
T: 020 7970 2700
F: 020 7970 2799
E: rail.enquiries@ hitachirail-eu.com
W: www.hitachirail-eu.com

HJ Skelton & Co Ltd
9 The Broadway,
Thatcham,
Berks, RG19 3JA
T: 01635 865256
F: 01635 865710
E: email@hjskelton.com
W: www.hjskelton.co.uk

HOCHTIEF (UK) Construction Ltd
Epsilon,
Windmill Hill Business Park,
Whitehill Way,
Swindon,
Wilts, SN5 6NX
T: 01793 755555
F: 01793 755556
E: enquiries@hochtief.co.uk
W: www.hochtief-construction.co.uk/

Hodge Clemco Ltd
36 Orgreave Drive,
Handsworth,
Sheffield,
South Yorks, S13 9NR
T: 0114 254 8811
F: 0114 254 0250
E: sales@hodgeclemco.co.uk
W: www.hodgeclemco.co.uk

Hodgson & Hodgson Group Ltd
Crown Business Park, Old Dalby, Melton Mowbray, Leics, LE14 3NQ
T: 01664 821810
F: 01664 821820
E: info@hodgsongroup.co.uk
W: www.acoustic.co.uk/h&h/rail.htm

Hogia Transport Systems Ltd
St James House, 13 Kensington Square, London, W8 5HD
T: 020 7795 8156
E: gary.umpleby@hogia.com
W: www.hogia.com/transport

HOK International Ltd
Qube, 90 Whitfield St, London, W1T 4EZ
T: 020 7636 2006
F: 020 7636 1987
E: samantha.davis@hok.com
W: www.hok.com

HOK International Ltd
Qube, 90 Whitfield St, London, W1T 4EZ
T: 020 7636 2006
F: 020 7636 1987
E: samantha.davis@hok.com
W: www.hok.com

Holdfast Level Crossings Ltd
Brockenhurst, Cheap St, Chegworth, Cheltenham, Glos, GL54 4AA
T: 01242 578801
F: 01285 720748
E: request@railcrossings.co.uk
W: www.railcrossings.co.uk

Holland Company
1000 Holland Drive, Crete, Illinois, 60417 USA, United States
T: 001 708 672 2300
F: 001 708 672 0119
E: sales@hollandco.com
W: www.hollandco.com

Holmar Rail Services
Kendal House, The Street, Shadoxhurst, Ashford, Kent, TN26 1LU
T: 01233 731007
F: 01233 733221
W: www.holmar.co.uk

Holmatro Group
Lissenveld 30, P.O. Box 66, 4940 AB, Raamsdonksveer, Netherlands
T: +31 (0) 162 751 480
E: info@holmatro.com
W: www.holmatro.com/

Holophane Rail Solutions
Bond Avenue, Bletchley, Milton Keynes, Bucks, MK1 1JG
T: 01908 649292
F: 01908 367618
E: info@holophane.co.uk
W: www.holophane.co.uk

Homegrown Timber (Rail) Ltd
Courtlands, Antlands Lane, Shipley Br, Surrey, RH6 9TE
T: 01293 821321
F: 01293 772319
E: rail@homegrowntimber.com
W: www.homegrowntimber.com

Hoppecke Industrial Batteries Ltd
Unit 2, Centre 500, Lowfield Drive, Wolstanton, Newcastle-under-Lyme, Staffs, ST5 0UU
T: 01782 667306
F: 01782 667314
E: sales@hoppecke.co.uk
W: www.hoppecke.co.uk

Horizon Utility Supplies Ltd
Unit 1, Windmill Business Park, Windmill Road, Clevedon, North Somerset, BS21 6SR
T: 01275 342700
E: enquiries@hor-i-zon.com
W: www.horizonutilitysupplies.com

Hosiden Besson Ltd
11 St Josephs Close, Hove, East Sussex, BN3 7EZ
T: 01273 861166
F: 01273 777501
E: info@hbl.co.uk
W: www.hbl.co.uk

Houghton International
Riverside Court, Fisher St, Walker, Newcastle upon Tyne, NE6 4LT
T: 0191 234 3000
F: 0191 263 7873
E: info@houghton-international.com
W: www.houghton-international.com

House of Commons Transport Commitee
7th Floor, 14 Tothill Street, House of Commons, London, SW1H 9NB
T: 020 7219 3266
E: transcom@parliament.uk
W: www.parliament.uk/business/committees/committees-a-z/commons-select/transport-committee

Howells Railway Products Ltd
Longley Lane, Sharston Ind. Est., Wythenshawe, Manchester, M22 4SS
T: 0161 945 5567
F: 0161 945 5597
E: info@howells-railway.co.uk
W: www.howells-railway.co.uk

HP Information Security
3200 Daresbury Park, Daresbury, Warrington, WA4 4BU
T: 01925 665500
F: 01925 667200
E: salessupport.infosec@hp.com
W: www.hp.com

HPR Consult
See Rendel Limited

HS Carlsteel Engineering Ltd
Crabtree Manorway South, Belvedere, Kent, DA17 6BH
T: 020 8312 1879
F: 020 8320 9480
E: sales@hscarlsteel.co.uk
W: www.hscarlsteel.co.uk

HS1 Ltd
12th Floor, One Euston Square, 40 Melton St, London, NW1 2FD
T: 020 7014 2700
E: wendy.spinks@highspeed1.co.uk
W: www.highspeed1.co.uk

HS2 Ltd
One Canada Square, London, E14 5AB
T: 020 7944 4908
E: hs2enquiries@hs2.org.uk
W: www.hs2.org.uk

HSBC Rail (UK)
See Eversholt Rail (UK) Ltd

HSS Training Ltd
Circle House, Lostock Rd, Davyhulme, Manchester, M41 0HS
T: 0845 766 7799
F: 0161 877 9074
E: training@hss.com
W: www.hsstraining.com

Huber + Suhner (UK) Ltd
Telford Rd, Bicester, Oxon, OX26 4LA
T: 01869 364100
F: 01869 249046
E: info.uk@hubersuhner.com
W: www.hubersuhner.co.uk

Hull Trains
See First Hull Trains

Human Reliability
1 School House, Higher Lane, Dalton, Lancs, WN8 7RP
T: 01257 463121
F: 01257 463810
E: dembrey@humanreliabilty.com
W: www.humanreliability.com

Hunslet Barclay
See Brush Barclay

Hunslet Engine Co
See LH Group Services

Husqvarna Construction Products
Unit 4, Pearce Way, Bristol Rd, Gloucester, GL2 5YD
T: 0844 844 4570
E: husqvarna.construction@husqvarna.co.uk
W: www.husqvarna.co.uk

Hutchinson Team Telecom Ltd
See Indigo Telecom Group

HV Wooding Ltd
Range Rd Industrial Estate, Hythe, Kent, CT21 6HG
T: 01303 264471
F: 01303 262408
E: sales@hvwooding.co.uk
W: www.hvwooding.co.uk

HW Martin (Fencing Contractors) Ltd
Fordbridge Lane, Blackwell, Alfreton, Derbys, DE55 5JY
T: 01773 813214
F: 01773 813339
E: fencing@hwmartin.com
W: www.hwmartin.com

Hyder Consulting (UK) Ltd
Manning House, 22 Carlisle Place, London, SW1P 1JA
T: 020 3014 9000
F: 020 7828 8428
E: mahmoud.alghita@hyderconsulting.com
W: www.hyderconsulting.com

HydraPower Dynamics Ltd
St Marks Street, Birmingham, B1 2UN
T: 0121 4565 656
F: 0121 4565 668
E: info@hdl.uk.net
W: www.hydrapower-dynamics.com

Hydraulic Pumps (UK) Ltd
Summit 2, Mangham Rd, Barbot Hill Ind. Est, Rotherham, S61 4RJ
T: 01709 360370
F: 01709 372913
E: sales@hydraulicpumps.co.uk
W: www.hydraulicpumps.co.uk

Hydrex Equipment UK Ltd
See TXM Plant Ltd

Hydrotech Europe Ltd
Beaufort Court, 11 Roebuck Way, Knowlhill, Milton Keynes, MK5 8HL
T: 01908 675244
F: 01908 397513
E: enquiries@hydro-usl.com
W: www.hydro-usl.com

Hydrotechnik UK Ltd
1 Central Park, Lenton Lane, Nottingham, NG7 2NR
T: 01159 003550
F: 01159 868875
E: sales@hydrotechnik.co.uk
W: www.hydrotechnik.co.uk

Hypertac UK
36-38 Waterloo Rd, London, NW2 7UH
T: 020 8450 8033
F: 020 8208 4114
E: info@hypertac.co.uk
W: www.hypertac.com

I C Consultants Ltd
58 Prince's Gate, Exhibition Rd, London, SW7 2QA
T: 020 7594 6565
F: 020 7594 6570
E: consultants@imperial.ac.uk
W: www.imperial-consultants.co.uk

IAD Rail Systems
See Network Rail Infrastructure Ltd

Ian Allan Publishing
Terminal House, Shepperton, Surrey, TW17 8AS
T: 01932 834950
E: info@ianallanpublishing.co.uk
W: www.ianallanpublishing.co.uk

Ian Catling Consultancy
Ash Meadow, Bridge Way, Chipstead, CR5 3PX
T: 01737 552225
F: 01737 556669
E: ic@catling.com
W: www.catling.com

Ian Riley
See Riley & Son (E) Ltd

IBI Group
87-91 Newman Street, London
T: +44 (0) 20 7079 9900
F: +44 (0) 20 7079 9901
E: enquiriesuk@ibigroup.com
W: www.ibigroup.com

ICEE
20 Arnside Rd, Waterlooville, Hants, PO7 7UP
T: 02392 230604
F: 02392 230605
E: sales@icee.co.uk
W: www.icee.co.uk

Icomera UK
Innovation Centre Medway, Maidstone Rd, Chatham, Kent, ME5 9FD
T: 0870 446 0461
E: sales@icomera.com
W: www.icomera.com

Icon Silentbloc UK Ltd
Wellington Rd, Burton upon Trent, Staffs, DE14 2AP
T: 01283 741741
F: 01283 741742
E: silentblocinfo@iconpolymer.com
W: www.iconpolymer.com

ID Computing Ltd
ID Centre, Lathkill House, rtc Business Park, London Rd., Derby, DE24 8UP
T: 01332 258880
F: 01332 258823
E: info@idcomputing.co.uk
W: www.idcomputing.co.uk

Ideas Limited (Integration Design Ergonomics Applications Solutions)
PO Box 193, Thame, Oxon, OX9 0BR
T: 01844 216896
F: 0970 460 6190
E: info@ideas.ltd.uk
W: www.ideas.ltd.uk

IET
See Institution of Engineering & Technology

IETG Ltd
Cross Green Way, Cross Green Ind. Est., Leeds, LS9 0SE
T: 0113 201 9700
F: 0113 201 9701
E: ietg.info@idexcorp.com
W: www.ietg.co.uk

iGuzzini Illuminazione UK Ltd
Astolat Business Park, Astolat Way, off Old Portsmouth Rd, Guildford, GU3 1NE
T: 01483 468000
F: 01483 468001
E: info@iguzzini.co.uk
W: www.iguzzini.co.uk

Ilecsys
Unit 4B, Tring Ind. Est, Upper Icknield Way, Tring, Herts, HP23 4JX
T: 01442 828387
F: 01442 828399
E: sales@ilecsysrail.co.uk
W: www.ilecsysrail.co.uk

iLine Technologies Ltd/ Channeline International
KG House, Kingsfield Way, Northampton, NN5 7QS
T: 01443 743402
E: hello@i-group.uk.com
W: www.iline.uk.com/

ILME UK Ltd
50 Evans Rd, Venture Point, Speke, Merseyside, L24 9PB
T: 0151 336 9321
F: 0151 336 9326
E: sales@ilmeuk.co.uk
W: www.ilmeuk.co.uk

Imagerail
Reservoir House, Wetheral Pasture, Carlisle, CA4 8HR
T: 01768 800208
E: andrew@imagerail.com
W: www.imagerail.com

Imetrum Ltd
Unit 4, Farleigh Court, Old Weston Road, Flax Bourton, Bristol, BS48 1UR
T: 01275 464443
E: sales@imetrum.com
W: www.imetrum.com/

IMI Precision Engineering
Blenheim Way, Fradley Park, Lichfield, Staffordshire, WS13 8SY
T: 01543 265000
E: advantage@imi-precision.com
W: www.imi-precision.com/

Imtech Traffic & Infra UK Ltd
Hazlewood House, Limetree Way, Chineham Business Park, Basingstoke, RG24 8WZ
T: 01256 891800
F: 01256 891870
E: info@imtech.uk.com
W: www.imtech.uk.com

In2rail Ltd
Hobbs Hill, Rothwell, Northants, NN14 6YG
F: 01536 711804
E: pm@in2rail.co.uk
W: www.in2rail.co.uk

Inbis Ltd
Club St, Bamber Bridge, Preston, Lancs, PR5 6FN
T: 01772 645000
F: 01772 645001
W: www.inbis.com

Inchmere Design
Swan Close Studios, Swan Close Way, Banbury, Oxon, OX16 5TE
T: 01295 661000
F: 01295 277939
E: mark@inchmere.co.uk
W: www.inchmere.co.uk

Incorporatewear
Edison Rd, Hams Hall National Distribution Park, C oleshill, B46 1DA
T: 0844 257 0530
F: 0844 257 0591
E: info@incorporatewear.co.uk
W: www.incorporatewear.co.uk

Independent Glass Co Ltd
540-550 Lawmoor St, Dixons Blazes Ind. Est, Glasgow, G5 0UA
T: 0141 429 8700
F: 0141 429 8524
E: toughened@ig-glass.co.uk
W: www.independentglass.co.uk

Independent Rail Consultancy Group (IRCG)
E: info@ircg.co.uk
W: www.ircg.co.uk

Indigo Telecom Group
Field House, Uttoxeter Old Rd, Derby, DE1 1NH
T: 01332 375570
F: 01332 375673
E: sales@indigotelecomgroup.com
W: www.indigotelecomgroup.com

Industrial Door Services Ltd
Adelaide St, Crindau Park, Newport, Gwent, NP20 5NF
T: 01633 853335
F: 01633 851989
E: enquiries@indoorserv.co.uk
W: www.indoorserv.co.uk

Industrial Flow Control Ltd
3 Ryder Way, Basildon, Essex, RM17 5XR
T: 01268 596900
F: 01268 728435
E: sales@inflow.co.uk
W: www.inflow.co.uk

Inflow
See Industrial Flow Control Ltd

Infodev EDI Inc.
1995 Rue Frank-Carrel, Suite 202, Quebec G1N 4H9, Canada
T: 001 418 681 3539
F: 001 418 681 1209
E: info@infodev.ca
W: www.infodev.ca

Infor
1 Lakeside Rd, Farnborough, Hants, GU14 6XP
T: 0800 376 9633
F: 0121 615 8255
E: ukmarketing@infor.com
W: www.infor.co.uk

informatica Software Ltd
6 Waltham Park, Waltham Rd, White Waltham, Maidenhead, Berks, SL6 3JN
T: 01628 511311
F: 01628 511411
E: ukinfo@informatica.com
W: www.informatica.com

Informatiq
Gresham House, 53 Clarendon Rd, Watford, WD17 1LA
T: 01923 224481
F: 01923 224493
E: permanent@informatiq.co.uk
W: www.informatiq.co.uk

Infotec Ltd
The Maltings, Tamworth Rd,
Ashby De La Zouch,
Leics, LE65 2PS
T: 01530 560600
F: 01530 560111
E: sales@infotec.co.uk
W: www.infotec.co.uk

Infra Safety Services
See ISS Labour

INIT Innovations in Transportation Ltd
49 Stoney St, The Lace Market,
Nottingham, NG1 1LX
T: 0870 890 4648
F: 0115 989 5461
W: www.init.co.uk

Initiate Consulting Ltd
9 Gainsford St, Tower Bridge,
London, SE1 2NE
T: 020 7357 9600
F: 020 7357 9604
E: info@initiate.uk.com
W: www.initiate.uk.com

Inline Track Welding Ltd
Ashmill Business Park,
Ashford Rd,
Lenham,
Maidstone, ME17 2GQ
T: 01622 854730
F: 01622 854731
E: david.thomson@fsmail.net

InnoTrans
Messe Berlin GmbH,
Messedamm 22, D-14055 Berlin,
Germany
T: 0049 303038 0
F: 0049 303038 2325
E: innotrans@messe-berlin.de
W: www.innotrans.com

Innovative Railway Safety Ltd
Ty Penmynydd,
Llangennith,
Swansea, SA3 1DT
M: 07974 065798
E: paul@inrailsafe.co.uk
W: www.inrailsafe.co.uk

Innovative Support Systems Ltd (ISS)
15 Fountain Parade,
Mapplewell,
Barnsley,
S Yorks, S75 6FW
T: 01226 381155
F: 01226 381177
E: enquiries@iss-eng.com
W: www.iss-eng.com

The Input Group
Input House,
101 Ashbourne Road,
Derby, DE22 3FW
T: 01332 348830
F: 01332 296342
E: info@inputgroup.co.uk
W: www.inputgroup.co.uk

Insight Security
Units 1 & 2, Cliffe Ind. Est,
South Street, Lewes,
E Sussex, BN8 6JL
T: 01273 475500
F: 01273 478800
E: info@insight-security.com
W: www.insight-security.com

Insituform Technologies Ltd
24-27 Brunel Close,
Park Farm Industrial Estate,
Wellingborough, Northants,
NN8 6QX
T: 01933 678266
F: 01933 678637
E: jbeech@insituform.com
W: www.insituform.co.uk

Inspectahire Instrument Co. Ltd
Unit 11,
Whitemyres Business Centre,
Whitemyres Ave,
Aberdeen, AB16 6HQ
T: 01224 789692
F: 01224 789462
E: enquiries@inspectahire.com
W: www.inspectahire.com

Install CCTV Ltd
10 Rochester Court,
Anthonys Way, Rochester,
Kent, ME2 4NW
T: 01634 717784
F: 01634 718085
W: www.installcctv.co.uk

Installation Project Services Ltd
53 Ullswater Crescent,
Coulsdon,
Surrey, CR5 2HR
T: 020 8655 6060
F: 020 8655 6070
E: sales@ips-ltd.co.uk
W: www.ips-ltd.co.uk

Institute of Rail Welding
Granta Park, Great Abington,
Cambridge, CB21 6AL
T: 01223 899000
E: iorw@twi.co.uk
W: www.iorw.org

Institute of Railway Research
University of Huddersfield,
Queensgate,
Huddersfield, HD1 3DH
T: 01484 472030
E: irr.info@hud.ac.uk
W: www.hud.ac.uk/irr

Institute Of Transport Studies, University Of Leeds
34-40 University Road,
University of Leeds,
Leeds, LS2 9JT
T: 0113 343 5325
F: 0113 343 5334
W: www.its.leeds.ac.uk

Institution of Civil Engineers (ICE)
One Great George St,
Westminster,
London, SW1P 3AA
T: 020 7222 7722
E: communications@ice.org.uk
W: www.ice.org.uk

Institution of Engineering & Technology
Michael Faraday House,
Six Hills Way, Stevenage,
Herts, SG1 2AY
T: 01438 313111
F: 01438 765526
E: postmaster@theiet.org
W: www.theiet.org

Institution of Mechanical Engineers (IMechE)
1 Birdcage Walk,
Westminster,
London, SW1H 9JJ
T: 020 7222 7899
F: 020 7222 4557
E: railway@imeche.org.uk
W: www.imeche.org/

Institution of Railway Operators
The Moat House,
133 Newport Rd,
Stafford, ST16 2EZ
T: 03333 440523
E: info@railwayoperators.co.uk
W: www.railwayoperators.co.uk

Institution of Railway Signal Engineers (IRSE)
4th Floor, 1 Birdcage Walk,
Westminster,
London, SW1H 9JJ
T: 020 7808 1180
F: 020 7808 1196
E: hq@irse.org
W: www.irse.org

Intamech Ltd
See Arbil Lifting Gear

Intec (UK) Ltd
York House,
76-78 Lancaster Rd,
Morecambe, Lancs, LA4 5QN
T: 01524 426777
F: 01524 426888
E: intec@inteconline.co.uk
W: www.inteconline.co.uk

Integrated Transport Planning Ltd
50 North Thirtieth St,
Milton Keynes, MK9 3PP
T: 01908 259718
F: 01908 605747
E: wheway@itpworld.net
W: www.itpworld.net

Integrated Utility Services
Unit 8, Brindley Way,
41 Industrial Estate,
Wakefield,
West Yorks, WF2 0XQ
T: 0800 0737373
E: enquiries@ius.co.uk
W: www.ius.co.uk

Integrated Water Services Ltd
Green Lane,
Walsall, WS2 7PD
T: 01543 445700
F: 01543 445717
E: contact@integrated-water.co.uk
W: www.integrated-water.co.uk

Intelligent Data Collection Ltd
4 Pocketts Yard, Cookham,
Berks, SL6 9SL
T: 0845 003 8747
E: info@intelligent-data-collection.com
W: www.intelligent-data-collection.com

Intelligent Glass Protection (IGP)
16 Hillbottom Rd,
High Wycombe,
Bucks, HP12 4HJ
T: 0800 448 8855
F: 01494 462675
E: sales@igpsolutions.com
W: www.igpsolutions.com

Intelligent Locking Systems
Bordesley Hall,
Alvechurch,
Birmingham, B48 7QA
T: 01527 68885
F: 01527 66681
E: info@ilslocks.co.uk
W: www.ilslocks.co.uk

Intelligent Radio Solutions (IRIS) Ltd
Networks House,
28 Earith Business Park,
Earith, Huntingdon,
Cambs, PE28 3QF
T: 01223 906052
E: info@intelligentradiosolutions.com
W: www.intelligentradiosolutions.com

Interface Fabrics Ltd
See Camira Fabrics Ltd

Interfaces
2 Valley Close,
Hertford, SG13 8BD
T: 01992 422042
E: reg.harman@ntlworld.com

Intermodal Logistics
Cedar House,
Glade Rd, Marlow,
Bucks, SL7 1DQ
T: 01234 822821
F: 01628 486800
E: derekbliss@intermodallogistics.co.uk
W: www.intermodallogistics.co.uk

Intermodality Ltd
6 Belmont Business Centre,
East Hoathly, Lewes,
East Sussex, BN8 6QL
T: 0845 130 4388
F: 01825 841049
E: info@intermodality.com
W: www.intermodality.com

International Engineering
314 W. Pitkin Ave, Pueblo,
Colorado 81004, United States
E: info@i-engr.com
W: www.i-engr.com/

International Rail
PO Box 153, Alresford,
Hants, SO24 4AQ
T: 0871 231 0790
F: 0871 231 0791
E: sales@internationalrail.com
W: www.internationalrail.com

International Transport Intermediaries Club Ltd
See ITIC

Interserve plc
Interserve House,
Ruscombe Park, Twyford,
Berks, RG10 9JU
T: 0118 932 0123
F: 0118 932 0206
E: info@interserve.com
W: www.interserve.com

Intertrain (UK) Ltd
Intertrain House, Union St,
Doncaster, DN1 3AE
T: 01302 815530
F: 01302 815531
E: intertraininfo@intertrain.biz
W: www.intertrain.biz

Invensys Rail Ltd
See Siemens Rail Automation

Invertec Interiors Ltd
Trimdon Grange Industrial Estate,
Trimdon Grange,
County Durham, TS29 6PE
T: 01429 882210
E: sales@invertec.co.uk
W: www.invertec.co.uk

Ionbond Ltd
Unit 36, Number One Ind Est,
Medomsley Rd, Consett,
Co Durham, DH8 6TS
T: 01207 500823
F: 01207 590254
E: maria.beadle@ionbond.com
W: www.ionbond.com

Iosis Associates
15 Good Shepherd Close,
Bishop Rd,
Bristol, BS7 8NF
T: 0117 370 6313
M: 07910 519247
E: pwt@iosis.org.uk
W: www.iosis.org.uk

Ipex Consulting Ltd
L33/N5, Euston Tower,
286 Euston Road,
London, NW1 3DP
T: 0203 463 8640
E: info@ipexconsulting.com
W: www.ipexconsulting.com

IQPC
129 Wilton Road,
London, SW1V 1JZ
T: 020 7368 9300
F: 020 7368 9301
E: enquire@iqpc.co.uk
W: www.iqpc.co.uk

Iridium Onboard
Clue House, Petherton Rd,
Hengrove, Bristol, BS14 9BZ
T: 01275 890140
W: www.iridiumonboard.com

iris-GMBH
Ostendstraße 1-14, Berlin, 12459,
Germany
E: mail@irisgmbh.de
W: www.irisgmbh.de

Irish Traction Group
31 Hayfield Rd, Bredbury,
Stockport, SK6 1DE
E: info@irishtractiongroup.com
W: www.irishtractiongroup.com

IRL Group Ltd
Unit C1, Swingbridge Rd,
Loughborough, Leics, LE11 5JD
T: 01509 217101
F: 01509 611004
E: info@irlgroup.com
W: www.irlgroup.com

Ironside Farrar
111 McDonald Rd,
Edinburgh, EH7 4NW
T: 0131 550 6500
E: mail@ironsidefarrar.com
W: www.ironsidefarrar.com

ISC Best Practice Consultancy Ltd
Lower Market Hall Offices,
Market St, Okehampton,
Devon, EX20 1HN
T: 01837 54555
E: isc.bestpractice@btconnect.com
W: www.isc-bestpracticeconsultancy.co.uk

Ischebeck Titan
John Dean House, Wellington Rd,
Burton upon Trent,
Staffordshire, DE14 2TG
T: 01283 515677
F: 01283 516126
E: sales@ischebeck-titan.co.uk
W: www.ischebeck-titan.co.uk

IS-Rayfast Ltd
2 Lydiard Fields,
Great Western Way,
Swindon,
Wilts, SN5 8UB
T: 01793 616700
F: 01793 644304
E: sales@israyfast.com
W: www.israyfast.com

ISS Labour
Unit 5,
Sidney Robinson Business Park,
Ascot Drive, Derby, DE24 8EH
T: 01332 37082
E: info@isslabour.co.uk
W: www.isslabour.co.uk

ITIC
90 Fenchurch St,
London, EC3M 4ST
T: 020 7338 0150
F: 020 7338 0151
E: itic@thomasmiller.com
W: www.itic-insure.com

itmsoil Group Ltd
Bell Lane, Uckfield,
E Sussex, TN22 1QL
T: 01825 765044
F: 01825 744398
E: sales@itmsoil.com
W: www.itmsoil.com

ITS United Kingdom
Suite 312,
Tower Bridge Business Centre,
46-48 East Smithfield,
London, E1W 1AW
T: 020 7709 3003
F: 020 7709 3007
E: mailbox@its-uk.org.uk
W: www.its-uk.org.uk

ITSO Ltd
Luminar House, Deltic Ave,
Milton Keynes, MK13 8LW
T: 01908 255455
F: 01908 255450
E: info@itso.org.uk
W: www.itso.org.uk

ITT Water & Wastewater UK Ltd
Colwick,
Nottingham, NG4 2AN
T: 0115 940 0111
F: 0115 940 0444
W: www.itwww.co.uk

ITW Plexus
Unit 3, Shipton Way,
Express Business Park,
Northampton Rd,
Rushden,
Northants, NN10 6GL
T: 01933 354550
F: 01933 354555
E: sales@itwppe.eu
W: www.staput.co.uk

IXC UK Ltd
Innovation Birmingham Campus,
Faraday Wharf, Holt St,
Birmimgham, B7 4BB
T: 0121 250 5717
E: connect@ixc-uk.com
W: www.ixc-uk.com

Ixthus Instrumentation Limited
The Stables, Williams Barns,
Tiffield Road, Towcester,
Northants, NN12 6JR
T: 01327 353437
F: 01327 353564
E: info@ixthus.co.uk
W: www.ixthus.co.uk

A J Paveley
416 Goldon Hillock Road,
Sparkbrook,
Birmingham, B11 2QH
T: 01217721739
E: sales@ajpaveley.com
W: www.ajpaveley.com

J.Boyle Associates Ltd
Bunch Meadows,
Woodway,
Princes Risborough,
Bucks, HP27 0NW
F: 0870 460244
E: info@jba.uk.net
W: www.jba.uk.net

Jabero Consulting Ltd
22 Church Rd,
Tunbridge Wells, TN1 1JP
T: 01892 535730
W: www.jaberoconsulting.com

Jacobs Consultancy UK Ltd
See LeighFisher

Jacobs UK Ltd
1180 Eskdale Rd, Winnersh,
Wokingham, RG41 5TU
T: 0118 946 7000
F: 0118 946 7001
W: www.jacobs.com

Jafco Tools Ltd
Access House,
Great Western St,
Wednesbury,
West Midlands, WS10 7LE
T: 0121 556 7700
F: 0121 556 7788
E: info@jafcotools.com
W: www.jafcotools.com

JB Corrie & Co Ltd
Frenchmans Rd, Petersfield,
Hants, GU32 3AP
T: 01730 237129
F: 01730 264915
E: mhickman@jbcorrie.co.uk
W: www.jbcorrie.co.uk

JBA Management Consultants
See J.Boyle Associates Ltd

JCB
World Headquarters,
Rocester,
Staffs, ST14 5JP
T: 01889 590312
F: 01889 593455
W: www.jcb.co.uk

Jeanette Bowden, Network PR
PO Box 173, Harrogate,
North Yorkshire, HG2 8YX
T: 01423 538699
E: jeanette@networkpr.co.uk
W: www.networkpr.co.uk

Jefferson Sheard Architects
Fulcrum, 2 Sidney St,
Sheffield, S1 4RH
T: 0114 276 1651
F: 0114 279 9191
E: contactus@jeffersonsheard.com
W: www.jeffersonsheard.com

Jestico + Whiles
1 Cobourg St, London, NW1 2HP
T: 020 7380 0382
E: jw@jesticowhiles.com
W: www.jesticowhiles.com/

Jewers Doors Ltd
Stratton Business Park,
Biggleswade, Beds, SG18 8QB
T: 01767 317090
F: 01767 312305
E: mjewers@jewersdoors.co.uk
W: www.jewersdoors.co.uk

Jigsaw M2M Ltd
Pemberton Business Centre,
Richmond Hill, P
emberton, Wigan,
Lancashire, WN5 8AA
T: 01942 621786
E: sales@jigsawm2m.com
W: www.jigsawm2m.com

JOBSON JAMESRAIL
THE RAIL BROKER
Specialist Insurance for Rail Industry Supply Chain Companies

• Infrastructure • Manufacturers • Rolling stock
• Maintenance • Contractors • Consultants
Jobson James Insurance Brokers Ltd
30 St Paul's Square Birmingham B3 1QZ
and 4-5 Park Place, London SW1A 1LP
Tel. 0121 452 8450
E. rail@jobson-james.co.uk
www.jobson-james.co.uk
INSURANCE BROKERS CII CHARTERED

KILBORN CONSULTING

Kilborn Consulting is an independent railway engineering consultancy business. We specialise in the design of new and altered railway signalling systems for the UK railway infrastructure. There are six defined areas for which we supply our services:
• Consultancy, including technical advice and support.
• Signalling Correlation, Condition Assessments and Surveys;
• Signalling & Level Crossing Risk Assessments;
• Feasibility, Concept and Outline Signalling Design;
• Detailed Signalling Design; and
• Competency Management and Assessment
Kilborn Consulting Limited, Kilborn House, 1 St Johns Street, Wellingborough, Northants, NN8 4LG.
T: 01933 279909 F: 01933 276629 E: pmcsharry@kilborn.co.uk
www.kilborn.co.uk

Jim Hailstone Ltd
Far End, Old Haslemere Rd,
Haslemere,
Surrey, GU27 2NN
T: 01428 641691
M: 07860 478197
E: jimhailstoneltd@gmail.com

JMJ Laboratories
See Synergy Health Plc

JMP Consultants Ltd
8th Floor,
3 Harbour Exchange Sq,
London, E14 9GE
T: 020 7536 8040
F: 020 7005 0462
E: docklands@jmp.co.uk
W: www.jmp.co.uk

Jobson James - Specialist Rail Supply Chain Insurance
4 Park Place,
St James,
London, SW1A 1LP
T: 020 7898 9100
E: rail@jobson-james.co.uk
W: www.jobson-james.co.uk

John Headon Ltd
Hivernia, Jackson's Hill,
St Mary's,
Isles of Scilly
T: 01720 423540
E: john@johnheadonltd.co.uk
W: www.johnheadonltd.co.uk

John Prodger Recruitment
The Courtyard, Alban Park,
Hatfield Rd, St Albans,
Herts, AL4 0LA
T: 01727 841101
F: 01727 838272
E: jobs@jprecruit.com
W: www.jprecruit.com

Johnson Rail
Orchard Ind Est, Toddington,
Glos, GL54 5EB
T: 01242 621362
F: 01242 621554
E: stephen.phillips@johnson-security.co.uk
W: www.4dji.com/products-services/security/

Jonathan Lee Recruitment
3 Sylvan Court,
Southfield Business Park,
Basildon,
Essex, SS15 6TU
T: 01268 455520
F: 01268 455521
E: southfields@jonlee.co.uk
W: www.jonlee.co.uk

Jones Garrard Move Ltd
7 Beaker Close,
Smeeton Westerby,
Leics, LE8 0RT
E: michael-rodber@jonesgarrardmove.com
W: www.jonesgarrardmove.com

Jotun Paints (Europe) Ltd
Stather Rd,
Flixborough,
Scunthorpe,
N. Lincs, DN15 8RR
T: 01724 400000
F: 01724 400100
E: decpaints@jotun.co.uk
W: www.jotun.com

Journeycall Ltd
3 James Chalmers Road,
Arbroath Enterprise Park,
Kirkton Industrial Estate,
Arbroath, DD11 3RQ
T: 01241 730300
E: journeycall@the-espgroup.com
W: www.journeycall.com

JourneyPlan
30 Canmore Street,
Dunfermline,
Fife, KY12 7NT
T: 01383 731048
F: 01383 731788
E: support@journeyplan.co.uk
W: www.journeyplan.co.uk

JSD Research & Development Ltd
Old Carriage Works,
Holgate Park Drive,
York, YO24 4EH
T: 01904 623500
F: 01904 352412
E: info@jsdrail.com
W: www.jsdrail.com

Judge 3d
34 New St, St Neots,
Cambs, PE19 1AJ
T: 01480 211080
F: 05601 152019
E: admin@judge3d.com
W: www.judge3dltd.com

JUMO Instrument Co Ltd
Temple Bank, Riverway,
Harlow,
Essex, CM20 2DY
T: 01279 635533
F: 01279 625029
E: info.uk@jumo.net
W: www.jumo.co.uk/

Kaba (UK) Ltd
Lower Moor Way,
Tiverton,
Devon, EX16 6SS
T: 01884 256464
F: 01884 234415
E: info@kaba.co.uk
W: www.kaba.co.uk

Kapsch Group
Unit 2 espace,
26 St Thomas Place,
Ely,
Cambs, CB7 4EX
T: 01353 644010
F: 01353 611001
E: ktc.uk.info@kapsch.net
W: www.kapsch.net/uk

Karcher Vehicle Wash
Karcher UK Ltd, Karcher House,
Beaumont Rd, Banbury,
Oxon, OX16 1TB
T: 01295 752172
F: 01295 752040
E: enquiries@karcher.co.uk
W: www.karchervehiclewash.co.uk

Kavia Moulded Products Ltd
Rochdale Rd, Walsden,
Todmorden,
West Yorks, OL14 6UD
T: 01706 816696
F: 01706 813822
E: enquiries@kavia.info
W: www.kavia.info

Kaymac Marine & Civil Engineering Ltd
Osprey Business Park, Byng St,
Landore, Swansea, SA1 2NX
T: 01792 301818
F: 01792 645698
E: claire.williamson@kaymacltd.co.uk
W: www.kaymacmarine.co.uk

Kee Systems
Thornsett Works, Thornsett Rd,
Wandsworth,
London, SW18 4EW
T: 0208 874 6566
F: 0208 874 5726
E: sales@keesystems.com
W: www.keesystems.com

Kelly Integrated Transport Services Ltd
Unit 21, Kynock Rd, Eley Ind. Est,
Edmonton,
London, N18 3BD
T: 020 8884 6605
F: 020 8884 6633
E: kitsenquiries@kelly.co.uk
W: www.kelly.co.uk

Keltbray
St Andrews House,
Portsmouth Rd, Esher,
Surrey, KT10 9TA
T: 020 7643 1000
F: 020 7643 1001
E: enquiries@keltbray.com
W: www.keltbray.com

Keltbray Aspire Rail Ltd
Unit 4a/5b,
Crewe Hall Enterprise Park,
Weston Lane, Crewe, CW1 6UA
T: 01270 254176
F: 01270 253267
W: www.keltbray.com

Kelvatek Ltd
Bermuda Innovation Centre,
St David's Way,
Bermuda Park, Nuneaton,
Warks, CV10 7SD
T: 02476 320100
F: 02476 641172
E: mail@kelvatek.com
W: www.kelvatek.com/

Kendall Poole Consulting
Pinewood Business Park – TS2,
Coleshill Rd,
Marston Green,
Solihull, B37 7HG
T: 0121 779 0934
E: scm@kendallpoole.com
W: www.kendallpoole.com

Kennedy Solutions
1 Bromley Lane,
Chislehurst,
Kent, BR7 6LH
T: 020 8468 1016
F: 01689 855261
E: martin@kennedy-solutions.com
W: www.kennedy-solutions.com

Kent Modular Electronics Ltd (KME)
621 Maidstone Rd,
Rochester,
Kent, ME1 3QJ
T: 01634 830123
F: 01634 830619
E: sales@kme.co.uk
W: www.kme.co.uk

Kent PHK Ltd
Kent House,
Lower Oakham Way,
Mansfield,
Notts, NG18 5BY
T: 01623 421202
F: 01623 421302
E: enquiries@kentphk.co.uk
W: www.kentphk.com/

Kent Stainless (Wexford) Ltd
Ardcavan,
Wexford,
Republic of Ireland
T: 0800 376 8377
F: 00353 53914 1802
E: info@kentstainless.com
W: www.kentstainless.com

Keolis (UK) Ltd
Evergreen Building North,
160 Euston Rd,
London, NW1 2DX
T: 020 3691 1715
E: comms@keolis.com
W: www.keolis.co.uk

KeTech Ltd
Glaisdale Drive East, Bilborough,
Nottingham, NG8 4GU
T: 0115 900 5600
F: 0115 900 5601
E: info@ketech.com
W: www.ketech.com

Key Publishing
Units 1-4,
Gwash Way Industrial Estate,
Ryhall Road,
Stamford,
Lincolnshire, PE9 1XP
T: 01780 755131
F: 01780 757261
W: www.keypublishing.com/

Keyline Builders Merchants
National Rail Office,
Unit 1, Electra Business Park,
160 Bidder St,
London, E16 4ES
T: 020 7473 5288
F: 020 7473 5171
E: rail@keyline.co.uk
W: www.keyline.co.uk

Keysight Technologies
610 Wharfedale Rd, IQ Winnersh,
Wokingham,
Berks, RG41 5TP
T: 0800 0260637
F: 01189 276855
E: contactcentre_uk@keysight.com
W: www.keysight.com

Kiel Seating UK Ltd
Regents Pavilion,
4 Summerhouse Road,
Moulton Park,
Northampton, NN3 6BJ
T: 01604 641148
F: 01604 641149
E: p.scott@kiel-seating.co.uk
W: www.kiel-sitze.de

Kier Rail
Tempsford Hall,
Sandy,
Beds, SG19 2BD
T: 01767 355000
F: 01767 355633
E: info@kier.co.uk
W: www.kier.co.uk

Kilborn Consulting Ltd
Kilborn House,
1 St Johns St,
Wellingborough,
Northants, NN8 4LG
T: 01933 279909
F: 01933 276629
E: pmcsharry@kilborn.co.uk
W: www.kilborn.co.uk

Kilfrost Ltd
4th Floor, Time Central,
32 Gallowgate,
Newcastle upon Tyne, NE1 4SN
T: 01434 320 332
F: 0191 230 0426
E: alex.stephens@kilfrost.com
W: www.kilfrost.com

Kilnbridge Construction Services Ltd
McDermott House,
Cody Rd. Business Park,
South Crescent,
London, E16 4TL
T: 020 7511 1888
F: 020 7511 1114
E: sales@kilnbridge.com
W: www.kilnbridge.com

Kimberley-Clark Professional
1 Tower View,
Kings Hill,
West Malling,
Kent, ME19 4HA
T: 01732 594000
F: 01732 594060
E: marta.longhurst@kcc.com
W: www.kcprofessional.com/uk

King Rail
King Trailers Ltd, Riverside,
Market Harborough,
Leics, LE16 7PX
T: 01858 467361
F: 01858 467161
E: info@kingtrailers.co.uk
W: www.kingtrailers.co.uk

Kingfisher Video
Felmersham, Mills Rd,
Osmington Mills,
Weymouth,
Dorset, DT3 6HE
T: 01305 832906
E: roger@kingfisher-prods.demon.co.uk
W: www.railwayvideo.com

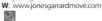

KNORR-BREMSE

Knorr-Bremse operates four major facilities in the UK to support rail customers based in the UK and Ireland.

Under the Knorr-Bremse brand, OE Systems sales and support is available from Melksham and Burton-upon-Trent (HVAC) and under the RailServices brand, train maintenance, overhaul and upgrades are available from Springburn and Wolverton.

ukrailenquires@knorr-bremse.com

www.knorr-bremse.co.uk

RAILSERVICES
always on track

Kingfisher Resources Management Ltd
First Floor,
Azrec Centre,
Aztec West,
Almondsbury,
Bristol, BS32 4TD
T: 01454 612799
E: mike@kingfisherlimited.com
W: www.kingfisherlimited.com

Kingston Engineering Co (Hull) Ltd
Pennington St,
Hull, HU8 7LD
T: 01438 325676
F: 01438 216438
E: sales@kingston-engineering.co.uk
W: www.kingston-engineering.co.uk

KJ Hall Chartered Land & Engineering Surveyors
30 Church Rd, Highbridge,
Somerset, TA9 3RN
T: 01278 794600
F: 01278 785562
E: admin@kjhsurvey.co.uk
W: www.kjhsurvey.co.uk

Klauke UK Ltd
Hillside Road East, Bungay,
Suffolk, NR35 1JX
T: 01986 891519
E: sales@klauke.textron.com
W: www.klauke.com

Klaxon Signals Ltd
Bradwood Court, St Crispin Way,
Haslingden,
Lancs, BB4 4PW
T: 01706 234800
E: sales@klaxonsignals.com
W: www.klaxonsignals.com

Kluber Lubrication GB Ltd
Longbow Close,
Pennine Business Park,
Bradley,
Huddersfield, HD2 1GQ
T: 01422 205115
F: 01422 206073
E: sales@uk.klueber.com
W: www.klueber.com

KLW - Wheelco SA
Via San Salvatore 13, PO Box 745,
CH-6902 Paradiso-Lugan,
Switzerland
T: 0041 91261 3910
F: 0041 91261 3919
E: info@klw-wheelco.ch
W: www.klw.biz

KM&T Ltd
The Techno Centre,
Coventry University
Technology Park,
Puma Way,
Coventry, CV1 2TT
T: 02476 236275
E: info@kmandt.com
W: www.kmandt.com

KMC International
7 Old Park Lane,
London, W1K 1QR
T: 020 7317 4600
F: 020 7317 4620
E: info@kmcinternational.com
W: www.kmcinternational.com

KME
See Kent Modular Electronics Ltd (KME)

Knorr-Bremse Rail UK
Westinghouse Way,
Hampton Park East, Melksham,
Wilts, SN12 6TL
T: 01225 898700
F: 01225 898705
E: ukrailenquiries@knorr-bremse.com
W: www.knorr-bremse.co.uk

Kone UK
Global House, Station Place,
Fox Lane North, Chertsey,
Surrey, KT16 9HW
T: 0870 770 1122
F: 0870 770 1144
E: sales.marketinguk@kone.com
W: www.kone.com

Konecranes UK Ltd
Unit 1B, Sills Road,
Willow Farm Business Park,
Castle Donington, Leics, DE74 2US
T: 0844 324 6599
F: 01332 697755
E: sales.uk@konecranes.com
W: www.konecranes.co.uk/

Kontron AG
Units 5&7, Sussex Business Village,
Lake Lane, Barnham,
West Sussex, PO22 0AL
T: 01243 533900
E: uksales@kontron.com
W: www.kontron.com

Korec Group
Blundellsands House,
34-44 Mersey View,
Brighton-le-Sands,
Liverpool, L22 6QB
T: 0845 603 1214
F: 0151 931 5559
E: info@korecgroup.com
W: www.korecgroup.com

Kroy (Europe) Ltd
Unit 2, 14 Commercial Rd,
Reading, Berks, RG2 0QJ
T: 0118 986 5200
F: 0118 986 5205
E: sales@kroyeurope.com
W: www.kroyeurope.com

KS Terminals Inc
21F-2, No 6, Lane 256, Sec 2,
Xitun Road, Xitun District,
407 Taichung City, Taiwan
T: 886 2706 6260
M: 886 4758 2786
E: exp@ksterminals.com.tw
W: www.ksterminals.com.tw

KV Mobile Systems Division
See Parker KV Division

Kwik-Step Ltd
Unit 5, Albion Dockside,
Hanover Place,
Bristol, BS1 6UT
T: 0117 929 1400
F: 0117 929 1404
E: info@kwik-step.com
W: www.kwik-step.com

L.E.K Consulting
40 Grosvener Place,
London, SW1X 7JL
T: 020 7389 7200
F: 020 7389 7440
E: surfacetransport@lek.com
W: www.lek.com

Laboursite Group Ltd (Rail)
See Wyse Rail Ltd

Lafarge Aggregates (UK) Ltd
Portland House, Bickenhill Lane,
Solihull,
West Midlands, B37 7BQ
T: 0800 1 218 218
F: 0870 336 8602
E: enquiries@lafargetarmac.com
W: www.lafarge.co.uk

Lafarge Tarmac
Portland House, Bickenhill Lane,
Solihull,
West Midlands, B37 7BQ
T: 0845 812 6400
F: 0845812 6200
E: enquiries@lafargetarmac.co.uk
W: www.lafargetarmac.com

Laing O'Rourke Infrastructure
Bridge Place, Anchor Blvd.,
Admirals Park, Crossways,
Dartford, Kent, DA2 6SN
T: 01322 296200
F: 01322 296262
E: info@laingorourke.com
W: www.laingorourke.com

Laing Rail
Western House, 14 Rickfords Hill,
Aylesbury,
Bucks, HP20 2RX
T: 01296 332108
F: 01296 332126
E: enquiries@laing.com
W: www.laing.com/

Lakesmere Ltd
The Ring Tower Centre,
Moorside Rd, Winnall, Winchester,
Hants, SO23 7RZ
T: 01962 826500
E: enquiries@lakesmere.com
W: www.lakesmere.com

Lanes Group Plc - Lanes For Drains
17 Parkside Lane, Parkside Ind. Est,
Leeds, LS11 5TD
T: 0800 526488
F: 0161 788 2206
E: sales@lanesfordrains.co.uk
W: www.lanesfordrains.co.uk

Lankelma Limited
Cold Harbour Barn,
Cold Harbour Lane, Iden,
East Sussex, TN31 7UT
T: 01797 280050
F: 01797 280195
E: info@lankelma.co.uk
W: www.lankelma.com

Lantern Engineering Ltd
Unit 4, Globe Court, Coalpit Road,
Denaby Main,
Doncaster, DN12 4LH
T: 01709 861008
F: 01709 863623
E: info@lantern.co.uk
W: www.lantern.co.uk

Largam
Unit 9, Oak Industrial Park,
Great Dunmow, Essex, CM6 1XN
T: 01371 876121
E: plant@largam.co.uk
W: www.largam.co.uk

Laser Rail
See Balfour Beatty Rail

LB Foster Rail Technologies (UK) Ltd
Stamford St, Sheffield, S9 2TX
T: 0114 256 2225
F: 0114 261 7826
E: uksales@lbfoster.com
W: www.lbfoster.co.uk

Leda Recruitment
See McGinley Support Services

Leewood Projects
38 Deacon Rd,
Kingston upon Thames,
Surrey, KT2 6LU
T: 020 8541 0715
F: 020 8546 4260
E: david.cockle@leewoodprojects.co.uk
W: www.leewoodprojects.co.uk

Legioblock (A Jansen B.V.)
Kanaaldojk Zuid 24, 5691 NL SON,
Netherlands
T: 0845 689 0036
F: 0845 689 0035
E: sales@legioblock.com
W: www.legioblock.com

Legion Limited
Hamilton House,
Mabledon Place,
London, WC1H 9BB
T: 020 7793 0200
F: 020 7793 8948
E: info@legion.com
W: www.legion.com

Legrand Electric Ltd
Great King St. North,
Birmingham, B19 2LF
T: 0121 515 0522
E: legrand.sales@legrand.co.uk
W: www.legrand.co.uk

Leica Geosystems Ltd
Hexagon House,
Michigan Drive, Tongwell,
Milton Keynes, MK15 8HT
T: 01908 513400
F: 01908 513401
E: uk.sales@leica-geosystems.com
W: www.leica-geosystems.co.uk

LeighFisher
65 Chandos Place,
London, WC2N 4HG
T: 020 7420 1770
E: david.bradshaw@leighfisher.com
W: www.leighfisher.com

LEM UK Ltd
West Lancs Investment Centre,
Suite 10,
Maple View,
White Moss Business Park,
Skelmersdale,
Lancs, WN8 9TG
T: 01942 388440
F: 01942 388441
E: luk@lem.com
W: www.lem.com

Lemon Consulting
See AMCL Systems Engineering Ltd

Lend Lease Consulting
20 Triton St, Regents Place,
London, NW1 3BF
T: 020 3430 9000
F: 020 3430 9001
E: marcus.woolmer@lendlease.com
W: www.lendlease.com

lexicraft

Interior train decals
Exterior train decals
Rail livery
Overlays
Nameplates, labels & badges

T +44 (0) 151 647 9281
E sales@lexicraft.co.uk
www.lexicraft.co.uk

Lesmac (Fasteners) Ltd
73 Dykehead St, Queenslie Ind. Est,
Queenslie, Glasgow, G33 4AQ
T: 0141 774 0004
F: 0141 774 2229
E: sales@lesmac.co.uk
W: www.lesmac.co.uk

Level 3 Communications
7th Floor, 10 Fleet Place,
London, EC4M 7RB
T: 0845 000 1000
F: 202 7954 2385
E: europe@level3.com
W: www.level3.com

Level Crossing Installations Ltd
Suite 9,
Canterbury Business Centre,
18 Ashchurch Rd, Tewkesbury,
Glos, GL20 8BT
T: 01684 278022
W: www.levelcrossinginstallations.co.uk

Lexicraft Ltd
Unit 32, Woodside Business Park,
Birkenhead, Wirral, CH41 1EL
T: 0151 647 9281
F: 0151 666 1079
E: jeff.davies@lexicraft.co.uk
W: www.lexicraft.co.uk

Ley Hill Solutions
Beech House, 9 Cheyne Walk,
Chesham, Bucks, HP5 1AY
T: 01494 772327
F: 0870 169 5984
E: graham.hull@leyhill.com
W: www.leyhill.com

LH Group Services
Graycar Business Park,
Barton-under-Needwood,
Burton upon Trent,
Staffs, DE13 8EN
T: 01283 722600
F: 01283 722622
E: lh@lh-group.co.uk
W: www.lh-group.co.uk

LH Safety Footwear
Greenbridge, Rawtenstall,
Rossendale,
Lancs, BB4 7NX
T: 01706 235100
F: 01706 235150
E: enquiries@lhsafety.co.uk
W: www.lhsafety.co.uk

Liebherr Transportation Systems UK
Liebherr Sunderland Works Ltd,
Ayres Quay, Deptford Terrace,
Sunderland, SR4 6DD
T: 0191 515 4930
F: 0191 515 4936
E: alan.lepatourel@liebherr.com
W: www.liebherr.com

Light Rail Transit Association (LRTA)
138 Radnor Ave, Welling,
Kent, DA16 2BY
T: 01179 517785
E: office@lrta.org
W: www.lrta.org

Linbrooke Services Ltd
Sheffield Business Park,
Churchill Way,
Chapeltown,
Sheffield, S35 2PY
T: 0114 232 8290
F: 0844 800 0984
E: ifo@linbrooke.co.uk
W: www.linbrooke.co.uk

Lindapter International
Lindsay House, Brackenbeck Rd,
Bradford, BD7 2NF
T: 01274 521444
F: 01274 521130
E: enquiries@lindapter.com
W: www.lindapter.com

Line Worx Ltd
2nd Floor, Afon Building,
Worthing Road, Horsham,
West Sussex, RH12 1TL
T: 0333 9000 939
W: www.lineworx.co.uk

Linbrooke
Total Network Solutions

Measurably safer with every shift

Telecommunications · Power · Signalling · Training · Resources
Design · Installation · Test · Commission

Birmingham / Glasgow / London
Manchester / Sheffield / Swindon / York

T / 0844 800 0983
E / info@linbrooke.co.uk

www.linbrooke.co.uk

HITACHI
Inspire the Next

Liniar Retaining Systems
Flamstead House,
Denby Hall Business Park,
Denby,
Derbyshire, DE5 8JX
T: 01332 883900
E: info@liniar.co.uk
W: www.liniar.co.uk

Link2 Ltd
2 Wortley Road,
Deepcar,
Sheffield, S36 2UZ
T: 0114 2180475
E: marketing@link-2.biz
W: www.link-2.biz

Linklite Systems Ltd
29 Waterloo Road,
Wolverhampton, WV1 4DJ
T: 0845 862 0236
F: 0203 0700 650
E: sales@linklite.co.uk
W: www.linklite.co.uk

Link-up
See Achilles Information Ltd (Link-Up)

LINSINGER Maschinenbau GmbH
Dr-Linsinger-Strasse 24,
A-466 Steyrermühl,
Austria
T: 0043 7613 8840 140
F: 0043 7613/8840-951
E: maschinenbau@linsinger.com
W: www.linsinger.com

Lionverge Civils Ltd
Unit 33,
Cornwell Business Park,
Salthouse Road,
Brackmills Industrial Estate,
Northampton, NN4 7EX
T: 01604 677227
F: 01604 677218
E: enquiries@lionverge.co.uk
W: www.lionverge.co.uk

Liquid Management Solutions Ltd
Creative Industries Centre,
Wolverhampton Science Park,
Glashier Drive,
Wolverhampton, WV10 9TG
T: 0845 450 7373
E: client.services@liquidms.co.uk
W: www.liquidms.co.uk

Lista (UK) Ltd
14 Warren Yard,
Wolverton Mill,
Milton Keynes, MK12 5NW
T: 01908 222333
E: info.uk@list.com
W: www.lista.co.uk

Llumar Anti-Grafitti Coating
See CP Films Solutia (UK) Ltd

LML Products Ltd
13 Portemarsh Rd,
Calne,
Wilts, SN11 9BN
T: 01249 814271
F: 01249 812182
E: sales@lmlproducts.co.uk
W: www.lmlproducts.co.uk

LNT Solutions Ltd
Helios 47,
Leeds, LS25 2DY
T: 0113 385 4187
F: 0113 385 3854
E: info@lntsolutions.com
W: www.lntsolutions.com

Lobo Systems Ltd
Centurion Way Business park,
Alfreton Rd,
Derby, DE21 4AY
T: 01332 365666
F: 01332 365661
E: sales@lobosystems.com
W: www.lobosystems.com

Logic Engagements Ltd
45-47 High St,
Cobham,
Surrey, KT11 3DP
T: 01932 869869
F: 01932 864455
E: info@logicrec.com
W: www.logicrec.com

LogiKal Ltd
27-29, Cursitor St,
London, EC4A 1LT
T: 020 7404 4826
E: admin@logikal.co.uk
W: www.logikalprojects.co.uk

London Midland
PO Box 4323,
Birmingham, B3 4JB
T: 0121 634 2040
F: 0121 654 1234
E: comments@londonmidland.com
W: www.londonmidland.com

London Overground Rail Operations Ltd (LOROL)
Customer Services Centre,
Overground House,
125 Finchley Rd,
London, NW3 6HY
T: 0203 031 9315
E: overgroundinfo@tfl.gov.uk
W: www.lorol.co.uk

London Rail
See Transport for London

London TravelWatch
169 Union Street,
London, SE1 0LL
T: 020 3176 2999
F: 020 3176 5991
E: info@londontravelwatch.org.uk
W: www.londontravelwatch.org.uk

London Underground Limited
See Transport for London

Look CCTV
Fleetwood Road North,
Blackpool,
Lancs, FY5 4QD
T: 01253 490399
E: enquiries@lookcctv.co.uk
W: www.look-cctv.co.uk/

Lordgate Engineering
1 Stonehill,
Stukeley Meadows Ind Est,
Huntingdon, Cambs, PE29 6ED
T: 01480 455600
F: 01480 454972
E: sales@lordgate.com
W: www.lordgate.com

Lorne Stewart Plc
Stewart House,
Orford Park, Greenfold Way,
Leigh,
Lancs, WN7 3XJ
T: 01942 683333
E: andy.vickers@lornestewart.co.uk
W: www.lornestewart.co.uk

LPA Group
Light & Power House, Shire Hill,
Saffron Walden,
Essex, CB11 3AQ
T: 01799 512800
F: 01799 512826
E: enquiries@lpa-group.com
W: www.lpa-group.com

LPDN - Luhn & Pulvermacher, Dittmann & Neuhaus
Voerder Strasse 38,
D-58135 Hagen,
Germany
T: 0039 0365 526213
E: giovannico.dore@sogefigroup.com
W: www.sogefigroup.com

Lucy Zodion Ltd
Chestnut Lodge,
3 Meeres Lane, Kirton,
Lincs, PE20 1PS
T: 01422 317337
E: pwpsales@lucyzodion.com
W: www.lucyzodion.com

Lundy Projects Ltd
195 Chestergate, Stockport,
Cheshire, SK3 0BQ
T: 0161 476 2996
F: 0161 476 3760
E: mail@lundy-projects.co.uk
W: www.lundy-projects.co.uk

LUR - Lucchini Unipart Rail Ltd
Ashburton Road West,
Trafford Park, Manchester,
M17 1GU
T: 0161 872 0492
F: 0161 872 2895
E: salesuk@lucchinirs.co.uk
W: www.lucchinirs.co.uk

Luxury Train Club
See The Train Chartering Company Ltd

Lynch Plant Hire
Lynch House, Parr Rd,
Stanmore,
London, HA7 1LE
T: 0845 400 0000
F: 020 8733 2020
E: brucel@l-lynch.com
W: www.l-lynch.com

Lynch Plant Hire
Lynch House, Parr Rd,
Stanmore,
Middx, HA7 1LE
T: 020 8900 0000
F: 020 8733 2020
E: brucel@l-lynch.com
W: www.l-lynch.com

M H Southern & Co Ltd
Church Bank Sawmills, Jarrow,
Tyne & Wear, NE32 3EB
T: 0191 489 8231
F: 0191 428 0146
E: timber@mhsouthern.co.uk
W: www.mhsouthern.co.uk

M.A.C. Solutions (UK) Ltd
Unit 6-7, Kingfisher Business Park,
Arthur St, Lakeside, Redditch,
Worcs, B98 8LG
T: 01527 529774
F: 01527 838131
E: sales@mac-solutions.co.uk
W: www.mac-solutions.net

Maber Architects
85 Tottenham Court Rd,
London, W1T 4TQ
T: 020 3402 2065
F: 020 7268 3100
E: info@maber.co.uk
W: www.maber.co.uk

Mabey Hire Ltd
Scout Hill, Ravensthorpe,
Dewsbury,
West Yorkshire, WF13 3EJ
T: 01942 460601
E: marketing@mabeyhire.co.uk
W: www.mabeyhire.co.uk

Mac Roberts LLP
Capella, 60 York St,
Glasgow, G2 8JX
T: 0141 303 1100
F: 0141 332 8886
E: lindsey.wright@macroberts.com
W: www.macroberts.com

Mace Group
153 Moorgate,
London, EC2M 6XB
T: 020 3522 3000
E: info@macegroup.com
W: www.macegroup.com

Macemain + Amstad Ltd
Boyle Rd, Willowbrook Ind. Est.,
Corby, Northants, NN17 5XU
T: 01536 401331
F: 01536 401298
E: sales@macemainamstad.com
W: www.macemainamstad.com

Mack Brooks Exhibitions Ltd
Romeland House, Romeland Hill,
St Albans, Herts, AL3 4ET
T: 01727 814400
F: 01727 814401
E: infrarail@mackbrooks.co.uk
W: www.mackbrooks.com

Macquarie European Rail
Ropemaker Place,
28 Ropemaker St,
London, EC2Y 9HD
T: 020 3037 2000
E: mfg.clientservice@macquarie.com
W: www.macquarie.com

MacRail Systems Ltd
Units One & Two, Morston Court,
Aisecome Way,
Weston Super Mare, BS22 8NG
T: 01934 319810
F: 01934 424139
E: info@macrail.co.uk
W: www.macrail.co.uk

Macrete Precast Concrete Engineers
50 Creagh Rd, Toomebridge,
Co. Antrim, BT41 3SE
T: 02879 650471
F: 02879 650084
E: info@macrete.com
W: www.macrete.com

Maddox Consulting Ltd
34 South Molton Street,
London, W1K 5RG
M: 0788 7575 254
E: info@maddoxconsulting.com
W: www.maddoxconsulting.com

MagDrill
Unit 11, Unthank Road, Bellshill,
North Lanarkshire, ML4 1DD
T: 01698 333200
F: 01698 749294
E: sales@magdrill.com
W: www.magdrill.com/

Mainframe Communications Ltd
Network House,
Journeymans Way,
Temple Farm Ind Est,
Southend on Sea,
Essex, SS2 5TF
T: 01702 443800
F: 01702 443801
E: info@mainframecomms.co.uk
W: www.mainframecomms.co.uk

Mainline Resourcing Ltd
Suite 214, Business Design Centre,
52 Upper St,
London, N1 0QH
T: 0845 083 0245
F: 020 7288 6685
E: info@mainlineresourcing.com
W: www.mainlineresourcing.com

Malcolm Rail
Fouldubs, Laurieston Rd,
Grangemouth,
Falkirk, FK3 8XT
T: 01324 668329
F: 01324 668312
E: turnerd@whm.co.uk
W: www.malcolmgroup.co.uk

Mammoet (UK) Ltd
The Grange Business Centre,
Belasis Ave, Billingham,
Cleveland, TS23 1LG
T: 0800 111 4449
E: saleseurope@mammoet.com
W: www.mammoet.com

MAN Diesel Ltd
1 Mirrlees Drive, Hazel Grove,
Stockport, Cheshire, SK7 5BP
T: 0161 483 1000
F: 0161 487 1465
E: primeserv-uk@mandiesel.com
W: www.mandieselturbo.com

Manbat Ltd
Lancaster House, Lancaster Road,
Shrewsbury, SY1 3NJ
T: 01743 218500
F: 01743 218511
E: sales@manbat.co.uk
W: www.manbat.co.uk

Mane Rail
UCB House, 3 St George St,
Watford, WD18 0UH
T: 01923 470720
E: rail@mane.co.uk
W: www.mane.co.uk

Mansell Recruitment Group
Mansell House, Priestley Way,
Crawley, West Sussex, RH10 9RU
T: 01293 404050
F: 01293 404122
E: neil@mansell.co.uk
W: www.mansell.co.uk

Maple Resourcing
Black Sea House, 72 Wilson Street,
London, EC2A 2DH
T: 020 7048 0775
F: 0845 052 9357
E: info@mapleresourcing.com
W: www.mapleresourcing.com

Marcroft Engineering Services
See Axiom Rail

Maritime and Rail
E-Business Centre,
Consett Business Park, Villa Real,
Consett, DH8 6BP
T: 01207 693616
F: 01207 693917
W: www.maritimeandrail.com

Marl International
Marl Business Park, Ulverston,
Cumbria, LA12 9BN
T: 01229 582430
F: 01229 585155
E: sales@marl.co.uk
W: www.marlrail.com

Marsh Bellofram Europe Ltd
9 Castle Park, Queens Drive,
Nottingham, NG2 1AH
T: 0115 993 3300
F: 0115 993 3301
E: bellofram@aol.com
W: www.marshbellofram.eu

Marshalls plc
Landscape House, Premier Way,
Lowfields Business Park, Elland,
West Yorkshire, HX5 9HT
T: 01422 312000
E: info@marshalls.co.uk
W: www.marshalls.co.uk/commercial

Martek Power Ltd
Glebe Farm Technical Campus,
Knapwell, Cambridge, CB23 4GG
T: 01954 267726
F: 01954 267626
E: pippa.keane@martekpower.co.uk
W: www.martekpower.com

Martin Higginson Transport Research & Consultancy
5 The Avenue, Clifton,
York, YO30 6AS
T: 01904 636704
M: 07980 874 126
E: mhrc@waitrose.com
W: www.martinhigginson.co.uk

Martineau
See SGH Martineau LLP

Masabi
56 Ayres St,
London, SE1 1EU
T: 020 7089 8860
E: kevin@masabi.com
W: www.masabi.com

Matchtech Group
1450 Park Way,
Solent Business Park,
Whiteley,
Fareham,
Hants, PO15 7AF
T: 01489 898989
F: 01489 898290
E: info@matchtech.com
W: www.matchtech.com

Matisa (UK) Ltd
PO Box 202,
Scunthorpe, DN15 6XR
T: 01724 877000
F: 01724 877001
E: melissa.carne@matisa.co.uk
W: www.matisa.ch

Maxim Power Tools (Scotland) Ltd
40 Couper St,
Glasgow, G4 0DL
T: 0141 552 5591
F: 0141 552 5064
E: akilpatrick@maximpower.co.uk
W: www.maximpower.co.uk

May & Scofield
Stroudley Road,
Basingstoke,
Hants, RG24 8UG
T: 01256 306800
F: 01256 306810
E: philj@may-scofield.co.uk
W: www.may-scofield.co.uk

May Gurney Rail Services
See Kier Rail

M-Brain Ltd
County House,
3rd Floor, Friar St,
Reading, RG1 1DB
T: 0118 956 5836
F: 0118 956 5850
E: response@esmerk.com
W: www.m-brain.com

MC Electronics
61 Grimsdyke Rd,
Hatch End, Pinner,
Middlesex, HA5 4PP
T: 020 8428 2027
F: 020 8428 2027
E: info@mcelectronics.co.uk
W: www.mcelectronics.co.uk

Sir Robert McAlpine Ltd
Eaton Court,
Maylands Avenue,
Hemel Hempstead,
Herts, HP2 7TR
T: 01442 233444
F: 01442 230024
E: information@sir-robert-mcalpine.com
W: www.sir-robert-mcalpine.com

McCulloch Rail
Craigiemains, Main St,
Ballantrae,
Girvan,
Ayrshire, KA26 0NB
T: 01465 831350
F: 01465 831350
E: enquiries@mccullochrail.com
W: www.mccullochrail.com

McGee Group Ltd
340-342 Athlon Rd,
Wembley,
Middx, HA0 1BX
T: 020 8998 1001
F: 020 8997 7689
E: mail@mcgee.co.uk
W: www.mcgee.co.uk

RAIL DEPOT
LIFTING & HANDLING
EQUIPMENT

Davy Industrial Park
Prince of Wales Road
Sheffield S9 4EX

E: info@mechan.co.uk
W: mechan.co.uk
T: +44 (0)114 257 0563

MADE IN SHEFFIELD
MECHAN

McGeoch LED Technology
86 Lower Tower Street,
Birmingham, B19 3PA
T: 01229 580180
F: 0121 333 3089
M: 07970 104390
E: debbie.albion@mcgeoch.co.uk
W: www.mcgeoch.co.uk

McGinley Support Services
Ground Floor,
Edward Hyde Building,
38 Clarendon Rd,
Watford,
Herts, WD17 1JW
T: 0845 543 5953
F: 0845 543 5956
E: info@mcginley.co.uk
W: www.mcginley.co.uk

B&M McHugh Ltd
429a Footscray Rd,
New Eltham,
London, SE9 3UL
T: 020 8859 7706
F: 020 8859 9999
E: msg@mchughltd.co.uk
W: www.mchughltd.co.uk

McKenzie Martin Partnership Ltd
126 Above Bar,
Southampton, SO14 7DW
T: 02380 216940
E: info@mmpartnership.co.uk
W: www.mmpartnership.co.uk

MCL (Martin Childs Ltd)
1 Green Way,
Swaffham,
Norfolk, PE37 7FD
T: 01760 722275
E: enquiries@martinchilds.com
W: www.martinchilds.com

McLellan & Partners
Sheer House,
West Byfleet,
Surrey, KT14 6NL
T: 01932 343271
F: 01932 348037
E: hq@mclellan.co.uk
W: www.mclellan.co.uk

McNealy Brown Limited - Steelwork
Prentis Quay,
Mill Way,
Sittingbourne,
Kent, ME10 2QD
T: 01795 470592
F: 01795 471238
E: info@mcnealybrown.co.uk
W: www.mcnealybrown.co.uk

McNicholas Rail
Lismirrane Industrial Park,
Elstree Road, Elstree,
Herts, WD6 3EA
T: 020 8953 4144
F: 01302 380591
E: mark.bugg@mcnicholas.co.uk
W: www.mcnicholas.co.uk

MCT Brattberg Ltd
Commerce St, Carrs Ind. Est,
Haslingden, Lancs, BB4 5JT
T: 01706 244890
F: 01706 244891
E: info@mctbrattberg.co.uk
W: www.mctbrattberg.co.uk

MDA Rail Ltd
Millbank House, Northway,
Runcorn, Cheshire, WA7 2SX
T: 01928 751000
F: 01928 751555
E: enquiries-runcorn@mdarail.com
W: www.mdarail.com

MDL Laser Measurement Systems
Acer House, Hackness Rd,
Northminster Business Park,
York, YO26 6QR
T: 01904 791139
F: 01904 791532
E: privers@mdl.co.uk
W: www.laserace.com

MDS Transmodal Ltd
5-6 Hunters Walk,
Canal St, Chester, CH1 4EB
T: 01244 348301
F: 01244 348471
W: www.mdst.co.uk

Mechan Ltd
Davy Industrial Park,
Prince of Wales Rd,
Sheffield, S9 4EX
T: 0114 257 0563
F: 0114 245 1124
E: info@mechan.co.uk
W: www.mechan.co.uk

Mechan Technology Ltd
See Zonegreen

MEDC Ltd
Unit B, Sutton Parkway,
Oddicroft Lane,
Sutton in Ashfield,
Notts, NG17 5FB
T: 01623 444400
F: 01623 444531
E: medcadmin@eaton.com
W: www.medc.com

Melford Electronics Ltd
Unit 14, Blenheim Rd,
Cressex Business Park,
High Wycombe, HP12 3RS
T: 01494 638069
F: 01494 463358
E: info@melford-elec.co.uk
W: www.melford-elec.co.uk

Mendip Rail Ltd
Merehead, East Cranmore,
Shepton Mallet,
Somerset, BA4 4RA
T: 01749 881202
F: 01749 880141
E: karen.taylor@mendip-rail.co.uk
W: www.aggregate.com/

Mennekes Electric Ltd
Unit 4, Crayfields Ind. Park,
Main Rd, St Pauls Cray, Orpington,
Kent, BR5 3HP
T: 01689 833522
F: 01689 833378
E: sales@mennekes.co.uk
W: www.mennekes.co.uk

Meon LLP
Railside, Northarbour Spur,
Portsmouth, PO6 3TU
T: 02392 200606
F: 02392 200707
E: mail@meonuk.com
W: www.meonuk.com

Merc Engineering UK Ltd
Lower Clough Hill, Pendle St,
Barrowford, Lancs, BB9 8PH
T: 01282 694290
F: 01282 613390
E: sales@merceng.co.uk
W: www.merceng.co.uk

Mercia Charters
PO Box 1926, Coventry, CV3 6ZL
T: 07535 759344
E: team@merciacharters.co.uk
W: www.merciacharters.co.uk

Merebrook Consulting Ltd
Suite 2B, Bridgefoot, Belper,
Derbys, DE56 2UA
T: 01773 829988
F: 01773 829393
E: consulting@merebrook.co.uk
W: www.merebrook.co.uk

Mermec
Via Oberdan 70,
I-70043 Monopoli (Bari), Italy
T: 0039 080 9171
F: 0039 080 9171 112
E: mermec@mermecgroup.com
W: www.mermecgroup.com

Merseyrail
Rail House, Lord Nelson St,
Liverpool, L1 1JF
T: 0151 702 2534
F: 0151 702 3074
E: comment@merseyrail.org
W: www.merseyrail.org

Merseytravel
PO Box 1976, Liverpool, L69 3HN
T: 0151 227 5181
E: comments@merseytravel.gov.uk
W: www.merseytravel.gov.uk

Merson Signs
2 Young Place, Kelvin Ind. Est.,
East Kilbride, Glasgow, G75 0TD
T: 01355 243021
E: web@merson-signs.com
W: www.railsignage.com

Met Systems Ltd
Cottis House, Locks Hill, Rochford,
Essex, SS4 1BB
T: 020 3246 1000
F: 020 7712 2146
E: info@metsystems.co.uk
W: www.metsystems.co.uk

Meteo Group UK Ltd
292 Vauxhall Bridge Rd,
London, SW1V 1AE
T: 020 7963 7575
F: 020 7963 7599
E: uk@meteogroup.com
W: www.meteogroup.com

Metham Aviation Design ltd (MADCCTV Ltd)
Unit 5, Station Approach,
Four Marks, Alton,
Hants, GU34 5HN
T: 01420 565618
F: 01420 565628
E: stuart@madcctv.com
W: www.madcctv.com

Metrail Construction Ltd
Unit 1, 70 Bell Lane,
Bellbrook Ind. Est.,
Uckfield, TN22 1QL
T: 01825 761360
E: nadia@metrail.co.uk
W: www.metrail.co.uk

Metrolink (Manchester)
Serco Metrolink, Metrolink House,
Queens Rd, Manchester, M8 0RY
T: 0161 205 8665
E: customerservices@metrolink.co.uk
W: www.metrolink.co.uk

Metronet
See Transport for London

Mettex Electronic Co Ltd
Beaumont Close,
Beaumont Road Ind Est, Banbury,
Oxon, OX16 1TG
T: 01295 250826
F: 01295 268643
E: sales@mettex.com
W: www.mettex.com

MF Hydraulics
See Centinal Group

MGB Electrical Ltd
See Ilecsys

MGB Engineering Ltd
MGB House, Unit D, Eagle Rd,
Langage Business Park, Plympton,
Plymouth, PL7 5JY
T: 0845 070 2490
F: 0845 070 2495
E: enquiries@mgbl.co.uk
W: www.mgbl.co.uk

MGF Trench Construction Ltd
Foundation House,
Wallwork Road, Astley,
Manchester, M29 7JT
T: 01942 402700
E: enquiries@mgf.ltd.uk
W: www.mgf.ltd.uk

Michael Evans & Associates Ltd
34 Station Rd, Draycott,
Derbys, DE72 3QB
T: 01332 871840
F: 01332 871841
E: mike@mevans.co.uk
W: www.mevans.co.uk

Micro-Epsilon UK Ltd
Dorset House, West Derby Rd,
Liverpool, L6 4BR
T: 0151 260 9800
F: 0151 261 2480
E: info@micro-epsilon.co.uk
W: www.micro-epsilon.co.uk

Micro-Mesh Engineering Ltd
Innovation House, Dabell Ave,
Blenheim Industrial Estate,
Nottingham, NG6 8WA
T: 01159 752929
F: 01159 751175
E: enquiries@micro-mesh.co.uk
W: www.micro-mesh.co.uk

Micromotive (A1 Results Ltd)
38 Coney Green Business Centre,
Wingfield View, Clay Cross,
Derbys, S45 9JW
T: 01246 252360
F: 01246 252361
E: a1micromotive@btopenworld.com
W: www.a1micromotive.co.uk

Middle Peak Railways Ltd
PO Box 71, High Peak,
Derbys, SK23 7WL
T: 0870 881 6743
F: 0870 991 7350
E: info@middlepeak.co.uk
W: www.middlepeak.co.uk

Midland Metro
Travel Midland Metro,
Metro Centre,
Potters Lane,
Wednesbury,
West Midlands, WS10 0AR
T: 0121 502 2006
F: 0121 556 6299
W: www.travelmetro.co.uk

Mid-West Services
44 Broadway,
Stratford,
London, E15 1XH
T: 020 3130 0466
F: 020 3070 0065
E: info@midwestservices.co.uk
W: www.midwestservices.co.uk

Mike Worby Survey Consultancy
37 Ramblers Way,
Welwyn Garden City,
Herts, AL7 2JU
T: 01707 333677
F: 01707 333677
E: survey@mw-sc.co.uk
W: www.mw-sc.co.uk

Millar Bryce Ltd
5 Logie Mill,
Beaverbank Office Park,
Logie Green Rd,
Edinburgh, EH7 4HH
T: 0131 556 1313
F: 0131 557 5960
E: marketing@millar-bryce.com
W: www.millar-bryce.com

Millcroft Services Plc
Salutation House,
1 Salutation Rd,
Greenwich,
London, SE10 0AT
T: 020 8305 1988
F: 020 8305 1986
E: sales@millcroft.co.uk
W: www.millcroft.co.uk

Millenium Site Services Ltd
Units 10/11, Riverside Park,
East Service Rd,
Raynesway,
Derby, DE21 7RW
T: 01332 820003
F: 01332 660081
E: millenium.site@btconnect.com
W: www.milleniumsiteservices.co.uk

Miller Construction
Miller House, 2 Lochside View,
Edinburgh, EH12 9DH
T: 0870 336 5000
E: mc.edinburgh@miller.co.uk
W: www.miller.co.uk

Mills Ltd
13 Fairway Drive,
Fairway Industrial Estate,
Greenford, Middlesex, UB6 8PW
T: 020 8833 2626
F: 020 8833 2600
E: sales@millsltd.com
W: www.millsltd.com

Mirror Technology Ltd
Redwood House,
Orchard Ind Est, Toddington,
Glos, GL54 5EB
T: 01242 621534
F: 01242 621529
E: malcolm@mirrortechnology.co.uk
W: www.mirrortechnology.co.uk

Mission Room Ltd
Kings Meadow Campus,
Lenton Lane,
Nottingham, NG7 2NR
T: 0115 951 6800
F: 0115 954 1002
E: info@missionroom.com
W: www.missionroom.com

Mita (UK) Ltd
See Schneider Electric Ltd

Mitchell Bridges Ltd
London Rd, Kingsworthy,
Winchester, Hants, SO23 7QN
T: 01962 885040
F: 01962 885040
E: chris@mitchellbridges.com
W: www.temporarybridges.com

MLM Rail Consulting Engineers Ltd
North Lodge, 25 London Rd,
Ipswich,
Suffolk, IP1 2HF
T: 01473 231100
F: 01473 231515
E: lee.bowker@mlm.uk.com
W: www.mlm.uk.com

MMRA
10 Fleet Place,
London, EC4M 7RB
T: 020 7651 0590
E: paul.bardsley@mottmac.com
W: www.mmra-cert.com

The Mobile Catering Group
The Monkey House, Kersoe,
Pershore,
Worcs, WR10 3JD
T: 01386 710123
F: 01386 710123
M: 07850 915959
E: fred@cateringcontracts.com
W: www.cateringcontracts.com

Mole Solutions
Alconbury, Huntingdon,
Cambridgeshire, PE28 4DA
T: 01480 413141
E: info@molesolutions.co.uk
W: www.molesolutions.co.uk/

Mono Design
4 St Andrews House,
Vernon Gate,
Derby, DE1 1UJ
T: 01332 361616
E: lynne@monodesign.co.uk
W: www.monodesign.co.uk

Moonbuggy Ltd
Solway Ind. Est, Maryport,
Cumbria, CA15 8NF
T: 01900 815831
F: 01900 815553
E: r.smith@moonbuggy.com
W: www.moonbuggy.com

Moore Concrete Products Ltd
Caherty House, 41 Woodside Rd,
Ballymena, Co. Antrim, BT42 4QH,
Northern Ireland
T: 028 2565 2566
F: 028 2565 8480
E: info@moore-concrete.com
W: www.moore-concrete.com

Morgan Advanced Materials
Upper Fforest Way,
Swansea Enterprise Park,
Swansea, SA6 8PP
T: 01792 763052
F: 01792 763167
E: meclsales@morganplc.com
W: www.morganelectricalmaterials.com

Morgan Hunt
5th Floor,
16 Old Bailey,
London, EC4M 7EG
T: 020 7419 8968
F: 020 7419 8999
E: rail@morganhunt.com
W: www.morganhunt.com

Morgan Marine Ltd
Llandybie,
Ammanford,
Carms, SA18 3GY
T: 01269 850437
F: 01269 850656
E: sales@morgan-marine.com
W: www.morgan-marine.com

HITACHI
Inspire the Next

Morgan Sindall
Corporation St, Rugby,
Warks, CV21 2DW
T: 01788 534500
F: 01788 534579
E: info@morgansindall.com
W: www.morgansindall.com

Mornsun Guangzhou Science & Technology Co Ltd
No 5, Kehui St 1,
Kehui Development Centre,
Science Avenue,
Guangzhou Science City 510660,
Luogang District, China
T: 0086 203860 1850 8810
F: 0086 203860 1272
E: info@mornsun.cn
W: www.mornsun-power.com

Morris Site Machinery
Station Rd, Four Ashes,
Wolverhampton, WV10 7DB
T: 0845 409 0280
F: 01902 790355
E: info@morrismachinery.co.uk
W: www.morrismachinery.co.uk

Morrison Utility Services Ltd
Fitzwilliam House, Middle Bank,
Doncaster,
South Yorkshire, DN4 5NG
T: 01302 898303
E: chris.ford@morrisonus.com
W: www.morrisonus.com

Mors Smitt UK Ltd (A Wabtec Company)
Graycar Business Park,
Barton-under-Needwood,
Burton upon Trent,
Staffordshire, DE13 8EN
T: 01283 722650
F: 01283 722651
E: info@morssmitt.co.uk
W: www.morssmitt.com

Morson International
Stableford Hall, Monton, Eccles,
Manchester, M30 8AP
T: 0161 707 1516
F: 0161 788 8372
E: rail@morson.com
W: www.morson.com

Morson Projects Ltd
Adamson House, Centenary Way,
Salford, Manchester, M50 1RD
T: 0161 707 1516
F: 0161 786 2360
E: andy.hassall@morson-projects.co.uk
W: www.morsonprojects.co.uk

Motorail Logistics
Quinton Rail Technology Centre,
Station Road, Long Marston,
Stratford upon Avon,
Warks, CV37 8PL
T: 01789 721995
F: 01789 721396
E: ruth.dunmore@motorail.co.uk
W: www.motorail.co.uk

Mott MacDonald Group
Mott Macdonald House,
8-10 Sydenham Rd,
Croydon, CR0 2EE
T: 020 8774 2000
F: 020 8681 5706
E: railways@mottmac.com
W: www.mottmac.com

Mouchel
4 Matthew Parker Street,
London, SW1H 9NP
T: 020 7227 6800
F: 020 7277 6801
E: consultingsales@Mouchel.com
W: www.mouchel.com

Movares
Mireille Ros,
Leidseveer 10,
3511 SB Utrecht,
Netherlands
T: 0031 30265 3101
F: 0031 30265 3111
E: info@movares.nl
W: www.movares.com

Movement Strategies
31-35 Kirby Street, Farringdon,
London, EC1N 8TE
T: 020 3540 8520
E: info@movementstrategies.com
W: www.movementstrategies.com/

Moveright International Ltd
Dunton Park, Dunton Lane,
Wishaw, Sutton Coldfield,
B76 9QA
T: 01675 475590
F: 01675 475591
E: andrew@moverightinternational.com
W: www.moverightinternational.com

Moxa Europe GmbH
Einsteinstrasse 7,
D-85716 Unterschleissheim,
Germany
T: 0049 893700 3940
F: 0049 893700 3999
E: europe@moxa.com
W: www.moxa.com/rail

MPEC Technology Ltd
Wyvern House, Railway Terrace,
Derby, DE1 2RU
T: 01332 363979
F: 08701 363958
E: andrew.whawell@mpec.co.uk
W: www.mpec.co.uk

MPI Ltd
International House,
Tamworth Rd,
Hertford, SG13 7DQ
T: 01992 501111
F: 01992 583384
E: info@mpi.ltd.uk
W: www.mpi.ltd.uk

MR Site Services Ltd
Unit 6,
Worcester Trading Estate,
Blackpole,
Worcester, WR3 8HR
T: 01905 755055
F: 01905 755053
E: welding@mrsiteservices.co.uk
W: www.mrsiteservices.co.uk

MRO Software Now part of IBM UK Ltd
PO Box 41,
North Harbour,
Portsmouth, PO6 3AU
T: 0870 542 6426
E: maximo@uk.ibm.com
W: www.maximo.com

MRX Technologies Ltd
22 Royal Scot Rd,
Pride Park,
Derby, DE24 8AJ
T: 01332 381418
F: 01332 381421
E: bww@mrxtech.co.uk
W: www.mrxtech.com

MSc Traction Oy
Alasniitynkatu 30,
FIN-33560 Tampere,
Finland
T: 358 050 532 1469
E: info@msc.eu
W: www.msc.eu

MSD Construction UK Ltd
Manvers House,
Pioneer Close,
Wath Upon Dearne,
Rotherham, S63 7JZ
T: 01709 878988
F: 01709 878918
E: enquiries@msdconstruction.com
W: www.msdconstruction.com

MTM Power Messtechnik Mellenbach GmbH
Edingerweg 6,
D-60320 Frankfurt am Main,
Germany
T: 0049 69154 2628
E: info@mtm-power.com
W: www.mtm-power.com

MTR Corporation
Finland House,
56 Haymarket,
London, SW1Y 4RN
T: 020 7766 3500
F: 020 7839 6217
E: europe@mtr.com.hk
W: www.mtr.com.hk

MTR Crossrail
E: enquiries@mtrcrossrail.co.uk
W: www.mtrcrossrail.co.uk

MTR Training Ltd
See HSS Training Ltd

MTU UK Ltd
Unit 29, The Birches Ind. Est,
East Grinstead,
West Sussex, RH19 1XZ
T: 01342 335450
F: 01342 335470
E: naomi.thornton@mtu-online.com
W: www.mtu-online.com

Multicell
Swannington Rd,
Broughton Astley,
Leicester, LE9 6TU
T: 01455 283443
F: 01455 284250
E: help@multicell.co.uk
W: www.multicell.co.uk

Multipulse
Units 1-2,
Goldsworth Park Trading Est,
Kestrel Way, Woking,
Surrey, GU21 3BA
T: 01483 713600
F: 01483 729851
E: sales@multipulse.com
W: www.multipulse.com

J Murphy & Sons Ltd
Hiview House, 81 Highgate Rd,
London, NW5 1TN
T: 020 7267 4366
F: 020 7428 3107
E: info@murphygroup.co.uk
W: www.murphygroup.co.uk

Murphy Surveys
Head Office UK,
9 Devonshire Square,
London, EC2M 4YF
T: 020 3178 6644
F: 020 3178 6642
E: london@murphysurveys.co.uk
W: www.murphysurveys.co.uk

MVA Consultancy
See Systra UK

MWH Treatment Ltd
Biwater Place, Gregge St,
Heywood, Lancs, OL10 2DX
T: 01706 626258
F: 01706 626294
E: info@mwhglobal.com
W: www.mwhglobal.com

Nacco (UK) Ltd
Office 3, The Dairy,
Crewe Hall Farm, Old Park Rd,
Crewe, Cheshire, CW1 5UE
T: 01270 254100
F: 0872 115 0919
E: sales@naccorail.co.uk
W: www.naccorail.com

Napier Turbochargers Limited
Ruston House, PO Box 1,
Waterside South, Lincoln,
Lincolnshire, LN5 7FD
T: 01522 516666
E: napier_enquiry@wabtec.com
W: www.napier-turbochargers.com

National Car Parks Ltd (NCP)
Saffron Court, 14B St Cross Street,
London, EC1N 8XA
T: 0345 050 70 80
E: derek.hulyer@ncp.co.uk
W: www.ncp.co.uk

National Composites Centre
Feynman Way Central,
Bristol & Bath Science Park,
Emersons Green, Bristol, BS16 7FS
T: 0117 370 7600
E: info@nccuk.com
W: www.nccuk.com

National Express East Anglia
See Abellio Greater Anglia

National Express Group Plc
75 Davies St, London, W1K 5HT
T: 020 7529 2000
F: 020 7529 2100
E: info@natex.co.uk
W: www.nationalexpressgroup.com

National Rail Enquiries
T: 08457 484950
W: www.nationalrail.co.uk

National Railway Museum
Leeman Rd, York, YO26 4XJ
T: 0844 815 3139
E: nrm@nrm.org.uk
W: www.nrm.org.uk

National Training Academy for Rail (NTAR)
Unit 5, Heathfield Way,
Kings Heath,
Northampton, NN5 7QP
T: 01604 594500
E: info@ntar.co.uk
W: www.ntar.co.uk

The Nationwide Accreditation Bureau Ltd
The Olympic Office Centre,
8 Fulton Rd, Wembley, HA9 0NU
T: 08458 902902
F: 08458 903903
E: enquiries@thenab.co.uk
W: www.thenab.co.uk

Nationwide Healthcare Connect
See Healthcare Connections Ltd

Navaho Technologies Ltd
8/9 Hayters Court, Grigg Lane,
Brockenhurst, Hants, SO42 7PG
T: 02380 000010
F: 02380 988598
E: sales@navaho.co.uk
W: www.navaho.co.uk

Nazeing Glass Works Ltd
Nazeing New Rd, Broxbourne,
Herts, EN10 6SU
T: 01992 464485
F: 01992 450966
E: sales@nazeing-glass.co.uk
W: www.nazeing-glass.com

NCH (UK) Ltd - Chemsearch
Landchard House,
Victoria St,
West Bromwich, B70 8ER
T: 0121 524 7300
F: 0121 500 5386
W: www.chemsearch.co.uk

Neale Consulting Engineers Ltd
Highfield,
Pilcot Hill,
Dogmersfield, Fleet,
Hants, RG27 8SX
T: 01252 629199
F: 01252 815625
E: ncel@tribology.co.uk
W: www.tribology.co.uk

Neary Rail
9 Coal Pit Lane,
Atherton,
Manchester, M46 0RY
T: 0845 217 7150
F: 0845 217 7160
E: alex.riley@neary.co.uk
W: www.neary.co.uk

NedRailways
See Abellio

Nedtrain BV
Kantorencentrum Katereine 9,
Stationshal 17, 3511 ED,
Utrecht,
Netherlands
T: 0031 30 300 4929
F: 0031 30 300 4647
W: www.nedtrain.nl

Nelsons Solicitors
Sterne House,
Lodge Lane,
Derby, DE1 3WD
T: 01332 372372
E: enquiries@nelsonslaw.co.uk
W: www.nelsonslaw.co.uk

Nemesis Rail Ltd
Burton Rail Depot,
Derby Rd,
Burton upon Trent,
Staffordshire, DE14 1RS
T: 01283 531562
E: enquiries@nemesisrail.com
W: www.nemesisrail.com

Nenta Traintours
Railtour House, 10 Buxton Rd,
North Walsham,
Norfolk, NR28 0ED
T: 01692 406152
F: 01692 406152
E: ray.davies@nentatraintours.co.uk
W: www.nentatraintours.co.uk

NES Track
Station House, Stamford New Rd,
Altrincham, Cheshire, WA14 1EP
T: 0161 942 4016
F: 0161 942 7969
E: nestrack.manchester@nes.co.uk
W: www.nestrack.co.uk

Network Certification Body

Enabling you to deliver

NCB (Network Certification Body) is *the choice* for rail conformity assessment.

01908 784 002

ncbenquiries@networkrail.co.uk

A NetworkRail Company

www.net-cert.co.uk

Network Certification Body Ltd
Ground Floor,
Caldecotte, The Quadrant,
Eldergate,
Milton Keynes, MK9 1EN
T: 01908 784002
E: ncbenquiries@networkrail.co.uk
W: www.net-cert.co.uk

Network Construction Services Ltd
Ercall House, Pearson Rd,
Central Park, Telford,
Shropshire, TF2 9TX
T: 01952 210243
F: 01952 290168
E: sales@ncsjob.co.uk
W: www.ncsjob.co.uk

Network Rail Consulting Ltd
Enterprise House,
167-169 Westbourne Terrace,
London, W2 6JX
T: 020 3356 0454
E: contactnrc@networkrail.co.uk
W: www.networkrailconsulting.co.uk

Network Rail Infrastructure Ltd
90 York Way,
London, N1 9AG
T: 020 7557 8000
W: www.networkrail.co.uk

Network Storage Systems Ltd
21 Leebrook Place,
Woodland Heights, Owlthorpe,
Sheffield, S20 6QL
T: 0800 633 5933
E: sales@networkstoragesystems.co.uk
W: www.networkstoragesystems.co.uk

Neway Training Solutions Ltd
Kelvin House, RTC Business Park,
London Rd,
Derby, DE24 8UP
T: 01332 360033
F: 01332 366367
E: artp@neway-training.com
W: www.neway-training.com

Newbury Data Recording Ltd
T: 0870 224 8110
F: 0870 224 8177
E: ndsales@newburydata.co.uk
W: www.newburydata.co.uk

Newby Foundries Ltd
Smith Road, Wednesbury,
West Midlands, WS10 0PB
T: 0044 (0) 121 556 4451
F: 0044 (0) 121 505 3626
E: sales@newbyfoundries.co.uk
W: www.newbyfoundries.co.uk

Newby Foundries Ltd
Steel Castings Division,
1 Cornwall Road,
Smethwick, B66 2JT
T: 0044 (0) 121 555 7615
F: 0044 (0) 121 505 3626
E: sales@newbyfoundries.co.uk
W: www.newbyfoundries.co.uk

Newey & Eyre
Eagle Court 2, Hatchford Brook,
Hatchford, Sheldon,
Birmingham, B26 3RZ
T: 0121 366 1000
F: 0121 366 1029
E: marc.roberts@rexel.co.uk
W: www.neweysonline.co.uk

NewRail Centre for Railway Research
Stephenson Building,
Newcastle University,
Claremont Rd,
Newcastle-upon-Tyne, NE1 7RU
T: 0191 208 8575
F: 0191 208 8600
E: newrail@ncl.ac.uk
W: www.newrail.org

Newton Europe Ltd
2 Kingston Business Park,
Kingston Bagpuize,
Oxon, OX13 5FE
T: 01865 601 300
F: 01865 601 348
E: info@newtoneurope.com
W: www.newtoneurope.com

Nexala Ltd
Suite 34, The Mall, Beacon Court,
Sandyford, Dublin 18,
Republic of Ireland
T: +353 (0) 1 4800 519
E: rail-lifecycle@trimble.com
W: www.trimble.com/rail-lifecycle

Nexans
Nexans House, Chesney Wold,
Bleak Hall,
Milton Keynes, MK6 1LF
T: 01908 250840
F: 01908 250841
E: iandi.sales@nexans.com
W: www.nexans.com

Nexus (Tyne & Wear Metro)
Nexus House, 33 St James Blvd,
Newcastle upon Tyne, NE1 4AX
T: 0191 203 3333
F: 0191 203 3180
E: contactus@twmetro.co.uk
W: ww.nexus.org.uk/metro

Nexus Alpha Low Power Systems Ltd
London House,
7 Prescott Place, Clapham,
London, SW4 6BS
T: 020 7622 6816
F: 020 7622 6817
E: commercialdept@lps.nexusalpha.com
W: www.lps.nexusalpha.com

Nexus Training
105 Sheffield Rd, Godley, Hyde,
Cheshire, SK14 2LT
T: 0161 339 2190
E: info@nexustraining.org.uk
W: www.nexustraining.org.uk

NG Bailey
Denton Hall, Ilkley,
West Yorkshire, LS29 0HH
T: 01943 601 933
E: enquiries@ngbailey.co.uk
W: www.ngbailey.co.uk

Nichols Group Ltd
53 Davies St, London, W1K 5JH
T: 020 7292 7000
F: 020 7292 5200
E: operations@nichols.uk.com
W: www.nicholsgroup.co.uk

Nigel Nixon Consulting
Suite 1, AD Business Centre,
Hithercroft Rd, Wallingford,
Oxon, OX10 9EZ
T: 01491 824030
F: 01491 824078
E: nigel@nigelnixon.com
W: www.nigelnixon.com

Nightsearcher Ltd
Unit 4, Applied House,
Fitzherbert Spur, Farlington,
Portsmouth, PO6 1TT
T: 023 9238 9774
F: 023 9238 9788
E: sales@nightsearcher.co.uk
W: www.nightsearcher.co.uk

Nitech Ltd
4-6 Highfield Business Park,
Churchfields Ind. Estate,
St Leonards on Sea,
East Sussex, TN38 9UB
T: 01424 852788
F: 01424 851008
E: sales@nitech.co.uk
W: www.nitech.co.uk

NMB Minebea UK Ltd
Doddington Rd, Lincoln, LN6 3RA
T: 01522 500933
F: 01522 500975
W: www.nmb-minebea.co.uk

No1 Scaffolding Service
Swinbourne Rd,
Burnt Mills Ind.Est., Basildon,
Essex, SS13 1EF
T: 01268 724793
F: 01268 725606
E: enquiries@no1scaffolders.co.uk
W: www.no1scaffolders.co.uk

Nomad Digital Limited
Second Floor, Baltic Chambers,
3 Broad Chare,
Newcastle-upon-Tyne, NE1 3DQ
T: 020 7096 6966
F: 0191 221 1339
E: europe@nomad-digital.com
W: www.nomad-digital.com

Nomad Digital

Leading global provider of connectivity solutions to the rail industry

- passenger WiFi
- on-board information systems
- intelligent fleet management with remote online condition monitoring

Second Floor, Baltic Chambers
3 Broad Chare, Newcastle Upon Tyne NE1 3DQ

T: +44 (0) 207 096 6966
E: europe@nomad-digital.com
W: nomad-digital.com

Nomix Enviro Ltd - A division of Frontier Agriculture Ltd
The Grain Silos,
Weyhill Rd, Andover,
Hants, SP10 3NT
T: 01264 388050
F: 01264 337642
E: nomixenviro@frontierag.co.uk
W: www.nomix.co.uk

Nord-Lock Ltd
Kingsgate House,
Newbury Road, Andover,
Wilts, SP10 4DU
T: 01264 355557
F: 01264 369555
E: enquiries@nord-lock.co.uk
W: www.nord-lock.com

Norgren Ltd
See IMI Precision Engineering

North East Railtours
See SRPS Railtours

North Star Consultancy Ltd
78 York St,
London, W1H 1DP
T: 020 7692 0936
F: 020 7692 0937
E: enquiries@northstarconsultancy.com
W: www.northstarconsultancy.com

Northern Ireland Railways
See Translink NI Railways

Northern Rail Ltd
Northern House, 9 Rougier St,
York, YO1 6HZ
T: 0333 222 0125
F: 0113 247 9059
E: firstname.lastname@northernrail.org
W: www.northernrail.org

Northsouth Communication
129 Main St, Lochgelly, KY5 9AF
T: 01592 782144
E: enquiries@northsouthcommunication.co.uk
W: www.northsouthcommunication.co.uk

Northston Engineering Consultancy Ltd
Northston, School Street,
Sulgrave, OX17 2RR
M: 07469 192830
E: graham@northstonengineering.com
W: www.northstonengineering.com

Northwood Railway Eng. Ltd
9 Scot Grove, Pinner,
Middx, HA5 4RT
T: 020 8428 9890
E: davidnbradley@btopenworld.com

Norton & Associates
32a High St, Pinner,
Middx, HA5 5PW
T: 020 8869 9237
F: 07005 964635
E: mail@nortonweb.co.uk
W: www.nortonweb.co.uk

Norton Rose Fulbright LLP
3 More London, Riverside,
London, SE1 2AQ
T: 020 7283 6000
F: 020 7283 6500
E: tim.marsden@nortonrosefulbright.com
W: www.nortonrose.com

Norwest Holst Construction
See Vinci Park Services UK Ltd

Nottingham Trams Ltd
NET Depot, Wilkinson St,
Nottingham, NG7 7NW
T: 0115 942 7777
E: info@thetram.net
W: www.thetram.net

Novacroft
Lakeside House, 9 The Lakes,
Bedford Road,
Northampton, NN4 7HD
T: 0845 330 0601
F: 0845 330 0745
E: projects@novacroft.com
W: www.novacroft.com

Novah Ltd
Unit 12, Jensen Court,
Astmoor Industrial Estate,
Runcorn, Cheshire, WA7 1SQ
T: 01928 242918
F: 01928 567838
E: sales@novah.co.uk
W: www.novah.co.uk

Novus Rail Ltd
Solaris Centre, New South Prom,
Blackpool, FY4 1RW
T: 01253 478027
F: 01253 478037
E: mmcm@novusrail.com
W: www.novusrail.com

NR Engineering Ltd
Duckworth Mill, Skipton Road,
Colne, Lancs, BB8 0RH
T: 01282 868500
F: 01282 868157
E: sales@nrengineering.co.uk
W: www.nrengineering.co.uk

NRL
Second Floor, Atlas House,
Caxton Close, Marus Bridge,
Wigan, Lancs, WN3 6XU
T: 01942 326727
F: 01942 829729
E: rail@nrl.co.uk
W: www.nrl.co.uk/rail

NSARE (National Skills Academy for Railway Engineering)
11 Carteret Street,
London, SW1H 9DJ
T: 0203 021 0575
E: enquiries@nsare.org
W: www.nsare.org

NTM Sales & Marketing Ltd
PO Box 2, Summerbridge,
Harrogate, HG3 4XN
T: 01423 781010
F: 01423 593953
E: info@xl-lubricants.com
W: www.xl-lubricants.com

NTRS (Network Training & Resource Solutions)
Unit 3&4, Churchill Way,
Chapeltown, Sheffield, S35 2PY
T: 0844 809 9902
F: 0844 809 9903
E: info@ntrs.co.uk
W: www.ntrs.co.uk

Nu Star Material Handling
Lakeside,
Ednaston Business Centre,
Ednaston, Derby, DE6 3AE
T: 0115 880 0070
F: 0115 880 0071
E: matt@nu-starmhl.com
W: www.nu-starmhl.com

NuAspect Ltd
The Gables, 47 Efflinch Lane,
Barton under Needwood,
Burton upon Trent, DE13 8EU
T: 020 7101 0800
E: enquiries@nuaspect.co.uk
W: www.nuaspect.co.uk

Nufox Rubber Ltd
Unit 1, Bentley Ave, Middleton,
Manchester, M24 2GP
T: 0161 655 8800
F: 0161 655 8801
E: info@nufox.com
W: www.nufox.com/

Nusteel Structures
Lympne, Hythe,
Kent, CT21 4LR
T: 01303 268112
F: 01303 266098
E: general@nusteelstructures.com
W: www.nusteelstructures.com

Nuttall Finchpalm
See BAM Nuttall Ltd

NVR Fleet UK
See Hitachi Capital Vehicle Solutions Ltd

Oce UK Ltd
Oce House, Chatham Way,
Brentwood,
Essex, CM14 4DZ
T: 0870 600 5544
F: 0870 600 1113
E: info@oce.com
W: www.oce.com

Odgers Ray & Berndtson
11 Hanover Square,
London, W1S 1JJ
T: 020 7529 1111
F: 020 7529 1000
E: info@rayberndtson.co.uk
W: www.odgers.com

Office of Rail and Road
One Kemble St,
London, WC2B 4AN
T: 020 7282 2000
F: 020 7282 2040
E: contact.cct@orr.gsi.gov.uk
W: www.orr.gov.uk

Ogier Electronics Ltd
Unit 13, Sandridge Park,
Porters Wood,
St Albans,
Herts, AL3 6PH
T: 01727 845547
F: 01727 852186
E: david.sproule@ogierelectronics.com
W: www.ogierelectronics.com

Oil Analysis Services Ltd
Unit 6/7, Blue Chalet Ind. Park,
London Rd,
West Kingsdown,
Kent, TN15 6BQ
T: 01474 854450
F: 01474 854408
E: ihbrown@oas-online.co.uk
W: www.oas-online.co.uk

Oldcastle Enclosure Solutions
IDA Industrial Est., Racecourse Rd,
Roscommon,
Republic of Ireland
T: 00353 9066 25922
F: 00353 9066 25921
W: www.oldcastleprecast.com/plants/enclosures/pages/default.aspx

HITACHI
Inspire the Next

Oleo International
Grovelands, Longford Rd, Exhall,
Coventry, CV7 9NE
T: 02476 645555
F: 02476 645900
E: sales@oleo.co.uk
W: www.oleo.co.uk

Omega Red Group Ltd
Dabell Ave, Blenheim Ind.Est.,
Bulwell, Nottingham, NG6 8WA
T: 0115 877 6666
F: 0115 876 7766
E: enquiries@
omegaredgroup.com
W: www.omegaredgroup.com

Omnicom Engineering Ltd
Eboracum House,
Clifton Park Avenue, York,
YO30 5PB
T: 01904 778100
F: 01904 778200
E: info@
omnicomengineering.co.uk
W: www.omnicom
engineering.co.uk

On Track Design Solutions Ltd
1st Floor Suite,
11 Pride Point Drive, Pride Park,
Derby, DE24 8BX
T: 01332 204450
F: 01332 204458
E: brianchadwick@
ontrackdesign.co.uk
W: www.ontrackdesign.co.uk

On Track Flooring Ltd
Unit E18, Langham Park,
Low's Lane, Stanton by Dale,
Derbys, DE7 4RJ
T: 0115 932 1691
F: 0115 930 9951
E: info@ontrackflooring.co.uk
W: www.ontrackflooring.co.uk/

Onboard Retail Solutions
See Iridium Onboard

One Way
26 Basepoint, Andersons Road,
Southampton,
Hampshire, SO14 5FE
T: 0845 644 8843
W: www.oneway.co.uk/

One-On Ltd
7 Home Farm Courtyard,
Meriden Rd, Berkswell,
West Midlands, CV7 7SH
T: 0845 505 1955
F: 0845 505 1977
E: info@one-on.co.uk
W: www.one-on.co.uk

Onyxrail Ltd
Scarborough House,
35 Auckland Rd,
Birmingham, B11 1RH
T: 0121 771 4219
E: enquiry@onyxrail.co.uk
W: www.onyxrail.co.uk

Open Technology Ltd
1 Woodlands Court,
Albert Drive,
Burgess Hill,
West Sussex, RH15 9TN
T: 0845 680 4004
F: 0845 680 4005
E: info@opentechnologyuk.com
W: www.opentechnologyuk.com

Opentree Ltd
Cabinet House,
Ellerbeck Court,
Stokesley Business Park,
North Yorkshire, TS9 5PT
T: 01642 714471
F: 01642 714451
E: info@opentree.co.uk
W: www.opentree.co.uk

Optilan Communication Systems
Sibree Rd,
Stonebridge Ind. Est,
Coventry, CV3 4FD
T: 01926 864999
F: 01926 851818
E: sales@optilan.com
W: www.optilan.com

Optimized Systems & Solutions Ltd
SIN D-7, PO Box 31,
Derby, DE24 8BJ
T: 01332 771700
F: 01332 770921
W: www.o-sys.com

Optimum Consultancy Ltd
Spencer House,
Mill Green Rd,
Haywards Heath,
West Sussex, RH16 1XQ
T: 020 3694 4100
F: 01444 448071
E: enquiries@
optimum.uk.com
W: www.optimum.uk.com

Opus International Consultants Ltd
Yale Business Village,
Wrexham Technology Park,
Wrexham, LL13 7YL
T: 01978 368100
F: 01978 368101
E: mark.valentine@
opusinternational.co.uk
W: www.opusinternational.co.uk

Oracle Recruitment
See Acorn People

Orchard Consulting
See Optimum Consultancy Ltd

Ordnance Survey
Romsey Rd,
Southampton, SO16 4GU
T: 02380 305030
F: 02380 792615
E: customerservice@
ordnancesurvey.co.uk
W: www.ordnancesurvey.co.uk

Orient Express
T: 020 7921 4028
F: 020 7805 5908
E: oesales.uk@orient-express.com
W: www.orient-express.com

Orion Electrotech
4 Danehill, Lower Earley,
Reading, RG6 4UT
T: 0118 923 9239
F: 0118 975 3332
E: rail@orion-group.co.uk
W: www.orionelectrotech.com

Orion Rail Services Ltd
30 Hepburn Road, Hillington Park,
Glasgow, G52 4RT
T: 0141 892 6666
F: 0141 892 6662
E: sales@orioneng.com
W: www.orionrail.co.uk/

Osborne Clarke
One London Wall,
London, EC2Y 5EB
T: 020 7105 7000
E: enquiries@osborneclarke.com
W: www.osborneclarke.com

Osborne Rail
Fonteyn House, 47-49 London Rd,
Reigate, Surrey, RH2 2PY
T: 01737 378200
F: 01737 378295
E: enquiries@osborne.co.uk
W: www.osborne.co.uk

OSL Rail
Unit 1.3, Alexander House,
19 Fleming Way, Swindon, SN1 2NG
T: 01793 600793
F: 08701 236249
E: enquiries@osl-rail.co.uk
W: www.osl-rail.co.uk

OTN Systems
Industrielaan 17b B-2250,
B-2250 Olen, Belgium
T: 003214252847
F: 003214252023
E: info@otnsystems.com
W: www.otnsystems.com

Owen Williams
See Amey

Oxford Hydrotechnics Ltd
Suite 2, The Great Barn,
Baynards Green, Bicester,
Oxon, OX27 7SR
T: 01869 346001
F: 01869 345455
E: info@h2ox.net
W: www.h2ox.net

Panasonic Computer Products Solutions
Panasonic House,
Willoughby Road, Bracknell,
Berks, RG12 8FP
T: 01344 853366
W: www.toughbook.eu

Panasonic Electric Works UK Ltd
Sunrise Parkway, Linford Wood,
Milton Keynes, MK14 6LF
T: 01908 231555
F: 01908 231599
E: info-uk@
eu.pewg.panasonic.com
W: www.panasonic-elec-
tric-works.co.uk

Pandrol UK Ltd
Gateford Rd, Worksop,
Notts, S81 7AX
T: 01909 476101
F: 01909 482989
E: info@pandrol.com
W: www.pandrol.com

Panolin
Ripon Way, Harrogate,
N Yorks, HG1 2AU
T: 01423 522911
F: 01423 530043
E: admin@cardev.com
W: www.cardev.com

Pantrak Transportation Ltd
G&S Building, 5, Sholto Cresc.,
Righead Ind. Est.,
Bellshill,
Lanarkshire, ML4 3LX
T: 01698 840465
F: 01698 749672
E: gavinroser@pantrak.com
W: www.pantrak.com

Parallel Project Training
Davidson House,
Forbury Sq,
Reading, RG1 3EU
T: 0845 519 2305
F: 0118 900 0501
E: withyoualltheway@
parallelprojecttraining.com
W: www.parallelproject
training.com

Parallel Studios
22 Balmoral Ave,
Bedford, MK40 2PT
F: 01234 217200
E: rick@parallelstudios.co.uk
W: ricktks.magix.net/website/
about_us.30.html#home

Park Signalling Ltd
3rd Floor,
Houldsworth Mill Business Centre,
Houldsworth St,
Reddish,
Stockport, SK5 6DA
T: 0161 219 0161
E: info@park-signalling.co.uk
W: www.park-signalling.co.uk

Parkeon Ltd
10 Willis Way, Fleets Ind Est,
Poole,
Dorset, BH15 3SS
T: 01202 339339
F: 01202 339369
E: sales_uk@parkeon.com
W: www.parkeon.com

Parker Hannifin (UK) Ltd
Tachbrook Park Drive,
Tachbrook Park,
Warwick, CV34 6TU
T: 01926 317878
F: 01926 317855
E: filtrationinfo@parker.com
W: www.parker.com

Parker KV Division
Presley Way, Crownhill,
Milton Keynes, MK8 0HB
T: 01908 561515
F: 01908 561227
E: saleskv@parker.com
W: www.parker.com

Parry People Movers Ltd
Overend Rd, Cradley Heath,
West Midlands, B64 7DD
T: 01384 569553
E: info@parrypeoplemovers.com
W: www.parrypeoplemovers.com

Parsons Brinckerhoff
6 Devonshire Square,
London, EC2M 4YE
T: 020 7337 1700
F: 020 7337 1701
E: railandtransit@pbworld.com
W: www.pbworld.com

Parsons Transportation Group
Holborn Gate, High Holborn,
London, WC1V 7QT
T: 020 7203 8440
F: 020 7203 8441
E: enquiries.pgil@parsons.com
W: www.parsons.com

Partex Marking Systems (UK) Ltd
Unit 61-64, Station Road, Coleshill,
Birmingham, B46 1JT
T: 01675 463670
E: sales@partex.co.uk
W: www.partex.co.uk

Partsmaster Ltd (NCH Europe)
NCH House,
Springvale Avenue, Bilston,
West Midlands, WV14 0QL
T: 01902 510335
E: victoria.summerfield@nch.com
W: www.partsmaster.com

Passcomm Ltd
Unit 24, Tatton Court,
Kingsland Garage,
Warrington,
Cheshire, WA1 4RR
T: 01925 821333
F: 01925 821321
E: info@passcomm.co.uk
W: www.passcomm.co.uk

Passenger Transport Networks
49 Stonegate,
York, YO1 8AW
T: 01904 611187
E: ptn@btconnect.com
W: www.passengertransport
networks.co.uk

Pathfinder Systems UK PTY Ltd
Unit 6, Bighams Park Farm,
Waterend,
Hemel Hempstead, HP1 3BN
T: 07711 189366
F: 020 7328 8818
E: cel@pathfindersystems.com.au
W: www.pathfindersystems.com.au

Pathfinder Tours
Stag House, Gydynap Lane,
Inchbrook, Woodchester,
Glos, GL5 5EZ
T: 01453 835414/834477
F: 01453 834053
E: office@pathfindertours.co.uk
W: www.pathfindertours.co.uk

Paypoint
1 The Boulevard, Shire Park,
Welwyn Garden City,
Herts, AL7 1EL
T: 08457 600633
E: areeves@paypoint.com
W: www.paypoint.com

PB – Consult GmbH
Am Plaerrer 12,
90429 Nuremburg,
Germany
T: 0049 911 32239 0
F: 0049 911 32239 10
E: info@pbconsult.de
W: www.pbconsult.eu

PB Design & Development
Unit 9/10, Hither Green Ind. Est.,
Clevedon, Bristol, BS21 6XT
T: 01275 874411
F: 01275 874428
E: sales@pbdesign.co.uk
W: www.pbdesign.co.uk

PBH Rail Ltd
The Old Coach House,
4a Custance Walk,
York, YO23 1BX
T: 01904 655666
F: 01904 655667
E: darren.pudsey@pbhrail.com
W: www.pbhrail.com

PBL Training
53 Guildford St, Bagshot,
Surrey, GU19 5NG
T: 01276 477499
F: 01276 562726
E: mike@pbl-training.co.uk
W: www.pbl-training.com

PCC.eu
Units 51/52, Llantarnam Ind. Park,
Cwmbran, NP44 3AW
T: 01633 214565
F: 01633 864752
E: info@pcc.eu.com
W: www.pcc.eu.com

PD Devices Ltd
Unit 1, Old Station Yard,
South Brent,
Devon, TQ10 9AL
T: 01364 649248
F: 01364 649250
E: marketing@pddevices.co.uk
W: www.pddevices.co.uk

Peacock Salt Ltd
North Harbour,
Ayr, KA8 8AE
T: 01292 292000
F: 01292 292001
E: info@peacocksalt.co.uk
W: www.peacocksalt.co.uk

Pearsons Engineering Services Ltd
17 Ilkeston Road, Heanor,
Derbys, DE75 7DR
T: 01773 763508
F: 01773 763508
E: nathan@pearsons
engineeringservices.co.uk
W: www.pearsons
engineeringservices.co.uk

A S Peck Engineering Ltd
116 Whitby Rd, Ruislip,
Middx, HA4 9DR
T: 01895 621398
F: 01895 613761
E: mark.jones@aspeckeng.co.uk
W: www.aspeckeng.co.uk

Peeping Ltd
See Tracsis Plc

PEI Genesis UK Ltd
George Curl Way,
Southampton, SO18 2RZ
T: 02380 621260
F: 02380 621270
E: peiuk@peigenesis.com
W: www.peigenesis.com

Peli Products (UK) Ltd
Peli House, Peakdale Rd, Brookfield,
Glossop, Derbys, SK13 6LQ
T: 01457 869999
F: 01457 869966
E: sales@peliproducts.co.uk
W: www.peliproducts.co.uk

Pell Frischmann
5 Manchester Square,
London, W1A 1AU
T: 020 7486 3661
F: 020 7487 4153
E: pflondon@pellfrischmann.com
W: www.pellfrischmann.com

Pelma Services and Autobuild Ltd
Chestnut Tree Cottage, One Pin Lane,
Farnham Common, Bucks, SL2 3QY
T: 01753 648484
E: pelma@btconnect.com
W: www.autobuildltd.co.uk

Peninsula Rail Task Force
Cllr Mark Coker (chair),
Plymouth City Council,
The Council House,
Plymouth, PL1 2AA
W: peninsularailtaskforce.co.uk/

Pennant Consulting Ltd
1 Sopwith Cres.,
Wickford Business Park, Wickford,
Essex, SS11 8YU
T: 01268 493495
E: enquiries@pennant-recruit.com
W: www.pennant-consult.com

Pennant Information Services Ltd
Parkway House, Palatine Rd,
Northenden,
Manchester, M22 4DB
T: 0161 947 6940
F: 0161 947 6959
E: john.churchman@pennantplc.co.uk
W: www.pennantplc.co.uk

Pennant International Group Plc
Pennant Court,
Staverton Technology Park,
Cheltenham, GL51 6TL
T: 01452 714914
F: 01452 714920
E: sales@pennantplc.co.uk
W: www.pennantplc.co.uk

People 1st
Hospitality House,
11-59 High Road, London, N2 8AB
T: 020 3074 1222
E: info@people1st.co.uk
W: www.people1st.co.uk

Perco Engineering Services Ltd
The Old Nurseries,
Nottingham Rd, Radcliffe on Trent,
Nottingham, NG12 2DU
T: 0115 933 5000
F: 0115 933 4692
E: info@perco.co.uk
W: www.perco.co.uk

Permali Gloucester Ltd
Permali Park, Bristol Rd,
Gloucester, GL1 5TT
T: 01452 528282
F: 01452 507409
E: fraser.rankin@permali.co.uk
W: www.permali.co.uk

Permalok Fastening Systems ltd
Plumtree industrial Estate,
Harworth, Doncaster, S Yorks,
DN11 8EW
T: 01302 711308
F: 01302 719823
E: info@permalokfastening.co.uk
W: www.permalokfastening.co.uk

Permanent Way Institution
5 Mount Crescent, Warley,
Brentwood, Essex, CM14 5DB
T: 01277 230031
E: info@thepwi.org
W: www.thepwi.org

Permaquip Ltd
Brierley Industrial Park,
Stanton Hill,
Sutton-in-Ashfield, NG17 3JZ
T: 01623 513349
F: 01623 517742
E: sales@permaquip.co.uk
W: www.permaquip.co.uk

Perpetuum Ltd
Epsilon House,
Southampton Science Park,
Southampton, SO16 7NS
T: 02380 765888
F: 02380 765889
E: info@perpetuum.com
W: www.perpetuum.com/rail

PESA
Zygmunta Augusta 11,
PL-85 082 Bydgoszcz, Poland
T: 0048 52339 1360
E: marketing@pesa.pl
W: www.pesa.pl

Petards Joyce-Loebl Ltd
390 Princesway North,
Team Valley Est., Gateshead,
Tyne & Wear, NE11 0TU
T: 0191 420 3000
F: 0191 420 3030
E: sales@petards.com
W: www.petards.com

Peter Brett Associates
Caversham Bridge House,
Waterman Place,
Reading, RG1 8DN
T: 0118 950 0761
F: 0118 959 7498
E: reading@pba.co.uk
W: www.pba.co.uk

Peter Davidson Consultancy
Brownlow House, Ravens Lane,
Berkhamsted,
Herts, HP4 2DX
T: 01442 891665
F: 01442 879776
E: mail@peter-davidson.com
W: www.peter-davidson.com

Peter Staveley Consulting
247 Davidson Rd, Croydon,
CR0 6DQ
T: 07973 168742
E: peter@peterstaveley.co.uk
W: www.peterstaveley.co.uk

Pfisterer
Unit 9, Ellesmere Business Park,
off Swingbridge Rd,
Grantham, Lincs, NG31 7XT
T: 01476 578657
F: 01476 568631
E: info.uk@pfisterer.com
W: www.pfisterer.co.uk

Pfleiderer
See RAIL.ONE GmbH

PFS Ltd
Unit 2-3, Wheaton Court,
Wheaton Road, Witham,
Essex, CM8 3UJ
T: 01376 535260
F: 01376 535268
E: trevor.mason@pfsfueltec.com
W: www.pfsfueltec.com

Phi Group Ltd
Hadley House, Bayshill Road,
Cheltenham,
Glos, GL50 3AW
T: 01242 707600
F: 0870 333 4127
E: marketing@phigroup.co.uk
W: www.phigroup.co.uk

Phoenix Contact Ltd
Halesfield 13, Telford,
Shropshire, TF7 4PG
T: 0845 881 2222
F: 0845 881 2211
E: info@phoenixcontact.co.uk
W: www.phoenixcontact.co.uk

Phoenix Systems UK Ltd
Unit 48, Standard Way,
Fareham Ind. Est.,
Fareham,
Hants, PO16 8XQ
T: 0845 658 6111
F: 0845 658 6222
E: sales@phoenixsystemsuk.com
W: www.phoenixsystemsuk.com

PHS Besafe incorporating Hiviz Laundries Ltd
PHS Group,
Western Industrial Estate,
Caerphilly, CF83 1XH
T: 02920 809120
F: 02920 863288
E: enquiries@phs.co.uk
W: www.phs.co.uk

Pilkington Glass Ltd
Prescot Rd, St Helens,
Merseyside, WA10 3TT
T: 01744 28882
F: 01744 692660
E: classics@pilkington.com
W: www.pilkington.com

Pilz Automation Technology
Pilz House, Little Colliers Field,
Corby, Northants, NN18 8TJ
T: 01536 460766
F: 01536 460866
E: sales@pilz.co.uk
W: www.pilz.co.uk

Pinsent Masons
City Point,
One Ropemaker St,
London, EC2Y 9AH
T: 020 7418 7000
F: 020 7418 7050
W: www.pinsentmasons.com

Pipeline Drillers Ltd
10 Kirkford, Stewarton,
Kilmarnock, KA3 5HZ
T: 01560 482021
F: 01560 484809
E: info@pipelinedrillers.co.uk

Pipex PX
Pipex House,
1 Belliver Way,
Roborough,
Plymouth,
Devon, PL6 7BP
T: 01752 581200
F: 01752 581209
E: sales@pipexpx.com
W: www.pipexpx.com

Pirtek (UK) Ltd
199 The Vale, Acton,
London, W3 7QS
T: 020 8749 8444
F: 020 8749 8333
E: info@pirtek.co.uk
W: www.pirtek.co.uk/

Pitchmastic PmB Ltd
Panama House,
184 Attercliffe Rd,
Sheffield, S4 7WZ
T: 0114 270 0100
F: 0114 276 8782
E: info@pitchmasticpmb.co.uk
W: www.pitchmasticpmb.co.uk

Plan Me Project Management
PO Box 281,
Malvern, WR14 9EP
T: 07906 439055
F: 0800 471 5332
E: info@planme.com
W: www.planme.com

Planet Platforms
Brunel Close, Century Park,
Wakefield 41 Ind. Est,
Wakefield, WF2 0XG
T: 0800 085 4161
F: 01924 267090
E: info@planetplatforms.co.uk
W: www.planetplatforms.co.uk

A Plant
See Ashtead Plant Hire Co Ltd
(APlant)

Plasser Machinery, Parts & Services Ltd
Manor Rd, West Ealing,
London, W13 0PP
T: 020 8998 4781
F: 020 8997 8206
E: info@plasser.co.uk
W: www.plasser.co.uk

Platipus Anchors Ltd
Unit Q, Philanthropic Rd,
Kingsfield Business Centre,
Redhill, Surrey, RH1 4DP
T: 01737 762300
F: 01737 773395
E: info@platipus-anchors.com
W: www.platipus-anchors.com

Plettac Security UK Ltd
Unit 39,
Sir Frank Whittle Business Centre,
Great Central Way, Rugby,
Warks, CV21 3XH
T: 0844 800 1725
F: 01788 544549
E: info@plettac.co.uk
W: www.plettac.co.uk

Plowman Craven Ltd
141 Lower Luton Rd, Harpenden,
Herts, AL5 5EQ
T: 01582 765566
F: 01582 765370
E: post@plowmancraven.co.uk
W: www.plowmancraven.co.uk

PM Safety Consultants Ltd
Suite D, 3rd Floor, Saturn Facilities,
101 Lockhurst Lane,
Coventry, CV6 5SF
T: 02476 665770
F: 02476 582401
E: info@pmsafety.com
W: www.pmsafety.com

PMA UK Ltd (Thomas & Betts Ltd)
Unit 4, Imperial Court,
Magellan Close,
Walworth Ind. Est., Andover,
Hants, SP10 5NT
T: 01264 333527
F: 01264 333643
E: sales@pma-uk.com
W: www.pma-uk.com

PMProfessional Learning
See Aikona Management Ltd

Pneumatrol
West End Business Park,
Blackburn Road, Oswaldtwistle,
Accrington, Lancs, BB5 4WZ
T: 01254 872277
F: 01254 390133
E: sales@pneumatrol.com
W: www.pneumatrol.com/

Pochins Ltd
Brookes Lane,
Middlewich,
Cheshire, CW10 0JQ
T: 01606 833333
F: 01606 833331
W: www.pochins.plc.uk/

Pod-Trak Ltd
Crove House,
14 Aintree Road, Perivale,
Middx, UB6 7LA
T: 0845 450 4190
F: 020 998 6901
E: enquiries@pod-trak.com
W: www.pod-trak.com

Polyamp AB
Box 229, Atvidaberg, 597 25,
Sweden
T: 0046 120 85410
F: 0046 120 85405
E: info@polyamp.se
W: www.polyamp.com

Polydeck Ltd
Unit 14, Burnett Ind Est,
Cox's Green, Wrington,
Bristol,
Somerset, BS40 5QS
T: 01934 863678
F: 01934 863683
E: sales@gripfast.co.uk
W: www.polydeck.co.uk/

Polyflor Ltd
Transport Flooring Division,
PO Box 3, Radcliffe New Rd,
Whitefield,
Manchester, M45 7NR
T: 0161 767 1111
F: 0161 767 1100
E: transport@polyflor.com
W: www.polyflor.com

Polypipe
Charnwood Business Park,
North Rd, Loughborough,
Leics, LE11 1LE
T: 01509 615100
F: 01509 610215
E: emma.thompson@polypipe.com
W: www.polypipe.com

Polyrack Tech-Group
Steinbeisstrasse 4,
D-75334 Straubenhardt,
Germany
T: 0800 7659 7225
E: sales@polyrack.com
W: www.polyrack.com

Polysafe Level Crossings
25 King St. Ind. Est., Langtoft,
Peterborough, PE6 9NF
T: 01778 560555
F: 01778 560773
E: sales@polysafe.co.uk
W: www.polysafe.co.uk

Pontoonworks
The Old Glove Factory,
Bristol Road, Sherborne,
Dorset, DT9 4HP
T: 01935 814950
F: 01935 815131
E: office@pontoonworks.co.uk
W: www.pontoonworks.co.uk

Portaramp UK Ltd
Units 3&4, Dolphin Business Park,
Shadwell, Thetford,
Norfolk, IP24 2RY
T: 01953 681799
F: 01953 688153
E: sales@portaramp.co.uk
W: www.portaramp.co.uk

Portastor
New Lane, Huntington,
York, YO32 9PR
T: 01904 624872
F: 01904 611760
E: action@portastor.com
W: www.portastor.com

Portec Rail Group
Stamford Street, Sheffield, S9 2TL
T: 0114 256 2225
F: 0114 261 7826
E: uk.sales@portecrail.co.uk
W: www.portecrail.com

Porterbrook Leasing Company Ltd
Ivatt House, 7 The Point,
Pinnacle Way, Pride Park,
Derby, DE24 8ZS
T: 01332 285050
F: 01332 285051
E: enquiries@porterbrook.co.uk
W: www.porterbrook.co.uk

Portwest Clothing Ltd
Commercial Rd,
Goldthorpe Ind. Est.,
Goldthorpe,
S.Yorks, S63 9BL
T: 01709 894575
F: 01709 880830
E: info@portwest.com
W: www.portwest.com

Postfield Systems
53 Ullswater Cres.,
Coulsdon,
Surrey, CR5 2HR
T: 020 8655 6080
F: 020 8655 6082
E: sales@postfield.co.uk
W: www.postfield.co.uk

Potensis Ltd
7th Floor, Froomsgate House,
Rupert St, Bristol, BS1 2QJ
T: 0117 910 7999
F: 0117 927 2722
E: office@potensis.com
W: www.potensis.com

Potter Logistics Ltd
Melmerby Ind. Est, Green Lane,
Melmerby, Ripon,
North Yorks, HG4 5HP
T: 01353 646703
E: sales@potterlogistics.co.uk
W: www.potterlogistics.co.uk

Power 4 from Fox & Cooper
See Stuart Group

Power Electrics Generators Ltd
St. Ivel Way,
Warmley,
Bristol, BS30 8TY
T: 0117 947 9700
F: 0117 947 9702
E: sales@powerelectrics.com
W: www.powerelectrics.com

Power Electronics (PE Systems Ltd)
Victoria St, Leigh,
Lancs, WN7 5SE
T: 01942 260330
F: 01942 261835
E: sales@pe-systems.co.uk
W: www.pe-systems.co.uk

Power Jacks Ltd
Balmacassie Commercial Park,
Ellon, Aberdeenshire, AB41 8BX
T: 01358 285100
E: sales@powerjacks.com
W: www.powerjacks.com

Powerbox Group
4/5 Knights Court,
Magellan Close,
Walworth Ind. Est, Andover,
Hants, SP10 5NT
T: 01264 384460
F: 01264 334337
E: warren.venn@powerboxgroup.co.uk
W: www.powerbox.info

Powernetics Systems Ltd
Jason Works, Clarence St,
Loughborough, Leics, LE11 1DX
T: 01509 214153 x205
F: 01509 262460
E: jag@powernetics.co.uk
W: www.powernetics.co.uk

Powertron Convertors Ltd
See Martek Power Ltd

Praxis
See Altran UK Ltd

Praybourne Ltd
Unit 2c, Eagle Road,
North Moons Moat, Redditch,
Worcs, B98 9HF
T: 0844 669 1860
F: 01527 543 752
E: enquiries@praybourne.co.uk
W: www.praybourne.co.uk

PRB Consulting
167 London Rd, Hailsham,
E.Sussex, BN27 3AN
T: 0845 557 6814
E: paul.brace@prbconsulting.co.uk
W: www.prbconsulting.co.uk

PRC Rail Consulting
7 Hunters Rise, Kirby Bellars,
Melton Mowbray, Leics, LE14 2DT
T: 01664 810118
E: piers.connor@railway-technical.com
W: www.railway-technical.com

Preformed Markings Ltd
Unit 6, Oyster Park,
109 Chertsey Rd,
Byfleet,
Surrey, KT14 7AX
T: 01932 359270
F: 01932 340936
E: info@preformedmarkings.co.uk
W: www.preformedmarkings.co.uk

Premier Calibration Ltd
Unit 3K/L, Lake Enterprise Park,
Sandall Stores Rd,
Kirk Sandall,
Doncaster, DN3 1QR
T: 01302 888448
F: 01302 881197
E: enquiries.premcal@btconnect.com
W: www.premiercalibration.co.uk/

Premier Pits
Town Drove, Quadring,
Spalding,
Lincs, PE11 4PU
T: 01775 821222
F: 01775 820914
E: info@premierpits.com
W: www.premierpits.com

Premier Stampings
Station St, Cradley Heath,
West Midlands, B64 6AJ
T: 01384 353100
F: 01384 353101
E: ashleyh@premierstampings.co.uk
W: www.premierstampings.co.uk

Premier Train Catering
See Creative Rail Dining

PremTech Solutions Ltd
9 Saffron Meadow,
Harrogate,
North Yorks, HG3 2NU
E: david@premtech.net
W: www.premtech.net

Preserved Traction Technical Services
3 No4 Pembroke Rd,
London, N15 4NW
E: markb754@aol.com
W: www.preservedtractiontechservice.com

Preston Trampower Ltd
1 Navigation Business Village,
Preston, Lancashire, PR2 2YP
T: 01772 730290
F: 01772 730291
E: lincoln.shields@trampower.co.uk
W: www.prestontrampower.co.uk

Price Tool Sales Ltd
See Birchwood Price Tools

PriceWaterhouseCoopers LLP
1 Embankment Place,
London, WC2N 6NN
T: 020 7583 5000
F: 020 7822 4652
E: julian.smith@uk.pwc.com
W: www.pwcglobal.com

Priestman Goode
150 Great Portland St,
London, W1W 6QD
T: 020 7580 3444
E: studio@priestmangoode.com
W: www.priestmangoode.com

Primat Recruitment
Lingfield Point, Darlington, DL1 1RW
T: 01325 744400
W: www.primatrecruitment.com

Prime Rail Solutions Ltd
Dartford Road, March,
Cambridgeshire, PE15 8AE
T: 01733 462420
M: 07934 899099
E: peter@primerailsolutions.com
W: www.primerailsolutions.com

Priority Vehicle Hire Ltd
Unit 1, Bestmans Lane Ind. Estate,
Bestmans Lane, Kempsey,
Worcester, WR5 3PZ
T: 01905 821843
E: enquiries@priorityhire.co.uk
W: www.priorityhire.co.uk/

Progress Rail Services
Eastfield, Peterborough, PE1 5NA
T: 01733 583000
E: mcdonald_michael@cat.com
W: www.progressrail.com

Prolec Ltd
25 Benson Rd, Nuffield Ind. Est.,
Poole, Dorset, BH17 0GB
T: 01202 681190
F: 01202 677909
E: info@prolec.co.uk
W: www.prolec.co.uk

Pro-Link Europe
Irene House,
Five Arches Business Park,
Maidstone Rd, Sidcup,
Kent, DA14 5AE
T: 020 8309 2700
F: 020 8309 7890
E: enquire@prolink-europe.com
W: www.prolink-europe.com

Prospects College of Advanced Technology (PROCAT)
Basildon Campus,
Luckyn Lane Entrance, Basildon,
Essex, SS14 3AY
T: 0800 389 3589
E: enquiries@procat.ac.uk
W: www.procat.ac.uk/

Prostaff Rail Recruitment
172 Buckingham Ave, Slough,
Bucks, SL1 4RD
T: 01753 575888
W: www.prostaff.com

Prostyle Ltd
Unit 7, Brindley Road,
Bayton Road Industrial Estate,
Coventry, Warks, CV7 9EP
T: 02476 367441
F: 02476 367145
E: info@pro-style.co.uk
W: www.pro-style.co.uk

Prostyle Ltd
Unit 7, Brindley Road,
Bayton Road Industrial Estate,
Coventry, Warks, CV7 9EP
T: 02476 367441
F: 02476 367145
E: info@pro-style.co.uk
W: www.pro-style.co.uk

Protec Fire Detection Plc
Protec House, Churchill Way,
Nelson, Lancs, BB9 6RT
T: 01282 717171
F: 01282 717273
E: sales@protec.co.uk
W: www.protec.co.uk

Proteq
Head Office, The Pinnacle Works,
Station Road, Epworth,
Doncaster, DN9 1JU
T: 01427 872572
F: 01427 875094
E: info@proteq.co.uk
W: www.proteq.co.uk

Provertha
21 Tarrant Wharf, Arundel,
West Sussex, BN18 9NY
E: service@provertha.com
W: www.provertha.com

PRV Engineering
Pegasus House, Polo Grounds,
New Inn, Pontypool, Gwent,
NP4 0TW
T: 01495 769697
F: 01495 769776
E: enquiries@prv-engineering.co.uk
W: www.prv-engineering.co.uk

Prysm Rail
See Archer Safety Signs

Prysmian Cables & Systems
Chickenhall Lane, Eastleigh,
Hants, SO50 6YU
T: 023 8029 5029
F: 023 8060 8769
E: marketing.telecom@prysmian.com
W: www.prysmiangroup.com

Psion Teklogix
Unit Q,
Bourne End Business Centre,
Cores End Rd, Bourne End,
Bucks, SL8 5AS
T: 01628 648800
F: 01628 648810
E: presales.info@motorolasolutions.com
W: www.psionteklogix.co.uk

PSV Glass
Hillbottom Rd, High Wycombe,
Bucks, HP12 4HJ
T: 01494 533131
T: 24/7 SERVICE 0845 600 9801
E: rail@psvglass.co.uk
W: www.psvglass.com

pteg
pteg Support Unit,
Wellington House,
40-50 Wellington Street,
Leeds, LS1 2DE
T: 0113 251 7204
F: 0113 251 7333
E: info@pteg.net
W: www.pteg.net/

PTH Group Ltd
See BHSF Occupational Health Ltd

PTM Design Ltd
Unit B2,
Sovereign Park Ind Est, Lathkill St,
Market Harborough, LE16 9EG
T: 01858 463777
F: 01858 463777
E: ptmdesign@aol.com
W: www.ptmdesign.co.uk/

PTP Associates
The Lodge, 21 Harcourt Rd.,
Dorney Reach, Berks, SL6 0DT
T: 01628 776059
E: ces@ptpassociates.co.uk
W: www.ptpassociates.co.uk

Pullman Rail
Train Maintenance Depot,
Leckwith Rd, Cardiff, CF11 8HP
T: 02920 368850
F: 02920 368874
E: sales@pullmanrail.co.uk
W: www.pullmanrail.co.uk

PULS UK Ltd
Unit 10, Ampthill Business Park,
Station Road, Ampthill,
Beds, MK45 2QW
T: 01525 841001
E: sales@puls.co.uk
W: www.puls.co.uk

Pulsarail
See Praybourne Ltd

Pyeroy Group
Kirkstone House, St Omers Rd,
Western Riverside Route,
Gateshead, Tyne & Wear, NE11 9EZ
T: 0191 493 2600
F: 0191 493 2601
E: mail@pyeroy.co.uk
W: www.pyeroy.co.uk

Pym & Wildsmith (Metal Finishers) Ltd
Bramshall Ind. Est, Bramshall,
Uttoxeter, Staffs, ST14 8TD
T: 01889 565653
F: 01889 567064
E: enquiries@pymandwildsmith.co.uk
W: www.pymandwildsmith.co.uk

Q'Straint
Unit 72-76,
John Wilson Business Park,
Whitstable, Kent, CT5 3QT
T: 01227 773035
F: 01227 770035
E: info@qstraint.co.uk
W: www.qstraint.com

QA-Aikona Ltd
Rath House, 55-65 Uxbridge Rd,
Slough, SL1 1SG
T: 0845 757 3888
E: info@qa.com
W: www.qa.com

QC Data Ltd
Park House, 14 Kirtley Drive,
Castle Marina, Nottingham, NG7 1LD
T: 0115 941 5806
F: 0115 947 2901
E: rjohnson@qcdata.com
W: www.qcdata.com

QHi Rail
City Park, Watchmead,
Welwyn Garden City, Herts, AL7 1LT
T: 01707 379870
E: info@qhirail.com
W: www.qhirail.com

The QSS Group Ltd
2 St Georges House, Vernon Gate,
Derby, DE1 1UQ
T: 01332 221400
F: 01332 221401
E: enquiries@theqssgroup.co.uk
W: www.theqssgroup.co.uk

QTS Plant
QTS Group, Rench Farm, Drumclog,
Strathaven, S. Lanarks, ML10 6QJ
T: 01357 440222
F: 01357 440364
E: enquiries@qtsgroup.com
W: www.qtsgroup.com

Qualitrain Ltd
Bridge House, 12 Mansfield Rd,
Tibshelf, Derbys, DE55 5NF
F: 01773 590671
E: richard.bates@qualitrain.co.uk
W: www.qualitrain.co.uk

Qualter Hall & Co Ltd
PO Box 8, Johnson St, Barnsley,
South Yorkshire, S75 2BY
T: 01226 205761
F: 01226 286269
E: admin@qualterhall.co.uk
W: www.qualterhall.co.uk

Quasar Associates
8 Flitcroft St, London, WC2H 8DJ
T: 020 7010 7700
F: 020 7010 7701
E: jonathan@quasarassociates.co.uk
W: www.quasarassociates.co.uk

Quattro Plant Ltd
Greenway Court, Canning Rd,
Stratford, London, E15 3ND
T: 020 8519 6165
F: 020 8503 0505
E: sales@quattroplant.co.uk
W: www.quattroplant.co.uk

Quest Diagnostics
Unit B1, Parkway West,
Cranford Lane, Heston, Middx,
TW5 9QA
T: 020 8377 3378
F: 020 8377 3350
E: uksales@questdiagnostics.com
W: www.questdiagnostics.com

Quickbuild (UK) Ltd
Imperial House, 1 Factory Rd,
Silvertown, London, E16 2EL
T: 020 7473 2712
F: 020 7476 2713
E: davidbrowne@hiremasters.co.uk
W: www.hiremasters.co.uk/www.quickbuild.uk.com

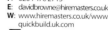

Quickway Buildings
Hardy's Yard, London Rd,
Riverhead, Sevenoaks,
Kent, TN13 2DN
T: 01304 612284
F: 01304 620012
E: sales@quickway-wingham.co.uk
W: www.quickway-wingham.co.uk

QW Rail Leasing
12 Plumtree Court,
London, EC4A 4HT

R&B Switchgear Services Ltd
Switchgear House,
The Courtyard, Green Lane,
Heywood,
Lancs, OL10 2EX
T: 01706 369933
F: 01706 364564
E: ian.penswick@rb-power.co.uk
W: www.rbswitch.co.uk

R&I Consulting
29 Marylebone Rd,
London, NW1 5JK
T: 020 3598 2479
E: info@raics.co.uk
W: www.raics.co.uk

R.S. Clare & Co Ltd
8-14 Stanhope St,
Liverpool, L8 5RQ
T: 0151 709 2902
F: 0151 709 0518
E: info@rsclare.co.uk
W: www.rsclare.com

Ra'alloy Ramps Ltd
A3 Stafford Park 15, Telford,
Shropshire, TF3 3BB
T: 01952 291224
E: enquiries@raalloy.co.uk
W: www.raalloy.co.uk/

RAICS
See R&I Consulting

Rail & Road Protec GmbH
Lise-Meitner-Strasse 4,
D-24941 Flensburg, Germany
T: 01628 635497
F: 00461 500 33820
E: info@r2protec.com
W: www.r2protec.com

Rail Academy
Newcastle College Rail Academy,
William St, Felling, Gateshead,
Tyne & Wear, NE10 0JP

Rail Accident Investigation Branch
The Wharf,
Stores Rd,
Derby, DE21 4BA
T: 01332 253300
F: 01332 253301
E: enquiries@raib.gov.uk
W: www.raib.gov.uk

Rail Alliance
The Control Tower,
Quinton Rail Technology Centre,
Station Rd, Long Marston,
Stratford upon Avon, Warks,
CV37 8PL
T: 01789 720026
E: info@railalliance.co.uk
W: www.railalliance.co.uk

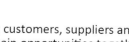

RMF

RMF is a leading provider of railway reservation based international settlement and clearing services, providing sophisticated revenue and cost allocation, including business critical management information.

Rail Manche Finance EEIG
Times House, Bravingtons Walk, Regent Quarter, London, N1 9AW
T: 00 44 (0) 20 7042 9961
F: 00 44 (0) 20 7833 3896
E: david.hiscock@rmf.co.uk

www.rmf.co.uk

Rail Positive Relations
Verba mea auribus

Rail Positive Relations is the UK's leading specialist communications consultancy for the railway industry. Services include Stakeholder & Government Relations, Lobbying and Media Management.

A: The Bothy, 18 Holloway Road
Duffield, Derbyshire DE56 4FE
M: +44 (0) 7973 950 923
E: rupert@railpr.com
W: www.railpr.com

Rail Audit & Assurance Services (RAAS)
54 Highfield Rd, Cheadle Hulme, Stockport, SK8 6EP
T: 0161 486 1237
E: stockport@raas.co.uk
W: www.raas.co.uk

Rail Delivery Group
200 Aldersgate, London, EC1A 4HD
T: 020 7841 8000
E: info@raildeliverygroup.com
W: www.raildeliverygroup.com

Rail Door Solutions Ltd
Blackhill Drive, Wolverton Mill, Milton Keynes, MK12 5TS
T: 01908 224140
F: 01908 224149
E: info@raildoorsolutions.co.uk
W: www.raildoorsolutions.co.uk

Rail Forum East Midlands
Lonsdale House, Quaker Way, Derby, DE1 3HB
T: 01332 593550
E: info@derbyrailforum.org.uk
W: www.derbyrailforum.org.uk

Rail Freight Group
7 Bury Place, London, WC1A 2LA
T: 020 3116 0007
F: 020 3116 0008
E: phillippa@rfg.org.uk
W: www.rfg.org.uk

Rail Gourmet Group
169 Euston Road, London, NW1 2AE
T: 020 7529 8330
F: 020 7922 6596
E: jfleet@railgourmetuk.com
W: www.railgourmet.com

Rail Images & Rail Images Video
5 Sandhurst Crescent, Leigh on Sea, E ssex, SS9 4AL
T: 01702 525059
F: 01702 525059
E: info@railimages.co.uk
W: www.railimages.co.uk

Rail Industry Contractors Association Ltd (RICA)
Gin Gan House, Thropton, Morpeth, Northumberland, NE65 7LT
T: 01669 620569
E: enquiries@rica.uk.com
W: www.rica.uk.com

Rail Industry First Aid Association (RIFAA)
Po Box 1152, Doncaster, DN1 9NL
T: 01302 329 729
F: 01302 320 590
E: bookings@rifaa.com
W: www.rifaa.com

Rail Insights Ltd
Highlands, St Andrews Rd, Henley-on-Thames, RG9 1PG
T: 01491 414218
E: info@railinsights.com
W: www.railinsights.com

Rail Manche Finance EEIG
Times House, Bravingtons Walk, Regent Quarter, London, N1 9AW
T: 020 7042 9961
F: 020 7833 3896
E: david.hiscock@rmf.co.uk
W: www.rmf.co.uk

Rail Measurement Ltd
The Mount, High St, Toft, Cambridge, CB23 2RL
T: 01223 264327
F: 01223 263273
E: enquiries@railmeasurement.com
W: www.railmeasurement.com

Rail Op UK Ltd
Gowers Farm, Tumblers Green, Braintree, Essex, CM77 8AZ
T: 0845 450 5232
F: 01376 388295
E: info@railop.co.uk
W: www.railop.co.uk

Rail Operations Developments Ltd
Electra House, Electra Way, Crewe Business Park, Crewe, CW1 6GL
T: 01270 588500
F: 01270 588500
E: enquiries@rodl.co.uk
W: www.railoperationaldevelopment.co.uk/

Rail Operations Group
6 Snow Hill, London, EC1A 2AY
M: 07712 329697
E: info@railopsgroup.co.uk
W: www.railopsgroup.co.uk

Rail Order
Unit 11, Billet Lane, Normanby Enterprise Park, Scunthorpe, DN15 9YH
T: 01724 292860
F: 01724 292242
E: sales@rail-order.co.uk
W: www.rail-order.co.uk

Rail Personnel Ltd
Level 26, Office Tower, Convention Plaza, 1 Harbour Rd, Wanchai, Hong Kong, China
T: 00 852 2753 5636
F: 00 852 2305 4512
E: info@railpersonnel.com
W: www.railpersonnel.com

Rail Photo Library
F: 0116 259 2068
E: studio@railphotolibrary.com
W: www.railphotolibrary.com

Rail Positive Relations
The Bothy, 18 Holloway Rd, Duffield, Derbys, DE56 4FE
M: 07973 950923
E: rupert@railpr.com
W: www.railpr.com

Rail Professional Development
Cranes House, 5 Paycocke Rd, Basildon, Essex, SS14 3DP
T: 01268 822842
F: 01268 822841
E: info@rpd.co.uk
W: www.rpd.co.uk

Rail Research UK Association (RRUKA)
Block 2, Angel Square, 1 Torrens St, London, EC1V 1NY
T: 02380 598454
F: 02380 677519
E: secretariat@rruka.org.uk
W: www.rruka.org.uk

Rail Restorations North East Ltd
8A Hackworth Industrial Park, Shildon, County Durham, DL4 1HF
T: 01388 777138
F: 01388 777138
E: enquiries@rail-restorations-north-east.co.uk
W: www.rail-restorations-north-east.co.uk

Rail Safety Solutions
Unit 27, Royal Scot Rd, Pride Park, Derby, DE24 8AJ
T: 01332 989593
F: 020 3142 5301
E: info@railsafetysolutions.com
W: www.railsafetysolutions.com

Rail Safety Systems BV
See Innovative Railway Safety Ltd

Rail Settlement Plan Ltd
See Association of Train Operating Companies (ATOC)

Rail Supply Group
E: secretariat@railsupplygroup.org
W: www.railsupplygroup.org

Rail Tech Group (Railway & Signalling Engineering) Ltd
91 Dales Rd, Ipswich, Suffolk, IP1 4JR
T: 01473 242344
F: 01473 242379
W: www.rttrainingsolutions.co.uk/railway-courses/

Rail Technology Ltd
Mill End Lane, Alrewas, Staffs, DE13 7BY
T: 01283 790012
F: 01283 792371
E: info@railtechnologyltd.com
W: www.railtechnologyltd.com

The Rail Technology Unit (RTU) at Manchester Metropolitan University
Rail Technology Unit, Manchester Metropolitan University, John Dalton Building, Chester St, Manchester, M1 5GD
T: 0161 247 6247
F: 0161 247 6840
E: j.grey@bham.ac.uk
W: www.mmu.ac.uk/business/our-expertise/expertise.php?area=sustainability_and_climate_change&expertise=railway_research_and_consultancy

Rail Training International Ltd
North Suite, Parsonage Offices, Church Lane, Canterbury, Kent, CT4 7AD
T: 01227 769096
F: 01227 479435
E: rtiuk@rti.co.uk
W: www.rti.co.uk

Rail Vision
2 Cygnus Court, Beverley Rd, Pegasus Business Park, East Midlands Airport, Castle Donnington, Leics, DE74 2UZ
T: 01509 672211
E: enquiries@rail-vision.com
W: www.rail-vision.com

Rail Waiting Structures
Unit 60, Dyffryn Business Park, Llantwit Major Rd, Llandow, Vale of Glamorgan, CF71 7PY
T: 01446 795444
F: 01446 773344
E: rail@shelters.co.uk
W: www.railwaitingstructures.com/

RAIL.ONE GmbH
Ingolstaedter Strasse 51, 92318 Neumarkt, Germany
T: 0049 9181 8952-0
F: 0049 9181 8952-5001
E: info@railone.com
W: www.railone.com

Rail-Ability Ltd
Tilcon Ave, Baswich, Stafford, ST18 0YJ
T: 01785 214747
F: 01785 214717
E: skelly@railability.co.uk
W: www.railability.co.uk

Railcare Ltd
See Knorr-Bremse Rail UK

Raileasy
10 Station Parade, High St, Wanstead, London, E11 1QF
T: 0906 2000 500
E: admin@raileasy.co.uk
W: www.raileasy.co.uk

Railex Aluminium Ltd
12/26 Dry Drayton Ind. Est., Dry Drayton, Cambridge, CB3 8AT
T: 0845 612 9555
F: 01954 210352
E: tony@railex.net
W: www.railex.net

Railfuture
24 Chedworth Place, Tattingstone, Suffolk, IP9 2ND
T: 0117 9272954
E: media@railfuture.org.uk
W: www.railfuture.org.uk

RailRoute Ltd
The Business and Innovation Centre, Enterprise Park East, Sunderland, SR5 2TA
T: 0191 516 6354
E: info@railroute.co.uk
W: www.railroute.co.uk

Railscape Ltd
15 Totman Cresc, Brook Rd Ind Est, Rayleigh, Essex, SS6 7UY
T: 01268 777795
F: 01268 777762
E: info@railscape.com
W: www.railscape.com

Railtex/Infrarail
See Mack Brooks Exhibitions Ltd

Railtourer Ltd
See West Coast Railway Co.

Railway Approvals Ltd
Derwent House, RTC Business Park, London Rd, Derby, DE24 8UP
T: 01332 483800
F: 01332 483800
E: sales@railwayapprovals.com
W: www.railwayapprovals.co.uk

Railway Civil Engineers Association
One Great George St, Westminster, London, SW1P 3AA
T: 020 7665 2233
F: 020 7799 1325
E: rcea@ice.org.uk
W: www.rcea.org.uk/

The Railway Consultancy Ltd
1st Floor, South Tower, Crystal Palace Station, London, SE19 2AZ
T: 020 8676 0395
F: 020 8778 7439
E: info@railwayconsultancy.com
W: www.railwayconsultancy.com

Railway Convalescent Home (RCH)
Bridge House, 2 Church St, Dawlish, Devon, EX7 9AU
T: 01626 863303
F: 01626 866676
E: sueg@rch.org.uk
W: www.rch.org.uk

Railway Drainage Ltd
The Steadings, Maisemore Court, Maisemore, Glos, GL2 8EY
T: 01452 422666
F: 01452 423516
E: info@rdlonline.co.uk
W: www.rdlonline.co.uk

Railway Employees & Public Transport Association
See REPTA (Railway Employees and Public Transport Association)

Railway Engineering Associates Ltd
68 Boden St, Glasgow, G40 3PX
T: 0141 554 3868
F: 0141 556 5091
E: postmaster@rea.uk.com
W: www.rea.uk.com

Railway Engineering Associates Ltd
125 Boden St, Glasgow, G40 3QF
T: 0141 556 0415
E: henry@rea.uk.com
W: www.rea.uk.com

Railway Engineers Forum (REF)
T: 020 7651 7910
M: 07766 496685
E: lwquinn@bechtel.com
W: www.theref.org.uk

Railway Finance Ltd
Barrow Rd, Wincobank, Sheffield, S9 1JZ
T: 01223 891300
F: 01223 891302
E: nick.preston@railwayfinance.co.uk
W: www.railwayfinance.co.uk

Railway Heritage Trust
1 Eversholt St, London, NW1 2DN
T: 020 7904 7354
E: rht@railwayheritagetrust.co.uk
W: www.railwayheritagetrust.co.uk

Railway Industry Association
22 Headfort Place, London, SW1X 7RY
T: 020 7201 0777
F: 020 7235 5777
E: ria@riagb.org.uk
W: www.riagb.org.uk

Railway Management Services Ltd
Kingfisher House, Suite 27, 21-23 Elmfield Rd, Bromley, Kent, BR1 1LT
T: 020 8315 6767
F: 020 8315 6766
E: peter.coysten@railwayms.com
W: www.railwayms.com

Railway Industry Association

Promoting and supporting UK railway suppliers

Call us or visit our website to see how we can help your business

ria@riagb.org.uk
020 7201 0777
www.riagb.org.uk

194

HITACHI
Inspire the Next

The Railway Mission
Rugby Railway Station,
Rugby, CV21 3LA
T: 0845 269 1881
E: office@railwaychaplain.net
W: www.railwaymission.org

Railway Projects Ltd
Lisbon House, 5-7 St Marys Gate,
Derby, DE1 3JA
T: 01332 349255
F: 01332 294688
E: enquiries@railwayprojects.co.uk
W: www.railwayprojects.co.uk

Railway Study Association (RSA)
PO Box 375, Burgess Hill,
West Sussex, RH15 5BX
T: 01444 246379
E: info@railwaystudyassociation.org
W: www.railwaystudyassociation.org

Railway Support Services
Montpellier House,
Montpellier Drive, Cheltenham,
Glos, GL50 1TY
T: 0870 803 4651
F: 0870 803 4652
E: info@railwaysupport services.co.uk
W: www.railwaysupport services.co.uk

Railway Systems Engineering & Integration Group
Birmingham Centre for Railway Reasearch & Education
College of Engineering Sciences,
University of Birmingham,
Edgbaston, Birmingham, B15 2TT
T: 0121 414 4342
F: 0121 414 4291
E: j.grey@bham.ac.uk
W: www.eng.bham.ac.uk/civil/study/postgrad/railway.shtml

Railway Touring Company
14a Tuesday Market Place,
Kings Lynn,
Norfolk, PE30 1JN
T: 01553 661500
F: 01553 661800
E: enquiries@railwaytouring.co.uk
W: www.railwaytouring.co.uk

Railway Vehicle Engineering Ltd (RVEL)
RTC Business Park,
London Rd, Derby, DE24 8UP
T: 01332 293035
F: 01332 331210
E: enquiries@rvel.co.uk
W: www.rvel.co.uk

Railways Pension Scheme
2nd Floor, Camomile Court,
23 Camomile St,
London, EC3A 7LL
T: 0800 234 3434
E: csu@rpmi.co.uk
W: www.railwayspensions.co.uk

Railweight
Foundry Lane,
Smethwick,
Birmingham, B66 2LP
T: 0845 246 6714
F: 0845 246 6715
E: sales@railweight.co.uk
W: www.averyweigh-tronix.com/railweight

Ramboll UK Ltd
Carlton House, Ringwood Rd,
Woodlands,
Southampton, SO40 7HT
T: 02380 817500
F: 02380 817600
E: tim.holmes@ramboll.co.uk
W: www.ramboll.co.uk

Ramtech Electronics Ltd
Abbeyfield House,
Abbeyfield Rd,
Nottingham, NG7 2SZ
T: 0115 957 8282
F: 0115 957 8299
E: matt.sadler@ramtech.co.uk
W: www.ramtech.co.uk

Ranstad CPE
Forum 4, Parkway,
Solent Business Park,
Whiteley,
Fareham, PO15 7AD
T: 01489 560000
F: 01489 560001
E: railteam@ranstadcpe.com
W: www.ranstadcpe.com/rail

Raspberry Software Ltd
9 Deben Mill Business Centre,
Old Maltings Approach,
Melton, Woodbridge,
Suffolk, IP12 1BL
T: 01394 387386
F: 01394 387386
E: info@raspberrysoftware.com
W: www.raspberrysoftware.com

Ratcliff Palfinger
Bessemer Rd,
Welwyn Garden City,
Herts, AL7 1ET
T: 01707 325571
F: 01707 327752
E: info@ratcliffpalfinger.co.uk
W: www.ratcliffpalfinger.com

Rayleigh Instruments
Raytel House, Brook Rd,
Rayleigh, Essex, SS6 7XH
T: 01268 749300
F: 01268 749309
E: sales@rayleigh.co.uk
W: www.rayleigh.co.uk

RE: Systems
Systems House,
Deepdale Business Park,
Bakewell,
Derbys, DE45 1GT
T: 01629 813961
F: 01629 813185
E: steve.england@re-systems.co.uk
W: www.re-systems.co.uk

REACT Beyond Cleaning
Stanhope Rd, Swadlincote,
Derbys, DE11 9BE
T: 08707 510422
F: 08707 510417
E: info@reactbeyond cleaning.co.uk
W: www.reactbeyond cleaning.co.uk

Readypower
Readypower House,
Molly Millars Bridge, Wokingham,
Berks, RG41 2WY
T: 01189 774901
F: 01189 774902
E: info@readypower.co.uk
W: www.readypower.co.uk

Real Time Consultants Plc
118-120 Warwick St,
Royal Leamington Spa,
Warks, CV32 4QY
T: 01926 313133
F: 01926 422165
E: contract@rtc.co.uk
W: www.rtc.co.uk

Rebo Systems
Beckeringhstraat 21,
NL-3762 EV Soest, Netherlands
T: 0031 0356 016 941
E: info@rebo.nl
W: www.rebosystems.com

Record Electrical Associates Ltd
Unit C1, Longford Trading Est.,
Thomas St., Stretford,
Manchester, M32 0JT
T: 0161 864 3583
F: 0161 864 3603
E: alanj@reauk.com
W: www.record-electrical.co.uk

Recruitrail (Recruit Engineers)
Bank Chambers,
36 Mount Pleasant Rd,
Tunbridge Wells, Kent, TN1 1RA
T: 01909 540825
F: 0870 443 0453
W: www.recruitrail.com

Red Plant Ltd
Red House, The Corner, Parkside,
Wootton, Canterbury,
Kent, CT4 6RR
T: 0845 838 7584
E: info@redplant.co.uk
W: www.redplant.co.uk

Redman Fisher Engineering Ltd
Marsh Road, Middlesbrough,
Teesside, TS1 5JS
T: 01952 685110
F: 01952 685117
E: sales@redmanfisher.co.uk
W: www.redmanfisher.co.uk

Rehau Ltd
Hill Court, Walford, Ross-on-Wye,
Herefordshire, HR9 5QN
T: 01989 762655
F: 01989 762601
E: anthonia.ifeany-okoro@rehau.com
W: www.rehau.co.uk

Reid Lifting Ltd
Unit 1, Severnlink,
Newhouse Farm Ind. Est,
Chepstow,
Monmouthshire, NP16 6UN
T: 01291 620796
F: 01291 626490
E: enquiries@reidlifting.com
W: www.reidlifting.com

Reinforced Earth Company
Innovation House, Euston Way,
Telford, Shropshire, TF3 4LT
T: 01952 204357
F: 01952 201753
E: info@reinforcedearth.co.uk
W: www.reinforcedearth.co.uk

Relec Electronics Ltd
Animal House, Justin Bus. Park,
Sandford Lane, Wareham,
Dorset, BH20 4DY
T: 01929 555700
F: 01929 555701
E: sales@relec.co.uk
W: www.relec.co.uk

Reliable Data Systems
March House, Lime Grove,
West Clandon, Guildford,
Surrey, GU4 7UH
T: 01483 225604
E: rdsintl@rdsintl.com
W: www.rdsintl.com

Renaissance Trains Ltd
4 Spinneyfield, Ellington,
Cambs, PE28 0AT
T: 07977 917148
E: peter.wilkinson@renaissancetrains.com
W: www.renaissancetrains.com

Rendel Limited
61 Southwark St, London, SE1 1SA
T: 020 7654 0500
F: 020 7654 0401
E: london@rendel-ltd.com
W: www.rendel-ltd.com

Rennsteig Werkzeuge GMBH
An der Koppel 1,
D-98547 Viernau,
Germany
T: 49 0368 474 410
E: info@rennsteig.com
W: www.rennsteig.com

Renown Railway Services
Brookside House,
Brookside Business Park,
Cold Meece, Staffs, ST15 0RZ
T: 01785 764484
F: 01785 760896
E: enquiries@renownrailway.co.uk
W: www.renownrailway.co.uk

Replin Fabrics
March St Mills, Peebles, EH45 8ER
T: 01721 724311
F: 01721 721893
E: enquiries@replin-fabrics.co.uk
W: www.replin-fabrics.co.uk

REPTA (Railway Employees and Public Transport Association)
c/o 4 Brackmills Close, Forest Town,
Mansfield, Notts, NG19 0PB
T: 01623 646789
E: candarolle@btinternet.com
W: www.repta.co.uk

Resourcing Solutions
Vector House, 5 Ruscombe Park,
Ruscombe, Berks, RG10 9JW
T: 0118 932 0100
F: 0118 932 1818
E: info@resourcing-solutions.com
W: www.resourcing-solutions.com

Rethinking Transport
E: jon@rethinkingtransport.com
W: www.rethinkingtransport.com

Retro Railtours Ltd
2 Brookfield Grove,
Ashton-under-Lyne,
Lancashire, OL6 6TL
T: 0161 330 9055
E: info@retrorailtours.co.uk
W: www.retrorailtours.co.uk

Revitaglaze
Unit 2, Swanwick Business Centre,
Bridge Road, Southampton,
Hants, SO31 7GB
T: 020 3384 0220
F: 01372 200881
E: marketing@revitaglaze.com
W: www.revitaglaze.com

Rexel UK
Eagle Court 2, Hatchford Brook,
Hatchford Way, Sheldon,
Birmingham, B26 3RZ
T: 0121 366 1000
E: sales@rexel.co.uk
W: www.rexel.com

Rexquote Ltd
Broadgauge Business Park,
Bishops Lydeard, Taunton,
Somerset, TA4 3RU
T: 01823 433398
F: 01823 433378
E: sales@rexquote.co.uk
W: www.rexquote.co.uk

RGS Rail
6 Clarendon St,
Nottingham, NG1 5HQ
T: 0115 959 9687
E: enquiries@rgsexecutive.co.uk
W: www.rgsexecutive.co.uk

Rhenus Lupprians (Romac)
Keiler House, Challenge Rd,
Ashford, Middx, TW15 1AX
T: 01784 422900
F: 01784 423105
E: sales@lupprians.com
W: www.lupprians.com

RIB Software (UK) Ltd
12 Floor, The Broadgate Tower,
20 Primrose St,
London, EC2A 2EW
T: 020 7596 2747
F: 020 7596 2701
W: www.rib-software.co.uk

Ricardo Rail Ltd
Edward Lloyd House,
8 Pinnacle Way, Pride Park,
Derby, DE24 8ZS
T: 01332 268700
F: 01332 268799
E: martin.hayhoe@ricardo.com
W: www.rail.ricardo.com

Ricardo UK Ltd
Midlands Technical Centre,
Southam Rd, Radford Semele,
Leamington Spa, Warks, CV31 1FQ
T: 01926 319319
F: 01926 319300
E: info@ricardo.com
W: www.ricardo.com

Riello UPS Ltd
Unit 50, Clywedog Rd North,
Wrexham Ind.Est.,
Wrexham, LL13 9XN
T: 01978 729297
F: 01978 729290
E: marketing@riello-ups.co.uk
W: www.riello-ups.co.uk

Riley & Son (E) Ltd
Baron St, Bury, Lancs, BL9 0TY
T: 0161 764 2892
F: 0161 763 5191
E: rileys@btconnect.com
W: www.rileyandson.co.uk/

RIQC Ltd
2 St Georges House, Vernon Gate,
Derby, DE1 1UQ
T: 01332 221421
F: 01332 221401
E: enquiries@riqc.co.uk
W: www.riqc.co.uk

RISC Ltd – Railway & Industrial Safety Consultants Ltd
Harlyn House,
3 Doveridge Rd, Stapenhill,
Burton Upon Trent, DE15 9GB
T: 0844 840 9420
F: 0871 247 2961
E: enquiries@railwaysafety.co.uk
W: www.railwaysafety.co.uk

Risk Solutions
Dallam Court, Dallam Lane,
Warrington, WA2 7LT
T: 01925 413984
E: enquiries@risksol.co.uk
W: www.risksol.co.uk

Risktec Solutions
Wilderspool Park,
Greenalls Ave,
Warrington, WA4 6HL
T: 01925 611200
F: 01925 611232
E: enquiries@risktec.co.uk
W: www.risktec.co.uk

Ritelite Systems Ltd
Meadow Park,
Bourne Rd,
Essendine,
Stamford,
Lincs, PE9 4LT
T: 01780 765600
F: 01780 765700
E: sales@ritelite.co.uk
W: www.ritelite.co.uk

Rittal Ltd
Braithwell Way,
Hellaby Ind Est,
Hellaby, Rotherham,
South Yorks, S66 8QY
T: 01709 704000
F: 01709 701217
E: information@rittal.co.uk
W: www.rittal.co.uk

Riviera Trains
116 Ladbroke Grove,
London, W10 5NE
T: 020 7727 4036
F: 020 7727 2083
E: enquiries@riviera-trains.co.uk
W: www.riviera-trains.co.uk

RJ Power Ltd
Unit 15, Lawson Hunt Ind. Park,
Guildford Road,
Broadbridge Heath,
Horsham,
West Sussex, RH12 3JR
T: 0845 034 1480
F: 0845 034 1481
E: info@rjpower.biz
W: www.rjpower.biz

Rittal is the world's largest manufacturer of enclosures and associated products for both indoor and outdoor applications with an extensive stock holding in the UK.

RITTAL

A: Rittal Ltd, Braithwell Way
Hellaby Industrial Estate
Hellaby, Rotherham
South Yorkshire S66 8QY

P: +44 (0)1709 704000
F: +44 (0)1709 701217
E: information@rittal.co.uk
W: www.rittal.co.uk

Rosehill Rail

ROAD CROSSING SYSTEMS
MADE FROM RUBBER · PROVEN ENGINEERING

+44 (0)1422 317 473 · www.rosehillrail.com

RMD Kwikform UK
Brickyard Road,
Aldridge,
Walsall, WS9 8BW
T: 01922 743743
F: 01922 743400
E: info@rmdkwikform.com
W: www.rmdkwikform.com/

RMS Locotec locomotive Hire
British American Railway Services,
Stanhope Station,
Stanhope, Bishop
Auckland, DL13 2YS
T: 01388 526203
E: documentcontroller@britamrail.com
W: www.rmslocotec.com

RMS Rail Projects Ltd
2 White House Close, New Road,
Laxey, Isle of Man, IM4 7BA
T: 01388 526203
E: mfairburn@britamrail.com
W: www.rmslocotec.com/#/rms-rail-projects/4534062441

RMT
National Union of Rail,
Maritime & Transport Workers,
Unity House,
39 Chalton St,
London, NW1 1JD
T: 020 7387 4771
F: 020 7387 4123
E: info@rmt.org.uk
W: www.rmt.org.uk

RNA Recruitment Ltd
Mere House, Brook St, Knutsford,
Cheshire, WA16 8GP
T: 01302 366003
W: www.rnarecruitment.com

Roan Building Solutions
First Floor, Unit 1,
Calder Close,
Calder Park,
Wakefield, WF4 3BA
T: 0845 1211687
M: 07972359917
E: predshaw@roanbuildings.co.uk
W: www.roanbuildings.co.uk

Robel Bahnbaumaschmen GmbH
Industriestrasse 31,
D 83395, Freilassing,
Germany
T: 0049 8654 6090
F: 0049 8654 609100
E: info@robel.info
W: www.robel.info

Robert West Consulting
Delta House, 175-
177 Borough High St,
London, SE1 1HR
T: 020 7939 9916
F: 020 7939 9909
E: london@robertwest.co.uk
W: www.robertwest.co.uk

Röchling Composites and Engineering Plastics
Waterwells Business Park,
Waterwells Drive,
Gloucester, GL2 2AA
T: 01452 727900
F: 01452 728056
E: sales@roechling-plastics.co.uk
W: www.roechling-plastics.co.uk

ROCOL
Rocol House, Wakefield Rd,
Swillington,
Leeds, LS26 8BS
T: 0113 232 2600
F: 0113 232 2740
E: customer-service.safety@rocol.com
W: www.rocol.com

Roevin Engineering
4th Floor,
Clydesdale Bank House,
33 Lower Regent St,
Piccadilly,
London, WC1Y 4NB
T: 0845 643 0486
F: 0870 759 8443
E: rail@roevin.co.uk
W: www.roevin.co.uk

Rollalong Ltd
Woolsbridge Ind. Park,
Three Legged Cross,
Wimborne,
Dorset, BH21 6SF
T: 01202 824541
F: 01202 826525
E: enquiries@rollalong.co.uk
W: www.rollalong.co.uk

Romag
Leadgate Ind. Est.,
Leadgate, Consett,
Co Durham, DH8 7RS
T: 01207 500000
F: 01207 591979
E: tiffany.sott@romag.co.uk
W: www.romag.co.uk

Romic House
A1/M1 Business Centre,
Kettering,
Northants, NN16 8TD
T: 01536 414244
F: 01536 414245
E: sales@romic.co.uk
W: www.romic.co.uk

Ronfell Ltd
Challenge House,
Pagefield industrial Est.,
Miry Lane, Wigan, WN6 7LA
T: 01942 492200
F: 01942 492233
E: sales@ronfell.com
W: www.ronfell.com

Rose Hill P&OD Ltd
1a Queen St, Rushden,
Northants, NN10 0AA
F: 01933 663846
E: info@rose-hill.co.uk
W: www.rose-hill.co.uk

Rosehill Rail
Spring Bank Mills, Watson Mill Lane,
Sowerby Bridge,
West Yorks, HX6 3BW
T: 01422 317482
F: 01422 316952
E: stuart.wilosn@rosehillrail.com
W: www.rosehillrail.com

Rosenqvist Rail AB
Hyggesvägen 4,
824 34 Hudiksvall, Sweden
T: 0046 650 16505
F: 0046 650 16501
E: info@rosenqvist-group.se
W: www.rosenqvistrail.se

Roughton Group
A2 Omega Park, Electron Way,
Chandlers Ford, Hants, SO53 4SE
T: 023 8027 8600
F: 023 8027 8601
E: hq@roughton.com
W: www.roughton.com

Rowe Hankins Ltd
Power House, Parker St, Bury,
Lancs, BL9 0RJ
T: 0161 765 3000
F: 0161 705 2900
E: sales@rowehankins.com
W: www.rowehankins.com

Roxtec Ltd
Unit C1, Waterfold Business Park,
Bury, Lancs, BL9 7BQ
T: 0161 761 5280
F: 0161 763 6065
E: russell.holmes@uk.roxtec.com
W: www.roxtec.com

Royal British Legion Industries (RBLI)
Royal British Legion Village,
Hall Rd, Aylesford, Kent, ME20 7NL
T: 01622 795900
F: 01622 795978
E: sales.office@rbli.co.uk
W: www.rbli.co.uk/manufacturing/services/19/

Royal Haskoning Ltd
Rightwell House, Bretton,
Peterborough, PE3 8DW
T: 01733 334455
F: 01733 262243
E: info@peterborough.royalhaskoning.com
W: www.royalhaskoning.com

RPS Planning and Development
T: 01636 605700
F: 01636 610696
E: alan.skipper@rpsgroup.com
W: www.rpsgroup.com

RS Components Ltd
Birchington Rd, Corby,
Northants, NN17 9RS
T: 0845 602 5226
W: www.rswww.com/purchasing

RSK STATS Health & Safety Ltd
Spring Lodge, 172 Chester Rd,
Helsby, Cheshire, WA6 0AR
T: 01928 726006
F: 01928 725633
E: info@rsk.com
W: www.rsk.com

RSK Ltd
18 Frogmore Rd,
Hemel Hempstead, Herts, HP3 9RT
T: 01442 437500
F: 01442 437550
E: info@rsk.co.uk
W: www.rsk.co.uk

RSL Cityspace
Unit 3, Fullwood Close,
Aldermans Green Industrial Estate,
Coventry, Warks, CV2 2SS
T: 02476 587894
E: support@rslcityspace.co.uk
W: www.rslcityspace.co.uk/

RSSB
Block 2, Angel Square,
1 Torrens St, London, EC1V 1NY
T: 020 3142 5300
E: enquirydesk@rssb.co.uk
W: www.rssb.co.uk

RTC Group
The Derby Conference Centre,
London Rd, Derby, DE24 8UX
T: 01332 861336
F: 0870 890 0034
E: info@rtcgroupplc.co.uk
W: www.rtcgroupplc.co.uk

RTI UK
35 Old Queen St, London, SW1H 9JD
T: 020 7340 0900
F: 020 7233 3411
E: rtiuk@rti.co.uk
W: www.rti.co.uk

RTS Infrastructure Services Ltd
The Rail Depot, Bridge Rd,
Holbeck, Leeds, LS11 9UG
T: 01132 344899
E: info@rtsinfrastructure.com
W: www.rtsinfrastructure.com

RTS Solutions Ltd
Atlantic House, Imperial Way,
Reading, RG2 0TD
T: 0118 903 6045
F: 0118 903 6100
E: stuart@rts-solutions.net
W: www.rts-solutions.net

RUGGED MOBILE Systems Ltd
Riverside, Mountbatten Way,
Congleton, Cheshire, CW12 1DY
T: 0845 652 0816
F: 0845 652 0817
E: info@rm-systems.co.uk
W: www.ruggedmobilesystems.co.uk

Rullion Engineering Personnel
2nd Floor, Unit 5 Bath Court,
Islington Row, Edgbaston,
Birmingham, B15 1NE
T: 0121 622 7720
F: 0121 622 7721
E: james.millward@rullion.co.uk
W: www.rullion.co.uk/rep

RWD Technologies UK Ltd
Furzeground Way, First Floor,
Stockley Park, Uxbridge, UB11 1AJ
T: 020 8569 2787
F: 020 8756 3625
E: info@gpstrategies.com
W: www.rwd.com

Rydon Signs
Unit 3, Peek House,
Pinhoe Trading Est, Exeter,
Devon, EX4 8JN
T: 01392 466653
F: 01392 466671
E: sales@rydonsigns.com
W: www.rydonsigns.com

S H Lighting
Salcmbe Rd,
Meadow Lane Ind. Est, Alfreton,
Derbys, DE55 7RG
T: 01773 522390
F: 01773 520693
E: sales@shlighting.co.uk
W: www.shlighting.co.uk

S M Consult Ltd
3 High St, Stanford in the Vale,
Faringdon, Oxon, SN7 8LH
T: 01367 710152
F: 01367 710152
E: info@smcsolar.co.uk
W: www.smconsult.co.uk

S.E.T. Ltd
Atlas Works, Litchurch Lane,
Derby, DE24 8AQ
T: 01332 346035
F: 01332 346494
E: sales@set.gb.com
W: www.set.gb.com

Sabre Rail Services Ltd
Grindon Way,
Heighington Lane Business Park,
Newton Aycliffe,
Co Durham, DL5 6SH
T: 01325 300505
F: 01325 300485
E: sales@sabrerail.com
W: www.sabrerail.com

Safeaid LLP
Signal House, 16 Arnside Rd,
Waterlooville, Hants, PO7 7UP
T: 02392 254442
F: 02392 257444
E: sales@safeaidsupplies.com
W: www.safeaidsupplies.com

Safeglass (Europe) Ltd
Nasmyth Building, Nasmyth Ave,
East Kilbride, G75 0QR
T: 01355 272438
F: 01355 272788
E: sales@safeglass.co.uk
W: www.safeglass.co.uk

Safeguard Pest Control Ltd
6 Churchill Bus. Park, The Flyers Way,
Westerham, Kent, TN16 1BT
T: 0800 195 7766
F: 01959 565888
E: info@safeguardpestcontrol.co.uk
W: www.safeguardpestcontrol.co.uk

Safestyle Security Services
Exe. Suite 1,
Cardiff International Arena,
Mary Ann St, Cardiff, CF10 2EQ
T: 02920 221711
F: 02920 234592
E: office@safestylesecurity.co.uk
W: www.safestylesecurity.co.uk

Safetell Ltd
Unit 46, Fawkes Ave,
Dartford Trade Park,
Dartford, DA1 1JQ
T: 01322 223233
F: 01322 277751
E: sales@safetell.co.uk
W: www.safetell.co.uk

Safetrack Baavhammar AB
1 Moleberga,
S-245 93 Staffanstorp,
Sweden
T: 0046 4044 5300
F: 0046 4044 5553
E: sales@safetrack.se
W: www.safetrack.se

Safetykleen UK Ltd
2 Heath Road, Weybridge,
Surrey, KT13 8AP
T: 01909 519300
E: skuk@sk-europe.com
W: www.safetykleen.co.uk

SAFT Ltd
1st Floor, Unit 5, Astra Centre,
Edinburgh Way,
Harlow, CM20 2BN
T: 01279 772550
F: 01279 420909
E: igb.info@saftbatteries.com
W: www.saftbatteries.com

SAFT Power Systems Ltd
See AEG Power Solutions Ltd

Saint Gobain Abrasives Ltd
Doxey Rd, Stafford, ST16 1EA
T: 01785 279550
F: 01785 213487
E: sonia.uppal@saint-gobain.com
W: www.saint-gobain.com

Saira Electronics
75 Chesterwood Road,
Kings Heath,
Birmingham, B13 0QQ
T: 0039 045 630 4558
E: saira@sairaelectronics.com
W: www.sairaelectronics.com

Saltburn Railtours
16 Bristol Ave,
Saltburn, TS12 1BW
T: 01287 626572
E: r.dallara@btinternet.com
W: www.saltburnrailtours.co.uk

Samsung Electronics Hainan Fibreoptics
c/o Go Tel Communications Ltd,
4 Hicks Close,
Wroughton,
Swindon, SN4 9AY
T: 01793 813600
F: 01793 529380
E: robindash@gtcom.co.uk
W: www.samsungfiberoptics.com

Samuel Taylor Ltd
Arthur Street,
Redditch,
Worcs, B98 8JY
T: 01527 504910
F: 01527 500869
E: sales@samueltaylor.co.uk
W: www.samueltaylor.co.uk

Santon Switchgear Ltd
Unit 9, Waterside Court,
Newport, NP20 5NT
T: 01633 854111
F: 01633 854999
E: sales@santonswitchgear.co.uk
W: www.santonswitchgear.com

Sapa Extrusions
Pantglas Ind. Est.,
Bedwas,
Caerphilly, CF83 8DR
T: 02920 854600
F: 02920 865229
E: sales.haeuk@hydro.com
W: www.sapagroup.com/en/extrusions-uk/

HITACHI
Inspire the Next

Sartoria Corporatewear
Gosforth Rd, Derby, DE24 8HU
T: 01332 342616
F: 01332 226940
W: www.sartorialtd.co.uk.co.uk

Savigny Oddie Ltd
Wallows Ind. Est, Wallows Rd,
Brierley Hill,
West Midlands, DY5 1QA
T: 01384 481598
F: 01384 482383
E: keith@oddiefasteners.com
W: www.savigny-oddie.co.uk

SB Rail (Swietelsky Babcock)
Kintail House, 3 Lister Way,
Hamilton International Park,
Blantyre, G72 0FT
T: 01698 203005
F: 01698 203006
E: shona.jamieson@babcock.co.uk
W: www.babcock.co.uk/rail

SBC Rail Ltd (Stanton Bonna)
Littlewell Lane, Stanton by Dale,
Ilkeston, Derbys, DE7 4QW
T: 0115 944 1448
F: 0115 944 1466
E: sbc@stanton-bonna.co.uk
W: www.stanton-bonna.co.uk

Scantec
Spinnaker House, Morpeth Wharf,
Twelve Quays, Wirral, CH41 1LF
T: 0151 666 8999
E: info@scantec.co.uk
W: www.scantec.co.uk/

SCCS
Hq1 Building, Phoenix Park,
Eaton Socon, St Neots,
Cambs, PE19 8EP
T: 01480 404888
F: 01480 404333
E: sales@sccssurvey.co.uk
W: www.sccssurvey.co.uk

SCG Solutions
335 Shepcote Lane,
Sheffield, S9 1TG
T: 0114 221 1111
E: sales@scgsolutions.co.uk
W: www.scgsolutions.co.uk

Schaltbau Machine Electrics
335/336 Springvale
Industrial Estate, Woodside Way,
Cwmbran, NP44 5BR
T: 01633 877555
F: 01633 873366
E: sales@schaltbau-me.com
W: www.schaltbau-me.com

Scheidt & Bachmann (UK) Ltd
7 Silverglade Business Park,
Leatherhead Rd, Chessington,
Surrey, KT9 2QL
T: 01372 230400
F: 01372 722053
E: info@scheidt-bachmann.de
W: www.scheidt-bachmann.de

Schenck Process UK
Carolina Court, Lakeside,
Doncaster, DN4 5RA
T: 01302 321313
F: 01302 554400
E: enquiries@schenckprocess.co.uk
W: www.schenckprocess.co.uk

Schneider Electric Ltd
Stafford Park 5, Telford,
Shropshire, TF3 3BL
T: 01952 209226
F: 01952 292238
E: gb-marcoms@gb.schneider.electric.com
W: www.schneider-electric.co.uk

Schoenemann Design Ltd
Friar Gate Studios, Studio 26,
Ford Street, Derby, DE1 1EE
T: 01332 258345
E: andrew@schoenemanndesign.co.uk
W: www.traindesign.co.uk

Schofield Lothian Ltd
Temple Chambers, 3-7 Temple Ave,
London, EC4Y 0DT
T: 020 7842 0920
F: 020 7842 0921
E: enquiries@schofieldlothian.com
W: www.schofieldlothian.com

Schroff UK Ltd
Maylands Ave, Hemel Hempstead,
Herts, HP2 7DE
T: 01442 240471
F: 01442 213508
E: schroff.uk@pentair.com
W: www.schroff.co.uk

Schweerbau GmbH & Co KG
UK Branch Office,
20 Beattyville Gardens,
Ilford, IG6 1JN
F: 020 7681 3971
E: verheijen@schweerbau.de
W: www.schweerbau.de

Schweizer Electronic
Peter House, Oxford Street,
Manchester, M1 5AN
T: 01827 289996
E: info@schweizer-electronic.co.uk
W: www.schweizer-electronic.co.uk

Schwihag AG
Lebernstrasse 3,
CH-8274 Tägerwilen, Switzerland
T: 0041 71 666 8800
F: 0041 71 666 8801
E: info@schwihag.com
W: www.schwihag.com

Scientifics
ESG House,
Bretby Business Park, Ashby Rd,
Burton upon Trent, DE15 0YZ
T: 0845 603 2112
F: 01283 554401
E: sales@esg.co.uk
W: www.esg.co.uk

Scisys
Methuen Park, Chippenham,
Wilts, SN14 0GB
T: 01249 466466
F: 01249 466666
E: marketing@scisys.co.uk
W: www.scisys.co.uk

ScotRail
See Abellio ScotRail

Scott Bader
Wollaston, Wellingborough,
Northants, NN29 7RL
T: 01933 663100
E: composites@scottbader.com
W: www.scottbader.com

Scott Brownrigg – Design Research Unit
77 Endell St, London, WC2H 9DZ
T: 020 7240 7766
F: 020 7240 2454
E: enquiries@scottbrownrigg.com
W: www.scottbrownrigg.com

Scott White & Hookings
Fountain House, 26 St Johns St,
Bedford, MK42 0AQ
T: 01234 213111
F: 01234 213333
E: bed@swh.co.uk
W: www.swh.co.uk

Scott Wilson Railways
See URS

Scotweld Employment Services
See SW Global Resourcing

Screwfast Foundations Ltd
1st Floor, 4 Sandridge Park,
Porters Wood,
St. Albans,
Herts, AL3 6PH
T: 01727 821282
F: 01727 828098
E: info@screwfast.com
W: www.screwfast.com

SCT Europe Ltd
See Wabtec Rail Group Ltd

SEA (Group) Ltd
SEA House,
PO Box 800,
Bristol, BS16 1SU
T: 01373 852000
F: 01373 831133
E: info@sea.co.uk
W: www.sea.co.uk

Search Consultancy
198 West George St,
Glasgow, G2 2NR
T: 0141 272 7777
F: 0141 272 7788
E: glasgow@search.co.uk
W: www.searchconsultancy.co.uk

Seaton Rail Ltd
Bridlington Business Centre,
Enterprise Way,
Bridlington, YO16 4SF
T: 01262 608313
F: 01262 604493
E: info@seaton-rail.com
W: www.seaton-rail.com

Secheron SA
Rue de pre-Bouvier 25,
Zimeysa 1217 Meyrin,
Geneva,
Switzerland
T: 0041 22 739 4111
F: 0041 22 739 4811
E: info@secheron.com
W: www.secheron.com

Sefac UK Ltd
1-6 Barton Rd,
Water Eaton,
Bletchley, MK2 3HU
T: 01908 821274
F: 01908 821275
E: info@sefac-lift.co.uk
W: www.sefac-lift.co.uk

Scott Cables
Painter Close, Anchorage Park,
Portsmouth, Hampshire, PO3 5RS
T: 02392 652552
F: 02392 655277
E: sales@scottcables.com
W: www.scottcables.com

Selectequip Ltd
Unit 7,
Britannia Way,
Britannia Enterprise Park,
Lichfield,
Staffs, WS14 9UY
T: 01543 416641
F: 01543 416083
E: sales@selectequip.co.uk
W: www.selectequip.co.uk

Selectrail (Australia) Pty Ltd
1/11 Trevi Crescent,
Tullamarine,
VIC 3043,
Australia
T: 6103 9335 0600
E: info@selectrail.com
W: www.selectrail.com

Selex ES Ltd
8-10 Great George St,
London, SW1P 3AE
F: 0207 340 6199
E: amanda.lachlan@selex-es.com
W: www.selex-es.com

Semikron Ltd
9 Harforde Court, John Tate Rd,
Foxholes Business Park,
Hertford, SG13 7NW
T: 01992 584677
F: 01992 503837
E: sales.skuk@semikron.com
W: www.semikron.com

Semmco Ltd
9 Kestrel Way,
Goldsworth Park Trading Est,
Woking, Surrey, GU21 3BA
T: 01483 757200
F: 01483 740795
E: sales@semmco.com
W: www.semmco.co.uk

Semperit Industrial Products
25 Cottesbrooke Park, Heartlands,
Daventry, Northants, NN11 8YL
T: 01327 313144
F: 01327 313149
E: ian.rowlinson@semperit.co.uk
W: www.semperit.at

Senator Security Services Ltd
1 The Thorn Tree,
Elmhurst Business Park,
Lichfield, Staffs, WS13 8EX
T: 01543 411811
F: 01543 411611
E: senatorgroup@senatorsecurity.co.uk
W: www.senatorsecurity.co.uk

Senceive Ltd
Hurlingham Studios,
Ranelagh Gardens,
London, SW6 3PA
T: 020 7731 8269
E: info@senceive.com
W: www.senceive.com

Serco Caledonian Sleepers Ltd
Basement and Ground Floor,
1-5 Union Street,
Inverness, IV1 1PP
T: 0330 060 0500
W: https://www.sleeper.scot/

Serco Transport services
Serco House,
16 Bartley Wood Bus. Park,
Bartley Way, Hook,
Hants, RG27 9UY
T: 01256 745900
F: 01256 744111
E: generalenquiries@serco.com
W: www.serco.com/markets/transport

Serco Rail Technical Services
Derwent House,
RTC Business Park, London Rd,
Derby, DE24 8UP
T: 01332 262672
F: 01332 264965
E: richard.hobson@serco.com
W: www.serco.com/srts

Rhomberg Sersa UK Ltd
Sersa House, Auster Rd,
Clifton Moor, York, YO30 4XA
T: 01904 479968
F: 01904 479970
E: carl.garrud@sersa-group.com
W: www.sersa-group.com

Setec Ltd
11 Mallard Way,
Derby, DE24 8GX
E: craig.king@setecltd.co.uk
W: www.setecltd.co.uk

Severn Lamb
Tything Rd, Alcester, B49 6ET
T: 01789 400140
F: 01789 400240
E: sales@severn-lamb.com
W: www.severn-lamb.com

The Severn Partnership Ltd
The Maltings, 59 Lythwood Rd,
Bayston Hill,
Shrewsbury,
Shropshire, SY3 0NA
T: 01743 874135
F: 01743 874716
E: mark.combes@severn-partnership.co.uk
W: www.severnpartnership.co.uk

Severn Valley Railway
Number One, Comberton Place,
Kidderminster, Worcs, DY10 1QR
T: 01562 757900
E: mktg@svr.co.uk
W: www.svr.co.uk

Seymourpowell
The Factory, 265 Merton Rd,
London, SW18 5JS
T: 020 7381 6433
E: lucy.kirby@seymourpowell.com
W: www.seymourpowell.com

SGA (Stuart Gray Associates)
88 Spring Hill, Arley,
Warks, CV7 8FE
T: 01676 541402
E: info@stuartgrayassociates.co.uk
W: www.stuartgrayassociates.co.uk

SGH Martineau LLP
No.1 Colmore,
Birmingham, B4 6AA
T: 0800 763 1000
F: 0800 763 1001
E: andrew.whitehead@sghmartineau.com
W: www.sghmartineau.com

SGS Correl Rail Ltd
Gee House, Holborn Hill,
Birmingham, B7 5PA
T: 0121 326 9900
F: 0121 328 5343
E: gary.winstanley@sgs.com
W: www.sgs.com

SGS Engineering (UK) Ltd
Unit 2, West Side Park,
Belmore Way,
Derby, DE21 7AZ
T: 01332 576850
F: 01332 753068
E: sales@sgs-engineering.com
W: www.sgs-engineering.com

SGS UK Ltd
Inward Way,
Rossmore Business Park,
Ellesmere Port, CH65 3EN
T: 0151 350 6666
F: 0151 350 6600
W: www.sgs.com

Shannon Rail Services Ltd
Orphanage Road Sidings,
Reeds Crescent, Watford,
Herts, WD17 1PG
T: 01923 254567
F: 01923 255678
E: info@shannonrail.co.uk
W: www.shannonrail.co.uk

Shay Murtagh Precast Ltd
Raharney, Mullingar,
Co Westmeath,
Republic of Ireland
T: 0844 202 0263
E: sales@shaymurtagh.co.uk
W: www.shaymurtagh.co.uk

Sheerspeed Shelters Ltd
Unit 3, Diamond House,
Reme Drive,
Heath Park Ind. Estate, Honiton,
Devon, EX14 1SE
T: 01404 46006
F: 01404 45520
E: sales@sheerspeed.com
W: www.sheerspeed.com

Shell UK Oil Products Ltd
Brabazon House,
Concord Business Park,
Threapwood Rd,
Manchester, M22 0RR
T: 08708 500924
F: 0161 499 8930
E: lubesenquiries-uk@shell.com
W: www.shell.co.uk/lubricants

Shere Ltd
See ATOS Origin

Sheridan Maine
Regus House,
George Curl Way,
Southampton, SO18 2RZ
T: 0871 218 0573
F: 0871 218 0173
E: southampton@sheridanmaine.com
W: www.sheridanmaine.com

Sherwin-Williams Protective & Marine Coatings
Tower Works, Kestor St,
Bolton, Lancs, BL2 2AL
T: 01204 521771
F: 01204 382115
E: enquiries.pm.emeas@sherwin.com
W: protectiveemea.sherwin-williams.com/

Shield Batteries
277 Stansted Rd,
Bishops Stortford,
Herts, CM23 2BT
T: 01279 652067
F: 01279 758041
E: info@shieldbatteries.co.uk
W: www.shieldbatteries.co.uk

Shorterm Rail
The Barn,
Philpots Close,
Yiewsley,
Middx, UB7 7RY
T: 01895 427900
E: info@shortermgroup.co.uk
W: www.shorterm.co.uk

Shotcrete Services Ltd
Old Station Yard,
Hawkhurst Rd, Cranbrook,
Kent, TN17 2SR
T: 01580 714747
E: stuart.manning@shotcrete.co.uk
W: www.shotcrete.co.uk

SICK (UK) Ltd
Waldkirch House,
39 Hedley Rd, St Albans,
Herts, AL1 5BN
T: 01727 831121
F: 01727 856767
E: info@sick.co.uk
W: www.sick.co.uk

Siegrist-Orel Ltd
Pysons Rd Ind. Est.,
Broadstairs,
Kent, CT10 2LQ
T: 01843 865241
F: 01843 867180
E: info@siegrist-orel.co.uk
W: www.siegrist-orel.co.uk

Siemens Rail Automation
Langley Park, Pew Hill,
Chippenham,
Wiltshire, SN15 1JD
T: 01249 441441
E: info.railautomation.gb@invensys.com
W: www.siemens.co.uk/rail

Siemens Rail Systems
Euston House,
24 Eversholt St,
London, NW1 1AD
T: 020 7227 0722
F: 020 7227 4435
E: info.railsystems.gb@siemens.com
W: www.siemens.co.uk/rail

SIEMENS

Siemens Rail Automation is a global leader in the design, supply, installation and commissioning of track-side and train-borne signalling and train control solutions.

This is delivered by over 10,000 people across a network of offices worldwide, with 1,650 UK-based employees.

Siemens Rail Automation, PO Box 79,
Pew Hill, Chippenham, SN15 1JD
Tel: +44 (0) 1249 441441
Info.railautomation.gb@siemens.com
www.siemens.co.uk/rail

Siemens Rail Systems provides expertise and technology in the full range of rail vehicles - from heavy rail to metros to trams and light-rail vehicles. In the UK, the Division employs around 700 people and maintains over 350 Siemens passenger trains for the First TransPennine Express, South West Trains, Heathrow Express, Great Anglia Franchise (Abellio), Northern Rail, London Midland and ScotRail. The company will also be supplying Eurostar with its new high speed fleet of trains.

Siemens Rail Systems, Euston House, 24 Eversholt Street, London, NW1 1AD

info.railsystems.gb@siemens.com
www.siemens.co.uk/rail

SIEMENS

Siemens RUGGEDCOM UK
Princess Road, Princess Parkway,
Manchester, M20 2UR
T: 0161 446 5000
F: 0161 446 5742
E: ianpoulett@ruggedcom.com
W: www.siemens.com/ruggedcom

Sig Cyclone
Unit 16 Gerald House,
Sherwood Network Centre,
Sherwood Energy Village,
Newton Hill, Ollerton,
Notts, NG22 9FD
T: 07833 433404
E: liane.launders@sigcyclone.co.uk
W: www.sig-ukgroup.com

SIG plc
Hillsborough Works,
Landsett Road, Sheffield, S6 2LW
T: 0114 285 6327
E: sigri@sigplc.co.uk
W: www.sigri.co.uk

SigAssure UK Ltd
Gerald House, Unit 4, Ebor Court,
Randall Park Way, Retford,
Notts, DN22 7WF
T: 01777 707809
E: info@sigassure-uk.com
W: www.sigassure-group.co.uk

Sigma Coachair Group UK Ltd
Unit 1, Queens Drive,
Newhall, Swadlincote,
Derbys, DE11 0EG
T: 01283 559140
F: 01283 225253
W: www.sigmacoachair.com

Signal House Ltd
Cherrycourt Way, Stanbridge Rd,
Leighton Buzzard, Beds, LU7 4UH
T: 01525 377477
F: 01525 850999
E: sales@signalhouse.co.uk
W: www.signalhousegroup.co.uk

Signalling Construction UK Ltd
Unit 56, Coleshill Industrial Estate,
Coleshill, Birmingham, B46 1JT
T: 01675 464746
E: info@sculktd.com
W: www.sculktd.com

Signalling Solutions Ltd
Bridgefoot House, Watling St,
Radlett, Herts, WD7 7HT
T: 01923 635000
E: info@signallingsolutions.com
W: www.signallingsolutions.com

Signature Aromas Ltd
Signature House,
65-67 Gospel End St, Sedgley,
West Midlands, DY3 3LR
T: 01902 678822
F: 01902 672888
E: enquiries@signaturearomas.co.uk
W: www.signaturearomas.co.uk

Signet Solutions
Kelvin House, RTC Business Park,
London Rd, Derby, DE24 8UP
T: 01332 343585
F: 01332 367132
E: enquiries@signet-solutions.com
W: www.signet-solutions.com

SignPost Solutions
Unit 5, Clarendon Drive,
The Parkway, Tipton,
West Midlands, DY4 0QA
T: 0121 506 4770
F: 0121 506 4771
E: i.thomas@signfix.co.uk
W: www.signfix.co.uk

Sill Lighting UK
3 Thame Park Bus. Centre,
Wenman Rd, Thame,
Oxon, OX9 3XA
T: 01844 260006
F: 01844 260760
E: sales@sill-uk.com
W: www.sill-uk.com

Silver Atena
Cedar House,
Riverside Business Park,
Swindon Rd, Malmesbury,
Wilts, SN16 9RS
T: 01666 580000
F: 01666 580001
E: info@silver-atena.com
W: www.silver-atena.com

Silver Fox Ltd
Swallow Court, Swallowfields,
Welwyn Garden City,
Herts, AL7 1SA
T: 01707 373727
F: 01707 372193
E: marketing@silverfox.co.uk
W: www.silverfox.co.uk

Silver Software
See Silver Atena

Simmons & Simmons
City Point, One Ropemaker St,
London, EC2Y 9SS
T: 020 7628 2020
F: 020 7628 2070
E: juliet.reingold@simmons-simmons.com
W: www.simmons-simmons.com

Simona UK
Telford Drive, Brookmead Ind. Park,
Stafford, ST16 3ST
T: 01785 222444
F: 01785 222080
E: mail@simona-uk.com
W: www.simona.de

SIMS
Fourth Floor, Roman Wall House,
1-2 Crutched Friars,
London, EC3N 2HT
T: 020 7481 9798
F: 020 7481 9657
E: inbox@sims-uk.com
W: www.simsrail.co.uk

Simulation Systems Ltd
Unit 12, Market Ind.Est, Yatton,
Bristol, BS49 4RF
T: 01934 838803
F: 01934 876202
W: www.simulation-systems.co.uk

Sinclair Knight Merz
See Jacobs UK Ltd

John Sisk & Sons Ltd
1 Curo Park, Frogmore, St Albans,
Herts, AL2 2DD
T: 01727 875551
F: 01727 875642
W: www.johnsiskandson.com/uk

Site Eye Time-Lapse Films
Unit 8D, Top Lands,
County Business Park,
Cragg Road, Cragg Vale, Halifax,
West Yorkshire, HX7 5RW
T: 01422 884477
E: info@site-eye.co.uk
W: www.site-eye.co.uk

signalling solutions

excellence in train control

Signalling Solutions offers turnkey solutions to the rail industry's train control and resignalling markets from conceptual design to full project delivery.

An Alstom company.

Signalling Solutions Limited
Bridgefoot House, Watling Street,
Radlett, Herts WD7 7HT

Tel: 01923 635000
Email:info@signallingsolutions.com

www.signallingsolutions.com

Site Vision Surveys
19 Warwick St, Rugby,
Warks, CV21 3DH
T: 01788 575036
F: 01788 576208
E: mail@svsltd.net
W: www.svsltd.net

SITECH UK & Ireland
Morgans Business Park,
Norton Canes, Cannock,
Staffs, WS11 9UU
T: 0845 600 5669
E: info@sitechukandireland.com
W: www.sitechukandireland.com

Skanska UK
Maple Cross House, Denham Way,
Maple Cross, Rickmansworth,
Herts, WD3 9SW
T: 01923 423100
F: 01923 423111
W: www.skanska.co.uk/

SKF UK Ltd
Railway Sales Unit,
Sundon Park Rd,
Luton, LU3 3BL
T: 01582 496490
F: 01582 496327
E: stewart.mclellan@skf.com
W: www.skf.com

Skills 4 Rail
35 Auckland Rd,
Birmingham, B11 1RH
T: 01217714219
E: sales@sills4rail.co.uk
W: www.skills4rail.co.uk

SKM Colin Buchanan
New City Court,
20 St. Thomas Street,
London, SE1 9RS
T: 020 7939 6160
E: acassidy@globalskm.com
W: www.skmcolinbuchanan.com

Skymasts Antennas
Unit 2, Clayfield Close,
Moulton Park Ind. Est,
Northampton, NN3 6QF
T: 01604 494132
F: 01604 494133
E: info@skymasts.com
W: www.skymasts.com

Slender Winter Partnership
The Old School,
London Rd, Westerham,
Kent, TN11 1DN
T: 01959 564777
F: 01959 562802
E: swp@swpltd.co.uk
W: www.swpltd.co.uk

Smart Component Technologies Ltd
3M Buckley Innovation Centre,
Firth St, Huddersfield, HD1 3BD
E: r.bromley@hud.ac.uk
W: www.hud.ac.uk

SMC Light & Power
Belchmire Lane, Gosberton,
Lincs, PE11 4HG
T: 01775 840020
F: 01775 843063
E: info@smclightandpower.com
W: www.smclightandpower.com

SMC Pneumatics Ltd
Vincent Ave, Crownhill,
Milton Keynes, Bucks, MK8 0AN
T: 0845 121 5122
F: 01908 555064
E: sales@smcpneumatics.co.uk
W: www.smcpneumatics.co.uk

SME Ltd
Unit 1, Lloyd St, Parkgate,
Rotherham, S62 6JG
T: 08444 930666
F: 08444 930667
W: www.sme-ltd.co.uk

SMI Conferences
SMI Group Ltd, Unit 122,
Great Guildford Business Square,
30 Great Guildford St,
London, SE1 0HS
T: 020 7827 6000
F: 020 7827 6001
E: info@smi-online.com
W: www.smi-online.co.uk

Smith Bros & Webb Ltd
Britannia House,
Arden Forest Ind.Est, Alcester,
Warks, B49 6EX
T: 01789 400096
F: 01789 400231
E: sales@sbw-wash.com
W: www.sbw-wash.com

Smith Cooper
Wilmot House, St Helen's House,
King St, Derby, DE1 3EE
T: 01332 332021
F: 01332 290439
E: janet.morgan@smithcooper.co.uk
W: www.smithcooper.co.uk

SML Resourcing
Unit 3.07, New Loom House,
101 Back Church Lane,
London, E1 1LU
T: 020 7423 4390
F: 020 7702 1097
E: jobs@sml-resourcing.com
W: www.sml-resourcing.com

SMP Electronics
Unit 6, Border Farm, Station Rd,
Chobham, Woking,
Surrey, GU24 8AS
T: 01276 855166
F: 01276 855115
E: sales@smpelectronics.com
W: www.samalite.com

Snap-On Rail Solutions
38A Telford Way, Kettering,
Northants, NN16 8SN
T: 01536 413904
F: 01536 413874
E: rail@snapon.com
W: www.snapon.com/industrialuk

SNC-Lavalin Group – Formally Interfleet Technology Ltd
Interfleet House, Pride Parkway,
Derby, DE24 8HX
T: 01332 223 000
F: 01332 223 001
E: groupcommunications@snclavalin.com
W: www.snclavalin.com

SNR Denton
One Fleet Place,
London, EC4M 7WS
T: 020 7242 1212
F: 020 7246 7777
E: info@dentonwildesapte.com
W: www.dentonwildesapte.com

Society of Operations Engineers (SOE)
22 Greencoat Place,
London, SW1P 1PR
T: 020 7630 1111
F: 020 7630 6677
E: soe@soe.org.uk
W: www.soe.org.uk

Socomec UPS (UK)
Units 7-9, Lakeside Business Park,
Broadway Lane,
South Cerney, Cirencester,
Glos, GL7 5XL
T: 01285 863300
F: 01285 862304
E: rail.ups.uk@socomec.com
W: www.socomec.co.uk/

Softech Global Ltd
Softech House,
London Rd, Albourne,
West Sussex, BN6 9BN
T: 01273 833844
F: 01273 833044
E: rail@softechglobal.com
W: www.softechglobal.com

Sogefi Rejna SpA
Via Nazionale 7,
Raffa di Puegnago (BS), I-25080,
Italy
T: 39 365 526 213
E: giovannico.dore@sogefigroup.com
W: www.sogefigroup.com

SOLID Applications Ltd
Old Market Place, Market St,
Oldbury, B69 4DH
T: 0121 544 1400
E: anton.plackowski@saplm.co.uk
W: www.solidapps.co.uk/

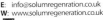

Solo Fabrications
Landor St, Saltley,
Birmingham, B8 1AE
T: 0121 327 3378
F: 0121 327 3757
E: sales@solorail.com
W: www.solorail.com

Solum Regeneration
6 Cavendish Place,
London, W1G 9NB
T: 020 7462 2759
E: info@solumregenration.co.uk
W: www.solumregeneration.co.uk

Solution Rail
22 Somers Way,
Bushey,
Herts, WD23 4HR
F: 0871 989 5700
E: enquiries@solutionrail.co.uk
W: www.solutionrail.co.uk

Solvay Speciality Polymers
Baronet Rd,
Warrington, WA4 6HA
T: 01925 943546
F: 01925 943548
E: shayel.ahmed@solvay.com
W: www.solvayplastics.com

Somers Totalkare
Unit 1, Coombs Wharf,
Chancel Way,
Halesowen,
West Midlands, B62 8PP
T: 0121 585 2700
F: 0121 585 2725
E: sales@somerstotalkare.co.uk
W: www.somerstotalkare.co.uk

Sonic Rail Service Ltd (SRS)
Unit 15, Springfield Ind. Est,
Springfield Rd,
Burnham-on-Crouch,
Essex, CM0 8UA
T: 01621 784688
F: 01621 786594
E: stewart.robinson@sonicrail.co.uk
W: www.sonicrail.co.uk

HITACHI
Inspire the Next

Sonic Windows Ltd
Unit 14/15, Beeching Park Ind.Est.,
Wainwright Rd, Bexhill on Sea,
E Sussex, TN39 3UR
T: 01424 223864
F: 01424 215859
E: enquiries@sonicwindows.co.uk
W: www.sonicwindows.co.uk

Sotera Risk Solutions Ltd
22 Glanville Rd, Bromley, BR2 9LW
F: 01737 551203
E: chris.chapman@sotera.co.uk
W: www.sotera.co.uk

SOUNDEX Solutions
The Old Dairy, Southfield Avenue,
Northampton, NN4 8AQ
T: 0800 814 4422
F: 0800 814 4423
E: enquiries@soundexsolutions.com
W: www.soundexsolutions.com

South West Trains
Stagecoach Group,
10 Dunkeld Rd, Perth, PH1 5TW
T: 0345 6000 650
F: 01738 643648
E: customerrelations@swtrains.co.uk
W: www.southwesttrains.co.uk/

South Yorkshire Passenger Transport Executive
11 Broad St West, Sheffield, S1 2BQ
T: 0114 276 7575
F: 0114 275 9908
E: comments@sypte.co.uk
W: www.sypte.co.uk

Southco Manufacturing Ltd
Touch Point, Wainwright Rd,
Warndon, Worcs, WR4 9FA
T: 01905 346722
F: 01905 346723
E: info@southco.com
W: www.southco.com

Southeastern
Friars Bridge Court,
41-45 Blackfriars Rd,
London, SE1 8PG
T: 020 7620 5000
W: www.southeasternrailway.co.uk

Southern Electric Contracting
55 Vastern Rd, Reading, RG1 8BU
T: 0118 958 0100
F: 0118 953 4755
E: marketing@sec.eu.com
W: www.sec.eu.com

Sovereign Planned Services On Line Ltd
Unit 3D, Forge Way,
Brown Lees Ind Est, Biddulph,
Stoke on Trent, Staffs, ST8 7DN
T: 01782 510600
F: 01782 510700
E: sales@sovonline.co.uk
W: www.sovonline.co.uk

Spartan Safety Ltd
Unit 3, Waltham Park Way,
Walthamstow,
London, E17 5DU
T: 020 8527 5888
F: 020 8527 5999
E: ryan@spartansafety.co.uk
W: www.spartansafety.co.uk

Specialist Engineering Services Ltd (SES)
SES House,
Harworth Business Park,
Blyth Road, Harworth,
Doncaster, DN11 8DB
T: 01302 756800
E: info@ses-rail.co.uk
W: www.ses-rail.co.uk/

Specialist Plant Associates
Airfield Rd, Hinwick,
Wellingborough,
Northants, NN29 7JG
T: 01234 781882
F: 01234 781992
E: info@specialistplant.co.uk
W: www.specialistplant.co.uk

Spectro
Palace Gate,
Odiham,
Hampshire, RG29 1NP
T: 01256 704000
F: 01256 704006
E: enquiries@spectro-oil.com
W: www.spectro-oil.com

Spectrum Freight Ltd
PO Box 105,
Chesterfield,
Derbys, S41 9XY
T: 01246 456677
F: 01246 456688
E: sales@spectrumfreight.co.uk
W: www.spectrumfreight.co.uk

Spectrum Technologies
Western Avenue, Bridgend,
Mid Glamorgan, CF31 3RT
T: 01656 655437
F: 01656 655920
E: ehardy@spectrumtech.com
W: www.spectrumtech.com

Speedy Hire Plc
Chase House, 16 The Parks,
Newton le Willows,
Merseyside, WA12 0JQ
T: 01942 720000
F: 01942 720077
E: admin@speedyhire.co.uk
W: www.speedyhire.co.uk

Spence Ltd
Parcel Deck, Barnby St,
Euston Station,
London, NW1 2RS
T: 020 7387 1268
F: 020 7380 1255
E: info@spenceltd.co.uk
W: www.spenceltd.co.uk

Spencer Group
One Humber Quays,
Wellington Street West,
Hull, East Yorkshire, HU1 2BN
T: 01482 766340
F: 01469 532233
E: mailbox@cspencerltd.co.uk
W: www.thespencergroup.co.uk

Speno International SA
26 Parc Chateau-Banquet POB 16,
1211 Geneva 21,
Switzerland
T: 0041 22906 4600
F: 0041 22906 4601
E: info@speno.ch
W: www.speno.ch

Sperry Rail International Ltd
Trent House,
RTC Business Park, London Rd,
Derby, DE24 8UP
T: 01332 262565
F: 01332 262541
E: jtansley@sperryrail.com
W: www.sperryrail.com

Spitfire Tours
PO Box 824,
Taunton, TA1 9ET
T: 0870 879 3675
E: info@spitfirerailtours.co.uk
W: www.spitfirerailtours.co.uk

SPL Powerlines UK Ltd
Unit 3A, Hagmill Cres,
East Shawhead Enterprise Park,
Coatbridge,
Lanarkshire, ML5 4NS
T: 01236 424666
F: 01236 426444
E: office@powerlines-group.com
W: www.powerlines-group.com

Spring Personnel
1 Canal Arm, Festival Park,
Stoke on Trent, ST1 5UR
T: 01782 221500
F: 01782 221600
E: personnel@spring.com
W: www.spring.com

SPX Rail Systems
Unit 7, Thames
Gateway Park, Choats Rd,
Dagenham,
Essex, RM9 6RH
T: 020 8526 7100
F: 020 8526 7151
E: brian.cannon@spx.com
W: www.spx.com/en/spx-rail-systems/

SRPS Railtours
3 South Cathkin Farm Cottages,
Glasgow, G73 5RG
T: 01698 263814/457777
E: railtours@srps.org.uk
W: www.srps.org.uk

SRS Rail Systems Ltd
3 Riverside Way,
Gateway Business Park, Bolsover,
Chesterfield, S44 6GA
T: 01246 241312
F: 01246 825076
E: info@srsrailuk.co.uk
W: www.srsrailuk.com

SSDM
See Aura Graphics Ltd

SSP
169 Euston Rd,
London, NW1 2AE
T: 020 7543 3300
F: 020 7543 3389
E: clare@templemerepr.co.uk
W: www.foodtravelexperts.com/uk/home/

St Leonards Railway Engineering Ltd
Bridgeway, St Leonards on Sea,
E Sussex, TN38 8AP
T: 01233 617001

Stadler Pankow GmbH
Lessingstrasse 102,
D-13158 Berlin,
Germany
T: 0049 309191 1616
F: 0049 309191 2150
E: stadler.pankow@stadlerrail.de
W: www.stadlerrail.com

Stadler Rail AG
Ernst-Stadler-Strasse 1,
9565 Bussnang,
Switzerland
T: +41 (0)71 626 21 20
F: +41 (0)71 626 21 28
E: stadler.rail@stadlerrail.com
W: www.stadlerrail.com/en/

Stagecoach Group
10 Dunkeld Rd,
Perth, PH1 5TW
T: 01738 442111
F: 01738 643648
E: info@stagecoachgroup.com
W: www.stagecoachgroup.com

Stagecoach Supertram
Nunnery Depot,
Woodbourn Rd,
Sheffield, S9 3LS
T: 0114 275 9888
F: 0114 279 8120
E: enquiries@supertram.com
W: www.supertram.com

Stahlwille Tools Ltd
Unit 2D, Albany Park Ind. Est,
Frimley Rd, Camberley,
Surrey, GU16 7PD
T: 01276 24080
F: 01276 24696
E: scottsheldon@stahlwille.co.uk
W: www.stahlwille.co.uk

Stanley Tools
Sheffield Business Park,
Sheffield City Airport, Europa Link,
Sheffield, S3 9PD
T: 0114 244 8883
F: 0114 273 9038

Stannah Lifts
Anton Mill, Andover,
Hants, SP10 2NX
T: 01264 339090
E: liftsales@stannah.co.uk
W: www.stannahlifts.co.uk

Stansted Express
See Abellio Greater Anglia

Star Fasteners (UK) Ltd
Unit 1, 44 Brookhill Road,, Pinxton,
Nottinghamshire, NG16 6RY
T: 0115 932 4939
F: 0115 944 1278
E: sales@starfasteners.co.uk
W: www.starfasteners.co.uk

Statesman Rail Ltd
PO Box 83, St Erth, Hayle,
Cornwall, TR27 9AD
T: 0345 310 2458
F: 0115 944 1278
W: www.statesmanrail.com

STATS
See RSK Ltd

Stauff Ltd
500 Carlisle St East,
Off Downgate Drive,
Sheffield, S4 8BS
T: 01142 518518
F: 01141 518519
E: sales@stauff.co.uk
W: www.stauff.co.uk

Staytite Ltd
Staytite House, Coronation Rd,
Cressex Bus. Park, High Wycombe,
Bucks, HP12 3RP
T: 01494 462322
F: 01494 464747
E: fasteners@staytite.com
W: www.staytite.com

Steam Dreams
PO Box 169, Albury, Guildford,
Surrey, GU5 9YS
T: 01483 209888
F: 01483 209889
E: info@steamdreams.co.uk
W: www.steamdreams.com

Steatite Ltd
Ravensbank Business Park,
Acanthus Rd, Redditch,
Worcs, B98 9EX
T: 01527 512400
F: 01527 512419
E: sales@steatite.co.uk
W: www.steatite.co.uk

Steelteam Construction (UK) Ltd
46 Goods Station Rd,
Tunbridge Wells, Kent, TN1 2DD
T: 01892 533677
F: 01892 511535
E: sales@steelteamconstruction.co.uk
W: www.steelteamconstruction.co.uk

Steelway Rail
Queensgate Works, Bilston Rd,
Wolverhampton,
West Midlands, WV2 2NJ
T: 01902 834911
F: 01902 452256
E: sales@steelway.co.uk
W: www.steelway.co.uk

Steer Davies Gleave
28-32 Upper Ground,
London, SE1 9PD
T: 020 7910 5000
F: 020 7910 5001
E: sdginfo@sdgworld.net
W: www.steerdaviesgleave.com

Stego UK Ltd
Unit 12, First Quarter Bus. Park,
Blenheim Rd, Epsom,
Surrey, KT19 9QN
T: 01372 747250
F: 01372 729854
E: info@stego.co.uk
W: www.stego.co.uk

Stent
See Balfour Beatty Ground Engineering

Step On Safety Ltd
Units 3-4, 122 Station Road,
Lawford, Manningtree,
Essex, CO11 2LH
T: 01206 396446
E: info@steponsafety.co.uk
W: www.steponsafety.co.uk

Stephenson Harwood LLP
1 Finsbury Circus,
London, EC2M 7SH
T: 020 7809 2618
F: 020 7003 8220
E: graeme.mclellan@shlegal.com
W: www.shlegal.com

Stewart Signs Rail
Trafalgar Close,
Chandlers Ford Ind. Est, Eastleigh,
Hants, SO53 4BW
T: 023 8025 4781
F: 023 8025 5620
E: sales@stewartsigns.co.uk
W: www.stewartsigns.co.uk

Stirling Maynard
Construction Consultants,
Stirling House, Rightwell, Bretton,
Peterborough, PE3 8DJ
T: 01733 262319
F: 01733 331527
E: enquiries@stirlingmaynard.com
W: www.stirlingmaynard.com

Stobart Rail
Solway Business Centre, Carlisle,
Cumbria, CA6 4BY
T: 01228 882300
F: 01228 882301
E: grant.mcnab@stobartrail.com
W: www.stobartrail.co.uk

Stock Redler Ltd
See Schenck Process UK

Stocksigns Ltd/ Burnham Signs
43 Ormside Way,
Holmethorpe Ind Est, Redhill,
Surrey, RH1 2LG
T: 01737 764764
F: 01737 763763
E: jgodden@stocksigns.co.uk
W: www.stocksigns.co.uk

Stockton Engineering Management Ltd
1 Warwick Row,
London, SW1E 5ER
T: 020 7808 7808
F: 020 7117 5253
E: info@stocktonlondon.com
W: www.stocktonlondon.com

Stored Energy Technology
See S.E.T. Ltd

Story Rail
Burgh Rd Ind Est, Carlisle,
Cumbria, CA2 7NA
T: 01228 590444
F: 01228 593359
E: info@storygroup.co.uk
W: www.storygroup.co.uk

Strabag
Donau-City-Str. 9,
1220 Vienna,
Austria
T: 0043 1 22422-0
E: pr@strabag.com
W: www.strabag.com/

STRAIL (UK) Ltd
Room 2, First Floor,
3 Tannery House, Tannery Lane,
Send, Woking,
Surrey, GU23 7EF
T: 01483 222090
F: 01483 222095
E: richard@srsrailuk.co.uk
W: www.strail.com

Strainstall UK Ltd
9-10, Mariners Way, Cowes, IOW,
PO31 8PD
T: 01983 203600
F: 01983 201335
E: enquiries@strainstall.com
W: www.strainstall.co.uk

Strataform
See TechnoRail (Technocover)

Strategic Team Group Ltd
Strategic Business Centre,
Blue Ridge Park,
Thunderhead Ridge,
Glasshoughton, Castleford,
West Yorks, WF10 4UA
T: 01977 555550
F: 01977 555509
E: contact@strategicteamgroup.com
W: www.strategicteamgroup.com

Strathclyde Partnership for Transport
Consort House,
12 West George St,
Glasgow, G2 1HN
T: 0141 332 6811
E: enquiry@spt.co.uk
W: www.spt.co.uk

Street Crane Co. Ltd
Chapel-en-le-Frith, High Peak,
Derbys, SK23 0PH
T: 01298 812456
F: 01298 814945
E: sales@streetcrane.co.uk
W: www.streetcrane.co.uk

Strukton Rail
Westkanaaldijk 2, NL-
3542 DA Utrecht,
Netherlands
T: 31 30 248 66 94
E: info@struktonrail.com
W: www.struktonrail.com

STS Rail
First Floor, 27 Cobham Road,
Ferndown Industrial Estate,
Wimborne, Dorset, BH21 7PE
T: 01202 950270
E: telecoms@sts-rail.com
W: www.sts-rail.com/

STS Signals
See Mors Smitt UK Ltd (A Wabtec Company)

Stuart Group
Middleplatt Road,
Immingham,
Lincs, DN40 1AH
T: 01469 551230
F: 01469 551239
E: enquiries@stuartgroup.info
W: www.stuartgroup.ltd.uk

Stuart Maher Ltd (SML)
Unit 3.07, New Loom House,
101 Back Church Lane,
London, SE1 1LU
T: 020 7423 4390
F: 07092 810 920
E: nick.stuart@stuart-maher.co.uk
W: www.stuart-maher.co.uk

Sulzer Dowding & Mills
193 Camp Hill, Bordesley,
Birmingham, B12 0JJ
T: 0121 766 6161
F: 0121 766 7247
E: engineering.birmingham@sulzer.com
W: www.sulzer.com

SYSTRA - World Leading Transport Planning, Rail and Urban Transport Engineers

Contact us:
Dukes Court, Duke Street,
Woking, Surrey GU21 5BH
T: +44 (0)1483 742941
E: sgulyvasz@systra.com

www.systra.co.uk

Superform Aluminium
Cosgrove Close, Worcester, WR3 8UA
T: 01905 874300
F: 01905 874301
E: enquiries@superform.net
W: www.superforming.com

Superjet London
Unit 5, Kennet Rd, Dartford,
Kent, DA1 4QN
T: 01322 554595
F: 01322 557773
E: chris@superjet.co.uk
W: www.jetchem.com

Supersine Duramark
See Aura Graphics Ltd

Surge Protection Devices Ltd
Unit 1, Ash Royd Farm, Royd Road,
Meltham, Holmfirth,
West Yorkshire, HD9 4BG
T: 01484 851747
F: 01484 852594
E: info@surgedevices.co.uk
W: www.surgedevices.co.uk

Survey Inspection Systems Ltd (SIS)
Green Lane Ind. Est, Enterprise House,
Meadowfield Ave, Spennymoor,
Co Durham, DL16 6JF
T: 01388 810308
F: 01388 819260
E: sales@survey-inspection.com
W: www.survey-inspection.com

Survey Systems Ltd
Willow Bank House, Old Road,
Handforth, Wilmslow, SK9 3AZ
T: 01625 533444
F: 01625 526815
E: enquiries@survsys.co.uk
W: www.survsys.co.uk/rail

SW Global Resourcing
270 Peters Hill Rd, Glasgow, G21 4AY
T: 0141 557 6133
F: 0141 557 6143
E: admin@sw-gr.com
W: sw-gr.com

Sweetnam & Bradley Ltd
Industrial Est, Gloucester Rd,
Malmesbury, Wilts, SN16 0DY
T: 01666 823491
F: 01666 826010
E: sales@sweetnam-bradley.com
W: www.sweetnam-bradley.com

Sweett Group
60 Grays Inn Rd,
London, W1X 8AQ
T: 020 7061 9000
F: 020 7430 0603
E: eryl.evans@sweettgroup.com
W: www.sweettgroup.com

Swietelsky Babcock
See SB Rail (Swietelsky Babcock)

Swietelsky Construction Company Ltd
7 Clairmont Gardens,
Glasgow, G3 7LW
T: 0141 353 1915
F: office@swietelsky.at
W: www.swietelsky.com

Sydac Ltd
Derwent Business Centre,
Clarke St, Derby, DE1 2BU
T: 01332 299600
F: 01332 299624
E: paul.williamson@sydac.co.uk
W: www.sydac.co.uk

Sylmasta Ltd
Unit 1, Dales Yard, Lewes Rd,
Scaynes Hill, W Sussex, RH17 7PG
T: 01444 831459
F: 01444 831971
W: www.sylmasta.co.uk

Synectic Systems Group Ltd
3-4 Broadfield Close, Sheffield,
South Yorkshire, S8 0XN
T: 0114 2552509
F: 0114 2582050
E: sales@synx.com
W: www.synecticsystems.com

Synergy Health Plc
Gavenny Court, Brecon Rd,
Abergavenny,
Monmouthshire, NP7 7RX
T: 01873 856688
F: 01873 585982
E: enquiries@synergyhealthplc.com
W: www.synergyhealthplc.com
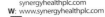

Syntax Conultancy
1 College Place, Derby, DE1 3DY
T: 01332 293605
F: 01332 296128
E: marketing@syntaxconsultancy.com
W: www.syntaxconsultancy.com

Systecon (UK) Ltd
PO Box 4612, Weymouth,
Dorset, DT4 9YY
T: 0871 641 2202
F: 01305 768480
E: phil.sturgess@systecon.co.uk
W: www.systecon.co.uk

System Store Solutions Ltd
Ham Lane, Lenham, Maidstone,
Kent, ME17 2LH
T: 01622 859522
F: 01622 858746
E: sales@systemstoresolutions.com
W: www.system-store.com

Systra UK
Fourth Floor, Dukes Court, Duke St,
Woking, Surrey, GU21 5BH
T: 01483 742941
F: 01483 755207
E: sgulyvasz@systra.com
W: www.systra.com

T & R Williamson Ltd
36 Stonebridgegate, Ripon,
N Yorks, HG4 1TP
T: 01765 607711
F: 01765 607908
E: info@trwilliamson.co.uk
W: www.trwilliamson.co.uk

T & RS Engineering Ltd
1st Floor, Gresley House,
Ten Pound Walk,
Doncaster, DN4 5HX
T: 01302 898645
E: mail@trsengineering.co.uk
W: www.trsengineering.co.uk

T J Thomson & Sons Ltd
Millfield Works, Grangefield Rd,
Stockton on Tees, TS18 4AE
T: 01642 672551
F: 01642 672556
E: postbox@tjthomson.co.uk
W: www.tjthomson.co.uk

TAC Europe
Matrix House, Basing View,
Basingstoke, Hants
T: 08700 600822
F: 01256 356371
E: enquiries@taceurope.com
W: www.taceurope.com

Talascend Ltd
First Floor, Broadway Chambers,
Hammersmith Broadway,
London, W6 7PW
T: 020 8600 1600
F: 020 8741 2001
E: info@talascend.com
W: www.talascend.com

Tammet Systems Ltd
Unit 1, Port Farm, Island Road,
Upstreet, Canterbury,
Kent, CT3 4DA
T: 01227 711072
E: info@tammetsystems.co.uk
W: www.tammetsystems.co.uk

Tanfield Engineering Systems
Tanfield Lea Ind. Est. North,
Stanley, Co Durham, DH9 9NX
T: 01207 521111
F: 01207 523355
W: www.tanfieldengineeringsystems.com/

The TAS Partnership Ltd.
Ross Holme, West End,
Long Preston, Skipton, BD23 4QL
T: 01729 840756
E: info@taspublications.co.uk
W: www.tas.uk.net

Tasty Plant Sales
Copsham House, 53 Broad St,
Chesham, Bucks, HP5 3EA
T: 0845 677 4444
E: info@tastyplant.co.uk
W: www.tastyplant.co.uk

Tata Steel Projects
Meridian House, The Crescent,
York, YO24 1AW
T: 01904 454600
F: 01904 454601
E: tatasteelprojects@tatasteel.com
W: www.tatasteelrail.com/en/

Tata Steel Rail
SRSM Area 3, PO Box 1,
Brigg Road,
Scunthorpe, DN16 1BP
T: 01724 405761
E: rail@tatasteel.com
W: www.tatasteelrail.com

Tate Rail Ltd
Station House, Station Hill,
Cookham, Berks, SL6 9BP
T: 0844 381 9956
F: 0844 381 9957
E: info@taterail.com
W: www.taterail.com

Taylor Precision Plastics / Commercial Vehicle Rollers Ltd
Mile Oak Ind. Est, Maesbury Rd,
Oswestry, Shropshire, SY10 8GA
T: 01691 679536
F: 01691 670538
E: sales@cvrollers.co.uk
W: www.cvrollers.co.uk

Taylor Technology Systems
Horizon Business Centre, Unit 25,
Alder Close, Erith, Kent, DA18 4AJ
T: 020 8320 9944
E: sales@taylortechnologysystems.com
W: www.taylortechnologysystems.com/

Taylor Woodrow
Astral House,
Imperial Way, Watford,
Herts, WD24 4WW
T: 01923 233433
F: 01923 800085
E: david.booker@taylorwoodrow.com
W: www.taylorwoodrow.com

Taziker Industrial Ltd t/a TI Protective Coatings
Unit 6, Lodge Bank,
Crown Lane, Horwich,
Bolton, BL6 5HY
T: 01204 468080
F: 01204 695188
E: sales@ti-uk.com
W: www.ti-uk.com

TBM Consulting Group
Unit 8, H2O Business Complex,
Sherwood Business Park,
Annesley,
Nottingham, NG15 0HT
T: 01623 758298
F: 01623 755941
E: nfletcher@tbmcg.com
W: www.tbmcg.com

TBM Rail
Marshfield Bank,
Crewe,
Cheshire, CW2 8UY
T: 01270 509243
F: 01270 580416
E: enquiries@tbmrail.com
W: www.tbmrail.com

TCP Ltd
Quayside Industrial Park,
Bates Road,
Maldon,
Essex, CM9 5FA
T: 01621 850777
F: 01621 843330
E: mail@tcp.eu.com
W: www.tcp.eu.com

TDK-Lambda UK
Kingsley Ave,
Ilfracombe,
Devon, EX34 8ES
T: 01271 856600
F: 01271 856741
E: powersolutions@emea.tdk-lambda.com
W: www.emea.tdk-lambda.com

TE Connectivity
1 rue Paul Martin,
F-21220 Gervey-Chambertin,
France
T: 33 03 80 58 32 13
E: rail@te.com
W: www.te.com/energy

TEAL Consulting Ltd
Deangate, Tuesley Lane,
Godalming, Surrey, GU7 1SG
T: 01483 420550
F: 01483 420550
E: info@tealconsulting.co.uk
W: www.tealconsulting.co.uk

Team Surveys Ltd
Team House,
St Austell Bay Business Park,
Par Moor Rd, St Austell, PL25 3RF
T: 01726 816069
F: 01726 814611
E: email@teamsurveys.com
W: www.teamsurveys.co.uk

Tecalemit Garage Equipment Co Ltd
Eagle Rd, Langage Business Park,
Plymouth, PL7 5JY
T: 01752 219111
F: 01752 219128
E: sales@tecalemit.co.uk
W: www.tecalemit.co.uk

Tecforce
Litchurch Lane, Derby, DE24 8AA
T: 01332 268000
F: 01332 268030
E: sales@tecforce.co.uk
W: www.tecforce.co.uk

Technical Cranes Ltd
Holmes Lock Works, Steel St,
Holmes, Rotherham, S61 1DF
T: 01709 561861
F: 01709 556516
E: info@technicalcranes.co.uk
W: www.technicalcranes.co.uk

Technical Cranes Ltd
Holmes Lock Works, Steel St,
Holmes, Rotherham, S61 1DF
T: 01709 561861
F: 01709 556516
E: info@technicalcranes.co.uk
W: www.technicalcranes.co.uk

Technical Programme Delivery
Systems House,
10 Heathfield Close,
Binfield Heath,
Henley on Thames, RG9 4DS
T: 01932 228710
F: 01932 228710
E: pac@tpd.uk.com
W: www.tpd.uk.com

Technical Resin Bonders
See TRB Lightweight Structures Ltd

Technocover
See TechnoRail (Technocover)

Technology Project Services Ltd
1 Warwick Row,
London, SW1E 5LR
T: 020 7963 1234
F: 020 7963 1299
E: mail@tps.co.uk
W: www.tps.co.uk

HITACHI Inspire the Next

Technology Resourcing Ltd
The Technology Centre,
Surrey Research Park,
Guildford, GU2 7YG
T: 01483 302211
F: 01483 301222
E: railways@tech-res.co.uk
W: www.railwayengineering jobs.co.uk

TechnoRail (Technocover)
Henfaes Lane,
Welshpool,
Powys, SY21 7BE
T: 01938 555511
F: 01938 555527
E: admin@technocover.co.uk
W: www.technocover.co.uk

Tecton Ltd
186 Main Road,
Fishers Pond,
Eastleigh,
Hants, SO50 7HG
T: 02380 695858
F: 02380 695702
E: admin@tectononline.com
W: www.tecton.co.uk

TEK Personnel Consultants Ltd
Norwich Union House,
Irongate,
Derby, DE1 3GA
T: 01332 360055
F: 01332 363345
E: derby@tekpersonnel.co.uk
W: www.tekpersonnel.co.uk

Telent Technology Services Ltd
Point 3, Haywood Rd,
Warwick, CV34 5AH
T: 01926 693564
F: 01926 693023
E: services@telent.com
W: www.telent.com

Telerail Ltd
Royal Scot Suite,
Carnforth Station Heritage Centre,
Warton Rd,
Carnforth,
Lancs, LA5 9TR
T: 01524 735774
F: 01524 736386
E: info@telerail.co.uk
W: www.telerail.co.uk

Telespazio VEGA UK
350 Capability Green,
Luton,
Beds, LU1 3LU
T: 01582 399000
E: info@vegaspace.com
W: www.telespazio-vega.com

Televic Rail
Leo Bakaertlaan 1,
B-8870 Izegem,
Belgium
T: 0032 5130 3045
E: rail@televic.com
W: www.televic-rail.com

Temple Group Ltd
Tempus Wharf,
33A Bermondsey Wall West,
London, SE16 4TQ
T: 020 7394 3700
F: 020 7394 7871
E: enquiries@templegroup.co.uk
W: www.templegroup.co.uk

Ten 47 Ltd
Unit 2B, Frances Ind. Park,
Wemyss Rd, Dysart,
Kirkcaldy, KY1 2XZ
T: 01592 655725
F: 01592 651049
E: sales@ten47.com
W: www.ten47.com

TenBroeke Company Ltd
Dorset House, Refent Park,
Kingston Rd, Leatherhead,
Surrey, KT22 7PL
T: 01372 824722
F: 01372 824332
E: paul.tweedale@tenbroekco.com
W: www.tenbroekeco.com/

TenCate Geosynthetics UK Ltd
PO Box 773, Telford,
Shropshire, TF7 9FE
T: 01952 588066
E: service.uk@tencate.com
W: www.tencategeo synthetics.com

Tenmat Ltd (Railko Ltd)
Ashburton Road West,
Trafford Park,
Manchester, M17 1RU
T: 0161 872 2181
F: 0161 872 7596
E: info@tenmat.com
W: www.tenmat.com

Tensar International
Cunningham Court,
Shadsworth Business Park,
Shadsworth,
Blackburn, BB1 2QX
T: 01254 262431
F: 01254 266868
E: info@tensar-international.com
W: www.tensar.co.uk

Tension Control Bolts
TCB House,
Clywedog Road South,
Wrexham Industrial Estate,
Wrexham, LL13 9XS
T: 01978 661122
E: info@tcbolts.co.uk
W: www.tcbolts.co.uk

Terram Ltd
Mamhilad Park Estate,
Pontypool,
Gwent, NP4 0YR
T: 01495 757722
F: 01495 762383
E: info@terram.co.uk
W: www.terram.com

Terrawise Construction Ltd
104 The Court Yard,
Radway Green Business Centre,
Radway Green, Crewe,
Cheshire, CW2 5PR
T: 01270 879011
F: 01270 875079
E: info@terrawise.co.uk
W: www.terrawise.co.uk

TES 2000 Ltd
TES House, Heath Industrial Park,
Grange Way, Colchester, CO2 8GU
T: 01206 799111
F: 01206 227910
E: info@tes2000.co.uk
W: www.tes2000.co.uk

Testo Ltd
Newman Lane, Alton,
Hants, GU34 2QJ
T: 01420 544433
F: 01420 544434
E: info@testo.co.uk
W: www.testo.co.uk

Tevo Ltd
Maddison house,
Thomas Rd,
Wooburn Green Ind Est,
Thomas Rd,
Wooburn Green, Bucks, HP10 0PE
T: 01628 528034
E: sales@tevo.eu.com
W: www.tevo.eu.com

Tew Engineering Ltd
6 The Midway, Lenton,
Nottingham, NG7 2TS
T: 0115 935 4354
F: 0115 935 4355
E: sales@tew.co.uk
W: www.tew.co.uk

Thales UK
4 Thomas More Square,
Thomas More St, London,
E1W 1YW
T: 020 3300 6000
F: 020 3300 6994
E: uk.enquiries@thalesgroup.com
W: www.thalesgroup.com/transportation

The Technical Strategy Leadership Group (TSLG)
Block 2, 1 Torrens St,
Angel Square,
London, EC1V 1NY
T: 0203 142 5300
E: innovations@futurerailway.org
W: www.futurerailway.org/leadership/pages

The Train Chartering Company Ltd
Benwell House, Preston,
Chippenham,
Wilts, SN15 4DX
T: 01249 890176
E: info@worldtraintravel.com
W: www.worldtraintravel.com/

ThermaCom Ltd
Farenheit House, New Line Rd,
Kirkby in Ashfield,
Notts, NG17 8JQ
T: 01623 758777
F: 01623 758444
E: sales@thermagroup.com
W: www.thermagroup.com

Thermal Economics Ltd
Thermal House, 8 Cardiff Rd,
Luton, Beds, LU1 1PP
T: 01582 450814
F: 01582 429305
E: info@thermal-economics.co.uk
W: www.thermal-economics.co.uk

Thermit Welding (GB) Ltd
87 Ferry Lane, Rainham,
Essex, RM13 9YH
T: 01708 522626
F: 01708 553806
E: rsj@thermitwelding.co.uk
W: www.thermit-welding.com/

Thomas & Betts Ltd
See PMA UK Ltd (Thomas & Betts Ltd)

Thomson Rail Equipment Ltd
Valley Rd, Cinderford,
Glos, GL14 2NZ
T: 01594 826611
F: 01594 825560
E: sales@thomsonrail.com
W: www.thomsonrail.com

Threeshires Ltd
Piper Hole Farm, Eastwell Rd,
Scalford, Leics, LE14 4SS
T: 01664 444604
F: 01664 444605
E: enquiries@threeshires.com
W: www.threeshires.com

Thurlow Countryside Management Ltd
2 Charterhouse Trading Est,
Sturmer Rd, Haverhill,
Suffolk, CB9 7UU
T: 01440 760170
F: 01440 760171
E: info@t-c-m.co.uk
W: www.t-c-m.co.uk

Thurrock Engineering Supplies Ltd
Unit 1, TES House,
Motherwell Way, West Thurrock,
Essex, RM20 3XD
T: 01708 861178
F: 01708 861158
E: info@thurrockengineering.com
W: www.thurrockengineering.com

Thursfield Smith Consultancy
25 Grange Rd, Shrewsbury,
SY3 9DG
T: 01743 246407
E: david@thursfieldsmith.co.uk
W: www.thursfieldsmith.co.uk

TI Protective Coatings
See Taziker Industrial Ltd t/a TI Protective Coatings

TICS Ltd
Oxford House,
Sixth Avenue,
Robin Hood Airport,
Doncaster, DN9 3GG
T: 01302 623074
F: 01302 623075
E: andrewmackenzie@tics-ltd.co.uk
W: www.tics-ltd.co.uk

Tidyco Ltd
Unit 2,
Pentagon Island,
Nottingham Road,
Derby, DE21 6BW
T: 01332 851301
F: 01332 290369
E: enquiries@tidyco.co.uk
W: www.tidyco.co.uk

Tiflex Ltd
Tiflex House,
Liskeard,
Cornwall, PL14 4NB
T: 01579 320808
F: 01579 320802
E: sales@tiflex.co.uk
W: www.tiflex.co.uk

Time 24 Ltd
19 Victoria Gardens,
Burgess Hill,
West Sussex, RH15 9NB
T: 01444 257655
F: 01444 259000
E: sales@time24.co.uk
W: www.time24.co.uk

Timeplan Ltd
12 The Pines,
Broad St,
Guildford,
Surrey, GU3 3BH
T: 01483 462340
F: 01483 462349
E: dave@timeplansolutions.com
W: www.timeplansolutions.com

TMD Friction UK Ltd
PO Box 18 Hunsworth Lane,
Cleckheaton,
West Yorks, BD19 3UJ
T: 01274 854000
F: 01274 854001
E: info@tmdfriction.com
W: www.tmdfriction.com

TMP Worldwide
Chancery House,
Chancery Lane,
London, WC2A 1QS
T: 020 7406 5075
E: contactus@tmpw.co.uk
W: www.tmpw.co.uk

Tolent Construction Ltd
Ravensworth House,
5th Avenue Business Park,
Team Valley,
Gateshead,
Tyne & Wear, NE11 0HF
T: 0191 487 0505
F: 0191 487 2990
E: tyneside@tolent.co.uk
W: www.tolent.co.uk/

Tony Gee and Partners LLP
Hardy House, 140 High St, Esher,
Surrey, KT10 9QJ
T: 01372 461600
F: 01372 461601
E: enquiries@tonygee.com
W: www.tonygee.com

TopDeck Parking
Springvale Business & Industrial Park, Bilston,
Wolverhampton, WV14 0QL
T: 01902 499400
F: 01902 494080
E: info@topdeckparking.co.uk
W: www.topdeckparking.co.uk

Topdrill
1 Seagrave Court, Walton Park,
Milton Keynes, MK7 7HA
T: 01908 666606
E: info@topdrill.co.uk
W: www.topdrill.co.uk

Toray Textiles Europe Ltd
Crown Farm Way, Forest Town, Mansfield,
Notts, NG19 0FT
T: 01623 415050
F: 01623 415070
E: sales@ttel.co.uk
W: www.ttel.co.uk

Torrent Trackside Ltd
Network House, Europa Way, Britannia Enterprise Park, Lichfield,
Staffs, WS14 9TZ
T: 01543 421900
F: 01543 421931
E: mail@torrent.co.uk
W: www.torrent.co.uk

Total Access (UK) Ltd
Unit 5, Raleigh Hall Ind. Est, Eccleshall, Staffs, ST21 6JL
T: 01785 850333
F: 01785 850339
E: enquiries@totalaccess.co.uk
W: www.totalaccess.co.uk

Total Rail Solutions
Crossway, Stephenson Road, Houndmills, Basingstoke,
Hants, RG21 6XR
T: 01962 711642
F: 01962 717330
E: info@totalrailsolutions.co.uk
W: www.totalrailsolutions.co.uk/

Totectors (UK) Ltd
9 Pondwood Close, Moulton Park Ind. Estate, Northampton, NN3 6RT
T: 0870 600 5055
F: 0870 600 5056
E: sales@totectors.net
W: www.totectors.net

Touchstone Renard Ltd
120 Pall Mall, London, SW1Y 5EA
T: 020 7101 0788
M: 07768 366 744
E: paustin@touchstonerenard.com
W: www.touchstonerenard.com

Tower Surveys Ltd
Vivian House, Vivian Lane, Nottingham, NG5 1AF
T: 0115 960 1212
F: 0115 962 1200
E: beverley.chiang@opusjoynespike.co.uk
W: www.towersurveys.co.uk

TPA Portable Roadways Ltd
TPA Head Office, Dukeries Mill, Claylands Industrial Estate, Worksop,
Notts, S81 7DJ
T: 0870 240 2381
F: 0870 240 2382
E: enquiries@tpa-ltd.co.uk
W: www.tpa-ltd.co.uk

TPK Consulting Ltd (RPS Group)
Centurion Court, 85, Milton Park, Abingdon, Oxon, OX14 4RY
T: 01235 438151
F: 01235 438188
E: rpsab@rpsgroup.com
W: www.rpsplc.co.uk

TQ Technical and Vocational
Pearson Academy of Vocational Training, Bangrave Road South, Corby, Northants, NN17 1NN
T: 01536 351300
E: technical@tq.com
W: www.tq.com/technical/

TRAC Engineering Ltd
Dovecote Rd, Eurocentral, North Lanarkshire, ML1 4GP
T: 01698 831111
F: 01698 832222
E: engineering@trac.com
W: www.tracengineering.com

TRaC Global
100 Frobisher Business Park, Leigh Sinton Road, Malvern, Worcs, WR14 1BX
T: 01684 571700
F: 01684 571701
E: quoteme@tracglobal.com
W: www.tracglobal.com

Track Maintenance Equipment Ltd
Witham Wood, Marley Lane, Haslemere, Surrey, GU27 3PZ
T: 01428 651114
F: 01428 644727
E: info@tmeltd.co.uk
W: www.tmeltd.co.uk

Track Safe Telecom (TST)
See Centregreat Rail Ltd

Tracklink UK Ltd
Unit 5, Miltons Yard, Petworth Rd, Witley, Surrey, GU8 5LH
T: 01428 685124
F: 01428 687788
E: enquiries@tklink.co.uk
W: www.tklink.co.uk

Tracksure
Wheelsure Holdings PLC, 8 Woburn Street, Ampthill, Beds, MK45 2HP
T: 01525 840557
F: 01525 403918
E: sales@wheelsure.co.uk
W: wheelsure.co.uk/tracksure/

Trackwork Ltd
PO Box 139, Kirk Sandall Lane, Kirk Sandall Ind. Est, Doncaster, DN3 1WX
T: 01302 888666
F: 01302 888777
E: sales@trackwork.co.uk
W: www.trackwork.co.uk

Tracsis Plc
Unit 6, The Point, Pinnacle Way, Pride Park, Derby, DE24 8ZS
T: 01332 226860
F: 01332 226862
E: info@tracsis.com
W: www.tracsis.com

Tractel UK Ltd
Old Lane, Halfway, Sheffield, S20 3GA
T: 0114 248 2266
F: 0114 247 3350
E: tracteluk.info@tractel.com
W: www.tractel.com

TracTruc Bi-modal
See Truck Train Developments Ltd (and TracTruc Bi-Modal)

Traffic Management Services Ltd
PO Box 10, Retford, Notts, DN22 7EE
T: 01777 705053
F: 01777 709878
E: info@traffic.org.uk
W: www.traffic.org.uk/

TrainFX Ltd
15 Melbourne Business Court, Millennium Way, Pride Park, Derby, DE24 8LZ
T: 01332 366175
E: enquiries@trainfx.com
W: www.trainfx.com

Train'd Up
Elmbank Mill, Menstrie Business Centre, Menstrie, Clackmannanshire, FK11 7BU
T: 0845 602 9665
F: 0870 850 3397
E: enquiries@traindup.org
W: www.traindup.org

Trainline
Trainline Holdings Ltd, 498 Gorgie Rd, Edinburgh, EH11 3AF
T: 08704 111111
W: www.thetrainline.com

Trainpassenger.com Ltd
Suite 364, 12 South Bridge, Edinburgh, EH1 1DD
T: 0131 235 2358
E: info@trainpassenger.com
W: www.trainpassenger.com

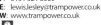

Traka plc
30 Stilebrook Road, Olney, Bucks, MK46 5EA
T: 01234 712345
W: www.traka.com/

Trakside Systems Ltd
See High Voltage Maintenance Services Ltd

TRAM Power Ltd
99 Stanley Rd, Bootle, Merseyside, L20 7DA
T: 0151 547 1425
F: 0151 521 5509
E: lewis.lesley@trampower.co.uk
W: www.trampower.co.uk

Tramlink (Croydon)
See Transport for London

Tranect Ltd
Unit 4, Carraway Rd, Gilmoss Ind. Est, Liverpool, L11 0EE
T: 0151 548 7040
F: 0151 546 6066
E: sales@tranect.co.uk
W: www.tranect.co.uk

Trans Pennine Express (TPE)
See First TransPennine Express

Transaction Systems Ltd
See Vossloh Kiepe

Transcal Ltd
Firth Rd, Houstoun Ind. Est, Livingston, West Lothian, EH54 5DJ
T: 01506 440111
F: 01506 442333
E: info@transcal.co.uk
W: www.transcal.co.uk

Translec Ltd
Saddleworth Business Centre, Huddersfield Rd, Delph, Oldham, OL3 5DF
T: 01457 878888
F: 01457 878887
E: mail@translec.co.uk
W: www.translec.co.uk

Translink NI Railways
Central Station, East Bridge St, Belfast, BT1 3PB
T: 02890 666630
F: 02890 899452
E: feedback@translink.co.uk
W: www.translink.co.uk

Transmitton
See Siemens Rail Systems

Transport & Travel Research Ltd (TTR)
Minster House, Minster Pool Walk, Lichfield, Staffs
T: 01543 416416
F: 01543 416681
E: enquiries@ttr-ltd.com
W: www.ttr-ltd.com

Transport 2000
See Campaign for Better Transport

Transport Benevolent Fund CIO
New Loom House, 101 Back Church Lane, London, E1 1LU
T: 0300 333 2000 (ETD 00 38571)
F: 0870 831 2882
E: help@tbf.org.uk
W: www.tbf.org.uk

Transport Focus
Fleetbank House, 2-6 Salisbury Square, London, EC4Y 8JX
T: 0300 123 0860
F: 020 7630 7355
E: info@transportfocus.org.uk
W: www.transportfocus.org.uk

Transport for Edinburgh
55 Annandale Street, Edinburgh, EH7 4AZ
W: transportforedinburgh.com/

Transport for Greater Manchester
2 Piccadilly Place, Manchester, M1 3BG
T: 0161 244 1000
E: customer.relations@tfgm.com
W: www.tfgm.com/

Transport for London
55 Broadway, London, SW1H 0BD
T: 020 7222 5600
E: enquire@tfl.gov.uk
W: www.tfl.gov.uk/rail

Transport for the North (TfN)
T: 0161 244 1055
E: mediarelations@tfgm.com
W: www.transportforthe north.com/

Transport iNet
SEIC, Holywell Business Park, Loughborough University, LE11 3TU
T: 01509 635270
F: 01509 635231
E: a.m.wilkinson@lboro.ac.uk
W: www.transport-inet.org.uk/

Transport Investigations Ltd
27-29 Margate Rd, Ramsgate, Kent, CT11 7SU
T: 01843 593595
F: 0845 280 2356
E: info@transport investigations.co.uk
W: www.transport nvestigations.co.uk

Transport Scotland
Buchanan House, 58 Port Dundas Rd, Glasgow, G4 0HF
T: 0141 272 7100
E: info@transportscotland.gsi.gov.uk
W: www.transportscotland.gov.uk

Transport Wales
The National Assembly for Wales, Cardiff Bay, Cardiff, CF99 1NA
T: 0300 200 6565
W: gov.wales/topics/transport/rail

Transportation Planning International
Crystal Court, Aston Cross, Rocky Lane, Aston, Birmingham, B6 5RH
T: 0121 333 3433
F: 0121 359 3200
E: info@tpi-bham.co.uk
W: www.tpi-world.com

Transsol Ltd
32 Buxton Rd West, Disley, Cheshire, SK12 2LY
F: 0870 052 5838
E: enquiries@transsol.net
W: www.transsol.net

Trans-Tronic Ltd
Whitting Valley Rd, Old Whittington, Chesterfield, Derbys, S41 9EY
T: 01246 264260
F: 01246 455281
E: sales@trans-tronic.co.uk
W: www.trans-tronic.co.uk

Transurb Technirail
Ravenstein Street 60/18, B-1000 Brussels, Belgium
T: 32 81 25 20 09
E: contact@transurb.com
W: www.transurb.com/simulation

Transys Projects Ltd
See Vossloh Kiepe

Trapeze Group Rail Ltd
Jervaulx House, 6 St Mary's Court, York, YO24 1AH
T: 01904 639091
F: 01904 639092
E: sales.railuk@trapezegroup.com
W: www.trapezegroup.com

Tratos Ltd
10 Eagle Court, Britton St, Farringdon, London, EC1M 5QD
T: 0845 413 9990
F: 020 3553 4815
E: john.light@tratos.co.uk
W: www.tratos.co.uk

Travel Info. Systems
Suite 3, Grand Union House, 20 Kentish Town Rd, London, NW1 9NX
T: 020 7284 8071
F: 020 7267 1133
E: enquiries@travelinfosystems.com
W: www.travelinfosystems.com

Traxsydes Training
Room 11, E.L.O.C, 80-86 St Mary Rd, Walthamstow, London, E17 9RE
T: 020 8223 1257
F: 020 8223 1258
E: bookings@traxsydes.co.uk
W: www.traxsydes.co.uk

TRB Lightweight Structures Ltd
12 Clifton Rd, Huntingdon, Cambs, PE29 7EN
T: 01480 447400
F: 01480 414992
E: sales@trbls.com
W: www.trbls.com

TRE Ltd
See Hitachi Information Control Systems Europe

Treadmaster Flooring
See Tiflex Ltd

Trelleborg Industrial AVS
1 Hoods Close, Leicester, LE4 2BN
T: 0116 267 0300
F: 0116 267 0510
E: rail@trelleborg.com
W: www.trelleborg.com/industrialavs

Tremco Illbruck Limited
Coupland Rd, Hindley Green, Wigan, WN2 4HT
T: 01942 251400
F: 01942 251410
E: uk.info@tremco-illbruck.com
W: www.tremco-illbruck.com

Trent Instruments Ltd
Unit 39, Nottingham South and Wilford Ind. Est, Ruddington Lane, Nottingham, NG11 7EP
T: 0115 969 6188
F: 0115 945 5696
E: phillip@trentinstruments.co.uk
W: www.trentinstruments.co.uk

Tribo Rail
Unit 36, Harpur Hill Business Park, Buxton, Derbys, SK17 9JL
T: 01298 214980
E: enquiries@triborail.com
W: www.triborail.com

Triforce Security Solutions Ltd
Westmead House, Westmead, Farnborough, Hants, GU14 7LP
T: 01252 373496
E: enquiries@triforcesecurity.co.uk
W: www.triforcesecurity.co.uk

Trimble UK
Trimble House, Meridian Office Park, Osborn Way, Hook, Hants, RG27 9HX
T: 01256 760150
F: 01256 760148
W: www.trimble.com

Triscan Systems Ltd
4 Petre Court, Clayton Business Park, Accrington, Lancs, BB5 5HY
T: 0845 225 3100
E: info@thetriscangroup.com
W: www.thetriscangroup.com

Tritech Rail/Tritech Rail Training
See AECOM

TRL
Crowthorne House, Nine Mile Ride, Wokingham, Berks, RG40 3GA
T: 01344 773131
F: 01344 770356
E: rail@trl.co.uk
W: www.trl.co.uk

Trojan Services Ltd
Curtis House, 34 Third Avenue, Hove, East Sussex, BN3 2PD
T: 0845 074 0407
F: 01243 783654
E: info@trojan-services.com
W: www.trojan-services.com

The experts in driver advisory systems for traffic management and energy savings

The iD Centre,
Lathkill House,
The rtc Business Park,
London Road,
Derby, DE24 8UP

Tel: +44 (0) 133 225 8867
Email: enquiries@ttgeurope.com

www.ttgtransportationtechnology.com

Trolex Ltd
Newby Rd, Hazel Grove,
Stockport, SK7 5DY
T: 0161 483 1435
F: 0161 483 5556
E: sales@trolex.com
W: www.trolex.com

Trough-Tec Systems Ltd (TTS)
Bennetthorpe,
Doncaster, DN2 6AA
T: 01302 343633
E: info@ttsrail.co.uk
W: www.ttsrail.co.uk

TRS Staffing Solutions
8th Floor, York House, Kingsway,
London, WC2B 6UJ
T: 020 7419 5800
F: 020 7419 5801
E: info-uk@trsstaffing.com
W: www.trsstaffing.com

Truck Train Developments Ltd (and TracTruc Bi-Modal)
4 Elfin Grove, Bognor Regis, W. Sussex, PO21 2RX
T: 01243 869118
M: 07748 550964
E: pmtrucktrain@tiscali.co.uk
W: www.trucktrain.co.uk

Trueform Engineering Ltd
Unit 12, Pasadena Trading Estate,
Pasadena Close, Hayes,
Middlesex, UB3 3NQ
T: 020 8280 8800
F: 020 8848 1397
E: sales@trueform.co.uk
W: www.trueform.co.uk

Truflame Welding
Truflame House, 56 Newhall Rd,
Sheffield, S9 2QL
T: 0114 243 3020
F: 0114 243 5297
E: sales@truflame.co.uk
W: www.truflame.co.uk

TS Components Ltd
Ladywood House,
Ladywood Works, Lutterworth,
Leics, LE17 4HD
T: 01455 553905
E: info@tscomponents.com
W: www.tscomponents.com

TSL Turton Ltd
PO Box 17, Effingham Street,
Sheffield, S4 7YP
T: 0114 270 1577
F: 0114 275 6947
E: sales@tslturton.com
W: www.tslturton.com

TSSA (Transport Salaried Staffs' Association)
Walkden House, 10 Melton St,
London, NW1 2EJ
T: 020 7387 2101
F: 0141 3329879
E: enquiries@tssa.org.uk
W: www.tssa.org.uk

TT Electronics plc
Clive House, 12-18 Queens Rd,
Weybridge, Surrey, KT13 9XB
T: 01932 825300
F: 01932 836450
E: info@ttelectronics.com
W: www.ttelectronics.com

TTCI UK
13 Fitzroy St, London, W1T 4BQ
T: 020 7755 4080
F: 020 7755 4203
E: michele_johnson@aar.com
W: www.ttc.aar.com

TTG Transportation Technology (Europe) Ltd
The iD Centre, Lathkill House,
rtc Business Park, London Rd,
Derby, DE24 8UP
T: 01332 258867
F: 01332 258823
E: enquiries@ttgeurope.com
W: www.ttgtransportation
technology.com

TTI Inc
Suite S06,
Business & Technology Centre,
Bessemer Drive, Stevenage,
Herts, SG1 2DX
T: 01438 794170
F: 01438 791139
E: kasey.sweetlove@
uk.ttiinc.com
W: www.ttieurope.com/page/
campbell-collins

TTR
See Transport & Travel Research
Ltd (TTR)

Tube Lines
15 Westferry Circus,
Canary Wharf,
London, E14 4HD
T: 0845 660 5466
E: enquiries@tubelines.com
W: www.tubelines.com

Tuchschmid Constructa AG
Langdorfstrasse 26, CH-8501,
Frauenfeld, Switzerland
T: 0041 52 728 8111
F: 0041 52 728 8100
E: w.luessi@tuchschmid.ch
W: www.intermodallogistics.co.uk

Tufnol Composites Ltd
76 Wellhead Lane, Perry Barr,
Birmingham, B42 2TN
T: 0121 356 9351
F: 0121 331 4235
E: sales@tufnol.co.uk
W: www.tufnol.com

Turbex Ltd
Unit 1, Riverwey Ind. Park,
Newman Lane, Alton,
Hants, GU34 2QL
T: 01420 544909
F: 01420 542264
E: sales@turbex.co.uk
W: www.turbex.co.uk

Turbo Power Systems Ltd
1 Queens Park, Queensway North,
Team Valley Trading Est,
Gateshead, Tyne & Wear,
NE11 0QD
T: 0191 482 9200
F: 0191 482 9201
E: sales@
turbopowersystems.com
W: www.turbopowersystems.com

Turkington Precast
James Park, Mahon Rd,
Portadown, Co. Armagh,
BT62 3EH, Northern Ireland
T: 028 38 332807
F: 028 38 361770
E: gary@turkington-precast.com
W: www.turkington-precast.com

Turner & Townsend
Low Hall, Calverley Lane,
Horsforth, Leeds, LS18 4GH
T: 0113 258 4400
F: 0113 258 2911
E: lee@turntown.com
W: www.turnerandtownsend.com

Turner Diesel Ltd
Unit 1A, Dyce Ind. Park, Dyce,
Aberdeen, AB21 7EZ
T: 01224 214200
F: 01224 723927
E: diesel.sales@turner.co.uk
W: www.turner-diesel.co.uk

Tusp Ltd
Ground Floor, Unit 7,
Highpoint Business Village,
Henwood, Ashford,
Kent, TN24 8DH
T: 01233 640257
E: enquiries@tusp.co.uk
W: www.tusp.co.uk

TUV Product Service Ltd
Octagon House, Concorde Way,
Segensworth, North Fareham,
Hants, PO15 5RL
T: 01489 558100
F: 01489 558101
E: info@tuvps.co.uk
W: www.tuvps.co.uk

TUV-SUD Rail GmbH
Westendstrasse 199, 80686,
Munich, Germany
T: 0049 89519 03537
F: 0049 89519 02933
W: www.tuv-sud.co.uk

TXM Plant Ltd
TXM Plant House,
Harbour Rd Trading Est,
Portishead, Bristol, BS20 7AT
T: 01275 399400
F: 01275 399500
E: info@txmplant.co.uk
W: www.txmplant.co.uk

TXM Projects Ltd
1 St Peters Court, Church Lane,
Bickenhill, Solihull, B92 0DN
T: 01675 446830
F: 01675 446839
E: simon.pitt@txmprojects.co.uk
W: www.txmprojects.co.uk

TXM Recruit Ltd
Blackhill Drive,
Wolverton Mill,
Milton Keynes,
Bucks, MK12 5TS
T: 0845 2263454
F: 0845 2262453
E: info@txmrecruit.co.uk

Tyne & Wear Metro
See Nexus (Tyne & Wear Metro)

Tyrolit
Eldon Close, Crick,
Northants, NN6 7UD
T: 01788 824500
E: gborder@tyrolit.com
W: www.tyrolit.co.uk

Tyrone Fabrication Ltd (TFL)
Goland Rd, Ballygawley,
Co Tyrone, BT70 2LA
T: 028 8556 7200
F: 028 8556 7089
E: sales@tfl.eu.com
W: www.tfl.eu.com

Tyseley Locomotive Works Limited
670 Warwick Rd, Tyseley,
Birmingham, B11 2HL
T: 0121 708 4960
F: 0121 708 4960
E: office@vintagetrains.co.uk

UK Accreditation Service (UKAS)
21-47 High St, Feltham,
Middx, TW13 4UN
T: 020 8917 8400
F: 020 8917 8500
E: info@ukas.com
W: info@ukas.com

UK Power Networks Services
237 Southwark Bridge Rd,
London, SE1 6NP
T: 0207 397 7695
E: rail@ukpowernetworks.co.uk
W: www.ukpowernetworks.
co.uk/internet/en/
infrastructure-services/rail/

UK Rail Leasing
Beal Street, Leicester, LE2 0AA
T: 0116 262 2783
E: info@ukrl.co.uk
W: www.ukrl.co.uk

UK Railtours
T: 01438 715050
E: john@ukrailtours.com
W: www.ukrailtours.com

UK Trade & Investment - Investment Services
1 Victoria St,
London, SW1H 0ET
T: 0845 539 0419/020 7333 5442
E: enquiries@ukti-invest.com
W: www.ukti.gov.uk

UK Ultraspeed
Warksburn House, Wark,
Hexham,
Northumberland, NE48 3LS
T: 020 7861 2497
F: 020 7861 2497
E: ncameron@
bell-pottinger.co.uk
W: www.500kmh.com

UKDN Waterflow
2480 Regents Court,
The Crescent,
Birmingham Business Park,
Solihull,
West Midlands, B37 7YE
T: 0121 788 4787
E: solutions@
ukdnwaterflow.co.uk
W: ukdnwaterflow.co.uk/

UKRS Projects Ltd
See Bowen Projects Ltd

Ultimate Hearing Protection
13 Moorfield Road,
Orpington,
Kent, BR6 0HG
T: 01689 876885
E: sales@ultimateear.com
W: www.ultimateear.com

Ultra Electronics PMES Ltd
Towers Business Park,
Wheelhouse Rd, Rugeley,
Staffs, WS15 1UZ
T: 01889 503300
F: 01889 572929
E: enquiries@ultra-pmes.com
W: www.ultra-pmes.com

Ultra Electronics-Electrics
Kingsditch Lane, Cheltenham,
Glos, GL51 9PG
T: 01242 221166
F: 01242 221167
E: info@ultra-electrics.com
W: www.ultra-electrics.com

Underground Pipeline Services Ltd
See Integrated Water Services Ltd

Unic Cranes Europe
See GGR Group Ltd

UNIFE
Avenue Louise 221,
B-1050 Brussels, Belgium
T: 0032 2642 2328
F: 0032 2626 1261
E: judit.sandor@unife.org
W: www.unife.org

Unilathe Ltd
Ford Green Business Park,
Ford Green Road, Smallthorne,
Stoke-on-Trent, Staffs, ST6 1NG
T: 01782 532000
F: 01782 532013
E: enquiries@unilathe.co.uk
W: www.unilathe.co.uk

Unilokomotive Ltd
Dunmore Rd, Tuam,
Co. Galway, Republic of Ireland
T: 00353 93 52150
F: 00353 93 52227
E: omcconn@unilok.ie
W: www.unilok.ie

Unipart Dorman
Wennington Rd,
Southport, Merseyside, PR9 7TN
T: 01704 518000
F: 01704 518001
E: dorman.enquiries@
unipartdorman.co.uk
W: www.unipartdorman.co.uk

Unipart Rail (infrastructure)
Gresty Rd,
Crewe, CW2 6EH
T: 01270 847600
F: 01270 847601
E: enquiries@unipartrail.com
W: www.unipartrail.com

Unipart Rail (infrastructure)
Leeman Rd, York, YO26 4ZD
T: 01904 544020
F: 01904 544021
E: enquiries@unipartrail.com
W: www.unipartrail.com

Unipart Rail (infrastructure)
Gresty Rd,
Crewe, CW2 6EH
T: 01270 847600
F: 01270 847601
E: enquiries@unipartrail.com
W: www.unipartrail.com

Unipart Rail (T&RS) Ltd
Jupiter Building,
First Point,
Balby Carr Bank,
Doncaster, DN4 5JQ
T: 01302 731400
F: 01302 731401
E: trsenquiries@unipartrail.com
W: www.unipartrail.com

Unite - The Union
Unite House,
128 St Theobald's Road,
Holborn,
London, WC1X 8TN
T: 020 7611 2500
E: executive.council@
unitetheunion.org
W: www.unitetheunion.com

United Kingdom Society for Trenchless Technology
Camden House,
Warwick Road,
Kenilworth,
Warks, CV8 1TH
T: 01926 513773
E: admin@ukstt.org.uk
W: www.ukstt.org.uk

United Springs Ltd
Mandale Park, Norman Road,
Rochdale, Lancs, OL11 4HP
T: 01706 644551
F: 01706 630516
E: sales@united-springs.co.uk
W: www.united-springs.com

Universal Heat Transfer Ltd
Well Spring Close,
Carlyon Rd, Atherstone,
Warks, CV9 1HU
T: 01827 722171
F: 01827 722174
E: sales@uhtltd.com
W: www.universalheat
transfer.com

The Universal Improvement Company
17 Knowl Ave, Belper,
Derbys, DE56 2TL
T: 01773 826659
F: 01773 826659
E: info@theuic.com
W: www.theuic.com

Universal Railway Equipment Ltd
Princess Royal Buildings,
Whitecroft Rd,
Bream, Lydney,
Glos, GL15 6LY
T: 01594 560555
E: unirail@btconnect.com
W: www.peeway.co.uk

University of Derby - Faculty of Arts, Design & Technology
Markeaton St,
Derby, DE22 3AW
T: 01332 593216
E: adtenquiry@derby.ac.uk
W: www.derby.ac.uk

Railway Education at The University of Birmingham
Postgraduate Taught Programmes
Doctoral Research and Short Courses
UNIVERSITY OF BIRMINGHAM
For Information: www.railway.bham.ac.uk
BCRRE, Gisbert Kapp Building, Pritchatts Road, Birmingham B15 2TT

Up & Cuming Consultancy Ltd (UCCL)
74 Chenies Mews,
London, WC1E 6HU
T: 020 7388 2232
F: 020 7388 3730
E: info@uccl.net
W: www.uccl.net

Urban Hygiene Ltd
Sky Business Park,
Robin Hood Airport, Doncaster,
South Yorks, DN9 3GN
T: 01302 623193
F: 01302 623167
E: enquiries@urbanhygiene.com
W: www.urbanhygiene.co.uk

Urbis Lighting Ltd
See Urbis Schreder Ltd

Urbis Schreder Ltd
Sapphire House, Lime Tree Way,
Hampshire International
Business Park, Chineham,
Basingstoke, Hants, RG24 8GG
T: 01256 354446
F: 01256 841314
E: sales@urbis-schreder.com
W: www.urbis-schreder.com

Uretek UK Ltd
Unit 6, Peel Rd, Skelmersdale,
Lancs, WN8 9PT
T: 01695 50525
F: 01695 555212
E: sales@uretek.co.uk
W: www.uretek.co.uk

URS
Scott House, Alencon Link,
Basingstoke, Hants, RG21 7PP
T: 01256 310200
F: 01256 310201
E: rail.marketing@scottwilson.com
W: www.urscorp.eu

URS Corporation Ltd
6-8 Greencoat Place,
London, SW1P 1PL
T: 0115 907 7086
F: 0115 907 7001
E: railways@scottwilson.com
W: www.urscorp.eu

VAE UK Ltd
Sir Harry Lauder Rd, Portobello,
Edinburgh, EH15 1DJ
T: 0131 550 2297
F: 0131 550 2660
E: jim.gemmell@vae.co.uk
W: www.voestalpine.com/vae

Vaisala Ltd
Elm House, 351 Bristol Rd,
Birmingham, B5 7SW
T: 0121 683 1200
F: 0121 683 1299
E: liz.green@vaisala.com
W: www.vaisala.com

Valmont Stainton Ltd
Unit 5, Dukesway,
Teesside Industrial Estate,
Thornaby, Cleveland, TS17 9LT
T: 01642 766242
F: 01642 765509
E: stainton@valmont.com
W: www.valmont-stainton.com

Van der Vlist UK Ltd
Burma Drive,
Kingston upon Hull, HU9 5SD
T: 01482 210100
F: 01482 216222
E: info@vandervlist.co.uk
W: www.vandervlist.com/en/european_offices/uk

Van Elle
Kirkby Lane, Pinxton,
Notts, NG16 6JA
T: 01773 580580
F: 01773 862100
E: mark.williams@van-elle.co.uk
W: www.van-elle.co.uk

Vapor Ricon Europe Ltd
Meadow Lane, Loughborough,
Leicestershire, LE11 1HS
T: 01509 635920
F: 01509 261939
E: riconuk@wabtec.com
W: www.ricon.eu

Variable Message Signs Ltd (VMS)
Unit 1,
Monkton Business Park North,
Mill Lane, Hebburn,
Tyne & Wear, NE31 2JZ
T: 0191 423 7070
F: 0191 423 7071
E: railsupport@vmslimited.co.uk
W: www.vmslimited.co.uk

Vector Management Ltd
Strathclyde House,
Green Man Lane,
London Heathrow Airport,
Feltham, Middx, TW14 0NZ
T: 020 8844 0444
F: 020 8844 0666
E: ju-liang.trigg@vecman.com
W: www.vecman.com

Vectra Group Ltd
See Arcadis EC Harris

Verint Systems
241 Brooklands Rd, Weybridge,
Surrey, KT13 0RH
T: 01932 839500
F: 01932 839501
E: marketing.emea@verint.com
W: www.verint.com

Veritec Sonomatic Ltd
Ashton House, The Village,
Birchwood Bus.Park,
Warrington, WA3 6FZ
T: 01925 414000
F: 01925 655595
E: jl@vsonomatic.com
W: www.vsonomatic.com/

Vertex Systems
See AMCL Systems Engineering Ltd

Veryards Opus
See Opus International Consultants Ltd

VGC Group
Cardinal House, Bury St, Ruislip,
Middx, HA4 7GD
T: 01895 671823
E: zena.wigram@vgcgroup.co.uk
W: www.vgcgroup.co.uk

Vi Distribution
Unit 7, Springvale Business Centre,
Millbuck Way, Sandbach,
Cheshire, CW11 3HY
T: 01270 750520
F: 01270 750521
E: sales@vidistribution.co.uk
W: www.vidistribution.co.uk

Video 125 Ltd
Glade House, High St, Sunninghill,
Berks, SL5 9NP
T: 01344 628565
E: sales@video125.co.uk
W: www.video125.co.uk

VINCI Construction UK Ltd
See Taylor Woodrow

Vinci Park Services UK Ltd
Oak House, Reeds Cres, Watford,
Herts, WD24 4QP
T: 01908 223500
F: 01923 231914
E: info@vincipark.co.uk
W: www.vincipark.co.uk

Vintage Trains Ltd
670 Warwick Rd, Tyseley,
Birmingham, B11 2HL
T: 0121 708 4960
F: 0121 708 4963
E: vintagetrains@btconnect.com
W: www.vintagetrains.co.uk

Virgin Trains (West Coast)
North Wing Offices,
Euston Station, London, NW1 2HS
T: 03331 031 031
E: firstname.lastname@virgintrains.co.uk
W: www.virgin.com/trains

Virgin Trains East Coast
East Coast House, 25 Skeldergate,
York, YO1 6DH
T: 03457 225 333
W: www.virgintrainseastcoast.com

Vision Infrastructure Services Ltd
Unit 7, Durham Lane,
West Moor Park, Doncaster,
DN3 3FE
T: 01302 831730
F: 01302 832671
E: ian@visioninfrastructureservices.com
W: www.visioninfrastructureservices.com

Vistorm Ltd
See HP Information Security

Visul Systems
Kingston House, 3 Walton Rd,
Pattinson North,
Washington,
Tyne & Wear, NE38 8QA
T: 0191 402 1960
F: 0191 402 1906
E: info@visulsystems.com
W: www.visulsystems.com

Vita Safety Ltd
1 Gillingham Rd, Eccles,
Manchester, M30 8NA
T: 0161 789 1400
F: 0161 280 2528
E: ian.hutchings@vitasafety.com
W: www.vitasafety.com

Vital Rail
The Mill, South Hall St,
Salford, M5 4TP
T: 0161 836 7000
F: 0161 836 7001
E: info@vital.uk.com
W: www.vital-rail.com

Vitec
3 Cae Gwrydd,
Greenmeadow Springs Bus. Park,
Cardiff, CF15 7AB
T: 02920 620232
F: 02920 624837
E: cardiff@vitecconsult.com
W: www.vitecwebberlenihan.com

Vivarail Ltd
Quinton Rail Technology Centre,
Station Road,
Long Marston,
Stratford upon Avon,
Warks, CV37 8PL
T: 01789 721922
M: 07815 010373
E: info@vivarail.co.uk
W: www.vivarail.co.uk/

VolkerFitzpatrick
As an industry leader in rail engineering and construction, we offer a fully integrated approach that delivers efficient and innovative solutions.
T: 01992 305000
E: enquiries@volkerfitzpatrick.co.uk
a VolkerWessels company
www.volkerfitzpatrick.co.uk

Voith Turbo Limited
Rail Division
Unit 49 Metropolitan Park,
Bristol Road, Greenford,
Middlesex. UB6 8UP
United Kingdom
Tel: +44 1629 821895
Fax: +44 1629 821895
Mob: +44 7971 794330
VOITH
Engineered Reliability

Vix Technology
ACIS House, 168 Cowley Rd,
Cambridge, CB4 0DL
T: 01223 728700
F: 01223 506311
E: uk.marketing@vixtechnology.com
W: www.vixtechnology.com

Viztek Ltd
North East Business & Innovation Centre, Wearfield,
Enterprise Park East,
Sunderland, SR5 2TA
T: 0191 516 6606
E: info@viztekltd.co.uk
W: www.viztekltd.co.uk

VMS
See Variable Message Signs Ltd (VMS)

Voestalpine UK Ltd
Voestalpine House, Albion Place,
Hammersmith, London, W6 0QT
T: 020 8600 5800
E: catherine.crisp@voestalpine.com
W: www.voestalpine.com

Vogelsang Ltd
Crewe Gates Ind. Est, Crewe,
Cheshire, CW1 6YY
T: 01270 216600
F: 01270 216699
E: sales@vogelsang.co.uk
W: www.vogelsang.co.uk

Voith Industrial Services Ltd
Tournament Court,
Tournament Fields,
Warwick, CV34 6LG
T: 01926 623585
E: viwa_enquiries@voith.com
W: www.voith.com

Voith Turbo Ltd
Unit 49 Metropolitan Park,
Bristol Road, Greenford,
Middlesex, UB6 8UP
T: 01629 821 895
E: rail.uk @voith.com
W: www.voith.com

VolkerFitzpatrick Ltd
Hertford Rd, Hoddesden,
Herts, EN11 9BX
T: 01992 305000
F: 01992 305001
E: enquiries@volkerfitzpatrick.co.uk
W: www.volkerfitzpatrick.co.uk

VolkerRail
Units 4 & 6, Carr Hill Road,
Doncaster, South Yorks, DN4 8DE
T: 01302 791100
F: 01302 791200
E: marketing@volkerrail.co.uk
W: www.volkerrail.co.uk

Volo TV & Media Ltd
Departure Side Offices,
Platform 1, Paddington Station,
Pread St, London, W2 1FT
T: 020 7706 4775
F: 020 7402 2498
E: findoutmore@volo.tv
W: www.volo.tv

Vortex Exhaust Technology
53 Tower Road,
Globe Industrial Estate, Grays,
Essex, RM17 6ST
T: 01375 372037
E: enq@vortexexhausttechnology.com
W: www.vortexexhausttechnology.com/

Vortok International
Innovation House,
3 Western Wood Way,
Langage Science Park, Plymouth,
Devon, PL7 5BG
T: 01752 349200
F: 01752 338855
E: gfermie@vortok.co.uk
W: www.vortok.co.uk

Vossloh AG
Vosslohstrasse 4, 58791 Werdohl,
Germany
T: 0049 2392 520
F: 0049 2392 520
W: www.vossloh.com

Vossloh Cogifer UK Ltd
80a Scotter Rd, Scunthorpe,
North Lincs, DN15 8EF
T: 01724 862131
F: 01724 295243
E: contact-uk@vossloh-cogifer.com
W: www.vossloh-cogifer.com

Vossloh Fastening Systems GmbH
Vosslohstrasse 4,
D-58791 Werdohl, Germany
T: 0049 2392 52 0
F: 0049 2392 52 375
E: info@vfs.vossloh.com
W: www.vossloh.com

Vossloh Kiepe
2 Priestley Wharf,
Birmingham Science Park, Holt St,
Aston, Birmingham, B7 4BN
T: 0121 359 7777
F: 0121 359 1811
E: enquiries@vkb.vossloh.com
W: www.vossloh-kiepe.co.uk

Voyager Leasing (a subsidiary of the Royal Bank Of Scotland)

VTG Rail UK Ltd
Sir Stanley Clarke House,
7 Ridgeway,
Quinton Business Park,
Birmingham, B32 1AF
T: 0121 421 9180
F: 0121 421 9192
E: sales@vtg.com
W: www.vtg-rail.co.uk

VTS Track Technology Ltd
See Vossloh Cogifer UK Ltd

Vulcanite UK and Europe
PO Box 456, Newcastle, NE3 9DR
T: 0191 490 6203
M: 07554 447 099
E: sales-uk@vulcanite.com
W: www.vulcanite.com

Vulcascot Cable Protectors Ltd
Unit 12, Norman-D-Gate,
Bedford Rd,
Northampton, NN1 5NT
T: 0800 035 2842
F: 01604 632344
E: sales@vulcascotcableprotectors.co.uk
W: www.vulcascotcableprotectors.com

W A Developments Ltd
See Stobart Rail

Wabtec Rail Group Ltd
PO Box 400, Doncaster Works,
Hexthorpe Rd,
Doncaster, DN1 1SL
T: 01302 340700
F: 01302 790058
E: wabtecrail@wabtec.com
W: www.wabtecgroup.com

vossloh
COGIFER
VOSSLOH COGIFER UK Limited
Manufacturers of all types of Switch and Crossing Systems and ancillary components for the Heavy Rail, High Speed and Light Rail markets.
Vossloh Cogifer UK Ltd
80A Scotter Road,
Scunthorpe DN15 8EF
Tel: +44 0 1724 862131
Fax: +44 0 1724 295243
Web: www.vossloh-cogifer-uk.com

HITACHI
Inspire the Next

Wabtec Rail Scotland
Caledonia Works,
West Langlands Street,
Kilmarnock,
Ayrshire, KA1 2QD
T: 01563 523573
F: 01563 541076
W: www.wabtecgroup.com

Wacker Neuson (GB) Ltd
Lea Rd, Waltham Cross,
Herts, EN9 1AW
T: 01992 707228
F: 01992 707201
E: chris.pearce@eu.wackergroup.com
W: www.wackerneuson.com

WAGO Ltd
Triton Park,
Swift Valley Industrial Estate,
Rugby, CV21 1SG
T: 01788 568008
E: ukmarketing@wago.com
W: www.wago.com

Wagony Swidnica S.A.
UL. Strzelinska 35,
58-100 Swidnica, Poland
T: 0048 74 856 2000
F: 0048 853 0323
E: secretariat@gbrx.com
W: www.gbrx.com

A N Wallis & Co Ltd
Greasley St, Bulwell,
Nottingham, NG6 8NG
T: 0115 927 1721
F: 0115 875 6630
E: mark.rimmington@an-wallis.com
W: www.an-wallis.com

Washroom Washroom
Units 1-10, Hill Farm,
Epping Lane, Abridge,
Essex, RM4 1TU
T: 0845 470 3000
F: 0845 470 3001
E: contact@washroom.co.uk
W: www.washroom.co.uk

Washtec UK Ltd
Unit 14A,
Oak ind. Park,
Great Dunmow,
Essex, CM9 1XN
T: 01371 878800
F: 01371 878810
W: www.washtec-uk.com

Waterflow
See UKDN Waterflow

Waterman Transport & Development Ltd
Pickfords Wharf,
Clink St,
London, SE1 9DG
T: 020 7928 7888
F: 020 7902 0992
E: paul.worrall@watermangroup.com
W: www.watermangroup.com/

Waverley Rail Project
See Borders Railway Project

Wavesight Ltd
Unit 13, Dencora Way,
Sundon Business Park,
Luton,
Beds, LU3 3HP
T: 01582 578160
F: 01582 578298
E: sales@wavesight.com
W: www.wavesight.com

WDS Component Parts Ltd
Richardshaw Road,
Grangefield Industrial Estate,
Pudsey, Leeds, LS28 6LE
T: 0113 290 9852
E: sales@wdsltd.co.uk
W: www.wdsltd.co.uk

Webasto AG
Kraillinger Strasse 5,
82131 Stockdorf,
Germany
T: 0049 89 857 948 444
F: 0049 89 899 217 433
E: tac3@webasto.com
W: www.rail.webasto.com

Webro Cable & Connectors Ltd
Vision House,
Meadow Brooks Business Park,
Meadow Lane, Long Eaton,
Nottingham, NG10 2GD
T: 0115 972 4483
F: 0115 946 1230
E: info@webro.com
W: www.webro.com

WEC Group Ltd
Spring Vale House,
Spring Vale Rd, Darwen,
Lancs, BB3 2ES
T: 01254 773718
F: 01254 771109
E: stevecooke@wecl.co.uk
W: www.welding-eng.com

Weedfree
Holly Tree Farm, Park Lane, Balne,
Goole, DN14 0EP
T: 01405 860022
F: 01405 862283
E: sales@weedfree.net
W: www.weedfree.net

Weidmuller Ltd
Klippon House,
Centurion Court Office Park,
Meridian East,
Meridian Business Park, Leicester,
LE19 1TP
T: 0116 282 1261
F: 0116 289 3582
E: marketing@weidmuller.co.uk
W: www.weidmuller.co.uk

Weightmans
High Holborn House,
52-54 High Holborn, London,
WC1V 6RL
T: 020 7822 1900
F: 020 7822 1901
E: sarah.seddon@weightmans.com
W: www.weightmans.com

Weighwell Ltd
Weighwell House,
Woolley Colliery Road, Darton,
Barnsley, South Yorks, S75 5JA
T: 0114 269 9955
F: 0114 269 9256
E: rwood@weighwell.co.uk
W: www.weighwell.co.uk

Weld-A-Rail Ltd
Lockwood Close,
Top Valley,
Nottingham, NG5 9JN
T: 0115 926 8797
F: 0115 926 4818
E: admin@weldarail.co.uk
W: www.weldarail.co.uk

The Welding Institute
See Institute of Rail Welding

Welfare Cabins UK (WCUK)
See Garic Ltd

A J Wells & Sons Vitreous Enamellers
Bishop's Way,
Newport, IOW, PO30 5WS
T: 01983 537766
F: 01983 537788
E: enamel@ajwells.co.uk
W: www.ajwells.com

Wentworth House Rail Systems Ltd
Vale House, Aston Lane North,
Preston Brook, Cheshire, WA7 3PE
T: 01270 448405
E: enquiries@railelectrification.com
W: www.railelectrification.com

Werther International SpA
Via F Brunelleschi 12F,
42124-Cadè (RE), Italy
T: 39 0522 9431
E: sales@wertherint.com
W: www.wertherint.com

West Coast Railway Co.
Jesson Way, Carnforth,
Lancs, LA5 9UR
T: 01524 732100
F: 01524 735518
E: info@wcrc.co.uk
W: www.wcrc.co.uk

West Midlands PTE
See Centro

West Yorkshire PTE (Metro)
Wellington House,
40-50 Wellington St,
Leeds, LS1 2DE
F: 0113 251 7272
E: metroline@westyorks-ca.gov.uk
W: www.wymetro.com/

Westcode Semiconductors
Langley Park Way, Langley Park,
Chippenham, Wilts, SN15 1GE
T: 01249 444524
F: 01249 659448
E: customerservices@westcode.com
W: www.westcode.com

Westermo Data Communications Ltd
Talisman Business Centre,
Duncan Rd, Park Gate,
Southampton, SO31 7GA
T: 01489 580585
F: 01489 580586
E: sales@westermo.co.uk
W: www.westermo.com

Western Rail Services
Unit 5H, Cricket Street, Wigan,
Lancs, WN6 7TP
T: 01942 245599
F: 01942 825544
E: info@railcable.co.uk
W: www.railcable.co.uk

Westinghouse Platform Screen Doors
Knorr-Bremse Rail Systems (UK) Ltd,
Westinghouse Way,
Hampton Park East, Melksham,
Wilts, SN12 6TL
T: 01225 898700
F: 01225 898705
E: wpsd.enquiries@knorr-bremse.com
W: www.platformscreendoors.com

Westinghouse Rail Systems
See Siemens Rail Automation

Westley Engineering Ltd
120 Pritchett St, Aston,
Birmingham, B6 4EH
T: 0121 333 1925
F: 0121 333 1926
E: g.dunne@westleyengineering.co.uk
W: www.westleyengineering.co.uk

Weston Williamson
43 Tanner St, London, SE1 3PL
T: 020 7403 2665
F: 020 7403 2667
E: chris@westonwilliamson.com
W: www.westonwilliamson.com

Westquay Trading Co. Ltd
3F Lyncastle Way, Appleton Thorn,
Warrington, WA4 4ST
T: 01925 265333
F: 01925 211700
E: enquiries@westquaytrading.co.uk
W: www.westquaytrading.co.uk

Westshield Ltd
Waldron House,
Greenwood Street, Oldham,
Lancs, OL4 2BB
T: 0161 682 6222
F: 0161 682 6333
E: mail@westshield.co.uk
W: www.westshield.co.uk

Wettons
Wetton House, 278-280 St James's Rd,
London, SE1 5JX
T: 020 7237 2007
F: 020 7252 3277
E: mark.hammerton@wettons.co.uk
W: www.wettons.co.uk

WH Davis Ltd
Langwith Rd, Langwith Junction,
Mansfield, Notts, NG20 9SA
T: 01623 741600
F: 01623 744474
W: www.whdavis.co.uk

Wheelsets (UK) Ltd
Unit 4B, Denby Way,
Hellaby Industrial Estate,
Rotherham, S66 8NZ
T: 01302 322266
F: 01302 322299
E: martin@wheelsets.co.uk
W: www.wheelsets.co.uk

White & Case LLP
5 Old Broad St, London,
EC2N 1DW
T: 020 7532 2310
F: 020 7532 1001
E: twinsor@whitecase.com
W: www.whitecase.com

White Young Green
See Amey

Whiteley Electronics Ltd
See Gemma Lighting

Whitmore Rail
Whitmore Europe, City Park,
Watchmead, Welwyn Garden City,
Herts, AL7 1LT
T: 01707 379870
E: info-uk@whitmores.com
W: www.whitmores.com

Wicek Sosna Architects
Unit 15, 21 Plumbers Row,
London, E1 1EQ
T: 020 7655 4430
E: office@sosnaarchitects.co.uk
W: www.sosnaarchitects.co.uk

Wilcomatic Ltd
Unit 5, Commerce Park,
19 Commerce Way,
Croydon, CR0 4YL
T: 020 8649 5760
F: 020 8680 9791
E: sales@wilcomatic.co.uk
W: www.wilcomatic.co.uk

Wilkinson Star Ltd
Shield Drive, Wardsley Ind Est,
Manchester, M28 2WD
T: 0161 793 8127
F: 0161 727 8538
E: steve.ross@wilkinsonstar.com
W: www.wilkinsonstar.com

WillB Brand Consultants
Studio 17,
Unit 201, Southbank House,
Black Prince Rd, London, SE1 7SJ
T: 020 7112 8911
E: will@willbaxter.com
W: www.willbaxter.com

William Bain Fencing Ltd
Lochin Works, 7 Limekilns Rd,
Blairlinn Ind. Est,
Cumbernauld, G67 2RN
T: 01236 457333
F: 01236 451166
E: sales@lochrin-bain.co.uk
W: www.lochrin-bain.co.uk/

William Cook Rail
Cross Green, Leeds, LS9 0SG
T: 0113 249 6363
F: 0113 249 1376
E: castproducts@william-cook.co.uk
W: www.william-cook.co.uk

Williamette Valley Company – WVCO Railroad Division
1075 Arrowsmith St, Eugene,
OR 97402, United States
T: 001 541 484 9621
F: 001 541 284 2096
E: sales@wilvaco.com
W: www.wvcorailroad.com

Willie Baker Leadership & Development Ltd
Aggborough Farm, College Rd,
Kidderminster, Worcs, DY10 1LU
E: willie@williebaker.co.uk
W: www.williebaker.co.uk

Wilmat Ltd
Wilmat House, 43 Steward Street,
Birmingham, B18 7AE
T: 0121 454 7514
F: 0121 456 1792
E: sales@wilmat-handling.co.uk
W: www.wilmat-handling.co.uk/

Winckworth Sherwood
Minerva House,
5 Montague Close, London,
SE1 9BB
T: 020 7593 5000
F: 0207 593 5099
E: info@wslaw.co.uk
W: www.wslaw.co.uk

Wind River UK Ltd
Oakwood House,
Grove Business Park,
White Waltham,
Maidenhead,
Berks, SL6 3HY
T: 01793 831831
F: 01793 831808
E: sue.woolley@windriver.com
W: www.windriver.com

Windhoff Bahn und Anlagentechnik GmbH
Hovestrasse 10, D-48431 Rheine,
Germany
T: 0049 5971 580
F: 0049 5971 58209
E: info@windhoff.de
W: www.windhoff.de

Winn & Coales (Denso) Ltd
Denso House, Chapel Rd,
London, SE27 0TR
T: 020 8670 7511
F: 020 8761 2456
E: mail@denso.net
W: www.denso.net

Winstanley & Co Ltd
See Transcal Ltd

Winsted Ltd
Units 7/8, Lovett Rd,
Hampton Lovett Ind Est,
Droitwich, Worcs, WR9 0QG
T: 01905 770276
F: 01905 779791
E: info@winsted.co.uk
W: www.winsted.com

Wintersgill
110 Bolsover St,
London, W1W 5NU
T: 020 7580 4499
F: 020 7436 8191
E: info@wintersgill.net
W: www.wintersgill.net

Wireless CCTV Ltd
Mitchell Hey Place, College Road,
Rochdale, Lancs, OL12 6AE
T: 01706 631166
E: sales@wcctv.com
W: www.wcctv.com

Witt O'Brien's Ltd
Trent House, RTC Business Park,
London Rd, Derby, DE24 8UP
T: 01332 222299
F: 01332 222298
E: info@wittobriens.com
W: www.wittobriens.co.uk

WM Plant Hire Ltd
Manor Farm Lane, Bridgnorth,
Shropshire, WV16 5HG
T: 01452 722200
F: 01452 769666
E: info@wmplanthire.com
W: www.wmplanthire.com

WMG Centre HVM Catapult
International Digital Laboratory,
The University of Warwick,
Coventry, Warks, CV4 7AL
T: 02476 572696
E: wmghvmcatapult@
warwick.ac.uk
W: www.wmghvmcatapult.org.uk

Woking Homes
Oriental Rd, Woking,
Surrey, GU22 7BE
T: 01483 763558
F: 01483 721048
E: administration@
woking-homes.co.uk
W: www.woking-homes.co.uk

Wood & Douglas Ltd
Lattice House, Baughurst, Tadley,
Hants, RG26 5LP
T: 0118 981 1444
F: 0118 981 1567
E: sales@woodanddouglas.co.uk
W: www.woodanddouglas.co.uk

Wood & Wood Signs
Heron Rd, Sowton Estate,
Exeter, EX2 7LX
T: 01392 444501
F: 01392 252358
E: info@wwsigns.co.uk
W: www.wwsigns.co.uk

Woodward Diesel Systems
Lancaster Centre,
Meteor Business Park,
Cheltenham Rd East,
Gloucester, GL2 9QL
T: 01452 859940
F: 01452 855758
E: corpinfo@woodward.com
W: www.woodward.com

Workmates Daniel Owen
1st Floor, Genesis House,
17 Godliman St,
London, EC4V 5BD
T: 0207 539 1660
W: www.wmdo.co.uk/sectors/rail

Workthing
Beaumont House,
Kensington Village, Avonmore Rd,
London, W14 8TS
T: 0870 898 0022
F: 0870 898 0033
E: info@workthing.com
W: www.workthing.com

Worldline
Triton Square, Regents Place,
London, NW1 3HG
T: 020 7830 4447
F: 020 7830 4445
W: www.uk.worldline.com/

Worlifts Rail Division
Guild House,
Sandy Lane,
Wildmoor, Bromsgrove,
Worcs, B61 0QU
T: 0121 460 1113
F: 0121 460 1116
E: rail@worlifts.co.uk
W: www.worlifts.co.uk

Wrekin Circuits Ltd
29/30 Hortonwood 33,
Telford,
Shropshire, TF1 7EX
T: 01952 670011
F: 01952 606565
E: sales@wrekin-circuits.co.uk
W: www.wrekin-circuits.co.uk

WRS Cable Ltd
MGB House,
Langage Business Park,
Plympton,
Plymouth,
Devon, PL7 5JY
W: www.wrscables.com

The WS Group (Tracksure)
8 Woburn St, Ampthill,
Beds, MK45 2HP
T: 01525 840557
F: 01525 403918
E: sales@tracksure.co.uk
W: www.tracksure.co.uk

WSP UK
Mountbatten House, Basing View,
Basingstoke, Hants, RG21 4HJ
T: 01256 318802
F: 01256 318700
W: www.wspgroup.com

**WVCO Railroad Division of
The Williamette Valley
Company**
1075 Arrowsmith St, PO Box 2280,
Eugene, OR 97402, United States
T: 001 541 484 9621
F: 001 541 284 2096
E: sales@wvcorailroad.com
W: www.wvcorailroad.com

WWP Consultants
5-15 Cromer St,
London, WC1H 8LS
T: 020 7833 5767
F: 020 7833 5766
W: www.wwp.co.uk

Wynnwith Rail
Wynnwith House, Church St,
Woking, Surrey, GU21 6DJ
T: 01483 748206
E: rail@wynnwith.com
W: www.wynnwith.com

Wyse Rail Ltd
Cressex Business Park,
Lancaster Rd, Bucks, HP12 3QP
T: 0870 145 0552
F: 01494 560929
E: wyserail@wysegroup.co.uk
W: www.wysegroup.com

WyvernRail Plc
Wirksworth Station, Station Rd,
Wirksworth, Derbys, DE4 4FB
T: 01629 821828
E: wirksworth_station@
wyvernrail.co.uk
W: www.mytesttrack.com

XEIAD
22 Lower Town, Sampford Peverill,
Tiverton, Devon, EX16 7BT
T: 01884 822899
E: info@bridgezoneltd.co.uk
W: www.xeiad.com/

Xervon Palmers Ltd
331 Charles St, Glasgow, G21 2QA
T: 0141 553 4040
F: 0141 552 6463
E: info@xervonpalmers.com
W: www.xervonpalmers.com

XiTRACK Ltd
See Dow Hyperlast

XL Lubricants Ltd
See NTM Sales & Marketing Ltd

**Yardene Engineering 2000
Ltd**
Daux Rd, Billingshurst,
West Sussex, RH14 9SJ
T: 01403 783558
F: 01403 783104
E: sales@yardene.co.uk
W: www.yardene.co.uk

Yellow Group Limited
The iD Centre, Lathkill House,
rtc Business Park, London Rd,
Derby, DE24 8UP
T: 01332 258865
F: 01332 258823
E: enquiries@yellowrail.org.uk
W: www.yellow-group.com

Yeltech Ltd
Upper Unstead Farm Cottage,
Unstead Lane, Bramley,
Guildford, GU5 0BT
T: 0845 052 3860
E: sales@yeltech.co.uk
W: www.yeltech.co.uk

YJL Infrastructure Ltd
39 Cornhill, London, EC3V 3ND
T: 020 7522 3220
F: 020 7522 3261
W: www.yjli.co.uk

York EMC Services Ltd
Market Square, University of York,
Heslington, York, YO10 5DD
T: 01904 324440
F: 01904 324434
E: enquiry@yorkemc.co.uk
W: www.yorkemc.co.uk

**Young Rail Professionals
(YRP)**
E: info@youngrailpro.com
W: www.youngrailpro.com

Zarges (UK) Ltd
Holdom Ave, Saxon Park Ind. Est,
Bletchley,
Milton Keynes, MK1 1QU
T: 01908 641118
F: 01908 648176
E: sales@zargesuk.co.uk
W: www.zargesuk.co.uk

ZEDAS GMBH
A-Hennecke-Strasse 37,
D-01968 Senftenberg,
Germany
T: 0049 3573 7075 0
E: info@zedas.com
W: www.zedas.com

Zep UK
PO Box 12, Tanhouse Lane,
Widnes, Cheshire, WA8 0RD
T: 0151 422 1000
F: 0151 422 1011
E: info@zep.uk.com
W: www.zep.uk.com

Zephir SpA
Via Salvador Allende N.85,
I-41122 Modena, Italy
T: 39 059 25 25 54
E: zephir@zephir.eu
W: www.zephir.eu

Zetica
Units 15/16,
Hanborough Business Park,
Long Hanborough,
Oxon, OX29 8LH
T: 01993 886682
F: 01993 886683
E: rail@zetica.com
W: www.zeticarail.com

ZF Services UK Ltd
Abbeyfield Rd,
Lenton,
Nottingham, NG7 2SX
T: 0333 240 1123
F: 0844 257 0666
E: mark.doughty@zf.com
W: www.zf.com/uk/rail

ZF UK Laser Ltd
9 Avacado Court,
Commerce Way,
Trafford Park,
Manchester, M17 1HW
T: 0161 871 7050
F: 0161 312 5063
E: info@zf-uk.com
W: www.zf-uk.com

**Zigma Ground
Solutions**
Unit 11,
M11 Business Link,
Parsonage Lane,
Stansted,
Essex, CM24 8TY
F: 0845 643734
E: amandacc@zigmaground
solutions.com
W: www.zigmaground
solutions.com

**Zircon Software
Ltd**
Bellefield House,
Hilperton Rd,
Trowbridge,
Wilts, BA14 7FP
T: 01225 764444
F: 01225 753087
E: info@
zirconsoftware.co.uk
W: www.zirconsoftware.co.uk

Zodiac Interconnect UK Ltd
220 Bedford Avenue, Slough,
Berks, SL1 4RY
T: 01753 896600
F: 01753 896601
E: cristophebigare@
zodiacaerospace.com
W: www.zodiacaerospace.com/
en/zodiac-interconnect-uk

Zollner UK Ltd
Clayton Business Ctr, Midland Rd,
Leeds, LS10 2RJ
T: 0113 270 3008
E: signal@zoellner.de
W: www.zoellner.de/

Zonegreen
Sir John Brown Building,
Davy Ind. Park, Prince of Wales Rd,
Sheffield, S9 4EX
T: 0114 230 0822
F: 0871 872 0349
E: info@zonegreen.co.uk
W: www.zonegreen.co.uk

**Zoppas Industries Heating
Element Technologies**
Via Podgora 26,
I-31029 Vittorio Veneto (TV), Italy
T: 39 0438 9101
E: rica@zoppas.com
W: www.zoppasindustries.com

ZTR Control Systems
8050 Country Rd, 101 East,
Shakopee, Minnesota, 55379,
United States
T: 001 952 233 4340
F: 001 952 233 4375
E: railinfo@ztr.com
W: www.ztr.com/rail

Zuken
1500 Aztec West,
Almondsbury, Bristol, BS32 4RF
T: 01454 207800
E: sales-uk@zuken.com
W: www.zuken.com

Zwicky Track Tools
See Arbil Lifting Gear